Visual Basic® .NET

Tips & Techniques

About the Author

Kris Jamsa, Ph.D., MBA, is the author of more than 90 computer books, with cumulative sales of several million copies. Jamsa holds a bachelor's degree in computer science from the United States Air Force Academy; a master's degree in computer science from the University of Nevada, Las Vegas; a Ph.D. in computer science with an emphasis in operating systems from Arizona State University; and an MBA from San Diego State University.

In 1992, Jamsa and his wife, Debbie, founded Jamsa Press, a computer-book publishing company. After expanding the company's presence to 70 countries and 28 languages, Jamsa sold Jamsa Press to a larger publishing house. Today Jamsa is President of the Jamsa Media Group, a company that provides content on a wide range of computer topics. Jamsa is also very active in analyzing emerging technologies.

Jamsa lives on a ranch in Houston, Texas, with his wife, their three dogs, and six horses. When he is not in front of his PC, Kris is riding and jumping his horse Robin Hood.

Visual Basic® .NET

Tips & Techniques

Kris Jamsa

McGraw-Hill/Osborne

New York / Chicago / San Francisco
Lisbon / London / Madrid / Mexico City / Milan
New Delhi / San Juan / Seoul / Singapore / Sydney / Toronto

McGraw-Hill/Osborne
2600 Tenth Street
Berkeley, California 94710
U.S.A.

To arrange bulk purchase discounts for sales promotions, premiums, or fund-raisers, please contact **McGraw-Hill**/Osborne at the above address. For information on translations or book distributors outside the U.S.A., please see the International Contact Information page immediately following the index of this book.

Visual Basic® .NET Tips & Techniques

1234567890 FGR FGR 0198765432

ISBN 0-07-222318-9

Publisher	Brandon A. Nordin
Vice President & Associate Publisher	Scott Rogers
Acquisitions Editor	Jim Schachterle
Project Editor	Jody McKenzie
Acquisitions Coordinator	Tim Madrid
Technical Editor	George Bullock
Copy Editor	Lunaea Weatherstone
Proofreader	Mike McGee
Indexer	Jack Lewis
Computer Designers	Carie Abrew, George Toma Charbak
Illustrators	Michael Mueller, Lyssa Wald
Series Design	Roberta Steele
Cover Series Design	Greg Scott

This book was composed with Corel VENTURA™ Publisher.

To Happy,
You will always be our very best friend. You taught us the meaning of
love and how to fully appreciate life.

Contents at a Glance

Contents

Acknowledgements

With each new title I write within the Osborne Tips & Techniques series, I more greatly appreciate the McGraw-Hill/Osborne team and their hard work and contributions. Their efforts make each book much easier to use and understand. The series owes its origin and high quality to Scott Rogers, Wendy Renaldi, and Jim Schachterle. Since our initial brainstorming meetings, these three have demanded content and presentation that constantly improves.

To begin, this book's copy editor, Lunaea Weatherstone, spent countless days improving this book's flow and cross-referencing text to the corresponding source code. Her attention to detail greatly improved the book's consistency and readability. I must also thank Tim Madrid for managing the manuscript flow and for keeping me going after long nights or weekends of coding. I greatly appreciate his humor and well-timed words of support.

I want to give special thanks to Jody McKenzie, this book's project editor. Jody's easygoing nature made our tight schedules a pleasure to meet. She is wonderful to work with. Please take time now to turn to the page near the front of the book that lists the Osborne team that brought this book together. As you look through this book's pages, the quality you will encounter is a direct result of everyone's hard work.

Introduction

Why You Should Read this Book

For years, Visual Basic has been the most widely used programming language. Visual Basic .NET extends programmer capabilities by introducing structured error handling, support for multiple threads of execution, the ability to quickly create and use Web services, a new model for interacting with databases (ADO.NET), and much more. For years, to perform many of these operations, a programmer had to be using a language such as C++ or Java.

In the past, many programmers claimed that for performance reasons, Visual Basic was not well suited for developing professional-quality applications. With the release of Visual Basic .NET, questions and concerns about performance should disappear. Within the .NET environment, programs written in Visual Basic .NET, C#, or Visual C++ .NET exploit the same methods and classes provided by the Common Language Runtime and Base Class Library to accomplish specific operations. Because each programming language uses the same libraries (and because of improvements to the Visual Basic compiler), .NET programs will have similar performance regardless of the programming language used to create the application.

With its technological advances and performance improvements, Visual Basic .NET is well positioned to remain the programming language of choice for years to come.

This book examines hundreds of ways you can exploit Visual Basic .NET capabilities and features built into the .NET environment. Each Tip provides ready-to-run source code that you can use to experiment with a programming concept or that you can cut and paste into your own programs. Further, each Tip provides step-by-step explanations of the processing the code performs. In this book's chapters, you will:

- Learn how to exploit Visual Basic .NET's object-oriented programming capabilities, such as classes, inheritance, interfaces, and reflection.

- Understand how your programs can use the Common Language Runtime and Base Class Library's thousands of programming-language independent methods and classes to accomplish specific tasks.

- Learn about the "common dialogs," which your programs can use to display standardized dialog boxes for operations that open, save, and print files and for selecting fonts and colors.

- See how Visual Basic .NET supports multiple threads of execution which create the illusion that your program is performing two or more tasks at the same time.

- Explore ways in which the .NET environment makes the forms-based user interface available to all programming languages through the use of Windows forms.

- Use the Try-Catch statement to detect and respond to an exception (which programmers refer to as structured error handling).

- Create an ASP.NET Web page using a compiled programming language such as Visual Basic .NET or C#.

- Create and use Web services (functions or subroutines a program can call remotely to accomplish a specific task) using Visual Studio.

- Learn how the .NET environment replaces the ADO model for database access with ADO.NET.

- Explore the many operations you can perform in Visual Basic .NET to quickly improve your program's performance and functionality.

- And much more!

What this Book Covers

This book contains 18 chapters. Each chapter examines a specific aspect of Visual Basic .NET or a key capability provided by the .NET environment. In each chapter, you will first examine the key "foundation" material and then you will learn how to put the concepts to use. Finally, you will learn how to leverage behind-the-scenes operations to maximize your program's performance and functionality. Each chapter is packed with dozens of ready-to-run programs. You can download each program's source code from the Osborne Web site at www.Osborne.com.

   Chapter 1, "Laying Your Visual Basic .NET Foundation":   Over the past ten years, Visual Basic has emerged as the programming language of choice for the vast majority of programmers. If you have not programmed in Visual Basic in the past, Chapter 1 will present the key data types, operators, and programming constructs (such as If and While statements) that you must know to create Visual Basic programs. You will also learn how to create console-based programs that display output to an MS-DOS–like window and Windows-based programs that use forms to provide the user interface. If you have programmed in Visual Basic, Chapter 1 presents Tips that cover the key differences between older versions of Visual Basic and Visual Basic .NET. By the time you finish Chapter 1, you will have the foundation in place upon which you can build your Visual Basic .NET expertise.

   Chapter 2, "Exploiting the .NET Environment":   If you are like most programmers who are moving to Visual Basic .NET, you not only face the task of learning a new programming language, but you also must understand the new features of the .NET environment and how to exploit those features within your programs. In Chapter 2, you will take a "crash course" in .NET technologies. You will examine the Common Language Runtime and common type system. You will create ASP.NET Web pages using Visual Basic .NET and C#. You will also exploit Web forms to build a user interface for your ASP.NET pages. You will examine how the .NET environment uses metadata

(data about data) to let programs query objects. Then you will learn about the .NET environment's use of intermediate-language (IL) code for executable programs and class libraries. Finally, you will learn how to exploit structured error handling with your Visual Basic .NET program to handle exceptions generated by your own source code as well as exceptions generated by a class method that resides in a class library. If you are trying to put your arms around the .NET environment, Chapter 2 provides the information you must know.

Chapter 3, "Programming Visual Basic .NET Classes": To create object-oriented programs, programmers make extensive use of classes to group an object's data (variables) and methods (functions and subroutines that operate on the variables). In Chapter 3, you will first examine the fundamentals of Visual Basic .NET classes. You will learn how to define a class and then how to create one or more instances of the class (objects). Next, you will learn how to use the dot operator to access class variables and methods and how you can restrict the class components a program can access directly by using access specifiers such as Public and Private. Then you will learn how to use the special New method (which programmers call the constructor method) to initialize an object's fields. You will then learn how the .NET environment uses "managed memory" to store the objects you create and the role of the .NET garbage collector and class-based destructor methods. By the time you finish Chapter 3, you will understand the ins and outs of Visual Basic .NET classes as well as the behind-the-scenes operations that affect the class objects you create and use.

Chapter 4, "Object-Oriented Programming in Visual Basic .NET": Visual Basic .NET programs make extensive use of classes to represent objects. Often, programmers can take advantage of the classes that are built into the .NET environment to perform key system operations, such as retrieving the system date and time, manipulating a file, and so on. When programmers create their own classes to represent an object, they often find that they can define a new object in terms of an existing class. For example, a programmer might define an Employee class using the variables and methods defined in an existing Person class. Or the programmer might define a ComputerBook class in terms of an existing Book class. To define a new class in terms of an existing class, programmers use inheritance. Chapter 4 examines inheritance in detail. You will learn how to take advantage of the constructor and destructor methods that reside in the existing class (which programmers call the base class) and how to override the processing a base-class method performs by defining a method with the same name with the new class (which programmers call the derived class). You will also learn how to create polymorphic objects that change forms as the program executes. A polymorphic Phone object, for example, might change from a cellular phone to a pay phone, depending on the processing the program performs. Finally, you will learn how to create and use interfaces within Visual Basic .NET programs.

Chapter 5, "Test Driving the Common Language Runtime and Base Class Library": The .NET environment provides the Common Language Runtime (CLR) and Base Class Library (BCL), which contain thousands of programming-language independent classes and routines your code can use to perform specific operations. In Chapter 5, you will examine several of the key classes that are used throughout this book's Tips on a regular basis. First, you will examine the DateTime class and ways you can use the class methods to determine the current system date and time, to compare dates, to determine dates in the future or past, and so on. Next, you will examine the String class, which implements many of the older Visual Basic string-manipulation functions. You will also learn why the "immutable" nature of the String class may reduce your program performance and how you can instead use StringBuilder objects to manipulate a string's contents in order to reduce overhead. Then you will examine the Math class and the methods it provides. Finally, you will learn how to send e-mail messages from within a Visual Basic .NET program or ASP.NET page.

Chapter 6, "Programming Visual Basic .NET File and Directory Operations":   To store information from one user session to the next, Visual Basic .NET programs make extensive use of files. In Chapter 6, you will examine key classes built into the .NET Common Language Runtime that your programs can use to perform key file and directory operations. To begin, you will learn how to create, select, move, and delete a directory. Next, you will learn how to retrieve a collection that contains a directory's files or subdirectories. You will then learn how to create, copy, move, and delete a file and how to exploit file attributes, such as the date and time the file was created or last accessed. Then you will learn how to store data, such as a form's contents, into a file and how to retrieve a file's contents using file stream operations. Finally, you learn how to monitor a directory for changes to files.

Chapter 7, "Leveraging the .NET Common Dialogs":   For years, Visual Basic programmers have made extensive use of forms to build user interfaces. To allow programs to perform key operations, such as opening, saving, or printing a file in a consistent manner, the .NET environment provides a set of classes that display dialog boxes programs can use to interact with the user. Programmers refer to this set of dialog boxes as the common dialogs. Chapter 7 examines the use of each class in detail. You will also learn how to preview and later print a document's contents.

Chapter 8, "Exploiting Multiple Threads of Execution":   Today, users commonly run two or programs at the same time using a multitasking operating system such as Windows or Linux. Although a multitasking operating system appears to run two or more programs at the same time, the CPU can only execute one program's instructions at any given time. A multitasking operating system creates the illusion that two or more programs are running at the same time by rapidly switching control of the CPU between each active program. Because the operating system switches the CPU so quickly, each program appears to be running at the same time. Using a similar CPU-switching technique, Visual Basic .NET allows programs to (appear to) perform two or more tasks at the same time through the use of threads of execution. In general, a thread of execution corresponds to a set of instructions, such as a subroutine. Within a Visual Basic .NET program, you can create multiple Thread objects that you direct to execute specific program instructions. As your program executes, it will switch control of the CPU between the Thread objects, creating the illusion that the threads are executing simultaneously. Chapter 8 examines threads of execution in detail. You will also learn how to synchronize thread operations to prevent one thread from interfering with another.

Chapter 9, "Taking Advantage of Structured Error Handling":   For years, Visual Basic programs and VBScript-based Active Server Pages have made extensive use of the ON ERROR statement to respond to errors. Using the ON ERROR statement, the program could specify the statements the program will execute when an operation generated an error. In the .NET environment, Visual Basic .NET programs make extensive use of methods and classes that are built into the Common Language Runtime. Many of these key methods respond to errors by generating exceptions. If a program does not detect and respond to the exception, the program will end, displaying a fatal error message that describes the exception. For years, C++ programmers have taken advantage of structured error handling to respond to exceptions. Visual Basic .NET now provides the same capabilities. In Chapter 9, you will learn how to detect and respond to exceptions in your Visual Basic .NET programs.

Chapter 10, "Responding to and Handling Events":   To build user interfaces, Visual Basic programmers write code that responds to form-based events, such as a mouse click. Visual Basic .NET changes the format that programmers must use to define the subroutines that handle events. Further, Visual Basic .NET provides the Delegate object to which your programs can assign the address of one or more subroutines you want the program to execute when a specific event occurs. Chapter 10 examines event handling and Delegate objects in detail.

Chapter 11, "Programming Windows Forms":   To quickly build user interfaces, Visual Basic programmers make extensive use of forms. To create a user interface using Visual Basic forms, programmers simply dragged and dropped controls onto a form. Compared to Visual Basic, building a user interface using other programming languages, such as C++, is quite difficult. In fact, the user interface is often one of the most time-consuming aspects of program development. The .NET environment, however, provides programming languages such as C# (as well as Visual Basic .NET) the ability create user interfaces using Windows Forms. In general, Windows forms are a programming language independent implementation of the form-based capabilities that Visual Basic programmers have exploited for years. Using Windows forms, you drag and drop controls onto a form. Behind the scenes, Visual Studio will include the code in your program that creates, displays, and interacts with each control. Chapter 11 examines Windows forms and the key controls in detail.

Chapter 12, "Looking Closer at .NET Assemblies and Versioning":   When you create an application in the .NET environment, the application resides in a special file called an assembly. The assembly may use the .exe extension for a program or the .dll extension for a class library. In addition to storing executable code, the assembly contains metadata (data about data) that describes the program and the components (the class libraries that reside in .dll files) the program requires. Further, the metadata provides version information about the program and about the version number the program requires for each of its components. The versioning information the assembly provides is key to the .NET's ability to reduce conflicts when new versions of a program or a .dll file release. In Chapter 12, you use several tools Visual Studio provides to closely examine and update the information an assembly contains. You will also learn how to create class libraries and the steps you must perform to share the library among Visual Basic .NET, C#, and ASP.NET applications.

Chapter 13, "Programming ASP.NET Solutions":   Today, programmers make extensive use of Active Server Pages to drive Web sites. By combining HTML tags within a script (normally written in VBScript), Active Server Pages let developers create dynamic content that can change on a per-user basis, pages that can interact with the user, as well as pages that utilize database content. The .NET environment extends the capabilities Web developers can use to build dynamic pages by introducing ASP.NET. An ASP.NET page, like an Active Server Page, combines HTML tags with programming code. Programmers can create an ASP.NET page using compiled programming languages such as Visual Basic .NET and C#. By letting programmers use a compiled language, ASP.NET pages provide programmers with all the features the programming language provides, as well those of the .NET Common Language Runtime. Within an ASP.NET page, programmers can create classes, use inheritance, leverage multiple threads of execution, handle errors via exceptions, and more. Because the ASP.NET pages use a compiled programming language, the scripts are faster than a scripted counterpart. Further, as you will learn in Chapter 15, ASP.NET pages support Web forms, which let programs build pages by dragging and dropping Web controls onto a page. Many of the Web controls are server-based, which means the server displaying the page responds to the controls, which greatly increases the processing each control can perform. This chapter examines ASP.NET pages in detail.

Chapter 14, "Programming Windows Services":   Within the Windows environment, a service is a special program that runs behind the scenes to perform a specific task. The print spooler, for example, oversees the output you send to a printer. Likewise, the Internet Information Services (IIS) server runs behind the scenes to send the Web pages and files that a user's browser request. Visual Studio makes it very easy for programmers to create Windows services. In Chapter 14, you will learn the key subroutines each server must provide in order to communicate with Windows, and you will learn the steps you must perform to install and start a service each time Windows boots.

Chapter 15, "Programming Web Forms":   The .NET environment brings with it the ASP.NET model for building dynamic Web pages. To create an ASP.NET page, programmers use a compiled programming language such as C# or Visual Basic .NET. A major advantage of using a compiled program to build Web pages is that the program can use routines built into the Common Language Runtime. Further, to simplify the process of building a user interface for Web pages, the .NET environment introduces Web forms. In general, using Web forms, you can drag and drop controls onto a Web page, much like you would build a form within a traditional Visual Basic program. Then you can assign a code to each control. Web controls are unique in that you can direct the control to perform its processing at the server, which lets the processing a control performs become quite complex. Chapter 15 examines Web forms and each of the Web-based controls in detail.

Chapter 16, "Programming Web Services":   For years, applications have evolved to make extensive use of networks and to support remote operations. Normally, within a distributed environment, applications running on a client computer will access data stored on a remote server computer, such as a company database. In the past, many network operating systems have supported remote procedure calls (RPC) that let a program call a function or procedure that resides on a remote system. Within the program's source code, the call to the remote procedure looks very much like a standard procedure call, including the subroutine or function name and parameters. Behind the scenes, however, the remote procedure call requires an exchange of messages between the program and the server. The program must send the server a message that specifies the subroutine or function it wants to call and messages that correspond to each parameter. After the remote procedure completes its processing, the server must send messages back to the program that contain the procedure's result. Across the Internet, Web services provide programmers with the ability to perform remote procedure calls. The .NET environment makes it easy to create Web services. Chapter 16 examines in detail the steps you must perform to create and to later call a Web service.

Chapter 17, "Getting Started with ADO.NET":   For years, programmers have made extensive use of Active Data Objects (ADO) to simplify database applications. The .NET environment brings with it a new model for database access called ADO.NET, which provides significant improvements over the ADO model. The ADO.NET model introduces the DataSet object that replaces the RecordSet object that programmers used in the past with ADO. In Chapter 17, you will learn how to connect to, query, and update databases using ADO.NET. You will also examine how the ADO.NET model exploits XML to provide structure to the data the DataSet object contains. Finally, you will perform ADO.NET operations from within an ASP.NET page and you will map data stored in a table to a DataGrid control for display.

Chapter 18, "Programming .NET Reflection and Program Attributes":   The .NET environment makes extensive use of metadata (data about data) to let objects become self-describing.

In other words, as a program executes, the program can query an object to learn about the capabilities the object provides. Programmers refer to the ability to query an object as reflection. Using reflection, a program can learn specifics about the methods a class provides, the class member variables, and more. Chapter 18 examines the steps you must perform to query an object's capabilities. You will learn how to query an assembly that contains an application or a class library about the classes it provides. Then you will retrieve information about those classes, such as each method's type (subroutine or function) as well as the number and type of parameters the method uses. With this information in hand, your programs can invoke the class methods, passing to the methods the correct parameter values. To provide programs with more information about entities, such as a class, method, or even an assembly itself, Visual Basic .NET supports attributes. You might use one set of attributes, for example, to influence compiler operations and a second set to control how the debugger performs various operations. In Chapter 18, you will examine attributes Visual Studio inserts into your programs and ways you can create and use your own custom attributes.

How to Use this Book

 USE IT — Although this book's chapters build on the information preceding chapters present, we have structured the book so that you can turn to any Tip and find the information you need. As you scan through the book's page, watch for the Use It icon, which highlights specific steps you can immediately perform to accomplish a task. For example, if you must save data to and later retrieve data from a file, you might turn directly to the Tip titled "Starting with File Streams," in Chapter 6, that tells you how to read and write files. Or if you must detect and handle a specific exception, you might turn to the Tip titled "Catching a Specific Exception," which appears in Chapter 9.

To help you quickly locate the information you need, at the start of each chapter, we have included a list of the specific Tips that chapter presents. If you need more information on a topic, each chapter provides introductory text that will give you a solid foundation.

If you have not programmed with Visual Basic in the past, you should turn first to Chapter 1, which provides the introductory information you must know. If you are an experienced Visual Basic programmer, Chapter 1 provides Tips that detail specific differences between older versions of Visual Basic and Visual Basic .NET. If you are new to the .NET environment, Chapter 2 examines many of the key .NET capabilities.

CHAPTER 1

Laying Your
Visual Basic .NET Foundation

TIPS IN THIS CHAPTER

Over the past ten years, Visual Basic has emerged as the programming language of choice for the vast majority of programmers. Many programmers site Visual Basic's ease of use as the key to its success. Others claim that the ability to drag and drop controls onto a form to quickly build a program's user interface lead to Visual Basic's widespread use.

While masses of programmers have used Visual Basic to implement solutions for a wide range of programming tasks, a large group of developers, many of whom have been programming with languages such as C and C++ for years, have refused to acknowledge Visual Basic's suitability as a professional programming language. Many such programmers have stated that while Visual Basic provides a convenient way to build a prototype, programmers should later rewrite the code using a language such as C++ to achieve better performance.

With the release of the .NET environment, Microsoft has included two new key programming languages, Visual Basic .NET and C# (Microsoft also included Visual C++ .NET as a part of the .NET environment). As you will learn, the .NET environment provides programming-language independent classes and routines that are used by both C# and Visual Basic .NET. This means whether a programmer is using Visual Basic .NET or C#, the programmer has the same .NET capabilities available for use. From a performance perspective, Visual Basic .NET applications will run neck and neck with identical programs written using C#. Although the .NET environment provides C# programmers with the ability to drag and drop controls onto a form to quickly build a user interface, the sheer number of Visual Basic programmers who migrate to Visual Basic .NET will make Visual Basic .NET the .NET programming language of choice.

Throughout this book's 18 chapters, you will examine Visual Basic .NET and the .NET environment in detail. This chapter exists to provide programmers who are new to Visual Basic with a foundation from which they can build their knowledge and understanding of the capabilities Visual Basic .NET and the .NET environment provide. If you are an experienced Visual Basic programmer, you may want to simply scan the titles of the Tips this chapter provides in search of topics you may find new and then turn to the chapter's final Tip, which summarizes key differences between Visual Basic and Visual Basic .NET. In either case, it's time to get started.

Creating Your First Console Application

Using Visual Basic .NET, you can create a variety of application types, such as a console-based program that displays its output in an MS-DOS-like window, as shown here, a Windows-based program that often displays a form-based interface, an ASP.NET page, and more.

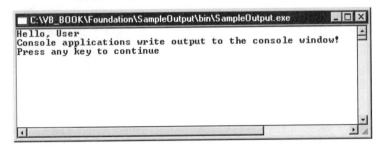

Because of the console-based application's ease of use (you can quickly create programs to display simple output without having to place controls onto a form), many of the Tips this book presents use console-based applications.

USE IT To create a console application using Visual Studio, perform these steps:

1. In Visual Studio, select File | New | Project. Visual Studio will display the New Project dialog box.

2. In the New Project dialog box, click the Console Application icon. In the Name field, type a project name that describes the program you are building, such as DemoProgram (do not type an extension). Then, in the Location field, type the name of the folder in which you want Visual Studio to place the project's folder and files. Click OK. Visual Studio will display a code window, as shown in Figure 1-1, in which you can type your program statements.

In the code window, type the following statements in the Main subroutine:

```
Sub Main()
    Console.WriteLine("My first VB.NET Program!")
    Console.ReadLine()
End Sub
```

Next, to run the program, select Debug | Start. Visual Studio will display your program's output in a console window. To end the program, which will direct Visual Studio to close the window, press ENTER.

As you type program statements in a Visual Basic .NET program, you must type the statements exactly as they appear in this book, making sure you include the quotes, commas, periods, and so on. Otherwise, your programs may violate one or more of the Visual Basic .NET syntax rules (the rules that define the language structure and the format you must use as you create programs). When a syntax

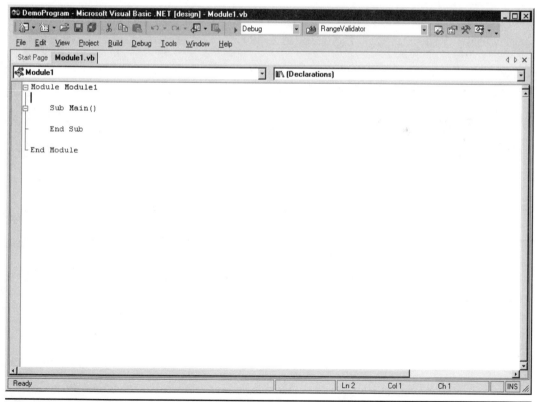

Figure 1-1 Displaying the code window in Visual Studio

error occurs, Visual Studio will display an error message that describes the error and the line number in your code where the error occurs. Before Visual Studio will build your program, you must locate and correct the syntax error.

Each time you make a change to your program code, you must direct Visual Studio to rebuild your program to put your change into effect. To rebuild your program, select Build | Build Solution. For example, in the previous program statements, change the code to display the message "Hello, user" by changing the Console.WriteLine method as follows:

```
Console.WriteLine("Hello, user")
```

Next, rebuild your program and then select Debug | Start to view your new output.

Building a Windows-Based Application

Using Visual Studio, you can create a variety of application types. Normally, to create a Windows-based application, programmers will drag and drop one or more controls onto a form to provide the user interface, as shown in Figure 1-2.

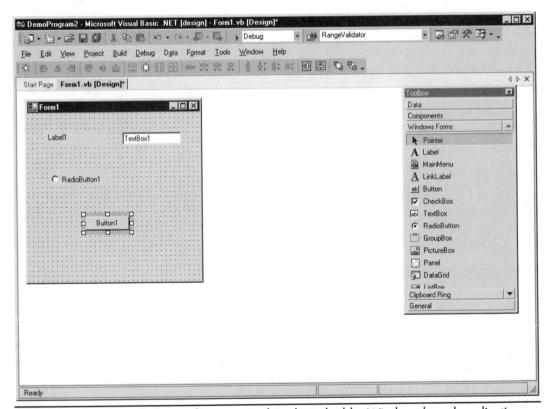

Figure 1-2 Placing controls on a form in Visual Studio to build a Windows-based application

USE IT   Chapter 11 examines in detail the controls you can place onto a form. To create a simple Windows-based application using Visual Studio, perform these steps:

1. In Visual Studio, select File | New | Project. Visual Studio will display the New Project dialog box.

2. In the New Project dialog box, click the Windows Application icon. In the Name field, type a project name that describes the program you are building, such as DemoProgram (do not type an extension). Then, in the Location field, type the name of the folder in which you want Visual Studio to place the project's folder and files. Click OK. Visual Studio will display a design window, similar to that previously shown in Figure 1-3, in which you can drag and drop controls onto your form.

3. To display the toolbox that contains the controls you can drag and drop onto the form, select View | Toolbox. Visual Studio will open the Toolbox window.

4. In the Toolbox window, locate the Label control. Drag and drop the control onto the form.

5. In the form, right-click the Label control and choose Properties. Visual Studio will display the Label control's properties in the Properties window.

6. In the Properties window, locate the Text property and type **Hello, user**.

To build your program, select Build | Build Solution. Then, to run your program, select Debug | Start. Visual Studio, in this case, will display your program's form in its own window as shown in Figure 1-3.

If you make changes to the program's form, a control that resides on the form, or your program code, you must direct Visual Studio to rebuild your program to put your changes into effect.

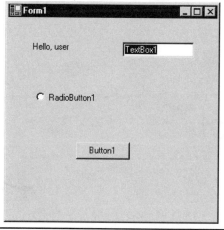

Figure 1-3   Creating and running a simple Windows-based application using Visual Studio

Choosing the Correct Visual Basic Types

To store information as they execute, programs place data into named storage locations that programmers refer to as variables—so named because the data a variable stores can change (vary) as the program executes. A program might use one variable to store a user's name, a second to store a user's e-mail address, and a third to store the user's age.

Each variable you create in your programs must be of a specific type. A variable's type defines the set of values a variable can store, such as counting or floating-point numbers (a number with a decimal point), or alphanumeric characters (such as the letters of the alphabet that make up a name). A variable's type also defines the set of operations a program can perform on a variable. It makes sense, for example, that a program can multiply two floating-point numbers, but it would not make sense to multiply two strings (such as two names). Table 1-1 briefly describes the Visual Basic data types. For each type, the table lists the range of values the type can store, along with the number of bytes of memory Visual Basic .NET must set aside to store the variable's value.

USE IT   As you select a data type for use in your programs, choose a type that best matches your data. Assume your program must store values in the range –10,000 to 20,000. The Visual Basic .NET data types Integer, Long, and Short can each store values in this range. However, by using the type Short, your programs will allocate less memory to store the value—which means your program can store and retrieve the value faster than it could with a larger data type. More importantly, however, by selecting the Short type, you provide another programmer who reads your code with insight into the variable's use. In the case of a variable defined as the type Short, another programmer who reads your code immediately knows the variable will store values in the range –32,768 to 32,767. Visual Basic .NET has "retired" (no longer supports) the Currency and Variant data types that existed in previous versions of Visual Basic.

Type	Values	Size
Boolean	Represents a True or False value.	2 bytes
Byte	Represents an 8-bit value in the range 0 to 255.	1 byte
Char	Represents a 16-bit Unicode character.	2 bytes
DateTime	Represents a date and time value.	8 bytes
Decimal	Represents a value with 28 significant digits in the range +/–79,228,162,514,264,337,593,543,950,335 with no decimal point to 7.9228162514264337593543950335 with 28 places to the right of the decimal point.	12 bytes
Double	Represents a floating-point value using 64 bits.	8 bytes
Integer	Represents a value in the range –2,147,483,648 to 2,147,483,647.	4 bytes
Long	Represents a value in the range –9,223,372,036,854,775,808 through 9,223,372,036,854,775,807.	8 bytes
Short	Represents a value in the range –32,678 to 32,677.	2 bytes
Single	Represents a floating-point value using 32 bits.	4 bytes

Table 1-1   The Visual Basic .NET Types

Declaring Variables in a Visual Basic .NET Program

Variables exist to let programs easily store and later retrieve information as the program executes. Programmers often describe a variable as "a named location in RAM" (a storage container) that holds a value. The size of the variable's storage container depends on the variable's type.

USE IT   To declare a variable in a Visual Basic .NET program, you use the Dim statement to specify the variable's name and type. The Dim statement is so named because it specifies the dimensions of the variable's storage container. The following Dim statement declares a variable named EmployeeNumber of type Integer:

```
Dim EmployeeNumber As Integer
```

In this case, by declaring the variable as type Integer, you direct Visual Basic .NET to allocate 4 bytes to store the variable's value, for which the type Integer can be in the range –2,147,483,648 to 2,147,483,647. Often, programs must declare several variables at one time. The following statements declare variables to store an employee's name, ID, salary, and phone number:

```
Dim EmployeeName As String
Dim EmployeePhoneNumber As String
Dim EmployeeNumber As Integer
Dim EmployeeSalary as Double
```

In the previous variable declarations, the first two statements declare variables of type String, which can store alphanumeric characters. When you declare variables of the same type, Visual Basic .NET lets you place the declarations in the same statement, as shown here:

```
Dim EmployeeName, EmployeePhoneNumber As String
```

The following statement is equivalent to that just shown—each declares two String variables:

```
Dim EmployeeName As String, EmployeePhoneNumber As String
```

In general, you should consider declaring variables on individual lines, so you can place a comment to the right of the declaration that describes the variable's purpose:

```
Dim EmployeeName As String         ' Employee first and last name
Dim EmployeePhoneNumber As String  ' 10 digits in the form ###-###-####
```

When you name variables, choose names that meaningfully describe the information the variable stores. In that way, another programmer who reads your code can better understand the variable's purpose and your code's processing simply by reading the variable's name. If you consider the following variable declarations, the first variable's name provides you with the variable's implied use, whereas the second variable does not:

```
Dim CityName As String
Dim X As String
```

After you declare a variable in Visual Basic .NET, you can then use the assignment operator (the equal sign) to assign a value to the variable, as shown here:

```
CityName = "Houston"
EmployeeName = "Smith"
EmployeeSalary = 60000
```

Often, programmers must assign an initial value to a variable. To do so, some programmers choose to declare the variables on one line and then initialize the variable on the next, as shown here:

```
Dim EmployeeName As String          ' Employee first and last name
EmployeeName = "Bill Smith"

Dim EmployeePhoneNumber As String  ' 10 digits in the form ###-###-####
EmployeePhoneNumber = "281-555-1212"
```

Visual Basic .NET, however, lets you combine these two operations into one statement, as shown here:

```
Dim EmployeeName As String = "Bill Smith"

Dim EmployeePhoneNumber As String  = "281-555-1212"
```

Visual Basic .NET is a case-independent programming language, which means it treats upper- and lowercase letters the same in a variable name. The following statements each assign the value 50000 to the variable named EmployeeSalary:

```
EmployeeSalary = 50000
employeesalary = 50000
EMPLOYEESALARY = 50000
eMpLoYeEsAlArY = 50000
```

If you do not assign an initial value to a variable, Visual Basic .NET will initialize your variables for you during compilation. Visual Basic .NET will use the initial values listed in Table 1-2 based on the variable's type.

Type	Value
Boolean	False
Date	12:00:00AM
Numeric types	0
Object	Nothing

Table 1-2   Default Values Visual Basic .NET Assigns to Variables of Specific Data Types

The following program, DeclareVariables.vb, declares and initializes several variables. The program then displays each variable's value using the Console.WriteLine method:

```
Module Module1

    Sub Main()
        Dim EmployeeName As String
        Dim EmployeePhoneNumber As String
        Dim EmployeeSalary As Double
        Dim NumberOfEmployees As Integer

        EmployeeName = "Buddy Jamsa"
        EmployeePhoneNumber = "555-1212"
        EmployeeSalary = 45000.0
        NumberOfEmployees = 1

        Console.WriteLine("Number of employees: " & NumberOfEmployees)
        Console.WriteLine("Employee name: " & EmployeeName)
        Console.WriteLine("Employee phone number: " & EmployeePhoneNumber)
        Console.WriteLine("Employee salary: " & EmployeeSalary)

        Console.ReadLine() ' Pause to view output
    End Sub

End Module
```

After you compile and execute this program, your screen will display the following output:

```
Number of employees: 1
Employee name: Buddy Jamsa
Employee phone number: 555-1212
Employee salary: 45000
```

▶ **NOTE**

In previous versions of Visual Basic, programmers used the LET statement to assign a value to a variable. Visual Basic .NET does not support the LET statement.

Displaying Screen Output Using Console.Write and Console.WriteLine

When you create a console-based application, your programs display their output to an MS-DOS window similar to that shown in Figure 1-4.

Figure 1-4   Displaying program output to a console window

To write output to the console window, your programs use the Console.Write and the Console.WriteLine methods. The difference between two methods is that Console.WriteLine will send a carriage-return and linefeed combination following your program output to advance the cursor to the start of the next line, whereas Console.Write will not.

To display a string message using Console.WriteLine, you simply pass the message as a parameter, placing the text in double quotes, as shown here:

```
Console.WriteLine("Hello, Visual Basic World!")
```

Similarly, to display a number or a variable's value, you pass the number or variable name to the method (without quotes) as shown here:

```
Console.WriteLine(1001)
Console.WriteLine(EmployeeName)
```

Often, programmers will precede a value with a text message, such as "The user's age is:". To display such output, the code will normally use the Visual Basic .NET concatenation operator (&) to append the value to the end of the string as shown here:

```
Console.WriteLine("The user's age is: " & UserAge)
```

USE IT   The following program, OutputDemo.vb, illustrates the use of the Console.Write and Console.WriteLine methods:

```
Module Module1

    Sub Main()
        Dim A As Integer = 100
        Dim B As Double = 0.123456789
        Dim Message As String = "Hello, VB World!"

        Console.WriteLine(A)
        Console.WriteLine("The value of A is " & A)
        Console.WriteLine(B)
```

```
        Console.WriteLine(B & " plus " & A & " = " & B + A)
        Console.WriteLine(Message)

        Console.ReadLine()
    End Sub

End Module
```

After you compile and execute this program, your screen will display the following output:

```
100
The value of A is 100
0.123456789
0.123456789 plus 100 = 100.123456789
Hello, VB World!
```

Note that the program places the Console.ReadLine() statement as the last statement in the program. When you run a console application in Visual Studio, the console window will immediately close after the program completes its processing. By placing the Console.ReadLine() statement at the end of the code, the program will pause, waiting for the user to press the ENTER key, before the program ends and the window closes.

Formatting Program Output Using Console.WriteLine

In the previous Tips, you used the Console.WriteLine and Write functions to display messages to the console window. In each example, your application simply wrote the character string:

```
Console.WriteLine("Hello, world!")
```

Using the Console.WriteLine and Write functions, you can display values by using placeholders in the method's text output in the form {0}, {1}, and so on, and then passing parameters for each placeholder. The following statement uses placeholders in the Console.WriteLine function:

```
Console.WriteLine("The number is {0}", 3 + 7)
```

In this case, the WriteLine function will substitute the value 10 for the placeholder {0}. The following statement uses three placeholders:

```
Console.WriteLine("The result of {0} + {1} = {2}",  3, 7, 3+7)
```

In this case, the function will substitute the value 3 for the placeholder {0}, the value 7 for the placeholder {1}, and the value 10 for the placeholder {2}.

Using placeholders such as {0} and {1}, you can display values and variables using the Console.WriteLine and Write functions. When you specify placeholders, you must make sure that you include values the function is to substitute for each placeholder. If you specify the placeholders {0} and {1}, for example, and only provide one value, the function will generate an exception. If your program does not handle the exception, your program will immediately end.

When your programs use the Console.WriteLine and Write functions to display output, your programs can place a format specifier after the placeholder number, such as {1, d} or {2, 7:f}. The format specifier can include an optional width value, followed by a colon and a character that specifies the value's type. Table 1-3 briefly describes the type specifiers.

In the previous Tip, you learned to use several different format specifiers in the Console.WriteLine and Console.Write functions. When your program displays floating-point values, there will be times, such as when the value represents currency, when you will want to specify the number of digits the functions display to the right of the decimal point. Assume your program must display the variable Amount, which contains the value 0.123456790. To control the number of digits the WriteLine and Write functions display, you specify the placeholder, width, format specifier, and number of digits, as shown here:

```
Console.WriteLine("See decimals {0, 12:f1}", _
    0.123456789)  ' 0.1
Console.WriteLine("See decimals {0, 12:f9}", _
    0.123456789)  ' 0.123456789
```

In addition to the width and format specifiers, the functions also let you use the pound sign (#) to format your data. The following statement directs Console.WriteLine to display a floating-point value with two digits to the right of the decimal point:

```
Console.WriteLine("The value is {0, 0:###.##}", Value)
```

Specifier	Value Type
C or c	Local currency format.
D or d	Decimal value.
E or e	Scientific notation.
F or f	Floating point.
G or g	Selects scientific or floating point depending on which is most compact.
N or n	Numeric formats which include commas for large values.
P or p	Percentage formats.
R or r	Called the "round-trip" specifier. Used for floating-point values to ensure that a value that is converted to a string and then back to floating point yields the original value.
X or x	Hexadecimal formats.

Table 1-3   Format Specifiers You Can Use with Console.WriteLine and Console.Write

When you use the pound-sign character to specify an output format, the WriteLine function will not display leading zeros. In other words, the function would output the value 0.123 as simply .123. When you want to display leading zeros, you can replace the pound sign with a zero, as shown here:

```
Console.WriteLine("The value is {0, 0:000.00}", Value)
```

The following program, ConsoleWriteLineDemo.vb, illustrates the use of the various Console.WriteLine formatting capabilities:

```
Module Module1

    Sub Main()
        Dim A As Double = 1.23456789
        Console.WriteLine("{0} {1} {2}", 1, 2, 3)
        Console.WriteLine("{0, 1:D} {1, 2:D} {2, 3:D}", 1, 2, 3)
        Console.WriteLine("{0, 7:F1} {1, 7:F3} {2, 7:F5}", A, A, A)
        Console.WriteLine("{0, 0:#.#}", A)
        Console.WriteLine("{0, 0:#.###}", A)
        Console.WriteLine("{0, 0:#.#####}", A)

        Console.ReadLine()
    End Sub

End Module
```

After you compile and execute this program, your screen will display the following output:

```
1 2 3
1   2   3
    1.2   1.235 1.23457
1.2
1.235
1.23457
```

Concatenating Characters to the End of a String

In Visual Basic .NET programs, the String type lets variables store alphanumeric characters (the upper- and lowercase letters of the alphabet, the digits 0 through 9, and punctuation symbols). To assign a value to a String variable, you must place the value in double quotes, as shown here:

```
Dim Name As String = "John Doe"
```

The following program, UseStrings.vb, assigns values to several different String variables, which the program later displays using Console.WriteLine:

```
Module Module1

    Sub Main()
        Dim Book As String = _
           "Visual Basic .Net Programming Tips & Techniques"
        Dim Author As String = "Jamsa"
        Dim Publisher As String = "McGraw-Hill/Osborne"

        Console.WriteLine(Book)
        Console.WriteLine(Author)
        Console.WriteLine(Publisher)

        Console.ReadLine()
    End Sub

End Module
```

After you compile and execute this program, your screen will display the following output:

```
Visual Basic .Net Programming Tips & Techniques
Jamsa
McGraw-Hill/Osborne
```

When your programs use String variables, a common operation your code will perform is to append characters to a String variable's existing contents. Programmers refer to operations that append characters to a String as concatenation operations.

USE IT   To concatenate one string to another, you use the ampersand (&), which is the Visual Basic .NET concatenation operator. The following statement assigns an employee's first name and last name to a variable called EmployeeName, by concatenating the FirstName and LastName variables and assigning the result to the EmployeeName variable:

```
Dim FirstName As String = "Bill"
Dim LastName As String = "Gates"
Dim EmployeeName As String
EmployeeName = FirstName & " " & LastName
```

As you can see, the code separates the first and last names with a space by concatenating the space to the end of the string the FirstName variable contains. Throughout this book, you will encounter Console.WriteLine statements that use the concatenation operator to append a value to a string:

```
Console.WriteLine("The result is " & SomeVariable)
```

The following program, ConcatenateDemo.vb, illustrates the use of the concatenation operator:

```
Module Module1

    Sub Main()
        Dim WebSite As String
        Dim Publisher As String = "Osborne"

        Console.WriteLine("This book's publisher: " & Publisher)

        WebSite = "www." & Publisher & ".com"
        Console.WriteLine("View their books at " & WebSite)

        Console.ReadLine()
    End Sub

End Module
```

After you compile and execute this program, your screen will display the following output:

```
This book's publisher: Osborne
View their books at www.Osborne.com
```

Forcing Programs to Specify a Variable's Type

To reduce possible errors that result from misspelled variable names, you should force programs to declare each variable the code uses to store data. By declaring a variable, your program specifies the variable's type, which, in turn, limits the range of values the program can assign to the variable and the operations the program can perform on the variable.

The following program, BadVariables.vb, does not declare the variables it uses. The program assigns values to several employee-based variables and then displays the employee's name:

```
Option Explicit Off   ' Lets the program use variables without
                       ' declaring the variables
Module Module1

    Sub Main()
        EmployeeName = "Buddy Jamsa"
        EmployeePhoneNumber = "555-1212"
        EmployeeSalary = 45000.0
        NumberOfEmployees = 1

        Console.WriteLine("Number of employees: " & NumberOfEmployees)
        Console.WriteLine("Employee name: " & EmployeName)
        Console.WriteLine("Employee phone number: " & EmployeePhoneNumber)
```

```
        Console.WriteLine("Employee salary: " & EmployeeSalary)

        Console.ReadLine() ' Pause to view output
    End Sub

End Module
```

Unfortunately, when you execute this program, the program does not display the employee's name. Instead, the program displays blank output for the name, as shown here:

```
Number of employees: 1
Employee name:
Employee phone number: 555-1212
Employee salary: 45000
```

If you examine the program statements closely, you will find that the Console.WriteLine statement that displays the employee's name misspells the variable name (it omits the ending *e* in Employee). Normally, Visual Studio requires that you declare each variable your program uses. By forcing the program to declare each variable, you eliminate such errors. In this case, the statement Option Explicit Off directs the compiler to let the program use a variable without first declaring the variable (an option you should not enable).

USE IT To force a program to declare variables, you place the following statement at the start of your program:

```
Option Explicit On
```

If you insert the statement at the start of the BadVariables.vb program, the Visual Basic .NET compiler will generate a syntax error message similar to those shown in Figure 1-5, that tells you

```
Output                                                                          [X]
Build                                                                            ▼
  ------ Build started: Project: BadVariables, Configuration: Debug .NET ------

  Preparing resources...
  Updating references...
  Performing main compilation...
  C:\VB_BOOK\Foundation\BadVariables\BadVariables.vb(6) : error BC30451: Name 'EmployeeName' is not declared.
  C:\VB_BOOK\Foundation\BadVariables\BadVariables.vb(7) : error BC30451: Name 'EmployeePhoneNumber' is not declared.
  C:\VB_BOOK\Foundation\BadVariables\BadVariables.vb(8) : error BC30451: Name 'EmployeeSalary' is not declared.
  C:\VB_BOOK\Foundation\BadVariables\BadVariables.vb(9) : error BC30451: Name 'NumberOfEmployees' is not declared.
  C:\VB_BOOK\Foundation\BadVariables\BadVariables.vb(11) : error BC30451: Name 'NumberOfEmployees' is not declared.
  C:\VB_BOOK\Foundation\BadVariables\BadVariables.vb(12) : error BC30451: Name 'EmployeName' is not declared.
  C:\VB_BOOK\Foundation\BadVariables\BadVariables.vb(13) : error BC30451: Name 'EmployeePhoneNumber' is not declared.
  C:\VB_BOOK\Foundation\BadVariables\BadVariables.vb(14) : error BC30451: Name 'EmployeeSalary' is not declared.
  Building satellite assemblies...



  ------------------- Done ---------------------

     Build: 0 succeeded, 1 failed, 0 skipped
```

Figure 1-5 Syntax-error messages that correspond to undeclared variables

the variables are not declared. As you declare variables to remove the syntax errors, you will likely discover the misspelled variable name.

Beware of Variable Overflow and Precision

As you learned, a variable's type specifies the range of values a variable can store and a set of operations a program can perform on the variable. If you assign a value to a variable that exceeds the range of values the variable can store, an overflow error occurs. Assume that your program is using a variable of type Short to store a value in the range –32,678 to 32,767. Further, assume that the variable contains the value 32,767 and your program adds the value 1 to the variable as shown here:

```
Dim Value As Short = 32767
Value = Value + 1
```

When the program executes this statement, the value 32,768 will fall outside of the range of values the variable can store. When the overflow error occurs, your program will generate an exception and will end, displaying an error message similar to that shown in Figure 1-6. Chapter 9 discusses exceptions and how your programs should respond to such errors.

USE IT Just as a variable's type limits the range of values a variable can store, it also limits the accuracy (or precision) of the value a variable can represent. Variables of type Single are generally precise to 7 digits to the right of the decimal point, whereas variables of type Double are precise to 15 digits. The following program, ShowPrecision.vb, illustrates the accuracy of single- and double-precision variables:

```
Module Module1

    Sub Main()
        Dim A As Single = 0.123456789012345
        Dim B As Double = 0.123456789012345

        Console.WriteLine("Single: " & A)
        Console.WriteLine("Double: " & B)

        Console.ReadLine()
    End Sub

End Module
```

After you compile and execute this program, your screen will display the following output:

```
Single: 0.1234568
Double: 0.123456789012345
```

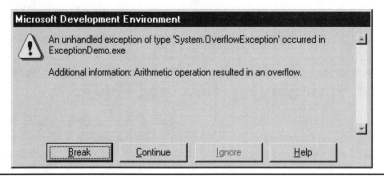

Figure 1-6   An exception (error) that occurs when the value a program assigns exceeds a type's acceptable range of values

As your programs manipulate floating-point numbers, a type's limited precision can lead to errors that are difficult to detect. The following program, PrecisionError.vb, uses a For loop to move through the values 0.01, 0.02, 0.03 up to 0.1. When the variable A contains the value 0.05, the program displays a message so stating:

```
Module Module1

    Sub Main()
        Dim A As Single

        For A = 0.01 To 0.1 Step 0.01
            If (A = 0.05) Then
                Console.WriteLine("Reached 0.05")
            End If
        Next

        Console.WriteLine("Done with loop")
        Console.ReadLine()
    End Sub

End Module
```

After you compile and execute the program, your screen will display the following output:

```
Done with loop
```

As you can see, the program does not display the message "Reached 0.05." That's because the computer's limited precision prevents the computer from exactly representing the value 0.05. For the loop to display the message, you must change the If statement to take the limited precision into account and test for the value being a few digits from 0.05, as shown here:

```
If (Math.Abs(A - 0.05) < 0.00001) Then
```

Performing Numeric Operations

To accomplish meaningful work, a program must perform operations on its variables. A program might multiply a variable that contains a user's total purchases by a sales tax amount, in order to determine the amount of tax the user must pay. Then the code may add the sales tax and shipping costs to the purchase amount in order to determine the total amount of money the user owes for his or her purchase of two items:

```
Purchases = 10.0 + 20.0
SalesTax = Purchases * 0.05
TotalDue = Purchases + SalesTax
```

To perform such operations, programs use arithmetic operations. Table 1-4 briefly describes the Visual Basic .NET arithmetic operators.

USE IT   The following program, OperatorDemo.vb, illustrates the use of the various Visual Basic .NET arithmetic operators:

```
Module Module1

    Sub Main()
        Console.WriteLine("1 + 2 = " & 1 + 2)
        Console.WriteLine("3 - 4 = " & 3 - 4)
        Console.WriteLine("5 * 4 = " & 5 * 4)
        Console.WriteLine("25 / 4 = " & 25 / 4)
        Console.WriteLine("25 \ 4 = " & 25 \ 4)
        Console.WriteLine("25 Mod 4 = " & 25 Mod 4)
        Console.WriteLine("5 ^ 2 = " & 5 ^ 2)

        Console.ReadLine()
    End Sub

End Module
```

Operator	Purpose
+	Addition
-	Subtraction
*	Multiplication
/	Division (standard)
\	Division (integer)
Mod	Modulo (remainder)
^	Exponentiation

Table 1-4   The Visual Basic .NET Arithmetic Operators

After you compile and execute this program, your screen will display the following output:

```
1 + 2 = 3
3 - 4 = -1
5 * 4 = 20
25 / 4 = 6.25
25 \ 4 = 6
25 Mod 4 = 1
5 ^ 2 = 25
```

When your programs perform arithmetic operations, you must understand that Visual Basic .NET assigns a precedence to each operator, which controls the order in which the program will perform the operations. Assume that your program must calculate the result of the following expression:

```
Result = 5 + 3 * 2
```

If Visual Basic .NET were to perform the operations from left to right, it would calculate the result 16, which is not correct. Instead, Visual Basic .NET will first perform the multiplication operation, because the multiplication operator has a higher precedence than addition:

```
Result = 5 + 3 * 2
Result = 5 + 6
Result = 11
```

Table 1-5 illustrates the precedence of Visual Basic .NET arithmetic operators.

If based only on operator precedence, the order in which Visual Basic .NET performs arithmetic operations often will not match the order you need. Assume that your program needs to determine the sales tax (using 5% for this example) for two items priced at $10 and $20. Consider the following expression:

```
SalesTax = 10 + 20 * 0.05
```

Arithmetic Operator	Purpose
^	Exponentiation.
-	Negation.
*, /	Multiplication and division.
\	Integer division.
Mod	Remainder.
+, -	Addition and subtraction. Note that string concatenation using + has equal precedence to addition and subtraction, whereas concatenation using & has lower precedence.
And, Or, Not, Xor	Bitwise operators.

Table 1-5   Operator Precedence with Visual Basic .NET

Because the multiplication operator has a higher precedence than the addition operator, Visual Basic .NET will perform the multiplication first, which results in the following incorrect result:

```
SalesTax = 10 + 20 * 0.05
         = 10 + 10
         = 20
```

USE IT To control the order in which Visual Basic .NET performs operations, you must group operations in parentheses. When Visual Basic .NET evaluates an expression, Visual Basic .NET will perform operations that appear in parentheses first. In the previous sales tax example, you can use parentheses as follows to ensure that the program adds the first two items and then performs the multiplication on the result:

```
SalesTax = (10 + 20) * 0.05
```

In this case, the program would calculate the sales tax as follows:

```
SalesTax = (10 + 20) * 0.05
         = (30) * 0.05
         = 1.50
```

The following program, PrecedenceDemo.vb, illustrates how using parentheses to force the order of an expression's evaluation can change the result:

```
Module Module1

    Sub Main()
        Dim Expression1 As Double
        Dim Expression2 As Double
        Dim Expression3 As Double
        Dim Expression4 As Double

        Expression1 = 5 ^ 2 + 1 * 3 - 4
        Expression2 = 5 ^ (2 + 1) * 3 - 4
        Expression3 = 5 ^ (2 + 1) * (3 - 4)
        Expression4 = 5 ^ ((2 + 1) * (3 - 4))

        Console.WriteLine(Expression1)
        Console.WriteLine(Expression2)
        Console.WriteLine(Expression3)
        Console.WriteLine(Expression4)

        Console.ReadLine()
    End Sub

End Module
```

After you compile and execute this program, your screen will display the following output:

```
24
371
-125
0.008
```

Casting a Value of One Variable Type to Another

A variable's type specifies a range of values a variable can store and a set of operations a program can perform on a variable. In your programs, there will be times when you must assign a value of one type of variable to a variable of a different type. Programmers refer to such operations as "casting" the variable's type.

When you assign a value of a "smaller type," such as a value of type Short, to a larger type, such as a variable of type Integer, Visual Basic .NET can perform the assignment because the smaller variable's value can fit into the larger variable's storage capacity. Programmers refer to an assignment operation that casts the value of a variable of a smaller type to a variable of a larger type as an implicit cast.

In contrast, if you reverse the assignment and assign a value of a larger type to a smaller type, Visual Basic .NET must discard bits that represent the larger variable's value. If you assign an Integer value (which Visual Basic .NET represents using 32 bits) to a variable of type Short (which uses 16 bits), Visual Basic .NET will discard the value's upper 16 bits, which obviously can lead to erroneous results.

 For such cases when your code must assign the value of a larger type to a variable of a smaller type and you do not care that Visual Basic .NET may discard part of the larger value, your code must perform an operation that programmers call an explicit cast. To perform an explicit cast, your program must use one of the built-in functions listed in Table 1-6.

Function	Purpose
ToBoolean	Converts a value to a Boolean (True or False).
ToByte	Converts a value to an 8-bit Byte in the range 0 to 255.
ToChar	Converts a value to a 2-byte Unicode character.
ToDateTime	Converts a value to a DateTime object.
ToDecimal	Converts a value to a 12-byte Decimal.
ToDouble	Converts a value to an 8-byte Double.
ToInt16	Converts a value to a 2-byte Short.
ToInt32	Converts a value to a 4-byte Integer.

Table 1-6   Type Conversion Routines Provided in the System.Convert Namespace

Function	Purpose
ToInt64	Converts a value to an 8-byte Integer.
ToSByte	Converts a value to an 8-bit signed value in the range –128 to 127.
ToSingle	Converts a value to a 4-byte Single.
ToString	Converts a value to its String representation.
ToUInt16	Converts a value to a 2-byte unsigned Short in the range 0 to 65,535.
ToUInt32	Converts a value to a 4-byte unsigned Integer in the range 0 to 4,294,967,295.
ToUInt64	Converts a value to an 8-byte unsigned long Integer in the range 0 to 18,446,744,073,709,551,615.

Table 1-6   Type Conversion Routines Provided in the System.Convert Namespace *(continued)*

The following program, CastDemo.vb, performs two simple cast operations. The first assigns a value of type Integer to a value of type Short. The second casts a value of type Double to a value of type Single:

```
Module Module1

    Sub Main()
        Dim BigInteger As Integer = 10000
        Dim LittleInteger As Short

        Dim BigFloat As Double = 0.123456789
        Dim LittleFloat As Single

        LittleInteger = BigInteger
        LittleFloat = BigFloat

        Console.WriteLine(LittleInteger)
        Console.WriteLine(LittleFloat)

        Console.ReadLine()
    End Sub

End Module
```

After you compile and execute this program, your screen will display the following output:

```
10000
0.1234568
```

In the case of the floating-point value 0.123456789, you can see that the assignment caused the operation to lose significant digits. The Integer to Short assign, in this case, was successful because the Integer variable contained a value in the range a variable of type Short can store. If, for example, you change the program to use the value 40000, the assignment will cause the program to generate an overflow exception. So, depending on the value that the Integer variable contains, this program may or may not work.

To reduce potential errors that can occur when your programs assign a value from a larger type to a smaller type, your code can demand that the Visual Basic .NET compiler not allow such assignments by placing the following statement at the start of your programs:

```
Option Strict On
```

After you enable strict type-conversion processing, the following assignment statement would cause the Visual Basic .NET compiler to generate a syntax error:

```
LittleInteger = BigInteger
```

Making Decisions Using Conditional Operators

A program is simply a set of instructions the CPU executes to perform a specific task. The programs this chapter has presented thus far have begun their execution with the first statement and then have continued to execute statements one following another, up to and including the last statement.

As your programs perform more complex operations, your code will often perform one set of operations for a given condition and a second set for a different condition. For example, a program that implements a Web-based shopping cart would use one sales tax for customers in Texas and another for customers in New York.

Programmers refer to the process of a program making decisions about which statements to execute as conditional processing. To perform conditional processing, programs make extensive use of the If and If-Else statements.

To use an If statement, programs must specify a condition that Visual Basic .NET evaluates to either True or False. A condition might, for example, use an If statement to determine whether a user's name is "Smith" or a student's test score was greater than or equal to 90:

```
If (Username = "Smith") Then
    ' Statements to execute
End If
```

```
If (TestScore > 90) Then
    ' Statements to execute
End If
```

When Visual Basic .NET encounters the If statement, Visual Basic .NET will evaluate the corresponding condition. If the condition evaluates to True, your program will execute the statements that appear between the If and End If statements. If, instead, the condition evaluates to False, your program will not execute the statements, continuing its execution at the first statement following the End If.

Often, programs must perform one set of statements when a condition is true and a second when the condition is false. In such cases, the programs can use the If-Else statement. The following statement displays a message that tells a student that he or she passed an exam (the student passes if his or her score is greater than or equal to 70). If the student did not pass the test, the code displays a message telling the student that he or she failed:

```
If (TestScore >= 70) Then
  Console.WriteLine("You passed!")
Else
  Console.WriteLine("You failed")
End If
```

To improve a program's readability, programmers normally indent the statements that appear in constructs, such as the If and Else statements. Using indentation, a programmer, at a glance, can determine which statements relate. To simplify the indentation process, Visual Studio will automatically indent the statements you type in an If statement.

Many times, a program must evaluate a variety of conditions. For example, rather than simply telling the student whether he or she passed or failed the exam, a better program would display the student's grade based on the following. One way to display a message that corresponds to the student's grade is to use several If statements, as shown here:

```
If (TestScore >= 90) Then
  Console.WriteLine("You got an A")
End If

If (TestScore >= 80) And (TestScore < 90)
  Console.WriteLine("You got a B")
End If

If (TestScore >= 70) And (TestScore < 80)
  Console.WriteLine("You got a C")
End If

If (TestScore < 70) Then
  Console.WriteLine("You failed")
End If
```

The problem with the previous series of If statements is that regardless of the user's test score, the program must evaluate each If statement, which adds unnecessary processing. A better solution is to use a series of If-Else statements as shown here:

```
If TestScore >= 90 Then
  Console.WriteLine("Test grade: A")
ElseIf TestScore >= 80 Then
  Console.WriteLine("Test grade: B")
```

```
ElseIf TestScore >= 70 Then
  Console.WriteLine("Test grade: C")
Else
  Console.WriteLine("Test grade: F")
End If
```

USE IT The following program, IfDemo.vb, illustrates the use of several different If and If-Else statements:

```
Module Module1

    Sub Main()
        Dim TestScore As Integer = 80

        If TestScore >= 90 Then
            Console.WriteLine("Test grade: A")
        ElseIf TestScore >= 80 Then
            Console.WriteLine("Test grade: B")
        ElseIf TestScore >= 70 Then
            Console.WriteLine("Test grade: C")
        Else
            Console.WriteLine("Test grade: F")
        End If

        Dim Language As String = "English"

        If (Language = "English") Then
            Console.WriteLine("Hello, world!")
        ElseIf (Language = "Spanish") Then
            Console.WriteLine("Hola, mundo")
        End If

        If (Now.Hour < 12) Then
            Console.WriteLine("Good morning")
        ElseIf (Now.Hour < 18) Then
            Console.WriteLine("Good day")
        Else
            Console.WriteLine("Good evening")
        End If
```

```
        Console.ReadLine()
    End Sub

End Module
```

After you compile and execute this program, your screen will display output similar to the following:

```
Test grade: B
Hello, world!
Good morning
```

Take time to experiment with this program by changing the values the program assigns to the TestScore and Language variables.

Taking a Closer Look at the Visual Basic .NET Relational and Logical Operators

In a condition, such as the test for an If or While statement, programs use relational operators to compare one value to another. Using relational operators, an If statement can test if one value is greater than, equal to, or less than another value. The result of the condition's test is always a Boolean (True or False) result. Table 1-7 briefly describes the Visual Basic .NET relational operators.

Depending on the condition a program examines, there are many times when a program must test two or more relationships. An If statement might test if a user's age is greater than or equal to 21 and

Operator	Relational Comparison
>	Greater than
<	Less than
>=	Greater than or equal to
<=	Less than or equal to
=	Equal
<>	Not equal
Like	Tests whether a string matches a specified pattern

Table 1-7 The Visual Basic .NET Relational Operators

if the user lives in the United States. To test two more or conditions, programs use logical operators. Visual Basic .NET supports the And, Or, Xor, and Not relational operators.

USE IT The following program, ConditionDemo.vb, illustrates the use of the And, Or, and Not logical operators:

```
Module Module1

    Sub Main()
        Dim OwnsAPet As Boolean = False
        Dim OwnsADog As Boolean = True
        Dim OwnsACat As Boolean = True

        If (Not OwnsAPet) Then
            Console.WriteLine("You need a pet")
        End If

        If (OwnsADog Or OwnsACat) Then
            Console.WriteLine("Dogs and Cats are great")
        End If

        If (OwnsADog And OwnsACat) Then
            Console.WriteLine("Do the dog and cat get along?")
        End If

        Console.ReadLine()
    End Sub

End Module
```

After you compile and execute this program, your screen will display the following output:

```
You need a pet
Dogs and Cats are great
Do the dog and cat get along?
```

Take time to experiment with this program by changing the True and False values the program assigns to each variable and then run the program to see how the change affects each condition.

Handling Multiple Conditions Using Select

USE IT When programmers discuss conditional processing, they often focus their solutions on If and If-Else statements. Visual Basic .NET, however, provides the Select control structure (construct) that your programs can use to simplify the code you must write to handle complex conditions. At first glance, the Select statement looks quite similar to a series of If-Else statements. For example, the following Select statement displays a message based on the current day of the week:

```
Dim DayOfWeek As Integer
DayOfWeek = Now.DayOfWeek

Select Case DayOfWeek
  Case 0
    Console.WriteLine("Sunday")
  Case 1
    Console.WriteLine("Monday")
  Case 2
    Console.WriteLine("Tuesday")
  Case 3
    Console.WriteLine("Wednesday")
  Case 4
    Console.WriteLine("Thursday")
  Case 5
    Console.WriteLine("Friday")
  Case 6
    Console.WriteLine("Saturday")
End Select
```

Using a Select statement, you can also specify a condition and a series of possible matching results. The following Select statement determines and displays a user's grades:

```
Dim TestScore As Integer
TestScore = 84

Select Case TestScore
  Case Is >= 90
    Console.WriteLine("Grade: A")
  Case Is >= 80
```

```
      Console.WriteLine("Grade: B")
   Case Is >= 70
      Console.WriteLine("Grade: C")
   Case Else
      Console.WriteLine("Grade: F")
End Select
```

As you can see, when you specify a condition in a Select statement, you must use the Is keyword. Also note that the Select statement supports an Else case that it executes when none of the specified cases match the selected value. In addition to using a condition in a Select statement as just shown, you can also specify a range of matching values, as shown here:

```
Dim TestScore As Integer
TestScore = 84

Select Case TestScore
   Case 90 To 100
      Console.WriteLine("Grade: A")
   Case 80 To 89
      Console.WriteLine("Grade: B")
   Case 70 To 79
      Console.WriteLine("Grade: C")
   Case Else
      Console.WriteLine("Grade: F")
End Select
```

In the first example, you learned how to use a Select statement to match one value. Depending on the processing your program performs, there may be times when you want to perform the same processing for a range of values. The following Select statement displays messages based on the current day. For several days of the week, the code displays the same message:

```
Dim DayOfWeek As Integer
DayOfWeek = Now.DayOfWeek

Select Case DayOfWeek
   Case 0, 6
      Console.WriteLine("Enjoy the weekend")
   Case 1, 2, 3
      Console.WriteLine("Too many days until the weekend")
   Case 4, 5
      Console.WriteLine("Almost the weekend!")
End Select
```

Repeating a Series of Instructions

Just as there may be times when your programs must perform conditional processing in order to make decisions, there will also be times when your programs must perform one or more statements as long as a specific condition is true, or you may want the statements to execute a specific number of times. Programmers refer to such repetitive processing as iterative processing. Visual Basic .NET provides four iterative constructions your programs can use to repeat one or more statements: the For, While, For Each, and Do While loops.

The For loop exists to let your programs repeat one or more statements a specific number of times. The following statement uses a For loop to display the numbers 1 to 5 on the screen using Console.WriteLine:

```
Dim I As Integer

For I = 1 To 5
   Console.WriteLine(I)
Next
```

When this loop executes, your screen would display the following output:

```
1
2
3
4
5
```

The For loop consists of three parts. The first part of the statement initializes the loop's control variable. The second part compares the control variable to an ending condition. The third part is optional and specifies the amount by which the loop increments or decrements the control variable with each iteration. The following loop displays the numbers 0, 10, 20, ... to 100 by incrementing the control variable by 10 with each iteration:

```
For I = 0 To 100 Step 10
   Console.WriteLine(I)
Next
```

When your programs use a For loop, Visual Basic .NET does not restrict you to using only counting numbers. You can also use variables of type Single and Double as a loop's control variable. The following statements use a For loop to display values 0.0 to 1.0 by incrementing the loop's control variable by 0.1 with each iteration:

```
Dim X As Double
For X = 0.0 To 1.0 Step 0.1
  Console.WriteLine(X)
Next
```

By using a negative step value, a For loop can move downward through a range of values. The following statements loop through the values 100 down to 0, decrementing the step value by 10 with each iteration:

```
For I = 100 To 0 Step -10
   Console.WriteLine(I)
Next
```

In contrast to the For loop, which repeats one or more statements a specific number of times, the While loop repeats statements as long as a specific condition is true. In your programs, you might use a While loop to read and display lines of a file. In this case, the statements in the loop would continue to read and display the file's content while (as long as) the file contains content the program has not yet read and displayed (meaning, you have not yet reached the end of the file). Or you might use a While loop to display and respond to a user menu's option selections until the user chooses the Quit option. The format of the While loop is as follows:

```
While (Condition)
   ' Statements to repeat
End While
```

Note that unlike previous versions of Visual Basic that used the Wend statement to mark the end of a While loop, Visual Basic .NET uses End While.

The For Each statement lets you repeat one or more statements for each element of an array. The following statements use a For Each statement to display the names of files that reside in the current directory:

```
Dim Files As String() = Directory.GetFiles(".")
Dim Filename As String

For Each Filename In Files
   Console.WriteLine(Filename)
Next
```

Finally, the Do loop is similar to the While loop in that it lets your programs repeat one or more statements while a specific condition is met. However, unlike the While loop, which places the test at the start of the loop, the Do loop places the test at the end of the loop. This means the statements a Do loop contains will always execute at least one time:

```
Do
   ' Statements to repeat
Loop While (Condition)
```

USE IT   The following program, LoopDemos.vb, uses the For, While, and Do While loops to iterate through a range of values. Then the code uses the For Each loop to display the names of files in the current directory:

```
Imports System.IO

Module Module1

    Sub Main()
        Dim I As Integer

        For I = 0 To 10
            Console.Write(I & " ")
        Next

        Console.WriteLine()

        Dim X As Double = 0.0      ← initialize
        While (X < 100)            ← condition
            Console.Write(X & " ")
            X = X + 25             ← incrementation.
        End While

        Console.WriteLine()

        Do
            Console.Write(X & " ")
            X = X - 10
        Loop While (X < 0)

        Console.WriteLine()

        Dim Files As String() = Directory.GetFiles(".")
        Dim Filename As String

        For Each Filename In Files
            Console.WriteLine(Filename)
        Next
        Console.ReadLine()
    End Sub
End Module
```

After you compile and execute this program, your screen will display the following output:

```
0 1 2 3 4 5 6 7 8 9 10
0 25 50 75
100
.\LoopDemo.exe
.\LoopDemo.pdb
```

Avoiding Infinite Loops

Iterative constructs such as the For and While statements exist to let your programs repeat a series of statements a specific number of times or as long as a specific condition is true. When your program uses iterative constructs, there may be times when a loop does not end (normally because of a programming error). Programmers refer to unending loops as infinite loops, because unless you can end the program by closing the program window, the loop will continue to execute forever. The goal of the following While loop, for example, is to display the values 0 through 99. However, if you examine the loop, you will find that it does not increment the variable I. As a result, after the loop starts, the loop will reach its ending condition (I equal to 100), so the code will repeat forever:

```
Dim I As Integer = 0

While I < 100
  Console.WriteLine(I)
End While
```

USE IT   To reduce the possibility of an infinite loop in your programs, you should examine each loop to ensure that the loop correctly performs the following four steps:

1. Initializes a control variable

2. Tests the control variable's value

3. Executes the loop's statements

4. Modifies the control variable

You can remember these four steps using the ITEM (Initialize, Test, Execute, Modify) acronym. Consider the previous While loop. The code initializes the variable I when it declares the variable. Then the first statement of the While loop tests the control variable. In the While loop, the code executes the Console.WriteLine statement. However, the code does not modify the control variable in the loop, which leads to the infinite loop.

Executing a Loop Prematurely

In a Visual Basic .NET program, loops let your code repeat a set of instructions a specific number of times or while a specific condition is met. Ideally, a loop should have one condition that determines if the code will perform (and later repeat) the loop's statements. In a For loop, the loop's processing ends when the loop's control variable's value is greater than the loop's ending value.

USE IT   That said, there may be times when your code must terminate a For loop's (or a For Each loop's) processing prematurely. In such cases, your code can use the Exit For statement, which directs Visual Basic .NET to end the loop's processing and to continue the program's execution at the first statement that follows the For statement (the first statement that follows Next). In a similar way, to exit a While loop prematurely, your code can execute the Exit While statement.

▶ **NOTE**

Later in this chapter, you will examine subroutines that let you group a set of related statements that perform a specific task. Normally, a subroutine will execute its statements in succession, from the first statement to the last. However, there may be times when you must end a subroutine's processing prematurely. In such cases, your code can issue the Exit Sub statement. However, as is the case of the For and While loops, to improve the readability of your code, you should avoid using Exit statements whenever possible.

Visual Basic .NET Supports Lazy Evaluation to Improve Performance

When your programs perform conditional and iterative processing, you can improve your program's performance by changing the way that Visual Basic .NET handles conditions that use the logical And and Or operators. In statements such as the If, Select, and While statements, your programs can use the logical And operator to specify two conditions that must evaluate to True before the program will perform the corresponding statements. The following statement uses the logical And operator to test if the employee is a programmer and if the programmer knows how to program using Visual Basic .NET:

```
If (UserIsProgrammer) And (UserKnowsVB) Then
   ' Statements
End If
```

Normally, when your code uses logical operators to evaluate a condition, Visual Basic will examine each part of the condition and then determine whether the condition is true. However, in the case of the And operator, if the first half of a condition evaluates to False, you know the entire condition will be False. In a similar way, in the case of the Or operator, if the first part of a condition evaluates to True, you know the entire condition will be True. To improve performance, you can take advantage of the AndAlso and OrElse operators. The AndAlso operator directs Visual Basic .NET to only evaluate the second part of a condition if the first part evaluates as a True. The OrElse operator directs Visual Basic .NET to evaluate the second part of a condition that uses OrElse should the first part of the condition evaluate to False.

 The following program, LazyEvaluation.vb, illustrates the use of AndAlso and OrElse operators:

```
Module Module1
    Sub Main()
        Dim OwnsDog As Boolean = True
        Dim OwnsCat As Boolean = False

        If OwnsDog AndAlso OwnsCat Then
            Console.WriteLine("Owns both a dog and a cat")
        End If
```

```
        If OwnsDog OrElse OwnsCat Then
            Console.WriteLine("Owns a dog or cat--maybe both")
        End If

        Console.ReadLine()
    End Sub
End Module
```

You may be wondering why Visual Basic .NET does not simply use lazy evaluation all the time. The reason is that there may be times when not executing the second half of a condition can introduce errors. Consider the following If statement that calls a function in each of the conditions:

```
If (IsAfterBusinessHours() And BuildingIsSecure()) Then
```

Depending on the processing the BuildingIsSecure function performs, you may not want the program to skip the function's execution simply because the IsAfterBusinessHours function returns a False result (which would end the statement's execution if you use lazy evaluation).

Wrapping Long Statements

As you examine the programs this book's Tips present, there will be many times when the code wraps a long statement onto two or more lines because of the limitations of the printed page. As you program, there may be times when you will want to wrap a long statement onto the next line so you do not have to continually scroll horizontally to see the program statements.

USE IT   To wrap a statement to the next line, you must place a space followed by an underscore (_) character at the end of the line, as shown here:

```
SomeVeryLargeVariableName = SomeLongSubroutineName(ParameterOne, _
    ParameterTwo, ParameterThree, ParameterFour)
```

Often, programmers will wrap long character strings over two or more lines. To wrap a character string, you must break the string into multiple strings, so that one string ends at the point you want to wrap the line and a new string begins at the location you want on the following line. Between each of the strings, you place the concatenation operator (&) as shown here:

```
Console.Writeline("The title of the book is: Visual Basic .Net" & _
    " Programming Tips and Techniques")
```

When you wrap a string in this way, you must remember to place a space character at either the end of one string or at the start of the new string if the strings were originally separated by a space.

Taking Advantage of the Visual Basic Assignment Operators

In programs, it is common to perform an arithmetic operation that uses a variable's current value and then assigns the result of the operation back to the variable. The following statement adds the value 1 to the variable Counter:

```
Counter = Counter + 1
```

USE IT To simplify operations that use a variable's value in an expression and then assign the result back to the variable, Visual Basic .NET provides the set of assignment operators listed in Table 1-8.

The following statement uses the addition assignment operator to increment the value of the Counter variable by 1:

```
Counter += 1
```

The following program, AssignmentDemo.vb, illustrates the use of the Visual Basic .NET assignment operators:

```
Module Module1

    Sub Main()
        Dim A As Integer

        A = 0
        A += 10
        Console.WriteLine("A += 10 yields " & A)

        A -= 5
        Console.WriteLine("A -=5 yields " & A)

        A *= 3
        Console.WriteLine("A *= 3 yields " & A)

        A /= 5
        Console.WriteLine("A /= 5 yields " & A)

        A ^= 2
        Console.WriteLine("A ^= 2 yields " & A)

        Console.ReadLine()
    End Sub

End Module
```

Operator	Purpose
+=	Adds the specified expression to a variable's current value.
-=	Subtracts the specified expression from a variable's current value.
*=	Multiplies a variable's current value by the specified expression and assigns the result back to the variable.
/= and \=	Divides a variable's value contents by the specified expression and assigns the result back to the variable.
^=	Raises a variable's current value to the power of the specified expression and assigns the result back to the variable.
&=	Concatenates the String to a variable's value and assigns the result back to the variable.

Table 1-8　The Visual Basic .NET Assignment Operators

After you compile and execute this program, your screen will display the following output:

```
A += 10 yields 10
A -=5 yields 5
A *= 3 yields 15
A /= 5 yields 3
A ^= 2 yields 9
```

Commenting Your Program Code

As you program, you should place comments throughout your code that explain the processing your program performs or a specific variable's use. Later, you or another programmer who is reviewing the code can read the comments to quickly understand the processing. To place a comment in a Visual Basic .NET program, you place a single quote on a line followed by the comment text. The Visual Basic .NET compiler will ignore any text that appears to the right of the single quote, treating the text as a comment.

USE IT　In a program, you can place comments on their own lines or to the right of a statement:

```
' The following subroutine displays the current date and time
Sub ShowDateTime()
  Console.WriteLine(Now())   'Now returns the current date and time
End Sub
```

As you test your programs, there may be times when you will want to disable one or more statements. Rather than removing the statements from your code, you can simply place the single-quote character in front of the statement. When Visual Basic .NET compiles your program, it will ignore the statement, which it will treat as a comment. If you later want the program to execute the statement, you can simply remove the single quote:

```
Console.WriteLine("This line will appear")
' Console.WriteLine("This line will not")
```

Reading Keyboard Input Using Console.Read and Console.ReadLine

When you create a console application, your programs can read keyboard input from the user using the Console.Read and Console.ReadLine methods. The difference between the methods is that Console.ReadLine returns all the characters up to the ENTER key, whereas Console.Read reads characters up to the first whitespace character, such as a space or tab. To assign the value a user types to a variable, you use the assignment operator as follows:

```
VariableName = Console.ReadLine()
```

Many of the Tips this book presents place the statement Console.ReadLine() at the end of the program code. When you run a console application in Visual Studio, the console window will immediately close after the program completes its processing. By placing the Console.ReadLine() statement at the end of the code, the program will pause, waiting for the user to press the ENTER key, before the program ends and the window closes.

USE IT The following program, KeyboardInputDemo.vb, illustrates the use of the Console.Read and Console.ReadLine methods:

```
Module Module1

    Sub Main()
        Dim Age As Integer
        Dim FirstName As String
        Dim Salary As Double

        Console.Write("Age: ")
        Age = Console.ReadLine()

        Console.Write("Name: ")
        FirstName = Console.ReadLine()

        Console.Write("Salary: ")
        Salary = Console.ReadLine()
        Console.WriteLine(Age & " " & FirstName & " " & Salary)
```

```
        Console.Write("Enter Age, Name Salary: ")
        Age = Console.Read()
        FirstName = Console.Read()
        Salary = Console.ReadLine()
        Console.WriteLine(Age & " " & FirstName & " " & Salary)
    End Sub

End Module
```

Take time to experiment with the program. You will find that if you type a value that does not correspond to the data type the program expects (such as if the program prompts for an age and you type your name instead), the program will generate an exception and will end. Chapter 9 examines exception processing in detail. To avoid such errors, many programs will read all keyboard input into character strings and then convert the string to an Integer or Double value as required.

Displaying a Message in a Message Box

Normally, console-based applications will display output to the console window using the Console.Write and Console.WriteLine methods. Likewise, a Windows-based program will display output using one or more controls that appear on a form. Both console- and Windows-based applications, however, can use a message box, similar to that shown here, to display a message to the user and to get a user's button response (such as OK or Cancel).

For years, Visual Basic programmers have used the MsgBox function to display a message box to the user:

```
MsgBox("Hello, User")
```

Although Visual Basic .NET supports the MsgBox function, most newer Windows-based programs will use the MessageBox class Show method to display a message box (as it turns out, behind the scenes, the MsgBox function itself calls MessageBox.Show):

```
MessageBox.Show("Hello, User")
```

To determine which message-box button a user selects, you assign the result of the MessageBox.Show (or MsgBox) method to a variable, as shown here:

```
VariableName = MessageBox.Show("Message", "Title", _
   MessageBoxButtons.OKCancel)
```

 The following program, MsgBoxDemo.vb, illustrates the use of the MsgBox function in a console application:

```
Module Module1
  Sub Main()
    MsgBox("Message")
    MsgBox("Message", MsgBoxStyle.AbortRetryIgnore, "Title")
  End Sub
End Module
```

The following program, MessageBoxDemo.vb, illustrates the use of the various message box types:

```
Public Class Form1
    Inherits System.Windows.Forms.Form

#Region " Windows Form Designer generated code "
    ' Code not shown
#End Region

  Private Sub Form1_Load(ByVal sender As System.Object, _
    ByVal e As System.EventArgs) Handles MyBase.Load
      MessageBox.Show("Message")
      MessageBox.Show("Message", "Title")
      MessageBox.Show("Message", "Title", MessageBoxButtons.OKCancel)
      MessageBox.Show("Message", "Title", _
        MessageBoxButtons.AbortRetryIgnore, MessageBoxIcon.Warning)
      Me.Close()
  End Sub
End Class
```

Prompting the User for Input Using an Input Box

Normally, console-based applications will get keyboard input from the user using the Console.Readline method. Likewise, Windows-based applications usually get input using one or more form-based controls. That said, both application types can use the InputBox function to prompt the user for input, as shown in Figure 1-7. Using the InputBox function, your code can assign the value the user enters to a variable, as shown here:

```
VariableName = InputBox("Enter name")
```

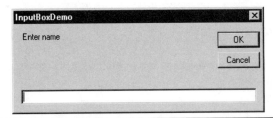

Figure 1-7   Using an input box to prompt the user for input

USE IT   Using the InputBox function, you can pass parameters that specify the prompt the box displays, the box title, as well as the x and y offsets (from the upper-left corner of the screen) at which the box appears. The following program, InputBoxDemo.vb, illustrates the use of the InputBox function:

```
Module Module1

    Sub Main()
        Dim Name As String
        Dim Age As Integer
        Dim Salary As Double

        Name = InputBox("Enter name")
        Age = InputBox("Enter age", 21)
        Salary = InputBox("Enter salary")

        Console.WriteLine(Name)
        Console.WriteLine(Age)
        Console.WriteLine(Salary)
        Console.ReadLine()
    End Sub

End Module
```

Again, when you use the InputBox function, the user must enter the value in the format that matches the type to which you are assigning a result. If, for example, you assign the result to an Integer value and the user enters a nonnumeric value, the program will generate an exception. Chapter 9 examines exceptions in detail. To avoid such errors, programs normally assign the InputBox result to a String variable and then convert that value to the format that matches the target variable's type.

Breaking a Programming Task into Manageable Pieces

As programs become larger and more complex, programmers often break the program into smaller, more manageable pieces of code, each of which performs a specific task. To organize the program statements by task, programmers use functions and subroutines.

The difference between a function and a subroutine is that after a function performs its processing, the function returns a value (a result) and a subroutine does not. For example, the MessageBox.Show function displays a dialog box and then returns a value that corresponds to the user's button selection. To use the function's return value, your code normally assigns the result to a variable, as shown here:

```
Variable = SomeFunctionName(OptionalParameters)
```

To create a subroutine, your code uses the keyword Sub, followed by a unique name (that should correspond to the processing the subroutine performs), followed by parentheses that contain optional variables that will store values the program passes to the subroutine (which programmers call parameters). If the subroutine does not use parameters, you will simply place empty parentheses after the subroutine name. Next, you place the statements that correspond to the processing the subroutine performs followed by the End Sub statement, as shown here:

```
Sub SubroutineName()
  ' Statements here
End Sub
```

The following statements create a subroutine named GreetUser that displays messages to the user using the Console.WriteLine method:

```
Sub GreetUser()
  Console.WriteLine("Hello, user")
  Console.WriteLine("The current date and time is: " & Now())
  Console.WriteLine("Have a nice day.")
End Sub
```

To use a subroutine in your program, you place the subroutine name, followed by the parentheses in your program code, as shown here:

```
GreetUser()
```

Programmers refer to the process of using a subroutine as "calling the subroutine." When your program encounters a subroutine call, your program will jump to the statements the subroutine contains. After the program completes the subroutine's processing, your program will resume its processing with the statement in your code that follows the subroutine call.

▶ **NOTE**

Visual Basic .NET no longer supports the GoSub statement which programmers used for many years to call a subroutine.

As your programs become larger, it is likely that they will contain many subroutines. A word processing program, for example, might use one subroutine to spell-check a document, another to save the document's contents to a file on disk, and yet another to print the document. In a console-based application, the program's execution will always begin with the first statement that appears in the subroutine called Main. (You can think of the Main subroutine as containing your main or primary program statements). From within the Main subroutine, your code can call other subroutines.

The following program, SubDemo.vb, creates and calls several subroutines:

```
Module Module1

    Sub ShowBookInformation()
        Console.WriteLine("Title: Visual Basic .Net " & _
            "Programming Tips & Techniques")
        Console.WriteLine("Author: Jamsa")
        Console.WriteLine("Publisher: McGraw-Hill/Osborne")
        Console.WriteLine("Price: 49.99")
    End Sub

    Sub GreetInEnglish()
        Console.WriteLine("Hello, world")
    End Sub

    Sub GreetInSpanish()
        Console.WriteLine("Hola, mundo")
    End Sub

    Sub ShowTime()
        Console.WriteLine("Current time is: " & Now)
    End Sub

    Sub Main()
        ShowTime()
        GreetInEnglish()
        GreetInSpanish()
        ShowBookInformation()
        Console.ReadLine()
    End Sub

End Module
```

As you can see, the program defines four subroutines, placing the statements for each between the Sub and End Sub statements. When the program runs, Visual Basic .NET will begin the program's execution in the subroutine named Main—a console application will always begin its execution in Main. When the program encounters the ShowTime subroutine call, the program will jump to the statements the ShowTime subroutine contains, which in this case is the Console.WriteLine statement that displays the current date and time. Then, after the subroutine completes its processing, the program will resume its execution back in Main at the first statement that follows the ShowTime subroutine call—the call to the GreetInEnglish subroutine. Again, the program will branch its execution to the statements the subroutine contains. The program will continue this process of calling a subroutine and then returning to Main until the program completes its statements.

After you compile and execute this program, your screen will display the following output:

```
Current time is: 4/9/2002 10:46:47 AM
Hello, world
Hola, mundo
Title: Visual Basic .Net Programming Tips & Techniques
Author: Jamsa
Publisher: McGraw-Hill/Osborne
Price: 49.99
```

As briefly discussed, a function differs from a subroutine in that, after the function completes its processing, the function will return a value that your programs can assign to a variable or use in an expression. In Chapter 5, you will examine the arithmetic functions provided by the Math class. The following statements illustrate the use of several of the Math class functions:

```
Dim SomeValue, SomeAngle As Double

SomeValue = Math.Sqrt(100)
SomeAngle = Math.Acos(2.225)
```

When the program encounters the Math.Sqrt function call, the program will branch its execution to the corresponding program statements. After the function completes its processing, the program will assign the value the function returns to the SomeValue variable. Then the program will continue its execution with the next statement, which in this case, calls the Math class Acos function.

To create a function, you use the Function keyword followed by a unique function name and parentheses that optionally declare variables to hold values the program passes to the function. You must also then specify the Returns keyword followed by the type (such as Integer or String) of the value the function returns. You place the function statements between the function header (which programmers also refer to as the function signature) and the End Function statement, as shown here:

```
Function UniqueFunctionName(OptionalParameters) As FunctionReturnType
    ' Function statements go here
End Function
```

The following statements create a function named GetBookPrice, which returns a value of type Double:

```
Function GetBookPrice() As Double
   ' Function statements go here
End Function
```

To return a value, a function can use the Return statement, or the function can assign the value to its own name. In a function named GetBookPrice, the following statements both return the value 49.99:

```
Return 49.99
```

```
GetBookPrice = 49.99
```

To call a function in your program code, you must specify the function name followed by the parentheses and optional parameters. Normally, your code will assign the function's result to a variable as shown here:

```
Dim Price As Double
```

```
Price = GetBookPrice()
```

However, you can use the value a function returns in any expression, such as A = B + SomeFunction(), or in a call to Console.WriteLine, as shown here:

```
Console.WriteLine("The price is: " & GetBookPrice())
```

The following program, FunctionDemo.vb, creates two functions, one that returns value of type Double and one that returns a String. The program first calls each function, assigning the value the function returns to a variable. Then the program calls each function from within a Console.WriteLine statement, displaying the value the function returns. Finally, the code uses the GetBookPrice function in an If statement:

```
Module Module1
    Function GetBookPrice() As Double
        GetBookPrice = 49.99
    End Function

    Function GetBookTitle() As String
        GetBookTitle = "Visual Basic .Net Programming Tips & Techniques"
    End Function

    Sub Main()
        Dim Price As Double
        Dim Title As String
```

```
        Price = GetBookPrice()
        Title = GetBookTitle()

        Console.WriteLine(Price)
        Console.WriteLine(Title)

        Console.WriteLine(GetBookPrice())
        Console.WriteLine(GetBookTitle())

        If (GetBookPrice() = 49.99) Then
            Console.WriteLine("The book is 49.99")
        End If

        Console.ReadLine()
    End Sub

End Module
```

After you compile and execute this program, your screen will display the following output:

```
49.99
Visual Basic .Net Programming Tips & Techniques
49.99
Visual Basic .Net Programming Tips & Techniques
The book is 49.99
```

▶ **NOTE**

As you read Visual Basic .NET books, you will often find that books use the terms function, subroutine, and method interchangeably. Keep in mind that a function differs from a subroutine in that the function returns a result. The term method is a general term that describes functions and subroutines that appear in a class. Chapter 3 discusses class variables in detail.

Passing Parameters to a Function or Subroutine

In a program, functions and subroutines exist to organize statements that perform a specific task. Often, to perform its processing, a function or subroutine will require that program pass it one or more values. The values a program passes to a function or subroutine are called parameters. Earlier in this chapter, for example, you passed values to the Console.WriteLine method for display:

```
Console.WriteLine("Values are {0}, {1}, {3}", 100, 200, 300)
Console.Writeline("The price is: " & GetBookPrice())
```

Similarly, your programs have passed values to the MessageBox.Show method:

```
MessageBox.Show("Hello, World")
```

To pass values to a subroutine or function, you must place the values in the parentheses that follow the routine's name, separating the values with a comma. Before a function or subroutine can use the values, the routine must declare variables in which Visual Basic .NET will place the values when the program calls the routine. You declare the variables between the parentheses that follow the function or subroutine name when you create the routine. The following statements create a subroutine called Greeting that lets programs pass a message (a parameter) to the routine that the subroutine will display:

```
Sub Greeting(ByVal Message As String)
   Console.WriteLine("Hello, user")
   Console.WriteLine("Today's message is: " & Message)
End Sub
```

To support parameters, you must declare a variable in the subroutine or function header that will hold the parameter's value as the function executes. In this case, the subroutine declares a Variable named Message of type String. For now, you can ignore the ByVal keyword, which you will examine in the following Tip. In the program code, you would call the Greeting subroutine as follows:

```
Greeting("Have a great day")
```

When a function or subroutine supports parameters, your program must pass the correct number and type of parameters to the routine. If a function expects a parameter of type Double, and your program passes a String value to the function, an error will occur. Likewise, if a routine expects three parameter values, your program must pass three parameters to the routine in the order the parameter expects the values.

The following program, ThreeSubs.vb, declares different subroutines, each of which uses a different number and type of parameter:

```
Module Module1
    Sub OneValue(ByVal Name As String)
        Console.WriteLine("Hello, " & Name)
    End Sub

    Sub TwoValues(ByVal Age As Integer, ByVal Name As String)
        Console.WriteLine("Age: " & Age)
        Console.WriteLine("Name: " & Name)
    End Sub

    Sub ThreeValues(ByVal Name As String, ByVal Age As Integer, _
        ByVal Salary As Double)
        Console.WriteLine("Name: " & Name)
        Console.WriteLine("Age: " & Age)
```

```
            Console.WriteLine("Salary: " & Salary)
        End Sub

        Sub Main()
            OneValue("Mr. Gates")
            Console.WriteLine()
            TwoValues(50, "Mr. Gates")
            Console.WriteLine()
            ThreeValues("Mr. Gates", 50, 250000.0)
            Console.ReadLine()
        End Sub

End Module
```

After you compile and execute this program, your screen will display the following output:

```
Hello, Mr. Gates

Age: 50
Name: Mr. Gates

Name: Mr. Gates
Age: 50
Salary: 250000
```

Declaring Local Variables in a Function or Subroutine

Depending on the processing a function or subroutine performs, there will be many times when the routine will require one or more variables to store values as the routine's statements execute. In a function or subroutine, you can declare variables, which programmers refer to as local variables, following the subroutine or function heading, as shown here:

```
Sub SomeFunction()
  Dim I As Integer
  Dim Sum As Double

  ' Statements go here
End Sub
```

Programmers refer to a subroutine or function's variables as "local" because the fact that the variables exist and the values the variables contain are known only to the function or subroutine. The code outside of the function or subroutine does not know about the routine's local variables, nor can the code use them. Because the variables are local, the names you use for the variables will not conflict with variables you have defined in other functions or subroutines.

The following program, LocalVarDemo.vb, defines local variables in a subroutine and function. Although the variables use the same names in each routine, the local variables are distinct and the values your code assigns to the variables in one routine do not affect the values of the variables in another:

```vb
Module Module1

    Sub YahooInfo()
        Dim Name As String = "Yahoo"
        Dim Price As Double = 17.45
        Dim I As Integer = 1001

        Console.WriteLine("In YahooInfo")
        Console.WriteLine("Name: " & Name)
        Console.WriteLine("Price: " & Price)
        Console.WriteLine("I: " & I)
    End Sub

    Sub BookInfo()
        Dim Name As String = "C# Programming Tips & Techniques"
        Dim Price As Double = 49.99
        Dim I As Integer = 0

        Console.WriteLine("In BookInfo")
        Console.WriteLine("Name: " & Name)
        Console.WriteLine("Price: " & Price)
        Console.WriteLine("I: " & I)
    End Sub

    Sub Main()
        YahooInfo()
        Console.WriteLine()
        BookInfo()
        Console.ReadLine()
    End Sub

End Module
```

After you compile and execute this program, your screen will display the following output:

```
In YahooInfo
Name: Yahoo
Price: 17.45
I: 1001


In BookInfo
```

```
Name: C# Programming Tips & Techniques
Price: 49.99
I: 0
```

Changing a Parameter's Value in a Subroutine

In the Tip titled "Passing Parameters to a Function or Subroutine," you learned how to pass a parameter to a function or subroutine. In each of the examples the Tip presented, the routines used, but did not change, the values of the parameters the routines received. Depending on the processing a subroutine or function performs, there may be times when you will want the subroutine to change a parameter's value. If you examine the previous functions and subroutines, you will find that each routine preceded its parameter declarations with the ByVal keyword:

```
Sub SomeSubroutineName(ByVal A As Integer)
```

The ByVal keyword specifies that Visual Basic .NET will pass the parameter to the function by value which means, when your program calls the routine, Visual Basic .NET will make a copy of the value the parameter contains. Then Visual Basic .NET will pass the copy of the value to the routine as opposed to the original variable. When you pass a parameter by value in this way, a subroutine or function cannot make a change to the parameter value that remains in effect after the routine ends. Consider the following program, ByValueDemo.vb, that passes the value of the Number parameter to a subroutine. In the subroutine, the code changes and displays the parameters value. After the subroutine ends and the program's execution resumes in the Main subroutine, the value of the variable number is unchanged from its original value of 100. That's because changes to a parameter that a program passes to a subroutine or function by value only remain in effect for the duration of the routine's processing:

```
Module Module1

    Sub NoChangeToParameter(ByVal A As Integer)
        A = 1001
        Console.WriteLine("Value of A in subroutine " & A)
    End Sub

    Sub Main()
        Dim Number As Integer = 100

        Console.WriteLine("Number before function call: " & Number)
        NoChangeToParameter(Number)
        Console.WriteLine("Number before function call: " & Number)
        Console.ReadLine()
    End Sub

End Module
```

After you compile and execute this program, your screen will display the following output:

```
Number before function call: 100
Value of A in subroutine 1001
Number before function call: 100
```

USE IT   In order for a subroutine or function to change the value of a variable you pass to the routine as a parameter, the routine must know the variable's memory location (so the routine can use the memory location to replace the value the variable stores). To provide the routine with the address of the parameter, you must pass the parameter to the routine by reference. To do so, you precede the parameter variable name with the ByRef keyword. The following program, ByRefDemo.vb, passes a parameter by reference to the subroutine named ParameterChange. In the subroutine, the code changes and then displays the parameter's value. However, because the program passes the value by reference, the change to the value remains in effect after the subroutine ends:

```
Module Module1

    Sub ParameterChange(ByRef A As Integer)
        A = 1001
        Console.WriteLine("Value of A in subroutine " & A)
    End Sub

    Sub Main()
        Dim Number As Integer = 100

        Console.WriteLine("Number before function call: " & Number)
        ParameterChange(Number)
        Console.WriteLine("Number before function call: " & Number)
        Console.ReadLine()
    End Sub

End Module
```

After you compile and execute this program, your screen will display the following output:

```
Number before function call: 100
Value of A in subroutine 1001
Number before function call: 1001
```

Using Scope to Understand the Locations in a Program Where a Variable Has Meaning

In a Visual Basic .NET program, you can declare variables in functions and subroutines, as parameters to a function or subroutine, or in a construct such as an If or While statement. Depending on where you declare a variable, the location in your program where the variable has meaning (in other words, the statements in your program where you can use the variable) will differ. Programmers refer to the program areas where a variable is known to the program as the variable's scope.

Assume that you have two subroutines that each use a variable named Counter, as shown here:

```
Sub BigLoop()
  Dim Counter As Integer

  For Counter = 1000 To 10000
    Console.WriteLine(Counter)
  Next
End Sub

Sub LittleLoop()
  Dim Counter As Integer

  For Counter = 0 To 5
    Console.WriteLine(Counter)
  Next
End Sub
```

When you declare a local variable in a subroutine (or function), the variable's scope (the locations where that variable is known) is limited to the subroutine. Outside of each of the subroutines, the program does not know that the subroutine uses a variable named Counter. In this case, the two variables named Counter each have different scope. If one subroutine changes the value of its Counter variable, the change has no effect on the second subroutine's variable. Because of each variable's limited scope, using the same variable name in different subroutines does not create a conflict.

When you create a console-based application, you can declare a variable outside of your subroutines and functions. The following statements declare a variable named Counter outside of the two subroutines:

```
Dim Counter As Integer

Sub BigLoop()
  For Counter = 1000 To 10000
    Console.WriteLine(Counter)
  Next
End Sub

Sub LittleLoop()
  For Counter = 0 To 5
    Console.WriteLine(Counter)
  Next
End Sub
```

When you declare a variable outside of the routines in this way, the variable has global scope—that is, the variable is known throughout your program code. Any function or subroutine in your program can change the value of a global variable (which can lead to errors that are very difficult to detect when you are not expecting a subroutine to change the variable's value). Because global variables can lead to such errors, you should not use (or you should severely limit the use of) global variables.

When a local variable has the same name as a global variable, the code will always use the local variable (ignoring the global variable). In this case, any changes the routines make to their local variables named Counter will not affect the global variable named Counter, and vice versa. However, because such conflicts can confuse a programmer who is reading your code, you should avoid the use of global variables. If a subroutine or function must change a variable's value, your code should pass the variable to the routine by reference (using the ByRef keyword in the routine's parameter declaration). That way, another programmer who reads your code can better track the fact that the routine changes the parameter's value.

USE IT   The following program, ScopeDemo.vb, illustrates how scope affects variables in a program. The program uses a global variable named Counter, a local variable in a subroutine named Counter, and a variable named Counter whose scope corresponds to an If statement:

```
Module Module1

    Dim Counter As Integer

    Sub BigLoop()
        For Counter = 1000 To 1005        ' Use global Counter
            Console.Write(Counter & " ")
        Next
        Console.WriteLine()
    End Sub

    Sub LittleLoop()
        Dim Counter As Integer

        For Counter = 0 To 5        ' Use local Counter
            Console.Write(Counter & " ")
        Next
        Console.WriteLine()
    End Sub

    Sub Main()
        Counter = 100

        Console.WriteLine("Starting Counter: " & Counter)
        BigLoop()
```

```
    Console.WriteLine("Counter after BigLoop: " & Counter)
    LittleLoop()
    Console.WriteLine("Counter after LittleLoop: " & Counter)

    If (Counter > 1000) Then
        Dim Counter As Integer = 0

        Console.WriteLine("Counter in If statement: " & Counter)
    End If

    Console.WriteLine("Ending Counter: " & Counter)

    Console.ReadLine()

  End Sub

End Module
```

After you compile and execute this program, your screen will display the following output:

```
Starting Counter: 100
1000 1001 1002 1003 1004 1005
Counter after BigLoop: 1006
0 1 2 3 4 5
Counter after LittleLoop: 1006
Counter in If statement: 0
Ending Counter: 1006
```

Storing Multiple Values of the Same Type in a Single Variable

In a program, variables let the program store and later retrieve values as the program executes. Normally, a variable stores only one value at a time. Many programs, however, must work with many related values of the same type. For example, a program many need to calculate the average of 50 test scores, or changes in the prices of 100 stocks, or the amount of disk space consumed by files in the current directory. To store multiple values of the same type (such as 50 Integer values) in one variable, your programs can use an array data structure.

To create an array, you declare a variable of a specific type and then specify the number of elements the variable will store. The following statement declares an array named TestScores that can store 50 Integer values (the first array entry is at offset 0 in the array and the 50th is at offset 49):

```
Dim TestScores(49) As Integer
```

To access values in an array, you use an index value to specify the array element (the specific value's location) you desire. The first value in an array resides at location 0. The following statement assigns the test score 91 to the first element in the array:

```
TestScores(0) = 91
```

The following statements assign values to the first five elements of the TestScores array:

```
TestScores(0) = 91
TestScores(1) = 44
TestScores(2) = 66
TestScores(3) = 95
TestScores(4) = 77
```

Normally, to access the values in an array, a program uses a For loop that increments a variable the code uses to specify array locations. The following For loop would display the values previously assigned to the first five array elements:

```
For I = 0 To 4
  Console.WriteLine(TestScores(I))
Next
```

As discussed, the first element in an array resides at location 0. Likewise, the last element resides at the array size. In the case of the 50-element TestScores array, the last element would reside at TestScores(49). If your program tries to assign a value to an element outside of the array bounds (such as TestScores(100) = 45), the program will generate an exception. Chapter 9 examines exceptions and exception handling in detail.

To assign values to an array, a program might read the values from a file, prompt the user for the values, or calculate the values based on program-specific processing. In addition, a program can initialize an array by placing the values in left and right braces, as shown here (when you initialize an array in this way, you do not specify the array size in the parentheses that follow the array name):

```
Dim Values() As Integer = {100, 200, 300, 400, 500}
Dim Prices() As Double = {25.5, 4.95, 33.4}
```

As your programs execute, there may be times when you find that an array does not provide enough storage locations to hold the values you require. In such cases, your program can use the ReDim statement to increase or decrease the array's size.

The following program, ArrayDemo.vb, creates an array that stores ten values. The program then uses a For loop to display the array's contents. In Chapter 3, you will examine classes that let you group information, functions, and methods in a data structure. When you create an array in Visual Basic .NET programs, the array is actually a class object that stores information about the array (such as the number of elements the array contains) and provides methods programs can use to manipulate the array. This program illustrates several of the properties and methods the class provides:

```vbnet
Module Module1

    Sub Main()
        Dim Values() As Integer = {100, 200, 300, 400, 500}
        Dim MyValues(5) As Integer
        Dim Prices() As Double = {25.5, 4.95, 33.4}

        Dim I As Integer

        For I = 0 To 4
            Console.Write(Values(I) & " ")
        Next
        Console.WriteLine()

        ' Copy one array to another
        Values.CopyTo(MyValues, 0)
        For I = 0 To 4
            Console.Write(MyValues(I) & " ")
        Next
        Console.WriteLine()

        Values.Reverse(Values)
        For I = 0 To 4
            Console.Write(Values(I) & " ")
        Next
        Console.WriteLine()

        Console.WriteLine("Array length: " & Values.Length)
        Console.WriteLine("Array lowerbound: " & _
          Values.GetLowerBound(0))
        Console.WriteLine("Array upperbound: " & _
          Values.GetUpperBound(0))

        For I = 0 To Prices.GetUpperBound(0)
            Console.Write(Prices(I) & " ")
        Next
        Console.WriteLine()

        Console.ReadLine()
    End Sub

End Module
```

After you compile and execute this program, your screen will display the following output:

```
100 200 300 400 500
100 200 300 400 500
500 400 300 200 100
Array length: 5
Array lowerbound: 0
Array upperbound: 4
25.5 4.95 33.4
```

Grouping Values in a Structure

In the Tip titled, "Storing Multiple Values of the Same Type in a Single Variable," you learned how to group multiple values of the same type into an array. In an array, you can only store values of the same type, such as all Integer values, all Double values, and so on. Depending on the processing your programs perform, there may be times when your programs can use a program-defined data type called a structure to group related pieces of information. Unlike an array, which can only store values of the same type, a structure can store several values of different types.

Assume that your program must store information about a book, such as the title, author, publisher, and price. To do so, your programs can declare the following variables:

```
Dim Title As String
Dim Author As String
Dim Publisher As String
Dim Price As Double
```

Next, assume that your program creates several functions and subroutines that use the book information. In your code, you can pass the variables to a subroutine or function as parameters:

```
ShowBook(Title, Author, Publisher, Price)
```

Although passing the variables as parameters in this way lets the subroutines and functions work with the book information, assume that the user changes the program's requirements and you must now also track the number of pages and chapters in each book. In such cases, you could declare two new variables to store the page and chapter information and then change each and every function and subroutine to accept the information as parameters:

```
Dim PageCount As Integer
Dim ChapterCount As Integer

ShowBook(Title, Author, Publisher, Price, PageCount, ChapterCount)
```

As an alternative, your program can define a Book data structure in which you specify the information the structure must hold:

```
Structure Book
   Dim Title As String
   Dim Author As String
   Dim Publisher As String
   Dim Price As Double
End Structure
```

A structure is simply a type that groups related information. After you define the Book structure, your program can declare a variable of the Book type:

```
Dim BookInfo As Book
```

Next, your program can use the dot operator (which separates the variable name from a member variable) to assign values to each member variable:

```
BookInfo.Title = "Visual Basic .NET Programming Tips & Techniques"
Book.Author = "Jamsa"
Book.Publisher = "McGraw-Hill/Osborne"
Book.Price = 49.99
```

Then, rather than passing the individual variables to the function or subroutine, your code can instead pass the structure variable:

```
ShowBook(BookInfo)
```

Should the user change the program's requirement in the future, so that the program must also track the book's copyright date and weight, you can simply add the variables to the Book definition without having to change the subroutine calls:

```
Structure Book
   Dim Title As String
   Dim Author As String
   Dim Publisher As String
   Dim Price As Double
   Dim Copyright As String
   Dim Weight As Double
End Structure
```

USE IT   The following program, StructureDemo.vb, creates the Book structure and then uses the structure to create a variable named BookInfo. Using the dot operator, the program then assigns values to each of the structure's members. Finally, the code passes the structure variable to a subroutine that uses the dot operator to display the member's values:

```
Module Module1

   Structure Book
```

```
      Dim Title As String
      Dim Author As String
      Dim Publisher As String
      Dim Price As Double
   End Structure

   Sub ShowBook(ByVal SomeBook As Book)
      Console.WriteLine(SomeBook.Title)
      Console.WriteLine(SomeBook.Author)
      Console.WriteLine(SomeBook.Publisher)
      Console.WriteLine(SomeBook.Price)
   End Sub

   Sub Main()
      Dim BookInfo As Book
      BookInfo.Title = "Visual Basic .Net Programming Tips & Techniques"
      BookInfo.Author = "Jamsa"
      BookInfo.Publisher = "McGraw-Hill/Osborne"
      BookInfo.Price = 49.99

      ShowBook(BookInfo)
      Console.ReadLine()
   End Sub
End Module
```

After you compile and execute this program, your screen will display the following output:

```
Visual Basic .Net Programming Tips & Techniques
Jamsa
McGraw-Hill/Osborne
49.99
```

Improving Your Code's Readability Using Constants

In most programs, you must often use numeric values in a variety of ways. You might use a numeric value to control a For loop's processing, as shown here:

```
For I = 0 To 50
   Console.WriteLine(I)
Next
```

Or you might use a numeric value in an If statement to perform a comparison:

```
If (I = 50) Then
  Console.WriteLine("Processing the last value")
End If
```

Further, you might use a numeric constant to define the size of an array variable (which stores multiple values of the same type in the same variable):

```
Dim Students(50) As Integer
```

The following program, UseNumbers.vb, uses numeric constants throughout the source code. If you examine the program statements, you will find that the code makes extensive use of the value 50:

```
Module Module1

    Sub Main()
        Dim Students(50) As Integer
        Dim I As Integer

        For I = 0 To 50
            Students(I) = I
        Next

        For I = 0 To 50
            Console.WriteLine(Students(I))
        Next

        Console.ReadLine() ' Pause to view output
    End Sub

End Module
```

Rather than use numeric values in this way, your programs should take advantage of constants that assign a meaningful name to the value, such as a constant named NumberOfStudents.

USE IT   To create a constant, place a Const statement in your code similar to the following:

```
Const NumberOfStudents As Integer = 50
```

Then, in your program, use the constant name everywhere you would normally use the numeric constant. For example, you might declare arrays as follows:

```
Dim Students(NumberOfStudents) As Integer
```

Likewise, in the For loop, you would use the constant to express the loop's ending value as shown here:

```
For I = 0 To NumberOfStudents
  Students(I) = I
Next
```

If you compare the For loops, you will find that the use of the constant gives another programmer who reads your code more insight into the program's processing. With a glance at the loop, the programmer knows that the array will iterate (loop) through each of the students.

Using constants also simplifies your program should the number of students change from 50 to 100. In the first program, you would need to change each occurrence of the value 50 to the value 100. Each time you make a change to a program, you increase the likelihood of introducing an error (such as a typo that places the value 10 instead of 100 in the code). If your code uses a constant, you need only change the following statement:

```
Const NumberOfStudents As Integer = 100
```

Behind the scenes, the Visual Basic .NET compiler as it compiles your source code will perform the constant substitution for you.

Summarizing the Differences Between Visual Basic and Visual Basic .NET

If you are an experienced Visual Basic .NET programmer, you may have skipped many of the foundation Tips this chapter provides. This Tip will summarize many of the key differences between Visual Basic and Visual Basic .NET.

- Visual Basic .NET does not support the Variant data type. In Chapter 4, you will learn that all .NET classes inherit the System.Object type.

- Visual Basic .NET does not support the Currency data type. Instead, programs should use the Decimal type.

- Visual Basic .NET does not support the use of the LET statement to assign a value to a variable. Instead, your programs should simply use the assignment operator.

- Visual Basic .NET does not support the DefType statement that previous versions of Visual Basic used to define the program's default data type. As a matter of good programming practices, your programs should declare each and every variable.

- Visual Basic .NET does not support user-defined types. Instead, your programs should use a Structure (or class) to group related information.

- Visual Basic .NET no longer supports the IsMissing function. Instead, your programs should use IsNothing to determine whether an object contains a value.

- Visual Basic .NET does not support the use of the GoSub statement to call a subroutine. Instead, your program should simply call the subroutine by referencing the subroutine name followed by parentheses, which may contain optional parameters.

- Visual Basic .NET does not support Static subroutines or functions. If a variable in a subroutine or function must maintain its value from one invocation to the next, the routine should declare the variable as Static.

- Visual Basic .NET does not let programmers declare fixed length String variables.

- Visual Basic .NET changes the type Integer to 32 bits, which lets Integer variables store values in the range –2,147,483,648 to 2,147,483,647.

- Visual Basic .NET uses the type Short to represent 16-bit values, which can store numbers in the range –32,768 to 32,767.

- Visual Basic .NET changes the lower bound of an array to element 0 (as opposed to element 1). A Visual Basic .NET program cannot use the Option Base statement to specify the default array base. Visual Basic .NET does not let you specify an array's lower and upper bounds when you declare an array. All Visual Basic .NET arrays use the lower bound 0.

- Visual Basic .NET uses Math class methods to perform arithmetic and trigonometric operations such as calculating a value's square root or an angle's sine or cosine.

- When a Visual Basic .NET program calls a function or subroutine, the program must specify parentheses after the routine's name, even if the routine does not use parameters.

- By default, Visual Basic .NET passes variables to functions and subroutines by value (using the ByVal keyword), which means the routine cannot change the original variable's value. If a subroutine or function must change a variable, you must pass the variable to the routine by reference (using the ByRef keyword).

- Although Visual Basic .NET supports the MsgBox function, most newer programs will use the MessageBox class Show method.

- Visual Basic .NET replaces the Wend statement that indicates the end of a While loop with the End While statement.

- Visual Basic .NET replaces the Debug.Print statement with Debug.Writeline.

- Visual Basic .NET lets a program declare variables in a construct, such as a While loop or If statement. The variable's scope, in turn, corresponds to the construct.

- Visual Basic .NET uses the value Nothing to indicate that an object does not contain a value. Visual Basic .NET does not support Null or Empty.

CHAPTER 2

Exploiting the .NET Environment

If you are like most programmers who are moving to Visual Basic .NET, you are not only facing the task of learning a new programming language, but you are also trying to understand the new features of the .NET environment and how to exploit those features in the programs you create. The .NET environment brings with it many new features:

- A programming-language-independent runtime library programmers call the Common Language Runtime, which programs written in C#, Visual Basic .NET, and JScript can use.

- A common type system that means .NET programming languages all use the same representation for common data types.

- The ASP.NET model for Web pages that is based on a compiled programming language (as opposed to VBScript) and which provides server-based support for scripts and controls.

- Web forms, which let developers build an interface for Web pages by dragging and dropping controls onto a form.

- ADO.NET, which extends database programming capabilities.

- Extensive use of metadata (data that describes data) that lets programs query objects about the capabilities they provide.

- Use of namespaces to organize classes and reduce name conflicts.

- Compilers that produce an intermediate language, which a special software called a just-in-time (JIT) compiler compiles to native mode code when the user runs the application.

- The use of a special file called an assembly to package applications and class libraries.

- The ability to create Web services, special network-based software, that is callable across the Internet by a remote application or ASP.NET page.

- The use of version information in an application's assembly file that reduces problems caused by multiple software versions (such as conflicts among DLL files). Because of the version information programs and components contain, different versions of the same components can exist and execute side by side.

- Support for the detection and processing of exceptions through the use of structured error handling.

Throughout this book, you will examine these .NET capabilities in detail. To get you started, this chapter introduces the key .NET features. By the time you complete this chapter's Tips, you will have a solid foundation upon which you can build your .NET knowledge.

Taking Advantage of the Common Language Runtime

For years, programmers have made extensive use of runtime library functions to perform operations in their programs, including manipulating files and directories, retrieving or setting the system date and

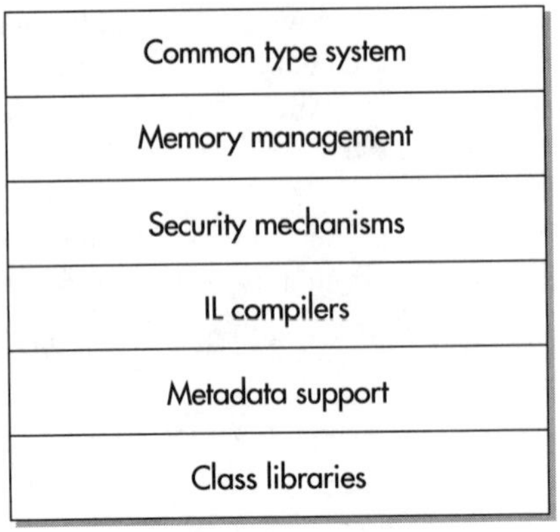

Common type system
Memory management
Security mechanisms
IL compilers
Metadata support
Class libraries

Figure 2-1   The key components of the Common Language Runtime

time, and performing arithmetic operations, such as calculating the sine of an angle or the square root of a value. Runtime libraries consist of hundreds to thousands of functions and subroutines programmers can use to perform common operations. In the past, most runtime libraries were programming-language-specific, meaning the runtime library routines available for Visual Basic programmers could be, and often were, different from those available to C++ programmers.

The .NET environment is built around two new and powerful language-independent runtime libraries called the Common Language Runtime (CLR) and a base-class library (BCL, which consists of thousands of class definitions). Because these libraries are programming-language independent, a Visual Basic .NET program has the same set of runtime library routines as a C# program. Although programmers often think of a runtime library in terms of the functions the library offers, the CLR also defines the .NET common types that specify a consistent set of language-independent data types for standard types such as integers and floating-point numbers.

In the Tip titled "Taking Advantage of Intermediate Language Code," you will learn that the .NET environment stores applications using an intermediate language (IL) form that the target system later compiles (using a just-in-time compiler) into a native mode application that matches the target system's instruction set. The Common Language Runtime itself actually resides in the intermediate language format. Figure 2-1 illustrates the key components of the .NET Common Language Runtime.

USE IT   The Common Language Runtime is programming-language independent. The following Visual Basic .NET and C# programs illustrate the use of the Directory class GetFiles runtime library routines to display the names of files that reside in the root directory on drive C. The code also uses the Console class WriteLine method to display the filenames to the screen and the ReadLine method to wait for the user to press the ENTER key before ending. The following statements implement the Visual Basic .NET program ShowRoot.vb:

```
Imports System.IO

Module Module1
```

```
    Sub Main()
        Dim Filename As String

        For Each Filename In Directory.GetFiles("C:\")
            Console.WriteLine(Filename)
        Next

        Console.ReadLine() ' Pause to view output
    End Sub
End Module
```

Likewise, the following statements implement the C# program CS_ShowRoot.cs:

```
using System;
using System.IO;
namespace CS_ShowRoot
{
  class Class1
    {
      static void Main(string[] args)
        {
           foreach (string Filename in Directory.GetFiles("C:\\"))
             Console.WriteLine(Filename);

           Console.ReadLine(); // Pause to view output
        }
    }
}
```

As you can see, using the Common Language Runtime, the Visual Basic .NET and C# programs are quite similar in form and identical in functionality.

Declaring Variables Based on Common Types

A variable's type defines a range of values a variable can store and a set of operations a program can perform on the variable. For example, a variable of type Integer can store values in the range –2,147,483,648 to 2,147,483,647. Likewise, a program can add, subtract, multiply, and divide integer values. In contrast, a Visual Basic .NET String variable holds character values (using a 2-byte Unicode format). A program can compare and concatenate two String variables, but a program could not multiply and divide a String variable's contents.

In the past, each programming language defined its own data types. Unfortunately, how one language defined a type was not always consistent with others. For example, the C++ programming

Type	Values
Char	Represents a 16-bit Unicode character
DateTime	Represents a date and time value
Decimal	Represents 0 through +/–79,228,162,514,264,337,593,543,950,335 with no decimal point; represents 0 through +/–7.9228162514264337593543950335 with 28 places to the right of the decimal
Double	Represents a floating-point value using 64 bits
GUID	Represents a globally unique identifier using 128 bits
Int16	Represents a value in the range –32,678 to 32,677
Int32	Represents a value in the range –2,147,483,648 to 2,147,483,647
Int64	Represents a value in the range –9,223,372,036,854,775,808 through 9,223,372,036,854,775,807
Single	Represents a floating-point value using 32 bits
TimeSpan	Represents a positive or negative time interval

Table 2-1   The .NET Common Types

language defined an integer using 32-bits (which meant an integer variable could store values in the range –2,147,483,648 to 2,147,483,647). Visual Basic defined an integer variable using 16 bits (which meant the variable could store values in the range –32,678 to 32,677).

In the .NET environment, the Common Language Runtime defines a set of types programmers refer to as the common types. Languages such as C# and Visual Basic .NET define their data types based on the common types. Table 2-1 briefly describes each of the .NET common types.

By taking advantage of the common types, the Common Language Runtime becomes programming-language independent. If a function in the CLR requires an integer parameter, for example, programs written in either C# or Visual Basic .NET will pass the same number of bits for the parameter value.

USE IT   When you create a program using Visual Basic .NET or C#, the compiler, behind the scenes, will map the programming language type names, such as Integer in Visual Basic .NET or int in C#, to the corresponding common type. The following Visual Basic .NET and C# programs illustrate how the compiler maps the programming language types to a common type. The following statements implement the Visual Basic .NET program VBShowCommonTypes.vb:

```
Module Module1
    Sub Main()
        Dim A As Short
```

```
        Dim B As Integer
        Dim C As Int64
        Dim D As Single
        Dim E As Double
        Dim F As Char

        Console.WriteLine("A: {0} ", A.GetType().FullName)
        Console.WriteLine("B: {0} ", B.GetType().FullName)
        Console.WriteLine("C: {0} ", C.GetType().FullName)
        Console.WriteLine("D: {0} ", D.GetType().FullName)
        Console.WriteLine("E: {0} ", E.GetType().FullName)
        Console.WriteLine("F: {0} ", F.GetType().FullName)
        Console.ReadLine()
    End Sub
End Module
```

After you compile and execute this program, your screen will display the following output:

```
A: System.Int16
B: System.Int32
C: System.Int64
D: System.Single
E: System.Double
F: System.Char
```

Likewise, the following statements implement the C# program ShowCommonType.cs:

```
using System;

namespace ShowCommonTypes
{
    class Class1
    {
        static void Main(string[] args)
        {
            short A = 0;
            int B = 0;
            long C = 0;
            float D = 0;
            double E = 0;
            char F = 'A';
```

```
        Console.WriteLine("A: {0} ", A.GetType().FullName);
        Console.WriteLine("B: {0} ", B.GetType().FullName);
        Console.WriteLine("C: {0} ", C.GetType().FullName);
        Console.WriteLine("D: {0} ", D.GetType().FullName);
        Console.WriteLine("E: {0} ", E.GetType().FullName);
        Console.WriteLine("F: {0} ", F.GetType().FullName);

        Console.ReadLine();
    }
  }
}
```

Migrating to ASP.NET

Across the World Wide Web, sites make extensive use of Active Server Pages to display dynamic (changing or customized) content. For years, Web developers have made extensive use of VBScript to implement Active Server Pages. Although tens of millions of Web pages are based on Active Server Pages and VBScript, the Active Server Page model has shortcomings, such as the limits of the VBScript language, which include interpreted as opposed to compiled code, a less powerful interface than Windows-based applications, and limitations on maintaining user state information.

The .NET environment brings with it a new model for creating dynamic Web pages, called ASP.NET. The first major change Web developers will encounter with ASP.NET is that VBScript is gone! To create an ASP.NET page, developers use a programming language such as Visual Basic .NET, C#, or JScript .NET. Unlike VBScript-based Active Server Pages, which the server first interprets and then executes, ASP.NET pages are compiled programs, which improves the pages' performance and security.

Because of the huge number of existing VBScript-based Active Server Pages, it is quite likely that ASP.NET pages and Active Server Pages will exist side by side within the same servers for years to come. Chapter 13 examines ASP.NET in detail. At that time, you will learn that an ASP.NET page can call an Active Server Page and vice versa.

Developers store Active Server Pages in files that use the .asp extension. ASP.NET pages use the .aspx extension. The server uses the different file extensions to distinguish an ASP.NET page from an Active Server Page. To support ASP.NET pages, a server must be running Microsoft Internet Information Services (IIS) version 5 or later.

For years, Web developers have used scripting languages such as VBScript and JavaScript to respond to client-side (browser-based) events. The ASP.NET environment introduces server-based support for events. In other words, within an ASP.NET page, many operations occur at the server. In addition, the .NET environment provides a new set of form-based controls that let programmers create traditional form-based user interfaces for Web pages, as shown in Figure 2-2. In general, you should think of a Web form as a server-side control that lets the server respond to events the ASP.NET page generates. Chapter 15 examines Web forms in detail.

USE IT   The following ASP.NET page, SimpleVBPage.aspx, uses Visual Basic .NET to implement a page that displays the current date and time and a random message:

```
<% @ Page Language="VB" %>

<script runat="server">
Sub GreetUser()
   Dim Seconds As Integer

   Seconds = Now.Second

   If ((Seconds Mod 3) = 0) Then
     Response.Write("Hello, World!<br/>")
   ElseIf (Seconds Mod 3) = 1 Then
     Response.Write("Hello, Visual Basic .NET World!<br/>")
   ElseIf (Seconds Mod 3) = 2 Then
     Response.Write("Hello, ASP.NET World!<br/>")
   End If
End Sub
</script>
<html>
<head>
   <title>ASP.NET Demo</title>
</head>
<body>
   <center><h1>Using Visual Basic .NET to Create an ASP.NET Page</h1></center><hr/>
The current date and time is
   <% =Now %>

   <b><br/>
   <%
     GreetUser()
   %>
   </b>
</body>
</html>
```

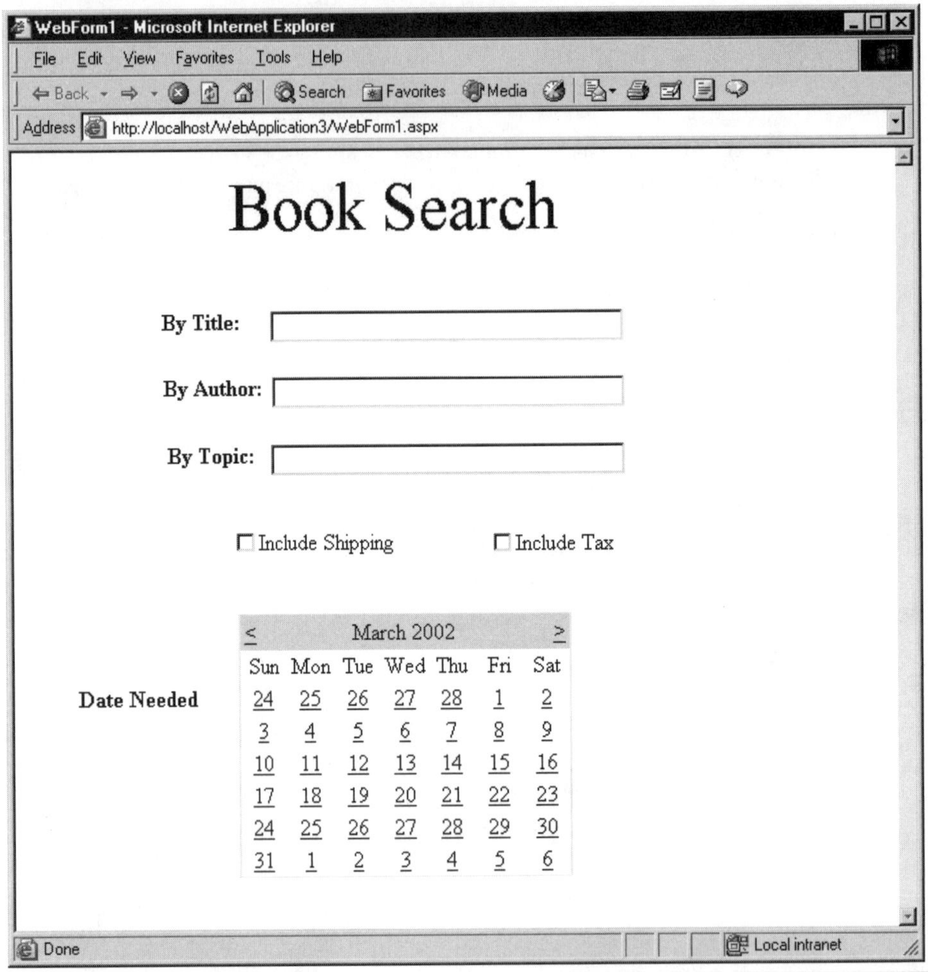

Figure 2-2   The .NET environment introduces Web forms, which developers can use to create form-based Web pages

When a user views this ASP.NET page, the user's browser will display output similar to that shown in Figure 2-3.

In a similar way, the following page, SimpleCsPage.aspx, implements the same page using the C# programming language:

```
<% @ Page Language="C#" %>

<script runat="server">
void GreetUser()
  {
    int Seconds;
```

```
   Seconds = DateTime.Now.Second;

   if ((Seconds % 3) == 0)
     Response.Write("Hello, World!<br/>");
   else if ((Seconds % 3) == 1)
     Response.Write("Hello, C# World!<br/>");
   else if ((Seconds % 3) == 2)
     Response.Write("Hello, ASP.NET World!<br/>");
 }
</script>
<html>
<head>
   <title>ASP.NET Demo</title>
</head>
<body>
  <center><h1>Using C# to Create an ASP.NET Page</h1></center><hr/>
The current date and time is
  <% =DateTime.Now %>

  <b><br/>
  <%
     GreetUser();
  %>
  </b>
</body>
</html>
```

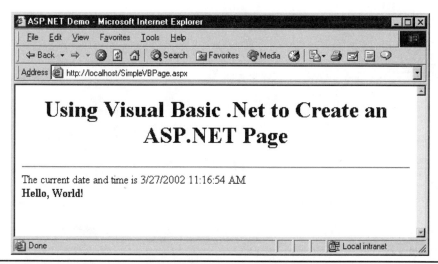

Figure 2-3   Displaying the output of the ASP.NET page SimpleVBPage.aspx

Exploiting Windows Forms

For years, Visual Basic programmers have exploited forms to quickly build consistent user interfaces. Many programmers will agree that the ability to drag and drop controls onto a form to build a user interface has been the key to Visual Basic's tremendous popularity and success. In contrast to the Visual Basic development environment, C and C++ programmers built user interfaces around the Microsoft Foundation Classes (MFC) and the Win32 application program interface (API). Building a user interface in languages other than Visual Basic was often one of the most time-consuming aspects of application development.

The .NET environment brings with it the Windows Forms user-interface development environment and controls that programmers using Visual Basic .NET, C#, or JScript can use to create form-based user interfaces by performing drag and drop operations. Figure 2-4 illustrates the process of building a form within the Visual Studio environment. As you would expect, programmers can drag and drop controls onto a form. Behind the scenes, Visual Studio generates the code the program can use to interact with the controls.

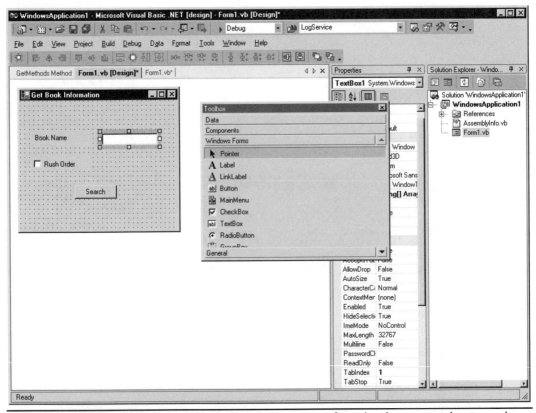

Figure 2-4   Windows forms extend drag-and-drop user interface development to the C# and JScript programming languages as well as Visual Basic .NET

USE IT The following source code (minus comments) illustrates the Visual Basic .NET code Visual Studio creates for the form shown in Figure 2-4:

```
Public Class Form1
    Inherits System.Windows.Forms.Form

#Region " Windows Form Designer generated code "

    Public Sub New()
        MyBase.New()

        InitializeComponent()
    End Sub

    Protected Overloads Overrides Sub Dispose(ByVal disposing As Boolean)
        If disposing Then
            If Not (components Is Nothing) Then
                components.Dispose()
            End If
        End If
        MyBase.Dispose(disposing)
    End Sub

    'Required by the Windows Form Designer
    Private components As System.ComponentModel.Icontainer

    Friend WithEvents Label1 As System.Windows.Forms.Label
    Friend WithEvents TextBox1 As System.Windows.Forms.TextBox
    Friend WithEvents CheckBox1 As System.Windows.Forms.CheckBox
    Friend WithEvents Button1 As System.Windows.Forms.Button
    <System.Diagnostics.DebuggerStepThrough()> Private Sub
InitializeComponent()
        Me.Label1 = New System.Windows.Forms.Label()
        Me.TextBox1 = New System.Windows.Forms.TextBox()
        Me.CheckBox1 = New System.Windows.Forms.CheckBox()
        Me.Button1 = New System.Windows.Forms.Button()
        Me.SuspendLayout()

        'Label1
        Me.Label1.Location = New System.Drawing.Point(24, 56)
        Me.Label1.Name = "Label1"
        Me.Label1.TabIndex = 0
        Me.Label1.Text = "Book Name"

        'TextBox1
```

```
    Me.TextBox1.Location = New System.Drawing.Point(144, 56)
    Me.TextBox1.Name = "TextBox1"
    Me.TextBox1.TabIndex = 1
    Me.TextBox1.Text = ""

    'CheckBox1
    Me.CheckBox1.Location = New System.Drawing.Point(24, 96)
    Me.CheckBox1.Name = "CheckBox1"
    Me.CheckBox1.TabIndex = 2
    Me.CheckBox1.Text = "Rush Order"

    'Button1
    Me.Button1.Location = New System.Drawing.Point(96, 144)
    Me.Button1.Name = "Button1"
    Me.Button1.TabIndex = 3
    Me.Button1.Text = "Search"

    'Form1
    Me.AutoScaleBaseSize = New System.Drawing.Size(5, 13)
    Me.ClientSize = New System.Drawing.Size(280, 221)
    Me.Controls.AddRange(New System.Windows.Forms.Control() _
       {Me.Button1, Me.CheckBox1, Me.TextBox1, Me.Label1})
    Me.Name = "Form1"
    Me.Text = "Get Book Information"
    Me.ResumeLayout(False)

  End Sub


#End Region
End Class
```

By integrating Windows forms into a language-independent platform, the .NET environment makes it very easy for programmers, regardless of their target programming language, to create a user interface by performing drag-and-drop operations.

Making Sense of Metadata

Metadata is a term programmers use to describe data about data. The .NET environment makes extensive use of metadata to describe objects, assemblies, ADO.NET data sets, and much more. Programmers state that one of the key benefits of the .NET environment is that objects are self-describing—in other words, a program can query an object to determine the methods, fields, and properties the object makes available for program use.

The .NET environment places metadata within the object itself. Each object contains data that describes the object. When you compile a .NET application, the compiler will create the metadata and include it in the application. As you will learn, every .NET application has a special file called an assembly that uses metadata to describe such information as the classes the application provides, as well as other components (such as DLL files) the application requires. When programmers discuss metadata, it doesn't take long before the conversation turns to Extensible Markup Language (XML). That's because XML provides an excellent way to structure metadata. Behind the scenes, the .NET environment makes extensive use of XML to format metadata.

USE IT The following program, ClassInfo.vb, creates a Book class that contains methods and properties. The code then uses the .NET reflection API to query the class about the capabilities it provides (in other words, the program asks a class, which is self-describing, to tell the program about itself):

```
Module Module1
    Class Book
        Public Title As String
        Public Author As String
        Public Price As Double

        Public Sub New(ByVal Title As String, ByVal Author As String, _
          ByVal Price As Double)
            Me.Title = Title
            Me.Author = Author
            Me.Price = Price
        End Sub

        Public Sub ShowTitle()
            Console.WriteLine("Title: " & Title)
        End Sub

        Public Sub ShowBook()
            Console.WriteLine("Title: " & Title)
            Console.WriteLine("Author: " & Author)
            Console.WriteLine("Price: " & Price)
        End Sub
    End Class

    Sub Main()
        Dim NetBook As _
          New Book("Visual Basic .NET Programming Tips & Techniques", _
          "Jamsa", 49.99)

        Console.WriteLine("Method Names")
        Dim Info As Reflection.MethodInfo
```

```
        For Each Info In NetBook.GetType.GetMethods()
            Console.WriteLine(Info.Name)
        Next

        Console.WriteLine()
        Console.WriteLine("Member Names")
        Dim Member As Reflection.MemberInfo

        For Each Member In NetBook.GetType.GetMembers()
            Console.WriteLine(Member.Name)
        Next

        Console.ReadLine()
    End Sub
End Module
```

After you compile and execute this program, your screen will display the following output:

```
Method Names
GetHashCode
Equals
ToString
ShowTitle
ShowBook
GetType

Member Names
Title
Author
Price
GetHashCode
Equals
ToString
ShowTitle
ShowBook
GetType
.ctor
```

Using the Reflection API, your programs can query any .NET class object about its capabilities. Chapter 18 examines reflection in detail.

Organizing Object Libraries Using Namespaces

In object-oriented programming environments, such as the .NET environment, programmers make extensive use of classes to describe objects. To better organize classes and to simplify class use, programmers often group classes into class libraries. Normally, the classes in a library will perform related tasks. You might, for example, have a Math class library that provides functions that perform key arithmetic operations. Or you might have a Network class library that programs can use to communicate with a remote server.

As the number of classes programmers add to a library increases, so too does the likelihood of name conflicts (two classes might use the same name). To reduce such potential name conflicts, programmers use namespaces to organize objects. In general, a namespace groups objects (which may reside in multiple assemblies) and assigns a name to the objects that can eliminate naming conflicts between two or more classes that do not share the same namespace. Assume, for example, that you use an Address class to store a site's dotted IP address (such as 111.212.211.112) and domain name (such as www.osborne.com):

```
Class Address
   Public DottedName As String
   Public DomainName As String
End Class
```

Likewise, assume that within your program, you use the following Address class to store an Employee's home address:

```
Class Address
   Public Street As String
   Public City As String
   Public State As String
   Public Zip As String
End Class
```

To eliminate the name conflict between the two Address classes, the programmer can place each class into a different namespace. The code might, for example, create a Network namespace into which it places the Address class that contains the IP information. Likewise, the program might create a Mailing namespace into which it places the Address class that stores street information. After you create a namespace, you then precede the corresponding class with the namespace followed by the dot operator, such as Mailing.Address or Network.Address. Using the namespace prefix, you create a unique name.

In the .NET environment, your programs will make extensive use of the Common Language Runtime and the Base Class Library. To better organize the thousands of runtime library routines, the .NET environment makes extensive use of namespaces. Table 2-2 briefly describes key .NET namespaces.

Namespace	Purpose
System.CodeDOM	Classes programs can use to represent a source code document
System.Collections	Classes that describe a variety of collection-based data structures, such as arrays, linked lists, and queues
System.Configuration	Classes programs can use to access .NET Framework configuration information
System.Data	Classes that support data input from sources such as ADO.NET
System.Diagnostics	Classes you can use to debug a .NET application by interacting with system counters, event logs, and performance counters
System.DirectoryServices	Classes that provide programs with an interface to the Active Directory
System.Drawing	Classes programs can use to achieve the GDI+ graphics functionality
System.Globalization	Classes that support international features, such as date, time, and currency formats
System.IO	Classes that support stream-based I/O operations
System.Management	Classes that interface with the Windows Management Instrumentation services
System.Messaging	Classes programs can use to send and receive messages across message queues
System.NET	Classes programs can use to perform network operations
System.Reflection	Classes programs can use to query an object about the object's capabilities
System.Runtime	Classes programs can call to interact with assemblies, COM objects, and remote objects, such as InteropServices and Remoting
System.Security	Classes programs can call for encryption, access control, and more
System.Text	Classes programs can call to manipulate ASCII, Unicode, UTF-7, and UTF-8 text
System.Timers	Classes that provide timer-event support
System.Web	Classes programs can call to interact with a browser
System.Windows.Forms	Classes programs can call to create Windows-based forms
System.XML	Classes that support XML-based operations, such as reading and writing XML-based content

Table 2-2   Key .NET Namespaces

USE IT   When your programs use classes that the Common Language Runtime defines, there will be times when your programs must specify the namespace within which the class resides (the compiler will automatically search several of the commonly used .NET namespaces). To direct the compiler to include classes that reside in a specific namespace, you must import the namespace into your program code using the Imports statement. The following statement, for example, directs the compiler to include the System.IO namespace that contains classes your programs can use to manipulate files and directories:

```
Imports System.IO
```

To define your own namespace in a program or a class library that you create, you place items between the Namespace and End Namespace statements:

```
Namespace YourNamepaceName
  ' Place classes here
End Namespace
```

The following program, NamespaceDemo.vb, creates two namespaces, one named Network and one named Mailing. In each namespace, the code defines a class named Address. The program then uses each class type to create an object. By preceding the class name with the namespace name followed by the dot operator, the code explicitly states to the compiler which Address class it desires:

```
Namespace Network
    Class Address
        Public DottedName As String
        Public DomainName As String

        Public Sub New(ByVal IPAddr As String, ByVal Domain As String)
            DottedName = IPAddr
            DomainName = Domain
        End Sub

        Public Sub ShowAddress()
            Console.WriteLine("IP: " & DottedName)
            Console.WriteLine("Domain: " & DomainName)
        End Sub
    End Class
End Namespace

Namespace Mailing
    Class Address
        Public Street As String
        Public City As String
        Public State As String
        Public Zip As String

        Public Sub New(ByVal Street As String, ByVal City As String, _
          ByVal State As String, ByVal Zip As String)
            Me.Street = Street
            Me.City = City
            Me.State = State
            Me.Zip = Zip
        End Sub

        Public Sub ShowAddress()
```

```
            Console.WriteLine("Street: " & Street)
            Console.WriteLine("City: " & City)
            Console.WriteLine("State: " & State)
            Console.WriteLine("Zip: " & Zip)
        End Sub
    End Class
End Namespace


Module Module1
    Sub Main()
        Dim PC_Address As New Network.Address("122.111.222.112", _
            "www.SomeSite.com")

        Dim Employee_Address As New Mailing.Address("122 Main", _
           "Houston", "Texas", "77469")

        PC_Address.ShowAddress()
        Console.WriteLine()
        Employee_Address.ShowAddress()
        Console.ReadLine()
    End Sub
End Module
```

Taking Advantage of Intermediate Language Code

Normally, when you compile a program, the compiler converts your program's source code from a high-level language, such as Visual Basic or C++, into machine code (ones and zeros) that is specific to a CPU's instruction set. Programmers refer to the CPU specific ones and zeros as native code. Because the native code for an Intel processor uses instructions specific to the Intel CPU's instruction set, that native code would not run on a Mac, which uses a Motorola processor.

To support the wide range of CPU types and operating systems connected to the Web, the Java programming language introduced the concept of a virtual machine language. Java applets do not contain instructions specific to any one processor. Instead, the applets contain a set of generic platform-independent instructions. When a browser downloads a Java applet, special software within the browser (which programmers often refer to as the Java virtual machine) converts the virtual machine code into the native mode instructions specific to the CPU and operating system the computer is using. Using the virtual machine language format, programmers can create one executable program that can run on all machine types. The disadvantage of the virtual machine language model is that before a computer can run the program, the computer must first convert the virtual machine code into native code, which introduces overhead and a delay before the program execution begins.

In a similar way, .NET applications do not compile to native mode instructions. Instead, the .NET compilers create intermediate language (IL) code. Later, when a user runs a .NET program, special software (called the just-in-time or JIT compiler) converts the intermediate language code to native mode instructions.

USE IT   To view a program's intermediate language code, you can run a special program called the IL Disassembler, as shown in Figure 2-5. To run the IL Disassembler, you must run the program ILDASM.EXE from the system prompt, specifying the name and directory of the program you want to disassemble:

```
C:\> ildasm   \ProgramPath\ProgramName.exe   <Enter>
```

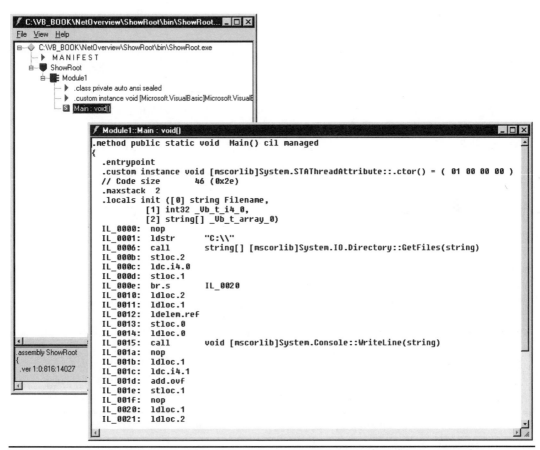

Figure 2-5   Using the IL Disassembler to view a program's intermediate language code

To run the IL Disassembler from the command line, you must move the program file ILDASM .EXE into a directory contained in your command path, or you must add the program's directory to the path.

Packaging .NET Solutions into Assemblies

In the .NET environment, the unit of program deployment is the assembly. An assembly may contain a program or a class library. In addition, the assembly contains information about the object (which programmers refer to as metadata). Figure 2-6 illustrates the common components of an assembly. Behind the scenes, an assembly can span multiple files (modules).

Every assembly contains a manifest that describes the assembly's contents. Within the manifest, you will find the assembly's name and version number, as well as a list of files that make up the assembly.

USE IT   Using the IL Disassembler program that is provided with Visual Studio, you can view a manifest's contents, as shown in Figure 2-7.

To view a manifest using the IL Disassembler, run the ILDASM program from the system prompt, specifying the name of the program you desire. To run the program, you will need to move the file ILDASM.EXE into a directory that is included in your command path, or you must add the file's directory to the path:

```
C:\> ildasm  \ProgramDirectory\ProgramName.exe  <Enter>
```

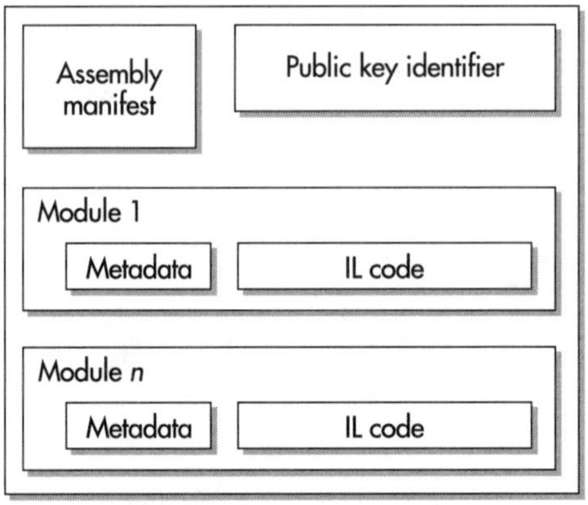

Figure 2-6   .NET applications deploy applications and class libraries using an assembly

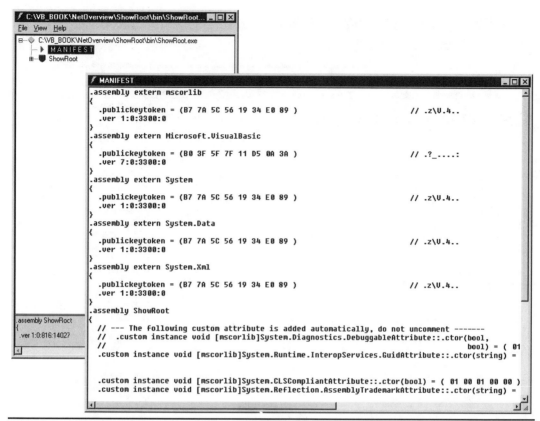

Figure 2-7   Using the IL Disassembler to view an assembly's manifest

An assembly may be application private, which means the assembly exists for and is used only by one application, or an assembly can be shared by two or more applications. In the Windows 2000 environment, shared assemblies reside in a special folder that programmers refer to as the global assembly cache (normally C:\WinNT\Assembly), as shown in Figure 2-8. Chapter 12 examines .NET assemblies in detail.

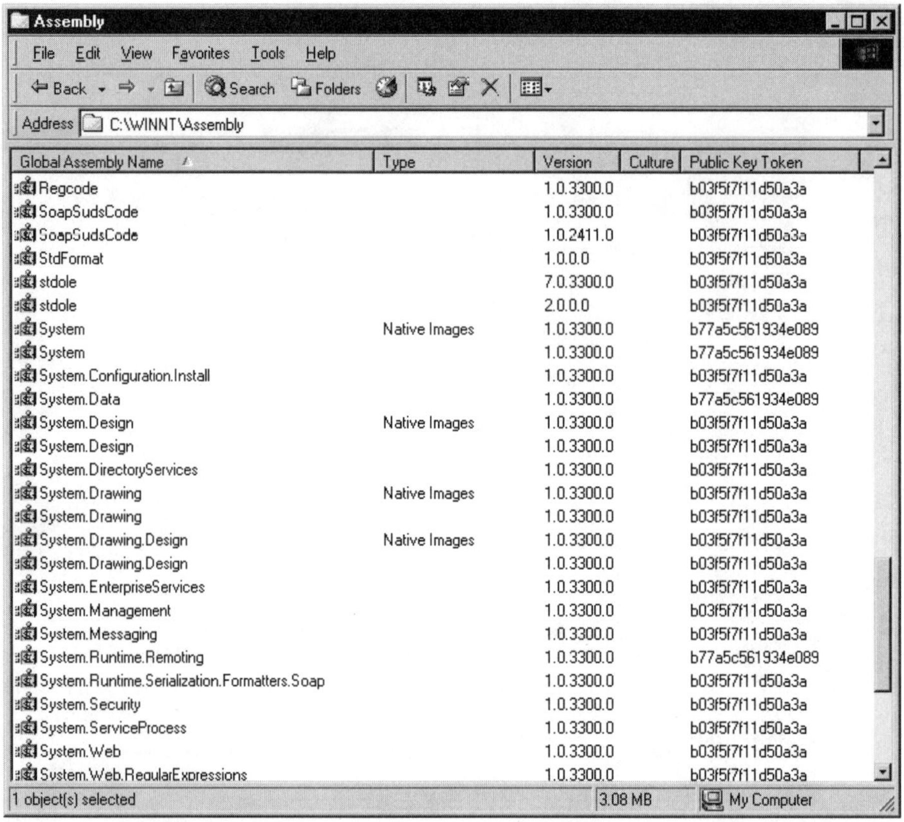

Figure 2-8 Viewing shared assemblies in the global assembly cache

Leveraging Managed Memory and Garbage Collection

In the .NET environment, program objects reside in a special memory location that programmers refer to as the heap. What makes the .NET heap special is that it is "managed memory." Behind the scenes, special .NET software called the garbage collector takes care of deleting objects and freeing the object's memory after the object is no longer in use.

In the past, allocating and releasing object memory was the program's responsibility. Unfortunately, many programs would allocate memory that they later failed to give back to the operating system. Even after the program ended, the memory remained allocated (and hence was unavailable for use by other programs). Programmers refer to such memory errors as "memory leaks," because over time, as such programs execute, the amount of memory available to the system becomes less and less.

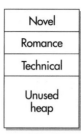

Figure 2-9   Allocating memory in the heap for three book objects

In the .NET environment, every object you create resides in the managed heap. The model the managed heap uses to allocate memory for an object is quite simple, and hence, quite fast. Assume, for example, that your code creates three Book class objects, named Novel, Romance, and Technical. The managed heap would allocate memory for the objects as shown in Figure 2-9.

Next, assume that program no longer uses the Romance object and that the program creates two new objects, named Business and Cooking. The heap management software will free the memory used by the Romance object and allocate space for the two new objects at the end of the heap, as shown in Figure 2-10. The heap management software does not try to find an unused area of memory that is large enough to hold the new object. Instead, it simply allocates the memory for the new object from the end of the heap, which it can do quickly.

Over time, as programs no longer use specific objects, the heap may have several gaps of available memory. At that time, the heap management software will run the garbage collector, which will move items around in the heap in a way that compacts the previously freed memory, making the memory available at the end of the heap, as shown in Figure 2-11.

USE IT   The following program, HeapUse.vb, first displays the amount of heap space the program has allocated. The program then allocates memory to store two different objects. The program then again displays the program's amount of allocated heap space. Next, the program discards one of the objects and requests that the garbage collector run and clean up the heap (by passing the value True to the GetTotalMemory method):

```
Module Module1

    Sub Main()
        Console.WriteLine("Starting Heap Space: " & _
          GC.GetTotalMemory(False))

        Dim BigArray(50000) As Byte
        Dim BiggerArray(250000) As Byte
```

allocates memory

```
        Console.WriteLine("Heap Space After Arrays: " & _
          GC.GetTotalMemory(False))

        BigArray = Nothing

        Console.WriteLine("Final Heap Space: " & _
          GC.GetTotalMemory(True))
        Console.ReadLine()
    End Sub
End Module
```

To indicate that it will no longer use the BigArray variable, the program sets the variable to Nothing, which marks the object as discardable for future garbage collection operations. When a program calls the GetTotalMemory method to determine the program's allocated memory, the program passes a Boolean value that indicates whether the garbage collector should first discard unused objects before returning the value. If the program passes the value True, the garbage collector will perform a collection and then determine the amount of heap space the program has allocated. If the program passes the value False, the garbage collector will not discard unused objects and will return the program's current heap allocation.

After you compile and execute this program, your screen will display the following output:

```
Starting Heap Space: 10216
Heap Space After Arrays: 322545
Final Heap Space: 268825
```

After the program ends, the .NET heap management software will release the remaining program objects.

Figure 2-10   The heap management software allocates memory for new objects from the end of the heap

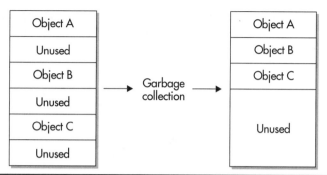

Figure 2-11   The garbage collector moves items in the heap and places unused memory at the end of the heap

Making Sense of .NET Versioning

In the Windows environment, large programs often consist of a .exe file and multiple dynamic link library (DLL) files. Unfortunately, when users install new programs on their systems, there are often times when a new program's installation replaces a DLL file with a newer (or in some cases, depending on the installation software, an older) DLL that causes other programs that worked before the installation to no longer run. Windows programmers refer to the conflicts that arise between various DLL files as "DLL hell."

To reduce the possibility of such conflicts with .NET applications, the assembly that packages an application provides versioning information. Applications can specify that they require a specific version of a class library (actually, the applications state that they require a specific version of an assembly that contains the class library). Further, two versions of an assembly can coexist on a system, and programs can select the assembly that corresponds to the version they need. In fact, a program can use each version of the assembly at the same time to reference different objects!

Within an assembly's manifest (the metadata that describes the assembly) is a four-digit version number that defines the assembly's major and minor version numbers, followed by a build number and a revision number of the build:

```
Major:Minor:Build:Revision
```

The following statement illustrates how a version number might appear in an assembly:

```
.ver 1:0:816:147
```

USE IT   Chapter 12 examines .NET versioning in detail. Using the IL Disassembler discussed in the Tip titled "Taking Advantage of Intermediate Language Code," you can view an assembly's version information as shown in Figure 2-12. As you examine the assembly, you will find that it specifies the version for each component (such as each DLL file) it requires.

```
┌─────────────────────────────────────────────────────────────────────────────────────┐
│ ✏ MANIFEST                                                               _ □ ✕ │
├─────────────────────────────────────────────────────────────────────────────────────┤
│ {                                                                               ▲ │
│   .publickeytoken = (B7 7A 5C 56 19 34 E0 89 )                 // .z\U.4..        │
│   .ver 1:0:3300:0                                                                │
│ }                                                                                │
│ .assembly extern System.Xml                                                       │
│ {                                                                                │
│   .publickeytoken = (B7 7A 5C 56 19 34 E0 89 )                 // .z\U.4..        │
│   .ver 1:0:3300:0                                                                │
│ }                                                                                │
│ .assembly ShowRoot                                                                │
│ {                                                                                │
│   // --- The following custom attribute is added automatically, do not uncomment ------- │
│   //  .custom instance void [mscorlib]System.Diagnostics.DebuggableAttribute::.ctor(bool, │
│   //                                                              bool) = ( 01   │
│   .custom instance void [mscorlib]System.Runtime.InteropServices.GuidAttribute::.ctor(string) = ( │
│                                                                                  │
│                                                                                  │
│   .custom instance void [mscorlib]System.CLSCompliantAttribute::.ctor(bool) = ( 01 00 01 00 00 ) │
│   .custom instance void [mscorlib]System.Reflection.AssemblyTrademarkAttribute::.ctor(string) = ( │
│   .custom instance void [mscorlib]System.Reflection.AssemblyCopyrightAttribute::.ctor(string) = ( │
│   .custom instance void [mscorlib]System.Reflection.AssemblyProductAttribute::.ctor(string) = ( 0 │
│   .custom instance void [mscorlib]System.Reflection.AssemblyCompanyAttribute::.ctor(string) = ( 0 │
│   .custom instance void [mscorlib]System.Reflection.AssemblyDescriptionAttribute::.ctor(string) = │
│   .custom instance void [mscorlib]System.Reflection.AssemblyTitleAttribute::.ctor(string) = ( 01  │
│   .hash algorithm 0x00008004                                                      │
│   .ver 1:0:816:14027                                                              │
│ }                                                                             ▼ │
│ ◄                                                                             ► │
└─────────────────────────────────────────────────────────────────────────────────────┘
```

Figure 2-12   Viewing an assembly's version information

Standardizing Error Handling

For years, Visual Basic programmers have made extensive use of the ON ERROR statement to
respond to errors and ERR.Number to determine specifics about an error. As you have learned,
in the .NET environment, routines in the Common Language Runtime are programming-language
independent, which means a C# program and a Visual Basic .NET program each call the
same routines.

The Common Language Runtime routines do not support the ON ERROR statement. Instead,
when a routine in the Common Language Runtime encounters an unexpected error, the routine will
generate an exception, for which the program must perform code to detect and respond to the error.
If the program does not handle the exception, the program will display an error message describing
the exception, as shown next, and the program will end.

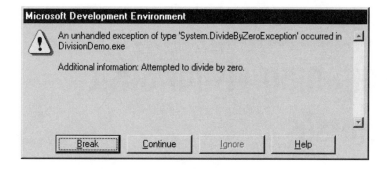

USE IT To detect and respond to an exception, Visual Basic .NET programs must perform operations that may generate an exception within a Try-Catch statement. The following statements, for example, try to open the text file Report.Txt that resides in the Temp directory on drive C. If the file does not exist, the StreamReader method will generate an exception. In this case, because the program calls the routine within a Try-Catch block, the program can detect and respond to the error:

```
Try
   SourceFile = New StreamReader("C:\Temp\Report.txt")
Catch Except As Exception
   MsgBox("Error opening the file C:\Temp\Report.txt")
End Try
```

Depending on the processing a routine performs, the routine may generate a variety of exceptions, each of which corresponds to a specific error. For example, when a program tries to open a file, the StreamReader method can encounter an error because the file does not exist, the directory specified does not exist, the file is locked, the file is read-only, and so on. Within a program, your code can use a Try-Catch block to handle specific errors, as shown here:

```
Try
    SourceFile = New StreamReader("C:\Temp\Report.txt")
Catch Except As DirectoryNotFoundException
   MsgBox("Error: Temp directory not found")
Catch Except As FileNotFoundException
   MsgBox("Error: Report.txt not found")
Catch Except As Exception
   MsgBox("Error: " & Except.Message)
End Try
```

Programmers refer to the use of Try-Catch statements as structured error handling. Chapter 9 examines exceptions and structured error handling in detail.

CHAPTER 3

Programming Visual Basic .NET Classes

To design programming solutions for complex operations, programmers first identify the objects (things) that make up a system. For example, to design an online banking system, a programmer might first identify the following objects:

- Accounts
- Customers
- Deposits
- Withdrawals
- Checks

Next, the programmer would identify each object's attributes (characteristics). For example, an account has a type, such as a checking or savings account. Likewise, an account has an account number, a balance, and customer-contact information. A check has a check number, an amount, a date, and so on.

After the programmer identifies each object's attributes, the programmer must determine the operations the system performs on each object. In the case of an account, for example, the system can open or close the account, balance (reconcile) the account, and let the user or teller look up account information.

Using a programming language, such as Visual Basic .NET, the programmer groups each object's attributes and operations within a class. The class begins with the Class keyword followed by a unique class name, and ends with the End Class statement:

```
Class UniqueClassName
    ' Attributes and operations
End Class
```

Within a class definition, the programmer defines operations, such as opening or closing an account, or using functions and subroutines. Programmers refer to the functions and subroutines that make up a class as the class methods:

```
Class BankAccount
   Sub OpenAccount()
     ' Statements
   End Sub

   Sub CloseAccount()
```

```
   ' Statements
  End Sub
End Class
```

Likewise, within a class definition, the programmer defines the class attributes using class-member variables. A class consists of subroutines, functions, and variable declarations:

```
Class BankAccount
  Dim AccountNumber As String
  Dim AccountBalance As Double
  Dim BankBranch As String

  Sub OpenAccount()
    ' Statements
  End Sub

  Sub CloseAccount()
    ' Statements
  End Sub
End Class
```

A class, therefore, consolidates an object's operations and attributes.

Using a Class

Within a program, a class defines a template the program can use to later declare a variable of the class type, which programmers refer to as an object or a class instance. A class definition, in and of itself, does not create a variable. Instead, after a program defines a class, the program can then declare one or more variables of the class type, using the New operator:

```
Dim CheckingAccount As New Account()
```

After a program creates a variable of a class type, the program uses the dot operator (the period) to reference specific class members. For example, the following statement would assign an account number to the CheckingAccount variable:

```
CheckingAccount.AccountNumber = "1234ABC56"
```

Using the dot operator, the programmer first specifies the class variable (in this case the CheckingAccount variable) and then the member variable within the class. To call the OpenAccount subroutine, the code would use the dot operator:

```
CheckingAccount.OpenAccount()
```

Putting an Existing Class to Use

Within the .NET environment, the Common Language Runtime provides a myriad of built-in classes your programs can use to perform a specific task. The following program, ClassDemo.vb, for example, uses the DateTime class. To start, the program creates a variable named DateInfo of the type DateTime:

```
Dim DateInfo As New DateTime(Now.Ticks)
```

In this case, to create a DateTime class variable that contains the current date and time, the program passes to function using Now.Ticks, which represents the current system date and time to a special function in the DateTime class (called the constructor) that initializes the class member variables. The code then uses the dot operator to access class members that include class variables and methods:

```
Module Module1
    Sub Main()
        Dim DateInfo As New DateTime(Now.Ticks)

        Console.WriteLine("Date: " & DateInfo.Month & "/" & _
            DateInfo.Day & "/" & DateInfo.Year)
        Console.WriteLine("Date: " & DateInfo.ToLongDateString())
        Console.WriteLine("Today is: " & DateInfo.DayOfWeek)
        Console.WriteLine("Days in April, 2002: " & _
            DateInfo.DaysInMonth(2002, 4))
        Console.ReadLine() ' Pause to view output
    End Sub
End Module
```

After you compile and run this program, your screen will display output similar to the following:

```
Date: 3/16/2002
Date: Saturday, March 16, 2002
Today is: 6
Days in April, 2002: 30
```

Creating Your Own Class

In a simplified online bookstore, users can look up or purchase books. Likewise, a simple Book object consists of a title, author name, publisher name, and price. The following Book class uses four member variables to store the book information:

```
Class Book
  Public Title As String
  Public Author As String
  Public Publisher As String
```

```
      Public Price As Double
End Class
```

For now, you can ignore the Public keyword that appears within the class definition. In general, the Public keyword lets a program access the corresponding class member using the dot operator. In addition to storing an object's attributes (which a class stores using variables) a class also defines the operations the program can perform on the class. The following statements extend the Book class to support the DisplayBookInfo subroutine:

```
Class Book
   Public Title As String
   Public Author As String
   Public Publisher As String
   Public Price As Double

   Public Sub DisplayBookInfo()
      Console.WriteLine("Title: " & Title)
      Console.WriteLine("Author: " & Author)
      Console.WriteLine("Publisher: " & Publisher)
      Console.WriteLine("Price: " & Price)
   End Sub
End Class
```

A class definition simply provides a template a program can use to later declare a variable of the class type. The following program, FirstBookClass.vb, defines the book class and then creates a variable named ComputerBook based on the Book class definition:

```
Dim ComputerBook As New Book()
```

After the program creates the object, the program uses the dot operator to assign values to the object's member variables. Then the code uses the dot operator to call the DisplayBookInfo subroutine:

```
Module Module1

    Class Book
        Public Title As String
        Public Author As String
        Public Publisher As String
        Public Price As Double

        Public Sub DisplayBookInfo()
            Console.WriteLine("Title: " & Title)
            Console.WriteLine("Author: " & Author)
            Console.WriteLine("Publisher: " & Publisher)
            Console.WriteLine("Price: " & Price)
```

```
        End Sub
    End Class


    Sub Main()
        Dim ComputerBook As New Book()

        ComputerBook.Title = "VB.NET Programming Tips & Techniques"
        ComputerBook.Author = "Jamsa"
        ComputerBook.Publisher = "McGraw-Hill/Osborne"
        ComputerBook.Price = 49.99

        ComputerBook.DisplayBookInfo()
        Console.ReadLine() ' Pause to display output
    End Sub
End Module
```

Note that to access the member variables outside of the class, the program code must use the dot operator to specify both the class name and that of the member variable. Within the DisplayBookInfo subroutine, in contrast, which the Book class defines, the code can simply refer to the member variable by name (because the class, Book, is implied). After you compile and execute this program, your screen will display the following output:

```
Title: VB.NET Programming Tips & Techniques
Author: Jamsa
Publisher: McGraw-Hill/Osborne
Price: 49.99
```

Using Scope Attributes to Restrict Access to Class Members

When you create a class, you should think of the class as a "black box," meaning, to use the class, you do not need to know how the class performs its processing, but rather, what processing the class performs. Your television, for example, is a good example of a black box. To watch TV, you do not need to understand how the TV's receiver converts the signals it receives into the images that appear on the screen. Instead, you simply must know how to turn the TV on, change channels, and increase or decrease the volume.

Likewise, to use your class, another programmer should only need to know the class's callable methods and usable member variables. The programmer does not need to understand how each of your class methods work, but rather, the programmer must only know which parameters his or her code must pass to the methods.

To help you better treat your classes as black boxes, Visual Basic .NET lets you hide class member variables and methods that are private to the class so that code outside of the class cannot access them. Assume, for example, that you have an Employee class that provides the CalcPay method that a program can call to determine an employee's paycheck amount. To perform its processing, the CalcPay function may call the GetPayScale, DetermineDeductions, and CheckVacationTime methods. Because you want to treat the Employee class as a black box, you do not want code outside of the Employee class to know that these other methods exist. Instead, you only want other code to be able to call the CalcPay function.

USE IT   To let you control which class members code outside of your class can access, Visual Basic .NET lets you precede class members (both variables and methods) with one of the access control modifiers described in Table 3-1.

The following program, PublicPrivateDemo.vb, creates an Employee class that uses both Public and Private members. Outside of the class, the code can access the Public members directly, using the dot operator. If code outside of the class tries to access a Private member directly, the compiler will generate a syntax error. Within the class, however, the code can access Private members directly:

```
Module Module1

    Class Employee
        Public Name As String
        Private Age As Integer
        Public OfficeNumber As String
        Private HomePhone As String

        Public Sub ShowEmployee()
            Console.WriteLine("Name: " & Name)
            Console.WriteLine("Age: " & Age)
            Console.WriteLine("Office Number: " & OfficeNumber)
            Console.WriteLine("Home Phone: " & HomePhone)
        End Sub

        Public Sub AssignAge(ByVal EmpAge As Integer)
            If (EmpAge > 18) And (EmpAge < 100) Then
                Age = EmpAge
            End If
        End Sub

        Public Sub AssignHomePhone(ByVal Phone As String)
            HomePhone = Phone
        End Sub
    End Class
```

```
    Sub Main()
        Dim Boss As New Employee()

        Boss.Name = "Jane Doe"
        Boss.OfficeNumber = "123A"
        Boss.AssignAge(35)
        Boss.AssignHomePhone("555-1212")

        Boss.ShowEmployee()
        Console.ReadLine()
    End Sub
End Module
```

Within the program that uses the class, the code can use the dot operator to directly access the Public class members. In contrast, if you try to use the dot operator to access a Private class member, the Visual Basic .NET compiler would generate a syntax error telling you the member is not accessible.

When your program defines a class, you can also precede the class name with one of the access control specifiers, to control how your program can use the class. The following statement, for example, precedes the Class definition with the Private specifier, which restricts use of the class to the current program:

```
Private Class Employee
    ' Member declarations
End Class
```

If you do not precede a class definition with an access control specifier, the default is Public.

Access Control Modifier	Meaning
Friend	The member is only available within the current project.
Private	The member is only available within the class.
Protected	The member is available within the class and classes that inherit the class.
Protected Friend	The member is available within the current project and within classes that inherit the class.
Public	The member is available to code outside of the class.

Table 3-1 Visual Basic .NET Access Modifiers that Programmers Can Use to Control Access to Class Members

Initializing Class Member Variables

When you create a class object, you will normally immediately assign values to specific class member variables. For example, the following code fragment defines a Book class that contains fields for a title, publisher, author, and price:

```
Class Book
    Public Title As String
    Public Pubilsher As String
    Public Author As String
    Public Price As Double
End Class
```

Within your program, you can create (instantiate) instances of the Book class, which programmers refer to as objects, using the following statement:

```
Dim ThisBook As New Book()
```

To simplify the process of initializing class member variables, you can place a special subroutine within your class definition (named New) that Visual Basic .NET automatically calls each time you create a class object. Programmers refer to this special subroutine as a "constructor" because it helps you build (construct) the class object.

The constructor method is special in that within any class definition, the constructor is always named New. Programmers use the constructor to initialize class member variables. The following code fragment, for example, extends the Book class to include the New constructor method:

```
Class Book
    Public Title As String
    Public Publisher As String
    Public Author As String
    Public Price As Double

    Sub New(ByVal BookTitle As String, _
        ByVal BookPublisher As String, _
        ByVal BookAuthor As String, ByVal BookPrice As Double)

        Title = BookTitle
        Publisher = BookPublisher
        Author = BookAuthor
        Price = BookPrice
    End Sub
End Class
```

When your code creates a Book object, your code can pass the initial values you want to assign to the class members as parameters to the constructor:

```
Dim ThisBook As New Book("Visual Basic .NET Programming Tips & Techniques",
    "McGraw-Hill/Osborne", "Jamsa", 49.95)
```

USE IT The following program, ConstructorDemo.vb, creates a TVShow class that contains Name, Day, and Time fields. The code uses a constructor method to initialize the class members:

```
Module Module1
    Class TVShow
        Public Name As String
        Public Day As String
        Public Time As String

        Sub New(ByVal ShowName As String, ByVal DayOfWeek As String, _
            ByVal ShowTime As String)
            MsgBox("Name: " & ShowName & " Day: " & DayOfWeek & _
                " Time: " & ShowTime)
            Name = ShowName
            Day = DayOfWeek
            Time = ShowTime
        End Sub
    End Class

    Sub Main()
        Dim Drama As New TVShow("West Wing", "Wednesday", "8:00PM")
        Dim Medical As New TVShow("ER", "Thursday", "9:00PM")
        Dim Comedy As New TVShow("Friends", "Thursday", "7:00PM")
    End Sub
End Module
```

To help you better understand the constructor method's processing, the constructor, in this case, displays a message box that describes the values the method receives as parameters, as shown here.

In this case, because the program creates three different TVShow objects, the program will display three message boxes, one for each object's parameters. When you run the program, you will see that Visual Basic .NET automatically calls the constructor method each time you create an object using the New keyword.

Using a constructor method, you can easily initialize a new object's member variables. After you use the constructor method to initialize member variables, your code can later change a Public member variable's value using the dot operator. The following statement, for example, changes the values the program assigns to the Drama object:

```
Dim Drama As New TVShow("West Wing", "Wednesday", "8:00PM")

Drama.Name = "NYPD Blue"
Drama.Day = "Tuesday"
```

Defining Multiple Constructors to Support Different Parameters

To initialize class member variables, programmers make extensive use of constructor methods. Normally, for a simple class, the constructor method will support a parameter for each key class member variable. Consider the following BookDetail class that provides support for the title, author, publisher, price, chapter count, and copyright date:

```
Class BookDetails
    Public Title As String
    Public Publisher As String
    Public Author As String
    Public Price As Double
    Public ChapterCount As Integer
    Public CopyrightDate As String
End Class
```

The key variable variables, in this case, may be the title and price. As such, the class might provide the following constructor method that initializes those two member variables:

```
Public Sub New(ByVal Title As String, ByVal Price As Double)
    Me.Title = Title
    Me.Price = Price
    Me.Author = ""
    Me.ChapterCount = 0
    Me.Publisher = ""
    Me.CopyrightDate = ""
End Sub
```

In this case, the constructor uses the two parameters to initialize the title and price variables and then the constructor assigns default values to the other members.

Often, the program will specify author and publisher information as well. As such, the class might provide a second constructor method that supports four parameters:

```
Public Sub New(ByVal Title As String, ByVal Author As String, _
   ByVal Publisher As String, ByVal Price As Double)
    Me.Title = Title
    Me.Author = Author
    Me.Publisher = Publisher
    Me.Price = Price
    Me.ChapterCount = 0
    Me.CopyrightDate = ""
End Sub
```

Finally, to allow the program to initialize each of the member variables, the class may provide yet a third constructor:

```
Public Sub New(ByVal Title As String, ByVal Author As String, _
   ByVal Publisher As String, ByVal Price As Double, _
   ByVal ChapterCount As Integer, ByVal CopyrightDate As Date)
    Me.Title = Title
    Me.Author = Author
    Me.Publisher = Publisher
    Me.Price = Price
    Me.ChapterCount = ChapterCount
    Me.CopyrightDate = CopyrightDate
End Sub
```

 The following program, MultipleConstructors.vb, illustrates the use of multiple constructors to initialize the BookDetail class:

```
Module Module1

    Class BookDetails
        Public Title As String
        Public Publisher As String
        Public Author As String
        Public Price As Double
        Public ChapterCount As Integer
        Public CopyrightDate As String

        Public Sub New(ByVal Title As String, ByVal Price As Double)
            Me.Title = Title
            Me.Price = Price
            Me.Author = ""
            Me.ChapterCount = 0
            Me.Publisher = ""
            Me.CopyrightDate = ""
        End Sub
```

```vb
Public Sub New(ByVal Title As String, ByVal Author As String, _
   ByVal Publisher As String, ByVal Price As Double)
    Me.Title = Title
    Me.Author = Author
    Me.Publisher = Publisher
    Me.Price = Price
    Me.ChapterCount = 0
    Me.CopyrightDate = ""
End Sub

Public Sub New(ByVal Title As String, ByVal Author As String, _
   ByVal Publisher As String, ByVal Price As Double, _
   ByVal ChapterCount As Integer, ByVal CopyrightDate As Date)
    Me.Title = Title
    Me.Author = Author
    Me.Publisher = Publisher
    Me.Price = Price
    Me.ChapterCount = ChapterCount
    Me.CopyrightDate = CopyrightDate
End Sub

Public Sub ShowInfo()
    Console.WriteLine(Title)

    If (Author.Length > 0) Then
        Console.WriteLine(Author)
    End If

    If (Publisher.Length > 0) Then
        Console.WriteLine(Publisher)
    End If

    If (Price > 0.0) Then
        Console.WriteLine(Price)
    End If

    If (ChapterCount > 0) Then
        Console.WriteLine(ChapterCount)
    End If

    If (CopyrightDate.Length > 0) Then
        Console.WriteLine(CopyrightDate)
    End If
End Sub
```

```
      End Class

   Sub Main()
        Dim Palm = New BookDetails("Instant Palm OS Applications", 49.99)
        Dim CSharp = New BookDetails("C# Programming Tips & Techniques", _
           "Wright", "McGraw-Hill/Osborne", 49.99)
        Dim VB = New BookDetails("VB.NET Programming Tips & Techniques", _
           "Jamsa", "McGraw-Hill/Osborne", 49.99, 18, "April 2002")

        Palm.ShowInfo()
        Console.WriteLine()
        VB.ShowInfo()
        Console.ReadLine()
   End Sub
End Module
```

After you compile and execute this program, your screen will display the following output:

```
Instant Palm OS Applications
49.99

VB.NET Programming Tips & Techniques
Jamsa
McGraw-Hill/Osborne
49.99
18
4/1/2002
```

Simplifying Object Member References

To reference an object's member variables or methods, Visual Basic .NET programs make extensive use of the dot operator:

```
Book.Title = "Visual Basic .NET Programming Tips & Techniques"
```

When your code must work with a large number of class members, as might well be the case within a constructor method that initializes class member variables, you can reduce the amount of typing you must perform by taking advantage of the Visual Basic .NET With statement. The following statements, for example, initialize several class member variables using the dot operator. As you can see, each statement must specify the class name followed by the dot operator and the class member name:

```
Book.Title = "Visual Basic .NET Programming Tips & Techniques"
Book.Publisher = "McGraw-Hill/Osborne"
```

```
Book.Author = "Jamsa"
Book.Price = 49.95
```

USE IT   Using the With statement, you can specify an object's class name one time and then simply specify the dot operator and member name. Visual Basic .NET, in turn, will assume that any member variable that appears between the With and End With statements correspond to the class name you specify. The following statements illustrate the use of With and End With:

```
With Book
  .Title = "Visual Basic .NET Programming Tips & Techniques"
  .Publisher = "McGraw-Hill/Osborne"
  .Author = "Jamsa"
  .Price = 49.95
End With
```

As you can see, within a With statement, you must still precede member variable names with the dot operator. The following program, WithDemo.vb, uses the With statement to assign values to a LunchOrder class:

```
Module Module1
    Class LunchOrder
        Public Salad As String
        Public Meal As String
        Public Beverage As String
        Public Dessert As String

        Public Sub New(ByVal SaladType As String, _
           ByVal MealType As String, ByVal BeverageType As String, _
           ByVal DessertType As String)

            Salad = SaladType
            Meal = MealType
            Beverage = BeverageType
            Dessert = DessertType
        End Sub
    End Class

    Sub Main()
        Dim MyLunch As New LunchOrder("Spinach", "Pasta", _
          "Red Wine", "Cookies")

        With MyLunch
            Console.WriteLine("Salad: " & .Salad)
            Console.WriteLine("Meal: " & .Meal)
            Console.WriteLine("Beverage: " & .Beverage)
```

```
            Console.WriteLine("Dessert: " & .Dessert)
        End With

        Console.ReadLine()
    End Sub
End Module
```

Taking Advantage of Static Class Members

Throughout this chapter, to use class methods, your programs have created an instance of a class object. As you examine various .NET classes throughout this book, you will periodically encounter the term "static class." A static class is unique in that your program can call the class methods without first creating an instance of the class (an object). The following program, MathClassDemo.vb, for example, uses several of the methods the Math class provides. The program does not, however, ever create a Math class object:

```
Module Module1
    Sub Main()
        Console.WriteLine("Absolute value of -1 is " & Math.Abs(-1))
        Console.WriteLine("Square Root of 144 is " & Math.Sqrt(144))
        Console.WriteLine("Value for PI is " & Math.PI)
        Console.WriteLine("10 raised to the power of 2 is " & _
            Math.Pow(10, 2))

        Console.ReadLine()
    End Sub
End Module
```

The program can use the Math class methods without creating an object because the Math class is a static class. As you create classes, there may be times when you build a class that simply groups a useful set of methods. In such cases, you can provide programs with access to the methods by making the class static.

 To create a static class within Visual Basic .NET, you simply place the Shared keyword before members within the class definition. The following class definition, for example, creates two static (shared) members that programs can use to calculate the area of a circle and the area of a square without having to create an instance of the Area object:

```
Class Area
    Public Shared Function Circle(ByVal Radius As Double) As Double
        Circle = (Math.PI * Radius * Radius)
    End Function
```

```
    Public Shared Function Square(ByVal Length As Double) As Double
        Square = (Length * Length)
    End Function
End Class
```

Within a class, you can specify either fields or methods as shared. The following program, StaticClassDemo.vb, creates a class named Today, that contains several shared fields which the user can use to get the current date in various formats. Because the class is static, the program can access the class member variables without creating a Today object:

```
Module Module1
    Class Today
        Public Shared TodayDate As DateTime = Now()
        Public Shared Day As Integer = Now.Day()
        Public Shared Month As Integer = Now.Month()
        Public Shared Year As Integer = Now.Year()
        Public Shared NumericDayOfWeek As Integer = Now.DayOfWeek()
        Public Shared StringDayOfWeek As String = Now.DayOfWeek.ToString()
    End Class

    Sub Main()
        Console.WriteLine("Today: " & Today.TodayDate)
        Console.WriteLine("Day: " & Today.Day)
        Console.WriteLine("Month: " & Today.Month)
        Console.WriteLine("Year: " & Today.Year)
        Console.WriteLine("Day of week: " & Today.NumericDayOfWeek)
        Console.WriteLine("Day of week: " & Today.StringDayOfWeek)

        Console.ReadLine()
    End Sub
End Module
```

When you compile and execute this program, your screen will display output similar to the following:

```
Today: 3/15/2002 7:10:32 PM
Day: 15
Month: 3
Year: 2002
Day of week: 5
Day of week: Friday
```

Taking Advantage of Properties to Control Values a Class Member Can Store

When you create a class, there will often be times when you will want your code to restrict the values a program can assign to a class variable. For example, within an Employee class, you may want to restrict the values the Age member can store to the range 18 to 80. Likewise, within a ContactInformation class, you might restrict the Email variable to storing only values in the form Name@SomeSite.com.

USE IT   To restrict the values a program can assign to a class variable, your code can define the variable as Private (which limits access to the variable to class member methods) and then create a property within the class that manipulates the Private member variable. In general, a property is a class member variable that, behind the scenes, uses two special functions named Get and Set to control access to the variable's value. The Get function returns the property's value. The Set function assigns a value to the property. A program can only assign a value to or retrieve the value of a property using the Set and Get functions. The following code fragment illustrates how you might declare the Age property within a class:

```
Public Property Age() As Integer
   Get
      Return AgeValue
   End Get

   Set (ByVal Age As Integer)
     If (Age >= 18) And (Age <= 80) Then
        AgeValue = Age
     Else
        MsgBox("Invalid age - using 0")
        AgeValue = 0
     End If
   End Set
End Property
```

As you have learned, a program that uses a class can directly access Public class members. Because the Age property is public, programs that use the class can access the field. Classes use a property to sit in front of a private class member, which programs cannot access directly. In this case, the Age property sits in front of a private class member named AgeValue. If the user specifies a valid age, the Set method will assign the private AgeValue member the corresponding value (a class can access its own private members, whereas code outside of the class cannot). Likewise, the Get method returns the value stored in the private AgeValue member.

What makes a property unique is that someone who is using the class may not know that the Get and Set functions exist. Instead, to assign a value to a property, the programmer simply uses an assignment statement similar to the following:

```
EmployeeName.Age = 27
```

Behind the scenes, however, when Visual Basic .NET compiles the code, it will convert the assignment into a function call:

```
EmployeeName.Age = Set(27)
```

Likewise, to retrieve the property's value, the code simply specifies the property name:

```
SomeVariable = EmployeeName.Age
```

Again, behind the scenes, the Visual Basic .NET compiler will create a reference to the Get function. When your class has a member for which you want to restrict the values, the program can assign to the variable, you should "wrap" the variable within a property. The following program, PropertyDemo.vb, creates a simple Book class that stores a title, author, price, and page count. To control the range of values the program can assign to the BookPrice and BookPages member variables, the class uses two properties, Price and Pages:

```vbnet
Module Module1
    Class Book
        Public Title As String
        Public Author As String
        Private BookPrice As Double
        Private BookPages As Integer

        Public Property Price() As Double
            Get
                Return BookPrice
            End Get
            Set(ByVal Value As Double)
                If (Value >= 0) And (Value <= 100) Then
                    BookPrice = Value
                Else
                    MsgBox("Invalid price for " & Title)
                    BookPrice = 0
                End If
            End Set
        End Property
```

```
        Public Property Pages() As Integer
            Get
                Return BookPages
            End Get

            Set(ByVal Value As Integer)
                If (Value >= 0) And (Value <= 1500) Then
                    BookPages = Value
                Else
                    MsgBox("Invalid page count for " & Title)
                    BookPages = 0
                End If
            End Set
        End Property

        Public Sub New(ByVal Title As String, ByVal Author As String)
            Me.Title = Title
            Me.Author = Author
        End Sub
    End Class

    Sub Main()
        Dim Palm As New Book("Instant Palm OS Applications", "Jamsa")
        Dim Upgrading As New _
          Book("PC Performance Tuning & Upgrading Tips & Techniques", _
          "Jamsa")

        Palm.Price = 49.99
        Palm.Pages = 2000

        Upgrading.Price = 119.99
        Upgrading.Pages = 600
        Console.WriteLine(Upgrading.Pages)
        Console.ReadLine()  ' Pause to view output
    End Sub
End Module
```

After you compile and execute this program, the Pages property Set function will detect that 2000 is an invalid number of pages and, in turn, will display a message box describing the error. Likewise, the Set function for the Pages property will detect that 119.99 falls outside of the price range and will display a message box describing the error.

Avoiding Parameter Name and Class Member Variable Name Conflicts

When your programs use a constructor method to initialize class-member variables, your code will normally pass parameters to the New subroutine. For example, the following constructor method initializes several class members:

```
Sub New(ByVal ShowName As String, ByVal DayOfWeek As String, _
   ByVal ShowTime As String)

    Name = ShowName
    Day = DayOfWeek
    Time = ShowTime
End Sub
```

As you can see, the constructor method uses names for the parameters that differ from those of the class member variables. If a parameter name matches that of a class member name, Visual Basic .NET will assume that each reference to the variable corresponds to the parameter, as opposed to the class member.

USE IT To differentiate between parameters and class member variables, many programmers often take advantage of the Me keyword that references the current instance of an object. The following constructor method, for example, uses the parameter names that match those of the class member variables. To distinguish between the class member variables and the parameters, the code precedes each class member variable name with the Me keyword followed by the dot operator:

```
Sub New(ByVal Name As String, ByVal Day As String, _
   ByVal Time As String)

    Me.Name = Name
    Me.Day = Week
    Me.Time = Time
End Sub
```

As you examine Visual Basic classes, you may encounter the Me keyword on a regular basis. As discussed, the Me keyword corresponds to the current instance of an object.

Performing "Cleanup" Processing Using a Destructor Method

Programs that use class objects normally make extensive use of constructor methods to initialize the object's member variables. When you create a class object, Visual Basic .NET automatically calls the class constructor method. In a similar way, when your code no longer uses an object, Visual Basic .NET will automatically call a special subroutine that programmers call the class "destructor" method, because the method lets you specify the processing you want your program to perform before the .NET environment discards the object (removes the object from memory). Depending on the object's purpose, for example, your program might use the destructor method to close an open reference to a file stream or database. Or your program might save the object's current settings (in the case of a form within which the user is entering values) to a file. Just as Visual Basic .NET programs use the New method to identify a class constructor method, your programs will use the Finalize subroutine to implement the destructor.

 The following program, FinalizeDemo.vb, creates a Contact class that contains information about a person's name, phone number, and e-mail address. The program uses a constructor method to initialize each object. In this case, the Finalize subroutine (the destructor) simply displays a message box that contains information about each object the class is destroying, as shown here.

```
Module Module1
    Class Contact
        Public Name As String
        Public Phone As String
        Public EMail As String

        Sub New(ByVal ContactName As String, _
          ByVal ContactPhone As String, ByVal ContactEmail As String)

            MsgBox("Name: " & ContactName & " Phone: " & ContactPhone & _
              " Email: " & ContactEmail)
            Name = ContactName
            Phone = ContactPhone
            EMail = ContactEmail
        End Sub

        Protected Overrides Sub Finalize()
            MsgBox("In Finalize for " & Name)
        End Sub
    End Class

    Sub Main()
        Dim Amanda As New Contact("Amanda", "281-555-1111", "Duh@aol.com")
```

```
          Dim Megan As New Contact("Megan", "713-555-1212", "Megan@Hotmail.com")
          Dim Sara As New Contact("Sara", "281-555-1212", "Sara@Yah.com")
     End Sub
End Module
```

In this case, the program creates and initializes three Contact objects. The program then simply ends. Behind the scenes, however, before the program ends, the program will call each object's Finalize method. Using the Finalize method, the code might perform specific "cleanup" processing. In this case, the Finalize method simply displays a message box telling you that it was called.

Mapping a Class Object to a Visual Basic .NET Form

USE IT Throughout this chapter, many of the tips have created simple classes to which the code then assigned hard-coded values. The following program, FormClassData.vb, displays the form shown in Figure 3-1, which the user can use to enter data about a book. When the user clicks the Submit button, the code creates a Book object, using a constructor method to initialize the class member variables with the specified values. After the program creates the object, it uses a message box to display the object's member values.

```
Public Class Form1
    Inherits System.Windows.Forms.Form

#Region " Windows Form Designer generated code "
    ' Code not shown
#End Region

    Class Employee
        Public Name As String
        Public Phone As String
        Public EMail As String

        Public Sub New(ByVal Name As String, ByVal Phone As String, _
          ByVal EMail As String)
            Me.Name = Name
            Me.Phone = Phone
            Me.EMail = Email
        End Sub
    End Class

    Private Sub Button1_Click(ByVal sender As Object, _
      ByVal e As System.EventArgs) Handles Button1.Click
```

```
        If (TextBox1.Text.Length = 0) Then
            MsgBox("Must specify employee name")
        ElseIf (TextBox2.Text.Length = 0) Then
            MsgBox("Must specify employee phone number")
        ElseIf (TextBox3.Text.Length = 0) Then
            MsgBox("Must specify employee e-mail address")
        Else
            Dim Worker As New Employee(TextBox1.Text, _
              TextBox2.Text, TextBox3.Text)

            MsgBox("Employee: " & Worker.Name & " Phone: " & _
              Worker.Phone & " Email: " & Worker.EMail)
        End If
    End Sub
End Class
```

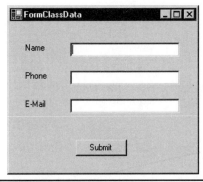

Figure 3-1   Using a form to provide class data

Taking a Closer Look at .NET Garbage Collection

In the .NET environment, the objects you create reside within a special "managed" memory region. When your program no longer needs an object, Visual Basic .NET will set an attribute for the object that marks the object as ready for deletion. Later, special software built into the .NET environment, which programmers refer to as the "garbage collector," will release the memory (back to Windows) that the object previously consumed, making the memory available for other uses.

Unfortunately, a program has no way of knowing when the garbage collector will actually perform its cleanup operations. However, before the garbage collector discards an object, it will call the object's Finalize method, which the Tip titled "Performing 'Cleanup' Processing Using a Destructor Method" discussed in detail. To provide your programs with access to the garbage collector, the .NET environment provides a Garbage Collector class, named GC. Table 3-2 briefly describes the Garbage Collector methods your programs can call.

Method	Purpose
Collect	Forces the garbage collector to collect unused objects. The Collect method is overloaded.
GetGeneration	Returns the garbage collector's current generation for an object. The GetGeneration method is overloaded.
GetTotalMemory	Returns the amount of memory (in bytes) the program has currently allocated.
KeepAlive	Marks the specified object as ineligible for garbage collection while the program is executing code from the start of the current routine to the location where KeepAlive is called.
ReRegisterForFinalize	Directs the system to call the specified object's finalizer method, following a call to the SuppressFinalizer method.
SuppressFinalize	Directs the system not to call the specified object's finalizer method.
WaitForPendingFinalizers	Suspends the current thread until the thread processing the finalizer methods for discard objects has finished its processing.

Table 3-2   Methods Within the GC Class Programs Can Call to Interact with the .NET Garbage Collector

USE IT   The following program, GarbageCollectorDemo.vb, displays the current allocated memory. It then creates three Employee objects and again displays the amount of allocated memory. The code then directs the system not to call the Finalize method for the last object:

```
Module Module1

    Class Employee
        Public Name As String
        Public Email As String

        Public Sub New(ByVal Name As String, ByVal Email As String)
            Me.Name = Name
            Me.Email = Email
        End Sub

        Protected Overrides Sub Finalize()
            MsgBox("In Finalize for " & Name)
        End Sub
    End Class

    Sub Main()
        MsgBox("Allocated memory " & GC.GetTotalMemory(True))

        Dim Boss As New Employee("Jones", "Bill@SomeCompany.com")
        Dim Worker As New Employee("Smith", "Debbie@SomeCompany.com")
```

```
        Dim Manager As New Employee("Davis", "Janet@SomeCompany.com")

        MsgBox("Allocated memory " & GC.GetTotalMemory(True))
        GC.SuppressFinalize(Manager)
    End Sub
End Module
```

After you compile and run this program, your system will display message boxes that contain the amount of memory (in bytes) the program has allocated. When a program begins, Visual Basic .NET has allocated memory to store program data (such as thread space, stack space, and so on). After the program creates the three objects, the amount of memory the program has allocated increases. The program calls the GC class SuppressFinalize method to prevent the garbage collector from calling the Manager object's Finalize method before the program executes the call to GC.SuppressFinalize.

Forcing the Garbage Collector to Collect Unused Memory

In the .NET environment, a special program called the garbage collector manages the heap (the special memory area from which .NET programs allocate memory for objects). The garbage collector runs behind the scenes. As your program no longer needs an object, the garbage collector will free up the memory the object consumed, making the memory available for other uses. Before the garbage collector discards an object, it will call the object's Finalize method, giving the object an opportunity to perform any cleanup processing it requires.

Within a Visual Basic .NET program, you can tell the garbage collector that your program will no longer be using an object by setting the object to "nothing" as shown here:

```
Employee = nothing
```

As the garbage collector performs its processing, it will identify the fact that you are no longer using the object and it will release the object's memory. As discussed, the garbage collector performs its processing behind the scenes. Normally, it wakes up at specific time intervals and then performs its collection operations. Depending on the processing your program performs, there may be times, however, when you will want your program to request that the garbage collector initiate a collection operation. For example, if your program must allocate a large amount of memory (perhaps to store an array of large objects), your program may want the garbage collector to free up available memory before your program allocates the array. Likewise, after your program is done with the array, your code may initiate a collection operation to give back the memory the array consumed. As a general rule, to avoid system overhead, your code should use the GC.Collect method with care and only as necessary.

USE IT   To force the garbage collector to run, your programs can call the GC class Collect method:

```
GC.Collect()
```

The following program, ForceGarbageCollection.vb, creates three Pet objects. The program then assigns the Bird object to nothing and uses the GC class Collect method to force a collection operation. Before the garbage collector frees the Bird object's memory, it will call the object's Finalize method. The program will then assign the Dog object to nothing and will use the GC class Collect method to force a second collection:

```
Module Module1

    Class Pet
        Public Type As String
        Public Name As String
        Public Price As Double

        Public Sub New(ByVal Type As String, ByVal Name As String, _
          ByVal Price As Double)
            Me.Type = Type
            Me.Name = Name
            Me.Price = Price
        End Sub

        Protected Overrides Sub Finalize()
            Console.WriteLine("In Finalize for " & Type)
        End Sub
    End Class

    Sub Main()
        Dim Dog As New Pet("Dog", "Buddy", 99.95)
        Dim Bird As New Pet("Bird", "Tweety", 199.95)
        Dim Cat As New Pet("Cat", "Sylvester", 39.95)

        Bird = Nothing ' Discard the object
        GC.Collect()
        Console.WriteLine("Started first collection")

        Dog = Nothing ' Discard the object
        GC.Collect()
        Console.WriteLine("Started second collection -- Press Enter")
        Console.ReadLine() ' Delay to view output
    End Sub
End Module
```

After you compile and execute this program, your screen may display output similar to the following:

```
Started first collection
In Finalize for Bird
```

```
Started second collection -- Press Enter
In Finalize for Dog
```

The output that your PC displays may differ slightly from that shown here due to the timing at
which the various threads execute. The garbage collector is a background task. Depending on how
your system allocates the CPU time slices, it is possible that the garbage collector will run and call
the object's Finalize method before the program displays the message that it has started the corresponding
collection. After you press the ENTER key to continue, the garbage collector will eventually run a
final time before your program ends, calling the Finalize method for the Cat object.

Providing Destructor-like Support for Dispose Operations

In the Tip titled "Performing 'Cleanup' Processing Using a Destructor Method," you learned that
before the .NET garbage collector releases an object, it will call the object's Finalize method, which
your program can use to perform cleanup processing. Depending on the processing an object
performs, there may be times when the time delay is simply too long between when your program
stops using an object and when the object's Finalize method runs. In such cases, you can include a
special method in your class named Dispose, within which you can perform the processing you need
for a discarded object. By calling the Dispose method, your code can immediately perform the
object's cleanup processing when you know that you will no longer be using the object's contents.

USE IT   If you examine the code that Visual Studio creates for a form, you will find that the code
creates a Dispose method within the form's class:

```
'Form overrides dispose to clean up the component list.
Protected Overloads Overrides Sub Dispose(ByVal disposing As Boolean)
   If disposing Then
     If Not (components Is Nothing) Then
        components.Dispose()
     End If
   End If
   MyBase.Dispose(disposing)
End Sub
```

In Chapter 4, you will examine Visual Basic interfaces (which you can think of as a class for
which the definition does not provide method definitions). To use the Dispose method, your code
must implement the IDisposable interface. However, as you talk with other programmers about
destructor methods and garbage collection, you may encounter discussions regarding the Dispose
method. For now, think of the Dispose method as a way an object can immediately release resources
(such as an open file). To invoke the Dispose method, the object must explicitly call the method:

```
SomeClass.Dispose()
```

Taking a Closer Look at Visual Basic .NET Forms

One of the primary reasons, if not the single most important reason, Visual Basic has been so successful is the ease with which programmers can build user interfaces by dragging and dropping objects onto forms. As you know, when you design a user interface using Visual Studio's toolset, Visual Studio will create the corresponding program code, behind the scenes, that actually creates and displays the form elements.

If you examine the code that Visual Studio creates for the various form elements, you will find that Visual Studio makes extensive use of class objects to implement and interact with each element. For example, Figure 3-2 shows a simple form within Visual Studio.

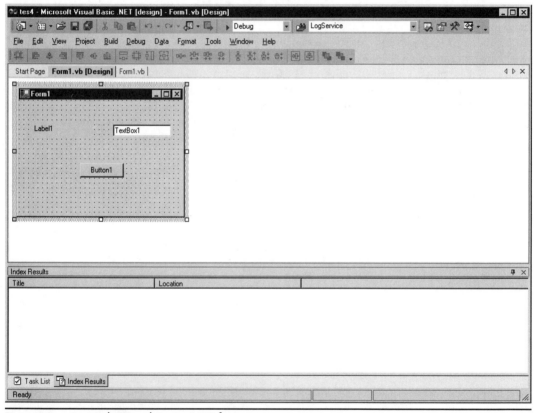

Figure 3-2   A simple Visual Basic .NET form

USE IT   If you examine the code that Visual Studio creates for the form, you will find the
following statements:

```
Public Class Form1
    Inherits System.Windows.Forms.Form

#Region " Windows Form Designer generated code "

    Public Sub New()
        MyBase.New()
        InitializeComponent()
    End Sub

    Protected Overloads Overrides Sub Dispose(ByVal _
      disposing As Boolean)
        If disposing Then
            If Not (components Is Nothing) Then
                components.Dispose()
            End If
        End If
        MyBase.Dispose(disposing)
    End Sub

    Private components As System.ComponentModel.Icontainer

    Friend WithEvents Label1 As System.Windows.Forms.Label
    Friend WithEvents TextBox1 As System.Windows.Forms.TextBox
    Friend WithEvents Button1 As System.Windows.Forms.Button
    <System.Diagnostics.DebuggerStepThrough()> Private Sub _
        InitializeComponent()
        Me.Label1 = New System.Windows.Forms.Label()
        Me.TextBox1 = New System.Windows.Forms.TextBox()
        Me.Button1 = New System.Windows.Forms.Button()
        Me.SuspendLayout()
        '
        'Label1
        '
        Me.Label1.Location = New System.Drawing.Point(24, 40)
        Me.Label1.Name = "Label1"
        Me.Label1.TabIndex = 0
```

```
        Me.Label1.Text = "Label1"
        '
        'TextBox1
        '
        Me.TextBox1.Location = New System.Drawing.Point(160, 40)
        Me.TextBox1.Name = "TextBox1"
        Me.TextBox1.TabIndex = 1
        Me.TextBox1.Text = "TextBox1"
        '
        'Button1
        '
        Me.Button1.Location = New System.Drawing.Point(104, 104)
        Me.Button1.Name = "Button1"
        Me.Button1.TabIndex = 2
        Me.Button1.Text = "Button1"
        '
        'Form1
        '
        Me.AutoScaleBaseSize = New System.Drawing.Size(5, 13)
        Me.ClientSize = New System.Drawing.Size(280, 189)
        Me.Controls.AddRange(New System.Windows.Forms.Control() _
          {Me.Button1, Me.TextBox1, Me.Label1})
        Me.Name = "Form1"
        Me.Text = "Form1"
        Me.ResumeLayout(False)
    End Sub
#End Region
End Class
```

As you can see, the code begins with a Class definition that defines the form. Within the class definition, you should see several common elements. For example, the class defines the New constructor method. Likewise, the class defines a Dispose method which it calls when the program discards the form. Further, the class makes extensive use of the Me keyword to refer to the current instance of the class. To create the Label, Textbox, and Button objects, the class defines three member variables (which the class precedes with the Friend access modifier that restricts access to the variables to the class itself):

```
Friend WithEvents Label1 As System.Windows.Forms.Label
Friend WithEvents TextBox1 As System.Windows.Forms.TextBox
Friend WithEvents Button1 As System.Windows.Forms.Button
```

As you will learn in Chapter 10, the WithEvents keyword lets the class respond to events, such as a button click. In Chapter 4, you will examine class inheritance, which lets you build a new class based on an existing class. At that time, you will examine the Inherits keyword in detail. For now, the first line of the class definition tells you that Visual Basic is building the Form1 class based on the definition of the System.Windows.Forms.Form class:

```
Public Class Form1
    Inherits System.Windows.Forms.Form
```

Taking a Closer Look at a Class Using the Visual Studio Class View

As the classes you create within your Visual Basic .NET programs become more complex, you may find that viewing the class structure visually, in Visual Studio's Class View, helps you quickly recall the class methods, properties, base classes, interfaces, and so on, as shown in Figure 3-3.

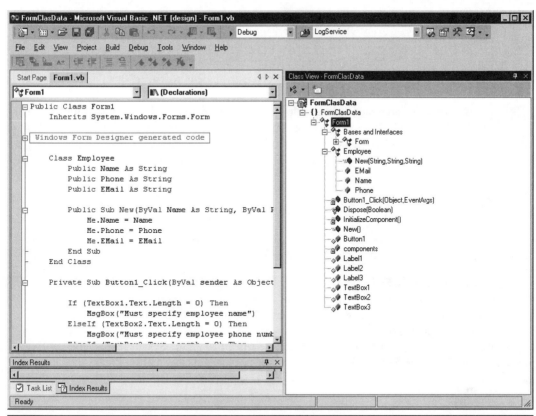

Figure 3-3   Viewing class information in Visual Studio Class View

USE IT To display a class using Visual Studio's Class View, perform these steps:

1. Within Visual Studio, select View | Class View. Visual Studio, in turn, will open the Class View window.
2. In the Class View window, click the plus sign that precedes the class you want to display. If the class contains a base class or interfaces (discussed in Chapter 4), you can click the plus sign that precedes the corresponding entries to display specifics about each.

Sharing a Class Member Variable Among Class Instances

Normally, when your program creates a class object (an instance of a class), the object gets its own set of member variables. In other words, if your program creates two or more instances of a class, the values that one object assigns to its member variables do not affect the values a different instance assigns to its fields.

There may be times, however, when you will want each object to share a specific member variable—meaning, when one object assigns a value to the variable, every object sees the same value. You might use a shared member variable, for example, to share a file with each instance of an object, or you might use a shared variable as a locking mechanism that controls access to a resource.

USE IT To create a shared member variable, simply precede the variable's name with the shared keyword. The following code fragment, for example, defines a class named Students that creates a shared member variable named StudentCount, which maintains a count of the current number of students:

```
Class Student
   Public Name As String
   Public Grade As Integer
   Public Shared StudentCount = 0
End Class
```

The following program, SharedCountMember.vb, uses a shared member variable named StudentCount to track the number of instances of the Student class. Within the class constructor method (which executes each time the program creates an instance of the class), the code increments the StudentCount variable. Each time the program creates a Student object, the program displays a message using each of the existing Student objects to show that all the objects display the same value for the StudentCount variable. Within the class destructor method (the Finalize method), the code decrements the StudentCount variable each time the program discards a Student object:

```
Module Module1

    Class Student
        Public Name As String
```

```
        Public Grade As Integer
        Public Shared StudentCount = 0

        Public Sub New(ByVal Name As String, ByVal Grade As Integer)
            Me.Name = Name
            Me.Grade = Grade
            StudentCount = StudentCount + 1
        End Sub

        Protected Overrides Sub Finalize()
            StudentCount = StudentCount - 1
        End Sub
    End Class

    Sub Main()
        Dim Joe = New Student("Joe Smith", 11)
        Console.WriteLine("Joe's student count {0}", Joe.StudentCount)

        Dim Bill = New Student("Bill Davis", 10)
        Console.WriteLine("Joe's student count {0}", Joe.StudentCount)
        Console.WriteLine("Bill's student count {0}", Bill.StudentCount)

        Dim Jill = New Student("Jill Willis", 11)
        Console.WriteLine("Joe's student count {0}", Joe.StudentCount)
        Console.WriteLine("Bill's student count {0}", Bill.StudentCount)
        Console.WriteLine("Jill's student count {0}", Jill.StudentCount)
        Console.ReadLine()
    End Sub
End Module
```

After you compile and execute this program, your screen will display the following output:

```
Joe's student count 1
Joe's student count 2
Bill's student count 2
Joe's student count 3
Bill's student count 3
Jill's student count 3
```

Inserting a Class Template Using Visual Studio

In a Visual Basic .NET program, you will normally create classes by dragging and dropping objects (such as form or control) onto your program's user interface or by defining the class statements as you have done throughout this chapter. As you have learned, when you drag and drop objects onto a form, for example, Visual Studio, behind the scenes, produces the class-based source code your program uses to interact with the object.

USE IT   In a similar way, Visual Studio provides software that you can use to add a class header and footer (the Class and End Class statements) to your code. Assume, for example, you want to add a Book class to your program. To add the class, you can simply type the program statements as you have done throughout this chapter. Or you can use Visual Studio to insert the template code by performing these steps:

1. Within Visual Studio, select View | Class View. Visual Studio will open the Class View window.

2. In the Class View window, select Project | Add Class. (If the Add Class option is not on the menu, select Project | Add Module and then choose VB Class.) Visual Studio will display the Add New Item dialog box.

3. In the Add New Item dialog box, type the class name **Book** and then click OK. Visual Studio will add a class item to your project.

4. In the class window, if you select the New and Finalize entries in the Declarations pull-down list, Visual Studio will place code within the class that provides a template you can use to complete the class constructor and destructor methods, as shown in Figure 3-4.

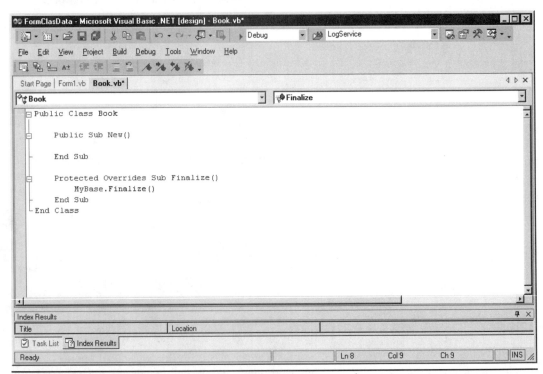

Figure 3-4   Building a class using the Visual Basic Class Wizard

Researching Classes Using the Visual Studio Object Browser

As you develop Visual Basic .NET programs, there will be many times when you must look up specifics about a class, such as the class methods, properties, namespace, and so on. To locate such information quickly, you can take advantage of Visual Studio's Object Browser. As shown in Figure 3-5, the Object Browser lets you display class specifics.

USE IT   To look up class information using the Object Browser, perform these steps:

1. Within Visual Studio, select View | Other Windows and then choose Object Browser. Visual Studio will open the Object Browser window.

2. In the Object Browser window, click the plus sign that precedes the System entry. The Object Browser will expand its display to show items that appear within the System namespace.

3. To locate the class you want, simply continue to open the corresponding namespaces by clicking the plus sign that precedes the namespace.

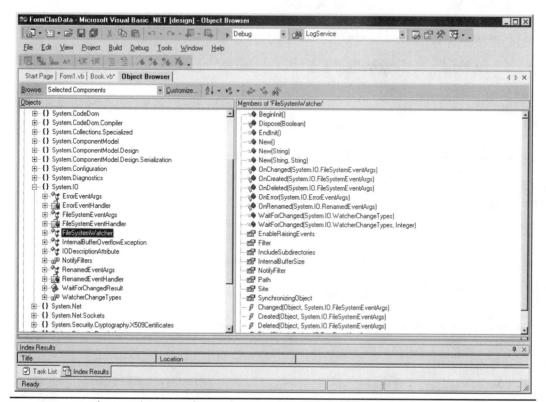

Figure 3-5   Displaying class specifics in the Visual Studio Object Browser

CHAPTER 4

Object-Oriented Programming in Visual Basic .NET

TIPS IN THIS CHAPTER

In Chapter 3, you learned how to group an object's methods (operations) and attributes (member variables and properties) within a Visual Basic class. In this chapter, you will learn how to create a new class that takes advantage of the methods and variables within an existing class. When you build a new class (which programmers refer to as the derived class), from an existing class (the base class), the new class is said to inherit the existing class's methods and variables. By taking advantage of an existing class, you can quickly create a new class without having to implement the programming the base class provides.

When programmers discuss object-oriented programming, they normally refer to the terms encapsulation, inheritance, polymorphism, and abstraction. Encapsulation is the process of grouping the methods and variables into a class that represents the fields an object stores and the operations the object performs to accomplish specific tasks. Inheritance is the ability to create a new class based on an existing class's methods and member variables. Polymorphism is the ability of an object to change forms as the program executes. A polymorphic computer object, for example, might change from a server to a workstation to a notebook PC as the program executes. Likewise, a polymorphic phone might change from a pay phone to a cellular phone, depending on the program's needs. Finally, abstraction provides a programmer with the ability to temporarily ignore an object's underlying details, while the programmer builds a solution.

In Chapter 3, you learned how to use a class to encapsulate an object. In this chapter, you will use inheritance to build a new class from an existing class. You will also learn how to build a polymorphic object that changes forms. Finally, you will learn how interfaces let a program ignore the underlying details of a class implementation.

Keeping Track of Constructor Methods

Within a class, constructor methods exist to simplify the process of initializing class member variables. When you use inheritance to build one class from another, two sets of constructors come into play: the base-class constructor and the derived-class constructor.

USE IT The following program, InheritanceConstructors.vb, illustrates how Visual Basic .NET uses the base- and derived-class constructors. In the Base class, the New method (the constructor) displays a message box stating "The Base Class Constructor is Running." Likewise, within the Derived class, the New method displays a message box stating "The Derived Class Constructor is Running." When you run the program, it will display a form that contains a button you can select to create an instance of the Derived class. When you click the button, the code will create the object which causes the Base class constructor to execute first, followed by the Derived class constructor:

```
Public Class Form1
    Inherits System.Windows.Forms.Form

#Region " Windows Form Designer generated code "
 ' Code not shown
```

```
#End Region

    Class Base
        Public Sub New()
            MsgBox("The Base Class Constructor is Running")
        End Sub
    End Class

    Class Derived
        Inherits Base
        Public Sub New()
            MsgBox("The Derived Class Constructor is Running")
        End Sub
    End Class

    Private Sub Button1_Click(ByVal sender As Object, _
      ByVal e As System.EventArgs) Handles Button1.Click
        Dim Sample As New Derived()
    End Sub
End Class
```

As you can see, in the Button1_Click subroutine, the code creates an instance of the Derived class, which it names Sample. When you compile and run the program, the Base class message box will first appear, followed by the Derived class message box. That's because, behind the scenes, when a base-class constructor does not require parameters, Visual Basic .NET automatically will call the Base-class constructor method when the Derived-class constructor method starts.

The following program, ThreeConstructors.vb, creates three classes named A, B, and C. Class B inherits class A, and class C inherits class B. When you run the program, your screen will first display class A's constructor message, followed by class B's constructor message, and finally class C's constructor message:

```
Public Class Form1
    Inherits System.Windows.Forms.Form

#Region " Windows Form Designer generated code "
  ' Code not shown
#End Region

    Class A
        Public Sub New()
            MsgBox("In class A constructor")
        End Sub
    End Class

    Class B
```

```
        Inherits A
        Public Sub New()
            MsgBox("In class B constructor")
        End Sub
    End Class

    Class C
        Inherits B
        Public Sub New()
            MsgBox("In class C constructor")
        End Sub
    End Class

    Private Sub Button1_Click(ByVal sender As Object, _
        ByVal e As System.EventArgs) Handles Button1.Click

        Dim objSample As New C()

    End Sub
End Class
```

Passing Parameters to the Base-Class Constructor

If a base-class constructor does not receive parameters, Visual Basic .NET automatically calls the base-class constructor when the derived-class constructor starts its execution. However, if the base-class constructor requires parameters, the derived class must explicitly call the base-class constructor, passing to the constructor the corresponding parameter values.

Because all classes use the New method as the constructor name, the derived class cannot simply call the New method—the Visual Basic .NET compiler would not be able to determine which New method the code was trying to call, its own or the base-class method. Instead, the derived class must precede the New method with the MyBase keyword, as shown here:

```
MyBase.New("Some Value")
```

In the derived-class constructor, the call to the base-class constructor must be the first statement. Otherwise, Visual Basic .NET will generate a syntax error when you try to compile your program. If the base-class constructor does not require parameters, the derived class can omit the call to MyBase.New. Visual Basic .NET, in turn, will automatically call the base-class constructor when the derived-class constructor starts. However, to improve the readability of their code, many programmers will include the following MyBase.New method call at the start of a derived-class constructor to remind other programmers (who may be reading the code) that the base class exists and that its constructor does execute:

```
MyBase.New()
```

USE IT   The following program, MyBaseDemo.vb, creates a base class named Person that has fields that store an individual's first and last names. Within the Person class, the New method assigns the names it receives as parameters to the FirstName and LastName fields:

```
Class Person
   Public FirstName As String
   Public LastName As String

   Public Sub New(ByVal First As String, ByVal Last As String)
      FirstName = First
      LastName = Last
   End Sub
End Class
```

Next, the code derives the Author class from the Person class by adding a book title and e-mail address:

```
Class Author
    Inherits Person

   Public Title As String
   Public Email As String

   Public Sub New(ByVal First As String, ByVal Last As String, _
      ByVal BookTitle As String, ByVal EmailAddr As String)

      MyBase.New(First, Last)

      Title = BookTitle
      Email = EmailAddr
   End Sub
End Class
```

Within the Author class, the constructor receives four parameters. The Author class constructor passes two of the parameters (FirstName and LastName) to the base-class (Person) constructor:

```
MyBase.New(First, Last)
```

The following code implements the MyBaseDemo.vb program:

```
Public Class Form1
    Inherits System.Windows.Forms.Form

#Region " Windows Form Designer generated code "
   ' Code not shown
#End Region
```

```vb
Class Person
    Public FirstName As String
    Public LastName As String

    Public Sub New(ByVal First As String, ByVal Last As String)
        FirstName = First
        LastName = Last
    End Sub
End Class

Class Author
    Inherits Person

    Public Title As String
    Public Email As String

    Public Sub New(ByVal First As String, ByVal Last As String, _
      ByVal BookTitle As String, ByVal EmailAddr As String)

        MyBase.New(First, Last)

        Title = BookTitle
        Email = EmailAddr
    End Sub
End Class

Private Sub Button1_Click(ByVal sender As Object, _
  ByVal e As System.EventArgs) Handles Button1.Click

    If (TextBox1.Text.Length = 0) Then
        MsgBox("Must specify first name")
    ElseIf (TextBox2.Text.Length = 0) Then
        MsgBox("Must specify last name")
    ElseIf (TextBox3.Text.Length = 0) Then
        MsgBox("Must specify book title")
    ElseIf (TextBox4.Text.Length = 0) Then
        MsgBox("Must specify e-mail address")
    Else
        Dim BookAuthor As New Author(TextBox1.Text, TextBox2.Text, _
          TextBox3.Text, TextBox4.Text)

        MsgBox("Name: " & BookAuthor.FirstName & " " & _
          BookAuthor.LastName & " Title: " & BookAuthor.Title & _
          " Email: " & BookAuthor.Email)
```

```
        End If
    End Sub
End Class
```

After you compile and execute this program, your screen will display a form that prompts you to enter information about the author. The code will then create an Author class object, assigning the values you enter to the corresponding fields, which the program will then display in a message box, as shown in Figure 4-1.

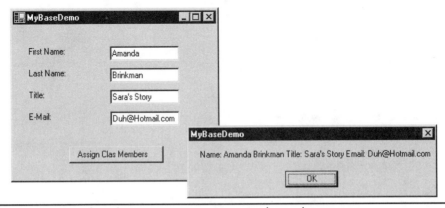

Figure 4-1   Deriving a class that passes parameters to a base-class constructor

Taking a Close Look at Inheritance and Destructor Methods

Within a class, a destructor method lets the class perform "cleanup" processing before the garbage collector releases the memory that holds an object. To specify the processing you want a program to perform before an object is released, you must define the Finalize method.

When you use inheritance to derive one class from another, the garbage collector will first call the derived-class destructor method (if the derived class defines the Finalize method). If the derived class does not define the Finalize method, the garbage collector will instead call the base-class destructor. Normally, within a destructor method, the last processing the code will perform is to call the base-class Finalize method, as shown here:

```
MyBase.Finalize()
```

USE IT   The following program, InheritDestructor.vb, illustrates how Visual Basic .NET uses the base- and derived-class destructors. Within the Base class, the Finalize method (the constructor) displays a message box stating "The Base Class Destructor is Running." Likewise, within the Derived class, the Finalize method displays a message box stating "The Derived Class Destructor is Running."

```
Public Class Form1
    Inherits System.Windows.Forms.Form

#Region " Windows Form Designer generated code "
  ' Code not shown
#End Region

    Class Base
        Public Sub New()
            MsgBox("The Base Class Constructor is Running")
        End Sub

        Protected Overrides Sub Finalize()
            MsgBox("The Base Class Destructor is Running")
        End Sub
    End Class

    Class Derived
        Inherits Base
        Public Sub New()
            MsgBox("The Derived Class Constructor is Running")
        End Sub

        Protected Overrides Sub Finalize()
            MsgBox("The Derived Class Destructor is Running")
            MyBase.Finalize()
        End Sub
    End Class

    Private Sub Button1_Click(ByVal sender As Object, _
      ByVal e As System.EventArgs) Handles Button1.Click
        Dim Sample As New Derived()
    End Sub
End Class
```

When you compile and run the program, the program will display a form that contains a button you can use to create a class. When you click the button, the code will create the class, causing the base-class and the derived-class constructor methods to run. The destructor methods, however, will not run until you close the program. As you will recall, the garbage collector calls the destructor method for an object that is no longer in use. In this case, the program does not discard the objects until it ends.

If you examine closely the definition of the Finalize method within a class, you will find that the definition must override the base-class definition of a function with a similar name:

```
Protected Overrides Sub Finalize()
  ' Subroutine code here
End Sub
```

The fact that a derived class overrides the base class Finalize method explains why Visual Basic .NET does not automatically call the base-class destructor function as it does a constructor. Instead, if a class defines the Finalize method, at the end of the method's processing, the class should call the base class implementation of the method.

The following program, ThreeDestructors.vb, creates three classes named A, B, and C. Class B inherits class A and class C inherits class B. When you run the program, your screen will first display class C's destructor message, followed by class B's destructor message, and finally class A's destructor message:

```
Public Class Form1
    Inherits System.Windows.Forms.Form

#Region " Windows Form Designer generated code "
  ' Code not shown
#End Region

    Class A
        Public Sub New()
            MsgBox("In class A constructor")
        End Sub

        Protected Overrides Sub Finalize()
            MsgBox("In class A destructor")
        End Sub
    End Class

    Class B
        Inherits A
        Public Sub New()
            MsgBox("In class B constructor")
        End Sub

        Protected Overrides Sub Finalize()
            MsgBox("In class B destructor")
            MyBase.Finalize()
        End Sub
    End Class
```

```
        Class C
            Inherits B
            Public Sub New()
                MsgBox("In class C constructor")
            End Sub

            Protected Overrides Sub Finalize()
                MsgBox("In class C destructor")
                MyBase.Finalize()
            End Sub
        End Class

        Private Sub Button1_Click(ByVal sender As Object, _
          ByVal e As System.EventArgs) Handles Button1.Click
            Dim objSample As New C()
        End Sub
End Class
```

As you can see, within each class, the Finalize method calls the corresponding base-class destructor.

Method Overloading and Inheritance

To improve the readability and functionality of your code, Visual Basic .NET lets you overload methods by defining two or more methods with the same name, but whose "method signatures" differ by the number or type of parameters. Assume, for example, that a class has an AssignName method that assigns the name it receives as a parameter to the class member variable Name, as shown here:

```
Class Worker
  Public Name As String
  Public Sub AssignName(ByVal Name As String)
    Me.Name = Name
  End Sub
End Class
```

In this case, the code treats first and last names as a single string. There may be times, however, when your programs must assign the first and last names to separate fields, while maintaining support for the single-string Name field. To do so, you might add the FirstName and LastName fields to the class. Then you might overload the AssignName method so that it supports the first and last name parameters as shown here:

```
Class Worker
    Public Name As String
    Public FirstName As String
    Public LastName As String
```

```
   Public Sub AssignName(ByVal Name As String)
      Me.Name = Name
   End Sub

   Public Sub AssignName(ByVal FirstName As String, _
      ByVal LastName As String)
      Me.FirstName = FirstName
      Me.LastName = LastName
      Me.Name = FirstName & " " & LastName
   End Sub
End Class
```

Because the two implementations of the AssignName methods differ by the number of parameters, the Visual Basic .NET compiler can distinguish between the two methods and between calls to each method. When you provide multiple definitions of a function or subroutine in this way, programmers state that you have overloaded the function's definition, meaning you have provided more than one implementation of the method. Based on the parameters you pass to the method, the Visual Basic .NET compiler will determine which method your code wants to use.

USE IT The following program, ConstructorOverload.vb, defines four different implementations of the New subroutine within the Book class. Each implementation of the method differs by the number of parameters it supports. Later, when the program creates Book class objects, the Visual Basic .NET compiler will determine which method to call, based, in this case, on the number of parameters the program is passing to the constructor. (Rather than differing by the number of parameters, the methods could differ based on the parameter type.)

```
Module Module1

    Class Book
        Public Title As String
        Public Author As String
        Public Publisher As String
        Public Price As Double

        Public Sub New(ByVal Title As String)
            Me.Title = Title
            Me.Author = "Unknown"
            Me.Publisher = "Unknown"
            Me.Price = 0
        End Sub

        Public Sub New(ByVal Title As String, ByVal Author As String)
            Me.Title = Title
            Me.Author = Author
            Me.Publisher = "Unknown"
```

```vbnet
            Me.Price = 0
        End Sub

        Public Sub New(ByVal Title As String, ByVal Author As String, _
          ByVal Publisher As String)
            Me.Title = Title
            Me.Author = Author
            Me.Publisher = Publisher
            Me.Price = 0
        End Sub

        Public Sub New(ByVal Title As String, ByVal Author As String, _
          ByVal Publisher As String, ByVal Price As Double)
            Me.Title = Title
            Me.Author = Author
            Me.Publisher = Publisher
            Me.Price = Price
        End Sub

        Public Sub ShowBook()
            Console.WriteLine("Title: " & Title)
            Console.WriteLine("Author: " & Author)
            Console.WriteLine("Publisher: " & Publisher)
            Console.WriteLine("Price: " & Price)
            Console.WriteLine()
        End Sub
    End Class

    Sub Main()
        Dim BookA As New Book("Palm OS Developer's Guide")
        Dim BookB As _
          New Book("Visual Basic .NET Programming Tips & Techniques", _
            "Jamsa")
        Dim BookC As New Book("C# Programming Tips & Techniques", _
            "Wright", "McGraw-Hill/Osborne")
        Dim BookD As New Book("HTML & Web Design Tips & Techniques", _
            "King", "McGraw-Hill/Osborne", 49.99)

        BookA.ShowBook()
        BookB.ShowBook()
        BookC.ShowBook()
        BookD.ShowBook()
        Console.ReadLine() ' Delay to view output
    End Sub
End Module
```

As you can see, the program creates four different Book class objects, using each of the different overloaded constructor methods. After you compile and execute this program, your screen will display the following output:

```
Title: Palm OS Developer's Guide
Author: Unknown
Publisher: Unknown
Price: 0

Title: Visual Basic .NET Programming Tips & Techniques
Author: Jamsa
Publisher: Unknown
Price: 0

Title: C# Programming Tips & Techniques
Author: Wright
Publisher: McGraw-Hill/Osborne
Price: 0

Title: HTML & Web Design Tips & Techniques
Author: King
Publisher: McGraw-Hill/Osborne
Price: 49.99
```

If you were to derive a new class named BookDetails using the Book class, the BookDetails class, in turn, could call each of the various Book constructors using the MyBase keyword:

```
MyBase.New("C# Programming Tips & Techniques")
MyBase.New("C# Programming Tips & Techniques", "Wright")
```

Method Overriding and Inheritance

In the .NET environment, all classes are derived from the System.Object class. As you know, the System.Object class provides the ToString method (which all classes inherit) which returns a string representation of the object's value. By default, when you call the ToString method for an object, such as the Person object, the ToString method will return a string that contains the object's class name.

Within a class definition, your code can implement its own ToString method, which overrides the base-class implementation of the method. If a class object calls the ToString method, the program will invoke the method definition that appears within the derived class, as opposed to the base class.

USE IT   In the following program, ToStringOverrides, the Phone class defines its own ToString method. When your program calls the ToString method for a Phone class object, the method will return a string that contains the object's phone number:

```
Module Module1
    Class Phone
        Public Number As String

        Public Sub New(ByVal Number As String)
            Me.Number = Number
        End Sub

        Public Overrides Function ToString() As String
            ToString = Number
        End Function
    End Class

    Sub Main()
        Dim MyPhone As New Phone("555-1212")

        Console.WriteLine(MyPhone)
        Console.WriteLine(MyPhone.ToString())
        Console.ReadLine() ' Pause to view output
    End Sub
End Module
```

To override a base-class function or subroutine, a derived class must place the Overrides keyword within the method definition to tell the Visual Basic .NET compiler that its goal is to replace the base-class method implementation with its own, as shown here:

```
Public Overrides Function ToString() As String
    ToString = Number
End Function
```

In a similar way, the following program, TitleOverload.vb, creates a Book class that contains Author, Publisher, and Title information. Then, using the Book class, the program derives the BestSeller class, which adds new fields and overloads the ShowTitle method by allowing the program to specify an additional message. To override the base-class method, the derived class must place the Overrides keyword within the subroutine definition, as shown here:

```
Public Overrides Sub ShowTitle()
  Console.WriteLine("Title: " & Title)
  Console.WriteLine("Author: " & Author)
  Console.WriteLine("Publisher: " & Publisher)
  Console.WriteLine("Price: " & Price)
  Console.WriteLine("Best seller list: " & List & " at # " & Position)
End Sub
```

Before a derived class can override a base-class method, the base-class must state that its method definition is overridable, by placing the Overridable keyword within the method definition, as shown here:

```
Public Overridable Sub ShowTitle()
    Console.WriteLine("Title: " & Title)
    Console.WriteLine("Author: " & Author)
    Console.WriteLine("Publisher: " & Publisher)
    Console.WriteLine("Price: " & Price)
End Sub
```

Programmers refer to a method that can be overridden by a derived-class method as a virtual function. The following statements implement the TitleOverload.vb program:

```
Module Module1

    Class Book
        Public Title As String
        Public Author As String
        Public Publisher As String
        Public Price As Double

        Public Sub New(ByVal Title As String, ByVal Author As String, _
          ByVal Publisher As String, ByVal Price As Double)
            Me.Title = Title
            Me.Author = Author
            Me.Publisher = Publisher
            Me.Price = Price
        End Sub

        Public Overridable Sub ShowTitle()
            Console.WriteLine("Title: " & Title)
            Console.WriteLine("Author: " & Author)
            Console.WriteLine("Publisher: " & Publisher)
            Console.WriteLine("Price: " & Price)
        End Sub
    End Class

    Class BestSeller
        Inherits Book
        Public List As String
        Public Position As Integer

        Public Sub New(ByVal Title As String, ByVal Author As String, _
            ByVal Publisher As String, ByVal Price As Double, _
            ByVal List As String, ByVal Position As Integer)
```

```
            MyBase.New(Title, Author, Publisher, Price)

            Me.List = List
            Me.Position = Position
        End Sub

        Public Overrides Sub ShowTitle()
            Console.WriteLine("Title: " & Title)
            Console.WriteLine("Author: " & Author)
            Console.WriteLine("Publisher: " & Publisher)
            Console.WriteLine("Price: " & Price)
            Console.WriteLine("Best seller list: " & List & " at # " & Position)
        End Sub
    End Class

    Sub Main()
        Dim ProgrammingBook As _
          New Book("C# Programming Tips & Techniques", "Wright", _
          "McGraw-Hill", 49.99)

      Dim BigSeller As New BestSeller("Oprah and .NET", "Big O", _
            "O Code", 9.99, "New York Times", 3)

        ProgrammingBook.ShowTitle()
        Console.WriteLine()
        BigSeller.ShowTitle()
        Console.ReadLine() ' Pause to view output
    End Sub
End Module
```

As you can see, within the BestSeller class, the New constructor method first calls the base-class constructor to initialize the member variables the base class defines. After you compile and execute this program, your screen will display the following output:

```
Title: C# Programming Tips & Techniques
Author: Wright
Publisher: McGraw-Hill
Price: 49.99

Title: Oprah and .NET
Author: Big O
Publisher: O Code
Price: 9.99
Best seller list: New York Times at # 3
```

Shadowing a Base-Class Method

Within a derived class, you can override a base-class method definition by implementing the method within the derived class, preceded by the Overrides keyword. Before a derived class can override a base-class method, the base class must essentially provide permission to override a method by placing the Overridable keyword within its method definition. When a derived class overrides a base-class method, the new method definition only applies to objects of the derived class. When your programs use inheritance, there may be times when you need greater control over which method an object invokes based on how the code defines and uses an object—what type of class your program uses to declare the object and the type of object the program later assigns the object. In such cases, a class can "shadow" the base-class method.

 To shadow (replace) a base-class method, a derived class defines the method using the Shadows keyword, as shown here:

```
Public Shadows Sub MethodName()
  ' Place code here
End Sub
```

This differs from overriding an object, which requires that the base class give permission to override the method by placing the Overridable keyword within the method definition. The base class does not have to provide a derived class with permission to shadow a method.

After you shadow a method, which method the program will invoke depends on how you declare the object (whether you use the base or derived class) and the value you assign to the object. For example, assume that you have two classes, named BaseClass and DerivedClass. In Visual Basic .NET, you can define objects using either class as follows:

```
Dim SomeObject As BaseClass
Dim SomeOtherObject As DerivedClass
```

Then you can use the New operator to assign the following values to each variable:

```
SomeObject = New BaseClass()
SomeObject = New DerivedClass()
SomeOtherObject = New DerivedClass()
```

As you can see, when you declare an object using the BaseClass type, Visual Basic will later let you assign a value of either the BaseClass or the DerivedClass to the object. If you are shadowing a method, the combination of the object type and the value assigned to the object dictates which method the code will invoke (the base class method or the shadowed derived class method). Table 4-1 describes how Visual Basic .NET determines which method to invoke.

The following program, ShadowDemo.vb, illustrates how shadowing impacts which method an object will invoke. The program declares a base class named Base and then derives a new class using the Base class named Derived. Within the Derived class, the code shadows one base class method and overrides a second. The code then creates the objects, one of the Base class to which the code

Object Type	Value Assigned	Method Invoked
BaseClass	New BaseClass()	BaseClass
DerivedClass	New DerivedClass()	DerivedClass
BaseClass	New DerivedClass()	BaseClass
DerivedClass	New BaseClass()	Invalid cast error

Table 4-1   How an Object's Type and Value Influences the Method the Object Invokes When Shadowing Is in Use

assigns a Base class object, one of the Derived class to which the program assigns a Derived class object, and one of the Base class to which the program assigns a Derived class object. The program then uses each object to invoke the shadowed and overridden class:

```
Module Module1

    Class Base
        Public Function Message() As String
            Message = "Hello, World from Base Class"
        End Function

        Public Overridable Function Message2() As String
            Message2 = "Base Class Message 2"
        End Function
    End Class

    Class Derived
        Inherits Base

        Public Shadows Function Message() As String
            Message = "Hi, from Derived Class"
        End Function

        Public Overrides Function Message2() As String
            Message2 = "Derived Class Message 2"
        End Function
    End Class

    Sub Main()
        Dim BaseObj As New Base()
        Dim DerivedObj As New Derived()

        Console.WriteLine("Base object Message: " & _
          BaseObj.Message())
```

```
        Console.WriteLine("Derived object Message:" & _
          DerivedObj.Message())

        Dim MixedObj As Base = New Derived()
        Console.WriteLine("Mixed message: " & MixedObj.Message())

        Console.WriteLine()
        Console.WriteLine("Base object Message2: " & _
          BaseObj.Message2())
        Console.WriteLine("Derived object Message2:" & _
          DerivedObj.Message2())
        Console.WriteLine("Mixed message2: " & _
          MixedObj.Message2())

        Console.ReadLine() ' Pause to view output
    End Sub
End Module
```

After you compile and execute this program, your screen will display the following output:

```
Base object Message: Hello, World from Base Class
Derived object Message:Hi, from Derived Class
Mixed message: Hello, World from Base Class

Base object Message2: Base Class Message 2
Derived object Message2:Derived Class Message 2
Mixed message2: Derived Class Message 2
```

As you can see, in the case of the MixedObj variable, the object called the base class method when the method was shadowed and the derived class method when the method was overridden.

▶ **NOTE**

In addition to using the Shadows keyword to replace a method, a derived class can also use the Shadows keyword to replace a base-class member variable.

Forcing a Specific Method's Invocation Using MyClass

When a derived class shadows a base class method, the method an object will invoke depends on the object's type and the type of object the variable stores. The Tip titled "Shadowing a Base-Class Method" examines method shadowing and method invocation in detail. There may be times, however, when you want to force an object to invoke the method its own class defines, as opposed to a shadowed method. In such cases, you can precede the method name with the MyClass keyword as shown here:

```
MyClass.SomeMethod()
```

USE IT   The following program, MyClassDemo.vb, extends the ShadowDemo.vb program
presented in the previous Tip to add a ShowMessages subroutine to the base class. Within
the subroutine routine, the code precedes the method calls with the MyClass keyword, to force the
object to call the methods that correspond to the object type:

```
Module Module1

    Class Base
        Public Function Message() As String
            Message = "Hello, World from Base Class"
        End Function

        Public Overridable Function Message2() As String
            Message2 = "Base Class Message 2"
        End Function

        Public Sub ShowMessages()
            Console.WriteLine(MyClass.Message())
            Console.WriteLine(MyClass.Message2())
        End Sub
    End Class

    Class Derived
        Inherits Base

        Public Shadows Function Message() As String
            Message = "Hi, from Derived Class"
        End Function

        Public Overrides Function Message2() As String
            Message2 = "Derived Class Message 2"
        End Function
    End Class

    Sub Main()
        Dim BaseObj As New Base()
        Dim DerivedObj As New Derived()

        Console.WriteLine("Base object Message: " & BaseObj.Message())
        Console.WriteLine("Derived object Message: " & DerivedObj.Message())

        Dim MixedObj As Base = New Derived()
        Console.WriteLine("Mixed message: " & MixedObj.Message())
        Console.WriteLine()
```

```
        Console.WriteLine("Base object Message2: " & BaseObj.Message2())
        Console.WriteLine("Derived object Message2: " & DerivedObj.Message2())
        Console.WriteLine("Mixed message2: " & MixedObj.Message2())

        Console.WriteLine()
        Console.WriteLine("Mixed using MyClass")
        MixedObj.ShowMessages()

        Console.ReadLine() ' Pause to view output
    End Sub
End Module
```

After you compile and execute this program, your screen will display the following output:

```
Base object Message: Hello, World from Base Class
Derived object Message: Hi, from Derived Class
Mixed message: Hello, World from Base Class

Base object Message2: Base Class Message 2
Derived object Message2: Derived Class Message 2
Mixed message2: Derived Class Message 2

Mixed using MyClass
Hello, World from Base Class
Base Class Message 2
```

As you can see, the methods the MixedObj variable calls change when the code uses the MyClass keyword from those the object calls using the shadowed method.

Preventing Class Inheritance

Normally, when you define a class, you will want to create the class in a manner that makes the class suitable for inheritance by another class. Depending on the processing a class performs, however, there may be times when you will not want any other classes to inherit the class. Perhaps the class performs processing that is unique to an internal operation at your company, and you do not want to export the class capability to other applications.

USE IT Programmers refer to the process of preventing a class from being inherited as "sealing" the class. To "seal" a class, you must place the NotInheritable keyword within the class definition, as shown here:

```
NotInheritable Class Book
  ' Class Members Here
End Class
```

If another class tries to inherit a sealed class, the Visual Basic .NET compiler will generate a syntax error.

Implementing Polymorphic Objects that Change Form as Your Program Executes

When programmers discuss object-oriented programming, they often include the term polymorphism in their discussion. In the simplest sense, polymorphism describes an object's ability to change forms. Assume, for example, that your code creates the following Phone object:

```
Class Phone
    Public Number As String

    Public Sub New(ByVal Number As String)
      Me.Number = Number
    End Sub

    Public Overridable Sub Dial()
      Console.WriteLine("Dialing: " & Number)
    End Sub
End Class
```

Depending on your program's purpose, you might want the Phone object to represent a rotary dial phone or a touch-tone phone. Or you may want the Phone object to represent a cellular phone or a pay phone. In other words, as a program executes, you may want the object to change forms.

USE IT To create a polymorphic object, a program derives classes based on the object. Within the derived class, the code overrides methods in the base class or adds methods to the derived class that change the processing the derived class performs (in other words, provides the object's new form). The following program, PolymorphicPhone.vb, derives TouchTonePhone and RotaryPhone classes from the Phone class. Each of the derived classes overrides the Phone class Dial method. In the main program, the code creates an object of type TouchTonePhone, one of type RotaryPhone, and one, which will be the program's polymorphic object, of type Phone:

```
Dim OldPhone As New RotaryPhone("555-1212")
Dim KidsPhone As New TouchTonePhone("800-555-1212")

Dim PolyPhone As Phone
```

By assigning the OldPhone object to the PolyPhone variable and later assigning the KidsPhone object to the PolyPhone variable, the program is able to change the PolyPhone variable's form. The following statements implement the PolymorphicPhone.vb program:

```
Module Module1

    Class Phone
        Public Number As String
```

```
        Public Sub New(ByVal Number As String)
            Me.Number = Number
        End Sub

        Public Overridable Sub Dial()
            Console.WriteLine("Dialing: " & Number)
        End Sub
End Class

Class TouchTonePhone
    Inherits Phone

        Public Sub New(ByVal Number As String)
            MyBase.New(Number)
        End Sub

        Public Overrides Sub Dial()
            Console.WriteLine("Beep, touch-tone phone calling: " & Number)
        End Sub
End Class

Class RotaryPhone
    Inherits Phone

        Public Sub New(ByVal Number As String)
            MyBase.New(Number)
        End Sub

        Public Overrides Sub Dial()
            Console.WriteLine("Rotary dialing: " & Number)
        End Sub
End Class

Sub Main()
    Dim OldPhone As New RotaryPhone("555-1212")
    Dim KidsPhone As New TouchTonePhone("800-555-1212")

    Dim PolyPhone As Phone

    Console.WriteLine("Using standard objects")
    OldPhone.Dial()
    KidsPhone.Dial()
```

```
        Console.WriteLine("Using polymorphic phone")
        PolyPhone = OldPhone
        PolyPhone.Dial()

        PolyPhone = KidsPhone
        PolyPhone.Dial()

        Console.ReadLine()
    End Sub
End Module
```

After you compile and execute the program, your screen will display the following output:

```
Using standard objects
Rotary phone calling: 555-1212
Beep, touch-tone phone calling: 800-555-1212
Using polymorphic phone
Rotary phone calling: 555-1212
Beep, touch-tone phone calling: 800-555-1212
```

As you can see, the program first uses the standard objects to call the Dial method. Then the code assigns a Phone object to the polymorphic Phone variable, which causes the object to call the Rotary dial method. Next, the code assigns the Phone variable a TouchTonePhone object, changing the Phone object's form (which causes the object to call the touch-tone-based Dial method).

Taking a Sneak Preview at Inheritance and Events

In Chapter 10, you will learn how to create and handle events in your programs, much like how your code responds to the event that a form raises when a user clicks a button. As you will learn, when you derive a new class from a base class that raises one or more events, the derived class inherits can handle (respond to) base-class events. The derived class cannot, however, raise a base-class event.

USE IT   To provide a derived-class object with the ability to respond to a base-class event, you must use the WithEvents keyword when you create the object, as shown here:

```
Dim WithEvents objectName As New DerivedClass("SomeParameter")
```

If you examine the code that Visual Studio creates when you place a button on a form, for example, you will find that the code contains the WithEvents keyword, which lets the button object respond to events:

```
Friend WithEvents Button1 As System.Windows.Forms.Button
```

Restricting a Class for Use Only as a Base Class

As you define class objects, you will find there are many times when assigning specific members to a base class makes the class well suited for inheritance by other classes in the future, but on its own, the class does not provide enough features to be useful for creating objects. For example, in the Tip titled "Implementing Polymorphic Objects that Change Form as Your Program Executes," you created the following Phone class:

```
Class Phone
   Public Number As String

   Public Sub New(ByVal Number As String)
     Me.Number = Number
   End Sub

   Public Overridable Sub Dial()
     Console.WriteLine("Dialing: " & Number)
   End Sub
End Class
```

Within the Phone class, the Dial method is not very useful. The programmer that created the Phone class assumed the class would serve as a base class that other classes would inherit and build upon to derive specific types of phones.

USE IT   When you create a class that you want only to serve as a base class—in other words, you do not want a program to create an object using the class itself—you can use the MustInherit keyword within the class definition, as shown here:

```
MustInherit Class ClassName
   ' Members here
End Class
```

Should a program later try to create an object using the class, the Visual Basic .NET compiler will generate a syntax error.

Forcing a Derived Class to Override a Base-Class Method

In the Tip titled "Method Overriding and Inheritance," you learned that by using the Overrides keyword, a derived class can replace the implementation of a base-class method. Likewise, in the Tip titled "Implementing Polymorphic Objects that Change Form as Your Program Executes," you learned that to implement a polymorphic object, a derived class normally overrides a base-class method in a way that causes the object to change forms.

USE IT   When you derive classes for which you specify the MustInherit keyword, which means the class can only serve as a base class, you can specify one or more methods in the class for which a derived class must provide method definitions. For example, several of the previous Tips have used the following Phone class as a base class:

```
Class Phone
   Public Number As String

   Public Sub New(ByVal Number As String)
     Me.Number = Number
   End Sub

   Public Overridable Sub Dial()
     Console.WriteLine("Dialing: " & Number)
   End Sub
End Class
```

Rather than specify the Dial method which provides no functionality, the base class can instead specify the MustOverride keyword, which tells Visual Basic .NET that a class that inherits this class must define the Dial method:

```
Class Phone
   Public Number As String

   Public Sub New(ByVal Number As String)
     Me.Number = Number
   End Sub

   Public MustOverride Sub Dial()

End Class
```

Programmers refer to a class method that does not provide a definition, but which instead specifies the MustOverride keyword as an abstract method. Further, programmers refer to a class that contains one or more abstract methods as an abstract class. Within an abstract class, programmers refer to the methods for which a derived class must provide an implementation as pure-virtual functions. (A virtual function, in contrast, is a method that can be overridden by a derived class.)

The following program, AbstractMethod.vb, creates the PageContent class as follows:

```
MustInherit Class PageContent
   Public PageData As String

   Public MustOverride Sub ShowPage()

   Public Sub New(ByVal Message As String)
```

```
    PageData = Message
  End Sub
End Class
```

As you can see, the PageContent class uses the MustInherit keyword to specify that the class can only be used as a base class from which other classes are derived, and that a program cannot create an instance of the class. Further, the class defines the ShowPage method as an abstract method using the MustOverride keyword, which means a class that inherits the PageContent class must define the ShowPage method.

Next, the program derives two classes from the PageContent class. The first class, WMLPage, implements the ShowPage method such that it shows the code necessary to display the page content using the Wireless Markup Language (WML). The second class, HTMLPage, implements the ShowPage method such that it shows the code necessary to display the page using HTML. The following statements implement the AbstractMethod.vb program:

```
Module Module1

    MustInherit Class PageContent
        Public PageData As String

        Public MustOverride Sub ShowPage()

        Public Sub New(ByVal Message As String)
            PageData = Message
        End Sub
    End Class

    Public Class HTMLPage
        Inherits PageContent

        Public Overrides Sub ShowPage()
            Console.WriteLine("<html>")
            Console.WriteLine("<body>")
            Console.WriteLine("<p>" & PageData & "</p>")
            Console.WriteLine("</body>")
            Console.WriteLine("</html>")
        End Sub

        Public Sub New(ByVal Message As String)
            MyBase.New(Message)
        End Sub
    End Class

    Public Class WMLPage
        Inherits PageContent
```

```vb
        Public Overrides Sub ShowPage()
            Console.WriteLine("<wml>")
            Console.WriteLine("<card id=""Demo"">")
            Console.WriteLine("<p>" & PageData & "</p>")
            Console.WriteLine("<do type=""accept"" label=""TGIF"">")
            Console.WriteLine("<go href=""www.fridays.com"" />")
            Console.WriteLine("</do>")
            Console.WriteLine("</card>")
            Console.WriteLine("</wml>")
        End Sub

        Public Sub New(ByVal Message As String)
            MyBase.New(Message)
        End Sub
    End Class

    Sub Main()
        Dim WebPage = New HTMLPage("<a href=""www.yahoo.com"">" & _
          "Yahoo</a>")

        Dim MobilePage = New WMLPage("TGI Fridays</a>")

        WebPage.ShowPage()
        Console.WriteLine()
        MobilePage.ShowPage()
        Console.ReadLine()
    End Sub
End Module
```

After you compile and run the program, your screen will display the following output, which corresponds to the HTML and WML pages to display the corresponding data:

```
<html>
<body>
<p><a href="www.yahoo.com">Yahoo</a></p>
</body>
</html>

<wml>
<card id="Demo">
<p>TGI Fridays</a></p>
<do type="accept" label="TGIF">
<go href="www.fridays.com" />
```

```
</do>
</card>
</wml>
```

Multiple Levels of Inheritance Differs from Multiple Inheritance

One of the terms programmers often use when they discuss object-oriented programming is multiple inheritance. Multiple inheritance is the ability to derive a class using two or more base classes. For example, assume you have an Author class and a Publisher class. Using multiple inheritance, you could derive a Book class by combining the two classes, as shown in Figure 4-2.

Although Visual Basic .NET does not support multiple inheritance, some programming languages, such as C++, do. (The new C# programming language, like Visual Basic .NET, does not support multiple inheritance.) Visual Basic .NET does not support multiple inheritance because of the complexities that can arise, both within the source code due to naming conflicts, and behind the scenes with the tables the compiler must support to represent the class interdependencies.

USE IT   Do not confuse multiple inheritance with multiple levels of inheritance, where a class inherits a base class which itself was derived from a second base class. Figure 4-3, for example, illustrates the AllStar class, which is derived from the Athlete class, which was derived from the Person class. Visual Basic .NET lets your programs take advantage of multiple levels of inheritance.

As you will learn in the Tip titled "Creating an Interface," using Visual Basic .NET interfaces, your classes can derive a class from one or more existing interfaces, which gives you many of the advantages of multiple inheritance without the various class interdependencies.

The following program, MultiLevelInheritance.vb, illustrates the use of multiple levels of inheritance. Within each derived class, the code calls the base-class constructor method to initialize

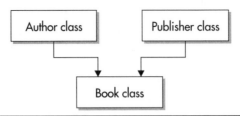

Figure 4-2   Multiple inheritance is the ability to derive a class using two or more base classes

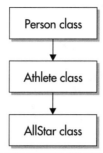

Figure 4-3   Visual Basic .NET supports multiple levels of inheritance

its member variables. The code first creates a Person class, which the code uses to derive the Athlete class. Using the Athlete class, the code then creates the AllStar class:

```
Module Module1
    Class Person
        Public Name As String
        Public Age As Integer

        Public Sub New(ByVal Name As String, ByVal Age As Integer)
            Me.Name = Name
            Me.Age = Age
        End Sub
    End Class

    Class Athlete
        Inherits Person

        Public Sport As String
        Public Team As String

        Public Sub New(ByVal Name As String, ByVal Age As Integer, _
          ByVal Sport As String, ByVal Team As String)
            MyBase.New(Name, Age)
            Me.Team = Team
            Me.Sport = Sport
        End Sub
    End Class
```

```
Class AllStar
    Inherits Athlete

    Public PointsPerGame As Double
    Public Rebounds As Double

    Public Sub New(ByVal Name As String, ByVal Age As Integer, _
      ByVal Sport As String, ByVal Team As String, _
      ByVal Points As Double, ByVal Rebounds As Double)

        MyBase.New(Name, Age, Sport, Team)
        Me.PointsPerGame = Points
        Me.Rebounds = Rebounds
    End Sub

    Public Sub Show()
        Console.WriteLine("Player: " & Name)
        Console.WriteLine("Age: " & Age)
        Console.WriteLine("Sport: " & Sport)
        Console.WriteLine("Team: " & Team)
        Console.WriteLine("Points: " & PointsPerGame)
        Console.WriteLine("Rebounds: " & Rebounds)
        Console.ReadLine() ' Pause to view output
    End Sub
End Class

Sub Main()
    Dim Kobe As New AllStar("Kobe Bryant", 23, "Basketball", _
        "Lakers", 25.5, 6.3)

    Kobe.Show()
End Sub
End Module
```

Creating an Interface

Throughout this chapter's Tips, you have used inheritance to derive a new class that uses the methods and properties of a base class. As the complexity of the classes you create increases, there may be times when you will want a class to use a set of members that do not reside in one base class. In such cases, your programs can use interfaces. You can think of an interface as an abstract class that contains only pure-virtual functions—in other words, a class that implements an interface must provide method definitions for each function or subroutine the interface specifies.

Within a program, an interface looks very similar to a class definition, in that the interface defines methods, properties, and even events (the interface does not define member variables). However, unlike a class definition, the interface does not implement any of the method. The following interface, for example, defines the signatures for three:

```
Interface InterfaceName
   Sub SomeMethod(ByVal A As Integer)
   Sub SomeOtherMethod(ByVal Name As String, _
     ByVal CurrentDate As DateTime)
   Function Calculate(ByVal A As Double, ByVal B As Double) As Double
End Interface
```

Within an interface, it is not necessary that you precede the method signatures with the MustOverride keyword. The fact that the methods appear in the interface implies that a class must define the methods. Likewise, you do not precede the method names with an access specifier such as Public or Private. Many programmers describe an interface as a template that defines the methods a programmer must include within a class that implements the interface. Some Microsoft documentation refers to an interface as a "contract" between a programmer who is creating a class and a programmer who is writing code that will use the class. By knowing that the class will implement specific methods, using specific types and parameters, the programmer whose code is using the class can create code that interacts with a class that implements the interface.

To "implement" an interface, a class uses the Implements keyword and provides statements that implement each of the specified functions and subroutines. In each function or subroutine signature, the code must use the Implements keyword to specify the routine within the interface that the method implements:

```
Class SomeClassName
   Implements InterfaceName

   Public Sub SomeMethod(ByVal A As Integer) _
     Implements InterfaceName.SomeMethod
     ' Statements
   End Sub

   Public Sub SomeOtherMethod(ByVal Name As String, ByVal _
     CurrentDate As DateTime) Implements InterfaceName.SomeOtherMethod
     ' Statements
   End Sub

   Public Function Calculate(ByVal A As Double, ByVal B As _
     Double) As Double Implements InterfaceName.Calculate
     ' Statements
   End Sub
End Interface
```

In this case, the class members are identical to those that appear within the interface definition. A class can include more members than the interface defines, but the class must implement each of the interface members.

To better understand the need for interfaces, assume that you have a class that groups the methods and member variables that define an object and that the object your class defines is very important and is thus widely used throughout many applications. As the number of applications using your class increases, it will become more difficult for you to make changes to the class without introducing errors in an existing program that uses the class. Depending on the number of programs that use your class, it may be impossible for you to locate and test each program should you make changes to the class.

An interface makes it easier for programmers to make changes to a class. In general, as long as the class continues to define the items that appear within the interface, using the same format of the original interface (the programmer cannot change the interface without causing errors to existing programs), the existing programs can continue to run, while the programmer extends the class functionality by adding new members that are not part of the interface upon which other applications are dependent.

USE IT   The following program, InterfaceDemo.vb, creates a sample interface. The program then creates two classes, each of which implements the interface. Although the classes perform different processing, the two classes provide methods that define each of the members that appear within the interface:

```
Module Module1

  Interface GreetUser
    Sub GoodMorning()
    Sub GoodEvening(ByVal CurrentDate As DateTime)
  End Interface

  Class English
    Implements GreetUser

    Public Sub GoodMorning() Implements GreetUser.GoodMorning
      Console.WriteLine("Good morning!")
    End Sub

    Public Sub GoodEvening(ByVal CurrentDate As _
        DateTime) Implements GreetUser.GoodEvening
      Console.WriteLine("Good evening -- it is now " & CurrentDate)
    End Sub
  End Class

  Class Spanish
    Implements GreetUser

    Public Sub GoodMorning() Implements GreetUser.GoodMorning
      Console.WriteLine("Buenos Dias!")
```

```
        Console.WriteLine(Now())
    End Sub

    Public Sub GoodEvening(ByVal CurrentDate As DateTime) _
        Implements GreetUser.GoodEvening
        Console.WriteLine("Buenas noches -- La fetcha y hora son " _
            & CurrentDate)
    End Sub
  End Class

  Sub Main()
    Dim Hello As New English()
    Dim Hola As New Spanish()

    Hello.GoodMorning()
    Hello.GoodEvening(Now())

    Hola.GoodMorning()
    Hola.GoodEvening(Now())
    Console.ReadLine() ' Pause to view output
  End Sub
End Module
```

Normally, when a class implements an interface, the class will use method names that match those that appear in the interface. However, Visual Basic .NET does not force your classes to use the same names. Instead, because your class specifies which interface routine each method implements, the class can use different method names. The previous program, for example, could define the Spanish class using the following methods:

```
Class Spanish
  Implements GreetUser

  Public Sub BuenosDias() Implements GreetUser.GoodMorning
    Console.WriteLine("Buenos Dias!")
    Console.WriteLine(Now())
  End Sub

  Public Sub BuenasNoches(ByVal CurrentDate As DateTime) _
    Implements GreetUser.GoodEvening
    Console.WriteLine("Buenas noches -- La fetcha y hora son " & CurrentDate)
  End Sub
End Class
```

Although the class does not use the same method names as the interface, the fact that the class specifies which of its interfaces correspond to the interface methods lets Visual Basic .NET map the methods as required.

In the .NET programming environment, you will encounter three built-in interfaces on a regular basis: ICloneable, IComparable, and IFormattable. The ICloneable interface provides the Clone method that lets an object create a copy of itself. Classes that implement the ICloneable interface include Array, ArrayList, and so on. The IComparable interface includes the CompareTo method, which programs can use to compare one value of the class type to another, a common operation in code that performs searching or sorting. Finally, the IFormattable interface includes the ToString method, which objects use to create a string representation of their current value.

Implementing Multiple Interfaces Within a Class

Depending on the processing a class performs, there may be times when the class implements more than one interface. Programmers often implement one or more interfaces within a class to simulate multiple inheritance. When a class implements more than one interface, the class must specify each of the interfaces it implements and define the methods each interface specifies.

 To specify the interfaces it implements, a class will use the Implements keyword, as shown here:

```
Class ClassName
   Implements FirstInterfaceName
   Implements SecondInterfaceName
   ' Statements
End Class
```

The following program, NetInterface.vb, creates a class named Demo that implements two of the common interfaces that are built into the .NET programming environment, IFormattable and IComparable. The IFormattable interface includes the ToString method that objects use to create a string representation of their current value. Likewise, the IComparable interface includes the CompareTo method that programs can use to compare one value of the class type to another:

```
Module Module1

    Class Demo
        Implements IFormattable
        Implements IComparable

        Public Value As String

        Public Overridable Overloads Function ToString(ByVal _
            Format As String, ByVal Provider As IFormatProvider) _
            As String Implements IFormattable.ToString

            ToString = Value
```

```
            End Function

            Public Overridable Overloads Function CompareTo(ByVal A _
                As Object) As Integer Implements IComparable.CompareTo
                If (Value = A.Value) Then
                    CompareTo = 0
                ElseIf (Value < A.Value) Then
                    CompareTo = -1
                Else
                    CompareTo = 1
                End If
            End Function

            Public Sub New(ByVal Value As String)
                Me.Value = Value
            End Sub
        End Class

    Sub Main()
        Dim A As New Demo("Hello")
        Dim B As New Demo("Hi")

        Console.WriteLine(A)
        Console.WriteLine(B)
        Console.WriteLine(A.CompareTo(B))
        Console.ReadLine() ' Pause to view output
    End Sub
End Module
```

As you can see, within the Demo class definition, the code defines the methods for each interface. After you compile and execute this program, your screen will display the following output:

```
Hello
Hi
-1
```

Inheriting a Class that Implements an Interface

When you inherit a base class to derive a new class, there may be times when you want the new class to override an interface method the base class defines. In such cases, the derived class may not care that the base class implements a specific interface. With respect to the syntax you must use to derive the class, the fact that the base class uses an interface makes no difference.

USE IT To replace the interface method within the derived class, you simply override the method, just as you would in any class that inherits methods from a base class. The following program, ReimplementInterface.vb, defines the Demo class that implements the IFormattable and IComparable interfaces. The code derives the DerivedDemo class from the Demo class. Within the derived class, the code overrides the ToString method, so that the function returns the object's value in uppercase:

```
Module Module1

    Class Demo
        Implements IFormattable
        Implements IComparable

        Public Value As String

        Public Overridable Overloads Function ToString(ByVal _
           Format As String, ByVal Provider As IFormatProvider) _
           As String Implements IFormattable.ToString

            ToString = Value
        End Function

        Public Overridable Overloads Function CompareTo(ByVal A _
           As Object) As Integer Implements IComparable.CompareTo
            If (Value = A.Value) Then
                CompareTo = 0
            ElseIf (Value < A.Value) Then
                CompareTo = -1
            Else
                CompareTo = 1
            End If
        End Function

        Public Sub New(ByVal Value As String)
            Me.Value = Value
        End Sub
    End Class

    Class DerivedDemo
        Inherits Demo

        Public Overrides Function ToString(ByVal _
           Format As String, ByVal Provider As IFormatProvider) _
           As String
            ToString = UCase(Value)
```

```
        End Function

        Public Sub New(ByVal Value As String)
            MyBase.New(Value)
        End Sub
    End Class

    Sub Main()
        Dim A As New Demo("Hello")
        Dim B As New DerivedDemo("Hi")

        Console.WriteLine(A)
        Console.WriteLine(B)
        Console.WriteLine(A.CompareTo(B))

        Console.ReadLine() ' Pause to view output
    End Sub
End Module
```

After you compile and execute this program, your screen will display the following output:

```
Hello
HI
-1
```

CHAPTER 5

Test Driving the Common Language Runtime and Base Class Library

TIPS IN THIS CHAPTER

hroughout this book's Tips, the programs will make extensive use of capabilities provided in the .NET Common Language Runtime (CLR) and Base Class Library (BCL). As you have learned, these libraries provide thousands of programming-language independent classes and routines your code can use to perform specific operations.

In this chapter, you will examine several of the key classes used throughout this book's Tips on a regular basis. To start, you will examine the DateTime class and ways you can determine the current system date and time, to compare dates, to determine dates in the future or past, and so on. You will also examine several related date and time properties your Visual Basic .NET programs and ASP.NET pages can exploit.

Next, you will examine the String class in detail. You will learn how the class implements many of the older string-manipulation functions and why the "immutable" nature of the class (meaning, after you assign a value to a string, you cannot change the string, you must replace it with a new string) may reduce your system performance. Then you will examine how you can use StringBuilder objects in programs that perform extensive manipulation of a string's contents in order to reduce overhead. After that, you will examine the Math class and the methods it provides. You will finish by learning how to send e-mail messages from within a Visual Basic .NET program or ASP.NET page.

The sheer size of the Common Language Runtime and Base Class Library prevents a book from covering each of the various classes and routines in detail. Instead, this chapter's goal is to improve your understanding of the classes that the programs in this book use extensively.

Retrieving the Current System Date and Time

Regardless of the processing your program performs, there will be many times when you must know the current system date and time. A billing program, for example, might retrieve the system date and then use the date in the invoices it prints. Likewise, a Web service might track the date and time the service was called by remote programs.

For years, programmers have used the Now function in Visual Basic programs and Active Server Pages to determine the current system date and time. The following Active Server Page, ShowDateTime.asp uses Now() to display the date and time:

```
<html>
<head>
  <title>Now Demo</title>
</head>
<body>
  <h1>
  <% =now() %>
  </h1>
</body>
</html>
```

In the Visual Basic .NET environment, Now corresponds to a property that returns a DateTime object. The following Tip, "Taking a Closer Look at the DateTime Class," examines the class methods and properties in detail. In addition to using the Now property to determine the current date and time, your programs can use the functions and properties described in Table 5-1 to determine specific date and time components.

USE IT The following program, DateTimeDemo.vb, illustrates the use of the date and time functions and properties Table 5-1 describes:

```
Module Module1

    Sub Main()
        Dim DT As DateTime = Now()
        Console.WriteLine("Day: " & Day(DT).ToString)
        Console.WriteLine("Month: " & Month(DT))
        Console.WriteLine("Year: " & Year(DT))
        Console.WriteLine("Hour: " & Hour(DT))
        Console.WriteLine("Minute: " & Minute(DT))
        Console.WriteLine("Second: " & Second(DT))
        Console.WriteLine("Today: " & Today)
        Console.WriteLine("TimeOfDay: " & TimeOfDay().ToString())

        Console.ReadLine() ' Pause to view output
    End Sub

End Module
```

Name	Purpose
Day function	Returns the current day of the month, from 1 to 31.
Month function	Returns the current month of the year, from 1 to 12.
Year function	Returns the current year, such as 2002.
Hour function	Returns the current hour, from 0 to 23.
Minute function	Returns the current minute, from 0 to 59.
Second function	Returns the current second, from 0 to 59.
Today property	Returns the current system date. The property ignores the time fields.
TimeOfDay property	Returns the current system time. The property ignores the date fields.

Table 5-1 Functions and Properties Your Programs Can Use to Manipulate Specific Date and Time Components

After you compile and execute this program, your screen will display the following output:

```
Day: 3
Month: 4
Year: 2002
Hour: 18
Minute: 21
Second: 22
Today: 4/3/2002
TimeOfDay: 1/1/0001 6:21:22 PM
```

Note that the TimeOfDay property ignores the current date, returning only a valid time.

Taking a Closer Look at the DateTime Class

In Visual Basic .NET applications, programmers make extensive use of DateTime objects to determine the current system date and time. Beyond simply determining the system date and time, DateTime objects provide a variety of methods your programs can use to compare dates, determine specifics about a date that occurred in the past or that will occur in the future, and more. Table 5-2 briefly describes the DateTime class methods. Table 5-3 briefly describes the class properties.

Method	Purpose
Add	Adds the value contained in a TimeSpan object to the date the object contains.
AddDays	Adds the number of days specified to the date the object contains.
AddHours	Adds the number of hours specified to the time the object contains.
AddMilliseconds	Adds the number of milliseconds specified to the time the object contains.
AddMinutes	Adds the number of minutes specified to the time the object contains.
AddMonths	Adds the number of months specified to the date the object contains.
AddSeconds	Adds the number of seconds specified to the time the object contains.
AddTicks	Adds the number of ticks specified to the object.
AddYears	Adds the number of years specified to the date the object contains.
Compare	Compares two DateTime and time objects.
CompareTo	Compares the object to the specified object.
DaysInMonth	Returns the number of days in the month specified for a given year.

Table 5-2 DateTime Class Methods

Method	Purpose
Equals	Compares an instance of a DateTime object to a specified object to determine if the objects are equal. The Equals method is an overloaded and overridden method.
FromFileTime	Returns a DateTime object that contains a date and time that corresponds to a file's timestamp.
FromOADate	Returns a DateTime object that contains a date and time that corresponds to the specified OLE Automation Date.
GetDateTimeFormats	Converts the object's date and time values to the string representations supported by the standard DateTime format specifiers. The GetDateTimeFormats method is an overloaded method.
GetHashCode	Returns the object's hash code. The GetHashCode method is an overridden method.
GetTypeCode	Returns the DateTime TypeCode.
IsLeapYear	Returns a Boolean value that specifies if the given year is a leap year.
Parse	Converts a string representation of a date and time to its DateTime equivalent. The Parse method is an overloaded method.
ParseExact	Converts a string representation of a date and time to its DateTime equivalent. The string's format must exactly match a specified date and time format. The ParseExact method is an overloaded method.
Subtract	Subtracts the specified time from the object's time. Subtract is an overloaded method.
ToFileTime	Converts the object's date and time value to a format suitable for use by the local file system.
ToLocalTime	Converts the object's coordinated universal time (UTC) to a local time.
ToLongDateString	Converts the object's date value to its equivalent long date string representation.
ToLongTimeString	Converts the object's time value to its equivalent long time string representation.
ToOADate	Converts the object's date and time value to the equivalent OLE Automation date format.
ToShortDateString	Converts the object's date value to its equivalent short date string representation.
ToShortTimeString	Converts the object's time value to its equivalent short time string representation.
ToUniversalTime	Converts the current local time to the corresponding coordinated universal time (UTC).

Table 5-2   DateTime Class Methods *(continued)*

Property	Purpose
Date	Returns the object's date component.
Day	Returns the day of the month that corresponds to the object's date (from 1 to 31).

Table 5-3   DateTime Class Properties

Property	Purpose
DayOfWeek	Returns the day of the week that corresponds to the object's date (from 1 Sunday to 7 Saturday).
DayOfYear	Returns the day of the year (from 1 to 365) that corresponds to the object's date.
Hour	Returns the hour that corresponds to the object's time.
Millisecond	Returns the millisecond that corresponds to the object's time.
Minute	Returns the minute that corresponds to the object's time.
Month	Returns the month that corresponds to the object's date.
Now	Returns a DateTime object that contains the computer's local date and time.
Second	Returns the second that corresponds to the object's time.
Ticks	Returns the number of ticks the object uses to represent the current date and time.
TimeOfDay	Returns the object's time of day components.
Today	Returns the current date.
UtcNow	Returns a DateTime object that contains the computer's current local date expressed using the coordinated universal time (UTC) format.
Year	Returns the year that corresponds to the object's date.

Table 5-3   DateTime Class Properties *(continued)*

 The following program, DateTimeClassDemo.vb, illustrates the use of many of the DateTime class properties and methods:

```
Module Module1

    Sub Main()
        Dim Dt As DateTime = Now()

        Dim NewDT As DateTime = Now()

        Console.WriteLine("Current date and time: " & Dt)

        NewDT = NewDT.AddHours(5)
        Console.WriteLine("Five hours from now is: " & NewDT)

        NewDT = Now()
        NewDT = NewDT.AddDays(45)
        Console.WriteLine("45 days from now is: " & NewDT)

        If (Dt.IsLeapYear(Dt.Year)) Then
            Console.WriteLine("This is a leap year")
```

```
        Else
            Console.WriteLine("This is not a leap year")
        End If

        Console.WriteLine("Long date: " & Dt.ToLongDateString)
        Console.WriteLine("Short date: " & Dt.ToShortDateString)

        Console.WriteLine("Long time: " & Dt.ToLongTimeString)
        Console.WriteLine("Short time: " & Dt.ToShortTimeString)

        Console.WriteLine("Universal time: " & Dt.ToUniversalTime)

        Console.ReadLine()
    End Sub

End Module
```

After you compile and execute this program, your screen will display the following output:

```
Current date and time: 4/3/2002 6:31:53 PM
Five hours from now is: 4/3/2002 11:31:53 PM
45 days from now is: 5/18/2002 6:31:53 PM
This is not a leap year
Long date: Wednesday, April 03, 2002
Short date: 4/3/2002
Long time: 6:31:53 PM
Short time: 6:31 PM
Universal time: 4/4/2002 12:31:53 AM
```

Taking a Closer Look at the String Class

Throughout this book, most of the programs the Tips present will make extensive use of String objects. In many cases, the programs will create a String object as follows:

```
Dim Message As String = "Hello, VB.NET World!"
```

More often than not, however, the programs will make use of the ToString method that every object inherits from the System.Object class:

```
Console.WriteLine(SomeObject.ToString())
```

In the .NET environment, String objects represent characters using a 2-byte Unicode format. Programmers describe String objects as "immutable," meaning, after you assign a value to a String object, you cannot change that object's value. Instead, when your program performs operations such as the following, which assign a new value to a String object, behind the scenes the .NET environment creates a new String object that it assigns to your variable:

```
SomeString = "ABC"
SomeString = SomeString & "DEF"
SomeString = SomeString.ToLower("ABC")
```

For years, Visual Basic programmers made extensive use of functions such as UCase, LCase, and Mid to manipulate a string's contents. Although Visual Basic .NET still supports these functions, most programs instead make use of the methods that are built into the String class itself. Table 5-4 briefly describes the String class methods and properties:

Method or Property	Purpose
Chars	A property that returns the character at a given character position with the string.
Length	A property that returns the number of characters in the string.
Clone	Creates an exact copy of the string.
Compare	Compares two specified String objects. The Compare method is an overloaded method.
CompareOrdinal	Compares two String objects based on each character's ordered value (without consideration for language or culture). The CompareOrdinal method is an overloaded method.
CompareTo	Compares the object to a specified object. The CompareTo method is an overloaded method.
Concat	Concatenates (appends) one or more String objects. The Concat method is an overloaded method.
Copy	Creates a new String object that contains the current object's value.
CopyTo	Copies the number of characters specified from a starting location in the string to a specified position in an array of Unicode characters.
EndsWith	Returns a Boolean value that specifies whether the string ends with the specified characters.
Equals	Returns a Boolean value that specifies whether two String objects have the same value. The Equals method is an overloaded and overridden method.
Format	Replaces each of a string's format specifications with the textual equivalent of an object's value. The Format method is an overloaded method.
GetEnumerator	Retrieves an object the program can use to iterate (loop) through the string's characters.
GetHashCode	Returns the String object's hash code. The GetHashCode method is an overridden method.
GetTypeCode	Returns the String class TypeCode.
IndexOf	Returns the character index of the first occurrence of a specified Unicode character or substring in a string. The IndexOf method is an overloaded method.

Table 5-4   String Class Methods and Properties

Method or Property	Purpose
IndexOfAny	Returns the character index of the first occurrence of any of the specified characters in an array of Unicode characters. The IndexOfAny method is an overloaded method.
Insert	Inserts a string at a specified index location in the string.
Intern	Returns a system reference that corresponds to the specified string.
IsInterned	Returns a reference to the specified string, or nothing if the string is not in the intern pool.
Join	Concatenates a specified separator string between each element in a string array producing a single string. The Join method is an overloaded method.
LastIndexOf	Returns the character index of the last occurrence of a specified Unicode character or substring in a string. The LastIndexOf method is an overloaded method.
LastIndexOfAny	Returns the character index in the string of the last occurrence of one or more characters specified in a Unicode array. The LastIndexOfAny method is an overloaded method.
PadLeft	Inserts spaces or a specified Unicode character before a string to achieve a specified total length. The PadLeft method is an overloaded method.
PadRight	Appends spaces or a specified Unicode character to a string to achieve a specified total length. The PadRight method is an overloaded method.
Remove	Deletes the number of characters specified starting at a given character position.
Replace	Replaces all occurrences of the specified Unicode character or substring in the string with another Unicode character or string. The Replace method is an overloaded method.
Split	Breaks a string into substrings based on a specified delimiter and then places the substrings into a String array. The Split method is an overloaded method.
StartsWith	Returns a Boolean value that specifies whether the string begins with the specified characters.
Substring	Returns a substring that begins at the specified character position from within a string. The Substring method is an overloaded method.
ToCharArray	Copies the string's characters to a Unicode character array. The ToCharArray method is an overloaded method.
ToLower	Returns a copy of the string in lowercase. The ToLower method is an overloaded method.
ToUpper	Returns a copy of the string in uppercase. The ToUpper method is an overloaded method.
Trim	Removes each occurrence of a set of specified characters (or whitespace) from the beginning and end of the string. The Trim method is an overloaded method.
TrimEnd	Removes each occurrence of a set of characters specified in a Unicode character array (or whitespace) from the end of the string.
TrimStart	Removes all occurrences of a set of characters specified in a Unicode character array (or whitespace) from the start of the string.

Table 5-4   String Class Methods and Properties *(continued)*

USE IT   The following program, StringDemo.vb, illustrates the use of the String class methods:

```
Module Module1

    Sub Main()
        Dim Alphabet As String = "abcdefghijklmnopqrstuvwxyz"

        Console.WriteLine("String: " & Alphabet)
        Console.WriteLine("Char at 5 is: " & Alphabet.Chars(5))
        Console.WriteLine("Length: " & Alphabet.Length)

        Console.WriteLine("Compare ABC & abc: " & _
           String.Compare("ABC", "abc"))

        Console.WriteLine("Hello & world! produces: " & _
           String.Concat("Hello ", "world!"))
        Console.WriteLine("Index of efg: " & Alphabet.IndexOf("efg"))
        Console.WriteLine(Alphabet & "ends with " & "efg" & " " & _
           Alphabet.EndsWith("efg"))

        Console.WriteLine(Alphabet & "starts with " & "abc" & " " & _
           Alphabet.StartsWith("abc"))
        Console.WriteLine("Padding with 5 A's: " & _
           Alphabet.PadLeft(31, "A"))

        Console.WriteLine(Alphabet.ToUpper())
        Console.WriteLine("Get efg substring: " & _
           Alphabet.Substring(4, 3))

        Dim Str As String = ".NET/VB/C#/ASP.NET/ADO.NET"
        Dim SplitArray() As String

        Console.WriteLine("Going to split: " & Str)
        SplitArray = Str.Split("/")

        For Each Str In SplitArray
            Console.WriteLine(Str)
        Next

        Console.ReadLine()
    End Sub

End Module
```

After you compile and execute this program, your screen will display the following output:

```
String: abcdefghijklmnopqrstuvwxyz
Char at 5 is: f
Length: 26
Compare ABC & abc: 1
Hello & world! produces: Hello world!
Index of efg: 4
abcdefghijklmnopqrstuvwxyzends with efg False
abcdefghijklmnopqrstuvwxyzstarts with abc True
Padding with 5 A's: AAAAAabcdefghijklmnopqrstuvwxyz
ABCDEFGHIJKLMNOPQRSTUVWXYZ
Get efg substring: efg
Going to split: .NET/VB/C#/ASP.NET/ADO.NET
.NET
VB
C#
ASP.NET
ADO.NET
```

Improving Performance Using a StringBuilder Object

In the .NET environment, String objects are immutable, meaning, after you assign a value to a String object, you cannot change the object's value. Instead, when you perform an operation that assigns a new value to a String object, the .NET environment, behind the scenes, will discard the original String object and will create a new object that contains the contents you desire.

Depending on the string-manipulation operations your program performs, the constant creating and discarding of objects can introduce considerable (behind the scenes) overhead. To reduce the impact on performance, many programmers will perform complex string-manipulation operations using a StringBuilder object. Unlike the immutable String object, the StringBuilder object is mutable, which means your programs can make changes to the object's value (without having to discard and create a new object). Table 5-5 briefly describes the StringBuilder class methods and properties.

Method or Property	Purpose
Capacity	A property that gets or sets the maximum number of characters the object can store.
Chars	A property that gets or sets the character at the specified character position in the object.
Length	A property that gets or sets the length (number of characters) in the object.

Table 5-5   StringBuilder Class Methods and Properties

Method or Property	Purpose
MaxCapacity	A property that gets the object's maximum capacity.
Append	Appends an object's string representation to the end of the object. The Append method is an overloaded method.
AppendFormat	Appends a formatted string, which contains zero or more format specifications, to the object, replacing each format specification with the string representation of the corresponding argument. The AppendFormat method is an overloaded method.
EnsureCapacity	Ensures that the object's capacity is greater than or equal to the specified value.
Equals	Returns a Boolean value that specifies whether the object is equal to a specified object. The Equals method is an overloaded method.
Insert	Inserts an object's string representation into the object at a specified character position. The Insert method is an overloaded method.
Remove	Removes the specified range of characters from the object.
Replace	Replaces each occurrence of a character or substring in the object with a different character or string. The Replace method is an overloaded method.
ToString	Converts the StringBuilder object to a String. The ToString method is an overloaded and overridden method.

Table 5-5   StringBuilder Class Methods and Properties *(continued)*

Normally, a program would only use a StringBuilder object for cases where the number of operations on the object are considerable. The following program, StringBuilderDemo.vb, creates a loop in which the code performs a variety of operations on the StringBuilder object. The code monitors the number of clock ticks required to perform the operations. Then the code performs the same operations using a String object. Again, the code monitors the clock ticks to provide you with an idea of the additional overhead creating and discarding String objects can place on your program:

```
Imports System.Text
Module Module1

    Sub ManipulateStringBuilderObject()
        Dim SB As StringBuilder = New StringBuilder(26)
        SB.Append("ABCDEFGHIJKLMNOPQRSTUVWYZ")

        Dim StartTicks As Int64 = Now().Ticks()
        Dim I As Integer

        For I = 0 To 1000000
            SB.Chars(4) = "e"
            SB.Chars(0) = "a"
            SB.Replace("aBCDe", "ABCDE")
        Next
```

```
            Dim EndTicks As Int64 = Now.Ticks()
            Dim Ticks = EndTicks - StartTicks

            Console.WriteLine("StringBuilder required: " & Ticks & " ticks")
            Console.WriteLine("Ending StringBuilder: " & SB.ToString())
        End Sub

        Sub ManipulateString()
            Dim Str As String = "ABCDEFGHIJKLMNOPQRSTUVWYZ"

            Dim StartTicks As Int64 = Now().Ticks()
            Dim I As Integer

            For I = 0 To 1000000
                Str = Str.Replace("A", "a")
                Str = Str.Replace("E", "e")
                Str = Str.Replace("aBCDe", "ABCDE")
            Next

            Dim EndTicks As Int64 = Now.Ticks()
            Dim Ticks = EndTicks - StartTicks

            Console.WriteLine("String required: " & Ticks & " ticks")
            Console.WriteLine("Ending String: " & Str)
        End Sub

        Sub Main()
            ManipulateStringBuilderObject()
            ManipulateString()

            Console.ReadLine()
        End Sub

End Module
```

After you compile and execute this program, your screen will display output similar to the following:

```
StringBuilder required: 9113104 ticks
Ending StringBuilder: ABCDEFGHIJKLMNOPQRSTUVWYZ
String required: 30143344 ticks
Ending String: ABCDEFGHIJKLMNOPQRSTUVWYZ
```

Exploiting the Math Class

For years, Visual Basic programmers have made extensive use of functions such as Sqrt, Tan, and Ceiling to perform arithmetic and trigonometric operations. In the .NET environment, these functions now reside in the Math class.

The Math class is a static class, which means, to use one of the class methods, your programs do not have to create an instance of a Math class object. Instead, your programs can simply call the method you require by preceding the method name with the Math class name and dot operator, such as Math.Sqrt(25). Table 5-6 briefly describes the methods the Math class provides.

Method	Purpose
Abs	Returns a value's absolute value. The Abs method is an overloaded method.
Acos	Returns the angle (in radians) whose cosine is the specified value.
Asin	Returns the angle (in radians) whose sine is the specified value.
Atan	Returns the angle (in radians) whose tangent is the specified value.
Atan2	Returns the angle (in radians) whose tangent is the quotient of two specified values.
Ceiling	Returns the smallest whole number whose value is greater than or equal to the specified value.
Cos	Returns the cosine of the specified angle (in radians).
Cosh	Returns the hyperbolic cosine of the specified angle (in radians).
Exp	Returns e raised to the specified power.
Floor	Returns the largest whole number whose value is less than or equal to the specified value.
IEEERemainder	Returns the remainder of the division of a specified numerator and denominator.
Log	Returns the logarithm of a specified value. The Log method is an overloaded method.
Log10	Returns the base 10 logarithm of a specified value.
Max	Returns the larger of two specified values. The Max method is an overloaded method.
Min	Returns the smaller of two specified values. The Min method is an overloaded method.
Pow	Returns the result of a specified value raised to a given power.
Round	Returns the whole number nearest the specified value. The Round method is an overloaded method.
Sign	Returns a value indicating the sign of a number. The Sign method is an overloaded method.
Sin	Returns the sine of the specified angle (in radians).

Table 5-6 Math Class Methods

Method	Purpose
Sinh	Returns the hyperbolic sine of the specified angle.
Sqrt	Returns the square root of a specified number.
Tan	Returns the tangent of the specified angle.
Tanh	Returns the hyperbolic tangent of the specified angle.

Table 5-6   Math Class Methods *(continued)*

USE IT   The following program, MathClassDemo.vb, illustrates the use of the Math class methods:

```
Module Module1

    Sub Main()
        Console.WriteLine("Abs(-1) = " & Math.Abs(-1))
        Console.WriteLine("Acos(0) = " & Math.Acos(0.0))
        Console.WriteLine("Acos(pi/4) = " & Math.Acos(Math.PI / 4))
        Console.WriteLine("Ceiling(1.1), Ceiling(0.9) = " & _
            Math.Ceiling(1.1) & " " & Math.Ceiling(0.9))
        Console.WriteLine("Cos(pi) = " & Math.Cos(Math.PI))
        Console.WriteLine("Exp(5) = " & Math.Exp(5))
        Console.WriteLine("Log10(100) = " & Math.Log10(100))
        Console.WriteLine("Max(1001, 100) = " & Math.Max(1001, 100))
        Console.WriteLine("Min(1001, 100) = " & Math.Min(1001, 100))
        Console.WriteLine("Floor(1.1), Floor(0.9) = " & _
            Math.Floor(1.1) & " " & Math.Floor(0.9))
        Console.WriteLine("Round(1.1), Round(0.9) = " & _
            Math.Round(1.1) & " " & Math.Round(0.9))
        Console.WriteLine("Pow(5, 2) = " & Math.Pow(5, 2))
        Console.WriteLine("Sqrt(25) = " & Math.Sqrt(25))

        Console.ReadLine()
    End Sub
End Module
```

After you compile and execute this program, your screen will display the following output:

```
Abs(-1) = 1
Acos(0) = 1.5707963267949
Acos(pi/4) = 0.667457216028384
Ceiling(1.1), Ceiling(0.9) = 2 1
Cos(pi) = -1
Exp(5) = 148.413159102577
```

```
Log10(100) = 2
Max(1001, 100) = 1001
Min(1001, 100) = 100
Floor(1.1), Floor(0.9) = 1 0
Round(1.1), Round(0.9) = 1 1
Pow(5, 2) = 25
Sqrt(25) = 5
```

Sending E-mail Messages from Within a Visual Basic .NET Program

Depending on the processing your programs perform, or the errors or events your programs may encounter, there may be times when your code needs to notify you (or possibly a system administrator) of a specific event. For example, in Chapter 14 you will learn how to create Windows services that can monitor system or network operations. Often, the easiest way for the program to notify an administrator of a specific event is simply to send an e-mail message. In the Windows 2000 environment, your programs can send an e-mail message using the Collaboration Data Object for Windows 2000 (CDOSYS).

USE IT   To send an e-mail message, your programs can use the Simple Mail Transport Protocol (SMTP) service built into Windows 2000, or you can specify a different SMTP server. To begin, your program should create an SmtpMail object to which you assign the SMTP server information to the SmtpServer property. Then your program can create a MailMessage object that you use to specify the message attributes (such as To, Subject, Body, and so on). Table 5-7 briefly describes the MailMessage class properties.

Property	Purpose
Attachments	Specifies a list of attachments to be sent with the message.
Bcc	Gets or sets a semicolon-delimited list of e-mail addresses that will receive a blind carbon copy of the message.
Body	Gets or sets the message body.
BodyEncoding	Gets or sets the message body encoding type.
BodyFormat	Gets or sets the message body content type.
Cc	Gets or sets a semicolon-delimited list of e-mail addresses that receive a carbon copy of the message.
From	Gets or sets the sender's e-mail address.
Headers	Gets or sets custom headers that are sent with the message.

Table 5-7   MailMessage Class Properties

Property	Purpose
Priority	Gets or sets the message priority.
Subject	Gets or sets the message subject.
To	Gets or sets a semicolon-delimited list of the message recipients.
UrlContentBase	Gets or sets the URL base of all relative URLs in an HTML-encoded message.
UrlContentLocation	Gets or sets the Content-Location HTTP header for an HTML-encoded message.

Table 5-7   MailMessage Class Properties *(continued)*

The following program, MailMessageDemo.vb, sends an e-mail message to the e-mail address Admin@SomeSite.com. By cutting and pasting the e-mail related code into your applications, you can quickly build e-mail support into your code. In the program code, assign the address of your SMTP server to the Smtp.SmtpServer variable:

```
Imports System.Web.Mail

Module Module1

    Sub Main()
        Dim Smtp As SmtpMail
        Smtp.SmtpServer = "Put Your STMP Server Address Here"

        Dim Msg As MailMessage = New MailMessage()

        Msg.Body = "Demo message from a program"
        Msg.From = "John@SomeSite.com"
        Msg.To = "Admin@SomeSite.com"
        Msg.Subject = "Demo Message"
        Smtp.Send(Msg)
    End Sub

End Module
```

To use the System.Web.Mail namespace, you must first add a reference to the System.Web.dll file to your project. To add the reference, select Project | Add Reference. Visual Studio will display the Add Reference dialog box. In the dialog box, click the System.Web.dll entry and choose OK.

CHAPTER 6

Programming Visual Basic .NET File and Directory Operations

TIPS IN THIS CHAPTER

To store information from one user session to the next, applications make extensive use of files. In this chapter, you will examine classes built into the .NET Common Language Runtime that your programs can use to perform key file and directory operations:

- Create, select, move, and delete a directory
- Retrieve a collection that contains a directory's files or subdirectories
- Create, copy, move, and delete a file
- Exploit file attributes, such as the date and time the file was created or last accessed
- Recursively traverse the directories on your disk to perform an operation on every file your disk contains
- Store a form's contents into a file or fill a form's text box using a file's contents
- Use file locks to protect shared data
- Store and retrieve text and binary data in a file
- Monitor a directory for changes to files and directories and then perform specific operations when such events occur

Each Tip this chapter presents provides sample source code that implements a key file or directory operation. By the time you finish this chapter, you will have the tools you need to take full advantage of the .NET file and directory manipulation classes. In Chapter 18, you will examine database operations using ADO.NET.

Getting Started with the Directory Class

As your programs store and retrieve information in files, you will often make extensive use of directories (folders) to organize related files. Within your program, you might, for example, need to create a directory, select a specific directory from which you will open existing files or into which you place files, or you may need to delete a directory and the files it contains. To perform such directory operations, your Visual Basic .NET programs can use the Directory class.

The Directory class is a static class, which means you do not have to create an instance of a Directory class object in order to use the class methods. As briefly discussed in Table 6-1, the Directory class provides methods you can use to perform common directory-manipulation operations.

Method	Purpose
CreateDirectory	Creates the specified directory.
Delete	Deletes a directory and the files and subdirectories the directory contains. The Delete method is an overloaded method.

Table 6-1   The Directory Class Methods

Method	Purpose
Exists	Determines if the specified directory exists.
GetCreationTime	Gets the date and time the specified file or directory was created.
GetCurrentDirectory	Gets the application's current directory.
GetDirectories	Gets a container that contains the names of subdirectories in the specified directory. The GetDirectories method is an overloaded method.
GetDirectoryRoot	Gets the volume information (disk letter) and root information for the specified directory.
GetFiles	Returns a collection that contains the names of files in the specified directory. The GetFiles method is an overloaded method.
GetFileSystemEntries	Returns a collection that contains the names of all files and subdirectories in the specified directory. The GetFileSystem method is an overloaded method.
GetLastAccessTime	Gets the date and time the specified file or directory was last accessed.
GetLastWriteTime	Gets the date and time the specified file or directory was last written to.
GetLogicalDrives	Returns a collection that contains the names of the system's logical drives.
GetParent	Gets the parent directory of the specified directory.
Move	Moves a file or directory.
SetCreationTime	Sets the creation date and time for the specified file or directory.
SetCurrentDirectory	Sets the application's current directory.
SetLastAccessTime	Sets the date and time the specified file or directory was last accessed.
SetLastWriteTime	Sets the date and time a file or directory was last written to.

Table 6-1   The Directory Class Methods *(continued)*

USE IT   Often, your program must create a directory to store user files. To create a directory, your code can use the Directory class CreateDirectory method. The following program, MakeDirectory.vb, uses the CreateDirectory method to create several different directories. By changing the path name the program passes to the CreateDirectory method, the program creates a directory in the root directory on a specific drive (C:\Sample01), in a specific directory on a drive (C:\Temp\Sample02), and in the current directory (Sample03):

```
Imports System.IO

Module Module1

    Sub Main()
        Console.WriteLine("Creating directories...")

        Directory.CreateDirectory("C:\Sample01")
```

```
        Directory.CreateDirectory("C:\Temp\Sample02")
        Directory.CreateDirectory("Sample03")

        Console.WriteLine("Directories created")
        Console.ReadLine() ' Delay to view output
    End Sub
End Module
```

When you use the Directory class CreateDirectory method to create a directory, the method will return a value of type DirectoryInfo that contains fields that describe the new directory's attributes. Several of the Tips this chapter presents examine the use of the DirectoryInfo class.

For purposes of simplicity, this program does not check for errors, such as a security exception that occurs when the user does not have permission to create the directory specified. A better solution would create the directories within a Try-Catch statement as shown here:

```
Try
  Directory.CreateDirectory("C:\Sample01")
  Directory.CreateDirectory("C:\Temp\Sample02")
  Directory.CreateDirectory("Sample03")

  Console.WriteLine("Directories created")
Catch E As Exception
  Console.WriteLine("Error creating a directory")
  Console.WriteLine("Error: {0}", E.Message)
End Try
```

The following program, DirectoryExists.vb, changes the previous program slightly to use the Directory class Exists method to determine if the specified directory exists. If the directory does not exist, the program will create the directory. Otherwise, the program will display a message box stating that the directory already exists:

```
Imports System.IO

Module Module1
    Sub Main()
        Console.WriteLine("Creating directories...")

        Try
            If (Directory.Exists("C:\Sample01")) Then
                Console.WriteLine("C:\Sample01 already exists")
            Else
                Directory.CreateDirectory("C:\Sample01")
            End If

            If (Directory.Exists("C:\Temp\Sample02")) Then
```

```
                Console.WriteLine("C:\Temp\Sample02 already exists")
            Else
                Directory.CreateDirectory("C:\Temp\Sample02")
            End If

            Console.WriteLine("Directories created")
        Catch E As Exception
            Console.WriteLine("Error creating directory")
            Console.WriteLine("Error: {0}", E.Message)
        End Try

        Console.ReadLine() ' Delay to view output
    End Sub
End Module
```

Just as there may be times when your programs must create a directory, there may also be times when your program must delete a directory and the files the directory contains. In such cases, your programs can call the Directory class Delete method. To delete a directory and, optionally, the files and subdirectories the directory contains, invoke the Delete method with the directory name and the value True:

```
Directory.Delete("DirectoryName", True)
```

If you do not want the Delete method to delete a directory that contains files or other subdirectories, invoke the method with the value False or simply omit the value:

```
Directory.Delete("DirectoryName", False)
Directory.Delete("DirectoryName")
```

The following program, DeleteDirectory.vb, uses the Directory class Delete method to delete the directories you created using the MakeDirectory.vb program:

```
Imports System.IO

Module Module1
    Sub Main()
        Console.WriteLine("Deleting directories...")

        Try
            Directory.Delete("C:\Sample01", True)
        Catch E As Exception
            Console.WriteLine("Error deleting directory C:\Sample01")
            Console.WriteLine("Error {0}", E.Message)
```

```
        End Try

        Try
            Directory.Delete("C:\Temp\Sample02", True)
        Catch E As Exception
            Console.WriteLine("Error deleting directory C:\Temp\Sample02")
            Console.WriteLine("Error {0}", E.Message)
        End Try

        Try
            Directory.Delete("Sample03", True)
        Catch E As Exception
            Console.WriteLine("Error deleting directory Sample03")
            Console.WriteLine("Error {0}", E.Message)
        End Try

        Console.WriteLine("Directories deleted")
        Console.ReadLine() ' Delay to view output
    End Sub
End Module
```

In addition to letting your programs delete a directory, the Directory class also provides the Move method that lets you move a directory and the files it contains. The following statement, for example, would move a directory named C:\Temp\Samples to the root directory:

```
Directory.Move("C:\Temp\Sample01", "C:\Sample01")
```

Finally, within your programs there will be many times when you must get or set the current directory. Using the Directory class SetCurrentDirectory and GetCurrentDirectory methods, your Visual Basic .NET programs can easily perform these operations. The following program, DirectoryInfo.vb, first uses the Directory class GetCurrentDirectory method to determine the current directory. Then, the program uses SetCurrentDirectory method to select the root directory on drive C as the current directory. The program then calls the GetCurrentDirectory method a second time to determine the new current directory:

```
Imports System.IO

Module Module1
    Sub Main()
        Console.WriteLine("Current directory is {0}", _
          Directory.GetCurrentDirectory())
```

```
        Directory.SetCurrentDirectory("C:\")

        Console.WriteLine("Current directory is {0}", _
           Directory.GetCurrentDirectory())

        Console.ReadLine()
    End Sub
End Module
```

After you compile and execute this program, your screen will display messages similar to those shown here:

```
Current directory is C:\VB_BOOK\Files\DirectoryInfo\bin
Current directory is C:\
```

Retrieving and Manipulating Directory Attributes

As your programs manipulate directories, there may be times when you will need to know information about specific directories, such as the date and time the directory was created, last written to, or last accessed. To help your programs determine directory attributes, the DirectoryInfo class provides the set of methods described in Table 6-2 that you can use to get or set various directory attributes. Table 6-3 discusses the class properties.

Method	Purpose
Create	Creates the corresponding directory.
CreateSubdirectory	Creates the specified subdirectory relative to the object's directory.
Delete	Deletes the object's directory and the files and subdirectories the directory contains. The Delete method is an overloaded method.
GetDirectories	Returns an array that contains the names of subdirectories in the directory. The GetDirectories method is an overloaded method.
GetFiles	Returns an array that contains the names of files in the directory. The GetFiles method is an overloaded method.
GetFileSystemInfos	Returns an array that contains FileSystemInfo objects in the directory. The GetFileSystemInfos method is an overloaded method.
MoveTo	Moves the directory and its contents to a new location.

Table 6-2 The DirectoryInfo Class Methods

Property	Purpose
Exists	Gets a Boolean value that indicates if the directory exists. The Exists method is an overloaded method.
Name	Gets the name of the directory that corresponds to the DirectoryInfo instance. The Name method is an overloaded method.
Parent	Gets the name of the parent directory that corresponds to the DirectoryInfo instance.
Root	Gets the root (drive letter and root) that corresponds to the DirectoryInfo instance.

Table 6-3   The DirectoryInfo Class Properties

 The following program, ShowDirectoryAttributes.vb, uses the DirectoryInfo class attribute methods to display information about the C:\WINNT\Temp directory:

```
Imports System.IO

Module Module1
    Sub Main()
        If (Directory.Exists("C:\WINNT\Temp")) Then
            Dim Dir As New DirectoryInfo("C:\WINNT\Temp")

            Console.WriteLine("Full name: {0}", Dir.FullName)
            Console.WriteLine("Creation time: {0}", Dir.CreationTime)
            Console.WriteLine("Last access time: {0}", Dir.LastAccessTime)
            Console.WriteLine("Last write time: {0}", Dir.LastWriteTime)
        Else
            Console.WriteLine("C:\WINNT\Temp does not exist")
        End If

        Console.ReadLine() ' Delay to view output
    End Sub
End Module
```

After you compile and execute this program, your screen will display output similar to the following:

```
Full name: C:\WINNT\Temp
Creation time: 3/5/2002 2:35:08 PM
Last access time: 3/5/2002 5:13:40 PM
Last write time: 3/5/2002 3:59:52 PM
```

Just as the DirectoryInfo class provides methods your programs can use to retrieve directory attributes, the class also provides methods your programs can use to set directory attributes. The following program, SetDirectoryAttributes.vb, sets each of the C:\WINNT\Temp attributes to the current date time and time:

```
Imports System.IO

Module Module1
    Sub Main()
        If (Directory.Exists("C:\WINNT\Temp")) Then
            Dim Dir As New DirectoryInfo("C:\WINNT\Temp")

            Dim DateTimeNow As DateTime = DateTime.Now()

            Try
                Dir.CreationTime = DateTimeNow
                Dir.LastAccessTime = DateTimeNow
                Dir.LastWriteTime = DateTimeNow

                Console.WriteLine("Directory attributes updated")
            Catch E As Exception
                Console.WriteLine("Error updating attributes")
                Console.WriteLine("Error {0}: ", E.Message)
            End Try
        Else
            Console.WriteLine("C:\WINNT\Temp does not exist")
        End If

        Console.ReadLine() ' Delay to view output
    End Sub
End Module
```

Compile and run the SetDirectoryAttributes program. Then run the ShowDirectoryAttributes program a second time to view the change in the attribute settings.

In addition to using the DirectoryInfo class to set and retrieve attributes for an instance of a DirectoryInfo class, your programs can also use Directory class methods to set and retrieve a directory's attributes (without creating an instance of the class), as shown here:

```
Imports System.IO

Module Module1
    Sub Main()
        Dim TargetDirectory As String = "C:\WINNT\Temp"

        If (Directory.Exists(TargetDirectory)) Then
            Console.WriteLine("Creation time: {0}", _
```

```
            Directory.GetCreationTime(TargetDirectory))
        Console.WriteLine("Last access time: {0}", _
           Directory.GetLastAccessTime(TargetDirectory))
        Console.WriteLine("Last write time: {0}", _
           Directory.GetLastWriteTime(TargetDirectory))
    Else
        Console.WriteLine("{0}does not exist", TargetDirectory)
    End If

    Console.ReadLine() ' Delay to view output
  End Sub
End Module
```

Creating a Unique Directory

Depending on the processing your program performs, there may be times when you must create a unique directory within which you can store a user's files. For example, in a server-based environment, you might create directories on a per-user basis.

USE IT Programmers use a myriad of techniques to generate a unique directory name. The following program, UniqueDirectory.vb, uses the Directory class CreateDirectory method to create a unique directory within the current directory. To generate a unique name, the program uses the DateTime class Ticks property that stores 100-nanosecond intervals since midnight January 1, 2001. The program uses the Ticks property within a loop that converts the ticks to a string representation and then checks if a directory exists with the same name. If not, the program uses the ticks as the new, unique directory name. Otherwise, the loop repeats and the program repeats the process using the new value stored in Ticks:

```
Imports System.IO

Module Module1
    Sub Main()
        Dim Name As String

        Do
            Name = DateTime.Now.Ticks

            Console.WriteLine("Testing Name: {0}", Name)
        Loop While (Directory.Exists(Name))

        Console.WriteLine("Unique name is {0}", Name)
        Console.ReadLine()  ' Delay to view output
    End Sub
End Module
```

After you compile and execute this program, your screen will show a message similar to the following that displays the unique directory name:

```
Testing Name: 631509539303926144
Unique name is 631509539303926144
```

Retrieving a Directory's Files and Subdirectories

USE IT   When your programs perform file operations, there may be times when you will want your code to perform a specific operation on each file or subdirectory a directory contains. In such cases, your programs can use the Directory class GetFiles and GetDirectories methods, each of which returns a container that contains the corresponding files or directories. After your program retrieves the files or directories, your code can use a For Each loop to process each of the files or directories:

```
Dim Files As String() = Directory.GetFiles("*.*")
Dim Filename As String

For Each Filename In Files
  Console.WriteLine(Filename)
Next
```

The following program, ShowRoot.vb, uses the GetFiles and GetDirectories methods to display the names of each file and directory in the root directory of drive C:

```
Imports System.IO

Module Module1
    Sub Main()
        Dim Files As String() = Directory.GetFiles("C:\")
        Dim Dirs As String() = Directory.GetDirectories("C:\")

        Console.WriteLine("Root Files")
        Dim Filename As String

        For Each Filename In Files
            Console.WriteLine(Filename)
        Next

        Console.WriteLine("Root Directories")

        Dim DirectoryName As String
```

```
        For Each DirectoryName In Dirs
            Console.WriteLine(DirectoryName)
        Next

        Console.WriteLine("Press Enter to Continue ...")
        Console.ReadLine()
    End Sub
End Module
```

In a similar way, the following program, ShowAllFiles.vb, displays all the files that reside on drive C:

```
Imports System.IO

Module Module1
    Sub DisplayTree(ByVal Dir As String)
        Dim Files As String() = Directory.GetFiles(Dir)
        Dim Dirs As String() = Directory.GetDirectories(Dir)

        Dim Filename As String

        For Each Filename In Files
            Console.WriteLine(Filename)
        Next

        Dim DirectoryName As String

        For Each DirectoryName In Dirs
            DisplayTree(DirectoryName)
        Next
    End Sub

    Sub Main()
        DisplayTree("C:\")
    End Sub
End Module
```

To display all the files on your disk, the program recursively calls the DisplayTree subroutine to display the files that reside in each directory. To start, the program will display the files that reside in your root directory. Then the program will retrieve a list of the root's subdirectories. With each subdirectory, the program will call the DisplayTree subroutine, which first displays the directory's files and then recursively examines the directory's subdirectories. By traversing the directory in this fashion, the program eventually displays the name of each file on your disk.

Determining a System's Logical Disk Drives

USE IT As your programs create, open, and manipulate files, there will be times when you will want to place files on specific disk drives. Using the Directory class GetLogicalDrives method, your code can retrieve a list of a system's disk drives. The GetLogicalDrives method returns a container that stores the drive letters for each disk in the system. After your program retrieves the logical drives, your programs can use a For Each loop to move through the container that contains the drive letters:

```
Dim Drive As String
For Each Drive In DriveList
   Console.WriteLine(Drive)
Next
```

The following program, ShowLogicalDrives.vb, uses the Directory class GetLogicalDrives method to display your system's disk drives:

```
Imports System.IO

Module Module1
    Sub Main()
        Dim DriveList As String() = Directory.GetLogicalDrives()
        Dim Drive As String

        Console.WriteLine("Logical Drives")

        For Each Drive In DriveList
            Console.WriteLine(Drive)
        Next

        Console.ReadLine()
    End Sub
End Module
```

After you compile and run the program, your screen will display messages that contain the disk drive letters for your system's drives, as shown here:

```
Logical Drives
A:\
C:\
F:\
```

Retrieving a Directory's Files and Subdirectories Using the DirectoryInfo Class

USE IT   Throughout this chapter, several Tips will use the Directory class to perform directory operations. Because the Directory class is a static class, your programs do not have to create an instance of the Directory class in order to use the class methods. As you have learned, in addition to the Directory class, Visual Basic .NET provides the DirectoryInfo class that your programs can use to perform operations on a specific directory instance. Many of the methods the Directory class provides are similar to those in the Directory class. For example, the following program, DirectoryInfoDemo.vb, illustrates the use of the DirectoryInfo class to display information about the subdirectories that reside in the Windows directory:

```
Imports System.IO

Module Module1
    Sub Main()
        Dim Root As New DirectoryInfo("C:\")

        Dim Files As FileInfo() = Root.GetFiles("*.*")
        Dim Dirs As DirectoryInfo() = Root.GetDirectories("*.*")

        Console.WriteLine("Root Files")

        Dim Filename As FileInfo

        For Each Filename In Files
            Try
                Console.Write(Filename.FullName)
                Console.Write(" Size: {0} bytes", Filename.Length)
                Console.WriteLine(" Last use: {0}", Filename.LastAccessTime)
            Catch E As Exception
                Console.WriteLine("*** Error accessing ***")
            End Try
        Next

        Console.WriteLine()
        Console.WriteLine("Root Directories")

        Dim DirectoryName As DirectoryInfo
```

```
      For Each DirectoryName In Dirs
          Try
              Console.Write(DirectoryName.FullName)
              Console.Write(" contains {0} files ", _
                 DirectoryName.GetFiles().Length)
              Console.WriteLine(" and {0} subdirectories ", _
                 DirectoryName.GetDirectories().Length)
          Catch E As Exception
              Console.WriteLine("*** Error accessing ***")
          End Try
      Next

      Console.WriteLine("Press Enter to Continue ...")
      Console.ReadLine()
   End Sub
End Module
```

After you compile and execute this program, your screen will display information about your root directory files and directories that reside in the root:

```
Root Files
C:\AUTOEXEC.nt Size: 52 bytes Last use: 8/26/2001 7:19:29 PM
C:\boot.ini Size: 192 bytes Last use: 9/5/2001 4:31:34 PM
::
C:\ntldr Size: 214432 bytes Last use: 8/26/2001 6:52:16 PM
C:\pagefile.sys Size: 603979776 bytes Last use: 3/2/2002 7:00:58 AM

Root Directories
C:\Borland contains 0 files  and 1 subdirectories
C:\Documents and Settings contains 0 files  and 10 subdirectories
 ::
C:\Temp contains 2 files  and 0 subdirectories
C:\WINNT contains 103 files  and 43 subdirectories
Press Enter to Continue ...
```

Retrieving a Directory's Parent or Root Directory

When your programs perform directory and file operations, there may be times when you must determine a directory's parent directory. For example, if a user specifies a path name such as "..\Subdir", your code may need to determine the current directory's parent (which corresponds to the double periods before the directory name) before your code can access the correct subdirectory.

USE IT To determine a directory's parent directory, your programs can use the Directory class GetParent method. The following program, GetParent.vb, uses the Directory class GetParent method to determine the current directory's parent. The program then displays a message that contains the current directory name and that of the parent:

```
Imports System.IO

Module Module1
    Sub Main()
        Dim Current As String
        Dim Parent As DirectoryInfo

        Try
            Current = Directory.GetCurrentDirectory()
            Parent = Directory.GetParent(Current)

            Console.WriteLine("Current directory {0}", Current)
            Console.WriteLine("Parent directory {0}", Parent.FullName)
        Catch E As Exception
            Console.WriteLine("Error determining parent directory")
            Console.WriteLine(E.Message)
        End Try

        Console.ReadLine()
    End Sub
End Module
```

After you compile and execute this program, your screen will display the name of the current directory and the directory's parent, as shown here:

```
Current directory C:\VB_BOOK\Files\GetParent\bin
Parent directory C:\VB_BOOK\Files\GetParent
```

In a similar way, there may be times when your programs must know a directory's root (which contains the drive letter, such as C:\). The following program, RootDirectory.vb, uses the Directory class GetRoot method to determine the current directory's root. The program then displays a message that contains the current directory name and that of the directory's root:

```
Imports System.IO

Module Module1
    Sub Main()
        Dim Current As String
        Dim Root As String
```

```
    Try
        Current = Directory.GetCurrentDirectory()
        Root = Directory.GetDirectoryRoot(Current)

        Console.WriteLine("Current directory {0}", Current)
        Console.WriteLine("Root directory {0}", Root)
    Catch E As Exception
        Console.WriteLine("Error determining root directory")
        Console.WriteLine(E.Message)
    End Try

    Console.ReadLine()
    End Sub
End Module
```

After you compile and execute this program, your screen will display your current directory and the directory's root, as shown here:

```
Current directory C:\VB_BOOK\Files\RootDirectory\bin
Root directory C:\
```

Manipulating a Directory Path

As your programs work with files and directories, there will be times when your code must parse directory-path information. For example, if your program prompts the user to enter a filename, your code may first parse the data the user entered to determine if the user specified a pathname that may contain a disk drive identifier, a subdirectory, and eventually a filename and extension.

USE IT   To manipulate a directory path, your code can use the Path class. The Path class is a static class, which means you do not have to create an instance of the class to use the class methods. Table 6-4 describes the Path class methods; Table 6-5 describes the Path class properties.

Method	Purpose
ChangeExtension	Changes a path's file extension.
Combine	Returns the result of one path concatenated to another.
GetDirectoryName	Returns a path's directory name.

Table 6-4   The Path Class Methods

Method	Purpose
GetExtension	Returns a path's file extension.
GetFileName	Returns a path's filename and extension.
GetFileNameWithoutExtension	Returns a path's filename without the extension.
GetFullPath	Returns a path's absolute path.
GetPathRoot	Returns a path's root directory information (the drive letter and root).
GetTempFileName	Creates a 0-byte file and returns a unique filename for the file in the directory.
GetTempPath	Returns the path to the current operating system's temporary directory.
HasExtension	Returns a Boolean value that specifies if a path includes a filename extension.
IsPathRooted	Returns a Boolean value that specifies if the path contains absolute or relative path information.

Table 6-4   The Path Class Methods *(continued)*

Property	Meaning
AltDirectorySeparatorChar	Gets a secondary operating system–specific alternate character that separates directory levels in a path.
DirectorySeparatorChar	Gets a primary operating system–specific character that separates directory levels in a path string.
InvalidPathChars	Returns an array that contains an operating system–specific set of characters that are not valid in path names.
PathSeparator	Gets an operating system–specific separator character that separates path strings in environment variables.
VolumeSeparatorChar	Gets an operating system–specific character that separates the volume from the path (disk drive letter from the path).

Table 6-5   The Path Class Properties

The following program, PathInfo.vb, uses the Path class to display specifics about several different path strings:

```
Imports System.IO

Module Module1
    Sub ShowPath(ByVal P As String)
        Try
            Console.WriteLine("Starting path: {0}", P)
            Console.WriteLine("Directory name: {0}", Path.GetDirectoryName(P))
            Console.WriteLine("Extension: {0}", Path.GetExtension(P))
            Console.WriteLine("Filename: {0}", Path.GetFileName(P))
            Console.WriteLine("Filename without extension: {0}", _
                Path.GetFileNameWithoutExtension(P))
            Console.WriteLine("Full path: {0}", Path.GetFullPath(P))
            Console.WriteLine("Root: {0}", Path.GetPathRoot(P))
        Catch E As Exception
            Console.WriteLine(" ** Error processing **")
            Console.WriteLine("Error: {0}", E.Message)
        End Try
        Console.WriteLine()
    End Sub

    Sub Main()
        ShowPath("C:\Folder\Subdir\Filename.ext")
        ShowPath("C:Filename.ext")
        ShowPath("C:Filename")
        ShowPath("C:\")
        ShowPath("\")
        Console.ReadLine() ' Delay to view output
    End Sub
End Module
```

After you compile and execute this program, your screen will display output similar to the following:

```
Starting path: C:\Folder\Subdir\Filename.ext
Directory name: C:\Folder\Subdir
Extension: .ext
Filename: Filename.ext
Filename without extension: Filename
Full path: C:\Folder\Subdir\Filename.ext
Root: C:\

Starting path: C:Filename.ext
```

```
Directory name: C:
Extension: .ext
Filename: Filename.ext
Filename without extension: Filename
Full path: C:\VB_BOOK\Files\PathInfo\bin\Filename.ext
Root: C:

Starting path: C:Filename
Directory name: C:
Extension:
Filename: Filename
Filename without extension: Filename
Full path: C:\VB_BOOK\Files\PathInfo\bin\Filename
Root: C:

Starting path: C:\
Directory name:
Extension:
Filename:
Filename without extension:
Full path: C:\
Root: C:\

Starting path: \
Directory name:
Extension:
Filename:
Filename without extension:
Full path: C:\
Root: \
```

Different operating systems support different characters in a directory path. Although the .NET environment is still a Windows-based environment, the Path class provides methods your code will use in the future to support environments such as Linux. The following program, PathProperies.vb, displays your system's settings for the Path class properties:

```
Imports System.IO

Module Module1
    Sub Main()
        Console.WriteLine("Alternate Directory Separator {0}", _
          Path.AltDirectorySeparatorChar)
        Console.WriteLine("Directory Separator {0}", _
          Path.DirectorySeparatorChar)
        Console.Write("Invalid Path Characters:")
```

```
      Dim C As Char
      For Each C In Path.InvalidPathChars
          Console.Write(" {0}", C)
      Next

      Console.WriteLine()
      Console.WriteLine("Path Separator {0}", Path.PathSeparator)
      Console.WriteLine("Volume Separator {0}", _
        Path.VolumeSeparatorChar)
      Console.ReadLine() ' Delay to view output
    End Sub
End Module
```

After you compile and execute this program, your screen will display output similar to the following:

```
Alternate Directory Separator /
Directory Separator \
Invalid Path Characters: "<>|▶◀↕¶§—↕↑↓
Path Separator ;
Volume Separator :
```

Performing Common File Operations

USE IT   One of the most common maintenance tasks programs perform is to copy, delete, and move files. To perform such operations, Visual Basic .NET programs can use the File class. Like the Directory class, the File class is a static class, which means your programs do not have to create an instance of a File class object in order to use the class methods. The File class methods support wildcard operations. The following code fragments, for example, illustrate how to use the File class to copy, move, and delete files:

```
File.Delete("*.bak")

File.Move("OldName", "NewName")

File.Copy("Source", "Destination")
```

Table 6-6 briefly describes the File class methods.

Method	Purpose
AppendText	Returns a StreamWriter object a program can use to append text to an existing file.
Copy	Copies the specified file to a new file. The Copy method is an overloaded method.

Table 6-6   The File Class Methods

Method	Purpose
Create	Creates the specified file within the directory given in a path. The Create method is an overloaded method.
CreateText	Creates or opens a new file for text output, returning a StreamWriter object the program can use to write to the file.
Delete	Deletes the specified file.
Exists	Returns a Boolean value that specifies if the file exists.
GetAttributes	Returns a FileAttributes object that contains the attributes for the specified file.
GetCreationTime	Returns the date and time the specified file or directory was created.
GetLastAccessTime	Returns the date and time the specified file or directory was last accessed.
GetLastWriteTime	Returns the date and time the specified file or directory was last written to.
Move	Moves the file to a new location.
Open	Opens the specified file, returning a FileStream object the program can use to read or write to the file.
OpenRead	Opens the specified file, returning a FileStream object the program can use to read the file.
OpenText	Opens the specified text file, returning a StreamReader object the program can use to read the file.
OpenWrite	Opens the specified file, returning a FileStream object the program can use to write to the file.
SetAttributes	Sets the attributes specified in a FileAttributes object for a given file.
SetCreationTime	Sets the date and time the file was created.
SetLastAccessTime	Sets the date and time the specified file was last accessed.
SetLastWriteTime	Sets the date and time the specified file was last written to.

Table 6-6   The File Class Methods *(continued)*

The following program, DeleteTmpFiles.vb, searches a user's current disk for files with the .tmp extension. The program then deletes the files using the File class Delete method:

```
Imports System.IO

Module Module1

    Sub ProcessTree(ByVal Dir As String)
        Dim DirObj As New DirectoryInfo(Dir)

        Dim Files As FileInfo() = DirObj.GetFiles("*.tmp")
```

```vbnet
        Dim Dirs As DirectoryInfo() = DirObj.GetDirectories("*.*")

        Dim Filename As FileInfo
        For Each Filename In Files
            Try
                If (Filename.Attributes And FileAttributes.ReadOnly) Then
                    Filename.Attributes = _
                    (Filename.Attributes And Not FileAttributes.ReadOnly)
                End If

                File.Delete(Filename.FullName)
                Console.WriteLine("Deleted {0}", Filename.FullName)
            Catch E As Exception
                Console.WriteLine("*** Error deleting {0}", _
                    Filename.FullName)
                Console.WriteLine("Error: {0}", E.Message)
            End Try
        Next

        Dim DirectoryName As DirectoryInfo
        For Each DirectoryName In Dirs
            Try
                ProcessTree(DirectoryName.FullName)
            Catch E As Exception
                Console.WriteLine("*** Error accessing {0}", _
                    DirectoryName.FullName)
                Console.WriteLine("Error: {0}", E.Message)
            End Try
        Next
    End Sub

    Sub Main()
        ProcessTree("C:\")

        Console.Write("Press Enter to Continue...")
        Console.ReadLine() ' Delay to view output
    End Sub
End Module
```

To process all the directories on drive C, the program calls the ProcessTree subroutine that uses recursion to move through a directory and its subdirectories. Within the ProcessTree subroutine, the code first retrieves all the files with the .tmp extension:

```
Dim Files As FileInfo() = DirObj.GetFiles("*.tmp")
```

Then the code uses a For Each loop to delete each of the files. Within the loop, the code first tests if the file's ReadOnly attribute is set. If so, the code removes the attribute:

```
If (Filename.Attributes And FileAttributes.ReadOnly) Then
   Filename.Attributes = _
      (Filename.Attributes And Not FileAttributes.ReadOnly)
End If
```

To remove the ReadOnly attribute, the program performs a bitwise And operation of the file's other attributes (some of which are set to 1 and some of which are 0) with the bitwise Not of the ReadOnly attribute value (which converts all the bits in the value to 1, with the exception of the bit that indicates the ReadOnly setting). The operation essentially turns off the ReadOnly attribute while leaving the others unchanged (which is not necessary, because the application later deletes the file, but you may want to perform a similar operation in a different program on a file you do not delete). After the program clears the ReadOnly attribute, the program uses the File class Delete method to delete the file:

```
File.Delete(Filename.FullName)
```

The subroutine then recursively calls itself for each of the subdirectories the directory contains.

Taking Advantage of File Attributes

In the Windows operating system, the file system tracks when a user creates, updates, and uses a file. Figure 6-1, for example, illustrates a Properties dialog box for a file. In the dialog box, you can view the file's size, date and time stamps, and other attributes.

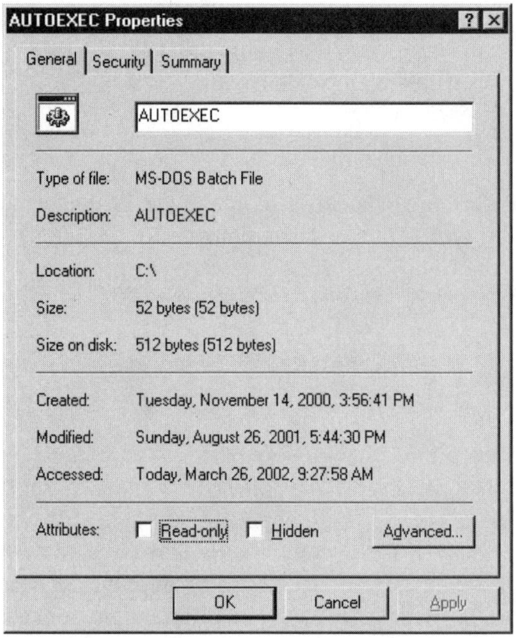

Figure 6-1 Viewing a file's creation, update, and access dates

---

USE IT Depending on the processing your program carries out, there may be times when you want
to perform specific processing based on the file attributes. To retrieve a file's creation,
update, and last access dates, your programs can use the File class GetCreationTime, GetLastAccessTime,
and GetLastWriteTime methods. The following program, TodaysFiles.vb, uses these attributes to
search your disk for files you created, changed, or accessed today:

```
Imports System.IO

Module Module1

    Public Today As DateTime

    Function SameDate(ByVal A As DateTime, _
        ByVal B As DateTime) As Boolean
```

```vb
        If (A.Year = B.Year) And (A.DayOfYear = B.DayOfYear) Then
            SameDate = True
        Else
            SameDate = False
        End If

    End Function

    Sub SearchTree(ByVal Dir As String)
        Dim Files As String() = Directory.GetFiles(Dir)
        Dim Dirs As String() = Directory.GetDirectories(Dir)

        Dim FileDateTime As DateTime
        Dim Filename As String
        For Each Filename In Files
            Try
                FileDateTime = File.GetCreationTime(Filename)

                If SameDate(FileDateTime, Today) Then
                    Console.WriteLine(Filename)
                End If
            Catch E As Exception
                Console.WriteLine("Error accessing {0}", Filename)
                Console.WriteLine("Error: {0}", E.Message)
            End Try
        Next

        Dim DirectoryDateTime As DateTime
        Dim DirectoryName As String
        For Each DirectoryName In Dirs
            Try
                DirectoryDateTime = _
                    Directory.GetCreationTime(DirectoryName)

                If SameDate(DirectoryDateTime, Today) Then
                    Console.WriteLine(DirectoryName)
                End If
```

```
                SearchTree(DirectoryName)
            Catch E As Exception
                Console.WriteLine("Error accessing {0}", DirectoryName)
                Console.WriteLine("Error: {0}", E.Message)
            End Try
        Next
    End Sub

    Sub Main()
        Today = DateTime.Today

        Console.WriteLine("Searching ...")
        SearchTree("C:\")
        Console.Write("Press Enter to Continue...")
        Console.ReadLine()
    End Sub
End Module
```

Just as you can retrieve a file's date and time attributes, your programs can also set the attributes using the File class SetCreationTime, SetLastAccessTime, and SetLastWriteTime methods. The following program, SetToday.vb, displays the Open dialog box shown in Figure 6-2, that lets the user

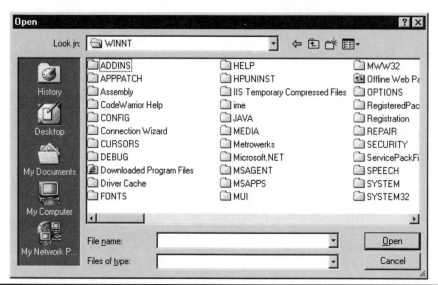

Figure 6-2   Using an Open dialog box to select a file

select a file on his or her disk. After the user selects a file, the program sets the file's date and time attributes to the current date and time:

```
Imports System.IO

Public Class Form1
    Inherits System.Windows.Forms.Form

#Region " Windows Form Designer generated code "
    ' Code not shown
#End Region

    Private Sub Button1_Click(ByVal sender As Object, _
        ByVal e As System.EventArgs) Handles Button1.Click

        Dim FileDB As New OpenFileDialog()
        Dim CurrentDateTime As DateTime = DateTime.Now

        If (FileDB.ShowDialog() = DialogResult.OK) Then
            Try
                File.SetCreationTime(FileDB.FileName, CurrentDateTime)
                File.SetLastAccessTime(FileDB.FileName, CurrentDateTime)
                File.SetLastWriteTime(FileDB.FileName, CurrentDateTime)

                MsgBox(FileDB.FileName & " date and time updated")
            Catch Ex As Exception
MsgBox("Error updating " & FileDB.FileName & _
                " " & Ex.Message)
            End Try
        Else
                MsgBox("User selected Cancel")
        End If
    End Sub
End Class
```

Chapter 7 examines the .NET common dialog boxes in detail. To display the Open dialog box, this program calls the OpenFileDialog class ShowDialog method. If the user selects the OK option, the program uses the FileName property the dialog box contains to set the attributes for the file the user has selected.

Figure 6-3   Using a FileInfo object to retrieve a file's attributes

Just as your programs can use the static File class to manipulate files, your programs can also use the FileInfo class, which works with a specific instance of a file. The following program, FileInfoGetAttributes.vb, uses a FileInfo object to display a file's attributes, as shown in Figure 6-3:

```
Imports System.IO

Public Class Form1
    Inherits System.Windows.Forms.Form

#Region " Windows Form Designer generated code "
  ' Code not shown
#End Region

    Private Sub Button1_Click(ByVal sender As Object, _
      ByVal e As System.EventArgs) Handles Button1.Click
        Dim FileDB As New OpenFileDialog()

      If (FileDB.ShowDialog() = DialogResult.OK) Then
          Try
              Dim FileObj As New FileInfo(FileDB.FileName)
              MsgBox(FileDB.FileName & " Created " & _
                FileObj.CreationTime & " Size " & FileObj.Length)
          Catch Ex As Exception
              MsgBox("Error updating " & FileDB.FileName & _
                " " & Ex.Message)
          End Try
      Else
          MsgBox("User selected Cancel")
      End If
    End Sub
End Class
```

Table 6-7 briefly explains the FileInfo class methods. Table 6-8 describes the FileInfo class properties.

Method	Purpose
AppendText	Returns a StreamWriter object a program can use to append text to the corresponding file.
CopyTo	Copies the corresponding file to a new file. The CopyTo method is an overloaded method.
Create	Creates a file, returning a FileStream object the program can use to read or write to the file.
CreateText	Creates a file, returning a StreamWriter object the program can use to write to the file.
Delete	Deletes the corresponding file. The Delete method is an overloaded method.
MoveTo	Moves the corresponding file to a new location.
Open	Opens a file, returning a FileStream object a program can use for shared read and write operations. The Open method is an overloaded method.
OpenRead	Returns a FileStream object for a file a program can use for read-only operations.
OpenText	Opens a file, returning a StreamReader object a program can use to read the file's contents.
OpenWrite	Opens a file, returning a FileStream object a program can use to write to the file.

Table 6-7   The FileInfo Class Methods

Property	Purpose
Directory	Gets a DirectoryInfo object that corresponds to the parent directory.
DirectoryName	Gets a directory's full path name.
Exists	Gets a Boolean value that specifies if a file exists.
Length	Gets the size of the current file (in bytes) or directory (in files).
Name	Gets a file's name. The Name property is an overloaded property.

Table 6-8   The FileInfo Class Properties

Starting with File Streams

To store information from one user session to the next, programs make extensive use of files. Because programs often read or write consecutive characters from or to a file up to the end of the data, programmers often refer to files as *streams* (meaning one character flows after another). To read information from, or write information to, a file, a program must first open an existing file or possibly create a new file. The File class provides programs with several methods that create or open file streams. When your programs use the File class methods, they create or open a file stream. Normally, programmers think of file streams in terms of text files. However, using the File class methods, a program can manipulate a stream that contains binary data, network data, or buffered data.

USE IT To simplify text file operations, your programs can use the StreamWriter and StreamReader classes. The following program, CreateTextFile.vb, uses the StreamWriter class to create a file named BookInfo.txt that contains the following specifics about this book:

```
Title: Visual Basic .NET Programming Tips & Techniques
Publisher: McGraw-Hill/Osborne
Author: Jamsa
```

Within the program, the following statement creates the file:

```
Dim TextFile As New StreamWriter("C:\BookInfo.txt")
```

For simplicity, this program does not perform any error checking. Instead, the program assumes the method is successful. Later in this chapter, you will learn how to verify that your file operations are successful. After the program creates the StreamWriter object, the code uses the WriteLine method to write the output to the file:

```
TextFile.WriteLine ("Title: Visual Basic .NET" _
    " Programming Tips & Techniques")
```

Finally, after the program writes the data to a file, the program closes the file, which directs the file system to flush any outstanding data to the file on disk and then update the file's directory entry:

```
TextFile.Close()
```

The following statements implement the CreateTextFile.vb program:

```
Imports System.IO

Module Module1
    Sub Main()
        Dim TextFile As New StreamWriter("C:\BookInfo.txt")

        TextFile.WriteLine("Title: Visual Basic .NET" & _
            "Programming Tips & Techniques")
        TextFile.WriteLine("Publisher: McGraw-Hill/Osborne")
        TextFile.WriteLine("Author: Jamsa")
        TextFile.Close()
```

```
        Console.WriteLine("Data written to file C:\BookInfo.txt")
        Console.ReadLine() ' Delay to view output
    End Sub
End Module
```

Next, the following program, DisplayTextFile.vb, creates a StreamReader object to read the contents of the BookInfo.txt file. To open the file, the code first creates a StreamReader object:

```
Dim TextFile As New StreamReader("C:\BookInfo.txt")
```

Again, for the sake of simplicity, the code assumes the file operations are successful. Then the code uses a Do loop to read and display each line of the file. When the StreamReader class ReadLine method successfully reads a line of input, the method will return a string that contains the corresponding text. When the ReadLine method encounters the end of the file, the method will return a Nothing object:

```
Do
  Content = TextFile.ReadLine()

  If (Content <> Nothing) Then
    Console.WriteLine(Content)
  End If
Loop While (Content <> Nothing)
```

After the program reads and displays the file's contents, the program uses the StreamReader class Close method to close the file. The following statements implement the DisplayTextFile.vb program:

```
Imports System.IO

Module Module1
    Sub Main()
        Dim TextFile As New StreamReader("C:\BookInfo.txt")

        Dim Content As String

        Do
            Content = TextFile.ReadLine()

            If (Content <> Nothing) Then
                Console.WriteLine(Content)
            End If
        Loop While (Content <> Nothing)
```

```
        TextFile.Close()
        Console.ReadLine() ' Delay to view output
    End Sub

End Module
```

The StreamReader class provides several methods your programs can use to read data from a file. When you work with small files (less than 64KB), you may want to use the ReadToEnd method to read the file's entire contents into a string variable in one step. The following program, ReadAllDemo.vb, uses the ReadToEnd method to read the contents of the BookInfo.txt file. The code also uses Try-Catch blocks to detect and respond to exceptions that occur during the file operations:

```
Imports System.IO

Module Module1
    Sub Main()
        Dim FileError As Boolean = False
        Dim TextFile As StreamReader

        Try
            TextFile = New StreamReader("C:\BookInfo.txt")
        Catch E As Exception
            Console.WriteLine("Error opening the file C:\BookInfo.txt")
            Console.WriteLine("Error {0}", E.Message)
            FileError = True
        End Try

        If (Not FileError) Then
            Dim Content As String

            Try
                Content = TextFile.ReadToEnd()
                Console.WriteLine(Content)
            Catch E As Exception
                Console.WriteLine("Error reading file")
                Console.WriteLine("Error {0}: ", E.Message)
            End Try

            TextFile.Close()
```

```
        End If
        Console.ReadLine() ' Delay to view output
    End Sub
End Module
```

Taking a Closer Look at the StreamWriter and StreamReader Classes

USE IT   When your programs manipulate files, your code will make extensive use of the StreamWriter and StreamReader classes. For example, the following program, SaveFormToFile.vb, displays a form as shown in Figure 6-4, within which you can type information into a form. When you click the form's Save To File button, the program will display the Save As dialog box, within which you can specify the file into which you want the program to store the form's text.

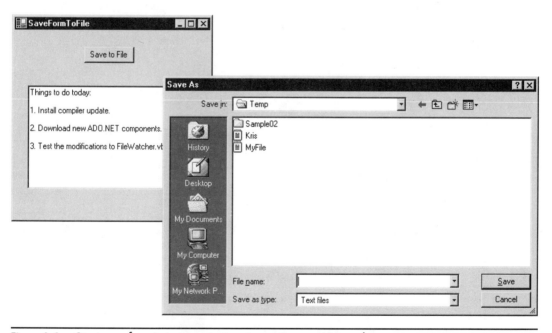

Figure 6-4   Storing a form's text contents using a StreamWriter class

```vbnet
Imports System.IO

Public Class Form1
    Inherits System.Windows.Forms.Form

#Region " Windows Form Designer generated code "
  ' Code not shown
#End Region

    Private Sub Button1_Click(ByVal sender As Object, _
      ByVal e As System.EventArgs) Handles Button1.Click
        Dim FileDB As New SaveFileDialog()
        FileDB.Filter = "All files | *.*| Text files | *.txt"

        FileDB.FilterIndex = 2
        FileDB.InitialDirectory = "C:\Temp"
        FileDB.AddExtension = True
        FileDB.DefaultExt = "txt"

        If (FileDB.ShowDialog() = DialogResult.OK) Then
            Dim TargetFile As StreamWriter

            Try
                TargetFile = New StreamWriter(FileDB.FileName)
            Catch
                MsgBox("Error opening " & FileDB.FileName)
            End Try

            Try
                TargetFile.Write(TextBox1.Text)
            Catch
                MsgBox("Error writing file")
            End Try

            TargetFile.Close()
            MsgBox("Text saved to " & FileDB.FileName)
        Else
            MsgBox("User selected Cancel")
        End If
    End Sub
End Class
```

Method	Purpose
Close	Closes the current StreamWriter object, flushing data buffers and updating the system settings. The Close method is an overridden method.
Flush	Forces the contents of a stream's buffers to the underlying file and then empties the buffer. The Flush method is an overridden method.
Write	Writes data to the stream. The Write method is an overloaded and overridden method.
WriteLine	Writes data to the stream followed by a line terminator.

Table 6-9   The StreamWriter Class Methods

The program uses a FileSaveDialog class object (discussed in Chapter 7) to display the Save As dialog box. After the user specifies the target filename, the program creates a StreamWriter object. Then, using the StreamWriter class Write method, the program writes the form's text to the file. Table 6-9 briefly describes the StreamWriter class methods. Table 6-10 describes the class properties.

In a similar way, the following program, FillFormContents.vb, displays an Open dialog box within which the user can select a text file for input. After the user selects a file, the program uses a StreamWriter class to read the file's contents into a form's text box:

```
Imports System.IO

Public Class Form1
    Inherits System.Windows.Forms.Form

#Region " Windows Form Designer generated code "
  ' Code not shown
#End Region

    Private Sub Button1_Click(ByVal sender As Object, _
      ByVal e As System.EventArgs) Handles Button1.Click
        Dim FileDB As New OpenFileDialog()

        FileDB.Filter = "All files | *.*| Text files | *.txt"

        FileDB.FilterIndex = 2
        FileDB.InitialDirectory = "C:\Temp"
        FileDB.AddExtension = True
        FileDB.DefaultExt = "txt"

        If (FileDB.ShowDialog() = DialogResult.OK) Then
            Dim SourceFile As StreamReader
```

```
        Try
            SourceFile = New StreamReader(FileDB.FileName)
        Catch
            MsgBox("Error opening " & FileDB.FileName)
        End Try

        Try
            TextBox1.Text = SourceFile.ReadToEnd()
        Catch
            MsgBox("Error reading file")
        End Try

        SourceFile.Close()
    Else
        MsgBox("User selected Cancel")
    End If
   End Sub
End Class
```

The program uses an OpenFileDialog class object (discussed in Chapter 8) to display the Open dialog box. After the user specifies the target filename, the program creates a StreamReader object. Using the StreamWriter class ReadToEnd method, the program reads the file's contents into the form. Table 6-11 briefly describes the StreamReader class methods. Table 6-12 describes the class properties.

Property	Purpose
AutoFlush	Gets or sets a Boolean value that indicates if the StreamWriter flushes its buffer after each call to Console.Write or Console.WriteLine.
BaseStream	Gets a Stream object that provides the StreamWriter with a backing store.
Encoding	Gets an Encoding object that corresponds to the stream's underlying encoding. The Encoding property is an overridden property.

Table 6-10   The StreamWriter Class Properties

Method	Purpose
Close	Closes the StreamReader object, releasing related system resources. The Close method is an overridden method.
DiscardBufferedData	Allows a StreamReader to discard data that is beyond the end of the stream.
Peek	Returns the next character in the stream, but does not consume the character. The Peek method is an overridden method.
Read	Reads the next character or specified number of characters from the stream. The Read method is an overridden method.
ReadLine	Reads characters from the stream up to the carriage return and linefeed characters that terminate the line. The ReadLine method is an overridden and overloaded method.
ReadToEnd	Reads the characters from the stream from the current position to the stream's end. The ReadToEnd method is an overridden method.

Table 6-11   The StreamReader Class Methods

Property	Method
BaseStream	Gets a Stream object that provides the StreamWriter with a backing store.
Encoding	Gets an Encoding object that corresponds to the stream's underlying encoding.

Table 6-12   The StreamReader Class Properties

Reading and Writing Binary Data

Throughout this chapter, you have used TextWriter objects to write text data to a file and TextReader objects to read text data from a file. Depending on the processing your program performs, there may be times when your programs must write or read binary data to or from a file, such as an integer or floating-point value. For such cases, your programs can use the BinaryWriter and BinaryReader classes. To create a BinaryWriter or BinaryReader object, your program first creates a FileStream object which it then passes to the BinaryWriter or BinaryReader constructor method:

```
Stream = New FileStream("C:\Binary.dat", FileMode.Create)

Dim BinaryStream As New BinaryWriter(Stream)
```

The following program, WriteBinaryData.vb, creates a root directory file named Binary.Dat. The program then uses the BinaryWriter class Write method to write several values to the file:

```vb
Imports System.IO

Module Module1
    Sub Main()
        Dim Stream As FileStream

        Try
            Stream = New FileStream("C:\Binary.dat", _
              FileMode.Create)

            Dim BinaryStream As New BinaryWriter(Stream)
        Catch E As Exception
            Console.WriteLine("Error creating C:\Binary.Dat")
            Console.WriteLine("Error {0}", E.Message)
        End Try

        Dim Age As Integer = 21
        Dim Salary As Double = 100000.0
        Dim Name As String = "Kris"

        Try
            BinaryStream.Write(Age)
            BinaryStream.Write(Salary)
            BinaryStream.Write(Name)
            BinaryStream.Close()

            Console.WriteLine("Data written to C:\Binary.Dat")
        Catch E As Exception
            Console.WriteLine("Error writing to C:\Binary.Dat")
            Console.WriteLine("Error {0}", E.Message)
        End Try

        Console.ReadLine() ' Delay to view output
    End Sub
End Module
```

Method	Purpose
Close	Closes the current StreamWriter object, flushing data buffers and updating the system settings.
Flush	Forces the contents of a stream's buffers to the underlying file and then empties the buffer.
Seek	Moves the stream pointer to the specified offset.
Write	Writes data to the stream. The Write method is an overloaded method.

Table 6-13   The BinaryWriter Class Methods

To help you make better use of the BinaryWriter class, Table 6-13 briefly describes the BinaryWriter class methods.

In a similar way, the following program, ReadBinaryData.vb, uses a BinaryReader object to read the binary values stored in the file Binary.Dat. After the program opens the file using a FileStream, the code then converts the FileStream object to a BinaryReader. Then the program uses various BinaryReader class read methods to read the binary data:

```
Imports System.IO

Module Module1
    Sub Main()
        Dim Stream As FileStream

        Try
            Stream = New FileStream("C:\Binary.dat", FileMode.Open)
            Dim BinaryStream As New BinaryReader(Stream)
        Catch E As Exception
            Console.WriteLine("Error opening C:\Binary.Dat")
            Console.WriteLine("Error {0}", E.Message)
        End Try

        Dim Age As Integer
        Dim Salary As Double
        Dim Name As String

        Try
            Age = BinaryStream.ReadInt32()
            Salary = BinaryStream.ReadDouble()
            Name = BinaryStream.ReadString()
            BinaryStream.Close()

            Console.WriteLine("Age: {0}", Age)
            Console.WriteLine("Salary: {0}", Salary)
            Console.WriteLine("Name: {0}", Name)
```

```
      Catch E As Exception
          Console.WriteLine("Error reading to C:\Binary.Dat")
          Console.WriteLine("Error {0}", E.Message)
      End Try

          Console.ReadLine() ' Delay to view output
      End Sub
End Module
```

As you can see, to read the binary data from the file, the program must use a read method specific to a particular data type, such as ReadInt32 or ReadDouble. Table 6-14 briefly describes the BinaryReader class methods.

Method	Purpose
Close	Closes the StreamReader object, releasing related system resources.
PeekChar	Returns the next character in the stream, but does not consume the character or advance the character pointer.
Read	Reads the next character or specified number of characters from the stream. The Read method is an overloaded method.
ReadBoolean	Reads a Boolean value from the stream, advancing the stream pointer 1 byte.
ReadByte	Reads a Byte value from the stream, advancing the stream pointer 1 byte.
ReadBytes	Reads the specified number of bytes from the stream into an array, advancing the stream pointer the same number of bytes.
ReadChar	Reads a Char value from the stream, advancing the stream pointer based on the stream's encoding.
ReadChars	Reads the specified number of characters from the stream into a character array, advancing the stream based on the stream's encoding.
ReadDecimal	Reads a decimal value from the stream, advancing the stream pointer by 16 bytes.
ReadDouble	Reads an 8-byte floating point value from the stream, advancing the stream pointer by 8 bytes.
ReadInt16	Reads a 2-byte signed integer from the stream, advancing the stream pointer by 2 bytes.
ReadInt32	Reads a 4-byte signed integer from the stream, advancing the stream pointer by 4 bytes.
ReadInt64	Reads an 8-byte signed integer from the stream, advancing the stream pointer by 8 bytes.

Table 6-14   The BinaryReader Class Methods

Method	Purpose
ReadSByte	Reads a signed byte from the stream, advancing the stream pointer by 1 byte.
ReadSingle	Reads a 4-byte floating point value from the stream, advancing the stream pointer by 4 bytes.
ReadString	Reads a String from the stream, advancing the stream pointer based on the string's encoded length. The string is prefixed with a length value encoded as an integer 7 bits at a time.
ReadUInt16	Reads a 2-byte unsigned integer from the stream, advancing the stream pointer by 2 bytes.
ReadUInt32	Reads a 4-byte unsigned integer from the stream, advancing the stream pointer by 4 bytes.
ReadUInt64	Reads an 8-byte unsigned integer from the stream, advancing the stream pointer by 8 bytes.

Table 6-14   The BinaryReader Class Methods (continued)

Getting Started with File Locks

In a multitasking or network environment, there may be times when two or programs must share the same file. Depending on how the programs access the file, there may be times when you must lock the file to prevent one program from reading the same file contents that a second program is updating. To lock and later unlock data in a file, your programs can use the FileStream class Lock and Unlock methods.

 USE IT   When you use the Lock and Unlock methods, your program specifies a byte range within the file that you want to lock. After you lock the data range, a second program cannot read or write to the range:

```
Fstream.lock(StartOffset, NumberOfBytes)

Fstream.Unlock(StartOffset, NumberOfBytes)
```

The following program, FileLockDemo.vb, displays a form that you can use to lock and unlock a file, as shown in Figure 6-5. After a program locks a region, another process cannot access the data. To better understand the locking and unlocking process, run two copies of the program at the same time. In one dialog box, lock the file. Then, in the other, try to update the file's contents. Because the other process has the file's content's locked, the second process cannot successfully update the file. However, the process that owns the lock can update the file. Take turns locking and unlocking the file in each process and trying to update the file's contents.

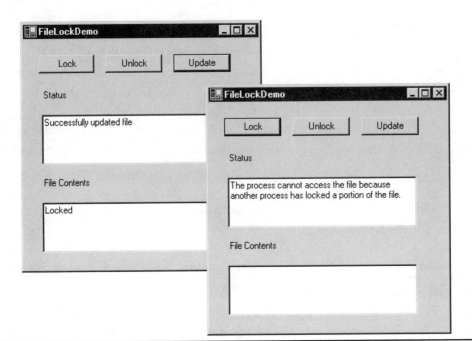

Figure 6-5 Using a lock to protect a file's contents

```
Imports System.IO

Public Class Form1
    Inherits System.Windows.Forms.Form

#Region " Windows Form Designer generated code "
  ' Code not shown
#End Region

    Public FileSt As FileStream = _
       New FileStream("C:\Data.dat", FileMode.Create, _
       FileAccess.Write, FileShare.Write)

    Public CrLf As String = Chr(13) & Chr(10)

    Private Sub Button1_Click(ByVal sender As Object, _
       ByVal e As System.EventArgs) Handles Button1.Click
         Try
```

```
            FileSt.Lock(0, 100)
            TextBox2.Text = "Locked"
        Catch Ex As Exception
            TextBox1.AppendText(Ex.Message & CrLf)
        End Try
    End Sub

    Private Sub Button2_Click(ByVal sender As Object, _
      ByVal e As System.EventArgs) Handles Button2.Click
        Try
            FileSt.Unlock(0, 100)
            TextBox2.Text = "Unlocked"
        Catch Ex As Exception
            TextBox1.AppendText(Ex.Message & CrLf)
        End Try
    End Sub

    Private Sub Button3_Click(ByVal sender As Object, _
      ByVal e As System.EventArgs) Handles Button3.Click
        Dim Values As Byte()
        Values = New Byte() {1, 2, 3, 4, 5}

        Try
            FileSt.Seek(0, SeekOrigin.Begin)
            FileSt.Write(Values, 0, 5)
            TextBox1.AppendText("Successfully updated file" & CrLf)
        Catch Ex As Exception
            TextBox1.AppendText(Ex.Message & CrLf)
        End Try
    End Sub
End Class
```

Responding to FileWatcher Events

Depending on the processing your program performs, there may be times when your code must know when a user changes a specific file's contents or when a user updates a directory in some way (by changing, deleting, or adding files or subdirectories to the directory). For example, assume your program must maintain up-to-the-minute backup copies of key files. In such cases, your code may want to back up a file each time the file's contents change. To perform such processing, your code can use a FileSystemWatcher object. Table 6-15 briefly describes the FileSystemWatcher class properties.

Property	Purpose
EnableRaisingEvents	Gets or sets a Boolean value that specifies if the component is enabled.
Filter	Gets or sets the filter (normally wildcards) that determines which files the object will monitor.
IncludeSubdirectories	Gets or sets a Boolean value that specifies if the object will monitor subdirectories in the target directory.
InternalBufferSize	Gets or sets the size of the internal buffer.
NotifyFilter	Gets or sets an object of type NotifyFilters that specifies the changes the object will monitor.
Path	Gets or sets the path the object will monitor.
SynchronizingObject	Gets or sets the object that marshals event handler calls issued due to a directory change.

Table 6-15   The FileSystemWatcher Class Properties

USE IT   In general, a FileSystemWatcher is an object that a program uses to monitor a specific directory or file. Using a FileSystemWatcher class properties, your program can specify the events you want the object to respond to. The following statement creates a FileSystemWatcher object:

```
Dim WithEvents Watcher As New FileSystemWatcher("C+:\")
```

After you create the object, you can assign values to the object's properties that specify the types of files you want to monitor, whether you want the object to monitor files that reside in subdirectories, and so on. In addition, your code must use the EnableRaisingEvents property before the object will respond to file changes:

```
Watcher.Filter = "*.*"
Watcher.IncludeSubdirectories = True
Watcher.EnableRaisingEvents = True
```

After you specify the FileSystemWatcher object's properties, your program must define event handlers to respond to the various events you have directed the object to monitor. The following program, FileWatcherDemo.vb, displays a form that contains a text box. The program then creates a FileSystemWatcher object that monitors the root directory on drive C as well as the subdirectories. Each time a file changes, the program places information about the file and the change into the text box, as shown in Figure 6-6.

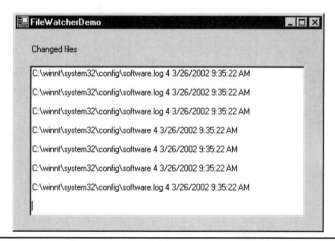

Figure 6-6   Using a FileSystemWatcher object to monitor file operations

```vb
Imports System.IO

Public Class Form1
    Inherits System.Windows.Forms.Form

#Region " Windows Form Designer generated code "
  ' Code not shown
#End Region

    Private WithEvents Watcher As New FileSystemWatcher("C:\")

    Protected Overrides Sub OnLoad(ByVal e As EventArgs)
        Watcher.Filter = "*.*"
        Watcher.IncludeSubdirectories = True
        Watcher.EnableRaisingEvents = True
    End Sub

    Protected Sub OnChanged(ByVal From As Object, _
      ByVal e As FileSystemEventArgs) Handles Watcher.Changed

        Dim DateAndTime As DateTime = DateTime.Now
        Dim CrLF As String = Chr(13) & Chr(10)
        TextBox1.AppendText(e.FullPath & " " _
            & e.ChangeType() & " " & DateAndTime & CrLF & CrLF)
    End Sub
End Class
```

CHAPTER 7

Leveraging the .NET Common Dialogs

TIPS IN THIS CHAPTER

For years, Visual Basic programmers have made extensive use of forms to build user interfaces. With the .NET environment, C# programmers now gain access to the same set of form capabilities through the use of Windows forms. In addition, the .NET environment provides a set of dialog boxes that programmers can use to open, save, and print files and to select a specific font or font attributes as well as color settings. Programmers refer to this set of dialog boxes as the common dialogs. By using the common dialogs in your applications, your programs can present the user with a familiar interface for key operations. Further, because .NET implements each dialog box as a class object, the only programming you must perform is to create an instance of the dialog box object you desire and then to interact with the object's methods and properties. Figure 7-1, for example, illustrates the use of the Open and Save As dialog boxes. Table 7-1 briefly describes the classes your programs will use to access the common dialogs. This chapter will examine the use of each class in detail.

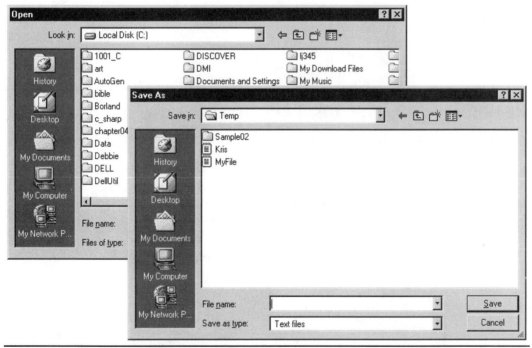

Figure 7-1 Using the .NET common dialogs to open and to save a file

Common Dialog Class	Purpose
ColorDialog	Displays standard and custom colors from which the user can select a color value. Also provides controls that let the user define custom colors.
FontDialog	Displays the available system fonts and key font attributes from which the user can select specific font settings.
OpenFileDialog	Displays the Open dialog box that the user can use to select an input file. The OpenFileDialog class cannot be inherited.
PageSetupDialog	Displays the Page Setup dialog box that the user can use to specify a document's page settings, such as margin and print orientation.
PrintDialog	Displays the Print dialog box which the user can use to select the target printer, number of copies, which portions of a document to print, and to initiate a print operation.
SaveFileDialog	Displays the Save As dialog box which the user can use to specify an output file's name and target directory.

Table 7-1   The .NET Common Dialog Classes

Prompting the User for a File to Open

In the Windows environment, programs make extensive use of the Open dialog box, shown in Figure 7-2, to open a specific file. In the Open dialog box, a user can browse folders on one or more disk drives (and network servers) to locate the file that he or she desires. The advantage of using the Open dialog box is that the user does not have to remember a filename or the folder in which he or she stored the file. Instead, the user can browse folders to locate the file. By using the Open dialog box with your Visual Basic .NET programs, you provide the user with a familiar interface.

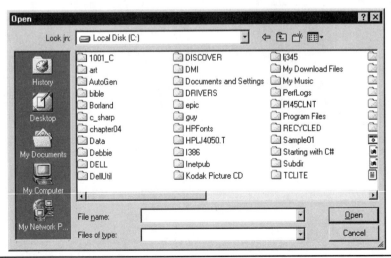

Figure 7-2   Using the Open dialog box to prompt the user for a file

Method	Purpose
OpenFile	Opens the file selected by the user, with read-only permission, returning a Stream object the program can use to access the file.
Reset	Resets all properties to their default values.

Table 7-2   The OpenFileDialog Class Methods

In the Open dialog box, programs will often limit the types of files that the dialog box displays. For example, Microsoft Word may limit the files that appear in the dialog box to document files that use the .doc extension. Likewise, a graphics-editing program may restrict the files that appear in the dialog box to those with the .jpg, .gif, .bmp, or .tif extensions.

To display the Open dialog box in your Visual Basic .NET programs, your code uses an OpenFileDialog class object. Table 7-2 briefly discusses the OpenFileDialog class methods, and Table 7-3 discusses the class fields and properties.

USE IT   The following program, OpenFileDemo.vb, uses the OpenFileClass to prompt the user to select the file that he or she wants to open. After the user selects the file, the program displays the file's name and path in a message box, as shown in Figure 7-3. If the user cancels the dialog box without selecting a file, the program displays a message so stating.

```
Public Class Form1
    Inherits System.Windows.Forms.Form

#Region " Windows Form Designer generated code "
  ' Not shown
#End Region

    Private Sub Button1_Click(ByVal sender As Object, _
       ByVal e As System.EventArgs) Handles Button1.Click
       Dim FileDB As New OpenFileDialog()

       If (FileDB.ShowDialog() = DialogResult.OK) Then
           MsgBox("File: " & FileDB.FileName)
       Else
           MsgBox("User selected Cancel")
       End If
    End Sub

End Class
```

Figure 7-3   Displaying the name and folder of a user's selected file

Property	Purpose
CheckFileExists	Gets or sets a Boolean value that specifies whether the dialog box will display a warning message if the user specifies a filename that does not exist.
Multiselect	Gets or sets a Boolean value that specifies whether the dialog box allows multiple files to be selected.
ReadOnlyChecked	Gets or sets a Boolean value that specifies whether the read-only check box is selected in the Open dialog box.
ShowReadOnly	Gets or sets a Boolean value that specifies whether the Open dialog contains a read-only check box.

Table 7-3   The OpenFileDialog class properties

The OpenFileDialog and the SaveFileDialog inherit the FileDialog class. The FileDialog class inherits its methods from the CommonDialog class and the Component and Object classes. Table 7-4 briefly describes the FileDialog class properties.

Property	Purpose
AddExtension	Gets or sets a Boolean value that specifies whether the dialog box automatically adds an extension to a filename should the user not specify an extension.
CheckFileExists	Gets or sets a Boolean value that specifies whether the dialog box displays a warning message if the user specifies a filename that does not exist.
CheckPathExists	Gets or sets a Boolean value that specifies whether the dialog box displays a warning message if the user specifies a path that does not exist.
DefaultExt	Gets or sets the default filename extension that the dialog box will automatically add to the filename should the user not specify an extension.
DereferenceLinks	Gets or sets a Boolean value that specifies whether the dialog box returns the location of the file referenced by a shortcut or whether the dialog box returns the location of the shortcut.
FileName	Gets or sets a string that contains the filename selected in the dialog box.
FileNames	Gets an array of strings that contain the filenames of all selected files in the dialog box.
Filter	Gets or sets the current filter string the dialog box uses to control which files it displays. The filter string appears in the Save As File Type pull-down list as well as the Open dialog box Files Of Type pull-down list.
FilterIndex	Gets or sets the index of the current filter string.
InitialDirectory	Gets or sets a string that contains the path of the initial directory the dialog box will display.

Table 7-4   The FileDialog Class Properties

Property	Purpose
RestoreDirectory	Gets or sets a Boolean value that specifies whether the dialog box restores the current directory before it closes.
ShowHelp	Gets or sets a Boolean value that specifies whether the dialog box displays a Help button.
Title	Gets or sets the dialog box title.
ValidateNames	Gets or sets a Boolean value that specifies whether the dialog box accepts only valid (Win32) filenames.

Table 7-4   The FileDialog Class Properties *(continued)*

Fine-Tuning OpenFileDialog Operations

When your programs use an OpenFileDialog object to prompt the user for a file, you will often want to specify the types of files the dialog box will display. In other words, you will want to filter the dialog box's file list based on file extensions. To limit the types of files that appear in the Open dialog box, you can assign a string that contains a pipe (|) delimited list of file types to the OpenFileDialog class Filter property, as shown here:

```
Db.Filter = "All files | *.*| Word files | *.doc| Text files | *.txt"
```

Within the pipe-delimited string, you specify pair values. The first half of the pair specifies the text that will appear in the dialog box Files Of Type pull-down list. The second half of the pair specifies a wildcard combination that corresponds to the file types. In the case of the filter just shown, the dialog box would display the file types shown in Figure 7-4 when the user opens the Files Of Type pull-down list.

When you specify file types using the Filter property, you can use the FilterIndex field to specify the dialog box's default file type. The FilterIndex value specifies an index from 1 to the number of entries in the list that selects a file type from your filter list. Given the previous list of filters, the value 1 would correspond to All Files, 2 to Word Files, and 3 to Text Files. The following statement uses the FilterIndex to select Word Files as the default filter:

```
Db.FilterIndex = 2
```

Often, your programs will want to specify the initial folder whose files appear when a program displays the Open dialog box. To specify the initial directory, your program can assign the corresponding directory path to the OpenFileDialog class InitialDirectory property. The following statement, for example, selects C:\Temp as the initial directory:

```
Db.InitialDirectory = "C:\Temp"
```

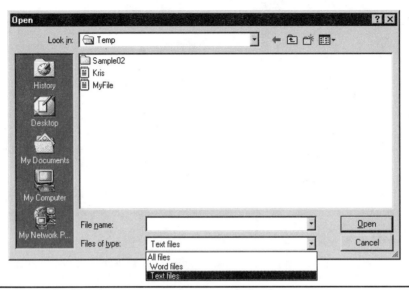

Figure 7-4 Filtering the files that appear in the Open dialog box

USE IT   The following program, InitializeOpenDB.vb, uses the FileOpenDialog class FilterIndex
and InitialDirectory properties to direct the Open dialog box to initially display text files
in the C:\Temp folder:

```
Public Class Form1
    Inherits System.Windows.Forms.Form

#Region " Windows Form Designer generated code "
  ' Code not shown
#End Region

    Private Sub Button1_Click(ByVal sender As Object, _
      ByVal e As System.EventArgs) Handles Button1.Click

        Dim FileDB As New OpenFileDialog()

        FileDB.Filter = "All files | *.*| Word files | *.doc" & _
            "| Text files | *.txt"

        FileDB.FilterIndex = 3
        FileDB.InitialDirectory = "C:\Temp"

        If (FileDB.ShowDialog() = DialogResult.OK) Then
            MsgBox("File: " & FileDB.FileName)
        Else
```

```
            MsgBox("User selected Cancel")
        End If
    End Sub
End Class
```

The program uses the OpenFileDialog class Filter property to specify the file types that appear in the dialog box's pull-down box. Then, using the FilterIndex property, the program selects text files as the default file filter. Finally, using the InitialDirectory property, the program selects the directory the dialog box will first display. If the initial directory you specify does not exist, the Open dialog box will display your default directory (often the My Documents folder).

USE IT   The following program, DisplayTextFile.vb, extends the previous program to open, read, and display the contents of a text file the user selects in the Open dialog box:

```
Imports System.IO

Public Class Form1
    Inherits System.Windows.Forms.Form

#Region " Windows Form Designer generated code "
  ' Code not shown
#End Region

    Private Sub Button1_Click(ByVal sender As Object, _
        ByVal e As System.EventArgs) Handles Button1.Click

        Dim FileDB As New OpenFileDialog()

        FileDB.Filter = "All files | *.*| Word files" & _
            " | *.doc| Text files | *.txt"

        FileDB.FilterIndex = 3

        FileDB.InitialDirectory = "C:\Temp"

        If (FileDB.ShowDialog() = DialogResult.OK) Then
            Dim FS As FileStream

            Try
               FS = FileDB.OpenFile()

               Dim TextData(1025) As Byte
               Dim BytesRead As Integer
               Dim I As Integer
               Dim NewText As String
```

```
            Do
              Try
                  BytesRead = FS.Read(TextData, 1, 1024)

                  NewText = ""
                  For I = 1 To BytesRead
                      NewText = NewText & Chr(TextData(I))
                  Next
                  TextBox1.AppendText(NewText)
              Catch
                  MsgBox("Error reading file")
              End Try
            Loop While (BytesRead <> 0)

              FS.Close()
          Catch
              MsgBox("Error opening " & FileDB.FileName)
          End Try
      Else
              MsgBox("User selected Cancel")
      End If
    End Sub
End Class
```

The OpenFileDialog class OpenFile method returns a FileStream that corresponds to a read-only file. Using the FileStream class Read method, the program reads the file's contents. Within the Read method call, the TextData parameter specifies the buffer into which the method will read the file data. The value 1 specifies an offset within the buffer at which the method places the data. As you know, Visual Basic .NET arrays are zero-based, which means the first storage location within the TextData byte array is TextData(0). This program, however, directs the Read method to place data into the buffer at offset 1 in order to simplify the For loop that follows. When the Read method reaches the end of the file stream, the method will return the value 0. The program could use the following If statement to test if the Read method encountered the end of the file:

```
BytesRead = FS.Read(TextData, 0, 1024)

If (BytesRead > 0) Then
  NewText = ""
  For I = 0 To BytesRead
    NewText = NewText & Chr(TextData(I))
  Next

  TextBox1.AppendText(NewText)
End If
```

However, by placing the data into the buffer at offset 1, the program can eliminate the If statement. If the Read method has encountered the end of the file, the Read method will return the value 0, which prevents the For loop from executing:

```
For I = 1 To BytesRead
  NewText = NewText & Chr(TextData(I))
Next
```

After the program reads the data into the buffer, the program appends the buffer's contents to the form's text box. When the Read method finally encounters the end of the stream, the code uses the FileStream class Close method to close the stream.

Saving Information in a User-Specified File

In the Windows environment, programs make extensive use of the Save As dialog box to let a user save information in a consistent manner. In your Visual Basic .NET programs, you can use SaveFileDialog to display a similar dialog box the user can use to specify a file's target disk, folder, and filename, as shown in Figure 7-5. Table 7-5 briefly describes the SaveFileDialog class methods. Table 7-6 briefly describes the class properties.

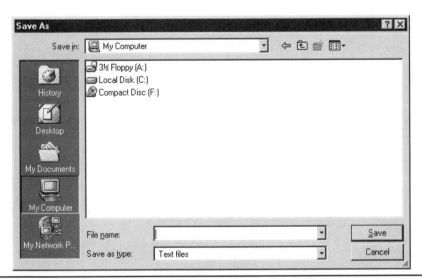

Figure 7-5   Using SaveFileDialog to prompt the user for an output file

Method	Purpose
OpenFile	Opens the file selected by the user, with read-write access, returning a FileStream object the program can use to access the file.
Reset	Resets all properties to their default values.

Table 7-5   The SaveFileDialog Class Methods

USE IT   The following program, ShowSaveFilename.vb, uses a Save dialog box to prompt the user for the location at which he or she wants to save information. After the user selects the target drive and folder, and then types a filename, the program displays a message box that specifies the user's selections, as shown in Figure 7-6. If the user cancels the dialog box operation without specifying a filename, the program will display a message so stating:

```
Public Class Form1
    Inherits System.Windows.Forms.Form

#Region " Windows Form Designer generated code "
    ' Code not shown
#End Region

    Private Sub Button1_Click(ByVal sender As Object, _
      ByVal e As System.EventArgs) Handles Button1.Click
        Dim FileDB As New SaveFileDialog()

        If (FileDB.ShowDialog() = DialogResult.OK) Then
            MsgBox("File: " & FileDB.FileName)
        Else
            MsgBox("User selected Cancel")
        End If
    End Sub
End Class
```

Figure 7-6   Displaying a user's target file information

Property	Purpose
CheckFileExists	Gets or sets a Boolean value that specifies whether the dialog box will display a warning message if the user specifies a filename that does not exist.
CreatePrompt	Gets or sets a Boolean value that specifies whether the dialog box prompts the user if it should create a file that does not exist.
Multiselect	Gets or sets a Boolean value that specifies whether the dialog box allows multiple files to be selected.
OverwritePrompt	Gets or sets a Boolean value that specifies whether the Save As dialog box displays a warning message if the user specifies a filename that already exists.
ReadOnlyChecked	Gets or sets a Boolean value that specifies whether the read-only check box is selected in the Open dialog box.
ShowReadOnly	Gets or sets a Boolean value that specifies whether the Open dialog contains a read-only check box.

Table 7-6   The SaveFileDialog Class Properties

Fine-Tuning File Save Operations

When your programs use the SaveFileDialog class to prompt the user to specify a target filename, there are several class properties your programs can use to simplify operations for the user. For example, you might use the AddExtension and DefaultExt fields to direct the dialog box to automatically append a specific file extension to the filename the user specifies. The following statements, for example, direct the dialog box to automatically append the .txt extension:

```
Dim FileDB As New SaveFileDialog()

FileDB.AddExtension = True
FileDB.DefaultExt = "txt"
```

You may also want to specify the initial folder the dialog box displays when the program opens the Save dialog box using the InitialDirectory field. The following statement directs the dialog box to display the folder C:\Program\Data as the Save dialog box's initial folder:

```
FileDB.InitialDirectory = "C:\Program\Data"
```

USE IT   The following program, SaveTextToFile.vb, displays a text box within which the user can type text, as shown in Figure 7-7. If the user selects Save To File, the program will display a Save As dialog box within which the user can specify the name and location of a text file into which the program will save the user's text. If the user specifies a filename, the program will

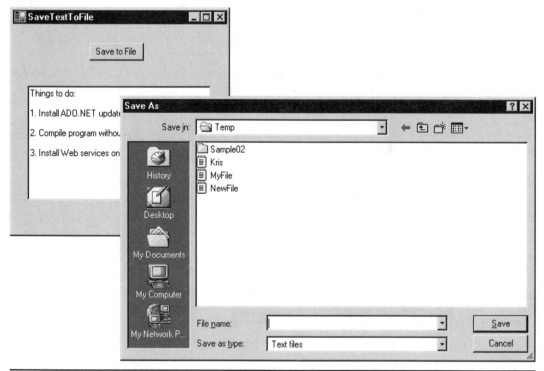

Figure 7-7   Letting the user save text to a file

save the text box contents into the file. If a file exists with the name the user specifies, the program will display a message box stating the file exists and asking the user if he or she wants to overwrite the existing file (actually, the SaveFileDialog class performs this processing on the program's behalf). After the program saves the text, the program displays a message box so stating:

```
Imports System.IO

Public Class Form1
    Inherits System.Windows.Forms.Form

#Region " Windows Form Designer generated code "
    ' Code not shown
#End Region

    Private Sub Button1_Click(ByVal sender As Object, _
      ByVal e As System.EventArgs) Handles Button1.Click
```

```
        Dim FileDB As New SaveFileDialog()

        FileDB.Filter = "All files | *.*| Word files" & _
            " | *.doc| Text files | *.txt"

        FileDB.FilterIndex = 3
        FileDB.InitialDirectory = "C:\Temp"
        FileDB.AddExtension = True
        FileDB.DefaultExt = "txt"

        If (FileDB.ShowDialog() = DialogResult.OK) Then
            Dim FS As FileStream

            Try
                FS = New FileStream(FileDB.FileName, FileMode.Create)
            Catch
                MsgBox("Error opening " & FileDB.FileName)
            End Try

            Dim I As Integer

            Try
                For I = 0 To TextBox1.Text.Length - 1
                    FS.WriteByte(Asc(TextBox1.Text.Chars(I)))
                Next
            Catch
                MsgBox("Error writing file")
            End Try

            FS.Close()
            MsgBox("Text saved to " & FileDB.FileName)
        Else
            MsgBox("User selected Cancel")
        End If
    End Sub
End Class
```

To output data, the program uses the Asc method to convert the text box contents one character at a time to an ASCII-byte value that it assigns to the byte array. The program then uses the FileStream class Write method to write the data to the file the user specifies. Because the program converts the text box's Unicode (double byte) data into a single ASCII character, the program only supports ASCII character sets. To support Unicode text, the program must store both bytes of each text box character. In Chapter 11, you can examine programs that write a text box's contents using Unicode format.

Selecting Font Attributes

Today, many Windows-based programs such as word processors, spreadsheets, and even e-mail applications make use of the Font dialog box, shown in Figure 7-8, to let the user select a specific font or change font attributes (such as bolding and italics). To provide similar support within your Visual Basic .NET programs, your code can take advantage of the FontDialog class. The FontDialog class inherits its methods from the CommonDialog, Component, and Object classes. Table 7-7 briefly describes the FontDialog class properties.

Property	Purpose
AllowScriptChange	Gets or sets a Boolean value that specifies whether the user can change the character set specified in the Script box to display a character set other than the current character set.
AllowSimulations	Gets or sets a Boolean value that specifies whether the dialog box supports GDI font simulations.
AllowVectorFonts	Gets or sets a Boolean value that specifies whether the dialog box lets the user select vector fonts.
AllowVerticalFonts	Gets or sets a Boolean value that specifies whether the dialog box displays both vertical and horizontal fonts or only horizontal fonts.
Color	Gets or sets the selected font color.
FixedPitchOnly	Gets or sets a Boolean value that specifies whether the dialog box only lets the user select fixed-pitch fonts.
Font	Gets or sets the selected font.
FontMustExist	Gets or sets a Boolean value that specifies whether the dialog box specifies an error condition if the user tries to select a font or style that does not exist.
MaxSize	Gets or sets the maximum point size the dialog box will let the user select.
MinSize	Gets or sets the minimum point size the dialog box will let the user select.
ScriptsOnly	Gets or sets a Boolean value that specifies whether the dialog box lets the user select fonts for all non-OEM and symbol character sets, as well as the ANSI character set.
ShowApply	Gets or sets a Boolean value that specifies whether the dialog box displays an Apply button.
ShowColor	Gets or sets a Boolean value that specifies whether the dialog box displays a color option.
ShowEffects	Gets or sets a Boolean value that specifies whether the dialog box contains strikethrough and underline options.
ShowHelp	Gets or sets a Boolean value that specifies whether the dialog box displays a Help button.

Table 7-7 The FontDialog Class Properties

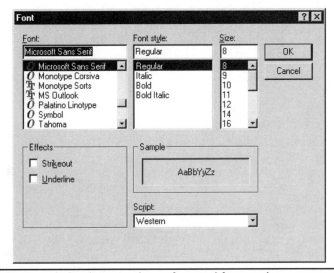

Figure 7-8   Using the Font dialog box to select a font and font attributes

USE IT   The following program, FontInfo.vb, displays the Font dialog box. After the user makes his or her font selections, the program uses a message box to display the user's choices, as shown in Figure 7-9. If the user cancels the dialog box without selecting a font, the program displays a message so stating:

```
Public Class Form1
    Inherits System.Windows.Forms.Form

    Dim FontDB As New FontDialog()

#Region " Windows Form Designer generated code "
  ' Code not shown
#End Region

    Private Sub Button1_Click(ByVal sender As Object, _
      ByVal e As System.EventArgs) Handles Button1.Click

        If (FontDB.ShowDialog() = DialogResult.OK) Then
            Dim CrLf As String = Chr(13) & Chr(10)

            TextBox1.Text = ""
            TextBox1.AppendText("Font Name: " & FontDB.Font.Name)
            TextBox1.AppendText(CrLf)
```

```
          TextBox1.AppendText("Bold: " & FontDB.Font.Bold)
          TextBox1.AppendText(CrLf)
          TextBox1.AppendText("Italic: " & FontDB.Font.Italic)
          TextBox1.AppendText(CrLf)
          TextBox1.AppendText("Size: " & FontDB.Font.Size)
          TextBox1.AppendText(CrLf)
          TextBox1.AppendText("Strikeout: " & FontDB.Font.Strikeout)
          TextBox1.AppendText(CrLf)
          TextBox1.AppendText("Underline: " & FontDB.Font.Underline)
          TextBox1.AppendText(CrLf)
      End If
    End Sub
End Class
```

The program's processing is actually quite straightforward. The code simply appends various FontDialog box class properties to the form's text box. To advance text to the start of the next line in the text box, the code appends a carriage-return and linefeed combination between each property.

Figure 7-9   Displaying information about a user's font selections

Putting a User's Font Selections to Use

USE IT   In the previous Tip, you learned how to use the FontDialog class to display a dialog box within which the user can select a font and specific font attributes. The following program, UseFont.vb, displays a text box, as shown in Figure 7-10, within which the user can enter text. If the user selects the Set Font button, the program will display the Font dialog box. After the user selects the font settings that he or she desires, the program uses the corresponding font and attributes to redisplay text the text box contains:

```
Public Class Form1
    Inherits System.Windows.Forms.Form

#Region " Windows Form Designer generated code "
  ' Code not shown
#End Region

    Private Sub Button1_Click(ByVal sender As Object, _
      ByVal e As System.EventArgs) Handles Button1.Click

        Dim FontDB As New FontDialog()

        If (FontDB.ShowDialog() = DialogResult.OK) Then
            TextBox1.Font = FontDB.Font
        End If
    End Sub
End Class
```

When you run the program and use the Font dialog box to change various settings, the form's text box will immediately apply your selections to the text box contents when you select the Font dialog box OK button.

Figure 7-10 Letting the user select a font and font attributes for user input

Selecting a Color

Just as many Windows-based programs let users select specific fonts and font attributes. Many programs let users select specific colors for text and screen objects. To prompt the user for color information, programs often use the Color dialog box shown in Figure 7-11. Using the Color dialog box, a user can select from one of 64 predefined colors (48 of which are defined by Windows and 16 of which are defined by the program or user). Or, as shown in Figure 7-12, the user can expand the Color dialog box to select a specific color from the color spectrum.

In your Visual Basic .NET programs, your code can use the ColorDialog class to display the Color dialog box. The ColorDialog class inherits its methods from the CommonDialog, Component, and Object classes. Table 7-8 briefly describes the class properties.

Property	Meaning
AllowFullOpen	Gets or sets a Boolean value that specifies whether the user can define custom colors using the dialog box.
AnyColor	Gets or sets a Boolean value that specifies whether the dialog box will display all available colors in the set of basic colors.
Color	Gets or sets the selected color.
CustomColors	Gets or sets the dialog box's custom colors.
FullOpen	Gets or sets a Boolean value that specifies whether the dialog box displays the custom colors when the dialog box opens.
ShowHelp	Gets or sets a value that specifies whether the dialog box displays a Help button.
SolidColorOnly	Gets or sets a Boolean value that specifies whether the dialog box limits the user to selecting only solid colors.

Table 7-8 The ColorDialog Class Properties

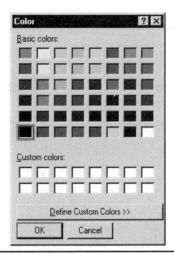

Figure 7-11   Using the Color dialog box to select 1 of 64 predefined colors

USE IT The following program, ColorDemo.vb, displays the Color dialog box. After the user makes his or her color choice, the program displays information about the user's selections in a message box:

```
Public Class Form1
    Inherits System.Windows.Forms.Form

#Region " Windows Form Designer generated code "
    ' Code not shown
#End Region

    Private Sub Button1_Click(ByVal sender As Object, _
      ByVal e As System.EventArgs) Handles Button1.Click

        Dim ColorDB As New ColorDialog()

        If (ColorDB.ShowDialog() = DialogResult.OK) Then
            MsgBox("Colors: " & ColorDB.Color.ToString())
        Else
            MsgBox("User selected Cancel")
        End If
    End Sub
End Class
```

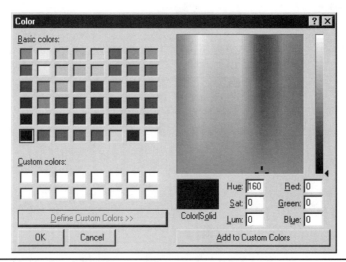

Figure 7-12   Using the Color dialog box to select a custom color

After you compile and run this program, your screen will display a message box containing either the color's constant name or red, green, and blue components, as shown here.

Fine-Tuning Color Dialog Box Operations

When your programs use a Color dialog box to prompt the user for a color value, there may be times when you will want to initialize (customize) one or more ColorDialog class properties before you display the dialog box. For example, you may want to define one or more of the 16 colors that appear in the dialog box. To specify the colors, you must specify each color's red, green, and blue (RGB) color values as a number (which you can specify as a decimal value, but which may be more meaningful to another programmer if you use hexadecimal) within an array of color values. When you specify RGB values, you essentially specify the intensity levels for the red, green, and blue colors that combine to create the color you desire. For each color you define, you must specify an intensity value in the range 0 to 255 (hexadecimal 0 to &HFF). For example, the following statements create an array of 16 colors, defining each color's RGB components using hexadecimal values:

```
ColorDB.CustomColors = New Integer() _
   {&HFF00FF, &HFF0000, &HF0F0F0, &HF0F0F0, _
    &HAAAAAA, &HBBBBBB, &HCCCCCC, &HDDDDDD, _
    &HEEEEEE, &HAAA0A0, &HBBB0B0, &HCCC0C0, _
    &HDDD0D0, &H111111, &H333333, &H888888}
```

USE IT   The following program, UseColors.vb, defines the 16 colors it wants the Color dialog box to display. The program then displays a text box, as shown in Figure 7-13, within which the user can enter text. If the user selects the Foreground or Background buttons, the program will display the Color dialog box. After the user selects the color that he or she desires, the program will immediately use the color to display the text box contents:

```vb
Public Class Form1
    Inherits System.Windows.Forms.Form

    Dim ColorDB As New ColorDialog()

#Region " Windows Form Designer generated code "

    Public Sub New()
        MyBase.New()

        'This call is required by the Windows Form Designer.
        InitializeComponent()

        ColorDB.CustomColors = New Integer() _
        {&HFF00FF, &HFF0000, &HF0F0F0, &HF0F0F0, _
         &HAAAAAA, &HBBBBBB, &HCCCCCC, &HDDDDDD, _
         &HEEEEEE, &HAAA0A0, &HBBB0B0, &HCCC0C0, _
         &HDDD0D0, &H111111, &H333333, &H888888}

    End Sub

    ' Remaining code not shown

#End Region

    Private Sub Button1_Click(ByVal sender As Object, _
      ByVal e As System.EventArgs) Handles Button1.Click
        If (ColorDB.ShowDialog() = DialogResult.OK) Then
            TextBox1.ForeColor = ColorDB.Color
        End If
    End Sub

    Private Sub Button2_Click(ByVal sender As Object, _
      ByVal e As System.EventArgs) Handles Button2.Click
        If (ColorDB.ShowDialog() = DialogResult.OK) Then
            TextBox1.BackColor = ColorDB.Color
        End If
    End Sub
End Class
```

Figure 7-13   Letting the user specify foreground and background colors for text input

Using the PrintDialog Class to Prompt the User for Printing Options

When a user selects the File menu Print option, most Windows-based programs display the Print dialog box, as shown in Figure 7-14, within which the user can specify settings such as whether or not he or she wants to print to a file, specific pages for printing, and whether or not the user can access network printers. In your Visual Basic .NET programs, your code can display the Print dialog box and process user selections using the PrintDialog class. The PrintDialog class inherits its methods from the CommonDialog, Components, and Objects classes. Table 7-9 briefly describes the class properties.

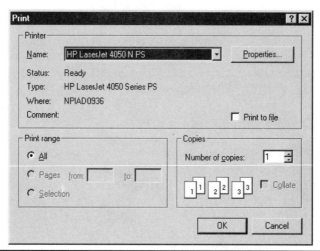

Figure 7-14   Using the Print dialog box to prompt the user for printing options

Property	Meaning
AllowPrintToFile	Gets or sets a Boolean value that specifies whether the dialog box displays the Print To File check box.
AllowSelection	Gets or sets a Boolean value that specifies whether the dialog box displays an option to let the user print specific pages.
AllowSomePages	Gets or sets a Boolean value that specifies whether the dialog box displays the Pages option button.
Document	Gets or sets a value that specifies the PrintDocument the dialog box used to obtain PrinterSettings.
PrinterSettings	Gets or sets the PrinterSettings the dialog box modifies.
PrintToFile	Gets or sets a Boolean value that specifies whether the dialog box displays the Print To File check box as checked.
ShowHelp	Gets or sets a Boolean value that specifies whether the dialog box displays a Help button.
ShowNetwork	Gets or sets a Boolean value that specifies whether the dialog box displays the Network button.

Table 7-9   The PrintDialog Class Properties

USE IT   The following program, ShowPrint.vb, displays a Print dialog box. After the user makes his or her selections, the program displays information about the user's choices:

```
Public Class Form1
    Inherits System.Windows.Forms.Form

    Dim PrintDB As New PrintDialog()

#Region " Windows Form Designer generated code "
  ' Code not shown
#End Region

    Private Sub Button1_Click(ByVal sender As Object, _
      ByVal e As System.EventArgs) Handles Button1.Click
        PrintDB.Document = New System.Drawing.Printing.PrintDocument()

        If (PrintDB.ShowDialog() = DialogResult.OK) Then
            Dim CrLf As String = Chr(13) & Chr(10)

            TextBox1.Text = ""
            TextBox1.AppendText("Printer: " & _
              PrintDB.PrinterSettings.PrinterName)
            TextBox1.AppendText(CrLf)
            TextBox1.AppendText("From Page: " & _
```

```
                    PrintDB.PrinterSettings.FromPage)
            TextBox1.AppendText(CrLf)
            TextBox1.AppendText("To Page: " & _
               PrintDB.PrinterSettings.ToPage)
            TextBox1.AppendText(CrLf)
            TextBox1.AppendText("Print Range: " & _
               PrintDB.PrinterSettings.PrintRange)
            TextBox1.AppendText(CrLf)
            TextBox1.AppendText("Copies: " & _
               PrintDB.PrinterSettings.Copies)
            TextBox1.AppendText(CrLf)
            If (PrintDB.PrinterSettings.LandscapeAngle = 90) Then
                TextBox1.AppendText("Landscape")
            Else
                TextBox1.AppendText("Portrait")
            End If
            TextBox1.AppendText(CrLf)
            TextBox1.AppendText("Allow Print to File: " & _
               PrintDB.AllowPrintToFile)
            TextBox1.AppendText(CrLf)
            TextBox1.AppendText("AllowSelection: " & _
               PrintDB.AllowSelection)
            TextBox1.AppendText(CrLf)
            TextBox1.AppendText("Allow Some Pages: " & _
               PrintDB.AllowSomePages)
            TextBox1.AppendText(CrLf)
            TextBox1.AppendText("Print to File: " & _
               PrintDB.PrintToFile)
            TextBox1.AppendText(CrLf)
            TextBox1.AppendText("Show Network: " & _
               PrintDB.ShowNetwork)
            TextBox1.AppendText(CrLf)
        End If
    End Sub
End Class
```

Before a program can display a Print dialog box, the program must provide the PrintDialog object with a PrinterSettings object that specifies information about how the program should print the document. One way to provide the PrinterSettings object is to assign a PrintDocument object to the PrintDialog class Document property, as shown here:

```
PrintDB.Document = New System.Drawing.Printing.PrintDocument()
```

After you select the printer settings and choose OK, the program will display output similar to that shown in Figure 7-15.

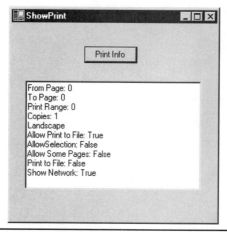

Figure 7-15   Displaying a user's printer settings

Determining Available Printers

As your programs provide print capabilities, they may need to know information about the printers available in the system. To get a list of printers available in the system, your programs can use the PrinterSettings class InstalledPrinters collection.

USE IT   The following program, ListPrinters.vb, displays a form that contains a List Printers button and a text box. When the user selects the List Printers button, the program will display the system's printers in the text box shown in Figure 7-16.

Figure 7-16   Displaying a list of the printers available in the system

```
Public Class Form1
    Inherits System.Windows.Forms.Form

#Region " Windows Form Designer generated code "
    ' Code not shown
#End Region

    Private Sub Button1_Click(ByVal sender As Object, _
      ByVal e As System.EventArgs) Handles Button1.Click

        Dim CrLf As String = Chr(13) & Chr(10)
        Dim PrinterName As String

        TextBox1.Text = ""

        For Each PrinterName In _
          System.Drawing.Printing.PrinterSettings.InstalledPrinters
            TextBox1.AppendText(PrinterName)
            TextBox1.AppendText(CrLf)
        Next
    End Sub
End Class
```

Using the PageSetupDialog Class to Prompt the User for Page Settings

When a user selects the File menu Page Setup option, most Windows-based programs display the Page Setup dialog box, as shown in Figure 7-17, within which the user can specify settings such as margin sizes, page orientation, and paper sources. In your Visual Basic .NET programs, your code can display the Page Setup dialog box and process user selections using the PageSetupDialog class. The PageSetupDialog class inherits its methods from the CommonDialog class which inherits methods from the Component class, which, in turn, inherits methods from the Object class. Table 7-10 describes the class fields and properties.

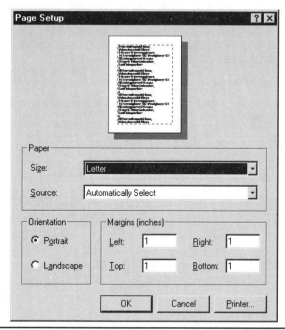

Figure 7-17   Using the Page Setup dialog box to prompt the user for printing options

Property	Method
AllowMargins	Gets or sets a Boolean value that specifies whether the dialog box enables the Margins section.
AllowOrientation	Gets or sets a Boolean value that specifies whether the dialog box enables the Orientation section.
AllowPaper	Gets or sets a Boolean value that specifies whether the dialog box enables the Paper section.
AllowPrinter	Gets or sets a Boolean value that specifies whether the dialog box enables the Printer button.
Document	Gets or sets a value that specifies the PrintDocument from which the dialog box gets the page settings.

Table 7-10   The PageSetupDialog Class Properties

Property	Method
MinMargins	Gets or sets a value that specifies the minimum margins (in hundredths of an inch) the user can select.
PageSettings	Gets or sets a value that specifies the page settings the dialog box will modify.
PrinterSettings	Gets or sets the printer settings the dialog box modifies if the user clicks the Printer button.
ShowHelp	Gets or sets a Boolean value that specifies whether the dialog box displays a Help button.
ShowNetwork	Gets or sets a Boolean value that specifies whether the dialog box displays the Network button.

Table 7-10   The PageSetupDialog Class Properties *(continued)*

USE IT   The following program, ShowPageSettings.vb, displays a Page Setup dialog box. After the user makes his or her selections, the program displays information about the user's choices:

```
Public Class Form1
    Inherits System.Windows.Forms.Form

#Region " Windows Form Designer generated code "
  ' Code not shown
#End Region

    Private Sub Button1_Click(ByVal sender As Object, _
      ByVal e As System.EventArgs) Handles Button1.Click

        Dim PageDB As New PageSetupDialog()

        PageDB.Document = New System.Drawing.Printing.PrintDocument()

        If (PageDB.ShowDialog() = DialogResult.OK) Then
            Dim CrLf As String = Chr(13) & Chr(10)

            TextBox1.Text = ""
            TextBox1.AppendText("Allow Margins: " & _
              PageDB.AllowMargins)
            TextBox1.AppendText(CrLf)
            TextBox1.AppendText("Allow Orientation: " & _
              PageDB.AllowOrientation)
```

```
            TextBox1.AppendText(CrLf)
            TextBox1.AppendText("Allow Paper: " & _
               PageDB.AllowPaper)
            TextBox1.AppendText(CrLf)
            TextBox1.AppendText("Allow Printer: " & _
               PageDB.AllowPrinter)
            TextBox1.AppendText(CrLf)
            TextBox1.AppendText("Minimum Margins: " & _
               PageDB.MinMargins.ToString())
            TextBox1.AppendText(CrLf)
            TextBox1.AppendText("Show Network: " & _
               PageDB.ShowNetwork)
            TextBox1.AppendText(CrLf)
            TextBox1.AppendText("Printer Settings: " & _
               PageDB.PrinterSettings.ToString())
            TextBox1.AppendText(CrLf)
        End If
    End Sub
End Class
```

After you compile and execute the ShowPageSettings program, the code will display a form that contains a button. If you select the Page Info button, the form will display information about the page, as shown in Figure 7-18.

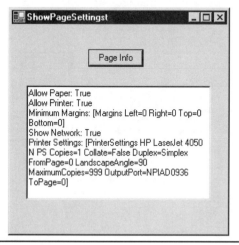

Figure 7-18   Displaying page settings

Performing Print Operations

Several of the previous Tips have presented dialog boxes your programs can use to perform various printer- and page-related operations. In this Tip, you will create a program that prints the contents of a form's text box.

 USE IT The following program, PrintFormText.vb, will use each of the printer-related dialog boxes you have examined. In addition, the program will use the Print Preview dialog box, similar to that shown in Figure 7-19, which you can use to preview how your document will appear before you print the document's contents.

```
Imports System.Drawing.Printing

Public Class Form1
    Inherits System.Windows.Forms.Form

    Private PrtSetupDB As New PrintDialog()
    Private WithEvents PrtDocument As _
        New System.Drawing.Printing.PrintDocument()
    Private PageSetupDB As New PageSetupDialog()
    Private PrintPreviewDB As New PrintPreviewDialog()
    Private PrinterSettings As _
        New System.Drawing.Printing.PrinterSettings()

#Region " Windows Form Designer generated code "
    ' Code not shown
#End Region

    Private Sub Button1_Click(ByVal sender As Object, _
      ByVal e As System.EventArgs) Handles Button1.Click
        PageSetupDB.Document = PrtDocument
        PageSetupDB.ShowDialog()
    End Sub

    Private Sub Button2_Click(ByVal sender As Object, _
      ByVal e As System.EventArgs) Handles Button2.Click
        PrintPreviewDB.Document = PrtDocument
        PrintPreviewDB.ShowDialog()
    End Sub
```

```
    Private Sub Button3_Click(ByVal sender As Object, _
       ByVal e As System.EventArgs) Handles Button3.Click
          PrtSetupDB.Document = PrtDocument
          PrtSetupDB.PrinterSettings = PrinterSettings

          If (PrtSetupDB.ShowDialog() = DialogResult.OK) Then
             PrtDocument.Print()
          End If
    End Sub

    Private Sub PrtDocument_PrintPage(ByVal sender As Object, _
       ByVal ev As PrintPageEventArgs) Handles PrtDocument.PrintPage
          ev.Graphics.DrawString(TextBox1.Text, TextBox1.Font, _
             Brushes.Black, 0, 0)
    End Sub
End Class
```

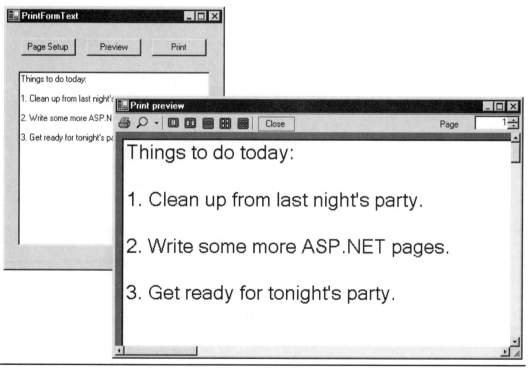

Figure 7-19   Using the Print Preview dialog box to preview printer output

The key to supporting the Print Preview dialog box and to printing the document is to define the PrintPage event handler. When you preview a page in the Print Preview dialog box, the dialog box will use the event handler to render the page contents. Likewise, when you call the PrintDocument class Print method to print the document, the code will call the event handler to oversee the actual printing. In this case, the code that prints the text box contents is actually quite simple. The code uses the DrawString method to render the text output:

```
ev.Graphics.DrawString(TextBox1.Text, TextBox1.Font, _
        Brushes.Black, 0, 0)
```

The code in this case only supports one page of output. If the text box content exceeds one page, the program will truncate the printed output. To support multiple pages of output, you must keep track of the output line in the PrintPage event handler and then create new pages as required.

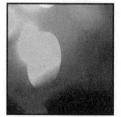

CHAPTER 8

Exploiting Multiple Threads of Execution

TIPS IN THIS CHAPTER

Operating systems such as Windows and Linux are multitasking systems that let you run multiple programs at the same time. As you know, a program is simply a list of instructions the CPU executes to perform a specific task. Before the CPU can execute a program's instructions, the instructions must reside within the computer's random access memory (RAM). To run multiple programs, the operating system loads each program's instructions into RAM.

When Windows loads two or more programs into memory, Windows must have a way to track each program's memory locations (and other items, such as which files a program has opened, whether the program is a foreground or background task, and so on). Windows keeps track of each program's resources by assigning each running program to a unique process. In general, you can think of a program as the list of instructions and a process as an object that contains information about a running program. Each time you run a program, Windows creates a new process to hold the program's resources and state information.

Within a PC, the CPU executes each program's instructions. It is important that you keep in mind that although the PC appears to be executing several programs at the same time, the CPU can only execute one program's instructions at any given time. A multitasking operating system creates the illusion that two or more programs are running at the same time by rapidly switching control of the CPU between each active process. If, for example, you have three programs running (processes 1, 2, and 3), Windows would execute process 1's instructions for a few milliseconds, then switch to process 2 for a few milliseconds, and then on to process 3. (In between running each process's instructions, Windows will assign the CPU to itself to perform its own behind-the-scenes operations, such as managing the active processes.) Today's GHz CPUs can perform tens of thousands of instructions during the millisecond time slice the program executes before Windows switches to a new program. Because the operating system switches the CPU so quickly, each program appears to be running at the same time.

In Windows 2000, you can monitor how Windows exchanges the CPU between processes (and the amount of CPU time each process has consumed) in the Windows Task Manager, shown in Figure 8-1. To display the Task Manager in Windows 2000 and Windows XP Professional, perform these steps:

1. Press the CTRL-ALT-DEL keyboard combination. Windows will display the Windows Security dialog box.

2. In the Windows Security dialog box, click the Task Manager button.

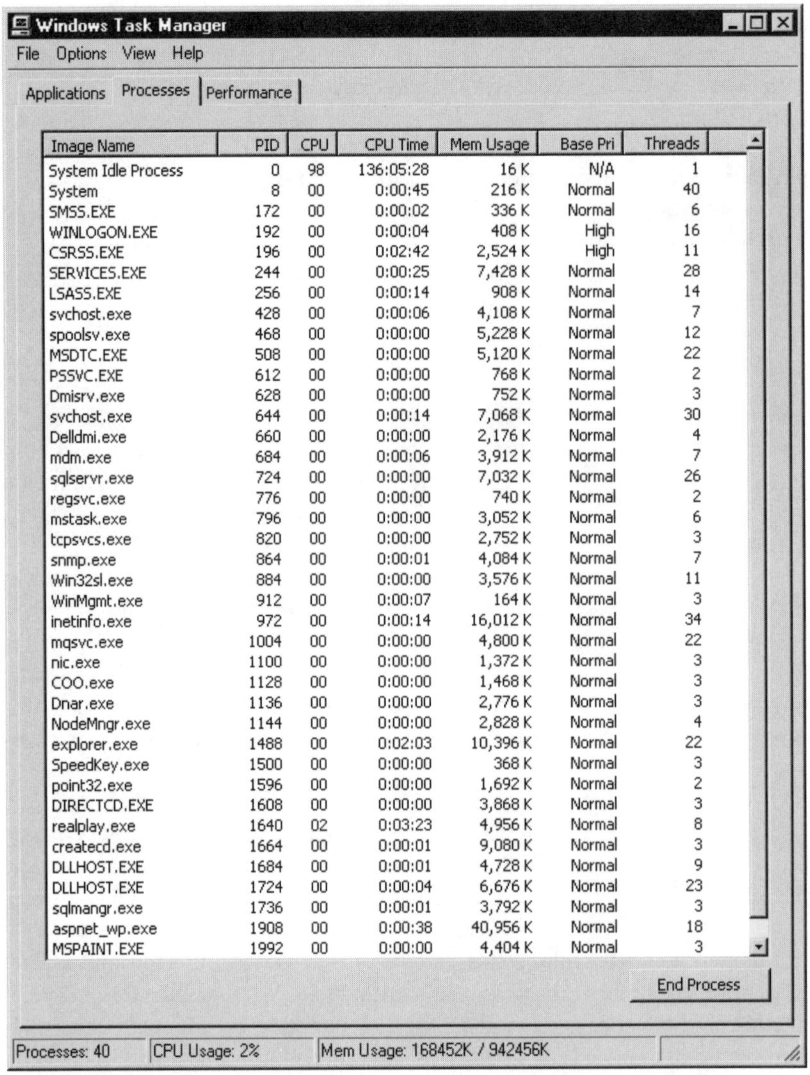

Image Name	PID	CPU	CPU Time	Mem Usage	Base Pri	Threads
System Idle Process	0	98	136:05:28	16 K	N/A	1
System	8	00	0:00:45	216 K	Normal	40
SMSS.EXE	172	00	0:00:02	336 K	Normal	6
WINLOGON.EXE	192	00	0:00:04	408 K	High	16
CSRSS.EXE	196	00	0:02:42	2,524 K	High	11
SERVICES.EXE	244	00	0:00:25	7,428 K	Normal	28
LSASS.EXE	256	00	0:00:14	908 K	Normal	14
svchost.exe	428	00	0:00:06	4,108 K	Normal	7
spoolsv.exe	468	00	0:00:00	5,228 K	Normal	12
MSDTC.EXE	508	00	0:00:00	5,120 K	Normal	22
PSSVC.EXE	612	00	0:00:00	768 K	Normal	2
Dmisrv.exe	628	00	0:00:00	752 K	Normal	3
svchost.exe	644	00	0:00:14	7,068 K	Normal	30
Delldmi.exe	660	00	0:00:00	2,176 K	Normal	4
mdm.exe	684	00	0:00:06	3,912 K	Normal	7
sqlservr.exe	724	00	0:00:00	7,032 K	Normal	26
regsvc.exe	776	00	0:00:00	740 K	Normal	2
mstask.exe	796	00	0:00:00	3,052 K	Normal	6
tcpsvcs.exe	820	00	0:00:00	2,752 K	Normal	3
snmp.exe	864	00	0:00:01	4,084 K	Normal	7
Win32sl.exe	884	00	0:00:00	3,576 K	Normal	11
WinMgmt.exe	912	00	0:00:07	164 K	Normal	3
inetinfo.exe	972	00	0:00:14	16,012 K	Normal	34
mqsvc.exe	1004	00	0:00:00	4,800 K	Normal	22
nic.exe	1100	00	0:00:00	1,372 K	Normal	3
COO.exe	1128	00	0:00:00	1,468 K	Normal	3
Dnar.exe	1136	00	0:00:00	2,776 K	Normal	3
NodeMngr.exe	1144	00	0:00:00	2,828 K	Normal	4
explorer.exe	1488	00	0:02:03	10,396 K	Normal	22
SpeedKey.exe	1500	00	0:00:00	368 K	Normal	3
point32.exe	1596	00	0:00:00	1,692 K	Normal	2
DIRECTCD.EXE	1608	00	0:00:00	3,868 K	Normal	3
realplay.exe	1640	02	0:03:23	4,956 K	Normal	8
createcd.exe	1664	00	0:00:01	9,080 K	Normal	3
DLLHOST.EXE	1684	00	0:00:01	4,728 K	Normal	9
DLLHOST.EXE	1724	00	0:00:04	6,676 K	Normal	23
sqlmangr.exe	1736	00	0:00:01	3,792 K	Normal	3
aspnet_wp.exe	1908	00	0:00:38	40,956 K	Normal	18
MSPAINT.EXE	1992	00	0:00:00	4,404 K	Normal	3

Figure 8-1 Viewing CPU switching in the Windows Task Manager

Windows is a preemptive multitasking operating system, which means that Windows itself determines when a process will begin to execute its CPU time slice and when that time slice will end. (Windows does not care which instructions the process is executing when it switches control of the CPU to another process.) When Windows later resumes a process's execution, Windows will continue the execution at the location where the processing left off before the last CPU switch. To keep track of each process's execution state (such as the instruction pointer and register contents), Windows assigns the state information to the process object before it begins the execution of the next process. When Windows is later ready to again execute the process, Windows restores the process information to the CPU.

Programmers refer to the instructions the CPU executes in a program as a thread of execution. Depending on the processing a program performs, there may be times when you will want to perform two or more operations at the same time. For example, in a word-processing application, you might want the program to spell-check your document behind the scenes as you type, or to print a copy of the document's current contents while you perform other tasks. To let a program perform multiple operations at the same time, you can create multiple threads in a program. In the case of the word processor, one thread might handle the user input, one thread the spell-checking, and a third the background printing.

When a program uses multiple threads, behind-the-scenes software in the process will exchange control of the CPU between the threads during the process's CPU time slice. In other words, after the operating system assigns the CPU to the process, software in the process will divide the time slice among its active threads. Because the software must preempt and later resume a thread's execution, the software must be able to store and later restore the thread's execution state (the thread's instruction pointer, register contents, and so on). To maintain thread state information, the software assigns the information to a thread object.

In this chapter, you will learn how to create and run multiple threads in a Visual Basic .NET program. You will also learn how to synchronize operations between threads and how to share resources in a multithreaded program.

Creating and Running Multiple Threads

A thread corresponds to a unit of execution. To use threads in a Visual Basic .NET program, you must first create a Thread object for each thread you plan to use. The following code fragment creates three Thread objects named, for simplicity, A, B, and C:

```
Dim A As System.Threading.Thread
Dim B As System.Threading.Thread
Dim C As System.Threading.Thread
```

A thread executes instructions in your program. When you create an instance of a Thread object, you must specify the address of the first statement the thread will execute, which normally corresponds to the address of a subroutine. The following statements assign different starting addresses to the three Thread objects. Thread A will begin its execution in the subroutine Display_A. Likewise, thread B will execute the subroutine Display_B, and thread C will execute Display_C:

```
A = New Threading.Thread(AddressOf Display_A)
B = New Threading.Thread(AddressOf Display_B)
C = New Threading.Thread(AddressOf Display_C)
```

Each subroutine, in this case, is quite simple, performing a loop that displays the thread's letter (such as "A", "B", or "C") 250 times. Then the subroutine ends, which also terminates and destroys the thread:

```
Sub Display_A()
  Dim I As Integer
  For I = 0 To 250
    Console.Write("A")
  Next
End Sub
```

To start a thread's execution, your code must call the Thread class Start method. The following statements, for example, will start each of the three threads:

```
A.Start()
B.Start()
C.Start()
```

 The following program, ThreadDemo.vb, creates and runs the three threads:

```
Module Module1

    Sub Display_A()
        Dim I As Integer
        For I = 0 To 250
            Console.Write("A")
        Next
    End Sub

    Sub Display_B()
        Dim I As Integer
        For I = 0 To 250
            Console.Write("B")
        Next
    End Sub

    Sub Display_C()
        Dim I As Integer
        For I = 0 To 250
            Console.Write("C")
        Next
    End Sub
```

```
Sub Main()
    Dim A As System.Threading.Thread
    Dim B As System.Threading.Thread
    Dim C As System.Threading.Thread

    A = New Threading.Thread(AddressOf Display_A)
    B = New Threading.Thread(AddressOf Display_B)
    C = New Threading.Thread(AddressOf Display_C)

    A.Start()
    B.Start()
    C.Start()

    Console.ReadLine()   ' Delay to view output
End Sub

End Module
```

After you compile and execute the program, your screen will display output similar to the following (the output will differ based on the programs your system is running and how Windows distributes CPU time slices among the programs):

```
AAAAAAAAAAAAAAAAAAAAAAAAAAAAAAAAAAAAAAAAAAAAAAAAAAAAAAAAAAAAAAA
AAAAAAAAAAAAAAAAAAAAAAAAAAAAAAAAAAAAAAAAAAAAAAAAAAAAAAAAAAAAAAA
AAAAAAAAAAAAAAAAAAAAAAAAAAAAAAAAAAAAAAAAAAAAAAAAAAAAAAAAAAAABC
CCCCCCCCCCCCCCCCCCCCCCCCCCCCCCCCCCCCCCCCCCCCCCCCCCCCCCCCCCCCCCC
CCCCCCCCCCCCCCCCCCCCCCCCCCCCCCCCCCCCCCCCCCCCCCCCCCCCCCCCCCCCCCC
CCCCCCCCCCCCCCCCCCCCCCCCCCCCCCCCCCCCCCCCCCCCCCCBBBBBBBBBBBBB
BBBBBBBBBBBBBBBBBBBBBBBBBBBBBBBBBBBBBBBBBBBBBBBBBBBBBBBBBBBBBBB
BBBBBBBBBBBAAAAAAAAAAAAAAAAAAAAAAAAAAAAAAAAAAAAAAAAAAAAAAAAAAA
AAAAAAAABBBBBBBBBBBBBBBBBBBBBBBBBBBBBBBBBBBBBBBBBBBBBBBBBBBBBBB
BBBBBBBBBBBBBBBBBBBBBBBBBBBBBBBBBBBBBBBBBBBBBBBBBBBBBBBBBBBBBBB
BBBBCCCCCCCCCCCCCCCCCCCCCCCCCCCCCCCCCCCCCCCCCCCCCCCCCCCCCCCCCCC
CCCCCCCCCCCCBBBBBBBBBBBBBBBBBBBBBBBBBBBBBBBBBBBBBBBBBB
```

As you can see, as the program executes, the process distributes its CPU time slice among the threads, which means thread A runs for a period of time, followed by thread B, then thread C. Then, after thread A completes its processing, the process distributes its time slices between threads B and C.

In this case, to better identify the namespaces within which each thread class resides, the code does not import various namespaces. In the programs that follow, the code will eliminate the need for the long class names by importing the System.Threading namespace:

```
Imports System.Threading
```

Putting a Thread to Sleep

Depending on the processing the threads within your program perform, there may be times when you must suspend a thread's execution for a specific period of time. Assume, for example, that you create a program that uses threads to monitor your server's resources. Within the program, you might use one thread to periodically check available memory, a second to examine free disk space, and a third to count the number of remote users connected to the server. Depending on your needs, you may want the threads to "wake up" and perform their processing every minute or possibly every ten minutes. To suspend a thread for a specific interval of time, your code can use the Thread class Sleep method. The following statement puts a thread to sleep for 60 seconds:

```
Threading.Thread.Sleep(60000)
```

When you put a thread to sleep using the Sleep method, the thread will not run and will consume only minimal CPU resources (those CPU cycles are required to determine when the program should wake up and resume the thread's execution).

USE IT The following program, ThreadSleep.vb, starts three threads. The program then uses the Sleep method to suspend one thread for 1 second, one for 0.5 seconds, and one for 0.1 seconds:

```
Imports System.Threading

Module Module1

    Sub Display_A()
        Dim I As Integer

        Thread.Sleep(1000)

        For I = 0 To 250
            Console.Write("A")
        Next
    End Sub

    Sub Display_B()
        Dim I As Integer

        Thread.Sleep(500)

        For I = 0 To 250
            Console.Write("B")
        Next
    End Sub

    Sub Display_C()
```

```
        Dim I As Integer

        Thread.Sleep(100)

        For I = 0 To 250
            Console.Write("C")
        Next
    End Sub

    Sub Main()
        Dim A As Thread
        Dim B As Thread
        Dim C As Thread

        A = New Thread(AddressOf Display_A)
        B = New Thread(AddressOf Display_B)
        C = New Thread(AddressOf Display_C)

        A.Start()
        B.Start()
        C.Start()

        Console.ReadLine()  ' Delay to view output
    End Sub

End Module
```

After you compile and execute this program, your screen will display the output shown here:

```
CCCCCCCCCCCCCCCCCCCCCCCCCCCCCCCCCCCCCCCCCCCCCCCCCCCCCCCCCCCCCCCCC
CCCCCCCCCCCCCCCCCCCCCCCCCCCCCCCCCCCCCCCCCCCCCCCCCCCCCCCCCCCCCCCCC
CCCCCCCCCCCCCCCCCCCCCCCCCCCCCCCCCCCCCCCCCCCCCCCCCCCCCCCCCCCCCCCCC
CCCCCCCCCCCCCCCCCCCCCCCCCCCCCCCCCCCCCCCCCCCCCCCCCCCCCCCCCCCCBBBBB
BBBBBBBBBBBBBBBBBBBBBBBBBBBBBBBBBBBBBBBBBBBBBBBBBBBBBBBBBBBBBBBBB
BBBBBBBBBBBBBBBBBBBBBBBBBBBBBBBBBBBBBBBBBBBBBBBBBBBBBBBBBBBBBBBBB
BBBBBBBBBBBBBBBBBBBBBBBBBBBBBBBBBBBBBBBBBBBBBBBBBBBBBBBBBBBBBBBBB
BBBBBBBBBBBBBBBBBBBBBBBBBBBBBBBBBBBBBBBBBBBBBBBBBBBBBBBBBBAAAAAAAAAA
AAAAAAAAAAAAAAAAAAAAAAAAAAAAAAAAAAAAAAAAAAAAAAAAAAAAAAAAAAAAAAAAA
AAAAAAAAAAAAAAAAAAAAAAAAAAAAAAAAAAAAAAAAAAAAAAAAAAAAAAAAAAAAAAAAA
AAAAAAAAAAAAAAAAAAAAAAAAAAAAAAAAAAAAAAAAAAAAAAAAAAAAAAAAAAAAAAAAA
AAAAAAAAAAAAAAAAAAAAAAAAAAAAAAAAAAAAAAAAAAAAAAAAAA
```

Because thread C sleeps the shortest amount of time, it is the first thread to execute. Further, because it does not require much processing time, thread C is able to complete before thread B awakens. Then, because thread B does not require much processing time, thread B can complete its processing before thread A finally wakes up.

Suspending, Resuming, and Aborting a Thread

When your programs use threads to perform specific processing, there will be times when you may need to temporarily halt and later resume a thread's processing. Using the Thread class Sleep method, you can suspend a thread's execution for a specific length of time. If, however, you do not know in advance the length of time for which you must suspend the thread, your programs can use the Thread class Suspend method to temporarily stop the thread. Later, when your code is ready for the thread to continue its processing, your code can call the Thread class Resume method:

```
SomeThread.Suspend()
' Other processing here
SomeThread.Resume()
```

Assume, for example, that your program uses a thread to validate the data a user enters in a form. If the user does not enter data for a specific interval of time (which means the user may be doing something else, such as running a different program), the program can suspend the validation thread's execution. Later, when the user again starts to input data, the program can resume the validation thread's processing.

Just as there may be times when your program must suspend a thread's execution, there may also be times when a program must end a thread's processing. To end a thread, your code can call the Thread class Abort method:

```
SomeThread.Abort()
```

USE IT   The following program, SuspendResumeAbort.vb, illustrates the use of the Thread class Suspend, Resume, and Abort methods. The program first starts three threads named A, B, and C. Then the code suspends thread A. After thread C completes its output, the thread's code resumes thread A's processing and then aborts thread B:

```
Imports System.Threading

Module Module1
    Public A As Thread
    Public B As Thread
    Public C As Thread

    Sub Display_A()
        Dim I As Integer
        Try
            A.Suspend()
```

```
        For I = 0 To 250
            Console.Write("A")
        Next
    Catch E As ThreadStateException
        Console.WriteLine()
        Console.WriteLine("Thread A Exception" & E.ToString())
        Console.WriteLine()
    End Try
End Sub

Sub Display_B()
    Dim I As Integer
    Try
        For I = 0 To 250
            Console.Write("B")
        Next
    Catch E As ThreadAbortException
        Console.WriteLine()
        Console.Write("Thread B has been aborted")
        Console.WriteLine()
    End Try
End Sub

Sub Display_C()
    Dim I As Integer
    Try
        If (B.IsAlive) Then
            B.Abort()
        End If

        For I = 0 To 250
            If (A.ThreadState = ThreadState.Suspended) Then
                A.Resume()
            End If

            Console.Write("C")
        Next
    Catch E As Threading.ThreadStateException
        Console.WriteLine()
        Console.WriteLine("Thread C Exception" &
          E.ToString())
        Console.WriteLine()
    End Try
End Sub
```

```
Sub Main()
    A = New Thread(AddressOf Display_A)
    B = New Thread(AddressOf Display_B)
    C = New Thread(AddressOf Display_C)

    A.Start()
    B.Start()
    C.Start()

    Console.ReadLine()   ' Delay to view output
End Sub

End Module
```

After you compile and execute this program, your screen will display the following output:

```
BBBBBBBBBBBBBBBBBBBBBBBBBBBBBBBBBBBBBBBBBBBBBBBBBBBBBBBBBBBBBBB
BBBBBBBBBBBBBBBBBBBBBBBBBBBBBBBBBBBBBBBBBBBBBBBBBBBBBBBBBBBBBBB
BBBBBBACCCCCCCCCCCCCCCCCCCCCCCCCCCCCCCCCCCCCCCCCCCCCCCCCCCCCCC
CCCCCCCCCCCCCCCCCCCCCCCCCCCCCCCCCCCCCCCCCCCCCCCCCCCCCCCCCCCCCC
CCCCCCCCCCCCCCCCCCCCCCCCCCCCCCCCCCCCCCCCCCCCCCCCCCAAAAAAAA
AAAAAAAAAAAAAAAAAAAAAAAAAAAAAAAAAAAAAAAAAAAAAAAAAAAAAAAAAAAAA
Thread B has been aborted
AAAAAAAAAAAAAAAAAAAAAAAAAAAAAAAAAAAAAAAAAAAAAAAAAAAAAAAAAAAAA
AAAAAAAAAAAAAAAAAAAAAAAAAAAAAAAAAAAAAAAAAAAAAAAAAAAAAAAAAAAAA
AAAAAAAAAAAAAAAAAAAAAAAAAAAAAACCCCCCCCCCCCCCCCCCCCCCCCCCCCCCC
CCCCCCCCCCCCCCCCCCCCCCCCCCCCCCCCCCCCCCCAAAAAAAAAAAAAAAAAAAA
```

As you can see, when thread A begins, it immediately suspends itself. In thread C, the code terminates thread B by calling B.Abort. Before thread C calls the Abort function, it uses the IsAlive method to ensure that thread B is running. If your program tries to abort a thread that is not running, an exception will occur. In thread B, the code uses a Try-Catch statement to detect that its thread has been aborted:

```
Try
  For I = 0 To 250
    Console.Write("B")
  Next
Catch E As ThreadAbortException
  Console.WriteLine()
  Console.Write("Thread B has been aborted")
  Console.WriteLine()
End Try
```

Later, thread C resumes thread A's processing. If you examine thread C's code, you will find that thread C first checks to be sure thread A is suspended before it resumes the thread's processing. If your code tries to resume a thread that is not suspended, an exception will occur.

Taking a Closer Look at the Thread Class

To use multiple threads of execution, your programs will make extensive use of the Thread class. Table 8-1 briefly describes the Thread class methods. Table 8-2 describes the Thread class properties.

Method	Purpose
Abort	Begins the process of terminating the thread. The thread may not terminate (see the ResetAbort method).
AllocateDataSlot	Allocates an unnamed data slot within which the thread can store thread-specific data for all threads.
AllocateNamedDataSlot	Allocates a named data slot for all threads.
FreeNamedDataSlot	Frees an allocated named data slot.
GetData	Retrieves the value from the current thread's specified named data slot.
GetDomain	Returns the current thread's domain. The domain specifies the environment within which an application executes.
GetDomainID	Returns the application's unique domain identifier.
GetNamedDataSlot	Returns the named data slot or a new data slot if the named slot does not exist.
Interrupt	Interrupts a thread that is blocked by a Wait, Sleep, or Join operation.
Join	Blocks the calling thread until the specified thread terminates. Join is an overloaded method.
ResetAbort	Cancels an Abort operation on the current thread.
Resume	Resumes a suspended thread.
SetData	Sets data in a current-thread data slot.
Sleep	Blocks the current thread for the specified number of milliseconds. Sleep is an overloaded method.
SpinWait	Causes a thread to wait the number of the iterations specified.
Start	Begins a thread's execution by directing the operating system to change the thread's state to ThreadStateRunning.
Suspend	Suspends the specified thread. If the thread is already suspended, the method has no effect.

Table 8-1   The Thread Class Methods

Property	Purpose
ApartmentState	Gets or sets the apartment state of this thread. The apartment state defines if the thread is running in a single-threaded or multithreaded apartment. By assigning each thread its own storage location (an apartment), the apartment model lets threads protect their resources from one another.
CurrentContext	Gets the thread's execution context. An object's context is a set of properties that defines the execution within which the object resides.
CurrentCulture	Gets or sets the thread's culture. The culture defines properties that control date, time and currency formats, sorting orders and so on.
CurrentPrincipal	Gets or sets the thread's current principal that specifies the thread's security context.
CurrentThread	Gets the thread that is currently running.
CurrentUICulture	Gets or sets the current culture identifier which the Resource Manager uses to look up culture information.
IsAlive	Returns True if the thread's state is not started, stopped, or aborted.
IsBackground	Returns True if the thread is a background thread.
IsThreadPoolThread	Returns True if the thread was allocated from the system thread pool.
Name	Gets or sets the thread's name.
Priority	Gets or sets the thread's scheduling priority.
ThreadState	Gets a value that specifies the thread's state.

Table 8-2   The Thread Class Properties

USE IT   The following program, ThreadInfo.vb, uses the Thread class properties to display information about the current thread:

```
Imports System.Threading

Module Module1
    Sub Main()
        Dim objThread As Thread
        objThread = Thread.CurrentThread

        With objThread
            Console.WriteLine("Apartment State: {0}", .ApartmentState)
            Console.WriteLine("Current Context: {0}", .CurrentContext)
            Console.WriteLine("Current Culture: {0}", .CurrentCulture)
            Console.WriteLine("Current Principal: {0}", .CurrentPrincipal)
            Console.WriteLine("Current Thread: {0}", .CurrentThread)
            Console.WriteLine("Current UI Culture: {0}", .CurrentUICulture)
            Console.WriteLine("Is Alive: {0}", .IsAlive)
```

```
            Console.WriteLine("Is Background: {0}", .IsBackground)
            Console.WriteLine("Is Thread Pool Thread: {0}", _
              .IsThreadPoolThread)
            Console.WriteLine("Name: {0}", .Name)
            Console.WriteLine("Priority: {0}", .Priority)
            Console.WriteLine("Thread State: {0}", .ThreadState)
        End With
        Console.ReadLine()
    End Sub
End Module
```

After you compile and execute this program, your screen will display the following output:

```
Apartment State: STA
Current Context: ContextID: 0
Current Culture: en-US
Current Principal: System.Security.Principal.GenericPrincipal
Current Thread: System.Threading.Thread
Current UI Culture: en-US
Is Alive: True
Is Background: False
Is Thread Pool Thread: False
Name:
Priority: Normal
Thread State: Running
```

Assigning Thread Names

When your programs use threads to perform specific processing, there may be times when your code must determine which thread is executing specific code. One way to distinguish between threads is to assign unique names to each thread's Name field:

```
Spell.Name = "Spell Checker"
Print.Name = "Background Printing"
```

USE IT   The following program, NameThreads.vb, uses the Thread class Name field to assign a unique name to each of the program's three threads. Next, the code directs each thread to execute the LoopName subroutine, which uses a For loop to display the thread's name, as shown here:

```
For I = 0 To 250
  Console.Write(Thread.CurrentThread.Name)
Next
```

By naming the threads A, B, and C, the code achieves the same output as the programs previously shown throughout this chapter:

```
Imports System.Threading

Module Module1
    Public A As Thread
    Public B As Thread
    Public C As Thread

    Sub Display()
        Dim I As Integer

        For I = 0 To 250
            Console.Write(Thread.CurrentThread.Name)
        Next
    End Sub

    Sub Main()
        A = New Thread(AddressOf Display)
        B = New Thread(AddressOf Display)
        C = New Thread(AddressOf Display)

        A.Name = "A"
        A.Start()

        B.Name = "B"
        B.Start()

        C.Name = "C"
        C.Start()

        Console.ReadLine()   ' Delay to view output
    End Sub
End Module
```

After you compile and execute this program, your screen will display output similar to the following:

```
AAAAAAAAAAAAAAAAAAAAAAAAAAAAAAAAAAAAAAAAAAAAAAAAAAAAAAAAAAAAAAAA
AAAAAAAAAAAAAAAAAAAAAAAAAAAAAAAAAAAAAAAAAAAAAAAAAAAAAAAAAAAAAAAA
AAAAAAAAAAAAAAAAAAAAAAAAAAAAAAAAAAAAAAAAAAAAAAAAAABCCCCCCCCCCCCCC
CCCCCCCCCCCCCCCCCCCCCCCCCCCCCCCCCCCCCCCCCCCCCCCCCCCCCCCCCCCCCCCC
CCCCCCCCCCCCCCCCCCCCCCCCCCCCCCCCCCCCCCCCCCCCCCCCCCCCCCCCCCCCCCCC
CCCCCCCCCCCCCCCCCCCCCCCCCCCCCCCCCCCBBBBBBBBBBBBBBBBBBBBBBBBBBBBB
BBBBBBBBBBBBBBBBBBBBBBBBBBBBBBBBBBBBBBBBBBBBBBBBBBBBBBBBBBBBBBAA
```

```
AAAAAAAAAAAAAAAAAAAAAAAAAAAAAAAAAAAAAAAAAAAAAAAAAAAAAAAAAAAAAAA
AAAAAAAABBBBBBBBBBBBBBBBBBBBBBBBBBBBBBBBBBBBBBBBBBBBBBBBBBBBBBBB
BBBBBBBBBBBBBBBBBBBBBBBBBBBBBBBBBBBBBBBBBBBBBBBBBBCCCCCCCCCCCCCC
CCCCCCCCCCCCCCCCCCCCCCCCCCCCCCCCCCCCCCCCCCCCCCCCCCCCCCCCCCBBBBB
BBBBBBBBBBBBBBBBBBBBBBBBBBBBBBBBBBBBBBBBBBBBBBBBBBB
```

The problem with using the Thread class Name field to distinguish between threads is that there is nothing to prevent a program from assigning the same name to two or more threads:

```
A.Name = "A"
B.Name = "A"
C.Name = "A"
```

USE IT For times when your code must distinguish between threads, your programs should use the Thread class GetHashCode method, which returns a value unique to each object instance (programmers refer to this as a hash value). The following program, GetHash.vb, creates three thread objects and then displays each thread's unique hash value:

```
Imports System.Threading

Module Module1
    Public A As Thread
    Public B As Thread
    Public C As Thread

    Sub DisplayHash()
        Dim O As Thread
        Dim hash As Integer
        O = Thread.CurrentThread

        hash = O.GetHashCode()

        Console.Write("Thread name: {0}", Thread.CurrentThread.Name)
        Console.WriteLine(" Thread hash: {0}", hash.ToString())

    End Sub

    Sub Main()
        A = New Thread(AddressOf DisplayHash)
        B = New Thread(AddressOf DisplayHash)
        C = New Thread(AddressOf DisplayHash)

        A.Name = "A"
        A.Start()
```

```
      B.Name = "B"
        B.Start()

        C.Name = "C"
        C.Start()

        Console.ReadLine()   ' Delay to view output
    End Sub

End Module
```

After you compile and execute this program, your screen will display output similar to the following (the hash values may differ based on the order in which the threads execute on your system):

```
Thread name: A Thread hash: 2
Thread name: B Thread hash: 3
Thread name: C Thread hash: 4
```

Suspending One Thread's Execution Until a Specific Thread Completes Its Processing

When your programs use threads to perform specific processing, there will be many times when you will want one thread to not perform its processing until a second thread has completed its tasks. In a word-processing program, for example, you may not want a thread to begin printing a document in the background until the SpellChecker thread has completed its processing.

To suspend a thread's execution until another thread has finished its processing, your code must call the Thread class Join method. The following statement, for example, directs a thread to wait for the SpellChecking thread to complete its processing:

```
SpellChecking.Join()
```

USE IT   The following program, JoinThreadsAB.vb, creates three threads named A, B, and C. Then the program uses the Thread class Join method to suspend thread A's processing until thread B completes its processing:

```
Imports System.Threading

Module Module1
    Public A As Thread
    Public B As Thread
    Public C As Thread

    Sub Display_A()
```

```
        Dim I As Integer

        B.Join()

        For I = 0 To 250
            Console.Write("A")
        Next
    End Sub

    Sub Display_B()
        Dim I As Integer

        For I = 0 To 250
            Console.Write("B")
        Next
    End Sub

    Sub Display_C()
        Dim I As Integer

        For I = 0 To 250
            Console.Write("C")
        Next
    End Sub

    Sub Main()
        A = New Thread(AddressOf Display_A)
        B = New Thread(AddressOf Display_B)
        C = New Thread(AddressOf Display_C)

        A.Start()
        B.Start()
        C.Start()

        Console.ReadLine()   ' Delay to view output
    End Sub

End Module
```

After you compile and execute this program, your screen will display output similar to the following:

```
BBBBBBBBBBBBBBBBBBBBBBBBBBBBBBBBBBBBBBBBBBBBBBBBBBBBBBBBBBB
BBBBBBBBBBBBBBBBBBBBBBBBBBBBBBBBBBBBBBBBBBBBBBBBBBBBBBBBBBBBB
BBBBBBBBBBBBBBBBBBBBBBBBBBBBBBBBBBBBBBBBBBBBBBBBBBBBBBBBBBBBBBB
BCCCCCCCCCCCCCCCCCCCCCCCCCCCCCCCCCCCCCCCCCCCCCCCCCCCCCCCCCCCC
```

```
CCCCCCCCCCCCCCCCCCCCCCCCCCCCCCCCCCCCCCCCCCCCCCCCCCCCCCCCCCCCCCC
CCCCCCCCCCCCCCCCCCCCCCCCCCCCCCCCCCCCCCCCCCCCCCCCCCCCCCCCCCCCCCC
CCCCCCCCCCCCCCCCCCCCCCCCCCCCCCCCCCCCCCBBBBBBBBBBBBBBBBBBBBBBBBB
BBBBBBBBBBBBBBBBBBBBBBBBBBBBBBBBBBBBCCCCCCCCCCCCCCCCCCCCCCCAAAAAAAAAA
AAAAAAAAAAAAAAAAAAAAAAAAAAAAAAAAAAAAAAAAAAAAAAAAAAAAAAAAAAAAAAA
AAAAAAAAAAAAAAAAAAAAAAAAAAAAAAAAAAAAAAAAAAAAAAAAAAAAAAAAAAAAAAA
AAAAAAAAAAAAAAAAAAAAAAAAAAAAAAAAAAAAAAAAAAAAAAAAAAAAAAAAAAAAAAA
AAAAAAAAAAAAAAAAAAAAAAAAAAAAAAAAAAAAAAAAAAAAAAAA
```

As you can see, because of the Join operation, thread A waits until thread B has completed its processing.

In a similar way, there may be times when you will want to suspend a thread's processing until multiple threads have completed their processing. To do so, the thread should call the Join method for each of the threads for which it wants to wait. For example, if thread A wants to wait for threads B and C to complete their processing, thread A would execute the following statements:

```
B.Join()
C.Join()
```

USE IT The following program, JoinMultipleThreads.vb, again creates three threads named A, B, and C. The program then uses two calls to Join methods to suspend thread A's processing until threads B and C finish their processing:

```
Imports System.Threading

Module Module1
    Public A As Thread
    Public B As Thread
    Public C As Thread

    Sub Display_A()
        Dim I As Integer
        B.Join()
        C.Join()

        For I = 0 To 250
            Console.Write("A")
        Next
    End Sub

    Sub Display_B()
        Dim I As Integer

        For I = 0 To 250
            Console.Write("B")
```

```
        Next
    End Sub

    Sub Display_C()
        Dim I As Integer

        For I = 0 To 250
            Console.Write("C")
        Next
    End Sub

    Sub Main()
        A = New Thread(AddressOf Display_A)
        B = New Thread(AddressOf Display_B)
        C = New Thread(AddressOf Display_C)

        A.Start()
        B.Start()
        C.Start()

        Console.ReadLine()   ' Delay to view output
    End Sub
End Module
```

After you compile and execute this program, your screen will display output similar to the following, showing that thread A delays its processing until threads B and C complete their processing:

```
BBBBBBBBBBBBBBBBBBBBBBBBBBBBBBBBBBBBBBBBBBBBBBBBBBBBBBBBBBBBBBBB
BBBBBBBBBBBBBBBBBBBBBBBBBBBBBBBBBBBBBBBBBBBBBBBBBBBBBBBBBBBBBBBB
BBBBBBBBBBBBBBBBBBBBBBBBBBBBBBBBBBBBBBBBBBBBBBBBBBBBBBBBBBBBBBBB
BBBBBBCCCCCCCCCCCCCCCCCCCCCCCCCCCCCCCCCCCCCCCCCCCCCCCCCCCCCCCCCC
CCCCCCCCCCCCCCCCCCCCCCCCCCCCCCCCCCCCCCCCCCCCCCCCCCCCCCCCCCCCCCCC
CCCCCCCCCCCCCCCCCCCCCCCCCCCCCCCCCCCCCCCCCCCCCCCCCCCCCCCCCCCCCCCC
CCCCCCCCCCCCCCCCCCCCCCCCCCCCCCCCCCCCCCCCCCCCCCBBBBBBBBBBBBBBBBBB
BBBBBBBBBBBBBBBBBBBBBBBBBBBBBBBBBCCCCCCCCCCCCCCCCCCCCAAAAAAAAAA
AAAAAAAAAAAAAAAAAAAAAAAAAAAAAAAAAAAAAAAAAAAAAAAAAAAAAAAAAAAAAAA
AAAAAAAAAAAAAAAAAAAAAAAAAAAAAAAAAAAAAAAAAAAAAAAAAAAAAAAAAAAAAAA
AAAAAAAAAAAAAAAAAAAAAAAAAAAAAAAAAAAAAAAAAAAAAAAAAAAAAAAAAAAAAAA
AAAAAAAAAAAAAAAAAAAAAAAAAAAAAAAAAAAAAAAAAAAAAAAAAA
```

Controlling Thread Priorities

When your Visual Basic .NET application uses multiple threads of execution, the .NET thread management software will assign each thread a small part (slice) of the CPU's processing time.

Normally, the thread management software will equally distribute the time slices across the threads. In other words, if three threads are running, the thread management software will give each thread 33 percent of the application's processing time. Keep in mind that in a multitasking operating system such as Windows, the operating system is already sharing CPU time slices among applications. The threads, in turn, divide the CPU time slice Windows has given the application.

USE IT Depending on the processing threads perform in your application, there may be times when the processing one thread performs is more important than that of the other threads. In such cases, your program can give the thread a higher priority, which causes the thread to execute more frequently than the lower priority threads. To increase (or decrease) a thread's priority, your programs can assign a value to the Thread class Priority field. The System.Threading.ThreadPriority namespace enumerates values for the following priority values: Lowest, BelowNormal, Normal, AboveNormal, and Highest. The following statement assigns a higher priority to the SpellChecker thread:

```
SpellChecker.Priority = ThreadPriority.Highest
```

USE IT The following program, ThreadPriority.vb, creates three threads named A, B, and C. The program then assigns thread A the priority BelowNormal and thread C the priority AboveNormal:

```
Imports System.Threading
Imports System.Threading.ThreadPriority

Module Module1
    Public A As Thread
    Public B As Thread
    Public C As Thread

    Sub Display_A()
        Dim I As Integer

        For I = 0 To 250
            Console.Write("A")
        Next
    End Sub

    Sub Display_B()
        Dim I As Integer

        For I = 0 To 250
            Console.Write("B")
        Next
    End Sub

    Sub Display_C()
```

```
        Dim I As Integer

        For I = 0 To 250
            Console.Write("C")
        Next
    End Sub

    Sub Main()
        A = New Thread(AddressOf Display_A)
        B = New Thread(AddressOf Display_B)
        C = New Thread(AddressOf Display_C)

        A.Priority = BelowNormal
        C.Priority = AboveNormal

        A.Start()
        B.Start()
        C.Start()

        Console.ReadLine()   ' Delay to view output
    End Sub
End Module
```

After you compile and execute this program, your screen will display the following output:

```
CCCCCCCCCCCCCCCCCCCCCCCCCCCCCCCCCCCCCCCCCCCCCCCCCCCCCCCCCCCCCC
CCCCCCCCCCCCCCCCCCCCCCCCCCCCCCCCCCCCCCCCCCCCCCCCCCCCCCCCCCCCCC
CCCCCCCCCCCCCCCCCCCCCCCCCCCCCCCCCCCCCCCCCCCCCCCCCCCCCCCCCCCCCC
CCCCCCCCCCCCCCCCCCCCCCCCCCCCCCCCCCCCCCCCCCCCCCCCCCCCCCCCCCCAAAAA
AAAAAAAAAAAAAAAAAAAAAAAAAAAAAAAAAAAAAAAAAAAAAAAAABBBBBBBBBBBB
BBBBBBBBBBBBBBBBBBBBBBBBBBBBBBBBBBBBBBBBBBBBBBBBBBBBBBBBBBBBBB
BBBBBBBBBBBBBBBBBBBBBBBBBBBBBBBBBBBBBBBBBBBBBBBBBBBBBBBBBBBBBB
BBBBBBBBBBBBBBBBBBBBBBBBBBBBBBBBBBBBBBBBBBBBBBBBBBBBBBBBBBBBBB
BBBBBBBBBBBBBBBBBBBBBBBBBBBBBBBBBBBBBBBBBBBBBBAAAAAAAAAAAAAAAA
AAAAAAAAAAAAAAAAAAAAAAAAAAAAAAAAAAAAAAAAAAAAAAAAAAAAAAAAAAAAA
AAAAAAAAAAAAAAAAAAAAAAAAAAAAAAAAAAAAAAAAAAAAAAAAAAAAAAAAAAAAA
AAAAAAAAAAAAAAAAAAAAAAAAAAAAAAAAAAAAAAAAAAAAAAAA
```

As you can see, because thread C has the highest priority, the thread completes its processing first. Likewise, because thread A has the lowest priority, its processing finishes last. Note, however, that just because a thread has a lower priority, that does not mean the thread will not run (thread A runs for a brief period of time after thread C completes its processing). Instead, the lower-priority thread will run less often.

Taking Advantage of the Thread Pool

Depending on the processing your threads perform, there may be times when you can improve your program's execution by taking advantage of a shared thread pool. In general, the thread pool consists of a group of existing threads that are simply sitting around waiting for something to do. By using the existing threads, your programs eliminate the overhead of creating and later discarding the thread objects.

The thread pool is well suited for threads that must wait for an asynchronous event or timer. Rather than creating your own thread that will then sit and wait for an event, you can take advantage of a thread-pool thread (which can sit and wait for a range of events). When you use the thread pool, you do not start the threads. Instead, your code calls the ThreadPool class QueueUserWorkItem method, passing to the method the address of the code the thread will execute and an event the thread can use to signal the program that the thread has completed its processing:

```
Dim AIsDone As New AutoResetEvent(False)

ThreadPool.QueueUserWorkItem(New _
   WaitCallback(AddressOf Display_A), AIsDone)
```

The following program, PoolDemo.vb, illustrates the use of thread-pool threads. The program changes the methods you have been using throughout this chapter so that a thread-pool thread can call the method. When the thread later completes its processing, the thread signals the main program:

```
Imports System.Threading

Module Module1

    Sub Display_A(ByVal state As Object)
        Dim I As Integer

        For I = 0 To 250
            System.Console.Write("A")
        Next

        Thread.Sleep(3000)

        CType(state, AutoResetEvent).Set()
    End Sub

    Sub Display_B(ByVal state As Object)
        Dim I As Integer

        For I = 0 To 250
            System.Console.Write("B")
        Next
```

```
        Thread.Sleep(3000)

        CType(state, AutoResetEvent).Set()
End Sub

Sub Display_C(ByVal state As Object)
        Dim I As Integer

        For I = 0 To 250
            System.Console.Write("C")
        Next

        Thread.Sleep(3000)

        CType(state, AutoResetEvent).Set()
End Sub

Sub Main()
        Dim AIsDone As New AutoResetEvent(False)
        Dim BIsDone As New AutoResetEvent(False)
        Dim CIsDone As New AutoResetEvent(False)

        ThreadPool.QueueUserWorkItem(New _
          WaitCallback(AddressOf Display_A), AIsDone)
        ThreadPool.QueueUserWorkItem(New _
          WaitCallback(AddressOf Display_B), BIsDone)
        ThreadPool.QueueUserWorkItem(New _
          WaitCallback(AddressOf Display_C), CIsDone)

        Dim ThreadCount, ThreadPorts As Integer

        ThreadPool.GetAvailableThreads(ThreadCount, ThreadPorts)
        Console.WriteLine("Thread pool size {0}", ThreadCount)
        Console.WriteLine()
        Console.WriteLine("Waiting for threads to complete")

        AIsDone.WaitOne()
        Console.WriteLine()
        Console.WriteLine("A is done")

        BIsDone.WaitOne()
        Console.WriteLine()
        Console.WriteLine("B is done")
```

```
        CIsDone.WaitOne()
        Console.WriteLine()
        Console.WriteLine("C is done")

        System.Console.ReadLine()   ' Delay to view output
    End Sub

End Module
```

After you compile and execute this program, your screen will display the following output:

```
Thread pool size 25

Waiting for threads to complete
AAAAAAAAAAAAAAAAAAAAAAAAAAAAAAAAAAAAAAAAAAAAAAAAAAAAAAAAAAAAAAA
AAAAAAAAAAAAAAAAAAAAAAAAAAAAAAAAAAAAAAAAAAAAAAAAAAAAAAAAAAAAAAA
AAAAAAAAAAAAAAAAAAAAAAAAAAAAAAAAAAAAAAAAAAAAAAAAAAAAAAAAAAAAAAA
AAAAAAAAAAAAAAAAAAAAAAAAAAAAAAAAAAAAAAAAAAAAAAAAAAAAAAAAAABBBBB
BBBBBBBBBBBBBBBBBBBBBBBBBBBBBBBBBBBBBBBBBBBBBBBBBBBBBBBBBBBBBBBB
BBBBBBBBBBBBBBBBBBBBBBBBBBBBBBBBBBBBBBBBBBBBBBBBBBBBBBBBBBBBBBBB
BBBBBBBBBBBBBBBBBBBBBBBBBBBBBBBBBBBBBBBBBBBBBBBBBBBBBBBBBBBBBBBB
BBBBBBBBBBBBBBBBBBBBBBBBBBBBBBBBBBBBBBBBBBBBBBBBBBBBBCCCCCCCCCC
CCCCCCCCCCCCCCCCCCCCCCCCCCCCCCCCCCCCCCCCCCCCCCCCCCCCCCCCCCCCCCC
CCCCCCCCCCCCCCCCCCCCCCCCCCCCCCCCCCCCCCCCCCCCCCCCCCCCCCCCCCCCCCC
CCCCCCCCCCCCCCCCCCCCCCCCCCCCCCCCCCCCCCCCCCCCCCCCCCCCCCCCCCCCCCC
CCCCCCCCCCCCCCCCCCCCCCCCCCCCCCCCCCCCCCCCCCCCCCCCCCC
A is done

B is done

C is done
```

Recognizing Potential Race Conditions Between Threads

When your Visual Basic .NET applications make use of multiple threads, there are times when the threads can actually interfere with each other because the threads get out of sync due to CPU switching. As you know, when your programs create multiple threads, each thread runs for a specific interval of time (the thread's CPU time slice). Assume, for example, that one thread, which you will name the Producer, must create (produce) an item before a second thread (the Consumer) can consume the object. Further, assume that the Producer cannot produce an item until the Consumer consumes the previous item. The Producer thread will execute the following code to produce an item:

```
Sub Producer()
  Dim Value As Integer = 0
```

```
    Do
      If (BufferEmpty) Then
        BufferEmpty = False
        Buffer = Value

        If (Value = 0) Then
          Value = 1
        Else
          Value = 0
        End If

        Console.WriteLine("Producer: " & Buffer)
      End If
    Loop While (True)
End Sub
```

As the Producer creates items, it will place, in order, an item with the value 0 followed by an item with the value 1, followed again by an item with value 0 and an item with the value 1, and so on. As the Producer creates a new item, the thread will write the item's value to the screen. Likewise, the Consumer thread will execute the following code to consume an item:

```
Sub Consumer()
  Dim Value As Integer

    Do
      If (Not BufferEmpty) Then
        BufferEmpty = True
        Thread.CurrentThread.Sleep(1000)

        Value = Buffer
        Console.WriteLine("Consumer: " & Value)
      End If
    Loop While (True)
End Sub
```

When the Consumer thread consumes an item, it will display the item's value on the screen. Ideally, when the two threads run, your screen should display output similar to the following:

```
Producer: 1
Consumer: 1
Producer: 0
Consumer: 0
Producer: 1
Consumer: 1
```

```
Producer: 0
Consumer: 0
Producer: 1
Consumer: 1
Producer: 0
Consumer: 0
Producer: 1
Consumer: 1
Producer: 0
Consumer: 0
```

USE IT   The following program, ProducerConsumer.vb, implements the producer-consumer model:

```
Imports System.Threading

Module Module1
    Public Buffer As Integer
    Public BufferEmpty As Boolean = True

    Sub Producer()
        Dim Value As Integer = 0

        Do
            If (BufferEmpty) Then
                BufferEmpty = False
                Buffer = Value

                If (Value = 0) Then
                    Value = 1
                Else
                    Value = 0
                End If

                Console.WriteLine("Producer: " & Buffer)
            End If
        Loop While (True)
    End Sub

    Sub Consumer()
        Dim Value As Integer

        Do
            If (Not BufferEmpty) Then
                BufferEmpty = True
```

```
            Thread.CurrentThread.Sleep(1000)

            Value = Buffer
            Console.WriteLine("Consumer: " & Value)
          End If
      Loop While (True)
    End Sub

    Sub Main()
      Dim ProducerThread As Thread
      Dim ConsumerThread As Thread

      ProducerThread = New Thread(AddressOf Producer)
      ConsumerThread = New Thread(AddressOf Consumer)

      ProducerThread.Start()
      ConsumerThread.Start()
    End Sub
End Module
```

Although the program's output appears correct, the program actually leaves open the opportunity for a very subtle bug that can cause the program to fail (hang), such that the Producer may produce an item before the previous item has been consumed, or the Consumer may consume the same item twice. If you examine the Producer code, you will find that when the If statement evaluates as True (meaning the buffer is empty), the Producer immediately sets a flag that indicates the buffer has a value:

```
If (BufferEmpty) Then
  BufferEmpty = False
```

The Producer assigns a value to the item buffer and then sleeps for 1 second (so that you have time to watch the output in a meaningful way). While the Producer thread is sleeping, however, the Consumer thread remains active, which means the Consumer will try to consume items. However, because the Consumer sets the buffer to empty after it consumes the first item, the Consumer code appears to prevent the Consumer from consuming items that have not yet been produced.

The potential error in the application exists because the code cannot control when the CPU will switch control between the two threads. Assume, for example, that the Producer thread has just completed the following statement when the CPU switches control to the Consumer class:

```
Buffer.Empty = False
```

In this case, although the Producer has set the flag to indicate the buffer has a new item, the Producer did not have time to place the item into the buffer before the CPU switch. When the Consumer thread runs, the thread's code will examine the Buffer.Empty field and will learn the buffer is not empty (although the Producer never placed the item into the buffer). At that time, the Consumer will consume an errant value. The error occurs because of when the CPU switches execution between the two threads.

Fortunately, Visual Basic .NET provides several tools you can use to better synchronize thread access to a shared resource.

To detect the error, change the Consumer method as follows, so the code compares the value it is consuming to the value it previously consumed (the values should be different). When the values are the same, an error has occurred:

```
Sub Consumer()
  Static OldValue As Integer
  Dim Value As Integer = -1

    Do
      If (Not BufferEmpty) Then
        BufferEmpty = True
        OldValue = Value
        Value = Buffer

        If (Value = OldValue) Then
          Console.WriteLine("Error in Consumer")
          Exit Do
        End If

        Console.WriteLine("Consumer: " & Value)
      End If
    Loop While (True)
End Sub
```

You may need to let the threads run for an extended period of time before the timing of the CPU switch becomes such that it generates the error. Programmers often refer to synchronization errors that occur in a multithreaded application as race conditions, because each thread is racing to gain access to a shared resource.

Using SyncLock to Protect a Shared Resource

When your Visual Basic .NET programs use multiple threads, the applications may encounter errors due to race conditions that occur when two or more threads require synchronized access to a shared resource. To prevent race conditions from leading to errors, your Visual Basic .NET programs can use the SyncLock statement to protect shared resources. Using the SyncLock statement, you can prevent one thread from accessing a shared resource until the current thread "unlocks" the object. To use the SyncLock statement, you must specify a variable, upon which you want your code to apply a lock. The following statement, for example, uses a variable named ProducerConsumerLock as the locking variable for SyncLock:

```
SyncLock ProducerConsumerLock
```

USE IT   The following program, SyncLockDemo.vb, illustrates the use of the SyncLock statement to eliminate the error caused by a race condition in a producer-consumer program:

```vb
Imports System.Threading

Module Module1
    Public Buffer As Integer
    Public BufferEmpty As Boolean = True
    Public ProducerConsumerLock As Object = New Object()

    Sub Producer()
        Dim Value As Integer = 0

        Do
            SyncLock ProducerConsumerLock
                If (BufferEmpty) Then
                    BufferEmpty = False
                    Buffer = Value

                    If (Value = 0) Then
                        Value = 1
                    Else
                        Value = 0
                    End If

                    Console.WriteLine("Producer: " & Buffer)
                End If
            End SyncLock
        Loop While (True)
    End Sub

    Sub Consumer()
        Dim Value As Integer

        Do
            SyncLock ProducerConsumerLock
                If (Not BufferEmpty) Then
                    BufferEmpty = True
                    Thread.CurrentThread.Sleep(1000)
                    Value = Buffer
                    Console.WriteLine("Consumer: " & Value)
                End If
            End SyncLock
        Loop While (True)
    End Sub
```

```
    Sub Main()
        Dim ProducerThread As Thread
        Dim ConsumerThread As Thread

        ProducerThread = New Thread(AddressOf Producer)
        ConsumerThread = New Thread(AddressOf Consumer)

        ProducerThread.Start()
        ConsumerThread.Start()
    End Sub
End Module
```

As you can see, before the Producer and Consumer threads try to use the shared buffer, the threads use SyncLock to try to lock the shared lock. If the lock is unlocked, the thread requesting the lock will lock it. If the lock is currently locked, the thread requesting the lock will block until the lock becomes available. Later, when the thread completes its use of the shared resource, the thread will unlock the shared lock when the thread encounters the End SyncLock statement.

Synchronizing Thread Resource Access Using the Monitor Class

When your Visual Basic .NET programs use multiple threads that access the same resources (variables and objects), race conditions between the threads can result in errors that are difficult to detect and debug. Using the Visual Basic .NET SyncLock statement, your programs can lock a shared object while a thread performs its processing. In addition, as you examine .NET applications, you may encounter programs that use the Monitor class to synchronize thread access to an object. Using the Monitor class, your code locks an object by calling the Monitor.Enter method. If the object specified is not currently in use, the thread will continue its processing. Otherwise, the thread will stop until the object is not in use. When a thread is done using a shared object, the thread calls the Monitor.Exit method, as shown here:

```
Monitor.Enter(MonitorLock)
  ' Thread processing that accesses a shared resource
Monitor.Exit(MonitorLock)
```

Table 8-3 briefly describes the methods the Monitor class provides.

As discussed, when a thread tries to use a shared object protected by a monitor, the Monitor.Enter method either grants the thread access to the object, which means the thread's execution can continue, or the monitor blocks the thread's execution. When two threads try to use an object protected by a monitor, the first thread to execute the Monitor.Enter method will gain access to the resource and the second thread will block. Later, after the first thread completes its processing, the monitor will resume the blocked thread's execution. When multiple threads try to use a resource protected by a monitor,

Method	Purpose
Enter	Lets a thread acquire an exclusive lock on an object. If the resource is currently locked, the thread blocks until the resource becomes available.
Exit	Releases a thread's exclusive lock on an object.
Pulse	Notifies a specific thread that is waiting for the shared object of a change in the locked object's state.
PulseAll	Notifies all waiting threads that are waiting for the shared object of a change in the object's state.
TryEnter	Lets a thread try to acquire an exclusive lock on the specified object. If the object is available, the thread gains an exclusive lock on the object. If the object is not available, the method returns False and the thread does not block. TryEnter is an overloaded method.
Wait	Releases a thread's lock on an object and blocks the thread until it reacquires the lock. Wait is an overloaded method.

Table 8-3   The Monitor Class Methods

the monitor will grant the threads access to the resource in the order the threads called the Monitor.Enter method.

USE IT   The following program, MonitorOrder.vb, creates four threads. Each thread tries to access the shared resource variable named Buffer that is protected by a monitor. The monitor will grant the threads access to the variable in the order the threads call the Monitor.Enter method:

```
Imports System.Threading

Module Module1
    Public MonitorLock As Object = New Object()

    Sub UseResource()
        Randomize()

        Thread.CurrentThread.Sleep(Int(1000 * Rnd()))

        Monitor.Enter(MonitorLock)

          Console.WriteLine("Thread: " & Thread.CurrentThread.Name)

        Monitor.Exit(MonitorLock)
    End Sub

    Sub Main()
        Dim A As Thread = New Thread(AddressOf UseResource)
        Dim B As Thread = New Thread(AddressOf UseResource)
```

```
        Dim C As Thread = New Thread(AddressOf UseResource)
        Dim D As Thread = New Thread(AddressOf UseResource)

        A.Name = "A"
        B.Name = "B"
        C.Name = "C"
        D.Name = "D"

        A.Start()
        B.Start()
        C.Start()
        D.Start(

        Console.ReadLine()   ' Delay to view output
    End Sub
End Module
```

After you compile and execute the program, your screen will display output similar to the following:

```
Thread: B
Thread: D
Thread: A
Thread: C
```

When a thread enters the UseResource subroutine, the thread will sleep for a random amount of time, which changes the order that the threads will reach the Monitor.Enter statement. As discussed, threads will gain access to the protected code in the order in which the threads perform the Monitor.Enter statement. If you run the program several times in succession, the use of the random thread delay will change the order that threads enter the monitor.

USE IT   The following program, MonitorProducerConsumer.vb, uses a monitor to protect the buffer variable used by the Producer and Consumer threads:

```
Imports System.Threading

Module Module1
    Public Buffer As Integer
    Public BufferEmpty As Boolean = True
    Public MonitorLock As Object = New Object()

    Sub Producer()
        Dim Value As Integer = 0

        Do
```

```vbnet
        Monitor.Enter(MonitorLock)

        If (BufferEmpty) Then
            BufferEmpty = False
            Buffer = Value

            If (Value = 0) Then
                Value = 1
            Else
                Value = 0
            End If

            Console.WriteLine("Producer: " & Buffer)
        End If

        Monitor.Exit(MonitorLock)
    Loop While (True)
End Sub

Sub Consumer()
    Dim Value As Integer

    Do
        Monitor.Enter(MonitorLock)
        If (Not BufferEmpty) Then
            BufferEmpty = True
            Thread.CurrentThread.Sleep(1000)

            Value = Buffer
            Console.WriteLine("Consumer: " & Value)
        End If
        Monitor.Exit(MonitorLock)
    Loop While (True)
End Sub

Sub Main()
    Dim ProducerThread As Thread
    Dim ConsumerThread As Thread

    ProducerThread = New Thread(AddressOf Producer)
    ConsumerThread = New Thread(AddressOf Consumer)

    ProducerThread.Start()
    ConsumerThread.Start()
```

```
      End Sub
End Module
```

Before the Producer and Consumer threads try to access the shared resource, the threads execute the Monitor.Enter statement. If the resource is not currently in use, the thread will gain immediate access to the resource. Otherwise, the thread will block until the monitor (and hence the shared resource) become available.

Preventing Thread Blocking with Monitor.TryEnter

When your programs use the Monitor class to protect a shared resource, the monitor will grant access to the first thread that executes the Monitor.Enter method. If a second thread calls the Monitor.Enter method before the first thread completes its processing (and executes the Monitor.Exit method) the Monitor class will block (suspend) the second thread. Later, when the first thread completes its processing, the Monitor class will resume the suspended thread. Depending on the processing the code performs between the Monitor.Enter and Monitor.Exit methods, the amount of time a thread can be blocked can become substantial. Depending on the processing the thread performs, there may be times when you want the thread to perform other tasks if the resource is in use, as opposed to simply blocking.

USE IT To prevent a Monitor class from blocking a thread, your code can use the Monitor class TryEnter method to determine if a resource is available. If the resource is free, the thread will gain immediate access to the resource. Otherwise, the TryEnter method will return the value False (which tells the thread that the object is in use) so the thread can perform other processing. The following program, MonitorTryEnter.vb, changes the producer-consumer application to use the TryEnter method to protect the shared buffer resource. If the resource is not in use, the Producer or Consumer class will gain access to the resource. If the resource is in use, the Producer or Consumer will do something else. In this case, the Producer will display the letter P to indicate it is performing other processing, and the Consumer will display the letter C to indicate it is performing other tasks waiting for the resource to become available:

```
Imports System.Threading

Module Module1
    Public Buffer As Integer
    Public BufferEmpty As Boolean = True
    Public MonitorLock As Object = New Object()

    Sub Producer()
        Dim Value As Integer = 0

        Do
            If (Monitor.TryEnter(MonitorLock)) Then
                If (BufferEmpty) Then
```

```
                    BufferEmpty = False
                    Buffer = Value

                    If (Value = 0) Then
                        Value = 1
                    Else
                        Value = 0
                    End If

                    Console.WriteLine()
                    Console.WriteLine("Producer: " & Buffer)
                End If

            Monitor.Exit(MonitorLock)
        Else
            Console.Write("P")
        End If
    Loop While (True)
End Sub

Sub Consumer()
    Dim Value As Integer

    Do
        If (Monitor.TryEnter(MonitorLock)) Then
            If (Not BufferEmpty) Then
                BufferEmpty = True

                Thread.CurrentThread.Sleep(10)

                Value = Buffer
                Console.WriteLine()
                Console.WriteLine("Consumer: " & Value)
            End If

            Monitor.Exit(MonitorLock)
        Else
            Console.Write("C")
        End If
    Loop While (True)
End Sub

Sub Main()
    Dim ProducerThread As Thread
```

```
        Dim ConsumerThread As Thread

        ProducerThread = New Thread(AddressOf Producer)
        ConsumerThread = New Thread(AddressOf Consumer)

        ProducerThread.Start()
        ConsumerThread.Start()
    End Sub
End Module
```

After you compile and execute this program, your screen will display output similar to the following:

```
Producer: 0
PPPPPPPPPPPPPPPPPPPPPPPPPPPPPPPPPPPPPPPPPPPPPPPPPPPPPPPPPP
PPPPPPPPPPPPPPPPPPPPPPPPPPPPPPPPPPPPPPPPPPPPPPPPPPPPPPPPPP
PPPPPPPPPPPPPPPPPPPPPPPPPPPPPPPPPPPPPPPPPPPPPPPPPPPPPPPPPP
PPPPPPPPPPPPPPPPPPPPPPPPPPPPPPPPPPPPPPPPPPPPPPPPPPPPPPPPPP
PPPPPPPPPPPPPPPPPPPPPPPPPPPPPPPPPPPPPPPPPPPPPPPPPPPPPPPPPP
PPPPPPPPPPPPPPPPPPPPPPPPPPPPPPPPPPPPPPPPPPPPPPPPPPPPPPPPPP
PPPPPPPPPP
Consumer: 0
Producer: 1
CCCCCCCCCCCCCCCCCCPPPPPPPPPPPPPPPPPPPPPPPPPPPPPPPPPPPPPPPP
PPPPPPPPPPPPPPPPPPPPPPPPPPPPPPPPPPPPPPPPPPPPPPPPPPPPPPPPPP
PPPPPPPPPPPPPPPPPPPPPPPPPPPPPPPPPPPPPPPPPPPPPPPPPPPPPPPPPP
PPPPPPPPPPPPPPPPPPPPPPPPPPPPPPPPPPPPPPPPPPPPPPPPPPPPPPPPPP
PPPPPPPPPPPPPPPPPPPPPPPPPPPPPPPPPPPPPPPPPPPPPPPPPPPPPPPPPP
PPPPPPPPPPPPPPPPPPPPPPPPPPPPPPPPPPPPPPPPPPP
Consumer: 1
PPPPPPPPPPPPPPPPPPPPPPPPPPPPPPPPPPPP
```

If your threads can perform useful work while waiting for a shared resource that is protected by a Monitor object, you should test if the Monitor is available by using Monitor.TryEnter. In this case, the Producer thread is able to perform significant processing (as indicated by the letter P in the output) while the Consumer is processing code protected by the Monitor object.

Protecting Shared Variable Increment and Decrement Operations Using InterLocked

When your programs use multiple threads of execution, your program will rapidly switch control of the CPU among the threads. As you have learned, depending on when your program preempts a thread, errors can occur if you do not protect resources the threads share. Using a Monitor object or SyncLock statement, your programs can control thread access to shared resources.

Often, in an application, programs must increment or decrement a variable's value:

```
X = X + 1
```

Although the operation appears as one statement, behind the scenes the statement creates multiple machine-level instructions. Because the thread management software can preempt the threads execution at any time, it is possible that the software can switch control of the CPU while a thread is in the middle of an increment or decrement operation.

USE IT   To let your programs perform safe increment and decrement operations (the operations are safe because they are "atomic" operations, which means the operations must complete before thread software can switch control of the CPU), your programs can use the Interlocked class. Using the Interlocked class, the following statements illustrate how your code can increment or decrement a shared variable:

```
NewValue = Interlocked.Increment(OldValue)

NewValue = Interlocked.Decrement(OldValue)
```

In addition to experiencing CPU-switching errors during an increment or decrement operation, your programs can also experience errors that occur when your code assigns values to or compares shared variables. For example, the following assignment statement again creates multiple machine-level instructions:

```
X = NewValue
```

If the thread management software interrupts the thread in the middle of the assignment operation, it is possible that the next thread that executes may change the value of the NewValue variable, which may cause an errant result in the first thread. Using the Interlocked class, your code can perform an assignment or compare a shared variable using an atomic operation:

```
Interlocked.Exchange(NewValue, OldValue)

Interlocked.CompareExchange(X, 10)
```

Taking a Closer Look at the Process Class

In the Windows environment, programs run in the context of a process. Many programmers use the terms program and process interchangeably. The difference between the two terms, however, is that a process is the environment within which a program runs, meaning the operating system has allocated resources, such as memory and CPU time, to the process.

To create the illusion that multiple programs are running at the same time, a multitasking operating system, such as Windows, rapidly switches control of the CPU between processes. The amount of time a process receives to execute is the process's CPU time slice. When a program uses multiple threads, the process breaks up and allocates its time slice between the threads.

As your programs execute, there may be times when you must start, stop, or monitor the state of other processes. In such cases, your code can use the Process class that resides in the System.Diagnostics namespace. Table 8-4 briefly describes the Process class methods. Table 8-5 describes the Process class properties.

Method	Purpose
Close	Frees all process resources.
CloseMainWindow	Sends a close message to the process's main window that ends the process.
EnterDebugMode	Lets the process interact with operating system debug processes.
GetCurrentProcess	Gets a new Process object and associates the object with the current process.
GetProcessById	Gets a new Process object and associates the object with the process that corresponds to the specified ID. GetProcessById is an overloaded method.
GetProcesses	Creates an array that contains new Process objects that correspond to processes that exist in the system. GetProcesses is an overloaded method.
GetProcessesByName	Creates an array that contains new Process objects that correspond to processes that have the specified process name. GetProcessesByName is an overloaded method.
Kill	Immediately stops the process.
LeaveDebugMode	Ends a process's ability to interact with operating system debug processes.
Refresh	Discards information about the specified process that has been cached inside the Process object.
Start	Starts a new process and associates the new process with a Process object.
WaitForExit	Blocks the current thread for a specified amount of time, or until the process has exited.
WaitForInputIdle	Blocks the process until it enters an idle state.

Table 8-4   The Process Class Methods

Property	Purpose
BasePriority	Gets the process's base priority.
EnableRaisingEvents	Gets or sets whether the exit event is raised when the process terminates.
ExitCode	Gets the value the process specifies when it terminates.
ExitTime	Gets the time the process exited.
Handle	Gets the process's handle.
HandleCount	Gets the number of handles the process has open.
HasExited	Returns True if the process has terminated.
Id	Gets the process's unique identifier.
MachineName	Gets the computer name on which the process is running.
MainModule	Gets the process's main module.
MainWindowHandle	Gets the window handle of the process's main window.
MainWindowTitle	Gets the caption that appears in the process's main window.
MaxWorkingSet	Gets or sets the process's maximum allowable working set size. The working set defines the set of virtual memory pages.
MinWorkingSet	Gets or sets the process's minimum allowable working set size.
Modules	Gets the modules the process has loaded.
NonpagedSystemMemorySize	Gets the size of the process's nonpaged system memory.
PagedMemorySize	Gets the size of page memory.
PagedSystemMemorySize	Gets the size of system paged memory.
PeakPagedMemorySize	Gets the size of peak paged memory.
PeakVirtualMemorySize	Gets the size of peak virtual memory.
PeakWorkingSet	Gets the size of the peak working set.
PriorityBoostEnabled	Gets or sets a value by which the operating system temporarily boosts the process priority when the process's main window has the focus.

Table 8-5   The Process Class Properties

Property	Purpose
PriorityClass	Gets or sets the process's priority category.
PrivateMemorySize	Gets the size of private memory.
PrivilegedProcessorTime	Gets the amount of privileged processor time the process has consumed.
ProcessName	Gets the process name.
ProcessorAffinity	Gets or sets the processors on which the process threads can be scheduled to run.
Responding	Returns True if the process's user interface of the process is responding.
StandardError	Gets a StreamReader your code can use to read the process's error output.
StandardInput	Gets a StreamWriter your code can use to redirect input to the process.
StandardOutput	Gets a StreamReader your code can use to redirect output from the process.
StartInfo	Gets or sets the properties used by the Process class Start method.
StartTime	Gets the time that the process execution began.
SynchronizingObject	Gets or sets the object used to marshal the process exit event the handler calls.
Threads	Gets the set of process threads.
TotalProcessorTime	Gets the total processor time the process has consumed.
UserProcessorTime	Gets the user processor time the process has consumed.
VirtualMemorySize	Gets the size of the process's virtual memory.
WorkingSet	Gets the total amount of physical memory the process is using.

Table 8-5 The Process Class Properties *(continued)*

USE IT   The following program, ProcessInfo.vb, uses the Process class properties to display information about the program's process, such as the amount of memory the process is using, the process priority, and the thread's CPU usage:

```
Module Module1
    Sub Main()
        Dim objProcess As New Process()

        objProcess = Process.GetCurrentProcess()

        With objProcess
            Console.WriteLine("Base Priority {0}", .BasePriority)
            Console.WriteLine("Handle count {0}", .HandleCount)
```

```vb
            Console.WriteLine("Process ID (PID) {0}", .Id)
            Console.WriteLine("Machine Name {0}", .MachineName)
            Console.WriteLine("Main Module {0}", .MainModule)
            Console.WriteLine("Main Window Title {0}", _
                .MainWindowTitle)
            Console.WriteLine("Max Working Set {0}", .MaxWorkingSet)
            Console.WriteLine("Min Working Set {0}", .MinWorkingSet)
            Console.WriteLine("Modules {0}", .Modules)
            Console.WriteLine("Nonpage System Memory Size {0}", _
                .NonpagedSystemMemorySize)
            Console.WriteLine("Paged Memory Size {0}", _
                .PagedMemorySize)
            Console.WriteLine("Paged System Memory Size {0}", _
                .PagedSystemMemorySize)
            Console.WriteLine("Peak Paged Memory Size {0}", _
                .PeakPagedMemorySize)
            Console.WriteLine("Peak Virtual Memory Size {0}", _
                .PeakVirtualMemorySize)
            Console.WriteLine("Peak Working Set {0}", _
                .PeakWorkingSet)
            Console.WriteLine("Priority Boost Enabled {0}", _
                .PriorityBoostEnabled)
            Console.WriteLine("Priority Class {0}", .PriorityClass)
            Console.WriteLine("Private Memory Size {0}", _
                .PrivateMemorySize)
            Console.WriteLine("Priviledged Processsor Time {0}", _
                .PrivilegedProcessorTime)
            Console.WriteLine("Name {0}", .ProcessName)
            Console.WriteLine("Processor Affinity {0}", _
                .ProcessorAffinity)
            Console.WriteLine("Start Time {0}", .StartTime)
            Console.WriteLine("Total Processor Time {0}", _
                .TotalProcessorTime)
            Console.WriteLine("User Processor Time {0}", _
                .UserProcessorTime)
            Console.WriteLine("Virtual Memory Size {0}", _
                .VirtualMemorySize)
            Console.WriteLine("Working Set {0}", .WorkingSet)
        End With

        Console.ReadLine() ' Delay to read output
    End Sub
End Module
```

After you compile and execute the ProcessInfo program, your screen will display output similar to the following. To end the program, press ENTER.

```
Base Priority 8
Handle count 265
Process ID (PID) 1700
Machine Name .
Main Module System.Diagnostics.ProcessModule (ProcessInfo.exe)
Main Window Title C:\Subdir\ProcessInfo\bin\ProcessInfo.exe
Max Working Set 1413120
Min Working Set 204800
Modules System.Diagnostics.ProcessModuleCollection
Nonpage System Memory Size 18372
Paged Memory Size 5472256
Paged System Memory Size 39420
Peak Paged Memory Size 6377472
Peak Virtual Memory Size 96440320
Peak Working Set 15794176
Priority Boost Enabled True
Priority Class Normal
Private Memory Size 5472256
Priviledged Processsor Time 00:00:00.1602304
Name ProcessInfo
Processor Affinity 1
Start Time 3/2/2002 1:50:44 PM
Total Processor Time 00:00:01.1115984
User Processor Time 00:00:00.9513680
Virtual Memory Size 86024192
Working Set 13746176
```

You might take time to compare your program's output to what the Windows Task Manager displays for the program, as shown in Figure 8-2.

Launching a Program Using the Process Class

As your programs execute, there may be times when one program must start another. To start a second application, your program can use the Process class Start method. The following program statement, for example, starts a program named Demo.exe that resides in the root directory of drive C:

```
Process.Start("C:\Demo.exe")
```

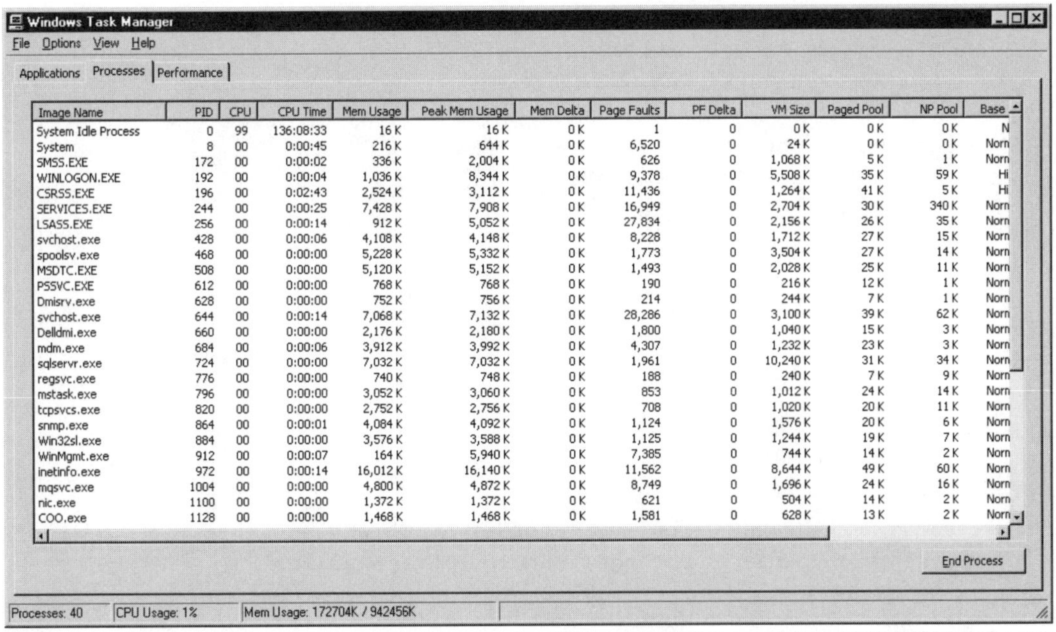

Figure 8-2   Using the Windows Task Manager to display process information

In addition to starting program files using the Start method, your code can also specify a document for which your system has a program association. The following statement, for example, would direct your system to start Microsoft Word and to load the document BookChapter.doc:

```
Process.Start("C:\Subdir\BookChapter.doc")
```

USE IT   The following program, LaunchProgram.vb, displays a form that contains two buttons. If the user selects the Launch a Program button, the program will display an Open dialog box similar to that shown in Figure 8-3, within which the user can specify the program (or document) he or she wants to open. After the user makes his or her selection, the program will run the corresponding program using the Process class Start method. If the user instead selects the End This Program button, the program will end.

```
Public Class Form1
    Inherits System.Windows.Forms.Form

#Region " Windows Form Designer generated code "
  ' Not shown
#End Region

    Private Sub Button1_Click(ByVal sender As Object, _
```

```
       ByVal e As System.EventArgs) Handles Button1.Click
         Dim OpenDB As New OpenFileDialog()
         Dim AppName As String

         If OpenDB.ShowDialog() = DialogResult.OK Then
             AppName = OpenDB.FileName
             If Not (AppName Is Nothing) Then
                Try
                    Process.Start(AppName)
                Catch
                    MsgBox("Error opening " & AppName)
                End Try
             End If
         End If
     End Sub

     Private Sub Button2_Click(ByVal sender As Object, _
       ByVal e As System.EventArgs) Handles Button2.Click
         Me.Close()
     End Sub
 End Class
```

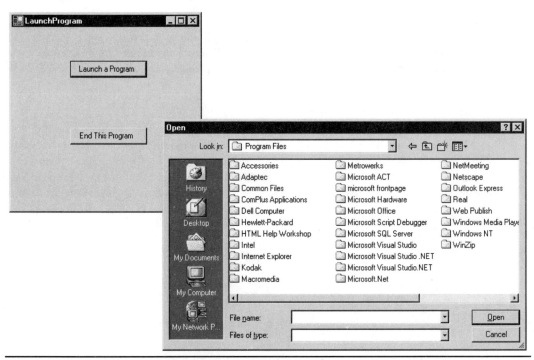

Figure 8-3   Using an Open dialog box to prompt the user for a program or document

After the program retrieves the filename from the dialog box, the program uses the Process class Start method to open the corresponding document or to run the specified program. The program calls the Start method in a Try-Catch block to detect and handle any exceptions that occur if the Start method cannot launch the specified file.

A common use of starting a second program is to open a window that contains online help or product information. The following program, CompanyInfo.vb, displays a form that contains buttons that correspond to different companies, as shown in Figure 8-4. When the user selects a button, the program launches Internet Explorer to display the company's Web site.

```
Public Class Form1
    Inherits System.Windows.Forms.Form

#Region " Windows Form Designer generated code "
  ' Not shown
#End Region

    Private Sub Button1_Click(ByVal sender As Object, _
      ByVal e As System.EventArgs) Handles Button1.Click
        Try
            Process.Start("IExplore.exe", "www.Microsoft.com")
        Catch
            MsgBox("Error launching Internet Explorer")
        End Try
    End Sub

    Private Sub Button2_Click(ByVal sender As Object, _
      ByVal e As System.EventArgs) Handles Button2.Click
        Try
            Process.Start("IExplore.exe", "www.Osborne.com")
        Catch
            MsgBox("Error launching Internet Explorer")
        End Try
    End Sub

    Private Sub Button3_Click(ByVal sender As Object, _
      ByVal e As System.EventArgs) Handles Button3.Click
        Try
            Process.Start("IExplore.exe", "www.yahoo.com")
        Catch
            MsgBox("Error launching Internet Explorer")
        End Try
    End Sub
End Class
```

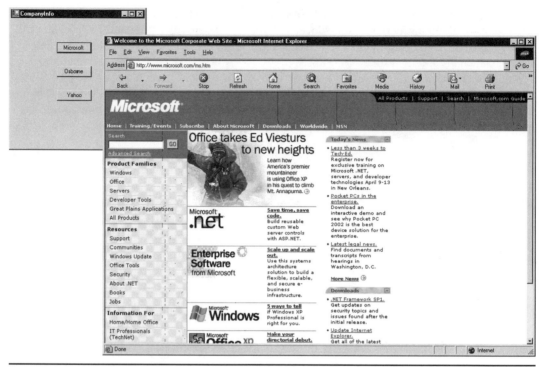

Figure 8-4   Using the Process class Start method to launch Internet Explorer

Terminating a Process

Just as there are times when your programs may launch a second application, there may also be times when your program must end a specific application. For example, assume that your application launches an application that displays online help information. If the user ends your application, you can direct the application to also end the program that is displaying the online help.

To end a second application, your code can call the Process class Kill method. Using the Kill method, you can end an application that corresponds to a Process object:

```
Process.GetCurrentProcessById(233).Kill()
Process.GetCurrentProcess.Kill()
```

You should use the Kill method as a "last effort" way to terminate a task. If, for example, you have a program that has stopped responding to user interactions, the program is a good candidate for termination using the Kill method.

USE IT   The following program, SpawnKill.vb, displays a form with two buttons, as shown in Figure 8-5. If the user clicks the Spawn button, the program launches another copy of itself. If the user clicks the Kill button, the program terminates (kills) itself.

```
Public Class Form1
    Inherits System.Windows.Forms.Form

#Region " Windows Form Designer generated code "
#End Region

    Private Sub Button1_Click(ByVal sender As Object, _
        ByVal e As System.EventArgs) Handles Button1.Click

        Process.Start(Process.GetCurrentProcess().MainModule.FileName)

    End Sub

    Private Sub Button2_Click(ByVal sender As Object, _
        ByVal e As System.EventArgs) Handles Button2.Click

        Process.GetCurrentProcess.Kill()

    End Sub
End Class
```

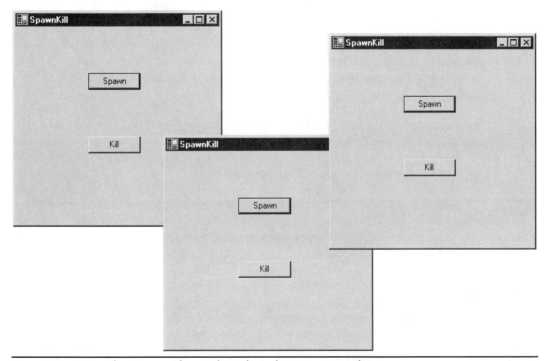

Figure 8-5   Using the Process class to launch and terminate applications

To launch a copy of itself, the program uses the Process class MainModule.Filename attribute that contains a path to the program's executable file. To end the current process, the program uses the Kill method.

Preventing Two Copies of the Same Program from Executing at the Same Time

Depending on the processing your program performs, there may be times when you will not want two (or more) copies of the program running at the same time. In such cases, your programs can use the Process class GetProcessesByName method to look for processes with the same name as your program. If another process with your program's unique name exists, another copy of the program is currently running:

```
TargetName = Process.GetCurrentProcess.ProcessName
MatchingNames = Process.GetProcessesByName(TargetName)
```

USE IT The following program, NoDuplicates.vb, performs the processing just described to ensure that only one copy of the program is running at any given time. If you try to run a second copy of the program, that program will display a message stating that the program is already running and then the program will end:

```
Module Module1
    Sub Main()
        Dim MatchingNames As Process()
        Dim TargetName As String

        TargetName = Process.GetCurrentProcess.ProcessName
        MatchingNames = Process.GetProcessesByName(TargetName)

        If (MatchingNames.Length = 1) Then
            Console.WriteLine("Started...")
            Console.ReadLine() ' Delay for input
        Else
            Console.WriteLine("Process already running")
        End If
    End Sub
End Module
```

To determine if a copy of the program is currently running, the code uses the Process class ProcessName field to determine the program's process name (which will be the same for each running copy of the program). Then the program uses the Process class GetProcessesByName method to locate processes with the specified name. If the GetProcessesByName method returns a collection that contains more than one entry, the program is already running.

Displaying Information About Each Process in Your System

Depending on the processing your program (or service) performs, there may be times when your code needs information about other processes that are running in the system. In such cases, your programs can call the Process class GetProcesses method, which returns a collection that contains the system's current processes:

```
Dim ProcessList As Process()
ProcessList = Process.GetProcesses()
```

USE IT The following program, ListProcesses.vb, uses the Process class GetProcesses method to retrieve the system's current processes. The program then loops through the collection displaying specifics about each process. To end the program, press ENTER.

```
Module Module1
    Sub Main()
        Dim ProcessList As Process()

        ProcessList = Process.GetProcesses()

        Dim Proc As Process

        For Each Proc In ProcessList
            Console.WriteLine("Name {0} ID {1}", _
                Proc.ProcessName, Proc.Id)
        Next

        Console.ReadLine() ' Delay to view output
    End Sub
End Module
```

After you compile and execute this program, your screen will display output similar to that shown here:

```
Name svchost ID 620
Name Dnar ID 1064
Name SpeedKey ID 1596
Name Delldmi ID 632
Name CSRSS ID 196
Name mqsvc ID 1016
Name WINLOGON ID 192
: : :
Name WinMgmt ID 912
```

```
Name ListProcesses ID 1712
Name explorer ID 752
Name NodeMngr ID 1072
Name Idle ID 0
```

Displaying Information About a Process's Threads

Just as there may be times when your programs (or services) need information about the processes running in your system, there may be times when your program needs information about its own threads. In such cases, your programs can call the Process class GetCurrentProcess method to determine the current process. Then your code can call the Process class Threads method, which returns a collection that contains the process's threads:

```
Dim List As ProcessThreadCollection
List = Process.GetCurrentProcess().Threads()
```

USE IT The following program, ListThreads.vb, creates three threads named A, B, and C that simply wait for the program's fourth thread, D, to complete its processing. In thread D, the code gathers and displays information about the process's current threads:

```
Imports System.Threading

Module Module1
    Public A As Thread
    Public B As Thread
    Public C As Thread
    Public D As Thread

    Sub Display()
        D.Join()
    End Sub

    Sub ThreadInfo()
        Dim List As ProcessThreadCollection
        List = Process.GetCurrentProcess().Threads()

        Dim objThread As ProcessThread

        For Each objThread In List
            Console.Write("Thread: {0:D5}", objThread.Id)
            Console.Write(" Start: {0}", objThread.StartTime)
            Console.WriteLine(" CPU Time: {0}", objThread.TotalProcessorTime)
            Console.Write(" State: {0}", objThread.ThreadState)
            If (objThread.ThreadState = System.Diagnostics.ThreadState.Wait) Then
                Console.Write("Reason: {0}", objThread.WaitReason())
```

```
            End If
            Console.WriteLine(" Address: {0}", objThread.StartAddress())
            Console.WriteLine()
        Next
    End Sub

    Sub Main()
        A = New Thread(AddressOf Display)
        B = New Thread(AddressOf Display)
        C = New Thread(AddressOf Display)
        D = New Thread(AddressOf ThreadInfo)

        A.Name = "A"
        B.Name = "B"
        C.Name = "C"
        D.Name = "D"

        A.Start()
        B.Start()
        C.Start()
        D.Start()

        Console.ReadLine()    ' Delay to view output
    End Sub
End Module
```

After you compile and execute this program, your screen will display output similar to the following. To end the program, press ENTER.

```
Thread: 01840 Start: 3/3/2002 7:53:52 AM CPU Time: 00:00:00.0500720
 State: WaitReason: LpcReply Address: 2011790534

Thread: 01852 Start: 3/3/2002 7:53:52 AM CPU Time: 00:00:00
 State: WaitReason: UserRequest Address: 2011723058

Thread: 00424 Start: 3/3/2002 7:53:52 AM CPU Time: 00:00:00
 State: WaitReason: UserRequest Address: 2011723058

Thread: 01728 Start: 3/3/2002 7:53:52 AM CPU Time: 00:00:00
 State: WaitReason: UserRequest Address: 2011723058

Thread: 01664 Start: 3/3/2002 7:53:52 AM CPU Time: 00:00:00
 State: WaitReason: UserRequest Address: 2011723058

Thread: 00972 Start: 3/3/2002 7:53:52 AM CPU Time: 00:00:00
 State: WaitReason: UserRequest Address: 2011723058
```

```
Thread: 01936 Start: 3/3/2002 7:53:52 AM CPU Time: 00:00:00.3204608
 State: Running Address: 2011723058

Thread: 01876 Start: 3/3/2002 7:53:52 AM CPU Time: 00:00:00
 State: WaitReason: EventPairLow Address: 2011723058

Thread: 01792 Start: 3/3/2002 7:53:52 AM CPU Time: 00:00:00
 State: WaitReason: UserRequest Address: 2011723058

Thread: 01776 Start: 3/3/2002 7:53:52 AM CPU Time: 00:00:00
 State: Ready Address: 2011723058
```

As you can see, when you run a Visual Basic .NET program, many threads actually run behind the scenes. If your program has debugging enabled, some of the threads will belong to the debugger. If your process uses multiple threads, some of the threads will correspond to thread management software. The following program, ThreadCount.vb, is a single-statement program that simply displays the number of threads in the process:

```
Module Module1
    Sub Main()
        Console.WriteLine("Thread Count: {0}", _
            Process.GetCurrentProcess().Threads.Count)
        Console.ReadLine()   ' Delay to view output
    End Sub
End Module
```

After you compile and execute this program, your screen will display the following output. To end the program, press ENTER.

```
Thread Count: 6
```

CHAPTER 9

Taking Advantage of Structured Error Handling

TIPS IN THIS CHAPTER

For years, programmers have made extensive use of runtime library functions to perform specific processing, such as opening a file, performing arithmetic operations such as calculating the sine of an angle, and determining the system date and time. Normally, to use the runtime library services, a program calls a specific function. If the function successfully performs the operation, the function would return a corresponding result. If, instead, an error occurred, a function would return an error status value. By examining the function's return value, a program could determine whether the function successfully performed the operation, as shown here:

```
Result = SomeFunction(parameters)

If (Result < 0) Then
  ' Handle an error
Else
  ' Function was successful
End If
```

Unfortunately, because of time constraints (or simply because of sloppy programming practices), many programs failed to test for error status values, instead assuming the function was successful and simply using the result. When errors later occurred, programmers had to add the code they (or another programmer) previously omitted to test the function's return value for an error status.

Depending on the error that occurred there were times when a function could not provide sufficient information using only a single error status value. For example, if a function could not open a file, the function might return the value 0, indicating that an error occurred. By testing for the value 0, a program could determine whether the function successfully opened the file. However, when an error occurred, the program did not know the cause of the error (which may have been that the file was not found, the directory path was invalid, or the file was locked). To provide additional error status information, many runtime library functions provided support for a special error status parameter. If the function's result indicated that an error occurred, the program could examine the error-status parameter to learn more about the cause of the error:

```
Result = SomeFunction(parameters, ErrorInfo)

If (Result < 0) Then
  ' Handle an error
  If (ErrorInfo = 1) Then
    MsgBox("File was not found")
  Else If (ErrorInfo = 2) Then
    MsgBox("Invalid directory path")
  Else If (ErrorInfo = 3) Then
    MsgBox("File currently locked"
  End IF
Else
```

```
' Function was successful
End If
```

For years, Visual Basic program and VBScript-based Active Server Pages have made extensive use of the ON ERROR statement to respond to errors. Using the ON ERROR statement, the program could specify how it wanted to respond when an operation generated an error. The program, for example, might branch to a specific subroutine, or it might simply continue its processing. To determine more information about an error, the programs examined the value contained in Err object's Number member:

```
On Error Resume Next
Dim FileNumber As Integer

FileNumber = FreeFil

Open "Data.dat" For Binary As #F
If Err.Number <> 0 Then
  MsgBox "An error happened here!" & vbCrLf & _
"Error number: " & Err.Number & vbCrLf & _
"Error Description" & Err.Description & vbCrLf)
  Err.Clear ' destroy the error and clean error settings
End If
End Function
```

Although Visual Basic .NET supports the On Error statement and Err object, it also supports structured error handling that is based on exceptions. In general, an exception is an error raised by your program (or an object) to indicate that an error occurred during an operation. In the .NET environment, the hundreds of different class types can generate thousands of different types of exceptions. Fortunately, most exceptions correspond to specific operations. When your code uses an object to perform a specific task, you must determine the possible exceptions that can occur as a result of the operation and then test for each exception's occurrence, much like program code should test a runtime library function's result in the past.

If your program does not detect and respond to an exception, it will end abruptly (the program will crash). To better understand how exceptions occur, create the following program, DivisionDemo.vb, which uses input boxes to prompt the user for two numbers that the code will use in a division operation. The code will first prompt the user to enter the numerator (often the larger number into which you are dividing another number). Then the code will prompt the user to enter the denominator:

```
Public Class Form1
    Inherits System.Windows.Forms.Form

#Region " Windows Form Designer generated code "
  ' Code not shown
#End Region
```

```
Private Sub Button1_Click(ByVal sender As Object, _
    ByVal e As System.EventArgs) Handles Button1.Click

    If (TextBox1.Text.Length = 0) Then
        MsgBox("Must specify numerator")
    ElseIf (TextBox2.Text.Length = 0) Then
        MsgBox("Must specify denominator")
    Else
        Dim A, B As Integer
        Dim C As Integer

        A = TextBox1.Text
        B = TextBox2.Text
        C = A Mod B
        TextBox3.Text = C
    End If
End Sub
End Class
```

Compile and run the program. When the program prompts you for a dividend, enter a number such as 100. Then, when the program prompts you for a divisor, enter the number 24. The program, in this case, will display the result 4 in a message box. Then run the program and enter the values 100 and 0. Because a number divided by zero is not defined, the program will crash due to a division-by-zero error. Your screen will display an error message similar to that shown in Figure 9-1.

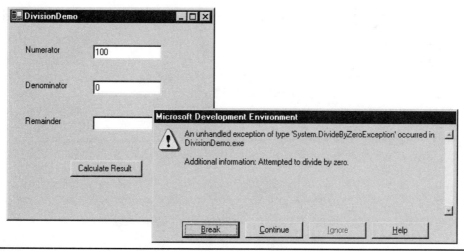

Figure 9-1   An error message that occurs due to a division-by-zero error

Next, create the following program, ShowTextFile.vb, that prompts you to enter the name of a text file, the contents of which the program will display in a text box:

```vb
Imports System.IO

Public Class Form1
    Inherits System.Windows.Forms.Form

#Region " Windows Form Designer generated code "
    ' Code not shown
#End Region

    Private Sub Button1_Click(ByVal sender As Object, _
      ByVal e As System.EventArgs) Handles Button1.Click

        Dim FileDB As New OpenFileDialog()

        FileDB.Filter = "All files | *.*| Text files | *.txt"
        FileDB.FilterIndex = 2
        FileDB.InitialDirectory = "C:\Temp"
        FileDB.AddExtension = True
        FileDB.DefaultExt = "txt"

        ' Prevent dialog box from validating file
        FileDB.CheckFileExists = False

        If (FileDB.ShowDialog() = DialogResult.OK) Then
            Dim SourceFile As StreamReader

            SourceFile = New StreamReader(FileDB.FileName)
            TextBox1.Text = SourceFile.ReadToEnd()
            SourceFile.Close()
        Else
            MsgBox("User selected Cancel")
        End If
    End Sub
End Class
```

Run the program and type in a text filename, such as the program's filename, ShowTextFile.vb. Then run the program a second time and enter the name of a file that does not exist, such as BadFilename.txt. When the program tries to open the nonexistent file, the program will generate a file not found exception that causes the program to crash. As before, the program will display an error message on the screen, as shown in Figure 9-2.

Finally, as you know, a variable's type specifies a range of values the variable can store and a set of operations the program can perform on the variable. When a program assigns a value to a

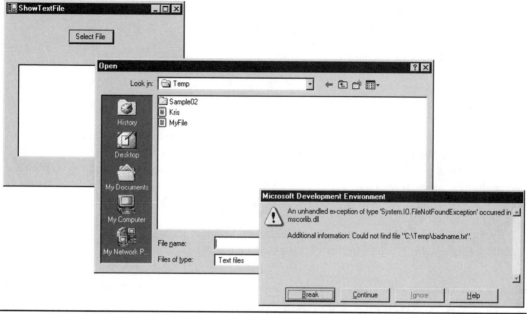

Figure 9-2   An error message that occurs due to a FileNotFound exception

variable that falls outside of the range of values the variable can store, the program will generate the OverflowException. To better understand this process, create the following program, OverflowException.vb, which prompts the user to enter two values. The program then adds the values and assigns the result to a variable of type integer which the program then displays in a message box:

```
Public Class Form1
    Inherits System.Windows.Forms.Form

#Region " Windows Form Designer generated code "
    ' Code not shown
#End Region

    Private Sub Button1_Click(ByVal sender As Object, _
      ByVal e As System.EventArgs) Handles Button1.Click

        If (TextBox1.Text.Length = 0) Then
            MsgBox("Must specify first value")
        ElseIf (TextBox2.Text.Length = 0) Then
            MsgBox("Must specify second value")
        Else
            Dim A, B As Integer
            Dim C As Integer
```

```
            A = TextBox1.Text
            B = TextBox2.Text
            C = A + B
            TextBox3.Text = C
        End If
    End Sub
End Class
```

Compile and run the program. When the program prompts you for the two numbers, enter the values 1000 and 5000. The program will display the value 6000. Then run the program again and enter two very large numbers (do not enter the commas), such as 2,000,000,000 and 1,000,000,000. When the program adds the numbers, the result 3,000,000,000 falls outside of the range of values a variable of type integer can store. As a result, the program generates an overflow exception and ends, displaying an error message as shown in Figure 9-3.

Throughout the Tips that follow, you will learn how to detect and respond to exceptions in ways that let your programs continue to run when an exception occurs.

Catching a Specific Exception

Exceptions exist to let your programs handle errors in a consistent way. When a program checks for and responds to an exception, programmers say that the program "catches" or "handles" the exception.

 To catch an exception, programs use a Try-Catch statement. In general, when the program is going to perform an operation that can generate an exception, the code groups the

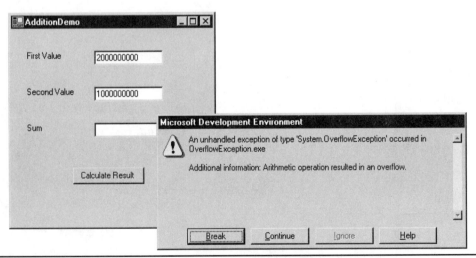

Figure 9-3   An error message that occurs due to an arithmetic overflow exception

operation's statements between the Try and End Try statements. Following the operation, the code uses Catch statements to detect specific exceptions:

```
Try
   C = A + B
Catch Ex As OverflowException
```

The Catch part of the Try-Catch statement lets the program detect and respond to a specific exception. For example, the following program, CatchDivideByZero.vb, changes the Button1_Click subroutine's processing to use a Try-Catch statement to detect and respond to a divide-by-zero exception:

```
Private Sub Button1_Click(ByVal sender As Object, _
    ByVal e As System.EventArgs) Handles Button1.Click

    If (TextBox1.Text.Length = 0) Then
        MsgBox("Must specify numerator")
    ElseIf (TextBox2.Text.Length = 0) Then
        MsgBox("Must specify denominator")
    Else
        Dim A, B As Integer
        Dim C As Integer

        A = TextBox1.Text
        B = TextBox2.Text

        Try
            C = A Mod B
            TextBox3.Text = C
        Catch Ex As DivideByZeroException
            MsgBox("Divide by Zero Exception")
            TextBox3.Text = "Infinity"
        End Try
    End If
End Sub
```

In a similar way, the following program, CatchOverflow.vb, uses a Try-Catch statement to detect and respond to an overflow exception:

```
Private Sub Button1_Click(ByVal sender As Object, _
    ByVal e As System.EventArgs) Handles Button1.Click

    If (TextBox1.Text.Length = 0) Then
        MsgBox("Must specify first value")
    ElseIf (TextBox2.Text.Length = 0) Then
        MsgBox("Must specify second value")
```

```
    Else
        Dim A, B As Integer
        Dim C As Integer

        Try
            A = TextBox1.Text
            B = TextBox2.Text
            C = A + B
            TextBox3.Text = C
        Catch Except As OverflowException
            MsgBox("Overflow error detected")
            TextBox3.Text = "Error"
        End Try
    End If
End Sub
```

In this case, the code places the Try-Catch block around the statements that assign the values to the variables A and B and the statement that assigns the sum of the two variables to C. The program places the statements that assign the values to A and B within the Try-Catch block to detect overflow errors that may occur if the user types in a very large number, such as 4,000,000,000 (do not enter the commas), which the program then tries to assign to one of the variables.

Finally, the following program, CatchBadFile.vb, uses a Try-Catch statement to detect and respond to an invalid filename:

```
Private Sub Button1_Click(ByVal sender As Object,
    ByVal e As System.EventArgs) Handles Button1.Click

    Dim FileDB As New OpenFileDialog()
    FileDB.Filter = "All files | *.*| Text files | *.txt"
    FileDB.FilterIndex = 2
    FileDB.InitialDirectory = "C:\Temp"
    FileDB.AddExtension = True
    FileDB.DefaultExt = "txt"

    ' Prevent dialog box from validating file
    FileDB.CheckFileExists = False

    If (FileDB.ShowDialog() = DialogResult.OK) Then
        Dim SourceFile As StreamReader
        Try
            SourceFile = New StreamReader(FileDB.FileName)

            TextBox1.Text = SourceFile.ReadToEnd()

            SourceFile.Close()
```

```
        Catch Except As FileNotFoundException
            MsgBox("File not found")
        End Try
    Else
        MsgBox("User selected Cancel")
    End If
End Sub
```

Testing for Different Exceptions

When an object performs an operation on a program's behalf, it is possible that the object may encounter a wide range of errors. Normally, the object's class definition will define unique exceptions for each error. In the object's documentation, you can normally determine which exceptions the object might generate for each operation the object performs. Then, in your program, you should use a Try-Catch statement to test for the corresponding exceptions.

For example, when your program tries to open a file, the operation can encounter a variety of errors. First, the file may simply not exist, in which case the object will generate the FileNotFoundException exception. Second, the folder specified in the file's directory path may not exist. In this case, the program will generate the DirectoryNotFoundException exception.

When an operation can result in several different exceptions, your code can specify a series of Catch statements, much like you might use a series of If-Else statements or multiple cases within a Select statement. The following program, CaptureFileExceptions.vb, uses the FileOpenDialog class to display the Open dialog box that prompts the user for a text file the user wants to display. The code then tries to open the files within a Try-Catch block that detects a variety of different exceptions:

```
Imports System.IO

Public Class Form1
    Inherits System.Windows.Forms.Form

#Region " Windows Form Designer generated code "
    ' Code not shown
#End Region

    Private Sub Button1_Click(ByVal sender As Object, _
      ByVal e As System.EventArgs) Handles Button1.Click
        Dim FileDB As New OpenFileDialog()

        FileDB.Filter = "All files | *.*| Text files | *.txt"
        FileDB.FilterIndex = 2
        FileDB.InitialDirectory = "C:\Temp"
        FileDB.AddExtension = True
        FileDB.DefaultExt = "txt"
```

```
    ' Prevent dialog box from validating file and path
    FileDB.CheckFileExists = False
    FileDB.CheckPathExists = False

    If (FileDB.ShowDialog() = DialogResult.OK) Then
        Dim SourceFile As StreamReader

        Try
            SourceFile = New StreamReader(FileDB.FileName)
            TextBox1.Text = SourceFile.ReadToEnd()
            SourceFile.Close()
        Catch Except As DirectoryNotFoundException
            MsgBox("Error: " & Except.Message)
        Catch Except As FileNotFoundException
            MsgBox("Error: " & Except.Message)
        Catch Except As Exception
            MsgBox("Error: " & Except.Message)
        End Try
    Else
        MsgBox("User selected Cancel")
    End If
  End Sub
End Class
```

Compile and run this program and type in the name of a file that does not exist. The program should detect and respond to the FileNotFoundException exception. Then run the program and type in a pathname to the file that includes a directory that does not exist. Again, the program should detect and respond to the DirectoryNotFoundException exception.

Handling Exceptions Using a Generic Catch Statement

When an object performs an operation on a program's behalf, the object may generate a range of exceptions. Depending on the processing your program performs, there may be times when you do not care which specific exception occurred, but rather, that an exception occurred. For example, when your program cannot open a file, you may not care if the cause of the problem is that the directory was invalid or the file was locked, but rather, that the program simply could not open the file.

USE IT To handle exceptions without regard for the exception's type, your code can use a Try-Catch statement that does not specify a specific exception, as shown here:

```
Catch Ex As Exception
```

The following program, FileError.vb, again displays an Open dialog box that prompts the user to select the file that he or she wants to open. The code then opens the file within a "generic" Try-Catch statement that tests only for an exception (not a specific exception):

```
Imports System.IO

Public Class Form1
    Inherits System.Windows.Forms.Form

#Region " Windows Form Designer generated code "
  ' Code not shown
#End Region

    Private Sub Button1_Click(ByVal sender As Object, _
      ByVal e As System.EventArgs) Handles Button1.Click

        Dim FileDB As New OpenFileDialog()

        FileDB.Filter = "All files | *.*| Text files | *.txt"
        FileDB.FilterIndex = 2
        FileDB.InitialDirectory = "C:\Temp"
        FileDB.AddExtension = True
        FileDB.DefaultExt = "txt"

        ' Prevent dialog box from validating file and path
        FileDB.CheckFileExists = False
        FileDB.CheckPathExists = False

        If (FileDB.ShowDialog() = DialogResult.OK) Then
            Dim SourceFile As StreamReader

            Try
                SourceFile = New StreamReader(FileDB.FileName)
                TextBox1.Text = SourceFile.ReadToEnd()
                SourceFile.Close()
            Catch Except As Exception
                MsgBox("Error: " & Except.Message)
            End Try
        Else
            MsgBox("User selected Cancel")
        End If
    End Sub
End Class
```

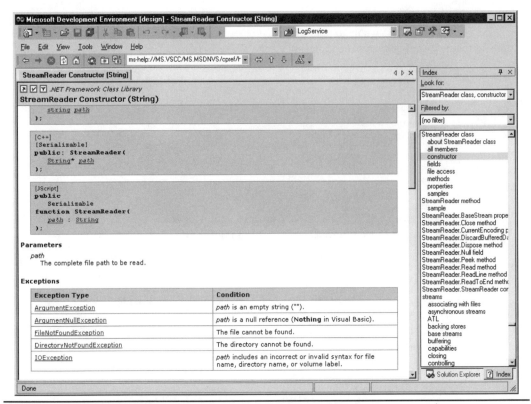

Figure 9-4   Viewing information about exceptions generated by the StreamReader constructor

Using a series of Try-Catch statements similar to those shown here, programs often handle one or two exceptions using specific exception names and all other exceptions less specifically. Compile and run the program. Again, try specifying the name of a file that does not exist as well as a pathname that contains an invalid directory. For each error type, the program will simply generate an error that states the program could not open the file.

When your programs use an object to perform specific task, you must determine the possible exceptions the object can generate so your code can test for and respond to each exception. If you examine a class description in the Visual Studio online help, you will find discussion of the exceptions various class methods generate. Figure 9-4 shows the online help for the StreamReader constructor method.

Performing "Cleanup" Processing After an Exception Occurs

When your programs use Try-Catch statements to respond to a series of exceptions, you will normally perform operations specific to each exception within the corresponding Catch statement.

Depending on the processing your program performs, there may be times when your code must perform specific processing any time an exception occurs, regardless of the exception type. For such times, you can place a Finally clause at the end of your Try-Catch statements that specifies the statements you want your program to perform for each and every exception:

```
Try
    SourceFile = New StreamReader(FileDB.FileName)
Catch Except As DirectoryNotFoundException
   MsgBox("Error: " & Except.Message)
Catch Except As FileNotFoundException
   MsgBox("Error: " & Except.Message)
Catch Except As Exception
   MsgBox("Error: " & Except.Message)
Finally
   ' Perform clean up processing here
   ' regardless of which exception was
   ' generated and even if no exception
   ' was generated
End Try
```

▶ *NOTE*

Within a Try-Catch statement, the Finally clause will execute even if no exception occurs.

Depending on the type of exception that occurs or your program's state of execution when the exception occurs, your program may need to perform what programmer's refer to as "cleanup" operations following an exception. By performing the operations within the Finally clause, you eliminate your program's need to duplicate the statements within each clause.

USE IT   The following program, FinallyClause.vb, displays an Open dialog box the user can use to select a text file. The code then opens the file within a Try-Catch block. If an error occurs during the file open operation, the code displays a message box that describes the error. Otherwise, the program reads the file's contents (again within a Try-Catch block). In the second Try-Catch block, the code uses a Finally clause in which it closes the file (regardless of whether an exception occurred during the read operation):

```
Imports System.IO

Public Class Form1
    Inherits System.Windows.Forms.Form

#Region " Windows Form Designer generated code "
   ' Code not shown
#End Region
```

```
Private Sub Button1_Click(ByVal sender As Object, _
    ByVal e As System.EventArgs) Handles Button1.Click

    Dim FileDB As New OpenFileDialog()
    FileDB.Filter = "All files | *.*| Text files | *.txt"
    FileDB.FilterIndex = 2
    FileDB.InitialDirectory = "C:\Temp"
    FileDB.AddExtension = True
    FileDB.DefaultExt = "txt"

    ' Prevent dialog box from validating file and path
    FileDB.CheckFileExists = False
    FileDB.CheckPathExists = False

    If (FileDB.ShowDialog() = DialogResult.OK) Then
        Dim SourceFile As StreamReader

        Try
            SourceFile = New StreamReader(FileDB.FileName)
        Catch Except As Exception
            MsgBox("Error: " & Except.Message)
        End Try

        If (Not SourceFile Is Nothing) Then
            Try
                TextBox1.Text = SourceFile.ReadToEnd()
            Catch Except As Exception
                MsgBox("Error: " & Except.Message)
            Finally
                MsgBox("In finally statements")
                SourceFile.Close()
            End Try
        End If
    Else
        MsgBox("User selected Cancel")
    End If
End Sub
End Class
```

Note that before the program reads the file's contents, the code examines the value of the SourceFile object to determine if the file was successfully opened. If the file open operation was successful, the SourceFile object will contain stream information. Otherwise, if an error occurred during the open, the SourceFile object will contain the value Nothing. By closing the file in the Finally clause, the program ensures that it closes the file should an exception occur during the read operation.

When your code uses a Finally clause, there may be times when you do not want your program to execute the Finally clause for a specific exception. In such cases, your code can exit using the Exit Try statement, which directs the program to continue its processing at the first statement that follows the End Try statement:

```
Try
   Catch Except As FileNotException
      MsgBox("Error: " & Except.Message)
      Exit Try

   Catch Except As DirectoryNotException
      MsgBox("Error: " & Except.Message)

   Finally
      MsgBox("In finally statements")
End Try
```

Taking a Closer Look at the System.Exception Class

When your programs catch specific exceptions, your code actually creates a variable that corresponds to the specific exception type. The following statement, for example, creates a variable named DivZero that corresponds to the DivideByZeroException error:

```
Catch DivZero As DivideByZeroException
```

In Visual Basic .NET, every exception type is derived from the System.Exception class. Like all classes, the System.Exception class has fields your programs can use. Table 9-1 briefly describes the System.Exception class properties.

Property	Purpose
HelpLink	Gets or sets a link to the exception's help file. An application that catches the exception can use the link to provide the user with online help to respond to the exception.
InnerException	Gets the Exception instance that caused the current exception. When an exception occurs as the result of the code processing another exception, the second exception will contain a reference to the previous (the inner) exception.
Message	Gets a string message that describes the current exception.
Source	Gets or sets the name of the object or application that generated the exception.
StackTrace	Gets a string containing the call stack at the time the exception occurred.
TargetSite	Gets a MethodBase object that corresponds to the method that generated the exception.

Table 9-1   The Exception Class Properties

Like all .NET objects, Exception objects have a ToString method that returns a character-string representation of the object's value. When you are debugging your programs, you may find it useful to display an exception's specifics by showing the ToString method's results in a message box:

```
Catch DivZero As DivideByZeroException
  MsgBox(DivZero.ToString())
End Try
```

USE IT   The following program, ShowException.vb, catches a divide-by-zero exception and then displays specifics about the Exception in a message box. When the program begins, it displays a form as shown in Figure 9-5. If you click the Show Exception.Message button, the program will display the contents of the Exception class Message property. If you instead click the Show Exception.ToString button, the program will display the result of the ToString method:

```
Public Class Form1
    Inherits System.Windows.Forms.Form

#Region " Windows Form Designer generated code "
    ' Code not shown
#End Region

    Private Sub Button1_Click(ByVal sender As System.Object, _
       ByVal e As System.EventArgs) Handles Button1.Click

        Dim A, B, C As Integer

        A = 3
        B = 0

        Try
            C = A Mod B
        Catch Except As Exception
            MsgBox(Except.Message())
        End Try
    End Sub

    Private Sub Button2_Click(ByVal sender As System.Object, _
       ByVal e As System.EventArgs) Handles Button2.Click

        Dim A, B, C As Integer

        A = 3
        B = 0

        Try
```

```
            C = A Mod B
        Catch Except As Exception
            MsgBox(Except.ToString())
        End Try
    End Sub
End Class
```

 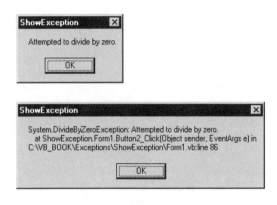

Figure 9-5   Using the Exception class ToString method to display specifics about an exception

Creating Your Own Custom Exceptions

Just as most Common Language Runtime classes make use of exceptions to support structured error handling, there may be times when the classes you create use their own exceptions. For example, a class that prompts the user for contact information might raise exceptions such as InvalidEMailException or InvalidZipCodeException. Using Try-Catch statements, programs that use your class can detect and respond to such exceptions.

 To create your own exception, you simply create a class that inherits the Exception class. For example, the following statements create an exception named InvalidEmailException:

```
Public Class InvalidEmailException
    Inherits System.Exception

    Sub New(ByVal Message As String)
        MyBase.New(Message)
    End Sub
End Class
```

Within the class, you can create methods and properties, as you require. In this case, the class simply calls the base-class (the Exception class) constructor to initialize the Message member. The following program, CustomException.vb creates a simple exception named MyException. The program then uses the Throw statement to generate the exception:

```
Public Class MyException
    Inherits System.Exception

    Sub New(ByVal Message As String)
        MyBase.New(Message)
    End Sub
End Class


Public Class Form1
    Inherits System.Windows.Forms.Form

#Region " Windows Form Designer generated code "
  ' Code not shown
#End Region

    Private Sub Button1_Click(ByVal sender As Object, _
      ByVal e As System.EventArgs) Handles Button1.Click

        Try
            MsgBox("About to generate custom exception")
            Throw (New MyException("** Custom Message **"))
        Catch Ex As MyException
            MsgBox("Custom Exception thrown " & Ex.Message)
        End Try
    End Sub
End Class
```

When your own classes use custom exceptions, the code within your class will use the Throw statement to generate the exception when an error occurs.

Testing Your Exception Handling by Throwing an Exception

When most .NET objects encounter an error, the object will generate an exception. Programmers refer to the process of generating an exception as "throwing" the exception. As you have learned, applications later detect and respond to the error by "catching" the exception.

When you implement exception handlers in your code, you can test your handler code by "throwing" the corresponding exceptions using the Throw statement. For example, the following code directs the program to test for a divide-by-zero exception thrown by the DoMod function:

```
Function DoMod(ByVal A As Integer, _
   ByVal B As Integer) As Integer

     Try
         DoMod = A Mod B

     Catch Except As Exception
        MsgBox(Except.Message)
        DoMod = 0
     End Try
End Function
```

USE IT   To test your exception handler, you can place a Throw statement in the DoMod function that directs the program to simulate the exception:

```
Try
     DoMod = A Mod B

     Throw New DivideByZeroException()

     Catch Except As Exception
        MsgBox(Except.Message)
        DoMod = 0
     End Try
```

The following program, ThrowException.vb, illustrates the use of the Throw statements to test for exceptions. The program uses a Try-Catch statement to monitor the processing of the AddNumbers and DoMod functions. In each function, the code uses a Throw statement to generate a specific exception:

```
Public Class Form1
     Inherits System.Windows.Forms.Form

#Region " Windows Form Designer generated code "
   ' Code not shown
#End Region

     Function AddNumbers(ByVal A As Integer, _
        ByVal B As Integer) As Integer

        Try
            AddNumbers = A + B

            Throw New ArithmeticException()

        Catch Except As Exception
```

```
            MsgBox(Except.Message)
            AddNumbers = 0
        End Try
End Function

Function DoMod(ByVal A As Integer, _
    ByVal B As Integer) As Integer

        Try
            DoMod = A Mod B

            Throw New DivideByZeroException()

        Catch Except As Exception
            MsgBox(Except.Message)
            DoMod = 0
        End Try
End Function

Private Sub Button1_Click(ByVal sender As System.Object, _
    ByVal e As System.EventArgs) Handles Button1.Click

        Dim A, B, C As Integer

        TextBox3.Text = ""

        If (TextBox1.Text.Length = 0) Then
            MsgBox("Must specify first value")
        ElseIf (TextBox2.Text.Length = 0) Then
            MsgBox("Must specify second value")
        Else
            Try
                TextBox3.Text = AddNumbers(TextBox1.Text, _
                    TextBox2.Text)
            Catch Except As Exception
                MsgBox("Call generated error: " & Except.Message)
            End Try
        End If
End Sub

Private Sub Button2_Click(ByVal sender As System.Object, _
    ByVal e As System.EventArgs) Handles Button2.Click

        TextBox3.Text = ""
```

```
        If (TextBox1.Text.Length = 0) Then
            MsgBox("Must specify first value")
        ElseIf (TextBox2.Text.Length = 0) Then
            MsgBox("Must specify second value")
        Else
            Try
                TextBox3.Text = DoMod(TextBox1.Text, TextBox2.Text)
            Catch Except As Exception
                MsgBox("Call generated error: " & Except.Message)
            End Try
        End If
    End Sub
End Class
```

After you compile and execute this program, your screen will display a form in which you can enter numbers you want to manipulate. When you click Add Numbers, the program will call the AddNumbers function. Likewise, if you click Calculate Remainder, the code will call the DoMod function. In this case, however, rather than completing the arithmetic operations, the functions use the Throw statements to test the exception handlers.

If your handler tests for multiple exceptions, you can simply edit the Throw statement to test each exception, one at a time. After you know your handler's processing is correct, you can remove the Throw statement from your function.

Chasing Down the Code Location that Caused an Exception

As your programs become more complex, there may be times when it becomes difficult to determine the specific code that caused the exception to occur. For example, one subroutine may call another that calls a function, which, in turn, calls a Common Language Runtime routine within which the exception occurs.

USE IT To determine the source of an exception, your program can use the System.Exception class Source, TargetSite, and StackTrace fields. The Source field contains the name of the object that generated the exception. The following program, ShowExceptionFields.vb, tries to open a nonexistent file. When the program catches the exception, the code uses the Source property to display the name of the object that caused the error. Likewise, the program uses the TargetSite field to determine the name of the method that caused the exception. Finally, the code uses the StackTrace field to display the call stack at the time the exception occurred:

```
Imports System.IO

Public Class Form1
```

```
    Inherits System.Windows.Forms.Form

#Region " Windows Form Designer generated code "
  ' Code not shown
#End Region

    Private Sub Button1_Click(ByVal sender As Object, _
      ByVal e As System.EventArgs) Handles Button1.Click

        Dim SourceFile As StreamReader

        Try
            SourceFile = New StreamReader("FilenameISBad.XXX")
        Catch Except As Exception
            MsgBox(Except.Message, MsgBoxStyle.Information, _
              "Message")
            MsgBox(Except.Source, MsgBoxStyle.Information, _
              "Source")
            MsgBox(Except.StackTrace, MsgBoxStyle.Information, _
              "StackTrace")
            MsgBox(Except.TargetSite.Name, MsgBoxStyle.Information, _
              "TargetSite")
        End Try
    End Sub
End Class
```

Within an Exception object, the StackTrace field maintains a list of the routines called prior to an exception. By examining the last function that appears in a stack trace, you can determine the location in your program where the exception occurred. The following program, ShowStackTrace.vb, calls a series of functions named First, Second, and Third. In the Third function, the code performs a division-by-zero operation. When the code catches the exception, the code displays the StackTrace field in a message box, as shown in Figure 9-6:

```
Public Class Form1
    Inherits System.Windows.Forms.Form

#Region " Windows Form Designer generated code "
    ' Code not shown
#End Region

    Private Function First() As Integer
        First = Second()
    End Function

    Private Function Second() As Integer
```

```
        Second = Third()
    End Function


    Private Function Third() As Integer
        Dim A As Integer = 0
        Third = 100 Mod A
    End Function


    Private Sub Button1_Click(ByVal sender As Object, _
      ByVal e As System.EventArgs) Handles Button1.Click

        Try
            Console.WriteLine("Result: ", First())
        Catch Except As Exception
            MsgBox(Except.StackTrace, MsgBoxStyle.Critical, _
                "StackTrace")
        End Try
    End Sub
End Class
```

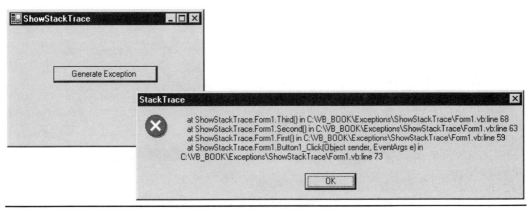

Figure 9-6   Displaying an exception's stack trace

Taking a Closer Look at the Debug Class

For years, programmers have made extensive use of "Debug-Write" statements throughout programs that display messages that contain intermediate status values the programmer can use to determine the source of an error. In a Visual Basic .NET program, a programmer might place Debug-Write statements throughout his or her programs that display messages to the console device. Or the programmer might write the debug messages to a text file using a StreamWriter object. Often, after a programmer believes that his or her program is working, the programmer will delete or "comment out" the debug statements.

Unfortunately, about the time the programmer removes each of the Debug-Write statements, the program encounters an error that requires additional debugging.

To help you debug program errors, Visual Basic .NET provides the Debug class, which contains methods you can use to write debug messages to a file. The advantage of using the Debug class to write messages (as opposed to writing console messages or performing StreamWriter operations) is that you can turn the messages on or off with one step. When you compile a release version of the program that disables the debugger, you will disable the Debug-Write statements (without having to comment out or delete the statements). Should you later need to use the Debug-Write messages, you simply need to compile the program with debugger support to re-enable the debug messages.

In Visual Studio, you use the Configuration Manager, shown in Figure 9-7, to control whether a program compiles with or without debugger support. To display the Configuration Manager, select Build | Configuration Manager.

When programmers use the Debug class to write status messages, the programmer can direct the Debug class to write the messages to a specific text file by binding a StreamWriter class to a Debug class Listener object:

```
Dim Str As New FileStream("C:\DebugMessages.txt", _
   System.IO.FileMode.Append)

Dim DebugFile As New StreamWriter(Str)

Dim Listener = New TextWriterTraceListener(DebugFile)
```

After the program assigns a StreamWriter object to a Listener object, the messages the Debug object writes will be stored in the text file:

```
Debug.WriteLine("About to enter processing loop")
```

Figure 9-7   Enabling or disabling debugger support in the Configuration Manager

The following program, FileDebugMessages.vb, displays the form shown in Figure 9-8, which you can use to generate and then view a series of debug messages. When you click Generate Messages, the code creates a StreamWriter object that corresponds to the file DebugMessages.txt. The code then assigns the stream to a Debug class listener. Then the code calls subroutines that write debug messages. If you click View Messages, the program opens the DebugMessages.txt file and reads the file's contents into the form's text box.

```vb
Imports System.IO

Public Class Form1
    Inherits System.Windows.Forms.Form

#Region " Windows Form Designer generated code "
    ' Code not shown
#End Region

    Private Sub First()
        Debug.WriteLine("In First")
        Debug.WriteLine("Calling Second")
        Second()
        Debug.WriteLine("Back in First")
    End Sub

    Private Sub Second()
        Debug.WriteLine("In Second")
    End Sub

    Private Sub Button1_Click(ByVal sender As Object, _
      ByVal e As System.EventArgs) Handles Button1.Click

        Dim Str As New FileStream("C:\DebugMessages.txt", _
            System.IO.FileMode.Append)

        Dim DebugFile As New StreamWriter(Str)

        Dim Listener = New TextWriterTraceListener(DebugFile)

        Debug.Listeners.Add(Listener)
        Debug.AutoFlush = True
        Debug.WriteLine("")
        Debug.WriteLine("Messages generated at " & Now())
        Debug.WriteLine("In Button Click")
        Debug.WriteLine("Calling First")
        First()
        Debug.WriteLine("Exiting Button Click")
```

```
        Debug.Listeners.Remove(Listener)
        Str.Close()
        TextBox1.Text = "Done"
    End Sub

    Private Sub Button2_Click(ByVal sender As Object, _
      ByVal e As System.EventArgs) Handles Button2.Click

        Dim SourceFile As StreamReader

        Try
            SourceFile = New StreamReader("C:\DebugMessages.txt")

            TextBox1.Text = SourceFile.ReadToEnd()

            If TextBox1.Text.Length = 0 Then
                TextBox1.Text = "No messages"
            End If

            SourceFile.Close()
        Catch Except As Exception
            MsgBox("Debug file does not yet exist")
        End Try
    End Sub
End Class
```

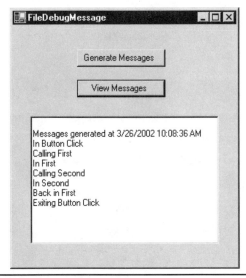

Figure 9-8   Generating and displaying debug messages

As discussed, the advantage of using the Debug class to write debug messages is that you can turn off the messages by compiling your program without debugger support. Using the Configuration Manager, compile the program without debugger support. Then run the program and click the Generate Messages button. Because the program has disabled debugging, the program will not write any new messages to the file.

To help you make better use of the Debug class, Table 9-2 briefly describes the class methods. Table 9-3 describes the class fields and properties.

Method	Purpose
Assert	Tests a specified condition displaying a message if the condition is false. The Assert method is an overloaded method.
Close	Flushes the output buffer and then closes the listeners.
Fail	Displays an error message that contains one or two strings. The Fail method is an overloaded method.
Flush	Flushes the output buffer to the listeners.
Indent	Increases the IndentLevel (that controls the spacing before Debug class output) by 1.
Unindent	Decreases the IndentLevel by 1.
Write	Writes a debug message to the trace listeners. The Write method is an overloaded method.
WriteIf	Evaluates a condition and, if the result is true, writes a debug message to the trace listeners. The WriteIf method is an overloaded method.
WriteLine	Writes a debug message to the trace listeners that contains a carriage-return and linefeed. The WriteLine method is an overloaded method.
WriteLineIf	Evaluates a condition and, if the result is true, writes a debug message to the trace listeners that contains a carriage-return and linefeed. The WriteLineIf method is an overloaded method.

Table 9-2   The Debug Class Methods

Property	Purpose
AutoFlush	Gets or sets a Boolean value that controls if the Flush method is automatically called after each Write operation.
IndentLevel	Gets or sets the indent level that controls the spacing that precedes the Debug class output.
IndentSize	Gets or sets the number of spaces the Debug class displays for each IndentLevel.
Listeners	Gets the collection that contains the listeners monitoring the Debug class output.

Table 9-3   The Debug Class Properties

Determining If the Debugger Is Active

In the previous Tip, you learned how to use the Debug class to write debug messages that you can enable or disable by compiling your program with or without debugger support. Depending on the processing your program performs, there may be times when your code must know whether or not the debugger is active. For example, the following statements use the Debug.WriteLine method to write debug messages to a file:

```
Dim Str As New FileStream("C:\DebugMessages.txt", _
   System.IO.FileMode.Append)

Dim DebugFile As New StreamWriter(Str)

Dim Listener = New TextWriterTraceListener(DebugFile)

Debug.Listeners.Add(Listener)
Debug.AutoFlush = True
Debug.WriteLine("Messages generated at " & Now())
Debug.WriteLine("In Button Click")
```

By compiling your program without debugger support, you can disable the Debug.WriteLine statements. However, in the previous statements, the code would still open the file DebugMessages.txt, regardless of whether the program is running with debugger support. A better solution would be for the program only to perform the statements when the debugger is active.

USE IT   To determine if the Debugger is running, your programs can use the Debugger class IsAttached property:

```
If (Debugger.IsAttached) Then
   MsgBox("Debugging")
Else
   MsgBox("Not debugging")
End If
```

The following program, TestDebugStatus.vb, changes the Button1_Click subroutine to use the Debugger class IsAttached property to determine if the debugger is active. If the debugger is running, the program executes the statements necessary to support the Debug class WriteLine statements. Otherwise, if the debugger is not active, the program does not execute the statements:

```
Private Sub Button1_Click(ByVal sender As Object, _
    ByVal e As System.EventArgs) Handles Button1.Click

    Dim Str As FileStream
    Dim Listener As TextWriterTraceListener

    If (Debugger.IsAttached) Then
        MsgBox("Debugging")
        Str = New FileStream("C:\DebugMessages.txt", _
            System.IO.FileMode.Append)
        Dim DebugFile As New StreamWriter(Str)
        Listener = New TextWriterTraceListener(DebugFile)
        Debug.Listeners.Add(Listener)
        Debug.AutoFlush = True
    Else
        MsgBox("Not debugging")
    End If

    Debug.WriteLine("")
    Debug.WriteLine("Messages generated at " & Now())
    Debug.WriteLine("In Button Click")
    Debug.WriteLine("Calling First")
    First()
    Debug.WriteLine("Exiting Button Click")

    If (Debugger.IsAttached) Then
        Debug.Listeners.Remove(Listener)
        Str.Close()
        TextBox1.Text = "Done"
    End If
End Sub
```

As you can see, by using the IsAttached property to determine if the debugger is running, the code only opens (and later closes) the file DebugMessages.txt when the debugger is running.

Using Debug Class Assertions to Locate Program Errors

To debug programs, programmers make extensive use of the Debug class WriteLine method to write debug messages. By using the Debug class to display messages, you can enable or disable the messages by compiling your program with or without debug support. In addition to using the Debug class WriteLine method, programmers often use the Debug class Assert method to test specific conditions and then to display an error message when the condition fails. For example, the following statement uses the Assert method to test if a stream object contains the value Nothing and if so, the statement displays an error message:

```
Debug.Assert(Not (FileStr Is Nothing), "The stream is NULL")
```

When you use the Assert method, keep in mind that the method will display its message only when your test fails. In the previous statement, for example, the Assert method will only display the message when the result of the test Not (FileStr is Nothing) returns false (meaning, when the FileStr object actually contains the value Nothing). The following program, DebugAssertDemo.vb, illustrates the use of the Assert method:

```
Imports System.IO

Module Module1

    Sub Main()
        Dim FileStr As StreamWriter

        Debug.Assert(Not (FileStr Is Nothing), "FileStr is NULL")

        Debug.Assert(Directory.Exists("\Temp"), "\Temp does not exist")

        Console.Write("Press Enter to continue...")
        Console.ReadLine()
    End Sub
End Module
```

After you compile and execute this program, the first Assert method call will execute, causing the program to display the window shown here.

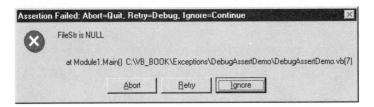

Using Event Logs to Track Program Operations

In the Windows 2000 and Windows NT environments, system administrators make extensive use of event logs to monitor various events. For example, by monitoring security-related events, an administrator may detect the fact that a hacker is trying to break into a server. Likewise, by monitoring application events, programmers can monitor an application's processing as users run the program. To view the Event logs in Windows 2000, perform these steps:

1. Select Start | Settings | Control Panel. Windows will open the Control Panel.

2. In the Control Panel, double-click the Administrative Tools icon. Windows will open the Administrative Tools window.

3. In the Administrative Tools window, double-click the Event Viewer icon. Windows will open the Event Viewer window, as shown in Figure 9-9.

4. In the Event Viewer window, click the Application Log, Security Log, or Security Log icon to display the corresponding events.

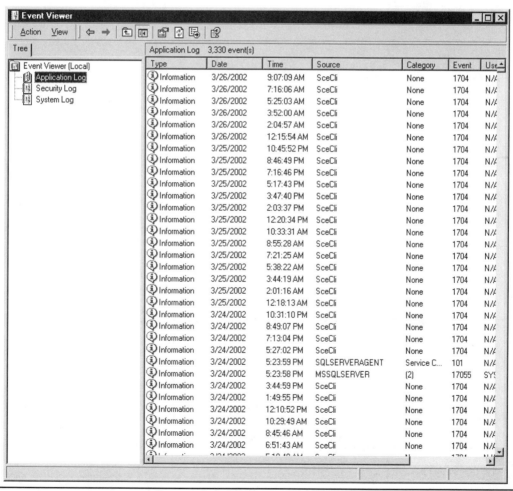

Figure 9-9   Viewing events in the Windows Event Viewer

To place an event into an event log, your program must first create an EventLog object. The following statement, for example, creates an object the program can use to access the Application event log:

```
Dim Log As New EventLog("Application")
```

Next, to place an entry into the log, the program uses the EventLog class WriteEntry method:

```
Log.WriteEntry("Application-specific message")
```

To help your programs make better use of the EventLog class, Table 9-4 briefly describes the class methods. Table 9-5 describes the class properties.

The following program, FormEventLog.vb, displays a form into which you can type a text message, as shown in Figure 9-10. If you click Store In Log, the program will add your message to the application event log:

```
Public Class Form1
    Inherits System.Windows.Forms.Form

#Region " Windows Form Designer generated code "
  ' Code not shown
#End Region

    Private Sub Button1_Click(ByVal sender As Object, _
      ByVal e As System.EventArgs) Handles Button1.Click

        Dim Log As New EventLog("Application")

        If (TextBox1.Text.Length > 0) Then
            Log.Source = "FormEventLog"
            Log.WriteEntry(TextBox1.Text)
            MsgBox("Event Stored")
            TextBox1.Text = ""
        Else
            MsgBox("You must specify event text")
        End If
    End Sub
End Class
```

Method	Purpose
BeginInit	Starts the initialization of an EventLog object used by another component.
Clear	Removes the event log's entries.
Close	Closes the event log and releases the corresponding handles.

Table 9-4   The EventLog Class Methods

Method	Purpose
CreateEventSource	Defines the application as a source of event information for a specific log. The CreateEventSource method is an overloaded method.
Delete	Deletes the log and its contents. The Delete method is an overloaded method.
DeleteEventSource	Removes the application as a source of event information for a specific log. The DeleteEventSource method is an overloaded method.
EndInit	Ends the initialization of an EventLog object used by another component.
Exists	Returns a Boolean value that specifies if the specified log exists. The Exists method is an overloaded method.
GetEventLogs	Returns an array that contains the available event logs. The GetEventLogs method is an overloaded method.
LogNameFromSourceName	Gets the name of the log for which the application is specified as an event source. The LogNameFromSourceName method is an overloaded method.
SourceExists	Returns a Boolean value that specifies whether a specific event source is registered.
WriteEntry	Writes an entry to the event log. The WriteEntry method is an overloaded method.

Table 9-4   The EventLog Class Methods *(continued)*

Just as your programs can place entries into an event log, your programs can also read a log's current entries. For example, the following program, ViewEvents.vb, displays the form shown in

Property	Purpose
EnableRaisingEvents	Gets or sets a Boolean value that controls if this instance of an EventLog receives EntryWritten events.
Entries	Gets the collection that contains the entries in the event log.
Log	Gets or sets the name of the event log (such as Application, System, or Security).
LogDisplayName	Gets the name by which the Event Viewer refers to the log.
MachineName	Gets or sets the name of the computer that contains the desired log.
Source	Gets or sets the source name (often the program) by which the log will register (categorize) the event.
SynchronizingObject	Gets or sets the object that marshals event handler calls that correspond to EventLog entry events.

Table 9-5   The EventLog Class Properties

Figure 9-10   Creating custom event-log entries

Figure 9-11 that you can use to view the Application events from a specific source. If you do not know the name of the source you desire, you can click the form's View Sources button to display a list of the sources that have placed entries in the log.

```
Public Class Form1
    Inherits System.Windows.Forms.Form

#Region " Windows Form Designer generated code "
  ' Code not shown
#End Region

    Private Sub Button1_Click(ByVal sender As Object, _
      ByVal e As System.EventArgs) Handles Button1.Click

      Dim Log As New EventLog("Application")
      Dim CrLF As String = Chr(13) & Chr(10)

      If (TextBox2.Text.Length = 0) Then
          MsgBox("Must specify a source event")
      Else
          TextBox1.Text = ""

          Dim Evt As EventLogEntry
          For Each Evt In Log.Entries
              If Evt.Source = TextBox2.Text Then
                  TextBox1.AppendText(Evt.Message & _
                      " " & Evt.TimeGenerated & CrLF)
              End If
```

```
        Next
    End If
End Sub

Private Sub Button2_Click(ByVal sender As Object, _
  ByVal e As System.EventArgs) Handles Button2.Click

    Dim Log As New EventLog("Application")
    Dim CrLF As String = Chr(13) & Chr(10)

    TextBox1.Text = ""

    Dim Evt As EventLogEntry
    For Each Evt In Log.Entries
        If (InStr(TextBox1.Text & CrLF, _
          Evt.Source & CrLF, CompareMethod.Binary) = 0) Then
            TextBox1.AppendText(Evt.Source & CrLF)
        End If
    Next
End Sub
End Class
```

In the program, the code that displays the events uses the EventLog class Entries property to retrieve a collection that contains each of the log's entries. The code then uses a For Each loop to compare each entry's source to that specified by the user.

To display the sources, the code again uses the Entries collection. Before the program adds a source name to the text box, the code uses the InStr function to check if the source name is already in the text box. If so, the code does not add the source to the box. If the source is not present in the text box, the program uses the AppendText method to add the source name to the box.

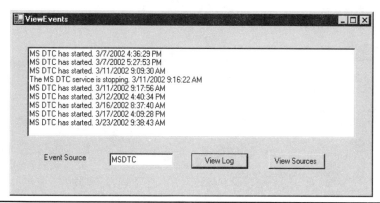

Figure 9-11   Viewing event log entries for a specific source

CHAPTER 10

Responding to and Handling Events

TIPS IN THIS CHAPTER

For years, Visual Basic programmers have used forms within programs to build an application's user interface. In the programs that display the forms, the programmers place code that responds to various form-related events, such as the user clicking a button, completing the context of a text box, changing the value of a checkbox, and so on. Programmers refer to the code the program executes in response to an event as an event handler.

Although the concept of creating a subroutine that executes in response to an event seems quite simple to Visual Basic programmers today, the use of event-driven code changed the "sequential program execution mindset" that had existed for the first 50 years of computing. In contrast to a program that executes statements sequentially, the execution of an event-driven program is often based on asynchronous operations. An event-driven program, for example, does not know which button a user might select or when. Instead, the program simply responds to the operation when the operation occurs.

Although programmers often associate the use of event-driven code with Visual Basic forms, the .NET introduction of Web- and Windows-based forms will extend the event model to ASP.NET pages and other Windows-based programming languages. Today, most programmers make extensive use of events to implement forms and respond to timers. In the future, events will notify programmers of the completion of database transactions, the termination of a network-based communication, and much more. The Tips this chapter presents will teach you how to create and respond to events in Visual Basic .NET and how to leverage the .NET Delegate class, which your programs can use to hold the address of one or more methods in order to implement a "call back" solution.

Defining and Raising an Event in a Class

Normally, in Visual Basic .NET programs, your code will respond to events that are defined by other objects. For example, many of the programs you have created in the previous chapters have responded to button click events that occur within a form. In such cases, the Button class defines the event, meaning the Button class specifies the number and type of parameters the event passes to the event handler when the event occurs. In addition, a button object later generates (raises) the event to notify the program of a specific operation. When the event occurs, Visual Basic automatically calls the subroutine you have specified to handle the event.

In a Visual Basic .NET class, you can define an event by declaring event class objects. The following statements, for example, define three different events, each of which passes a different number of parameters to its handler when the event occurs:

```
Class SomeClassName

    Public event BurglarAlarm()
```

```
Public event FireAlarm(ByVal Temperature As Integer)

Public event MotionAlarm(ByVal Room As String, ByVal Duration As Integer)

' Other class members

End Class
```

As you can see, when you define an event, you specify whether the event receives zero or more parameters. After a class defines an event, code within the class can later generate the event using the RaiseEvent statement. When a class raises an event, your code must specify values for each of the event's parameters, as shown here:

```
RaiseEvent BurglarAlarm()

RaiseEvent FireAlarm(200)

RaiseEvent MotionAlarm("Living room", 10)
```

USE IT   As discussed, Visual Basic .NET forms make extensive use of events. In fact, most of the controls you place on a form generate a wide range of events. A Button control, for example, inherits numerous events from the Control class. Table 10-1 briefly describes a few of the Button control's more common events.

In Visual Studio, create the program, EventDemo.vb, which defines a simple form that contains a button, as shown in Figure 10-1. Next, to display the Button object's events, open the control's drop-down list and select Button1. Then open the Declarations drop-down list.

Event	Occurs When
BackColorChanged	Occurs when the value of the button's BackColor property changes
BackgroundImageChanged	Occurs when the value of the button's BackgroundImage property changes
Click	Occurs when the user clicks the button
EnabledChanged	Occurs when the button's Enabled property value changes
FontChanged	Occurs when the button's Font property value changes
GotFocus	Occurs when the button receives the input focus
Leave	Occurs when the button loses the input focus
MouseDown	Occurs when the mouse pointer is over the button and the user clicks the mouse button
MouseEnter	Occurs when the mouse pointer enters the button's screen area

Table 10-1   A Sample of the Events Generated by a Button Control

Event	Occurs When
MouseHover	Occurs when the mouse pointer hovers over the button
MouseLeave	Occurs when the mouse pointer leaves the button's screen area
MouseMove	Occurs when the mouse pointer is moved within the button's screen area
MouseUp	Occurs when the mouse pointer is over the button and the user releases a mouse button

Table 10-1   A Sample of the Events Generated by a Button Control *(continued)*

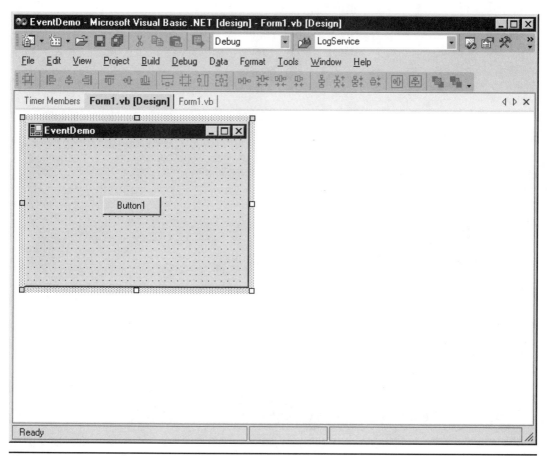

Figure 10-1   A Visual Basic .NET form containing a button

To add code to handle a specific event, simply click the event in the drop-down event list. For example, if you select the Click event, Visual Studio will place the following event handler code template in your code:

```
Private Sub Button1_Click(ByVal sender As Object, _
   ByVal e As System.EventArgs) Handles Button1.Click


End Sub
```

Within the subroutine, you can place the code you want the handler to perform each time the event occurs. By clicking events in the Declarations drop-down list, you can add code to handle the Click and TextChanged events. The Click event occurs when a user clicks the button. The TextChanged event occurs when the text the button displays changes. Then, within each of the corresponding subroutines, place the following statements:

```
Private Sub Button1_Click(ByVal sender As Object, _
   ByVal e As System.EventArgs) Handles Button1.Click

   MsgBox("Click event occurred")

   If (Button1.Text = "Button1") Then
     Button1.Text = "Clicked"
   Else
     Button1.Text = "Button1"
   End If
End Sub

Private Sub Button1_TextChanged(ByVal sender As Object, _
   ByVal e As System.EventArgs) Handles Button1.TextChanged

   MsgBox("Textchanged event occurred")

End Sub
```

Within the Click event handler, the code displays a message box stating that the event occurred. Then the code changes the button's label, which triggers the TextChanged event.

Handling an Event Using the Handles Clause

To respond to an event, your program must specify a subroutine whose purpose is to handle the specific event type. Each time the event occurs, Visual Basic .NET will automatically call the subroutine to handle the event. Programmers refer to such subroutines as event handlers. To define an event handler, you must place the Handles keyword after the subroutine's signature and then specify the event the subroutine handles. For example, to handle a form's button click event, you would define a subroutine similar to the following:

```
Private Sub Button1_Click(ByVal sender As Object, _
  ByVal e As System.EventArgs) Handles Button1.Click

    MsgBox("Click event occurred")

End Sub
```

As you can see, following the subroutine's signature (the name and parameters), the code uses the Handles clause to specify the event to which the subroutine responds. The Handles clause is new to Visual Basic .NET. In previous versions of Visual Basic, the subroutine's name identified the event the subroutine handled. For example, to handle the MouseDown event created by the Button1 object, you would create a subroutine named Button1_MouseDown. (Actually, Visual Basic's integrated development environment created the subroutine for the programmer and the program then added the statements to the subroutine that corresponded to the event.) In Visual Basic .NET, you must specify the object and event using the Handles keyword.

The following code fragment, for example, implements handlers for the FireAlarm, BurglarAlarm, and MotionAlarm events:

```
Sub Burglar() Handles Alarms.BurglarAlarm
   MsgBox("Burglar alarm occurred")
End Sub

Sub Fire(ByVal Temp As Integer) Handles Alarms.FireAlarm
   MsgBox("Fire alarm occurred: Temp: " & Temp)
End Sub

Sub Motion(ByVal Room As String, _
  ByVal Duration As Integer) Handles Alarms.MotionAlarm
   MsgBox("Motion alarm occurred: " & Room & " " & Duration)
End Sub
```

As you can see, each event handler uses the Handles clause to specify the object and the event for which the code implements a handler.

USE IT The following program, EventHandlerDemo.vb, creates an Alarms class that creates and later raises the Burglar, Fire, and Motion events:

```
Module Module1

    Class AlarmGroup
        Public Event BurglarAlarm()
        Public Event FireAlarm(ByVal Temp As Integer)
```

```
    Public Event MotionAlarm(ByVal Room As String, _
        ByVal Duration As Integer)

    Public Sub GenerateEvents()
        RaiseEvent BurglarAlarm()
        RaiseEvent FireAlarm(212)
        RaiseEvent MotionAlarm("Living Room", 25)
    End Sub
End Class

Dim WithEvents Alarms As New AlarmGroup()

Sub Burglar() Handles Alarms.BurglarAlarm
    Console.WriteLine("Burglar alarm occurred")
End Sub

Sub Fire(ByVal Temp As Integer) Handles Alarms.FireAlarm
    Console.WriteLine("Fire alarm occurred: Temp: " & Temp)
End Sub

Sub Motion(ByVal Room As String, ByVal Duration As Integer) _
  Handles Alarms.MotionAlarm
    Console.WriteLine("Motion alarm occurred: " & _
        Room & " " & Duration)
End Sub

Sub Main()

    Alarms.GenerateEvents()

    Console.ReadLine()    ' Delay to view output

End Sub
End Module
```

As you can see, to generate the events, the program uses the RaiseEvents statement, passing the correct parameters to each event handler. After you compile and run this program, your screen will display the following output:

```
Burglar alarm occurred
Fire alarm occurred: Temp: 212
Motion alarm occurred: Living Room 25
```

Within the program, note that the code declares the Alarms object using the WithEvents keyword:

```
Dim WithEvents Alarms As New AlarmGroup()
```

If you do not specify WithEvents when you declare the object, Visual Basic will not send any events to the object. If you examine the code that Visual Studio creates for controls you place on a form, such as a button, you will find that the code uses the WithEvents keyword to ensure the object can raise and respond to events:

```
Friend WithEvents Button1 As System.Windows.Forms.Button
```

Specifying an Event Handler Using AddHandler

For years, Visual Basic programmers have successfully handled events by specifying the event handler within the program code using a format similar to the following:

```
Private Sub Button1_Click(ByVal sender As Object, _
  ByVal e As System.EventArgs)

   MsgBox("Click event occurred")

End Sub
```

Visual Basic .NET, however, changes the event format slightly to include the Handles keyword followed by the event name, as shown here:

```
Private Sub Button1_Click(ByVal sender As Object, _
  ByVal e As System.EventArgs) Handles Button1.Click

   MsgBox("Click event occurred")

End Sub
```

When you specify an event handler in this way, your code statically binds the event handler to the event, much like a compiler or linker statically links a function or subroutine call to a specific memory address. For many applications, such as handling common form-based events, static binding is fine. Depending on the processing your application performs there may be times when you can improve your application's functionality by dynamically binding handlers to events at runtime. For example, assume that your program uses a security object that monitors the network for possible hacker attacks. When the monitor detects that a hacker is trying to break into the system, the monitor generates a HackerAttempt event. Under normal conditions, when a hacker tries to break into the system, your code responds to the break-in with a handler that simply sends an e-mail message to the system administrator:

```
Private Sub Hacker_15( ByVal Port As Integer) Handles HackerAttempt

  Dim Mail As New MailMessage()
```

```
Dim SendMsg As SmtpMail

Mail.To = "Admin@somesite.com"
Mail.Subject = "Hacker Attack"
Mail.Body = "Check port " & Port & " for a hacker attack"

SendMsg.Send(Mail)

End Sub
```

Assume that on the 15th of each month the server processes payroll information. If a hacker breaks into the system on the 15th, you not only want your program to notify the system administrator, but you also want the code to lock down all databases. To implement such processing, your code might define two event handlers for the HackerAttempt event. On the 15th, your code may dynamically (meaning, at runtime) install the high-security handler. Then, after the 15th, the code can reinstall the lower-security handler.

USE IT To dynamically link a handler to an event, your code must use the AddHandler statement to assign the address of the subroutine you want your program to use to handle the event, as shown here:

```
AddHandler HackerAttack, AddressOf Hacker_15
```

The following program, AddHandlerDemo.vb, creates a stock class that generates three different events. Within the Main subroutine, the code uses the AddHandler statement to assign a handler to each event. The code then calls the GenerateEvents method that directs the class to raise each of the events:

```
Module Module1

  Class Stock
      Public Event PriceUp(ByVal Amount As Double)
      Public Event PriceDown(ByVal Amount As Double)
      Public Event Earnings(ByVal Amount As Double, _
        ByVal AnnounceDate As DateTime)

      Public Sub GenerateEvents()
          RaiseEvent PriceUp(2)
          RaiseEvent PriceDown(-5.5)
          RaiseEvent Earnings(1.25, Now())
      End Sub
  End Class

  Dim WithEvents StockInfo As New Stock()
```

```
    Sub PriceGoingUp(ByVal Price As Double)
        Console.WriteLine("Good News! Price up: " & Price)
    End Sub

    Sub PriceGoingDown(ByVal Price As Double)
        Console.WriteLine("Don't Panic! Price down: " & Price)
    End Sub

    Sub EarningsAnnouncement(ByVal Amount As Double, _
       ByVal AnnounceDate As DateTime)
        Console.WriteLine("Earnings Announcement: " & Amount & _
          " " & AnnounceDate)
    End Sub

    Sub Main()
       AddHandler StockInfo.PriceUp, AddressOf PriceGoingUp
       AddHandler StockInfo.PriceDown, AddressOf PriceGoingDown
       AddHandler StockInfo.Earnings, AddressOf EarningsAnnouncement

       StockInfo.GenerateEvents()

       Console.ReadLine()    ' Delay to view output
    End Sub
End Module
```

When your code uses the AddHandler statement to assign a handler to an event, the signature of the subroutine you specify must match the signature of the event handler. Otherwise, the compiler will generate a syntax error. After you compile and execute this program, your screen will display the following output:

```
Good News! Price up: 2
Don't Panic! Price down: -5.5
Earnings Announcement: 1.25 3/19/2002 7:10:56 PM
```

Calling Multiple Handlers for an Event

Using the AddHandler method, your code can bind the address of an event handler to an event during the program's runtime execution:

```
AddHandler SomeClass.Event, AddressOf HandlerSubroutine
```

Depending on your program's purpose (and how the program wants to handle the event), there may be times when you will want multiple handlers to respond to an event. In such cases, your

code can call the AddHandler method for each of the methods you desire (and in the order you want
the programs to invoke the handlers). For example, in the case of a FireAlarm, you may want the
CallFireDepartment handler to respond first to the event. Then you may want the LogFireAlarm
method to respond. Finally, you may want the NotifyNewsMedia handler to execute. To assign all
the methods to the event, you would use the AddHandler method as follows:

```
AddHandler Alarm.FireAlarm, AddressOf CallFireDepartment

AddHandler Alarm.FireAlarm, AddressOf LogFireAlarm

AddHandler Alarm.FireAlarm, AddressOf NotifyNewsMedia
```

USE IT   The following program, MultipleEventHandlers.vb, creates a Morning class that defines
and raises three events, which the program then might use to trigger events within an
automated house. The program uses the same handler, the AutomatedHouse subroutine, to handle
each event. To assign the handler to the events, the code uses the AddHandler statement:

```
Module Module1

    Class Morning
        Public Event StartCoffee(ByVal Item As String, _
           ByVal StartTime As DateTime)
        Public Event TurnOnTV(ByVal Item As String, _
           ByVal StartTime As DateTime)
        Public Event StartShower(ByVal Item As String, _
           ByVal StartTime As DateTime)

        Public Sub GenerateEvents()
            RaiseEvent StartCoffee("Coffee", Now())
            RaiseEvent TurnOnTV("TV", Now().AddMinutes(5.0))
            RaiseEvent StartShower("Shower", Now.AddMinutes(10.0))
        End Sub
    End Class

    Dim WithEvents ThisMorning As New Morning()

    Sub AutomateHouse(ByVal Item As String, _
      ByVal StartTime As DateTime)
        Console.WriteLine("Starting " & Item & " at: " & StartTime)
    End Sub

    Sub Main()
      AddHandler ThisMorning.StartCoffee, AddressOf AutomateHouse
      AddHandler ThisMorning.TurnOnTV, AddressOf AutomateHouse
      AddHandler ThisMorning.StartShower, AddressOf AutomateHouse
```

```
      ThisMorning.GenerateEvents()
      Console.ReadLine()    ' Delay to view output
   End Sub
End Module
```

After you compile and execute this program, your screen will display the following output:

```
Starting Coffee at: 3/19/2002 6:29:49 AM
Starting TV at: 3/19/2002 6:34:49 AM
Starting Shower at: 3/19/2002 6:39:49 AM
```

Adding and Removing Event Handlers

When your program handles events, you can specify event handlers statically when you compile the application, or you can use the AddHandler method to specify a handler during runtime. Depending on the processing your program performs, your code will normally use a single method to respond to and handle an event. However, as you learned in the Tip titled "Calling Multiple Handlers for an Event," there may be times when you will want two or more methods to respond to an event. In such cases, your code can use the AddHandler method to specify the methods and the method invocation order:

```
AddHandler ClassName.Event, AddressOf FirstToExecute
AddHandler ClassName.Event, AddressOf SecondToExecute
AddHandler ClassName.Event, AddressOf LastToExecute
```

As your program executes, there may be times when you will want to add one or more handlers to an event, or when you will want to remove an event handler or replace an existing handler with another. In such cases, your code can call the RemoveHandler method to remove a handler from an event's method invocation list.

 Assume, for example, your program creates a NotifyFireChief method, which the program adds to the FireAlarm event's method list:

```
AddHandler Alarm.FireAlarm, AddressOf NotifyFireChief

AddHandler Alarm.FireAlarm, AddressOf CallFireDepartment

AddHandler Alarm.FireAlarm, AddressOf LogFireAlarm

AddHandler Alarm.FireAlarm, AddressOf NotifyNewsMedia
```

Normally, the Fire Chief wants immediate notification of all fire alarms. On Thursday nights between 6:00 and 7:00, however, the Fire Chief has dinner out with his wife and does not want to be disturbed. In your program code, you can remove the NotifyFireChief method from the FireAlarm event during dinner hours using the RemoveHandler method, as follows:

```
RemoveHandler Alarm.FireAlarm, AddressOf NotifyFireChief
```

Taking Advantage of Events and Class Inheritance

In Chapter 4, you learned how to use inheritance to derive a new object based on an existing object. When you derive a new class, the new class inherits the base class methods, properties, and events. Although the derived class can handle (respond to) base-class events, the derived class cannot raise a base-class event using the Raise statement.

USE IT   The following program, InheritEvent.vb, creates a DailyEvents class that defines three event types and later generates a series of events. Next, the code creates the TodaysActivities class that inherits DailyEvents. The code then creates an object of the TodaysActivities class that uses the WithEvents keyword, which makes the class events (and those of a base class the class inherits) available to the object. Then the code uses the AddHandler statement to assign an event handler to each of the object's events:

```
Module Module1

    Public Class DailyEvents
        Public Event Meeting(ByVal Item As String, _
            ByVal StartTime As String)
        Public Event Meals(ByVal Item As String, _
            ByVal StartTime As String)
        Public Event Family(ByVal Item As String, _
            ByVal StartTime As String)

        Public Sub GenerateEvents()
            RaiseEvent Meeting("Sales Presentation", "9:30AM")
            RaiseEvent Meeting("Client", "11:30AM")
            RaiseEvent Meeting("Production Scheduling", "2:30PM")
            RaiseEvent Meals("Lunch with Debbie", "12:30PM")
            RaiseEvent Family("Ball Game", "5:30PM")
        End Sub
    End Class

    Public Class TodaysActivities
        Inherits DailyEvents

        Public StartDay As DateTime
```

```
        Public EndDay As DateTime

        Public Sub New(ByVal StartDay As DateTime, ByVal EndDay As DateTime)
            MyBase.New()
            Me.StartDay = StartDay
            Me.EndDay = EndDay
        End Sub
    End Class

    Dim WithEvents Today As New TodaysActivities(Now(), Now.AddHours(8))

    Sub ScheduleHandler(ByVal Item As String, _
      ByVal StartTime As String)
        Console.WriteLine(Item & " at: " & StartTime)
    End Sub

    Sub Main()
        AddHandler Today.Meeting, AddressOf ScheduleHandler
        AddHandler Today.Meals, AddressOf ScheduleHandler
        AddHandler Today.Family, AddressOf ScheduleHandler

        Today.GenerateEvents()
        Console.ReadLine()    ' Delay to view output
    End Sub
End Module
```

After you compile and execute this program, your screen will display the following output:

```
Sales Presentation at: 9:30AM
Client at: 11:30AM
Production Scheduling at: 2:30PM
Lunch with Debbie at: 12:30PM
Ball Game at: 5:30PM
```

Using a .NET Delegate to Point to a Function

Using the AddHandler and RemoveHandler methods, your programs can dynamically add and remove a handler from an event during runtime. When you use the AddHandler, your programs use the AddressOf statement to determine the address of the method that handles the event. The .NET environment provides a special object called a delegate that can store the address of one or more methods. .NET applications make extensive use of delegate objects to "call back" specific code, such as an event handler.

In general, to define a delegate within your program, you specify a method signature that corresponds to the method type your program can use the delegate to reference. The following statements, for example, declare a delegate for a subroutine that receives a single string parameter:

```
Delegate Sub StringProcedure(ByVal S As String)
```

The Delegate keyword generates a class with which your program can create an object that is capable of storing the address of a method. The signature of the method you assign to an object of the delegate class must correspond to the delegate's method signature. In this case, the delegate object can only store the address of subroutines that use one parameter of type String, such as following:

```
Sub DisplayMessage(ByVal Message As String)
   Console.WriteLine(Message)
End Sub

Sub ShowTime(ByVal TimeStr As String)
   Console.WriteLine(TimeStr)
End Sub
```

Using the delegate class, you create an object that is capable of storing a method address. The following statement, for example, creates an object of the StringProcedure delegate class type and uses the delegate class constructor to initialize the object to the address of the DisplayMessage method:

```
Dim MethodAddressObj As New StringProcedure(AddressOf DisplayMessage)
```

In the Tips that follow, the purpose and use of delegates will begin to make more sense. For now, however, simply understand that the delegate exists to store a method's address. Further, remember that a delegate can only store the address of a method that matches the delegate's signature. The following program, DelegateDemo.vb, creates two delegates. The first delegate defines a class capable of storing the address of a method that receives one string as a parameter. The second delegate defines a class capable of holding the address of a function that returns two parameters of type Double and that returns a value of type Double:

```
Delegate Sub StringMethod(ByVal S As String)

Delegate Function Numbers(ByVal A As Double, _
   ByVal B As Double) As Double
```

The following statements implement the DelegateDemo.vb program:

```
Module Module1
```

```vbnet
    Delegate Sub StringMethod(ByVal S As String)

    Sub DisplayString(ByVal S As String)
        Console.WriteLine(S)
    End Sub

    Sub UpperString(ByVal S As String)
        Console.WriteLine(UCase(S))
    End Sub

    Delegate Function Numbers(ByVal A As Double, _
      ByVal B As Double) As Double

    Function SubtractNumbers(ByVal A As Double, _
      ByVal B As Double) As Double
        SubtractNumbers = A - B
    End Function

    Function AddNumbers(ByVal A As Double, _
      ByVal B As Double) As Double
        AddNumbers = A + B
    End Function

    Sub Main()
        Dim MyMethod As New StringMethod(AddressOf DisplayString)
        MyMethod.Invoke("Visual Basic .Net Programming")

        MyMethod = AddressOf UpperString
        MyMethod.Invoke("Visual Basic .Net Programming")

        Dim DoNumbers As New Numbers(AddressOf SubtractNumbers)
        Console.WriteLine(DoNumbers.Invoke(100, 50))

        DoNumbers = AddressOf AddNumbers
        Console.WriteLine(DoNumbers.Invoke(100, 50))
        Console.ReadLine()   ' Pause to view output
    End Sub
End Module
```

As you can see, the program first creates an object named MyMethod of the delegate class type StringMethod. The code then uses delegate object to invoke two different string methods. Then the code creates a second delegate object named DoNumbers that can store a function that returns type Double. The code next uses the delegate to perform two arithmetic operations. After you compile and execute this program, your screen will display the following output:

```
Visual Basic .Net Programming
VISUAL BASIC .NET PROGRAMMING
50
150
```

Taking Advantage of a Delegate in a Subroutine Call

In Visual Basic .NET, a delegate is an object that can store the address of a subroutine or function. A convenient use of a delegate is to change the processing your code performs by assigning a different subroutine or function to the delegate. Assume, for example, that your program has a subroutine that displays a greeting to the user based on the current time of day, such as "Good morning," "Good afternoon," or "Good evening." Further, assume that based on the user's preferences, the subroutine displays the message using English or Spanish. Within the subroutine that greets the user, you might use the following series of If-Else statements:

```
If (UseEnglish) Then
  If (IsMorning) Then
    MsgBox("Good morning")
  Else If (IsAfternoon) Then
    MsgBox("Good afternoon")
  Else
    MsgBox("Good evening")
Else
  If (IsMorning) Then
    MsgBox("Buenas dias")
  Else If (IsAfternoon) Then
    MsgBox("Buenos tardes")
  Else
    MsgBox("Buenos noches")
End If
```

Next, assume that you want to support several additional languages, such as German, French, and so on. To simplify your code, you might create a series of subroutines that correspond to time period and language, as shown here:

```
Sub MorningEnglish()
   MsgBox("Good morning")
End Sub
```

In the subroutine that greets the user, you might call the subroutines as follows:

```
If (UseEnglish) Then
  If (IsMorning) Then
    MorningEnglish()
  Else If (IsAfternoon) Then
    AfternoonEnglish()
  Else
    EveningEnglish()
Else
  If (IsMorning) Then
    MorningSpanish()
  Else If (IsAfternoon) Then
    AfternoonSpanish()
  Else
    EveningSpanish()
End If
```

Although this code accomplishes your goal of greeting the user with an appropriate message, the code may replicate processing that you performed elsewhere to determine the time and language. As an alternative to the processing shown here, you can define a delegate that will store the address of the subroutine that corresponds to the correct greeting:

```
Delegate Sub GreetingMethod()

Dim Greeting As New GreetingMethod(AddressOf MorningEnglish)
```

Then, in your code that determines the time of day and the user's language preference, you can assign the corresponding subroutine to the delegate:

```
Greeting = AddressOf EveningSpanish
```

Finally, in your subroutine that greets the user, your code can simply call the delegate:

```
Greeting.Invoke()
```

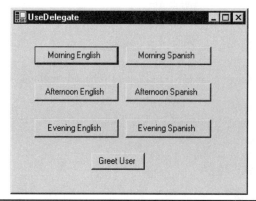

Figure 10-2   Using a Visual Basic form to control a delegate's value

USE IT   The following program, UseDelegate.vb, creates a form, as shown in Figure 10-2, that contains buttons you can use to specify a time of day and language. Each time you click a button, the code assigns the corresponding message subroutine to the Greeting delegate object. Then, when you click the Greet User button, the code uses the Greeting variable's current method to display a message box with the appropriate text.

```
Public Class Form1
    Inherits System.Windows.Forms.Form

#Region " Windows Form Designer generated code "
    ' Code not shown
#End Region

    Delegate Sub GreetingMethod()

    Dim Greeting As New GreetingMethod(AddressOf MorningEnglish)

    Sub MorningEnglish()
        MsgBox("Good morning")
    End Sub

    ' To reduce space, similar subroutines are not shown

    Sub EveningSpanish()
        MsgBox("Buenos noches")
    End Sub
```

```
    ' To reduce space, similar subroutines are not shown

    Private Sub Button1_Click(ByVal sender As Object, _
      ByVal e As System.EventArgs) Handles Button1.Click
        Greeting = AddressOf MorningEnglish
    End Sub

    Private Sub Button6_Click(ByVal sender As Object,
      ByVal e As System.EventArgs) Handles Button6.Click
        Greeting = AddressOf EveningSpanish
    End Sub

    Private Sub Button7_Click(ByVal sender As Object,
      ByVal e As System.EventArgs) Handles Button7.Click
        Greeting.Invoke()
    End Sub
End Class
```

Sorting Data Using Delegates

In the Tip titled "Taking Advantage of a Delegate in a Subroutine Call," you learned how to use a .NET delegate object in a subroutine to pass the address of the subroutine or function a second method can use to perform a specific task. In this Tip, you will use a delegate in a simple sort routine to let the subroutine sort an array of objects based on a variety of fields. To begin, the program will create an array of Book objects that store information, as shown here:

Title	Author	Price
C# Programming Tips & Techniques	Wright	$49.99
Visual Basic .Net Programming Tips & Techniques	Jamsa	$49.99
HTML & Web Design Tips & Techniques	King	$49.99
PC Performance Tuning & Upgrading Tips & Techniques	Jamsa	$39.99

The program will use the following Book class to store individual records:

```
Class Book
  Public Title As String
  Public Author As String
  Public Price As Double

  ' Methods not shown
End Class
```

After the program creates the array of book items, it will sort the array by title, author, and price. To sort the array based on different fields, the code implements the CompareAuthor, CompareTitle, and ComparePrice functions that the code assigns to the CompareMethod delegate object that the SortList method uses to compare different fields.

USE IT   The following code implements the DelegateSort.vb program:

```
Module Module1

  Class Book
    Public Publisher As String
    Public Title As String
    Public Author As String
    Public Price As Double

    Public Sub New(ByVal Title As String, ByVal Publisher As String, _
      ByVal Author As String, ByVal Price As Double)
        Me.Publisher = Publisher
        Me.Title = Title
        Me.Author = Author
        Me.Price = Price
      End Sub
  End Class

  Delegate Function Compare(ByVal A As Book, _
    ByVal B As Book) As Boolean

  Dim CompareMethod As New Compare(AddressOf CompareAuthor)

  Function CompareAuthor(ByVal A As Book, ByVal B As Book) As Boolean
    If (A.Author < B.Author) Then
      CompareAuthor = False
    Else
      CompareAuthor = True
    End If
  End Function

  Function CompareTitle(ByVal A As Book, ByVal B As Book) As Boolean
    If (A.Title < B.Title) Then
      CompareTitle = False
    Else
      CompareTitle = True
    End If
```

```
End Function

Function ComparePrice(ByVal A As Book, ByVal B As Book) As Boolean
  If (A.Price < B.Price) Then
    ComparePrice = False
  Else
    ComparePrice = True
  End If
End Function

Public Sub SortList(ByVal Booklist() As Book)
  Dim I, J As Integer
  Dim Temp As Book

  For I = 0 To Booklist.Length - 2
    For J = I + 1 To Booklist.Length - 1
      If (CompareMethod(Booklist(I), Booklist(J))) Then
        Temp = Booklist(I)
        Booklist(I) = Booklist(J)
        Booklist(J) = Temp
      End If
    Next
  Next
End Sub

Sub Main()
  Dim BookList(3) As Book
  BookList(0) = New Book("C# Programming Tips & Techniques", _
    "McGraw-Hill/Osborne", "Wright", 49.99)

  BookList(1) = _
    New Book("Visual Basic .Net Programming Tips & Techniques", _
    "McGraw-Hill/Osborne", "Jamsa", 49.99)

  BookList(2) = New Book("HTML & Web Design Tips & Techniques", _
    "McGraw-Hill/Osborne", "King", 49.99)

  BookList(3) =
    New Book("PC Performance Tuning & Upgrading Tips & Techniques", _
    "McGraw-Hill/Osborne", "Jamsa", 39.99)

  SortList(BookList)
  Console.WriteLine("By Author")
```

```
    Dim BookEntry As Book
    For Each BookEntry In BookList
       Console.WriteLine(BookEntry.Title & " " & BookEntry.Author & _
          " " & BookEntry.Price)
    Next

    Console.WriteLine()
    Console.WriteLine("By Title")

    CompareMethod = AddressOf CompareTitle
    SortList(BookList)
    For Each BookEntry In BookList
      Console.WriteLine(BookEntry.Title & " " & BookEntry.Author & _
         " " & BookEntry.Price)
    Next

    Console.WriteLine()
    Console.WriteLine("By Price")

    CompareMethod = AddressOf ComparePrice
    SortList(BookList)
    For Each BookEntry In BookList
       Console.WriteLine(BookEntry.Title & " " & BookEntry.Author & _
          " " & BookEntry.Price)
    Next

    Console.ReadLine() ' Delay to view output
  End Sub
End Module
```

After you compile and run this program, your screen will display the following output:

```
By Author
PC Performance Tuning & Upgrading Tips & Techniques Jamsa 39.99
Visual Basic .Net Programming Tips & Techniques Jamsa 49.99
HTML & Web Design Tips & Techniques King 49.99
C# Programming Tips & Techniques Wright 49.99

By Title
C# Programming Tips & Techniques Wright 49.99
HTML & Web Design Tips & Techniques King 49.99
PC Performance Tuning & Upgrading Tips & Techniques Jamsa 39.99
Visual Basic .Net Programming Tips & Techniques Jamsa 49.99
```

```
By Price
PC Performance Tuning & Upgrading Tips & Techniques Jamsa 39.99
Visual Basic .Net Programming Tips & Techniques Jamsa 49.99
HTML & Web Design Tips & Techniques King 49.99
C# Programming Tips & Techniques Wright 49.99
```

Assigning Multiple Methods to a Delegate

In the Tip titled "Calling Multiple Handlers for an Event," you learned how to assign multiple methods to an event using the AddHandler method. When you create a Delegate object, you actually create an instance of an object that inherits the System.MulticastDelegate class. As its name implies, the MulticastDelegate class lets you assign multiple methods to a delegate. To assign multiple methods to a delegate, your code can use the Delegate class Combine method that assigns the delegates stored in an array to a delegate object.

USE IT The following program, MultipleDelegates.vb, creates an array of delegate objects to which the code then assigns the addresses of three methods. The code then creates a new delegate object to which it assigns the methods contained in the array. When your code later calls the delegate's Invoke method, the program will call each of the delegate's methods:

```
Module Module1

    Delegate Sub NotifyInfo()
    Dim ListOfDelegates(3) As NotifyInfo

    Sub EmailNotify()
        Console.WriteLine("Email Bill at BG@Microsoft.com")
    End Sub

    Sub PhoneNotify()
        Console.WriteLine("Call Bill at 555-1212")
    End Sub

    Sub FaxNotify()
        Console.WriteLine("Fax Bill at 800-555-1212")
    End Sub

    Sub Main()
        ListOfDelegates(0) = New NotifyInfo(AddressOf PhoneNotify)
        ListOfDelegates(1) = New NotifyInfo(AddressOf EmailNotify)
        ListOfDelegates(2) = New NotifyInfo(AddressOf FaxNotify)
```

```
        Dim NotifyAll As New NotifyInfo(AddressOf PhoneNotify)
        NotifyAll = NotifyInfo.Combine(ListOfDelegates)

        NotifyAll.Invoke()
        Console.ReadLine() ' Pause to view output
    End Sub
End Module
```

After you compile and execute this program, your screen will display the following output:

```
Call Bill at 555-1212
Email Bill at BG@Microsoft.com
Fax Bill at 800-555-1212
```

Just as your code can use the Delegate class Combine method to add a method to the delegate's method invocation list, your code can use the Delegate class Remove method to remove a method from the list. The following statement, for example, removes the EmailNotify method from the NotifyAll delegate object:

```
NotifyAll = NotifyInfo.Remove(NotifyAll, ListOfDelegates(1))
```

Viewing a Delegate's Invocation List

In the .NET environment, a delegate is an object that stores the address of one or more methods. Depending on the processing your program performs, there may be times when you will want to know which methods are in a delegate's list. In such cases, your code uses the GetInvocationList method to return a collection of delegate objects that correspond to each of the methods the delegate will call.

 The following code fragment uses the NotifyAll delegate object that you created in the previous Tip to display the methods the object contains:

```
Dim Del As NotifyInfo
For Each Del In NotifyAll.GetInvocationList()
   Console.WriteLine(Del.Method)
Next
```

If you add the code fragment to the MultipleDelegates.vb program, your screen displays the following output:

```
Void PhoneNotify()
Void EmailNotify()
Void FaxNotify()
```

Responding to Timer Events

As your programs begin to perform more sophisticated processing, there will be times when you will want them to perform specific operations at specific times. In such cases, your programs can make use of a Timer control. Using a Timer control, for example, your programs can "wake up" to perform processing at specific intervals. In Visual Studio, you can add a timer to your program by dragging and dropping a Timer control onto your application as shown in Figure 10-3. Then, within your source code, you can define a subroutine that handles the Timer control's Tick event, which occurs when the time expires.

Although the Timer class inherits a number of methods, your programs will normally only use the Start and Stop methods. Similarly, your programs will likely only use the Enabled and Interval properties. The Enabled property lets you set or determine whether the timer is enabled (running).

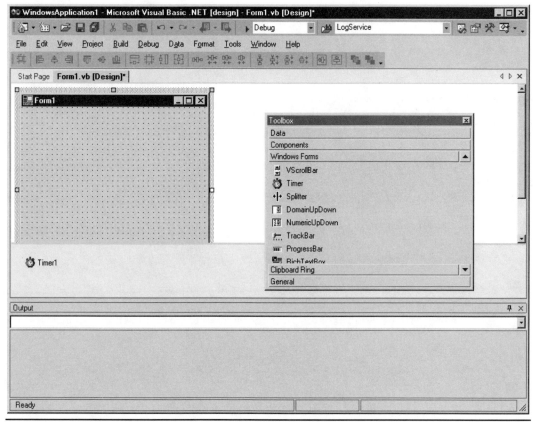

Figure 10-3   Adding a Timer control to a Visual Basic .NET program

The Interval property specifies the number of milliseconds until the timer occurs. When your programs use a Timer control, you must define an event handler similar to the following that handles the Timer control's Tick event:

```
Private Sub Timer1_Tick(ByVal sender As Object, _
  ByVal e As System.EventArgs) Handles Timer1.Tick
    ' Code to handle the event here
End Sub
```

The following program, TimerDemo.vb, displays a form with a button you can use to initiate a timer. After you click the button, the program will direct the timer to occur in 10 seconds. In the code that handles the Timer control's Tick event, the program displays a message box and then resets the timer to occur 15 seconds later. The program will continue this processing until you end the program:

```
Public Class Form1

  Inherits System.Windows.Forms.Form

#Region " Windows Form Designer generated code "
    ' Code not shown
#End Region

    Private Sub Timer1_Tick(ByVal sender As Object, _
      ByVal e As System.EventArgs) Handles Timer1.Tick

    Dim objTimer As Timer

      MsgBox("Timer Occurred--Resetting for 15 seconds")
      objTimer = sender
      objTimer.Interval = 15000
      objTimer.Start()
    End Sub

    Private Sub Button1_Click(ByVal sender As Object, _
      ByVal e As System.EventArgs) Handles Button1.Click
      MsgBox("Timer will occur 10 seconds after you close this box")
      Timer1.Interval = 10000
      Timer1.Start()
    End Sub
End Class
```

Taking a Closer Look at the EventArgs Class

When your Visual Basic .NET programs respond to form-based events, your event handlers receive two parameters, as shown here:

```
Private Sub Button1_Click(ByVal sender As Object, _
  ByVal e As System.EventArgs) Handles Button1.Click

    MsgBox("Click event occurred")

End Sub
```

The first parameter to the event handler is the object that generated the event. The second parameter is an object of type System.EventArgs. Normally, the EventArgs class does not contain any data that is useful to an event handler. However, often, a program will use the EventArgs class as a base class from which it derives a new class that holds more specifics about the event.

USE IT The following program, ExpandEventArgs.vb, creates a class named MoreArgs that inherits the System.EventArgs class. In this case, the MoreArgs class adds a message and time field to a new class. The code then generates the HackerMonitor class that raises the HackerAttack event. When the event occurs, the code passes a reference to the object that raised the event and a reference to a MoreArgs object that contains the time the hacker attack occurred, as well as a frantic message:

```
Module Module1

    Class MoreArgs
        Inherits System.EventArgs

        Public Message As String
        Public Time As DateTime

        Public Sub New(ByVal S As String, ByVal DT As DateTime)
            MyBase.New()
            Message = S
            Time = DT
        End Sub
    End Class

    Class HackerMonitor
```

```
        Public Event HackerAttack(ByVal E As Object, _
          ByVal Args As MoreArgs)

        Public Sub GenerateEvent()
            Dim Args As New MoreArgs("Hacker, Hacker", Now())
            RaiseEvent HackerAttack(Me, Args)
        End Sub
    End Class

    Dim WithEvents HackerAlarm As New HackerMonitor()

    Sub Attack(ByVal O As Object, ByVal Args As MoreArgs) _
        Handles HackerAlarm.HackerAttack

        Console.WriteLine("Hack Attack in progress")
        Console.WriteLine(Args.Message)
        Console.WriteLine(Args.Time)

    End Sub

    Sub Main()
        HackerAlarm.GenerateEvent()

        Console.ReadLine() ' Delay to view output
    End Sub

End Module
```

After you compile and execute this program, your screen will display the following output:

```
Hack Attack in progress
Hacker, Hacker
3/19/2002 4:42:25 PM
```

CHAPTER 11

Programming Windows Forms

TIPS IN THIS CHAPTER

For years, Visual Basic programmers have made extensive use of forms to build user interfaces. Most programmers will argue that the ability to drag and drop controls onto a form to quickly construct a user interface was the critical driving force behind Visual Basic's widespread adoption by the programming community.

In contrast to Visual Basic, other programming languages, such as C++, had to build user interfaces using the Microsoft Foundation Classes (MFC) and the WIN32 application program interface (API). Often, building the user interface became one of the most time-consuming aspects of program development. The .NET environment, however, provides programming languages such as C# (as well as Visual Basic .NET) the ability to create user interfaces using Windows Forms.

In general, you can think of Windows forms as a programming-language-independent implementation of the form-based capabilities that Visual Basic programmers have exploited for years. Figure 11-1 illustrates the process of building a user interface in Visual Studio, by dragging and dropping controls onto a form.

Behind the scenes, Visual Studio automatically creates the program code that builds and interacts with each control. If the programming is creating a Visual Basic .NET application, Visual Studio will implement the form's code using Visual Basic .NET. Likewise, if the programmer is creating a C# program, Visual Studio will create the code using C#.

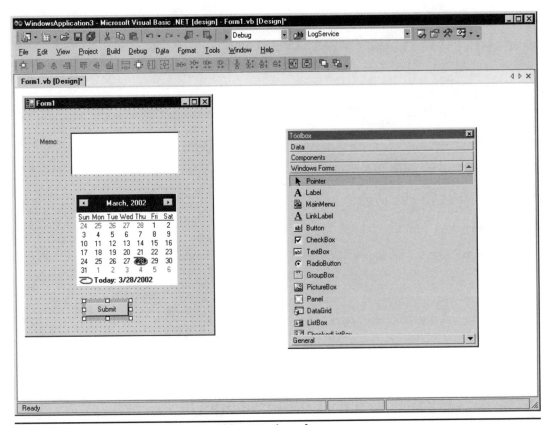

Figure 11-1 Using Visual Studio to build a Windows form

Each time you create a Windows application, Visual Studio will display a blank form, onto which you can drag and drop controls from the Visual Studio Toolbox window. If Visual Studio is not currently displaying the Toolbox window, select View | Toolbox.

After you drag and drop a control onto the form, you can then use the control's property settings to customize the control (perhaps by changing the control's name, the text the control displays, the control's border, exact screen position, and so on). If Visual Studio is not currently displaying a control's properties, right-click the control and then select Properties from the pop-up menu which Visual Studio displays. Visual Studio will open a Properties window that contains attribute settings specific to the control, as shown in Figure 11-2.

For many of the controls that you place on a form, you may not have to write any code at all, except possibly to set or retrieve the control's current value (such as the text that appears in a TextBox control or the state of a checkbox). For other controls, such as a Button, you will normally implement one or more event handlers (subroutines) that execute when a specific event occurs (such as a button click). To implement an event handler for a control, switch from design view to code view by selecting

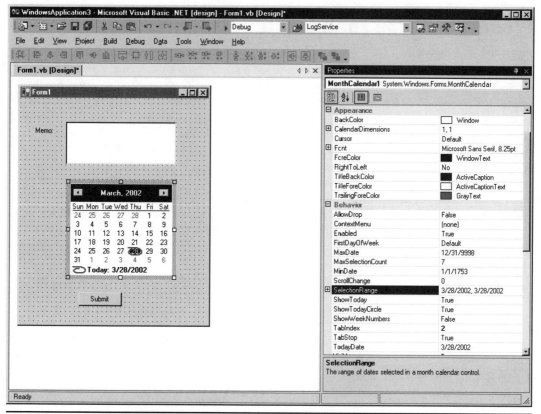

Figure 11-2   Displaying a control's properties in Visual Studio

View | Code. Then use the object pull-down list to select the object you desire. Use the pull-down Declarations list to select the event you want to handle. Visual Studio will place template code for the event handler in your source code that you can customize to handle the event:

```
Private Sub Button1_Click(ByVal sender As Object, _
  ByVal e As System.EventArgs) Handles Button1.Click

  ' Place your code here

End Sub
```

The following Tips examine each of the controls supported by .NET Windows Forms, with the exception of the DataGrid control, the use of which Chapter 17 examines in detail in applications that use ADO.NET.

Programming the Form Control

Each time you create a Windows application, Visual Studio will display a blank form onto which you can drag and drop other controls. The Windows-based programs you create using Visual Basic .NET run in the context of a form. When you close the form, the application ends. To use Visual Studio to create a simple Windows application, one that contains a form with no controls, select File | New | Project. Visual Studio will display a New Project dialog box. In the dialog box, select the Windows Application icon and then type the project name and directory location you desire. Visual Studio will then display your application's blank form. Behind the scenes, Visual Studio has already placed statements into your source code that create and display the form. To build the current program, select Build | Build Solution. Then to run the program, select Debug | Start. Windows will open your application's blank form. To close the form and to end the application, click the form's close button (the X that appears in the upper-right corner). To display the program statements Visual Studio created for your program, select View | Code. Then click the plus sign that precedes the line containing the text Windows Form Designer–generated code. Visual Studio will display the following program statements (minus the comments):

```
Public Class Form1
    Inherits System.Windows.Forms.Form

#Region " Windows Form Designer generated code "

    Public Sub New()
       MyBase.New()

       InitializeComponent()
    End Sub

    Protected Overloads Overrides Sub Dispose(ByVal _
      disposing As Boolean)
       If disposing Then
           If Not (components Is Nothing) Then
               components.Dispose()
           End If
       End If
       MyBase.Dispose(disposing)
    End Sub

    Private components As System.ComponentModel.IContainer
```

```
<System.Diagnostics.DebuggerStepThrough()> _
    Private Sub InitializeComponent()
      components = New System.ComponentModel.Container()
      Me.Text = "Form1"
  End Sub
#End Region
End Class
```

As you can see, Visual Studio implements the form as a class. In the class, Visual Studio provides the New constructor method and the Dispose method the program can call to discard the form object. The code that appears between the Region and End Region directives is created by Visual Studio. Normally, you will place your program statements beyond the #End Region directive.

Throughout this chapter, the programs perform very few operations that affect the Form object itself. When you create a program, you may use the Form object's Text field to change the name that appears in the form's title bar. Likewise, as you have learned, when you close a form, the application will end. Several of the programs the following Tips present will close a form using the following statement:

```
Me.Close()
```

USE IT If you examine the Form class in Visual Studio's online help, you will find that the class provides a myriad of methods and properties you can use to customize the form's processing. Further, like other controls, the Form class generates many different events. By responding to the Form events, your programs can perform specific processing when the program first loads a form, or each time a user switches (activates) the form, and so on. To view the Form class events in Visual Studio code view, select the pull-down object list and choose Base-Class Events. Then select the Declarations drop-down list. Visual Studio will display the Form events as shown in Figure 11-3.

In the pull-down list, select the Load event which the program will generate as it loads a form (before it displays the form). Visual Studio will place an event handler in your code. In the event handler, place the following MsgBox call to display a message telling you the form is being loaded:

```
Private Sub Form1_Load(ByVal sender As Object, _
    ByVal e As System.EventArgs) Handles MyBase.Load
      MsgBox("Form is being loaded")
  End Sub
```

Then build and run the program. Before the program displays the form, the program will display the message box telling you that it is loading the form. By taking advantage of Form class events, your programs can initialize program variables when a program loads a form, or perform cleanup operations when a program prepares to close the form.

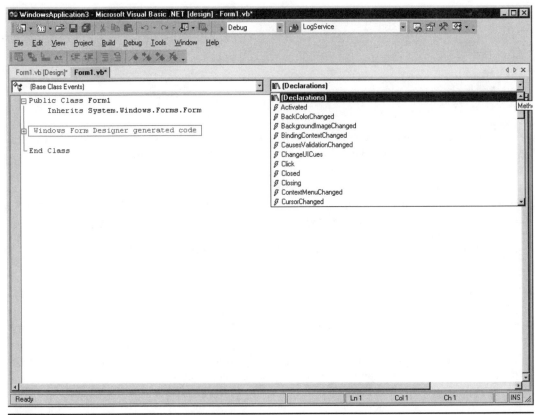

Figure 11-3   Displaying Form class events

Programming the Button Control

In a form, one of the simplest, yet most often used controls is the Button control. Depending on a form's purpose, the form might contain one Button control with the OK label, one with Cancel, and one with Help. Figure 11-4 illustrates a text box that contains a Next button.

USE IT   Throughout this book, programs make extensive use of Button objects. Normally, the objects simply respond to the Click event. Depending on the processing your program performs, there may be times when you will want to add buttons to a form "on the fly" as the program executes. The following program, ButtonDemo.vb, examines the root directory on drive C for files with the .txt extension. If the program locates a text file, the program will display the file in the form. If multiple text files exist, the program will add a Next button to the form. After the user

Figure 11-4   Using a Next button to move through text files in a form

views the last text, the program removes the Next button, displaying the Done button. When the user clicks the Done button, the program will end:

```
Imports System.IO

Public Class Form1
    Inherits System.Windows.Forms.Form

#Region " Windows Form Designer generated code "
  ' Code not shown
#End Region

    Public TextFiles() As FileInfo
    Public FileIndex As Integer

Private Sub Form1_Load(ByVal sender As System.Object, _
      ByVal e As System.EventArgs) Handles MyBase.Load
        Dim DirObj As New DirectoryInfo("C:\")
        TextFiles = DirObj.GetFiles("*.txt")

        If TextFiles.Length = 0 Then
            Me.Close()
        Else
            If TextFiles.Length = 1 Then
                Button1.Text = "Done"
            Else
                Button1.Text = "Next"
            End If

            FileIndex = 0
```

```
            RichTextBox1.LoadFile(TextFiles(FileIndex).FullName, _
               RichTextBoxStreamType.PlainText)
            Me.Text = TextFiles(FileIndex).FullName
        End If
    End Sub

    Private Sub Button1_Click(ByVal sender As Object, _
       ByVal e As System.EventArgs) Handles Button1.Click
        FileIndex = FileIndex + 1
        If FileIndex = TextFiles.Length Then
            Me.Close()
        Else
            If FileIndex = (TextFiles.Length - 1) Then
                Button1.Text = "Done"
            End If
            RichTextBox1.LoadFile(TextFiles(FileIndex).FullName, _
               RichTextBoxStreamType.PlainText)
            Me.Text = TextFiles(FileIndex).FullName
        End If
    End Sub
End Class
```

To simplify the file operations, the program loads the file's contents into a RichTextBox control that provides the LoadFile method. To access form attributes (such as the title, or to close the form), the code uses the Me keyword.

Programming the Label Control

In a form, a Label control lets you place descriptive text. As shown in the following illustration, forms normally use the Label control to precede another control with text that describes the second control's use. Typically, a programmer will drag and drop a Label control onto a form, assign the text he or she wants to appear in the label to the control's Text property, and then simply use the control's remaining default property settings.

Depending on your design preference, your code can create a label without a border, with a double-line border, or with a 3-D border, using the Label class BorderStyle property:

```
Label1.BorderStyle = BorderStyle.Fixed3D
```

The following image illustrates labels on a form with each border style.

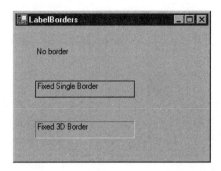

USE IT   Also, as your program executes, there may be times when you will want to add a label to a form "on the fly," or you may want to remove a label. The following program, DynamicLabels.vb, displays a form that displays three buttons titled Date, Time, and Clear. When you click the Date button, the program will display the current date on the form as a label. Likewise, when you click the Time button, the code will use a label to display the current time. Finally, when you click the Clear button, the code will remove the labels (by disabling each label's display). Figure 11-5 illustrates how the labels appear on the form. To start, use Visual Studio to design a form that contains three buttons and two blank labels. You should make the labels each 150×20. You can place the first label at the coordinates 30, 40 and the second at 30, 90. Then in the program code, place the following event handlers:

```
Public Class Form1
    Inherits System.Windows.Forms.Form

#Region " Windows Form Designer generated code "
  ' Code not shown
#End Region

    Private Sub Button1_Click(ByVal sender As Object, _
      ByVal e As System.EventArgs) Handles Button1.Click
        Label1.Text = "Date: " & Now.Date
        Label1.Visible = True
    End Sub

    Private Sub Button2_Click(ByVal sender As Object, _
      ByVal e As System.EventArgs) Handles Button2.Click
        Label2.Text = "Time: " & Now.TimeOfDay.ToString()
```

```
        Label2.Visible = True
    End Sub

    Private Sub Button3_Click(ByVal sender As Object, _
      ByVal e As System.EventArgs) Handles Button3.Click
        Label1.Visible = False
        Label2.Visible = False
    End Sub
End Class
```

As you can see, the program responds to the three different button events. When the user clicks the Date button, the code assigns the current date to the Label1 object and then sets the object's Visible property to True, which displays the label on the form. Likewise, if the user clicks the Time button, the code assigns the current time of day to the Label2 object and then displays the label by setting the object's Visible property to True. If the user clicks the Clear button, the program simply sets each label's Visible property to False to remove the label from view.

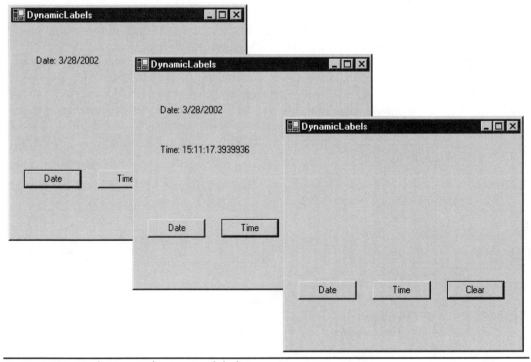

Figure 11-5 Displaying and removing labels as a program executes

Adding Images to a Form's Label

Most labels that appear forms normally contain only text. Using the Form class Image property, your programs can display an image in a Label control. Depending on your design goals, you can specifically size the label (which may or may not let the entire image appear), or you can use the AutoSize property to size the label to display the image.

USE IT   The following program, LabelImage.vb, uses images in a Label control. The program displays a form that contains two Label controls, each of which contains a fixed-size image, as shown in Figure 11-6:

```
Imports System.Drawing

Public Class Form1
    Inherits System.Windows.Forms.Form

#Region " Windows Form Designer generated code "
  ' Code not shown
#End Region

    Public Image1 As Image
    Public Image2 As Image

    Private Sub Form1_Load(ByVal sender As System.Object, _
      ByVal e As System.EventArgs) Handles MyBase.Load

        Image1 = Image.FromFile("lab.jpg")
        Image2 = Image.FromFile("dal.jpg")

        Label1.Image = Image1
        Label2.Image = Image2
    End Sub

    Private Sub Button1_Click(ByVal sender As Object, _
      ByVal e As System.EventArgs) Handles Button1.Click

        Me.Close()

    End Sub
End Class
```

To display an image in a label, the code first creates an Image object, loading the corresponding image from a file by calling Image class FromFile method. Then the code directs each Label object to autosize

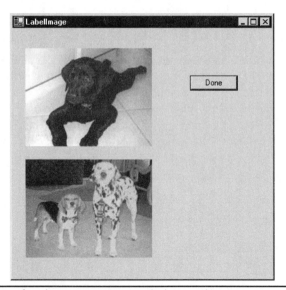

Figure 11-6   Displaying a fixed-size image in a Label control

itself as necessary (however, the images in this case were presized to 200×150 pixels). When the user clicks the Done button, the code closes the form, by using the Me keyword to refer to the current form.

In addition to assigning a single image to a Label control using the Image property, your programs can assign multiple images to the control's ImageList property. Then using the ImageIndex property, you can select the image from the image list that you want the label to display.

Programming the LinkLabel Class

To make your forms more "user friendly," there may be times when you will want to place a hyperlink onto the form that, for example, might let the user connect to an online help page that resides on your Web server, or that may link the user to an ASP.NET page that checks for updates to the program. To place a hyperlink on a form, you can use a LinkLabel control. The next illustration, for example, shows a form that contains a LinkLabel control that prompts the user to check for product updates.

When a user clicks a LinkLabel control that appears in a form, the only thing that happens is that Visual Basic .NET generates a Click event for the control, to which the program can respond. The event handler will receive two parameters, one that specifies the object that generated the event (the specific control) and the second the event arguments:

```
Private Sub LinkLabel1_LinkClicked(ByVal sender As System.Object, _
   ByVal e As System.Windows.Forms.LinkLabelLinkClickedEventArgs) _
   Handles LinkLabel1.LinkClicked
     ' Place Statements here
End Sub
```

In the event handler, the code must perform the actual processing that corresponds to the link, such as displaying an online Help page.

USE IT The following program, LinkLabelDemo.vb, creates a form that contains information about a book. The form also contains a LinkLabel control you can select to view the publisher's Web site in a browser, as shown in Figure 11-7:

```
Public Class Form1
    Inherits System.Windows.Forms.Form

#Region " Windows Form Designer generated code "
  ' Code not shown
#End Region

    Private Sub LinkLabel1_LinkClicked(ByVal sender As System.Object, _
       ByVal e As System.Windows.Forms.LinkLabelLinkClickedEventArgs) _
       Handles LinkLabel1.LinkClicked

        Try
            Process.Start("IExplore.exe", "www.Osborne.com")
        Catch
            MsgBox("Error launching Internet Explorer")
        End Try
    End Sub
End Class
```

As you can see, the code simply implements one event handler that responds when the user clicks the LinkLabel control. In this case, the event handler uses the Process class Start method to launch the Internet Explorer, directing IE to display the Osborne Web site. Chapter 8 examines the use of the Process class.

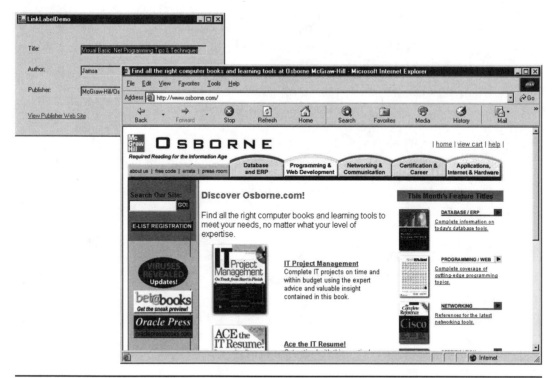

Figure 11-7   Using a LinkLabel control to launch the display of a Web page

Programming Menu Controls

Depending on the processing your program performs, there may be times when you will want to provide a menu of options from which the user can select to initiate a specific operation. In such cases, your programs can use a Menu control. The image here illustrates a form that contains several common menus.

USE IT   To place a menu onto a form in Visual Studio, drag and drop a MainMenu control onto the form. Visual Studio will display a box labeled Type Here on the form. In the box, type the first menu name, such as File. Visual Studio will expand the menu, letting you add items beneath the menu name or another menu to the right of the menu name. Using the boxes, type the options to build your menu (or menus).

To process a user's menu selections, your code must provide an event handler for each menu option. When the user selects a menu item, the program will generate the corresponding event. The following program, MenuDemo.vb, creates the menu previously shown. The program then provides event handlers that respond to the menu option selections. In this case, the program simply displays a message box stating the option the user selected:

```
Public Class Form1
    Inherits System.Windows.Forms.Form

#Region " Windows Form Designer generated code "
    ' Code not shown
#End Region

    Private Sub MenuItem1_Click(ByVal sender As Object, _
      ByVal e As System.EventArgs) Handles MenuItem1.Click
        MsgBox("File menu")
    End Sub

    Private Sub MenuItem2_Click(ByVal sender As Object, _
      ByVal e As System.EventArgs) Handles MenuItem2.Click
        MsgBox("Edit menu")
    End Sub

    Private Sub MenuItem4_Click(ByVal sender As Object, _
      ByVal e As System.EventArgs) Handles MenuItem4.Click
        MsgBox("Help menu about option")
    End Sub
End Class
```

Programming the PictureBox Control

In the Tip titled "Adding Images to a Form's Label," you learned how to place an image in a Label control that appears in a form. The most common (and proper) way to display an image on a form is to use a PictureBox control. Figure 11-8 illustrates a form that uses a PictureBox control to display images.

Figure 11-8   Using a PictureBox control to display images in a form

The following program, MyPhotos.vb, displays an Open dialog box in which the user can select a directory and multiple image files. The program then uses a picture box to display each image one after the other for five seconds. The program will continue to cycle through the images until you end the program:

```
Public Class Form1
    Inherits System.Windows.Forms.Form

#Region " Windows Form Designer generated code "
  ' Code not shown
#End Region

    Public ImageFiles() As String
    Public FileIndex As Integer

    Public Sub ShowImages()
        Dim FileDB As New OpenFileDialog()
        FileDB.Multiselect = True

        If (FileDB.ShowDialog() = DialogResult.OK) Then
            ImageFiles = FileDB.FileNames

            Me.Refresh()

            If ImageFiles.Length = 0 Then
                MsgBox("No files selected")
                Me.Close()
```

```
Else
    Dim IsImageFile As Boolean
    Button1.Text = "End"

    Dim MyImage As Image
    FileIndex = 0
    Do
        IsImageFile = False

        If (UCase(ImageFiles(FileIndex)).EndsWith("JPG")) Then
            IsImageFile = True
        End If

        If (UCase(ImageFiles(FileIndex)).EndsWith("BMP")) Then
            IsImageFile = True
        End If

        If (UCase(ImageFiles(FileIndex)).EndsWith("GIF")) Then
            IsImageFile = True
        End If

        If (IsImageFile) Then

            Me.Text = ImageFiles(FileIndex)
            Try
                MyImage = Image.FromFile(ImageFiles(FileIndex))

                PictureBox1.Image = _
                    Image.FromFile(ImageFiles(FileIndex))
                Display.Sleep(5000)
            Catch Ex As Exception
            End Try
        End If

        FileIndex = FileIndex + 1

        If (FileIndex = ImageFiles.Length) Then
            FileIndex = 0
        End If

    Loop While (True)
    End If
Else
    MsgBox("User selected Cancel")
```

```
            Me.Close()
        End If
    End Sub

    Dim Display As System.Threading.Thread

    Private Sub Button1_Click(ByVal sender As Object, _
        ByVal e As System.EventArgs) Handles Button1.Click
        Dim FileDB As New OpenFileDialog()
        FileDB.Multiselect = True

        If (Button1.Text = "End") Then
            Display.Abort()
            Me.Close()
        Else
            Button1.Text = "End"

            Display = New System.Threading.Thread(AddressOf ShowImages)
            Display.Start()
        End If
    End Sub
End Class
```

To display the images, the program starts a second thread, which executes the ShowImages subroutine. The program uses a second thread so that it can use the Sleep method to delay between the display of each image. If the program instead used the primary thread, the program would not respond to button click operations while the thread was sleeping, which would prevent the user from ending the program properly. Chapter 8 discusses threads in detail.

In the ShowImages function, the program retrieves the filenames the user selected in the Open dialog box. The program then simply loops through the array of names. Each time the program retrieves a name, the program checks if the filename ends with the JPG, BMP, or GIF extension. If you want the program to support additional graphics types, you must include additional If statements. Then the program creates an Image object that corresponds to the filename that the program then assigns to the PictureBox control. If an error occurs during the image retrieval and assignment, the program detects and then ignores the error using a Try-Catch statement. Rather than displaying an error message, the program simply continues with the next file.

Programming the NumericUpDown Control

Depending on the input a form requires, there may be times when you can simplify the coding you must perform to get a numeric value by using a NumericUpDown control, similar to that shown here.

Using the NumericUpDown control, you assign the control a range of values, such as 1 to 10 or 1 to 10,000 as well as an increment. The user can click the control to increment or decrement the control's value.

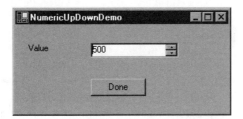

USE IT   The following program, NumericUpDownDemo.vb, creates a form containing a NumericUpDown control (previously shown). Using the control, the user can select a number between 0 and 1,000 (incrementing or decrementing the value, in this case, by 5). When the user clicks the form's Done button, the program displays a message box that states the NumericUpDown control's current value:

```
Public Class Form1
    Inherits System.Windows.Forms.Form

#Region " Windows Form Designer generated code "
  ' Code not shown
#End Region

    Private Sub Button1_Click(ByVal sender As Object, _
       ByVal e As System.EventArgs) Handles Button1.Click
        MsgBox("Value is " & NumericUpDown1.Value)
    End Sub

    Private Sub Form1_Load(ByVal sender As System.Object, _
      ByVal e As System.EventArgs) Handles MyBase.Load
        NumericUpDown1.Increment = 5
        NumericUpDown1.Maximum = 1000
        NumericUpDown1.Value = 500
    End Sub
End Class
```

As you can see, when the program first loads the form, the code initializes the NumericUpDown control's Increment, Maximum, and Value properties.

Programming the ComboBox Control

The .NET Windows Forms controls provide several controls you can use to prompt the user to select an entry from a list. The ComboBox control lets you create a drop-down list similar to that shown in Figure 11-9. When the form first displays the list, the form will show an entry that your program can use to describe the list contents, such as Select a State or Select a Book.

The following program, ComboBox.vb, displays the pull-down list shown in Figure 11-9. To create this program in Visual Studio, drag and drop a ComboBox control and a Button control onto a form. Then select the ComboBox control and display the control's properties. In the Property window, click the Text property and type **Pets** (the label the control will show when the form first displays). Then locate and select the Items property. Click the button that appears in the property. Visual Studio will display the String Collection Editor window, in which you can type the entries that you want to appear in the control. Finally, place the following statements in the program:

```
Public Class Form1
    Inherits System.Windows.Forms.Form

#Region " Windows Form Designer generated code "
  ' Code not shown
#End Region

    Private Sub Button1_Click(ByVal sender As Object, _
      ByVal e As System.EventArgs) Handles Button1.Click
        If (ComboBox1.SelectedItem <> "") Then
            MsgBox("You selected: " & ComboBox1.SelectedItem)
        Else
            MsgBox("You must select an item")
        End If
    End Sub
End Class
```

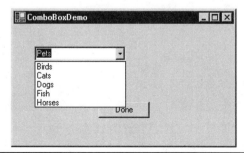

Figure 11-9   Using a ComboBox control to select items in a form

Displaying an Operation's Status Using a ProgressBar and the StatusBar

When your programs perform time-consuming tasks, such as calculating a complex result, downloading a large file from the Web, or searching a disk for files, your program should provide the user with status information about the operation's progress.

USE IT The Windows Forms class provides two controls your programs can use to provide the user with meaningful feedback regarding an operation's progress: the StatusBar and the ProgressBar. The StatusBar control normally appears at the bottom of a form or window. In the status bar, you display a text message to the user. The ProgressBar control lets your programs display a graphic indicator of the percentage of a task a program has completed, as shown in Figure 11-10.

The following program, UseProgressBar.vb, calculates the factorial of the numbers 10, 20, and 30 using a recursive function. To compute the factorial of the value 10, you would multiply 10*9*8*7*6*5*4*3*2*1. As the program calculates its results, it uses a ProgressBar control to indicate the amount of processing it has completed:

```
Public Class Form1
    Inherits System.Windows.Forms.Form

#Region " Windows Form Designer generated code "
 ' Code not shown
#End Region

    Function Factorial(ByVal Value As Double) As Double
        If (Value = 0) Then
            Factorial = 1.0
            System.Threading.Thread.Sleep(3000)
        Else
            Factorial = Value * Factorial(Math.Ceiling(Value - 1))
        End If
    End Function

    Private Sub Button1_Click(ByVal sender As Object, _
      ByVal e As System.EventArgs) Handles Button1.Click
        Label1.Text = Label1.Text & Factorial(10)
        Label1.Refresh()
        ProgressBar1.Value = 33
        Label2.Text = Label2.Text & Factorial(20)
        Label2.Refresh()
        ProgressBar1.Value = 66
        Label3.Text = Label3.Text & Factorial(30)
        Label3.Refresh()
        ProgressBar1.Value = 100
    End Sub
End Class
```

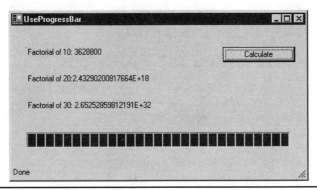

Figure 11-10 Using a ProgressBar to indicate completed processing

To delay the program briefly so that you can view changes in the progress bar, the Factorial function sleeps for three seconds before it returns the value 1 result. Note that after the code updates a Label control's Text property, the code calls the Label class Refresh method to immediately display the control's new value.

A StatusBar control is a text message box that you can place at the bottom of a form. As your program executes, you can display messages to the user in the status box by assigning a message to the control's Text property. In Visual Studio, drag and drop a status bar onto the current form. Then change the previous code slightly to display status messages in the box as the program executes:

```
Private Sub Button1_Click(ByVal sender As Object, _
    ByVal e As System.EventArgs) Handles Button1.Click

    StatusBar1.Text = "Calculating Factorial(10)"
    Label1.Text = Label1.Text & Factorial(10)
    Label1.Refresh()
    ProgressBar1.Value = 33

    StatusBar1.Text = "Calculating Factorial(20)"
    Label2.Text = Label2.Text & Factorial(20)
    Label2.Refresh()
    ProgressBar1.Value = 66

    StatusBar1.Text = "Calculating Factorial(30)"
    Label3.Text = Label3.Text & Factorial(30)
    Label3.Refresh()
    ProgressBar1.Value = 100
    StatusBar1.Text = "Done"
End Sub
```

Programming the TextBox Control

In Visual Basic programs, programmers make extensive use of the TextBox control to let the user view or enter large amounts of text. In a TextBox control that a program uses for input operations, the program can set the control's Readonly property to False. In a text box, a user can type data or paste it into the control from the clipboard. When a program wants to display data in a control, preventing the user from changing the data, the program can set the Readonly property to True.

USE IT   The following program, TextBoxInput.vb, displays a form that lets a user enter a memo as shown in Figure 11-11, to which the program assigns a date and time stamp. When the user clicks Save, the program will append the memo's contents to the root-directory file C:\Memos.txt:

```
Imports System.IO

Public Class Form1
    Inherits System.Windows.Forms.Form

#Region " Windows Form Designer generated code "
  ' Code not shown
#End Region

    Private Sub Button1_Click(ByVal sender As Object, _
      ByVal e As System.EventArgs) Handles Button1.Click
        Dim TargetFile As StreamWriter

        Try
            TargetFile = New StreamWriter("C:\Memos.txt", True)
        Catch
            MsgBox("Error opening " & "C:\Memos.txt")
        End Try

        Try
            TargetFile.WriteLine(Now())
            TargetFile.Write(TextBox1.Text)
            TargetFile.WriteLine()
            TargetFile.WriteLine()
        Catch
            MsgBox("Error writing file")
        End Try

        TargetFile.Close()
        MsgBox("Text saved to " & ("C:\Memos.txt"))
    End Sub
End Class
```

Figure 11-11   Using a TextBox control to enter text

As discussed, when a program wants to prevent a user from changing the text that appears in a text box, the program can set the control's Readonly property to True. The following program, ShowMemos.vb, uses a read-only text box to display the memos the user has saved into the file C:\Memos.txt:

```
Imports System.IO

Public Class Form1
    Inherits System.Windows.Forms.Form

#Region " Windows Form Designer generated code "
  ' Code not shown
#End Region

    Private Sub Button1_Click(ByVal sender As Object, _
      ByVal e As System.EventArgs) Handles Button1.Click
        Dim SourceFile As StreamReader

        Try
            SourceFile = New StreamReader("C:\Memos.txt")
        Catch
            MsgBox("Error opening " & "C:\Memos.txt")
        End Try

        Try
```

```
        TextBox1.Text = SourceFile.ReadToEnd()
        SourceFile.Close()
    Catch
        MsgBox("Error reading file")
    End Try


End Sub
End Class
```

To create the program in Visual Studio, drag and drop a TextBox control onto the form and then display the control's properties. In the Property window, set the Multiline property to True. Visual Studio will then let you size the control's height and width on the form. In the Property window, locate the Text property and delete the contents it contains, so the box will appear empty when the program begins. Because the program does not let the user change the file's contents, you should set the control's Readonly property to True. Also, by default, a TextBox control does not display scrollbars. In Visual Studio, you can use the Scrollbars property to select the type of scrollbar (horizontal, vertical, or both), or you can also enable and disable the display of scrollbars in your program code. To complete this program, you must also drag and drop a Button control onto the form, to which you assign the Text property the string Load Memos.

Programming the RichTextBox Control

For years, Visual Basic programmers have made extensive use of TextBox controls to display text in a form and to prompt the user for information. As applications increase their functionality, there are many times when the application must format the text that appears in a form, perhaps by bolding, italicizing, or highlighting the text in some other way. When your application must display formatted text, your programs can use a RichTextBox control.

USE IT   The following program, ShowRTF.vb, uses the Open dialog box to let the user select a rich text format (RTF) file. (To create an RTF file that contains formatting, you can use a word processor such as Microsoft Word.) The program opens the file the user specifies and displays the file's contents in a RichTextBox control, as shown in Figure 11-12.

```
Public Class Form1
    Inherits System.Windows.Forms.Form

#Region " Windows Form Designer generated code "
  ' Code not shown
#End Region

    Private Sub Button1_Click(ByVal sender As Object, _
      ByVal e As System.EventArgs) Handles Button1.Click
```

```
    Dim FileDB As New OpenFileDialog()

    FileDB.Filter = "All files|*.*|RTF files|*.rtf"
    FileDB.FilterIndex = 2
    FileDB.InitialDirectory = "C:\Temp"

    If (FileDB.ShowDialog() = DialogResult.OK) Then
        Try
            RichTextBox1.LoadFile(FileDB.FileName)
        Catch
            MsgBox("Error reading file")
        End Try
    Else
        MsgBox("User selected Cancel")
    End If
End Sub
End Class
```

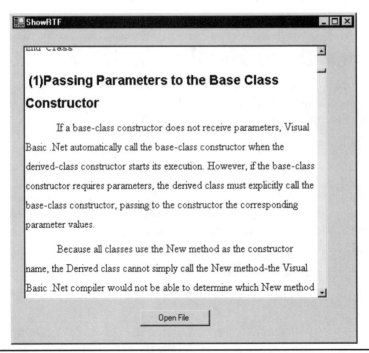

Figure 11-12   Displaying formatted text in a RichTextBox control

Programming ScrollBar Controls

In a window, programs often provide horizontal and vertical scrollbars which the user can use to move (scroll) content into view. When your program uses a TextBox control or a RichTextBox control, you can enable the display of horizontal and vertical scrollbars for the control using the Scrollbars property. Depending on other controls you place on your form, you may want to place a horizontal or vertical scrollbar onto the scrollbar itself. In such cases, you can use a ScrollBar control.

 The following program, ScrollBarDemo.vb, demonstrates the use of horizontal and vertical scrollbars in a form. When you run the program, it will display a form that contains two scrollbars as shown here.

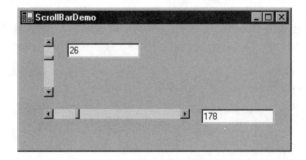

As you move the scrollbar sliders, the program will respond to the event and display the corresponding value.

```
Public Class Form1
    Inherits System.Windows.Forms.Form

#Region " Windows Form Designer generated code "
  ' Code not shown
#End Region

    Private Sub VScrollBar1_ValueChanged(ByVal sender As Object, _
      ByVal e As System.EventArgs) Handles VScrollBar1.ValueChanged
        TextBox1.Text = VScrollBar1.Value
    End Sub

    Private Sub HScrollBar1_Scroll(ByVal sender As Object, _
      ByVal e As System.Windows.Forms.ScrollEventArgs) _
      Handles HScrollBar1.Scroll
        TextBox2.Text = HScrollBar1.Value
    End Sub
End Class
```

To create the program in Visual Studio, drag a VScrollbar control and an HScrollbar control onto the form, as well as two TextBox controls. Using each control's Property window, set the vertical scrollbar's range of values to 1 to 100 and the horizontal scrollbar range of values to 1 to 1,000. Also, change each scrollbar's LargeChange property to 10 and the value to 1. The LargeChange property controls the amount by which the scrollbar increments or decrements its value when you click the scrollbar itself or press the PAGE UP or PAGE DOWN key.

Programming the TrackBar Control

In the Tip titled "Programming ScrollBar Controls," you learned how to program vertical and horizontal scrollbars. As shown in Figure 11-13, a TrackBar control is similar to a scrollbar in that it lets the user slide the bar's control to select a setting from a range of values. To help the user select intermediate values, the TrackBar control provides tick marks at set intervals.

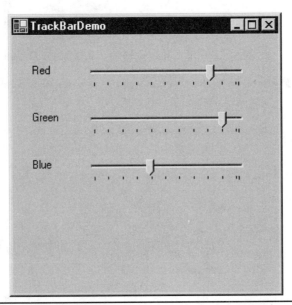

Figure 11-13 A TrackBar control provides tick marks to help the user select intermediate values

USE IT   The following program, TrackBarDemo.vb, displays three TrackBar controls the user
can use to select the form's red, green, and blue background color settings. As the user
changes a setting on the TrackBar, the program responds by changing the form's background color:

```vb
Public Class Form1
    Inherits System.Windows.Forms.Form

#Region " Windows Form Designer generated code "
  ' Code not shown
#End Region

    Public Red As Byte
    Public Green As Byte
    Public Blue As Byte
    Public Background As Color

    Private Sub TrackBar1_ValueChanged(ByVal sender As Object, _
      ByVal e As System.EventArgs) Handles TrackBar1.ValueChanged
        Red = TrackBar1.Value
        Background = Color.FromArgb(Red, Green, Blue)

        Form1.ActiveForm.BackColor = Background
        Form1.ActiveForm.Refresh()
    End Sub

    Private Sub TrackBar2_ValueChanged(ByVal sender As Object, _
      ByVal e As System.EventArgs) Handles TrackBar2.ValueChanged
        Green = TrackBar2.Value
        Background = Color.FromArgb(Red, Green, Blue)

        Form1.ActiveForm.BackColor = Background
        Form1.ActiveForm.Refresh()
    End Sub

    Private Sub TrackBar3_ValueChanged(ByVal sender As Object, _
      ByVal e As System.EventArgs) Handles TrackBar3.ValueChanged
        Blue = TrackBar3.Value
        Background = Color.FromArgb(Red, Green, Blue)
```

```
        Form1.ActiveForm.BackColor = Background
        Form1.ActiveForm.Refresh()
    End Sub

    Private Sub Form1_Activated(ByVal sender As System.Object, _
      ByVal e As System.EventArgs) Handles MyBase.Activated
        Red = Form1.ActiveForm.BackColor.R
        Green = Form1.ActiveForm.BackColor.G
        Blue = Form1.ActiveForm.BackColor.B
        TrackBar1.Value = Red
        TrackBar2.Value = Green
        TrackBar3.Value = Blue
    End Sub
End Class
```

To create this program in Visual Studio, drag and drop three TrackBar controls onto a form. Then, using each control's Property window, set the range of values each control supports to a minimum value 0 and a maximum value of 255. Next, set the TickFrequency property to 25 to put tick marks on the track bar every 25 values.

Programming the ToolBar Control

In the Windows environment, users have become accustomed to using toolbars in a window to quickly perform common operations. In Microsoft Word, for example, you might use toolbar buttons to start print, file save, or spell-check operations. In a form, you can create a toolbar using the ToolBar control.

USE IT In a ToolBar control, you place ToolBarButton objects. The following program, ToolBarDemo.vb, creates a ToolBar object and then assigns five ToolBarButton objects to the ToolBar. When you click one of the buttons in the toolbar, the program will display a message box that corresponds to the button, as shown here.

To create this program, use Visual Studio to place an empty toolbar onto a form. You can assign toolbar buttons in Visual Studio, however, this program creates and assigns the buttons itself:

```
Public Class Form1
    Inherits System.Windows.Forms.Form

#Region " Windows Form Designer generated code "
   ' Code not shown
#End Region

    Public MondayButton = New ToolBarButton("Monday")
    Public TuesdayButton = New ToolBarButton("Tuesday")
    Public WednesdayButton = New ToolBarButton("Wednesday")
    Public ThursdayButton = New ToolBarButton("Thursday")
    Public FridayButton = New ToolBarButton("Friday")

    Private Sub Form1_Load(ByVal sender As System.Object, _
        ByVal e As System.EventArgs) Handles MyBase.Load
ToolBar1.Buttons.Add(MondayButton)
        ToolBar1.Buttons.Add(TuesdayButton)
        ToolBar1.Buttons.Add(WednesdayButton)
        ToolBar1.Buttons.Add(ThursdayButton)
        ToolBar1.Buttons.Add(FridayButton)
End Sub

    Private Sub ToolBar1_ButtonClick(ByVal sender As Object, _
        ByVal e As System.Windows.Forms.ToolBarButtonClickEventArgs) _
        Handles ToolBar1.ButtonClick
        Dim ButtonPicked As ToolBarButton = e.Button

        If (ButtonPicked.Equals(MondayButton)) Then
            MsgBox("You picked Monday")
        ElseIf (ButtonPicked.Equals(TuesdayButton)) Then
            MsgBox("You picked Tuesday")
        ElseIf (ButtonPicked.Equals(WednesdayButton)) Then
            MsgBox("You picked Wednesday")
        ElseIf (ButtonPicked.Equals(ThursdayButton)) Then
            MsgBox("You picked Thursday")
        ElseIf (ButtonPicked.Equals(FridayButton)) Then
            MsgBox("You picked Friday")
        End If
    End Sub
End Class
```

Most Windows applications provide a pop-up ToolTip for each button in a ToolBar control, which displays a text message that briefly describes the button's purpose. To add a ToolTip to a button, simply add the text you desire to the ToolbarButton object's ToolTipText field:

```
MondayButton.ToolTipText = "View Monday's Events"
```

The previous program added buttons to the ToolBar control one button at a time. Using the AddRange method, the following code fragment creates an array of ToolbarButton objects that the code then assigns to a ToolBar object

```
Dim Buttons() As ToolBarButton = { _
  MondayButton, TuesdayButton, FridayButton}

ToolBar1.Buttons.AddRange(Buttons)
```

Normally, a button in a ToolBar control will contain an icon and text. To assign an image to a ToolBarButton object, you assign the images to the ToolBar object's ImageList property and then assign the index value that corresponds to the image you desire to the ToolbarButton object's ImageIndex property.

Programming the RadioButton Control

In a form, radio buttons let a user select one option from a set of choices. Radio buttons are so named because, like the buttons of an automobile radio, you can only select one radio button from a set of buttons at any one time. A form that uses radio buttons to restrict the user to selecting only one operating system is shown here.

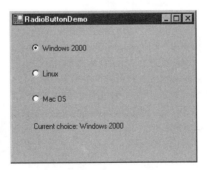

Normally, most programs do not respond to RadioButton control events. Instead, the program waits until the user completes the form and then simply tests each RadioButton object's Checked field to determine if the user has selected the button:

```
If RadioButton1.Checked Then
  MsgBox("You selected: " & RadioButton1.Text)
End If
```

USE IT   The following program, RadioButtonDemo.vb, displays three radio buttons. As the
           user selects a button, the program responds to the Click event by displaying a label that
corresponds to the selected button:

```
Public Class Form1
    Inherits System.Windows.Forms.Form

#Region " Windows Form Designer generated code "
  ' Code not shown
#End Region

    Private Sub RadioButton1_Click(ByVal sender As Object, _
      ByVal e As System.EventArgs) Handles RadioButton1.Click
        Label1.Text = "Current choice: " & RadioButton1.Text
        Label1.Refresh()
    End Sub

    Private Sub RadioButton2_Click(ByVal sender As Object, _
      ByVal e As System.EventArgs) Handles RadioButton2.Click
        Label1.Text = "Current choice: " & RadioButton2.Text
        Label1.Refresh()
    End Sub

    Private Sub RadioButton3_Click(ByVal sender As Object, _
      ByVal e As System.EventArgs) Handles RadioButton3.Click
        Label1.Text = "Current choice: " & RadioButton3.Text
        Label1.Refresh()
    End Sub

End Class
```

To create this program in Visual Studio, drag and drop the three RadioButton controls onto
the form. Using each control's Property window, assign the text you want the button to display
to the Text property.

Using a GroupBox to Group Radio Buttons

If your form contains two or more different sets of RadioButton controls, you must place each set of
buttons into its own GroupBox control in order for Visual Basic .NET to know how the buttons relate
to one another.

USE IT   In Visual Studio, you simply drag and drop a GroupBox control onto your form. Then,
           after you place and size the GroupBox control, you can drag and drop the related

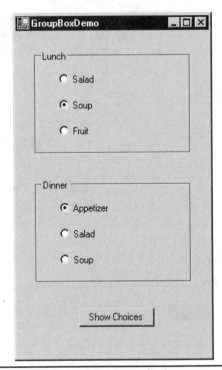

Figure 11-14 Using GroupBox controls to separate radio-button groups

RadioButton controls into the GroupBox. The following program, GroupBoxDemo.vb, creates a form that contains two GroupBox controls, as shown in Figure 11-14. In each GroupBox control, the code places three RadioButton controls.

By placing the GroupBox controls using Visual Studio, your program code can ignore the fact that the GroupBox controls exist, and can, instead, simply manipulate the radio buttons:

```
Public Class Form1
    Inherits System.Windows.Forms.Form

#Region " Windows Form Designer generated code "
  ' Code not shown
#End Region

    Private Sub Button1_Click(ByVal sender As System.Object, _
      ByVal e As System.EventArgs) Handles Button1.Click
        If (RadioButton1.Checked) Then
            MsgBox("Salad for lunch")
        ElseIf (RadioButton2.Checked) Then
            MsgBox("Soup for lunch")
        ElseIf (RadioButton3.Checked) Then
```

```
            MsgBox("Fruit for lunch")
        End If

        If (RadioButton4.Checked) Then
            MsgBox("Appetizer for dinner")
        ElseIf (RadioButton5.Checked) Then
            MsgBox("Salad for dinner")
        ElseIf (RadioButton6.Checked) Then
            MsgBox("Soup for dinner")
        End If
    End Sub
End Class
```

Programming the CheckBox Control

In a form, checkboxes let a user select multiple options—unlike radio buttons that restrict the user
to choosing only one item from several possible choices. Figure 11-15 illustrates a form that uses
checkboxes that correspond to the C#, Visual Basic .NET, and JScript .NET programming languages.
To place a checkbox in a form, your programs use the CheckBox control. Unlike traditional checkbox
objects that returned the value True if the box was selected and False otherwise, you can use the
CheckBox control ThreeState property (set the property to True) to direct the control to return the
Checked, Unchecked, and Indeterminate values. When your program uses a three-state checkbox,
the control will toggle between checked, indeterminate (dimmed in appearance), and not checked.
Figure 11-15 shows all three.

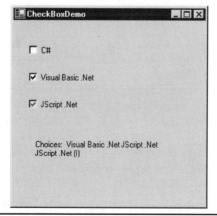

Figure 11-15   The .NET environment supports three-state checkboxes

Like RadioButton controls, programs normally do not respond to the events a CheckBox control generates. Instead, programs normally wait until a user completes a form and then examine the checkbox settings. The following program, CheckBoxDemo.vb, displays three checkbox controls. Each time the user changes a checkbox setting, the program updates a label that contains the current selections. If the box is checked, the program will display the checkbox text in the label. If the box is indeterminate, the program will display the checkbox text followed by the letter (I):

```
Public Class Form1
    Inherits System.Windows.Forms.Form

#Region " Windows Form Designer generated code "
    ' Code not shown
#End Region

    Private Sub CheckBox1_Click(ByVal sender As Object, _
      ByVal e As System.EventArgs) Handles CheckBox1.Click, _
      CheckBox2.Click, CheckBox3.Click

        Label1.Text = "Choices: "

        If (CheckBox1.Checked) Then
            Label1.Text = Label1.Text & " " & CheckBox1.Text
        End If

        If (CheckBox1.CheckState = CheckState.Indeterminate) Then
            Label1.Text = Label1.Text & " " & CheckBox1.Text & " (I)"
        End If

        If (CheckBox2.Checked) Then
            Label1.Text = Label1.Text & " " & CheckBox2.Text
        End If

        If (CheckBox2.CheckState = CheckState.Indeterminate) Then
            Label1.Text = Label1.Text & " " & CheckBox2.Text & " (I)"
        End If

        If (CheckBox3.Checked) Then
            Label1.Text = Label1.Text & " " & CheckBox3.Text
        End If

        If (CheckBox3.CheckState = CheckState.Indeterminate) Then
            Label1.Text = Label1.Text & " " & CheckBox3.Text & " (I)"
        End If

        Label1.Refresh()
    End Sub
End Class
```

As you can see, the program code uses one event handler to handle each of the checkbox events. To create this program in Visual Studio, drag and drop three CheckBox controls onto a form along with a Label control. Use each checkbox's Property window to set the ThreeState property to True.

Programming the DomainUpDown Control

Many forms contain a list of items, such as city or state names, from which the user can select a value. Often, forms use pull-down lists to let users select the item. However, if your form's "real estate" is limited, you may want to use a DomainUpDown control that lets the user move through the list of values by clicking the control's up and down arrows, as shown here.

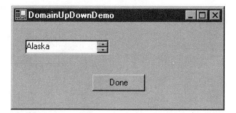

To use the DomainUpDown class, your program assigns the list entries to a collection, which you can do in Visual Studio or in your program code. The following program, DomainUpDownDemo.vb, displays a form that contains a DomainUpDown control from which a user can select a state (previously shown). After the user selects a state and clicks Done, the code displays the user's selection:

```
Public Class Form1
    Inherits System.Windows.Forms.Form

#Region " Windows Form Designer generated code "
  ' Code not shown
#End Region

    Private Sub Button1_Click(ByVal sender As Object, _
      ByVal e As System.EventArgs) Handles Button1.Click
        If (DomainUpDown1.SelectedItem = "") Then
            MsgBox("You must select a state")
        Else
            MsgBox("You choose: " & DomainUpDown1.SelectedItem)
        End If
    End Sub
End Class
```

To create this program, use Visual Studio to drag and drop and a DomainUpDown control onto a form, along with a Button control. Then select the DomainUpDown control and display the control's properties. In the Property window, locate and select the Items property. Then click the small button that appears in the property entry. Visual Studio will display the String Collection Editor window, in which you can type the list entries.

Depending on the processing your program performs, there may be times when you will want to add items to a DomainUpDown control object on the fly. In such cases, your program can use the object's Add method, as shown here:

```
DomainUpDown1.Items.Add("Alaska")
DomainUpDown1.Items.Add("Arizona")
DomainUpDown1.Items.Add("California")
```

Programming the ListBox Control

In a form, a list box provides a way to present items, such as product names, company locations, and other text-based items in a control through which the user can scroll to select an item (or multiple items if the list supports two or more selections). Figure 11-16 shows a form that uses a ListBox control to let the user select an operating system from a list of options.

To determine which item in the list a user selected, your code uses the ListBox object SelectedItem property. Depending on how your program uses the list, there may be times when you will want a list box to let a user select two or more items. In such cases, your code must set the object's SelectionMode property to enable multiple selections.

USE IT The following program, ListBoxDemo.vb, creates the form with a list box, previously shown in Figure 11-16, that contains a list of operating systems. After the user clicks Done, the program uses a MsgBox to display the user's selection. To create the list box in Visual Studio, drag and drop a ListBox control onto a form, along with a Button control. Then select the ListBox control and display its properties. In the control's Property window, locate and select the Items entry. Then click the small button that appears in the entry. Visual Studio will display the

Figure 11-16   Using a ListBox control to let users select items from a list

String Collection Editor dialog box, in which you can type the list of operating systems the control will display:

```
Public Class Form1
    Inherits System.Windows.Forms.Form

#Region " Windows Form Designer generated code "
  ' Code not shown
#End Region

    Private Sub Button1_Click(ByVal sender As Object, _
      ByVal e As System.EventArgs) Handles Button1.Click

        If (ListBox1.SelectedItem <> "") Then
            MsgBox("You selected: " & ListBox1.SelectedItem)
        Else
            MsgBox("You must select an item")
        End If
    End Sub
End Class
```

Depending on your list's contents, there may be times when you will want to add or remove items to or from a ListBox control as the program executes. In such cases, you can assign a new array of entries to the ListBox class DataSource method, as shown here:

```
Dim NewList() As String = {"Osborne", "Sybex", "Wrox", "Delmar" }
ListBox1.DataSource = NewList
```

In a similar way, using the AddRange method, your code can add choices to the current list as follows:

```
ListBox1.Items.AddRange(NewList)
```

Likewise, you can add a single item to the list by using the Add method:

```
ListBox1.Items.Add("New Item")
```

To remove an item from the list, you can use the Remove method:

```
ListBox1.Items.Remove("New Item")
```

Before your program changes a list's contents, your code should call the ListBox class BeginUpdate method, which delays the painting of the control until your program calls the EndUpdate method:

```
ListBox1.BeginUpdate
ListBox1.DataSource = NewList
ListBox1.EndUpdate
```

Programming the CheckedListBox Control

In the Tip titled "Programming the ListBox Control," you learned that a ListBox control makes it easy for a user to select a text-based item from a group (list) of items. When your form lets a user select more than one item from a list, you may want to use the CheckedListBox control that places a checkbox next to each item in the list.

 The following program, CheckedListBoxDemo.vb, displays the form shown here, which contains a CheckedListBox control that the user can use to select specific books.

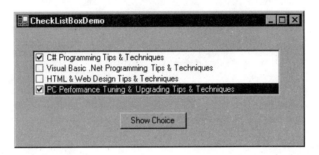

After the user makes his or her selections and clicks the Show Choice button, the program displays a message box for each selected title.

```
Public Class Form1
    Inherits System.Windows.Forms.Form

#Region " Windows Form Designer generated code "
  ' Code not shown
#End Region

    Public List() As String = _
      {"C# Programming Tips & Techniques", _
        "Visual Basic .Net Programming Tips & Techniques", _
        "HTML & Web Design Tips & Techniques", _
        "PC Performance Tuning & Upgrading Tips & Techniques"}

    Private Sub Form1_Load(ByVal sender As System.Object, _
      ByVal e As System.EventArgs) Handles MyBase.Load
        CheckedListBox1.BeginUpdate()
        CheckedListBox1.DataSource = List
        CheckedListBox1.EndUpdate()
    End Sub

    Private Sub Button1_Click(ByVal sender As Object, _
```

```
        ByVal e As System.EventArgs) Handles Button1.Click
        If (CheckedListBox1.SelectedItem <> "") Then
            Dim Entry As Object
            For Each Entry In CheckedListBox1.CheckedItems
                MsgBox(Entry.ToString())
            Next
        Else
            MsgBox("You must select an item")
        End If
    End Sub
End Class
```

Programming the DateTimePicker Control

Regardless of their processing, many applications require a user to enter a date and time. A travel-agent program, for example, might schedule a customer's flights based on a specific date and time. Likewise, a bill-pay program might prompt the user for the date (and possibly the time) he or she wants to send a payment. To simplify date and time operations, your programs can use the DateTimePicker control that expands to a calendar from which the user can select the date he or she desires, as shown in Figure 11-17.

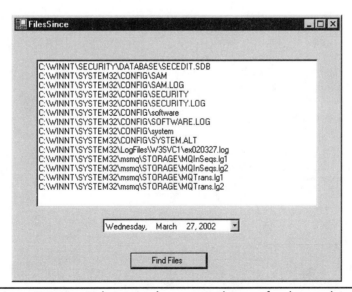

Figure 11-17   Using a DateTimePicker control to prompt the user for date and time information

The following program, FilesSince.vb, uses a DateTimePicker control to prompt the user to enter a date. The program then searches the user's disk for files the user has created since the given date and time. The program places each file's path in a text box:

```vb
Imports System.IO

Public Class Form1
    Inherits System.Windows.Forms.Form

#Region " Windows Form Designer generated code "
    ' Code not shown
#End Region

    Public SearchDate As Date

    Sub FindFiles(ByVal Dir As String)
        Dim DirObj As New DirectoryInfo(Dir)

        Dim Files As FileInfo() = DirObj.GetFiles("*.*")
        Dim Dirs As DirectoryInfo() = DirObj.GetDirectories("*.*")

        Dim Filename As FileInfo

        For Each Filename In Files
            If (Filename.LastWriteTime > SearchDate) Then
                TextBox1.AppendText(Filename.FullName & vbCrLf)
            End If
        Next

        Dim DirectoryName As DirectoryInfo

        For Each DirectoryName In Dirs
            Try
                FindFiles(DirectoryName.FullName)
            Catch E As Exception
                MsgBox("*** Error accessing " & _
                    DirectoryName.FullName)
            End Try
        Next
    End Sub

    Private Sub Button1_Click(ByVal sender As Object, _
        ByVal e As System.EventArgs) Handles Button1.Click
        SearchDate = DateTimePicker1.Value
        FindFiles("C:\")
    End Sub
End Class
```

Programming the MonthCalendar Control

In the Tip titled "Programming the DateTimePicker Control," you learned how to display a system date and time on a form that the user could select to display a monthly calendar with which he or she could choose a new date. Depending on your form's purpose and layout, there may be times when you will want to immediately display the calendar on the form. In such cases, you can place a MonthCalendar control.

USE IT   The following program, MonthlyCalendarDemo.vb, creates a form that contains a MonthCalendar control. After the user clicks Done, the program displays a message box containing the date (or range of dates) the user selected (to select a range of dates, hold down the SHIFT key and click the start and end dates you desire), as shown in Figure 11-18:

```
Public Class Form1
    Inherits System.Windows.Forms.Form

#Region " Windows Form Designer generated code "
  ' Code not shown
#End Region

    Private Sub Button1_Click(ByVal sender As Object, _
      ByVal e As System.EventArgs) Handles Button1.Click
        MsgBox("You selected: " & _
          MonthCalendar1.SelectionRange.ToString())
    End Sub
End Class
```

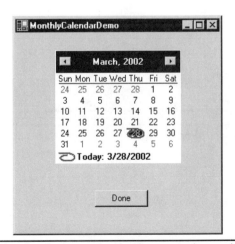

Figure 11-18   Using a MonthCalendar control to let the user select a date

Programming a Tab Control

Depending on the amount of information a form must display, there may be times when you will want to organize the form's content into individual sheets on a Tab control, as shown in Figure 11-19. When you use a Tab control, you can place various controls on each of the Tab control's sheets. You might, for example, use one sheet on a Tab control to prompt the user for address information, another for emergency contact information, another for important dates, and so on.

The following program, TabControlDemo.vb, uses a Tab control to display information about four different books. Each time you select a tab, the program will display the corresponding book's information. Using Visual Studio, you can build each tab's contents. In this case, to create the program, drag and drop a Tab control onto a form. Then, using the control's Property window, use

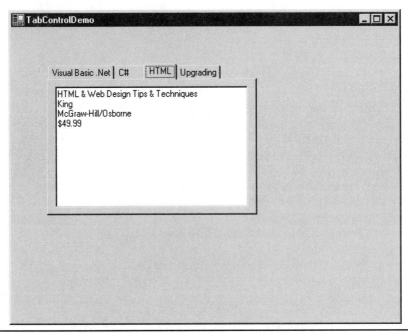

Figure 11-19   Using a Tab control on a form to group related controls

the TabPages property to add four pages to the control. Then in each page, drag and drop a TextBox control onto the page. The program code will place the text contents in each TextBox control:

```
Public Class Form1
    Inherits System.Windows.Forms.Form

#Region " Windows Form Designer generated code "
  ' Code not shown
#End Region

    Private Sub Form1_Activated(ByVal sender As System.Object, _
      ByVal e As System.EventArgs) Handles MyBase.Activated
        TextBox1.Text = _
          "Visual Basic .Net Programming Tips & Techniques" & vbCrLf
        TextBox1.AppendText("Jamsa" & vbCrLf)
        TextBox1.AppendText("McGraw-Hill/Osborne" & vbCrLf)
        TextBox1.AppendText("49.99" & vbCrLf)

        TextBox2.Text = "C# Programming Tips & Techniques" & vbCrLf
        TextBox2.Text &= "Wright" & vbCrLf
        TextBox2.Text &= "McGraw-Hill/Osborne" & vbCrLf
        TextBox2.Text &= "$49.99" & vbCrLf

        TextBox3.Text = "HTML & Web Design Tips & Techniques" & vbCrLf
        TextBox3.Text &= "King" & vbCrLf
        TextBox3.Text &= "McGraw-Hill/Osborne" & vbCrLf
        TextBox3.Text &= "$49.99" & vbCrLf

        TextBox4.Text = _
          "PC Performance Tuning & Upgrading Tips & Techniques" & vbCrLf
        TextBox4.Text &= "Jamsa" & vbCrLf
        TextBox4.Text &= "McGraw-Hill/Osborne" & vbCrLf
        TextBox4.Text &= "$39.99" & vbCrLf
    End Sub
End Class
```

Using a Panel Control to Group Controls

Depending on the entries a form contains, there may be times when you will want to visually separate items on a form. In such cases, you can place one or more Panel controls onto the form, into which you later drag and drop other controls. In Visual Studio (or in your program code) you can then change each Panel control's attributes, as shown in Figure 11-20.

USE IT   To group form controls using a Panel control, use Visual Studio to drag and drop a Panel control onto the form. Then size the form as you require to make space for the panel's controls. Using the Panel control's Property window, you can then change the panel's color, font, and other attributes, to graphically distinguish one set of controls on a form from another.

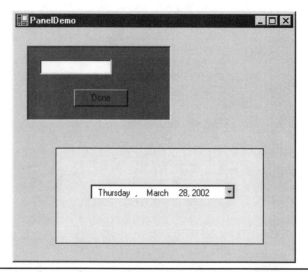

Figure 11-20   Using a Panel control to visually group controls on a form

Programming the TreeView Control

In the Windows programming environment, applications such as Windows Explorer use a tree-like display to present the file and directories on a disk. Depending on the information a form presents, there may be times when you will want to use a tree-like presentation to show the relationship between objects. In such cases, you can place a TreeView control onto your form.

USE IT The following program, TreeViewDemo.vb, uses a TreeView control to display the directories that reside on drive C, as shown in Figure 11-21. To create the program, use Visual Studio to drag and drop a TreeView control onto a form, as well as a Button control. To perform its processing, the program will recursively search each of the directories on drive C. Each time the program finds a directory, the program will add a new node to the tree that corresponds to the current directory.

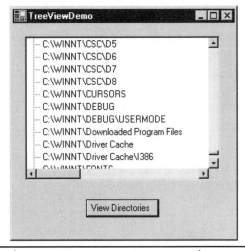

Figure 11-21   Displaying a directory tree in a TreeView control

```vb
Imports System.IO

Public Class Form1
    Inherits System.Windows.Forms.Form

#Region " Windows Form Designer generated code "
    ' Code not shown
#End Region

    Sub ProcessTree(ByVal Dir As String)
        TreeView1.BeginUpdate()
        TreeView1.Nodes.Add(New TreeNode(Dir))
        TreeView1.EndUpdate()
        TreeView1.Refresh()

        Dim DirObj As New DirectoryInfo(Dir)

        Dim Dirs As DirectoryInfo() = DirObj.GetDirectories("*.*")

        Dim DirectoryName As DirectoryInfo

        For Each DirectoryName In Dirs
            Try
                ProcessTree(DirectoryName.FullName)
            Catch E As Exception
                MsgBox("*** Error accessing " & _
                DirectoryName.FullName)
            End Try
        Next
    End Sub

    Private Sub Button1_Click(ByVal sender As Object, _
      ByVal e As System.EventArgs) Handles Button1.Click
        ProcessTree("C:\")
    End Sub
End Class
```

As you can see, before the program adds a node to the current tree, the program calls the TreeView class BeginUpdate method, which prevents the control from refreshing its screen contents until the program calls the EndUpdate method. By using the BeginUpdate and EndUpdate methods, a program will reduce flickering that would otherwise appear as the program tries to display a control whose content is changing.

Programming the ListView Control

In the previous Tip, you learned how to use a TreeView control to display data in a way that illustrates hierarchical relationships between the values. Often, your programs will simply need to display lists of items, such as a list of files in a directory. In such cases, your programs can use a ListView control. Figure 11-22, for example, illustrates the use of a ListView control to display the files that reside in the root directory on drive C.

USE IT The following program, ListViewDemo.vb, uses a ListView control to display the root-directory files on drive C, as shown in Figure 11-22. To create the program, use Visual Studio to drag and drop a ListView control and a Button control onto a form. Depending on the contents you plan to place in the ListView control, you can place entries into the control from within Visual Studio, or you can use the control's Add method to insert a new item. In the case of this program, when the user clicks the button, the program will search the root directory on drive C, using the Add method to append the name of each file it finds to the ListView object:

```
Imports System.IO

Public Class Form1
    Inherits System.Windows.Forms.Form

#Region " Windows Form Designer generated code "
  ' Code not shown
#End Region

    Private Sub Button1_Click(ByVal sender As Object, _
       ByVal e As System.EventArgs) Handles Button1.Click
        Dim Files() As String = Directory.GetFiles("C:\")

        ListView1.View = System.Windows.Forms.View.List

        Dim Filename As String

        For Each Filename In Files
            ListView1.BeginUpdate()
            ListView1.Items.Add(Filename)
            ListView1.EndUpdate()
            ListView1.Refresh()
        Next
    End Sub
End Class
```

Figure 11-22   Using a ListView control to display a list of files

To add an item to the ListView object, the code first calls the BeginUpdate method, which suspends repainting of the control until the code calls the EndUpdate method. In this way, the program reduces flickering that might appear as the form tries to repaint the control that the program is currently updating.

CHAPTER 12

Looking Closer at .NET Assemblies and Versioning

TIPS IN THIS CHAPTER

Throughout this book's chapters, you have created hundreds of executable programs. On the surface, these programs appear to reside in a traditional .exe file. Behind the scenes, however, .NET applications reside in an assembly. In addition to storing the program's executable code, the assembly contains metadata (data about data) that describes the program and the components (DLL files) the program requires. In addition, the metadata provides version information about the program and about the version number the program requires for each of its components. The versioning information the assembly provides is key to the ability of .NET applications to reduce conflicts when new versions of a program or DLL file release.

This chapter examines .NET assemblies and versioning. You will learn how to use several tools Visual Studio provides to closely examine and update the information an assembly contains. You will also learn how to create class libraries and the steps you must perform to share the library among Visual Basic .NET, C#, and ASP.NET applications.

Revisiting .NET Assemblies

In the .NET environment, the assembly is the unit of deployment for programs and class libraries. An assembly is simply a file with the .exe extension (for executable programs) or the .dll extension (for class libraries that reside in a dynamic-link library).

An assembly consists of one or more modules (files such as an executable program and the dynamic link libraries the program requires). Each module in an assembly has a corresponding manifest that provides metadata (information about the module). The assembly itself holds a master manifest that describes each of the modules the assembly contains as well as assembly-specific attributes, such as the assembly's version number, or the version number the assembly requires for each of its components.

In the assembly, the code resides in an intermediate language (IL) format. Before the assembly's code executes, a just-in-time (JIT) compiler on the target system compiles the IL code into native-mode code.

Assemblies can be private to an application or shared among multiple programs. A private assembly resides in the application's subdirectory. A shared assembly resides in the Global Assembly Cache (normally the directory C:\WinNT\Assembly). To place a shared assembly into the Global Assembly Cache, programmers use the GACUTIL command-line utility. A shared assembly differs from a private assembly in that the shared assembly contains a public key that uniquely identifies the assembly with what programmers refer to as a "strong name."

USE IT   To view an assembly's contents, you can run the ILDASM (the intermediate language disassembler) program from the command line as shown here:

```
C:\Subdir> ildasm  AssemblyFilename.ext  <Enter>
```

To run the ILDASM utility, you must place the utility into a directory defined within your command path, or you must add the utility's directory to the path. In the ILDASM program,

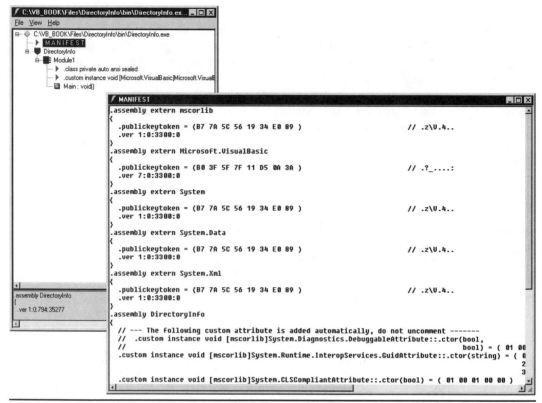

Figure 12-1 Using the ILDASM utility to view an assembly's contents

you can view an assembly's version number, list of required components (and their version numbers), the intermediate-language code, as well as type information, as shown in Figure 12-1.

To help you better understand the assembly's contents, Table 12-1 briefly describes the entries you may encounter in the assembly.

Entry	Purpose
.assembly	Specifies the name of this assembly
.assembly extern	Specifies other assemblies referenced by this assembly
.class extern	Specifies classes the assembly exports (makes available to programs) that are defined in a different module
.exeloc	Specifies the directory path for the assembly's executable program
.hash algorithm	Specifies the hash algorithm used to generate the assembly's hash values
.manifestres	Specifies resources that reside in the manifest

Table 12-1 Common Assembly Entries

Entry	Purpose
.module	Specifies the names of modules that make up the assembly
.module extern	Specifies the names of modules the assembly uses that do not reside in the assembly
.publickey	Specifies the bits that define the assembly's public key
.publickey token	Specifies the token value that corresponds to the assembly's public key
.subsystem	Specifies the assembly's runtime environment
.ver	Specifies the assembly's version

Table 12-1   Common Assembly Entries *(continued)*

Creating a Class Library

One of the best ways to understand .NET assemblies is to create a class library that you later convert into a shared assembly for use by multiple programs. Throughout this book, your programs have made extensive use of the Common Language Runtime (CLR) class libraries. As you create your own classes, there will be times when you will want to make a class available for use by two or more applications. In such cases, you can create a class library (a .dll file) that holds the class definition. The programs that must use the class can then create a reference to the class library and declare objects of the class type.

USE IT   In this Tip, you will create a class library named Book.dll that contains the following BookInfo class:

```
Public Class BookInfo
    Public Title As String
    Public Author As String
    Public Publisher As String
    Public Price As Double

    Public Sub New(ByVal Title As String, ByVal Author As String, _
      ByVal Publisher As String, ByVal Price As Double)
        Me.Title = Title
        Me.Author = Author
        Me.Publisher = Publisher
        Me.Price = Price
    End Sub

    Public Sub ShowBook()
        MsgBox("Title: " & Title & vbCrLf & _
          "Author:" & Author & vbCrLf & _
          "Publisher: " & Publisher & vbCrLf & _
          "Price: " & Price)
    End Sub
End Class
```

To create the class library in Visual Studio, perform these steps:

1. In Visual Studio, select File | New | Project. Visual Studio will display the New Project dialog box.

2. In the New Project dialog box, select the Class Library icon and type the class name **Book** and the directory location you desire. Click OK. Visual Studio will display a code template within which you can define the BookInfo class.

3. In the code template, enter the code previously shown.

4. Select Build | Build Solution. Visual Studio will create a class library file named Book.dll.

Next, to use the class library in a program, create the following UseBookInfo.vb program:

```
Imports Book

Public Class Form1
    Inherits System.Windows.Forms.Form

#Region " Windows Form Designer generated code "
  ' Code not shown
#End Region

    Private Sub Form1_Load(ByVal sender As System.Object, _
      ByVal e As System.EventArgs) Handles MyBase.Load

        Dim Book As New _
          BookInfo("Visual Basic .Net Programming Tips & Techniques", _
          "Jamsa", "McGraw-Hill/Osborne", 49.99)

        Book.ShowBook()
        Me.Close()
    End Sub
End Class
```

Note that the program imports the Book namespace at the start of the code. Before the program can use the class library, you must add a reference to the library file in the application's project. To add the reference in Visual Studio, perform these steps:

1. Select Project | Add Reference. Visual Studio will display the Add Reference dialog box.

2. In the Add Reference dialog box, select the Projects tab. The dialog box will display the Projects sheet.

3. In the Projects sheet, click Browse. Visual Studio will open a Browse dialog box.

4. In the Browse dialog box, locate the Book.dll file you created to hold your class library. After you select the Book.dll file, click OK.

If you use the ILDASM utility to examine the program file UseBookInfo.exe, you will see references to the Book.dll assembly, as shown in Figure 12-2.

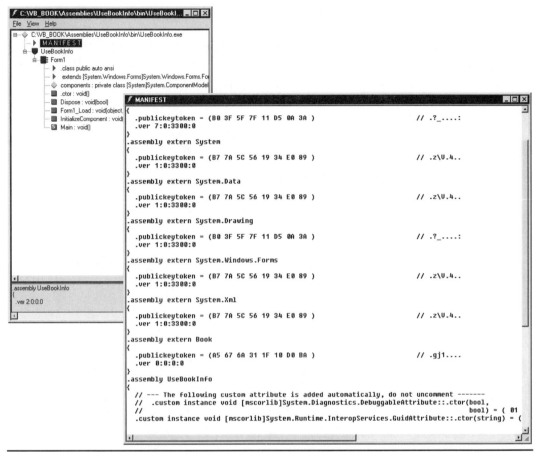

Figure 12-2   Viewing assembly information about a class library

Leveraging a Class Library's Programming-Language Independence

When you create a class library in the .NET environment, the class library is programming-language independent. In other words, if you use Visual Basic .NET to create a class library, you can later use the library from within a Visual Basic .NET program as well as from within a C# program. The programming language that references the class library does not matter.

USE IT   The following C# program, BookInfoDemo.cs, for example, uses the Book class library that you created using Visual Basic .NET in the previous Tip:

```
using System;
using System.Drawing;
```

```
using System.Collections;
using System.ComponentModel;
using System.Windows.Forms;
using System.Data;
using Book;

namespace BookInfoDemo
{
    public class Form1 : System.Windows.Forms.Form
    {
        // Code not shown

        private void Form1_Load(object sender, System.EventArgs e)
        {
            BookInfo ThisBook = new
                BookInfo("Visual Basic .Net Programming Tips & Techniques",
                "Jamsa", "McGraw-Hill/Osborne", 49.99);

            ThisBook.ShowBook();
            this.Close();
        }
    }
}
```

To create and run this program, perform these steps:

1. In Visual Studio, select File | New | Project. Visual Studio will display the New Project dialog box.

2. In the New Project dialog box, first select the Visual C# Projects. Then select the Class Library icon and type the program name **UseBookInfo** and the directory location you desire. Click OK. Visual Studio will open a project within which you can place the C# statements previously shown.

3. Select Project | Add Reference. Visual Studio will display the Add Reference dialog box.

4. In the Add Reference dialog box, select the Projects tab. The dialog box will display the Projects sheet.

5. In the Projects sheet, click Browse. Visual Studio will open a Browse dialog box.

6. In the Browse dialog box, locate the Book.dll file you created to hold your class library. After you select the Book.dll file, click OK.

7. Select Build | Build Solution. Visual Studio will compile your program.

8. To run the program, select Debug | Start.

Taking a Closer Look at a Shared Assembly's Public Key

If you use Windows Explorer to display the shared assemblies that reside in the Global Assembly Cache, you will find that Explorer displays public key information for each assembly, as shown in Figure 12-3.

To create a shared assembly, you must assign a public key to the assembly that uniquely identifies you (or your company). Because private assemblies are not shared, they do not require public key information. The .NET environment uses the public keys to create what programmers refer to as a "strong name" that uniquely identifies the assembly. Should two companies create a shared assembly named Book.dll, the .NET environment uses the public key to distinguish references between different Book.dll assemblies.

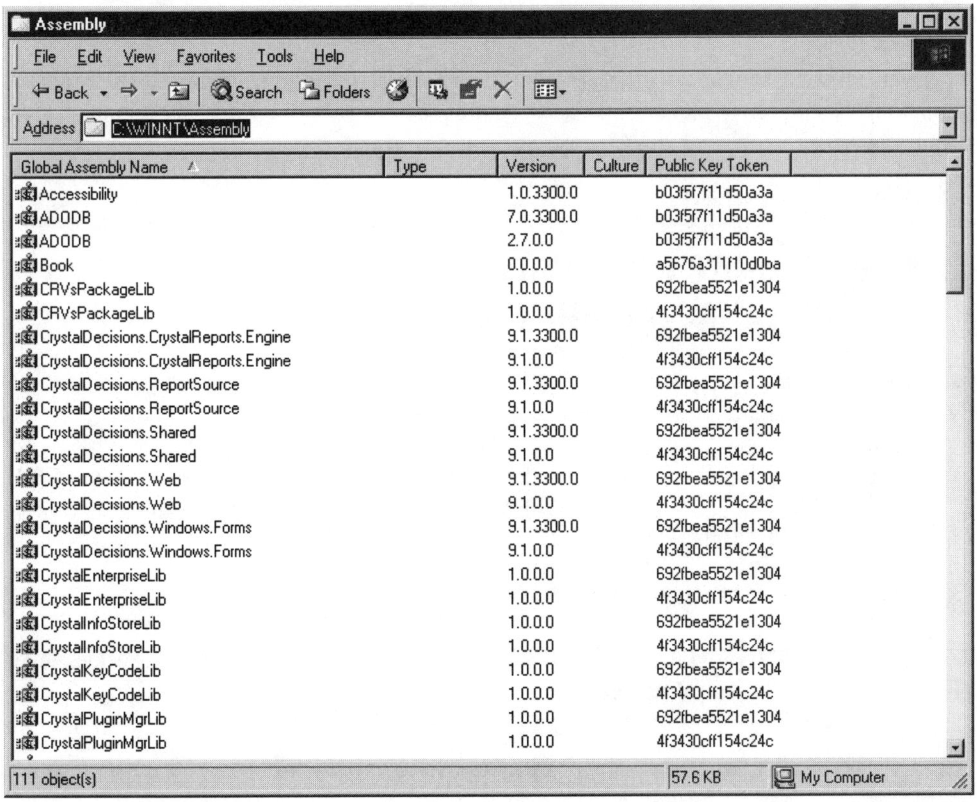

Figure 12-3   Using Windows Explorer to display public keys for shared assemblies in the Global Assembly Cache

USE IT To create a public key that you can assign to an assembly, you can use the SN (strong name) command line utility provided with Visual Studio. The SN utility places your public key in the key file you specify, as shown here:

```
C:\SomeDir> sn -k MyKeyFile.snk  <Enter>
```

To use the SN utility, you must first move the utility program to a directory defined in your command path, or you must add the utility's directory to the path.

After you create the file that contains your public key, you must assign the key to each assembly that you want to share. You can assign a public key to an assembly by editing the assembly's AssemblyInfo.vb file, which you can open in Visual Studio. In the file, you must place an AssemblyKeyFile attribute entry that specifies your file's full pathname, as shown here:

```
<Assembly: AssemblyKeyFile("C:\Path\KeyFilename.snk") >
```

After you edit and save the AssemblyInfo.vb file's contents, you must rebuild the program or class file to put your change into effect. Then you are ready to place the assembly into the Global Assembly Cache.

Installing a Shared Assembly into the Global Assembly Cache

After you assign a public key (a strong name) to an assembly, making the assembly sharable, you are ready to place the assembly into the Global Assembly Cache.

USE IT To place a shared assembly into the Global Assembly Cache, you use the GACUTIL command line utility provided with Visual Studio. To install the assembly into the cache, you must invoke GACUTIL using the -i switch, as shown here:

```
C:\> GACUTIL -i C:\Path\AssemblyName.dll   <Enter>
```

To run the GACUTIL program, you must place the program into a directory that resides in your command path, or you must add the program's directory to the path.

Exploiting .NET Versioning

A .NET assembly contains two types of version information. First, the assembly contains version information about itself that describes the assembly's major, minor, build, and revision number in the form:

```
.ver major.minor.build.revision
```

Second, the assembly specifies the version numbers that it requires for each of its components (the .dll files the assembly uses). Using the ILDASM utility, you can view an assembly's version information as shown in Figure 12-4. Each time you compile an application or a class library, the compiler will increment the assembly's revision number.

USE IT To manually change an assembly's version number, you can edit the assembly's AssemblyInfo.vb file, changing the AssemblyVersion attribute in the file to reflect the version number you desire, as shown here:

```
<Assembly: AssemblyVersion("2.0.0.0")>
```

You can edit the AssemblyInfo.vb file in Visual Studio. After you make and save your changes to the AssemblyInfo.vb file, you must rebuild the application to put your change into effect. Using the ILDASM utility, you can view your assembly to verify the version update.

When your application uses components such as a class library, the compiler will place the component's version-number information in the application's assembly. When you later run the program, the loader will use the version information to locate and use the correct assembly. If you change the version number of a class library you are using within a shared assembly, you can then use the GACUTIL to place the new version of the class library into the Global Assembly Cache, so that the code sits side by side with the previous version, as shown in Figure 12-5.

```
MANIFEST                                                              _ □ ×
.assembly BookInfoDemo
{
  .custom instance void [mscorlib]System.Reflection.AssemblyCopyrightAttribute::.ctor(str
  .custom instance void [mscorlib]System.Reflection.AssemblyKeyNameAttribute::.ctor(strin
  .custom instance void [mscorlib]System.Reflection.AssemblyKeyFileAttribute::.ctor(strin
  .custom instance void [mscorlib]System.Reflection.AssemblyDelaySignAttribute::.ctor(boo
  .custom instance void [mscorlib]System.Reflection.AssemblyTrademarkAttribute::.ctor(str
  .custom instance void [mscorlib]System.Reflection.AssemblyConfigurationAttribute::.ctor
  // --- The following custom attribute is added automatically, do not uncomment -------
  //  .custom instance void [mscorlib]System.Diagnostics.DebuggableAttribute::.ctor(bool,
  //                                                                              bool)
  .custom instance void [mscorlib]System.Reflection.AssemblyCompanyAttribute::.ctor(strin
  .custom instance void [mscorlib]System.Reflection.AssemblyProductAttribute::.ctor(strin
  .custom instance void [mscorlib]System.Reflection.AssemblyDescriptionAttribute::.ctor(s
  .custom instance void [mscorlib]System.Reflection.AssemblyTitleAttribute::.ctor(string)
  .hash algorithm 0x00008004
  .ver 1:0:818:26591
}
```

Figure 12-4   Viewing an assembly's version information

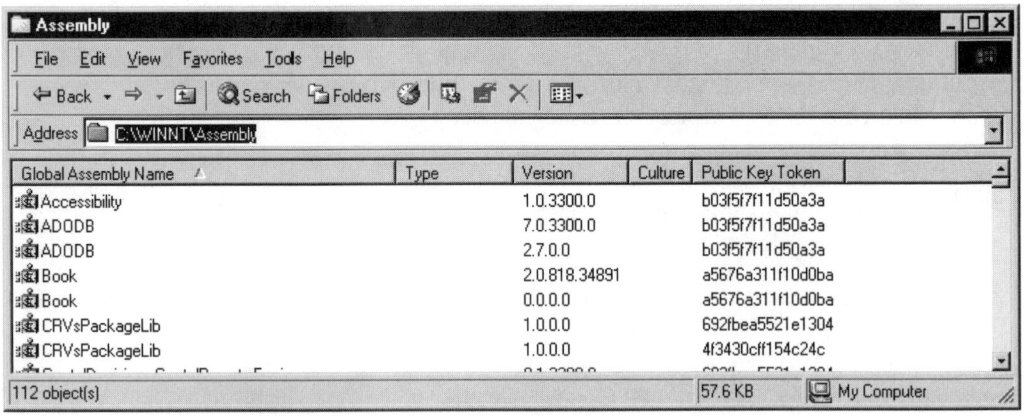

Figure 12-5   Different versions of an assembly residing side by side in the Global Assembly Cache

Precompiling a Shared Assembly to Reduce Load Time

In an assembly, the program code resides in an intermediate language (IL) format. Before the code executes, a special program called the just-in-time (JIT) compiler compiles the code into native-mode instructions that can execute on the target machine. If you have a shared assembly file that you anticipate many applications using on a regular basis, you can eliminate the overhead of the just-in-time compilation by precompiling the assembly's code.

USE IT   To precompile an assembly's code, you use the ngen command line utility provided with Visual Studio:

```
C:\SomeDir> ngen  AssemblyPath\AssemblyFilename  <Enter>
```

To use the ngen utility, you must move the program into a directory that resides within your command path, or you must place the utility's folder into the path. After you compile the assembly, Windows Explorer will list the assembly in the Global Assembly Cache with the Native Images type attribute, as shown in Figure 12-6.

The ngen utility stores the compiled assembly in a native-mode cache. To view the contents of the native-mode cache, invoke the ngen utility with the /Show switch:

```
C:\SomeDir> ngen  /Show  <Enter>
```

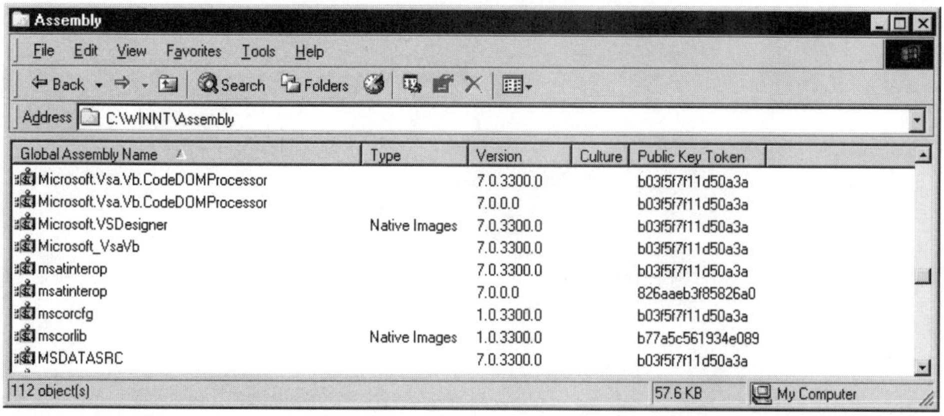

Figure 12-6   A precompiled assembly with the Native Images attribute in a Global Assembly Cache listing

Using the @Assembly Directive in an ASP.NET Page

After you create a class library, such as the Book class you created earlier in this chapter, you can use the library in ASP.NET pages you create by placing an @Assembly directive in your page as follows:

```
<% Assembly name="Book" %>
```

Note that the directive does not specify the .dll extension or a path to the file. When a user views the page, the server will examine several specific directories in \inetpub\wwwroot for the file. In this case, you can place the Book.dll file in a directory named Bin, Book, or Book\Bin (such as \inetpub\wwwroot\Book\Bin).

USE IT   The following ASP.NET page, AssemblyDemo.aspx, uses the Book assembly to create a BookInfo object. The page then displays the object's fields, as shown in Figure 12-7:

```
<% @ Page language="VB" %>
<% @Assembly name="Book" %>

<html>
<head>
   <title>Assembly Demo</title>
```

```
</head>
<body>
  <center><h1>Show Book Information</h1></center><hr/>
  <%
      Dim ThisBook As New _
        Book.BookInfo("Visual Basic .Net Programming Tips & Techniques", _
        "Jamsa", "McGraw-Hill/Osborne",49.99)

      Response.Write(ThisBook.Title & "<br/>")
      Response.Write(ThisBook.Author & "<br/>")
      Response.Write(ThisBook.Publisher & "<br/>")
      Response.Write(ThisBook.Price)
  %>
</body>
</html>
```

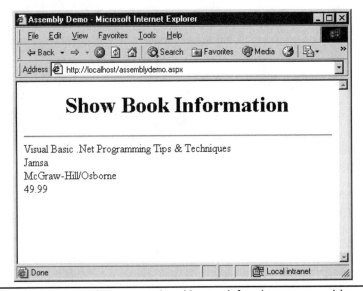

Figure 12-7   An ASP.NET page that uses a class library defined in an assembly

Taking Advantage of the Microsoft .NET Framework Configuration

Earlier in this chapter's Tips, to place a shared assembly into Global Assembly Cache, you used the GACUTIL command line utility. When you install Visual Studio, the installation normally installs a "snap-in" named the Microsoft .NET Framework Configuration which you can use to display, add, or remove assemblies from the Global Assembly Cache. Figure 12-8 illustrates the Global Assembly Cache in the Microsoft .NET Framework Configuration.

USE IT   To run the Microsoft .NET Framework Configuration, perform these steps:

1. Select Start | Settings | Control Panel. Windows will open the Control Panel window.
2. In the Control Panel, double-click the Administrative Tools icon. Windows will open the Administrative Tools window.
3. In the Administrative Tools window, click the Microsoft .NET Framework Configuration shortcut.

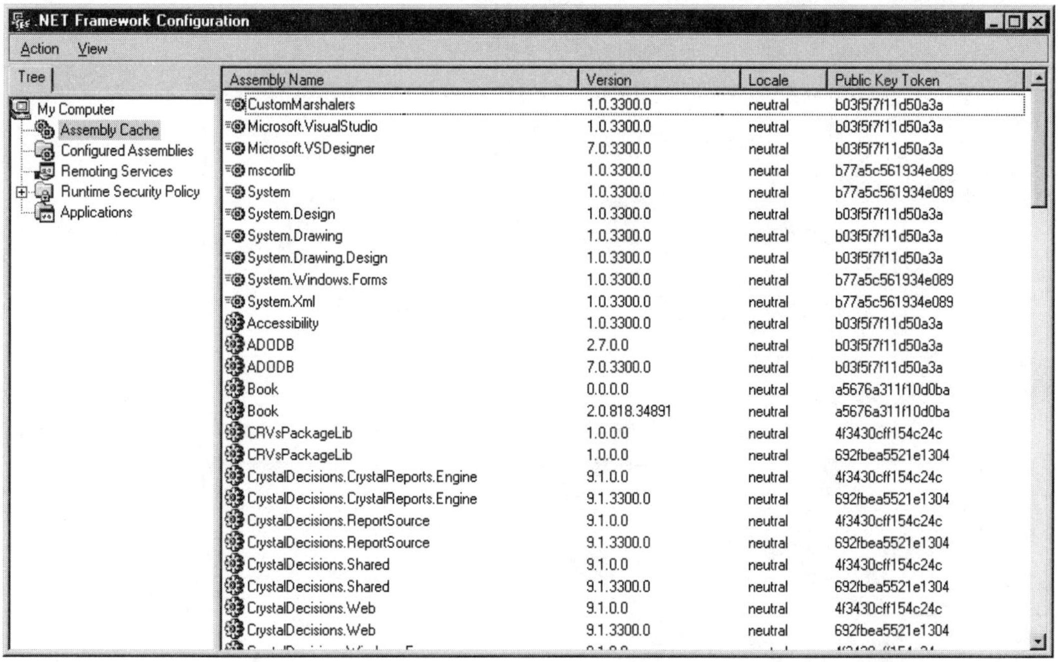

Figure 12-8   Using the Microsoft .NET Framework Configuration to display the Global Assembly Cache

Before you can add an assembly to the Global Assembly Cache, you must first assign a public key to the assembly, as previously discussed. Using the Microsoft Network Framework Configuration, you can assign a public key to an assembly (as opposed to having to edit the assembly's AssemblyInfo.vb file) by performing these steps:

1. In the Microsoft Network Framework Configuration, click the Configured Assemblies folder.
2. Select Action | Add. Your screen will display the Configure An Assembly window, as shown in Figure 12-9, that you can use to assign the public key token to a specific assembly. If you have previously assigned your public key to an assembly, you can view the public key token in the Global Assembly Cache.

After you assign a public key token to an assembly, your screen will display a dialog box for the assembly within which you can specify version information for the assembly, such as the code base of programs that correspond to a specific version number, or a version redirection information (that lets you redirect requests for one version to another).

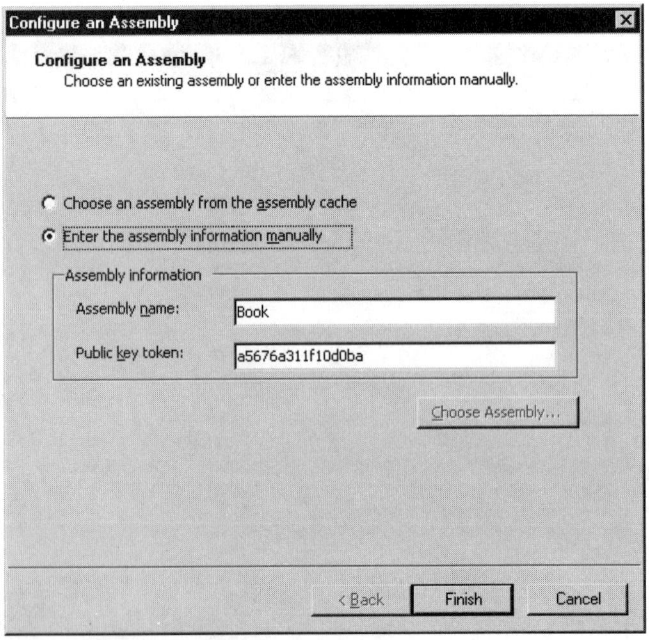

Figure 12-9   Assigning a public key token to an assembly

Viewing an Application's Assembly Specifics

In an assembly, the manifest provides metadata that describes the assembly's contents. In Chapter 18, you will learn how to use reflection to query an object about the capabilities it provides. To perform such queries, the Reflection API makes use of metadata that describes an object.

USE IT   As a sampling of the types of queries you can perform using reflection, the following program, QueryAssembly.vb, uses reflection to determine several different attributes of the program's assembly:

```
Imports System.Reflection
Module Module1

    Sub Main()
        Dim thisAssembly As [Assembly] = _
          [Assembly].GetExecutingAssembly()

        Console.WriteLine("Code base: " & thisAssembly.CodeBase)
        Console.WriteLine("Full name: " & thisAssembly.FullName)
        Console.WriteLine("Entry point: " & _
            thisAssembly.EntryPoint.ToString())
        Console.WriteLine("From Global Assembly Cache: " & _
            thisAssembly.GlobalAssemblyCache)
        Console.WriteLine("Location: " & thisAssembly.Location)

        Console.Write("Types: ")
        Dim TypeObj As Type
        For Each TypeObj In thisAssembly.GetTypes()
            Console.Write(TypeObj.Name & " ")
        Next

        Console.WriteLine()

        Console.WriteLine("Referenced Assemblies: ")
        Dim RefAssembly As AssemblyName

        For Each RefAssembly In thisAssembly.GetReferencedAssemblies()
            Console.WriteLine(RefAssembly.FullName)
        Next
        Console.ReadLine()
    End Sub
End Module
```

After you compile and execute this program, your screen will display the following output:

```
Code base: file:///C:/ShowAssemblies/bin/ShowAssemblies.exe
Full name: ShowAssemblies, Version=1.0.818.30056, Culture=neutral,
PublicKeyToken=null
Entry point: Void Main()
From Global Assembly Cache: False
Location: C:\ ShowAssemblies\bin\ShowAssemblies.exe
Types: Module1
Referenced Assemblies:
mscorlib, Version=1.0.3300.0, Culture=neutral,
    PublicKeyToken=b77a5c561934e089
Microsoft.VisualBasic, Version=7.0.3300.0, Culture=neutral,
PublicKeyToken=b03f5f7f11d50a3a
System, Version=1.0.3300.0, Culture=neutral,
    PublicKeyToken=b77a5c561934e089
System.Data, Version=1.0.3300.0, Culture=neutral,
    PublicKeyToken=b77a5c561934e089
System.Xml, Version=1.0.3300.0, Culture=neutral,
    PublicKeyToken=b77a5c561934e089
```

CHAPTER 13

Programming
ASP.NET Solutions

TIPS IN THIS CHAPTER

Across the Web, sites make extensive use of Active Server Pages to implement Web content. By combining HTML tags within a script, Active Server Pages let developers create dynamic content that can change on a per-user basis, pages that can interact with the user, and pages that utilize database content. Behind the scenes, when a user displays an Active Server Page in his or her browser, special software on the server that contains the page executes the programming statements that are defined in scripts the page contains. As the scripts perform their processing, the scripts create output that the page combines with HTML statements to present the page to the user. The majority of Active Server Pages are written using VBScript.

Although Active Server Pages have driven much of the Web's content for the past several years, Active Server Pages are not perfect. First, because most scripts are written using VBScript, programmers do not have the full range of features available to create pages as they would with a programming language, such as Visual Basic .NET (such as a larger set of data types, event handling, structured exception handling, and so on). Further, because Active Server Pages use a scripting language, the server must interpret (convert the script to machine code) on each user visit, which introduces overhead that would not exist with the use of a compiled language. Finally, one of the largest challenges developers face when implementing complex Active Server Page solutions is maintaining state information about the user (such as a username and password or user preferences) as the user moves from page to page possibly across multiple servers within a Web farm.

The .NET environment brings with it a new model, called ASP.NET, that developers can use to create Web pages. An ASP.NET page, like an Active Server Page, combines HTML tags with programming code. However, unlike an Active Server Page that uses VBScript, programmers can create an ASP.NET page using compiled programming languages such as Visual Basic .NET and C#. By letting programmers use a compiled language, ASP.NET pages provide programmers with all the features the programming language provides, as well as those of the .NET Common Language Runtime. In an ASP.NET page, programmers can create classes, use inheritance, leverage multiple threads of execution, handle errors via exceptions, and more. Because the ASP.NET pages use a compiled programming language, the scripts are faster than a scripted counterpart.

In addition, as you will learn in Chapter 15, ASP.NET pages can use Web forms to build user interfaces similar to those the user would encounter in a Visual Basic .NET application. Using Visual Studio, programmers can define the forms that implement an ASP.NET page's user interface by performing drag-and-drop operations. Then, behind the scenes, the programmer writes code to handle the form's events, just as he or she would do to create a C# or Visual Basic .NET program. When a user later displays a Web form, the form's processing (the code that handles each of the form's events) occurs within the server. In addition, the form can provide validation controls an ASP.NET page can use to ensure the user has completed the form correctly before he or she submits the form across the Web.

Like other .NET programs, ASP.NET compiles to an intermediate language. When a user first requests an ASP.NET page, the server will compile the page to an intermediate language, which the server then caches. When other users view the page, the server can use cached contents, avoiding the need to compile the code on a per-request basis.

As you get started with ASP.NET pages, you will find that the pages look very similar to Active Server Pages. In fact, for simple pages, the biggest difference between an ASP.NET page and an equivalent Active Server Page is the fact that ASP.NET pages use the .aspx extension as opposed to the .asp file extension that is predominant on the Web. This chapter's Tips are designed to get you up and running with ASP.NET pages. In Chapter 15, you will expand your capabilities as you integrate Web forms into your ASP.NET solutions.

Creating and Running a Simple ASP.NET Page

As the processing your ASP.NET pages perform becomes more complex, you will likely use Visual Studio to create your pages. In Chapter 15, you will learn how to build Web forms that provide your ASP.NET pages with a graphic user interface much like that found in Visual Basic form-based programs. At that time, you will use Visual Studio to drag-and-drop objects onto a form. When you use Visual Studio to create your ASP.NET pages, Visual Studio will automatically create several configuration files you can use to fine-tune your ASP.NET operations.

USE IT For simple ASP.NET pages, however, you can use a text editor such as Windows Notepad to create the file. Using Notepad, create a file named Showtime.aspx, that contains the following statements that display the current date and time (save the file in your \inetpub\wwwroot folder to make the file accessible to the Web server):

```
<% @ Page language="vb" %>
<html>
<head>
   <title>ShowTime</title>
</head>
<body>
   <center><h1>ASP.NET ShowTime Demo</h1></center><hr/>

   The current date and time is <% =now() %>
```

```
</body>
</html>
```

As you can see, the code looks very much like a traditional Active Server Page. In fact, the only differences between this page and an Active Server Page is the .aspx file extension and the first line of the file, which specifies that the script's programming language is Visual Basic .NET:

```
<% @ Page language="vb" %>
```

As you would with an Active Server Page, in an ASP.NET page you distinguish the script's code from the HTML statements by grouping the program statements (in this case, the call to the now function that returns the current date and time) between the <% and %> tags:

```
The current date and time is <% =now() %>
```

To test the ASP.NET page, you can enter the URL http://localhost/ShowTime.aspx in your browser, as shown in Figure 13-1.

If your server is connected to the Internet and has a domain name, you can specify your server's complete domain name. Likewise, others across the Web can test your script as well (this ASP.NET page should run in any browser). If your system is connected to the Net but does not have a domain name, you can use a URL similar to the following that replaces the IP address shown here with the IP address that corresponds to your system: http://111.222.121.123/ShowTime.aspx.

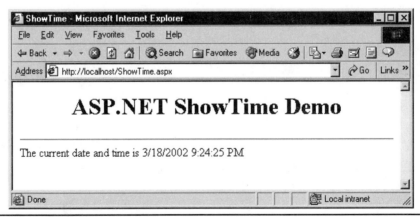

Figure 13-1   Displaying an ASP.NET page on your PC using localhost in the URL

Implementing a Simple ASP.NET Page Using C# and Visual Basic .NET

Unlike Active Server Pages that programmers normally create using VBScript, ASP.NET pages use compiled programs written in a programming language such as Visual Basic .NET or C#. To specify the programming language you are using to create an ASP.NET page, place a Page directive at the start of your page similar to the following:

```
<% @ Page Language="VB" %>
```

or

```
<% @ Page Language="C#" %>
```

The following ASP.NET page, VBLoop.aspx, uses Visual Basic .NET to display a message using different font sizes, as shown in Figure 13-2.

```
<% @ Page Language="VB" %>

<html>
<head>
   <title>Font Size Demo</title>
</head>
<body>
  <center><h1>Using ASP.NET to Change Font Sizes</h1></center><hr/>
  <% Dim I As Integer
      For I = 1 to 7
              Response.Write("<font size=")
              Response.Write(I)
              Response.Write(">")
              Response.Write("VB.Net Programming Tips & Techniques<br/>")
      Next I
  %>
</body>
</html>
```

In a similar way, the following ASP.NET page, CSLoop.aspx, uses the C# programming language to perform the identical processing, displaying a message using seven different font sizes:

```
<% @ Page Language="C#" %>

<html>
<head>
   <title>Font Size Demo</title>
</head>
```

```
<body>
  <center><h1>Using ASP.NET to Change Font Sizes</h1></center><hr/>
  <% int i;

     for (i = 1; i < 8; i++)
       {
         Response.Write("<font size=");
         Response.Write(i);
         Response.Write(">");
         Response.Write("VB.Net Programming Tips & Techniques<br/>");
       }
  %>
</body>
</html>
```

If you load either ASP.NET page in your browser and then select Edit | View Source, your browser will display the HTML statements shown in Figure 13-3.

▶ *NOTE*

Although you can create ASP.NET pages using C#, Visual Basic .NET, and JScript .NET, you must use the same programming language within the page. However, a page that you create using Visual Basic .NET, for example, can call a page that you created using C#. Within a page, however, you must use the same programming language throughout.

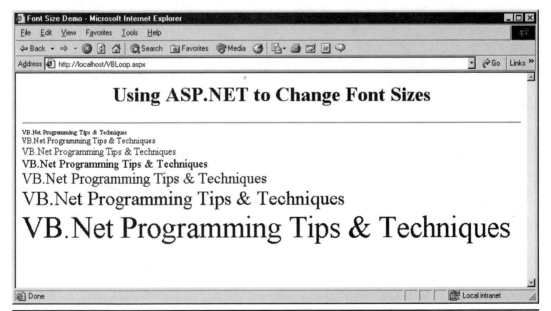

Figure 13-2   Using a loop to change a message's font size

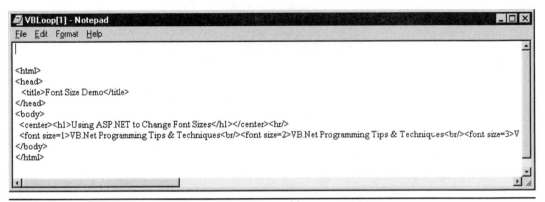

Figure 13-3   Displaying the HTML statements created by an ASP.NET page

Creating and Running an ASP.NET Project in Visual Studio

As your ASP.NET pages become more complex, or when you want to take advantage of server-based Web forms, which Chapter 15 discusses in detail, you will normally create your pages in Visual Studio. When you use Visual Studio to create an ASP.NET page, Visual Studio will create a project that it stores in a subdirectory that resides beneath your Web server folder (normally \inetput\wwwroot). Just as you can build and run Visual Basic .NET programs in Visual Studio, the same is true for ASP.NET pages. When you run an ASP.NET page in the Visual Studio environment, Visual Studio will automatically launch your Web browser, loading the corresponding ASP.NET page—which makes the process of creating and testing an ASP.NET page quite easy.

USE IT   In this Tip, you will first use Visual Studio to create a simple ASP.NET page that displays a Calendar control, as shown in Figure 13-4. Using the page, a user can scroll though the months of the year. The page, in this case, will simply display the control. It will not process the date the user selects.

To create the ShowCalendar.aspx page in Visual Studio, perform these steps:

1. In Visual Studio, select File | New Project. Visual Studio will display the New Project dialog box.

2. In the New Project dialog box, select an ASP.NET Web Application, and in the location field, type the project name **ShowCalendar** (the field should read http://localhost/ShowCalendar). When you click OK, Visual Studio will display a grid layout (similar to a form), onto which you can drag controls, such as the Calendar control.

3. In Visual Studio, select View | Toolbox. Visual Studio will display the Toolbox window.

4. In the Toolbox window, locate the Calendar control. Drag and drop the control onto the grid as shown in Figure 13-5.

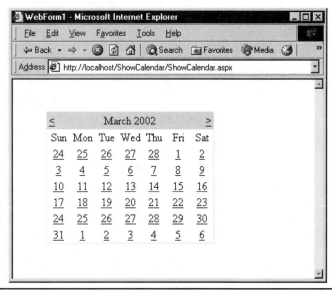

Figure 13-4   Using a Calendar control in an ASP.NET page

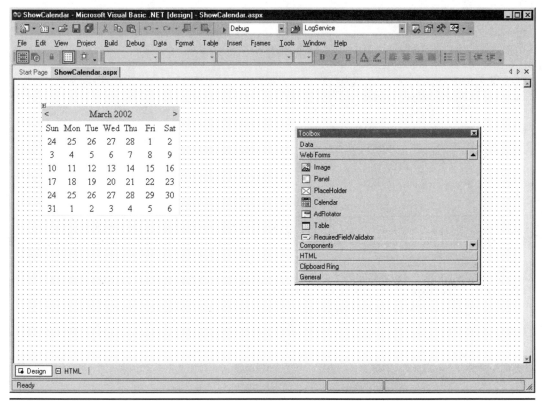

Figure 13-5   Placing a Calendar control on the design grid

5. Select Build | Build Solution. Visual Studio will create your ASP.NET page.

6. Select Debug | Start. Visual Studio will launch your browser, displaying your new page within the browser.

Just as Visual Studio automatically creates Visual Basic .NET source code when you create forms within Design View, Visual Studio also builds the HTML statements that correspond to ASP.NET pages. In Visual Studio, you can view your page's HTML code by right-clicking the design grid and then selecting View HTML. In this case, Visual Studio will create the following HTML entries, shown in Figure 13-6. For now, do not concern yourself with the HTML statements, you will examine each in detail in Chapter 15, when you create Web forms.

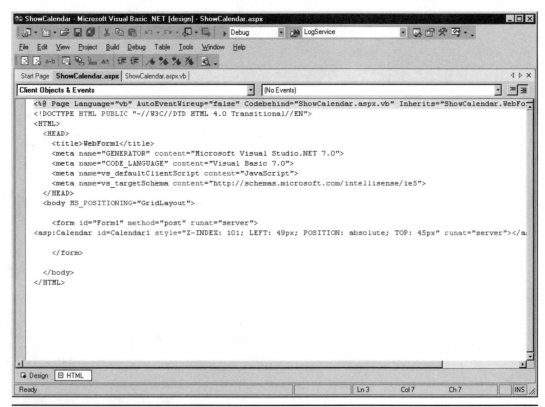

Figure 13-6   The HTML statements Visual Studio creates for an ASP.NET page

Coding Changes You Must Make as You Migrate from ASP to ASP.NET

If you ignore, for the moment, the support of Web forms, multithreading, structured error handling, and server-side processing, the code you write to create an ASP.NET page is quite similar to what you would use to create a traditional Active Server Page. This Tip summarizes key changes you must make as you get started with ASP.NET pages.

USE IT   To begin, ASP.NET pages no longer support LET and SET statements that VBScript programmers use to assign values to variables and objects. In ASP.NET pages, your code simply assigns values using the assignment operator.

In an ASP page that did not use the Option Explicit statement, programmers could use variables without first declaring the variable. VBScript, in turn, would create a Variant to store the variable's value (a Variant is so named because the object's type can vary with the value the object is storing). Unfortunately, the practice of not forcing scripts to declare variables often led to errors when a programmer used the wrong variable name (or misspelled a variable name). The following code fragment illustrates such an error. The code first assigns the result of the Form.Request ("File") method call to the Filename variable. Then, within the If statement, the code incorrectly examines the value of the Filepath variable, as opposed to Filename:

```
Filename = Form.Request("File")

If (FilePath = "") Then
   Response.Write("Filename not specified")
End If
```

To eliminate errors related to using an invalid variable name, programmers often placed the Option Explicit statement at the start of their scripts:

```
<% Option Explicit %>
```

Then, if a script tried to use a variable that had not yet been declared, a syntax error would occur which the programmer could use to quickly identify the invalid name.

In an ASP.NET page, the Option Explicit setting is the default. Further, Visual Basic .NET has eliminated the Variant type, which means your scripts must explicitly specify each variable's type, such as Integer, String, and so on. Many scripts also use the Option Strict On directive, which directs the Visual Basic .NET compiler to generate a syntax warning for variable assignments which may result in an incorrect assignment (such as the assignment of a value of one object type to another):

```
<% Option Strict On %>
```

In Active Server Pages, scripts make extensive use of methods such as Response.Write. The following Active Server Page, WriteDemo.asp, uses the Response.Write method to display two messages on a page:

```
<html>
<head>
  <title>Page Title</title>
</head>
<body>
  <%
      Response.Write "Hello, world! <br/>"
      Response.Write("ASP and ASP.NET are cool <br/>")
  %>
</body>
</html>
```

As you can see, the first call to the Response.Write method does not place the message text within parentheses, whereas the second call to Response.Write does. In an ASP.NET page, when your code calls a method, you must always place the parameters you pass to the method within parentheses:

```
<%
   Response.Write("Hello, world! <br/>")
   Response.Write("ASP and ASP.NET are cool <br/>")
%>
```

Further, in an Active Server Page, you can declare a subroutine or function between the <% and %> tags, as shown here:

```
<%
   Sub Demo(Value)
     Response.Write(Value)
   End Sub
%>
```

In an ASP.NET page, in contrast, you must declare functions and subroutines within the <script> and </script> tags:

```
<script runat="server">
   Sub Demo(ByVal Value As Integer)
```

```
      Response.Write(Value)
   End Sub
</script>
```

Your code can call the methods by placing the subroutine or function calls between the <% and %> tags, but you must declare the method between <script> and </script>:

```
<% Demo(1001) %>
```

When your code passes a parameter to a function, it can pass either the parameter's value or the parameter's address. By default, Visual Basic .NET passes parameters by value (ByVal). When you pass a parameter by value, Visual Basic .NET makes a copy of the value (or variable) you are passing to the subroutine as a parameter. Should the code within the subroutine change the value, the change does not affect the original variable passed to the subroutine, because the subroutine is using a copy of that variable's value. To change a parameter's value within a subroutine, you must use the ByRef keyword for the parameter, which directs Visual Basic .NET to pass the address of the original value (not a copy) as shown here:

```
<script runat="server">
   Sub Demo(ByRef DateVar As DateTime)
      DateVar = Now()
   End Sub
</script>
```

Taking Advantage of Cookies in an ASP.NET Page

Across the Web, Active Server Pages make extensive use of cookies to store cookies on a user's hard disk that contain a user's preferences and possibly historical data regarding the user's previous visits to the site. To store and retrieve cookie data using an ASP.NET page, your code performs identical processing that you would use in a traditional Active Server Page. To create a cookie, your scripts use the Response.Cookie method as shown here:

```
Response.Cookies("CookieName")("Variable") = "Value"
```

Likewise, to retrieve a Cookie's value, your code uses the Request.Cookie method:

```
Value = Request.Cookies("CookieName")("Variable")
```

USE IT The following ASP.NET page, StoreCookie.aspx, creates cookies that contain information about this book. The page also provides the link to the RetrieveCookie.aspx page that displays the cookie's contents, as shown in Figure 13-7:

```
<% @ Page language="vb" %>
<html>
<head>
  <title>StoreCookie</title>
</head>
<body>
  <center><h1>Cookies Stored</h1></center><hr/>
  <%
   Response.Cookies("VB_Book")("Title") = _
       "VB.Net Programming Tips & Techniques"
   Response.Cookies("VB_Book")("Publisher") = "McGraw-Hill/Osborne"
   Response.Cookies("VB_Book")("Author") = "Jamsa"
  %>
  <a href="RetrieveCookie.aspx">View the Cookies</a>
</body>
</html>
```

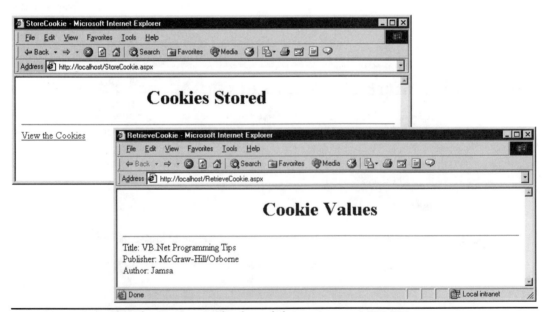

Figure 13-7   Storing and retrieving cookie-based data using an ASP.NET page

The following ASP.NET page implements RetrieveCookie.aspx:

```
<% @ Page language="vb" %>
<html>
<head>
  <title>RetrieveCookie</title>
</head>
<body>
  <center><h1>Cookie Values</h1></center><hr/>
  <%
    Response.Write("Title: " & _
       Request.Cookies("VB_Book")("Title") & "<br/>")
    Response.Write("Publisher: " & _
       Request.Cookies("VB_Book")("Publisher") & "<br/>")
    Response.Write("Author: " & _
       Request.Cookies("VB_Book")("Author") & "<br/>")
  %>
</body>
</html>
```

Determining a Browser's Capabilities

As the processing your ASP.NET pages perform becomes more complex, there will be times when you will want to know the capabilities that a user's browser supports, which may let your code perform an operation in a more optimal way. In such cases, your ASP.NET pages can use the Request.Browser object.

USE IT   The following ASP.NET page, BrowserSnoop.aspx, displays specifics about the user's browser and target operating system capabilities:

```
<% @ Page Language="VB" %>

<html>
<head>
   <title>Browser Snoop</title>
</head>
<body>
  <center><h1>Browser Capabilities</h1></center><hr/>
  <%
     Response.Write("ActiveX Controls: " & _
```

```
                Request.Browser.ActiveXControls & "<br/>")
        Response.Write("AOL: " & Request.Browser.AOL & "<br/>")
        Response.Write("Background Sounds: " & _
            Request.Browser.BackgroundSounds & "<br/>")
        Response.Write("Beta: " & Request.Browser.Beta & "<br/>")
        Response.Write("CDF: " & Request.Browser.CDF & "<br/>")
        Response.Write("CLR Version: " & _
            Request.Browser.ClrVersion.ToString() & "<br/>")
        Response.Write("Cookies: " & Request.Browser.Cookies & "<br/>")
        Response.Write("Crawler: " & Request.Browser.Crawler & "<br/>")
        Response.Write("ECMA Script Version: " & _
            Request.Browser.EcmaScriptVersion.ToString() & "<br/>")
        Response.Write("Frames: " & Request.Browser.Frames & "<br/>")
        Response.Write("Java Applets: " & _
            Request.Browser.JavaApplets & "<br/>")
        Response.Write("JavaScript: " & _
            Request.Browser.JavaScript & "<br/>")
        Response.Write("Major Version: " & _
            Request.Browser.MajorVersion & "<br/>")
        Response.Write("Minor Version: " & _
            Request.Browser.MinorVersion & "<br/>")
        Response.Write("MS DOM Version: " & _
            Request.Browser.MSDomVersion.ToString() & "<br/>")
        Response.Write("Platform: " & _
            Request.Browser.Platform & "<br/>")
        Response.Write("Tables: " & Request.Browser.Tables & "<br/>")
        Response.Write("Tag Writer: " & _
            Request.Browser.TagWriter.ToString() & "<br/>")
        Response.Write("Type: " & Request.Browser.Type & "<br/>")
        Response.Write("VBScript: " & _
            Request.Browser.VBScript & "<br/>")
        Response.Write("W3C DOM Version: " & _
            Request.Browser.W3CDomVersion.ToString() & "<br/>")
        Response.Write("Win16: " & Request.Browser.Win16 & "<br/>")
        Response.Write("Win32: " & Request.Browser.Win32 & "<br/>")
    %>
</body>
</html>
```

When a user visits the page, the user's browser will display output similar to that shown in Figure 13-8.

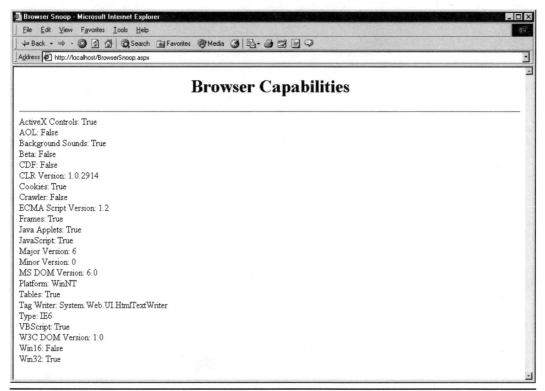

Figure 13-8   Determining a user's browser and operating system capabilities

Maintaining ASP and ASP.NET Pages Side by Side

Across the Web, sites make extensive use of Active Server Pages. Over time, programmers will migrate many ASP-based pages to ASP.NET. In many cases, however, programmers may decide that existing ASP implementations are fine. In either case, within many sites, ASP and ASP.NET pages will eventually reside side by side within a Web server.

Because the server can use the .asp and .aspx file extensions to distinguish between ASP and ASP.NET pages, the two page types can successfully coexist on the same server. In fact, an ASP page can link to an ASP.NET page and vice versa.

USE IT   To illustrate the capability of ASP and ASP.NET pages to coexist and interact, the following ASP page, LinkToASPNET.asp, creates a link to an ASP.NET page on the same server:

```
<html>
<head>
   <title>Active Server Page</title>
```

```
</head>
<body>
  <center><h1>ASP to ASP.NET Link</h1></center><hr/>
  The current date and time is
  <%
     =Now()
  %>
<br/><br/>
<a href="LinktoASP.aspx">Link to an ASP.NET Page</a>
</body>
</html>
```

Likewise, the following ASP.NET page, LinkToASP.aspx, creates a link back to the ASP page:

```
<% @ Page language="VB" %>

<html>
<head>
   <title>ASP.NET Page</title>
</head>
<body>
  <center><h1>ASP.NET to Active Server Page Link</h1></center><hr/>
  The current date and time is
  <%
     =Now()
  %>
<br/><br/>
<a href="LinktoASPNET.asp">Link to an Active Server Page</a>
</body>
</html>
```

If you open one of the pages in your browser, you can click the link to move between the two pages, as shown in Figure 13-9.

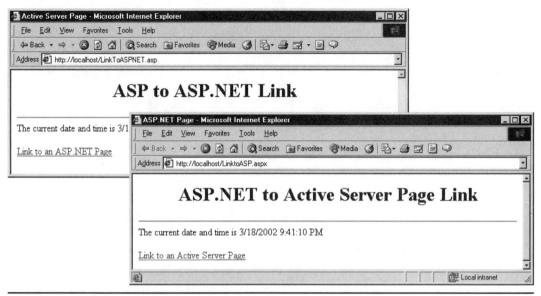

Figure 13-9   Linking ASP and ASP.NET pages

ASP and ASP.NET Cannot Share Application and Session Objects

Within a Web server, ASP and ASP.NET pages can exist side by side. In fact, an ASP page can link to an ASP.NET page and vice versa. If your application uses both ASP and ASP.NET pages (which may be quite common as you migrate ASP pages to ASP.NET), you must be aware that ASP and ASP.NET pages cannot share Session and Application objects. In an Active Server Page or ASP.NET page, a script can store values specific to a user's current visit (the session) using session variables. As a user moves from page to page within an application, scripts can use session variables to store such information as a user's login information, current shopping cart items, and so on. One user cannot access the session variables of a different user. In contrast, to store information that each user can access (shared information), scripts use the application variables.

USE IT The following ASP page, StoreVariables.asp, stores data within Session and Application objects. The code then creates a link to an ASP page named ShowVariables.asp and an ASP.NET page, named LookForVariables.aspx:

```
<html>
<head>
   <title>Store Variables</title>
</head>
<body>
  <center>
    <h1>Store Session and Application Variables</h1>
  </center><hr/>
  <%
    Session("Book") = "VB.NET Programming Tips & Techniques"
    Session("Chapter") = "Chapter 13"
    Application("Publisher") = "McGraw-Hill/Osborne"
    Application("Author") = "Jamsa"
  %>
<br/><br/>
<a href="ShowVariables.asp">
  Link to an ASP Page: ShowVariables.asp</a><br/><br/>
<a href="LookForVariables.aspx">
  Link to an ASP.NET Page: LookForVariables.aspx</a>
</body>
</html>
```

The following ASP page, ShowVariables.asp, retrieves the session information created by the page StoreVariables.asp. When you link to the page from the StoreVariables.asp page, your browser will display output similar to that shown in Figure 13-10.

```
<html>
<head>
   <title>Show Variables</title>
</head>
<body>
  <center><h1>Show Session and Application Variables</h1></center><hr/>
  <%
    Dim Book, Chapter, Publisher, Author
    Book = Session("Book")
    Chapter = Session("Chapter")
    Publisher = Application("Publisher")
    Author = Application("Author")

    If (Book <> "") Then
      Response.Write("Book: " & Book & "<br/>")
```

```
      Else
        Response.Write("Book: Unknown <br/>")
      End If

      If (Chapter <> "") Then
        Response.Write("Chapter: " & Chapter & "<br/>")
      Else
        Response.Write("Chapter: Unknown <br/>")
      End If

      If (Publisher <> "") Then
        Response.Write("Publisher: " & Publisher & "<br/>")
      Else
        Response.Write("Publisher: Unknown <br/>")
      End If

      If (Author <> "") Then
        Response.Write("Author: " & Author & "<br/>")
      Else
        Response.Write("Author: Unknown <br/>")
      End If
    %>

</body>
</html>
```

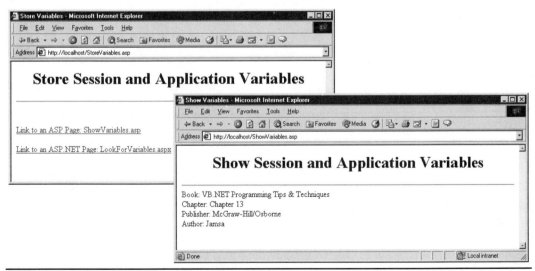

Figure 13-10   Displaying session information stored by an ASP page

In a similar way, the following ASP.NET page, LookForVariables.aspx, tries to retrieve the same session data:

```
<% @ Page Language="VB" %>
<html>
<head>
   <title>Look for Variables</title>
</head>
<body>
  <center><h1>Look for Session and Application Variables</h1></center><hr/>
  <%
    Dim Book, Chapter, Publisher, Author As String

    Book = Session("Book")
    Chapter = Session("Chapter")
    Publisher = Application("Publisher")
    Author = Application("Author")

    If (Book = Nothing) Then
      Response.Write("Book: Unknown <br/>")
    Else
      Response.Write("Book: " & Book & "<br/>")
    End If

    If (Chapter = Nothing) Then
      Response.Write("Chapter: Unknown <br/>")
    Else
      Response.Write("Chapter: " & Chapter & "<br/>")
    End If

    If (Publisher = Nothing) Then
      Response.Write("Publisher: Unknown <br/>")
    Else
      Response.Write("Publisher: " & Publisher & "<br/>")
    End If
```

```
  If (Author = Nothing) Then
    Response.Write("Author: Unknown <br/>")
  Else
    Response.Write("Author: " & Author & "<br/>")
  End If
%>
</body>
</html>
```

However, because ASP and ASP.NET pages cannot share session data, the variables are undefined within the ASP.NET page, as shown in Figure 13-11.

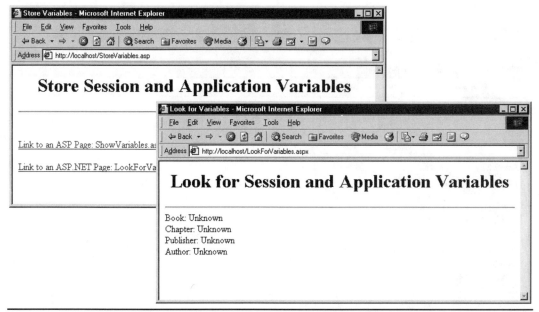

Figure 13-11 An ASP.NET page cannot retrieve session information stored by an ASP

Viewing HTTP Header Information

Depending on the processing your ASP.NET page performs, there may be times when your code must determine specifics about the request, such as whether the connection is secure, the user's previous Web site (which programmers call the referrer site), or the encoding types the user's browser will accept. In such cases, your scripts can examine the various Request object fields to view the HTTP request's header values.

USE IT The following ASP.NET page, HeaderInfo.aspx, uses the Request object to display specifics about an HTTP connection. When a user connects to the script, the user will see output similar to that shown in Figure 13-12.

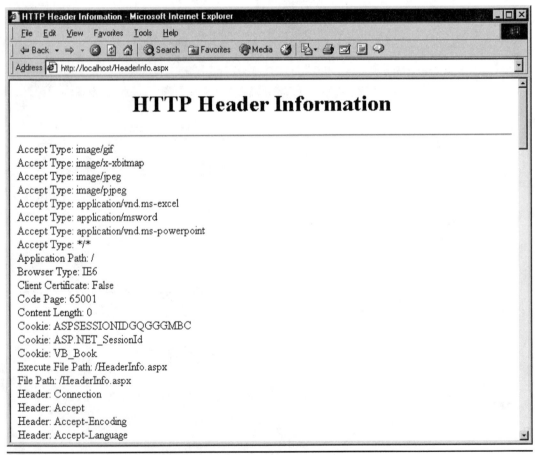

Figure 13-12 Displaying HTTP header information using an ASP.NET page

```
<% @ Page Language="VB" %>
<html>
<head>
   <title>HTTP Header Information</title>
</head>
<body>
  <center><h1>HTTP Header Information</h1></center><hr/>
  <%
  With Response
    Dim AcceptType As String
    For Each AcceptType In Request.AcceptTypes
      Response.Write("Accept Type: " & AcceptType & "<br/>")
    Next

    .Write("Application Path: " & Request.ApplicationPath & "<br/>")
    .Write("Browser Type: " & Request.Browser.Type & "<br/>")
    .Write("Client Certificate: " & _
       Request.ClientCertificate.IsPresent & "<br/>")
    .Write("Code Page: " & _
       Request.ContentEncoding.CodePage & "<br/>")
    .Write("Content Length: " & Request.ContentLength & "<br/>")

    Dim Cookie As String
    For Each Cookie In Request.Cookies
      Response.Write("Cookie: " & Cookie & "<br/>")
    Next

    .Write("Execute File Path: " & _
       Request.CurrentExecutionFilePath & "<br/>")
    .Write("File Path: " & Request.FilePath & "<br/>")

    Dim Filename As String
    For Each Filename In Request.Files
      Response.Write("File: " & Filename & "<br/>")
    Next

    Dim Header As String
    For Each Header In Request.Headers
      Response.Write("Header: " & Header & "<br/>")
    Next

    .Write("HTTP Method: " & Request.HttpMethod & "<br/>")
    .Write("Is Authenticated: " & Request.IsAuthenticated & "<br/>")
```

```vbnet
        .Write("Is Secure Connection: " & _
           Request.IsSecureConnection & "<br/>")

    Dim Param As String
    For Each Param In Request.Params
        Response.Write("Param: " & Param & "<br/>")
    Next

    .Write("Path: " & Request.Path & "<br/>")
    .Write("Path Info: " & Request.PathInfo & "<br/>")
    .Write("Application Path: " & _
       Request.PhysicalApplicationPath & "<br/>")
    .Write("Physical Path: " & Request.PhysicalPath & "<br/>")
    .Write("Raw URL: " & Request.RawUrl & "<br/>")
    .Write("Request Type: " & Request.RequestType & "<br/>")

    Dim ServerVar As String
    For Each ServerVar In Request.ServerVariables
        Response.Write("Server Variable: " & ServerVar & "<br/>")
    Next

    .Write("Total Bytes: " & Request.TotalBytes & "<br/>")
    .Write("URL: " & Request.Url.ToString() & "<br/>")

    If (Request.URLReferrer is Nothing) Then
        .Write("Referrer not defined<br/>")
    Else
        .Write("Referrer: " & Request.UrlReferrer.ToString() & "<br/>")
    End If

    .Write("User Agent: " & Request.UserAgent & "<br/>")
    .Write("Host Address: " & Request.UserHostAddress & "<br/>")
    .Write("Host Name: " & Request.UserHostName & "<br/>")

    Dim Lang As String
    For Each Lang In Request.UserLanguages
        Response.Write("Language: " & Lang & "<br/>")
    Next
  End With
  %>
</body>
</html>
```

Taking Advantage of Key ASP.NET Page-Based Methods

In an ASP.NET page, you place subroutine and function definitions within the <script> and </script> tags. In addition to defining your own functions and subroutines between the <script> and </script> tags, you may also want to provide functions that handle events related to the page itself. For example, each time the server loads an ASP.NET page, the server will generate a Load event. By defining a Page_Load subroutine within your script, your script can perform any preprocessing it requires, such as loading a data grid control with values from a database. In a similar way, when the server is done with the page, it generates an Unload method. Likewise, before the server renders a page's contents, the server generates a PreRender event. Finally, if a page encounters an error that is not detected, the server will generate an Error event.

The following ASP.NET page, PageEventDemo.aspx, implements several simple event handlers. Many of the handler subroutines simply place messages in the Application event log (as discussed in Chapter 10). Depending on the processing your script requires, the code you will place in each method will differ. In the Page_Unload method, for example, you might close any open files or databases. When you view this script, your browser will display a message that states Hello, ASP.NET World! The message appears in an italic font. If you examine the Page_PreRender subroutine, which the server calls before it begins to render the page's contents, you will find that the subroutine enables the use of italics. As such, the page displays its message using an italic font:

```vb
<% @ Page language="vb" %>
<% @ Import namespace="System.Diagnostics" %>

<script language="vb" runat="server">

  Protected Sub Page_Load(Sender As Object, E as EventArgs)
      Dim Log As New EventLog("Application")

      Log.Source = "PageDemo.aspx"

      Log.WriteEntry("Page loaded at " & Now())
      Log.Close()

      Session("LoadTime") = Now()
  End Sub

  Protected Sub Page_Error(Sender As Object, E as EventArgs)
      Dim Log As New EventLog("Application")

      Log.Source = "PageDemo.aspx"
```

```
      Log.WriteEntry("Error on the page")
      Log.Close()
  End Sub

  Protected Sub Page_Unload(Sender As Object, E as EventArgs)
      Dim Log As New EventLog("Application")

      Log.Source = "PageDemo.aspx"
      Log.WriteEntry("Page unloaded at " & Now())
      Log.Close()
  End Sub

  Protected Sub Page_PreRender(Sender As Object, E as EventArgs)
      Response.Write("<i>")
  End Sub
</script>
<html>
<head>
   <title>Page Event Demo</title>
</head>
<body>
  <center><h1>Hello ASP.NET World!</h1></center>
</body>
</html>
```

▶ *NOTE*

Depending on your system's security settings, you may need to change the application's trust level in the application's configuration file before the application can place entries into the event log.

ASP and ASP.NET Treat Form.Request and Form.QueryString Differently

When a page submits a form to a remote site using GET or POST operations, or when a URL contains arguments (www.SomeSite.com?Name=John), the script that processes the data uses either the Form.Request or Form.QueryString method to retrieve the data. Normally, for simple form objects, you can use the same code to retrieve values in an Active Server Page or ASP.NET page. For example, the following HTML file, FormDemo.html, creates a form that prompts a user to enter his or her first name, last name, and e-mail address:

```
<html>
<head>
```

```
    <title>FormDemo</title>
</head>
<body>
  <center><h1>Get User Information</h1></center><hr/>

  <form action="http://localhost/ShowForm.asp" method="POST">
    First Name: <input type="text" maxlength="50" name="Firstname"/>
    <br/>
    Last Name: <input type="text" maxlength="50" name="Lastname"/>
    <br/>
    Email: <input type="text" maxlength="50" name="Email"/><br/>
    <br/></br>
    <input type="submit" value="Submit">
  </form>
</body>
</html>
```

If you click the form's Submit button, the browser will submit the data to the Active Server Page, ShowForm.asp, which uses the Form.Request method to display the form's values:

```
<html>
<head>
    <title>ShowForm</title>
</head>
<body>
  <center><h1>Show User Information</h1></center><hr/>
  <%
        Dim First, Last, Email
        First = Request.Form("Firstname")
        Last = Request.Form("Lastname")
        Email = Request.Form("Email")

        Response.Write("Name: " & First & " " & Last & "<br/>")
        Response.Write("E-mail: " & Email)
  %>
</body>
</html>
```

To display the form's content using an ASP.NET page, you can use the following script, ShowForm.aspx, whose processing is nearly identical (the bold text illustrates the additional statements in the ASP.NET page):

```
<% @ Page language="VB" %>
<html>
<head>
```

```
   <title>ShowForm</title>
</head>
<body>
  <center><h1>Show User Information</h1></center><hr/>
  <%
     Dim First, Last, Email As String
     First = Request.Form("Firstname")
     Last = Request.Form("Lastname")
     Email = Request.Form("Email")

     Response.Write("Name: " & First & " " & Last & "<br/>")
     Response.Write("E-mail: " & Email)
  %>
</body>
</html>
```

To create a link to the ShowForm.aspx file, edit FormDemo.html and locate the following HTML <form> tag:

```
<form action="http://localhost/ShowForm.asp" method="POST">
```

Within the tag, change ShowForm.asp to ShowForm.aspx as shown here:

```
<form action="http://localhost/ShowForm.aspx" method="POST">
```

In an Active Server Page or ASP.NET page, a script uses the Response.Form method to retrieve values a browser submits to the form using a POST operation. In contrast, if the browser uses a GET operation to submit the data, the code must use the Response.QueryString method. Using the Request.HttpMethod property, a script can determine if the remote application performed a GET or POST operation. Then the code can use either the Response.Form or Response.QueryString, as appropriate to retrieve the form's data. The following ASP.NET page, GenericFormView.aspx, first determines if the remote application used a GET or POST operation and then displays the data submitted to the form:

```
<% @ Page language="VB" %>
<html>
<head>
   <title>ShowForm</title>
</head>
<body>
  <center><h1>Show User Information</h1></center><hr/>
  <%
      If Request.HTTPMethod = "POST" Then
        Dim I as Integer
```

```
      For I = 0 to Request.Form.Count - 1
        Response.Write(Request.Form.GetKey(I) & " " & _
           Request.Form(I) & "<br/>")
      Next
    Else
      Dim I as Integer

      For I = 0 to Request.QueryString.Count - 1
        Response.Write(Request.QueryString.GetKey(I) & " " & _
           Request.QueryString(I) & "<br/>")
      Next
    End If
  %>
</body>
</html>
```

As before, within the FormDemo.html file, change the HTML <form> tag to link to the ASP.NET page GenericFormView.aspx as shown here:

```
<form action="http://localhost/GenericFormView.aspx" method="POST">
```

As you migrate from Active Server Pages to ASP.NET, you must note that in ASP.NET array indexes begin at 0 (not 1, as is the case in Active Server Pages). The following script, ASPGenericFormView.asp, illustrates how you would perform the equivalent processing in an Active Server Page. Note how the For loops differ. Also, note that the script uses the Key method to get an item's name, as opposed to the GetKey method used in the ASP.NET page. Finally, because Active Server Pages do not support the Request.HTTPMethod property, the code must determine the operation type by using Request.ServerVariables("Request_Method"):

```
<html>
<head>
   <title>ShowForm</title>
</head>
<body>
  <center><h1>Show User Information</h1></center><hr/>
  <%
    Dim I

    If Request.ServerVariables("Request_Method") = "POST" Then
      For I = 1 to Request.Form.Count
        Response.Write(Request.Form.Key(I) & " " & _
           Request.Form(I) & "<br/>")
      Next
    Else
```

```
         For I = 1 to Request.QueryString.Count
            Response.Write(Request.QueryString.Key(I) & " " & _
               Request.QueryString(I) & "<br/>")
         Next
      End If
   %>
</body>
</html>
```

Again, in the FormDemo.html file, change the HTML <form> tag to link to the Active Server Page, ASPGenericFormView.asp, as shown here:

```
<form action="http://localhost/ASPGenericFormView.asp" method="POST">
```

Handling Exceptions in ASP.NET Pages

For years, programmers have made extensive use of ON ERROR statements in Active Server Pages to detect an error and the Err object's Number field to determine specifics about the error. Although ASP.NET pages still support the ON ERROR statement, you instead use exception handling (as discussed in Chapter 10) to detect and respond to errors.

For example, the following ASP.NET page, DivZero.aspx, uses the Mod operator to return the remainder of a division operation. However, in this case, the program divides the value 10 by 0, causing the script to encounter a division-by-zero error. When a user views this page, they will see a page similar to that shown in Figure 13-13, which explains that the script has encountered a division-by-zero error:

```
<% @ Page Language="VB" %>
<html>
<head>
   <title>Divide by Zero</title>
</head>
<body>
   <center><h1>Divide by Zero</h1></center><hr/>
   <%
         Dim A As Integer = 10
         Dim B As Integer = 0
         Dim Remainder As Integer

         Remainder = A Mod B

         Response.Write("Remainder: " & Remainder & "<br/>")
   %>
</body>
</html>
```

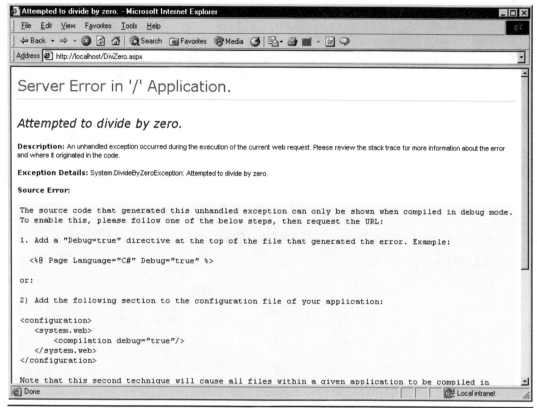

Figure 13-13   An error page describing an uncaught division-by-zero error

USE IT   To detect and handle the division-by-zero error, the script should use a Try-Catch statement to handle the division-by-zero exception, as discussed in Chapter 9. The following ASP.NET page, CatchDivisionException.aspx, uses a Try-Catch statement to detect and respond to the division error:

```
<% @ Page Language="VB" %>
<html>
<head>
   <title>Catch Divide by Zero</title>
</head>
<body>
  <center><h1>Catch Divide by Zero Exception</h1></center><hr/>
  <%
     Dim A As Integer = 10
     Dim B As Integer = 0
     Dim Remainder As Integer
```

```
      Try
         Remainder = A Mod B

         Response.Write("Remainder: " & Remainder & "<br/>")
      Catch Ex As DivideByZeroException
         Response.Write("<h1>Error in processing--Divide by 0</h1>")
      End Try
   %>
</body>
</html>
```

In a similar way, the following ASP.NET page, ShowFile.aspx, illustrates the use of exception handling. The code opens the text file that a user specifies within a form that, in turn, submits the filename to the script. If the script successfully opens the file, the page will display the file's contents. If an error occurs, the script will use exception handling to detect and respond to the error:

```
<% @ Page language="VB" %>
<% @ Import Namespace="System.IO" %>

<html>
<head>
   <title>ShowFile</title>
</head>
<body>
  <center><h1>ASP.NET File Demo</h1></center><hr/>
  <pre>
  <%
      Dim Filename As String
      Filename = Request.Form("Filename")

      If (Filename <> "") Then
        Try
            Dim TextFile As New StreamReader(Filename)

            Dim Content As  String
            Response.Write("<br/>")

            Content = TextFile.ReadToEnd()
            Response.Write(Content & "<br/>")
            TextFile.Close()
```

```
        Catch Ex As Exception
            Response.Write("Error opening or reading file")
        End Try
    Else
        Response.Write("Filename not specified")
    End If
  %>
 </pre>
</body>
</html>
```

The script uses a StreamReader object to read the file's contents, which means the script must import the System.IO namespace. The script retrieves the filename the user specifies in the form using the Request.Form method. Then, if the script successfully opens the file, it uses the ReadToEnd method to read the file's entire contents into the string variable Content. The code then displays the string using Response.Write. If an error occurs when the script tries to open the file, the code detects and responds to the error using a Try-Catch statement. Note that the code uses the <pre> and </pre> HTML tags to specify that the file's format is preformatted. Without these tags, the page would ignore the carriage-return and linefeed characters that appear within the file as well as various whitespace characters.

To test the ASP.NET page, create the following HTML file, GetFilename.html, which prompts the user for a filename and then submits the filename to the script:

```
<html>
<head>
   <title>Get File Name</title>
</head>
<body>
  <center><h1>ASP.NET File Demo</h1></center><hr/>

  <form action="http://localhost/ShowFile.aspx" method="POST">
      Filename: <input type="text" maxlength="50" name="Filename"/>
      <br/></br>
      <input type="submit" value="Submit Filename">
  </form>
</body>
</html>
```

As you can see, the HTML tags create a form that contains an input field within which the user can type the filename that he or she desires. The form also contains a Submit button. When the user clicks the Submit button, the browser will send the form's data to the ASP.NET page ShowFile.aspx which resides on the local host. When you type in a filename, you must specify a complete pathname. Depending on your server's file protections, you may need to create a test folder within which you place a file with permissions that let the script open and display the file's contents.

Taking Advantage of ASP.NET Configuration Files

Throughout this chapter, you have likely created the majority of the ASP.NET pages using an editor such as Windows Notepad. When you use Visual Studio to create an ASP.NET page, Visual Studio will place the application in its own folder, within which Visual Studio will place several files you can use to customize the application's processing. Table 13-1 briefly describes the various file types Visual Studio creates for your application.

USE IT For example, to specify startup and shutdown processing, place subroutines similar to the following in the Global.asax.vb file. In this case, the application creates a variable named StartTime that contains the date and time the application started:

```
<Script language="VB" runat="server">
    Sub Application_OnStart()
        Application("StartTime") = Now()
    End Sub
</script>
```

File	Contents
AppName.aspx, AppName.aspx.vb, AppName.aspx.resx	Contains the page's design template and the corresponding code-behind file that performs the form's processing. The AppName corresponds to the page's application name. The .resx file is a resource file used for Web forms.
AppName.vsdisco	Contains entries remote applications can use to discover the service.
Assembly.vb	Contains the assembly attributes. Visual Studio creates the Assembly.vb file for all .NET projects.
Global.asax, Global.asax.vb, Global.asax.resx	Provide support for application (and error, request, response, and session) event handling.
Styles.css	Defines the application's cascading style sheets.
Web.config	Defines and application's runtime attributes.

Table 13-1   The File Types Visual Studio Creates for an ASP.NET Project

Implementing a Custom-Error Page

By default, when an error (such as a syntax error or an unhandled exception) occurs in an ASP.NET page, the server will display an error page similar to that shown in Figure 13-14.

Before you release your ASP.NET application for use on the Web, you may want to direct the server to display a different error page that provides the user with fewer specifics about why the error occurred and the page crashed, and more information the user can use to continue as well as to contact your technical support team.

USE IT   Using the Page directive, you can specify the URL of the page the server should display in the event of an error:

```
<% @ Page ErrorPage="http://www.Somesite.com/ErrorPage.html" %>
```

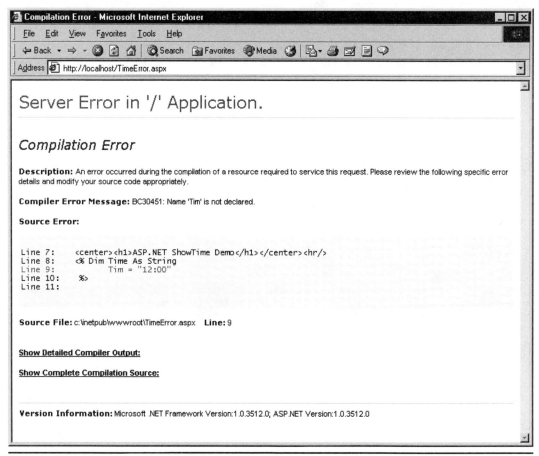

Figure 13-14   Displaying a standard error page for an "unhandled" error in an ASP.NET page

Likewise, using the application's Web.config file, you can specify the URL for a page the server displays in the event of an error, as follows:

```
<configuration>
  <system.web>
    <customErrors defaultredirect='Somepage.html' mode='on'>
    </customErrors>
  </system.web>
</configuration>
```

In addition to directing the server to redirect the user to a new page when an error occurs, your application can also use the Page_Error subroutine to define and handle an error. Each time an ASP.NET page generates an exception that the application does not catch, the server calls the Page class Page_Error method. By overriding the method within a page, your application can handle errors on a page-by-page basis. The following ASP.NET code fragment, for example, defines the Page_Error method, within which you can place the processing you want the page to perform when an error occurs:

```
<Script language="VB" runat="server">
  Protected Sub Page_Error(Sender As Object, E as EventArgs)
     ' Place your error-handling code here.
  End Sub
</script>
```

In addition to catching errors on a page basis, you can also define an application-wide error handler by overriding the Application_Error method by defining the method within the Global.asax.vb file:

```
<Script language="VB" runat="server">
    Sub Application_Error()
        ' Place your error-processing code here.
    End Sub
</script>
```

Improving Performance by Disabling Debug Operations

By default, when an error occurs in an ASP.NET page, the server displays a page that contains information you can use to debug the error. As shown in Figure 13-15, the debug information contains such data as the stack contents at the time of the error and the line number in your script that caused the error.

Although the debugging information can be very useful in helping you track down errors as you test your ASP.NET pages, forcing the server to maintain such information as users execute your pages places significant overhead on the server. Before you make your ASP.NET pages available for use on the Web, you should turn off debugging for the page.

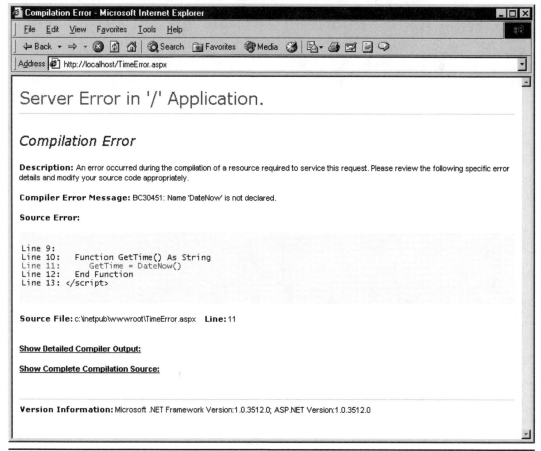

Figure 13-15   Using debug information to locate errors in an ASP.NET page

USE IT   To turn off debug mode on a page-by-page basis, you can place the following Page directive at the start of each page:

```
<% @ Page Debug="False" %>
```

You can also disable debug mode on an application basis by placing the following entry in the application's Web.config file:

```
<configuration>
    <system.web>
        <compilation debug="false"/>
    </system.web>
</configuration>
```

Specifying Application- and Session-Specific Processing

Depending on the processing your ASP.NET page performs, there will often be times when you must perform specific operations when the application begins or ends, or when a session begins or ends. To specify such processing, you can override the following methods by declaring the methods within the application's Global.asax.vb file.

USE IT For example, to specify startup and shutdown processing, you can place a subroutine with the names shown in the following code fragment within the Global.asax.vb file. Within the subroutines, you can place statements that perform the processing you want your pages to perform on startup and shutdown:

```
<Script language="VB" runat="server">
    Sub Application_OnStart()
        ' Place your start-up code here.
    End Sub

    Sub Application_OnEnd()
        ' Place your clean-up code here.
    End Sub
</script>
```

Likewise, you can place the following statements in the file to control the processing the page performs when a session starts or ends:

```
<Script language="VB" runat="server">
    Sub Session_OnStart()
        ' Place your start-up code here.
    End Sub

    Sub Session_OnEnd()
        ' Place your clean-up code here.
    End Sub
</script>
```

Taking a Closer Look at the Page Directive

All the ASP.NET pages this chapter's Tips have presented have used the following Page directive to specify the page's programming language:

```
<% @ Page Language ="VB" %>
```

In addition to letting your pages use the Language attribute to specify the programming language, the Page directive supports a myriad of attributes, as described in Table 13-2.

Attribute	Purpose
AspCompat	A Boolean value that when True allows the page to be executed on a single-threaded apartment (STA) thread. This allows the page to call STA components, such as a component developed with Microsoft Visual Basic 6.0. Setting this attribute to True also allows the page to call COM+ 1.0 components that require access to the unmanaged Active Server Pages (ASP) built-in objects. These are accessible through the ObjectContext object or the OnStartPage method. The default is False. Setting the AspCompat attribute to True may degrade your page's performance. The default is False.
AutoEventWireup	A Boolean value that specifies if the page's events are autowired. The default is True.
Buffer	A Boolean value that specifies whether HTTP response buffering is enabled. The default is True.
ClassName	Specifies the page's class (do not include a namespace) name for the page the compiler will create dynamically when a user requests the page.
ClientTarget	Specifies a user agent for which ASP.NET server controls should target the content they render.
CodePage	Specifies the code page value for the response output.
CompilerOptions	Specifies string options the compiler will use when it compiles the page.
ContentType	Specifies a standard MIME type used to format the HTTP response content.
Culture	Specifies the page's culture setting, which defines currency formats and so on.
Debug	A Boolean value that specifies if the compiler should include debug symbols when it compiles the page. The default is False.
Description	Specifies a text description of the page. The compiler does not use the description.
EnableSessionState	Specifies the page's session-state requirements. True enables session state. ReadOnly creates a session state that cannot be changed. False disables the session state. The default is True.
EnableViewState	A Boolean value that specifies whether the server maintains view-state information across page request. The default is True.
EnableViewStateMac	A Boolean value that specifies if ASP.NET should run a machine authentication check (MAC) on the page's view state when a client posts the page back. The default is False.
ErrorPage	Specifies a URL to which the server redirects the user if the page encounters an unhandled exception.
Explicit	A Boolean value that specifies whether the compiler compiles a Visual Basic .NET page using the Visual Basic Option Explicit mode. The default is False.
Inherits	Specifies a code-behind class that the page inherits.
Language	Specifies the programming language the compiler will use to compile the page.
LCID	Specifies the locale identifier for the Web Forms page.

Table 13-2   Attributes Supported by the Page Directive

Attribute	Purpose
ResponseEncoding	Specifies the encoding the page will use when it generates the response.
Src	Specifies the name of the source file of the code-behind class the compiler will dynamically compile when a user requests the page.
SmartNavigation	A Boolean value that specifies whether the page supports the smart navigation feature built into IE 5 and later.
Strict	A Boolean value that specifies whether the compiler should compile a Visual Basic .NET page using Option Strict mode. The default is False.
Trace	A Boolean value that specifies whether tracing is enabled. The default is False.
TraceMode	Specifies how trace messages are displayed: SortByTime or SortByCategory. The default is SortByTime.
Transaction	Specifies whether the page supports transactions: Disabled, NotSupported, Supported, Required, and RequiresNew. The default is Disabled.
UICulture	Specifies the page's culture setting.
WarningLevel	Specifies the compiler warning level (in the range 0 to 4) at which you want the compiler to end the page's compilation.

Table 13-2   Attributes Supported by the Page Directive (continued)

USE IT   The following Page directive, for example, specifies that the page uses Visual Basic .NET as the programming language, disables debugging for the page, and provides a URL to which the server should redirect the user if an error occurs:

```
<% @ Page language="vb" debug="false" ErrorPage="ShowError.html" %>
```

Fine-Tuning ASP.NET Cache Attributes

USE IT   In an ASP.NET page, your code can control caching using the OutputCache directive. For example, the following directive specifies that a page's contents should remain in the cache for no longer than two minutes (120 seconds):

```
<% @ OutputCache Duration="120" %>
```

In addition to the Duration attribute, the OutputCache directive supports the attributes specified in Table 13-3.

Attribute	Meaning
Duration	Specifies, in seconds, the length of time the page is cached. You must specify the duration attribute.
Location	Specifies the cache location: Any, Client, Downstream, Server, None. The default is Any. The Location attribute is not supported for @ OutputCache directives included in user controls.
VaryByCustom	Specifies custom output caching requirements. If specified, you must override the HttpApplication.GetVaryByCustomString method within the application's Global.asax file.
VaryByHeader	Specifies a list of semicolon-separated HTTP headers the application can use to vary the output cache. If you set VarByHeader to two or more headers, the output cache will maintain a different version of the document for each header. The VaryByHeader attribute is not supported for @ OutputCache directives in user controls. Note: The VaryByHeader attribute enables caching items in all HTTP/1.1 caches, not just the ASP.NET cache. The VaryByHeader attribute is not supported for @ OutputCache directives for user controls.
VaryByParam	Specifies a list of semicolon-separated parameter strings the application can use to vary the output cache. The parameter strings correspond to values sent to the page via a GET or POST operation. You can also specify "*" and "none". If you set VaryByParam to two or more strings, the output cache will maintain a different version of the document for each parameter. You must specify this attribute when you cache ASP.NET pages. You must specify the VaryByParam attribute for user controls unless you have used the VaryByControl attribute.
VaryByControl	Specifies a list of comma-separated control strings the application can use to vary the output cache. The strings correspond to fully qualified property names within a user control. If you set VaryByControl to two or more controls, the output cache will maintain a different version of the document for each control. You must specify this attribute for a user control OutputCache directive. You must specify a VaryByControl attribute for user controls, unless you have specified the VaryByParam attribute.

Table 13-3   Attributes Supported by the OutputCache Directive

Importing a Namespace Using the Imports Directive

As you have learned, namespaces exist to help you better organize classes and reduce name conflicts. The .NET environment makes extensive use of namespaces to organize the classes that make up the Common Language Runtime. Depending on the classes your Visual Basic .NET programs use, there are times when you must direct the compiler to import the namespace that contains a specific class. By default, an ASP.NET page will automatically import the following namespaces:

- System
- System.Collections
- System.Collections.Specialized
- System.IO
- System.Text
- System.Text.RegularExpressions
- System.Web
- System.Web.Caching
- System.Web.Security
- System.Web.Sessionstate
- System.UI
- System.UI.HTMLControls
- System.WebControls

USE IT If your ASP.NET page requires a different namespace, you can use the Import directive as shown here:

```
<% @ Import Namespace="System.Diagnostics" %>
```

The following ASP.NET page demonstrates an ASP.NET page's support of multiple threads. Chapter 8 discusses threads of execution in detail. The script, ThreadDemo.aspx, creates three threads, named A, B, and C, that simply write the letters "AAAA", "BBBB", and "CCCC" to the page within a loop. Depending on the processing your page performs, your threads will likely perform more valuable processing. However, by examining the concepts this Tip presents, you may get your thread-based pages up and running more quickly. To perform thread operations, the script must import the System.Threading namespace:

```
<% @ Import namespace="System.Threading" %>
```

When a user views the page, his or her browser will display the output similar to that shown in Figure 13-16.

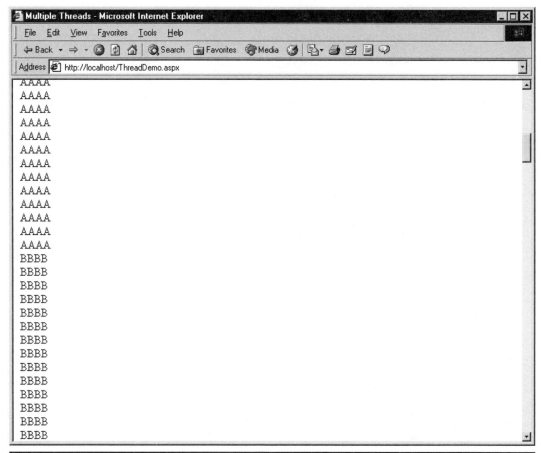

Figure 13-16   Using multiple threads of execution in an ASP.NET page

The following statements implement the ThreadDemo.aspx ASP.NET page:

```
<% @ Page language="vb" %>
<% @ Import namespace="System.Threading" %>

<html>
<head>
```

```
   <title>Multiple Threads</title>
</head>
<body>
  <script runat="server">
    Sub Display_A()
        Dim I As Integer

        For I = 0 To 50
            Response.Write("AAAA<br/>")
        Next

      Thread. Sleep(500)

        For I = 0 To 50
            Response.Write("AAAA<br/>")
        Next
    End Sub

    Sub Display_B()
        Dim I As Integer

        For I = 0 To 50
            Response.Write("BBBB<br/>")
        Next

        Thread.Sleep(100)

        For I = 0 To 50
            Response.Write("BBBB<br/>")
        Next
    End Sub

    Sub Display_C()
        Dim I As Integer

        For I = 0 To 50
            Response.Write("CCCC<br/>")
        Next

        Thread.Sleep(10)

        For I = 0 To 50
            Response.Write("CCCC<br/>")
        Next
```

```
    End Sub
</script>

  <%
        Dim A As System.Threading.Thread
        Dim B As System.Threading.Thread
        Dim C As System.Threading.Thread

        A = New Threading.Thread(AddressOf Display_A)
        B = New Threading.Thread(AddressOf Display_B)
        C = New Threading.Thread(AddressOf Display_C)

        A.Start()
        B.Start()
        C.Start()

        A.Join()
        B.Join()
        C.Join()
  %>
</body>
</html>
```

As you can see, the page defines each of the thread functions between the <script> and </script> tags. In each of the functions, the code writes 50 lines of output and then uses the Thread class Sleep method to suspend the thread's execution (which better illustrates the thread time slices in the program output). Note that after the code starts the threads, the code then uses the Join methods to wait for each thread to complete its processing. If the thread does not wait for the threads to complete their processing in this way, the page will have ended its rendering and the output the threads display will not appear.

CHAPTER 14

Programming Windows Services

TIPS IN THIS CHAPTER

I n the Windows environment, a service is a program that extends the capabilities the operating system provides. The Internet Information Services (IIS), for example, is a service that provides a system with Web server capabilities. IIS is not built into Windows. Instead, each time a Windows-based server boots, it installs and starts the IIS service. As you create real-world applications, you can exploit Windows services for a myriad of tasks. A Windows service, for example, might monitor an application's processing behind the scenes, providing developers with insights into how users are exploiting the application's capabilities. Or a Windows service may authenticate an application's users.

In Windows 2000, you can view the services your system is running in the Windows Services application shown in Figure 14-1.

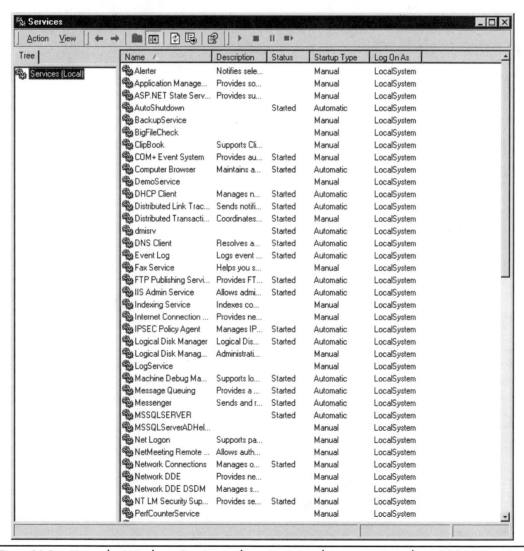

Figure 14-1   Using the Windows Services utility to monitor the services Windows 2000 is running

Subroutine	Purpose
OnStart	Executes each time Windows starts the service. Windows can load a service without starting the service.
OnStop	Executes each time Windows stops a service.
OnPause	Executes each time Windows suspends a service. You must enable the services you create to respond to pause operations.
OnContinue	Executes each time Windows resumes a service. You must enable the services you create to respond in order to continue operations.
OnShutdown	Executes each time Windows begins to shut down. You must enable the services you create to respond to shutdown operations.
OnPowerEvent	Executes each time Windows generates a change in the system's power status. You must enable the services you create to respond to power events.

Table 14-1   Subroutines that Control a Windows Service's Processing

To view services in Windows Services, perform these steps:

1. Select Start | Settings | Control Panel. Windows will display the Control Panel window.
2. In the Control Panel, double-click the Administrative Tools icon. Windows will display the Administrative Tools window.
3. In the Administrative Tools window, double-click the Services icon.

As it turns out, Visual Studio makes it very easy for you to create a Windows service. To start, you simply create a Windows Services project. Visual Studio will create a program template you can use to get your service up and running quickly.

Within the code template Visual Studio creates, you will define subroutines the service calls when it starts, stops, pauses, continues, and when the operating system later shuts down. Table 14-1 briefly discusses the subroutines you will implement in a Windows service.

Building a Simple Windows Service

Regardless of the processing a Windows service performs, the steps to create and install the service are quite similar. In this Tip, you will create and then install your first Windows service. To help you get started with Windows services, Visual Studio provides the Windows Service project type, which has a code template you can use to quickly create a simple service. In this Tip, you will use Visual Studio to create a service named DemoService. The service, in this case, will not perform any significant processing per se. Instead, the service will record various service-based events in a root-directory file named DemoEvents.log. In the file, the service will append a message that states when the service starts and later ends:

```
Service started at 3/7/2002 10:36:51 AM
Service stopped at 3/7/2002 11:57:25 AM
```

 To create a Windows service using Visual Studio, perform these steps:

1. In Visual Studio, select File | New Project. Visual Studio will display the New Projects dialog box.

2. In the New Projects dialog box, select the Windows Service icon. Then, in the dialog box Name field, type in the name of your service and select OK. Visual Studio will display a design view for the service as shown in Figure 14-2.

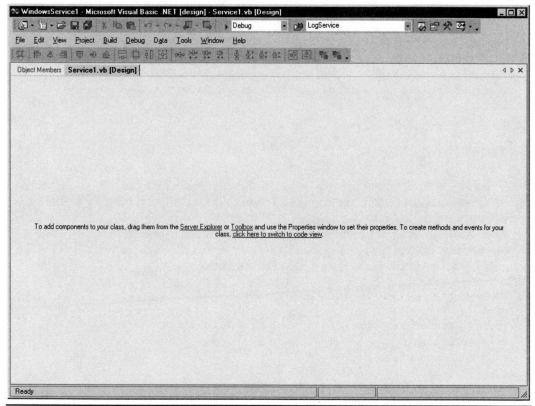

Figure 14-2   Displaying a Windows service in design view

3. In the Design View screen, right-click the project information. Visual Studio will display a pop-up menu.

4. In the pop-up menu, select Properties. Visual Studio will display the service's properties.

5. In the property list, assign the name DemoService to the Service name property (not the Name property).

6. Click the code view option to display the service's source code.

As discussed, each time DemoService starts, the service will append a message to the root-directory file DemoEvents.log. To perform this startup processing, place the following Imports statement at the start of the program code:

```
Imports System.IO
```

Then place the following statements in the OnStart method:

```
Private FileSt As StreamWriter

Protected Overrides Sub OnStart(ByVal args() As String)
  Try
     FileSt = New StreamWriter("C:\DemoEvents.log", True)
     FileSt.WriteLine("Service started at " & DateTime.Now)
     FileSt.Flush()
  Catch E As Exception
  End Try
End Sub
```

As you can see, the statements open the file and then use the StreamWriter class WriteLine method to write the message and current time to the file. To make the file easily accessible for use during other events, the code does not close the file.

In a similar way, when you end the service, the code will append a message to the file. Then, because the file is shutting down, the code will close the file. To perform the service's shutdown processing, place the following statements in the OnStop method:

```
Protected Overrides Sub OnStop()
  Try
    FileSt.WriteLine("Service stopped at " & DateTime.Now)
    FileSt.Close()
  Catch E As Exception
  End Try
End Sub
```

Before you can install a service, you must add special "installer code" to your project. The installer software provides information Windows needs to successfully install the service. To add installer code to the DemoService project, perform these steps:

1. Select design view and then right-click the design view window. Visual Studio will display a pop-up menu.

2. In the pop-up menu, select Add Installer. Visual Studio will add two components to your project, a service process installer and a service installer.

When Windows installs a service, Windows performs the installation using a given context that defines the privileges the service can use. Using the service process installer that Visual Studio adds to your project, you must specify an account on the system (such as a user account or special account you create for the service) that defines the service's context. To start, you must first select the account type. Table 14-2 briefly describes the available account types. Then you must specify the account's corresponding username and password. If you do not specify the account context information, Windows cannot install the service.

To specify the service's installer information, right-click the service process installer and select Properties from the pop-up menu. In the installer's properties fields, use the pull-down list to specify the account type as shown in Figure 14-3 and then type in the corresponding username and password.

Next, compile and build the service. At this stage, your service should contain the statements that follow. Because this is your first Windows service, the following statements include those created by

Account Type	Purpose
Local Service	Directs Windows to run the service in the context of an account on the local system that may have extended privileges.
Network Service	Directs Windows to run the service in the context of a non-privileged account on the local system. The service will present the computer's credentials to a remote server.
Local System	Directs Windows to run the service in the context of a non-privileged account on the local system. The service will present anonymous credentials to a remote server.
User	Directs Windows to prompt the user for a valid username and password each time the service runs. Windows will run the service in the context of the account the user enters.

Table 14-2   Account Settings that Define a Windows Service's Security Context

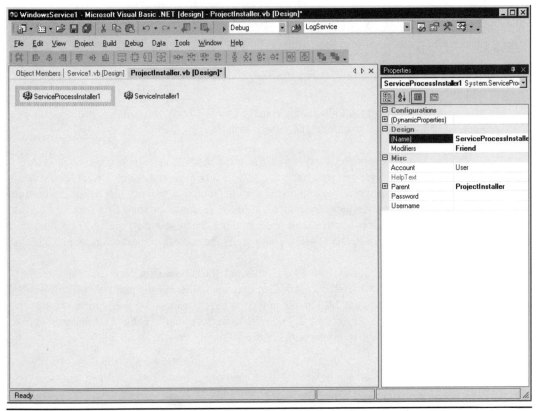

Figure 14-3 Specifying a service's account type, username, and password

Visual Studio when you create a Windows service project. The statements Visual Studio creates on your behalf appear between the #Region and #End Region directives:

```
Imports System.ServiceProcess
Imports System.IO

Public Class Service1
    Inherits System.ServiceProcess.ServiceBase

#Region " Component Designer generated code "

    Public Sub New()
        MyBase.New()
```

```vb
    ' This call is required by the Component Designer.
    InitializeComponent()

    ' Add any initialization after the InitializeComponent() call
End Sub

'UserService overrides dispose to clean up the component list.

Protected Overloads Overrides Sub Dispose(ByVal disposing As Boolean)
    If disposing Then
        If Not (components Is Nothing) Then
            components.Dispose()
        End If
    End If
    MyBase.Dispose(disposing)
End Sub

' The main entry point for the process
<MTAThread()> _
Shared Sub Main()
    Dim ServicesToRun() As System.ServiceProcess.ServiceBase

    ' More than one NT Service may run within the same process.
    ' To add another service to this process, change the following
    ' line to create a second service object. For example,
    '
    '   ServicesToRun = New System.ServiceProcess.ServiceBase () _
    '       {New Service1, New MySecondUserService}
    '

    ServicesToRun = New System.ServiceProcess.ServiceBase() _
      {New Service1()}
    System.ServiceProcess.ServiceBase.Run(ServicesToRun)
End Sub

'Required by the Component Designer
Private components As System.ComponentModel.Icontainer

' NOTE: The following is required by the Component Designer
' It can be modified using the Component Designer.
' Do not modify it using the code editor.
```

```
    <System.Diagnostics.DebuggerStepThrough()> _
      Private Sub InitializeComponent()
         '
         'Service1
         '
         Me.ServiceName = "DemoService"
    End Sub
#End Region

    Private FileSt As StreamWriter

    Protected Overrides Sub OnStart(ByVal args() As String)
        Try
            FileSt = New StreamWriter("C:\DemoEvents.log", True)
            FileSt.WriteLine("Service started at " & DateTime.Now)
            FileSt.Flush()
        Catch E As Exception
        End Try
    End Sub

    Protected Overrides Sub OnStop()
        Try
            FileSt.WriteLine("Service stopped at " & DateTime.Now)
            FileSt.Close()
        Catch E As Exception
        End Try
    End Sub
End Class
```

To create a Windows service, the code template creates a SystemBase object that corresponds to the process Windows runs on the service's behalf. The template code provides the object's constructor and destructor methods and also creates and launches the service process. The service itself, however, will not automatically start unless you direct it to do so by right-clicking the project's service installer (not the process service installer) and selecting Properties. In the service installer's properties fields, use the pull-down list to select the start option you desire, as shown in Figure 14-4.

In this case, the only code you must provide are the statements that appear within the OnStart and OnStop subroutines that the service automatically calls. As you can see, the subroutines override the methods that the base class provides.

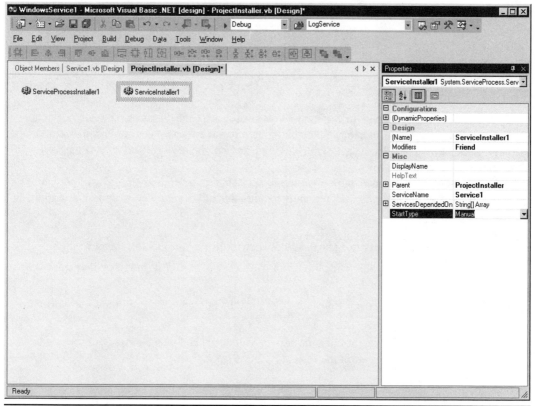

Figure 14-4   Controlling service startup options in the project's service installer properties

Installing and Removing a Service in Windows 2000

In the previous Tip, you created a Windows service named DemoService.exe. After you create a service, you must direct Windows to install the service (run the service program as a background task) each time your system starts. One of the easiest ways to install the service is to use the InstallUtil program (provided with Visual Studio) that you run from the command line.

USE IT To install the DemoService.exe program, open the command window and issue the following InstallUtil command, replacing the directory path shown here with the path on your system that contains the DemoService.exe program (the command assumes that you have placed the directory that contains the InstallUtil command in the command path):

```
C:\> InstallUtil  C:\SomeDirectoryPath\DemoService.exe  <Enter>
```

When you execute the InstallUtil command, you must specify the directory path on your system that contains the DemoServices.exe file. Pay close attention to the messages the InstallUtil program displays. If the utility cannot successfully install your service, the utility will display a message describing the cause of the error.

After the InstallUtil command ends, your service is installed in Windows, but it will not yet be running (you will learn later in this chapter how to automatically start a service upon installation). To view and start your service, perform these steps:

1. Select Start | Settings | Control Panel. Windows will display the Control Panel window.

2. In the Control Panel, double-click the Administrative Tools icon. Windows will display the Administrative Tools window.

3. In the Administrative Tools window, double-click the Service's icon. Windows will open the Services window.

4. In the Services window, right-click the service you desire and then choose Start. (You can also use the Action menu to control the selected service's processing.)

In addition to using the Windows Services application to control a service, you can view your services from within Visual Studio using the Server Explorer, as shown in Figure 14-5, by performing these steps:

1. In Visual Studio, select View | Server Explorer. Visual Studio will open the Server Explorer window.

2. In the Server Explorer, click the server that corresponds to your system and then select Services. The Server Explorer will display a list of the services running on the system.

3. In the list of services, right-click the service you desire and then select the menu option that corresponds to the operation you want to perform, such as starting or stopping the service.

When you no longer require a service, you will again use the InstallUtil command to remove the service. In this case, however, you will include the /U switch that directs the utility to remove the service as shown here:

```
C:\> InstallUtil  /U C:\SomeDirectoryPath\DemoService.exe  <Enter>
```

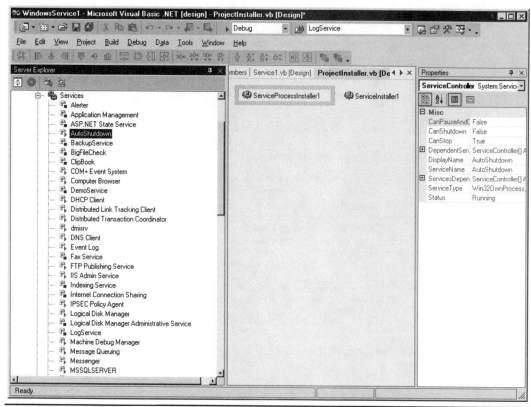

Figure 14-5   Using the Server Explorer to control Windows services

Taking a Closer Look at the ServiceBase Class

When you create a Windows service, your service uses the ServiceBase class that resides in the System.ServiceProcess namespace:

```
Public Class Service1
    Inherits System.ServiceProcess.ServiceBase
```

The ServiceBase class corresponds to the process that Windows creates to execute the service's processing. By overriding base-class methods within your source code, you can define the operations the service performs when it starts, stops, pauses, and later continues its operations. Table 14-3 briefly describes the ServiceBase class properties.

Property	Purpose
AutoLog	Gets or sets a Boolean value that specifies whether the service automatically reports Start, Stop, Pause, and Continue operations in the event log.
CanHandlePowerEvent	Gets or sets a Boolean value that specifies whether the service can respond to events that correspond to power status changes. If your service provides an OnPowerEvent method, set this property to True.
CanPauseAndContinue	Gets or sets a Boolean value that specifies whether the service can be paused and resumed. If your service provides the OnPause and OnContinue methods, set this property to True.
CanShutdown	Gets or sets a Boolean value that specifies whether the service can respond to an event that occurs when Windows shuts down. If your service provides an OnShutdown method, set this property to True.
CanStop	Gets or sets a Boolean value that specifies whether the service can be stopped. If your service provides an OnStop method, set this property to True.
EventLog	Gets an event log object your code can use to write entries into the application event log.
MaxNameLength	Returns the maximum size length you can use to name a service.
ServiceName	Gets or sets the name that identifies the service to the system.

Table 14-3   The ServiceBase Class Properties

In the DemoService service that you created in the Tip titled "Building a Simple Windows Service," you used the OnStart and OnStop methods to define the processing the service performs each time it begins and ends. Within the Windows Services application, in addition to starting and stopping a service, you can pause and later resume the service's processing. If your service must perform specific processing in response to a pause or continue operation, your service can define the processing in the OnPause and OnContinue methods. Further, there may be times when your service must perform specific processing when the system shuts down. To do so, you can define the processing in the OnShutDown method.

USE IT   In the DemoService.vb source code, place the following statements that direct the service to log pause, continue, and shut down events to the DemoEvents.log file:

```
Protected Overrides Sub OnPause()
    Try
        FileSt.WriteLine("Service paused at " & DateTime.Now)
        FileSt.Flush()
    Catch E As Exception
    End Try
End Sub
```

```
Protected Overrides Sub OnContinue()
   Try
      FileSt.WriteLine("Service continued at " & DateTime.Now)
      FileSt.Flush()

      Catch E As Exception
   End Try
End Sub

Protected Overrides Sub OnShutdown()
   Try
      FileSt.WriteLine("Service shutdown at " & DateTime.Now)
      FileSt.Close()
   Catch E As Exception
   End Try

End Sub
```

Next, before the service can respond to pause, continue, and shutdown operations, you must enable such operations in the service, which you can do with Visual Studio by performing these steps:

1. In design mode, right-click the service and select Properties from the pop-up menu.
2. In the service's property list, use the pull-down list to enable or disable the events to which you want the service to respond.

Behind the scenes, Visual Studio will place statements similar to the following in your source code:

```
Me.CanHandlePowerEvent = True
Me.CanPauseAndContinue = True
Me.CanShutdown = True
```

Then compile and build the service. Because the service has changed, you must use the InstallUtil program to uninstall the existing service before you can install the new service. In the Windows Services program, start, pause, continue, stop, and then shut down your service. The log file DemoEvents.log will contain entries similar to the following:

```
Service started at 3/12/2002 4:50:15 PM
Service paused at 3/12/2002 4:50:28 PM
Service continued at 3/12/2002 4:50:32 PM
```

Writing Service Events to the Windows Event Log

For simplicity, the DemoService program used a file to record information about the events it received. A better way to record service information is to place the entries into one of the Windows event logs. In Chapter 9, you learned how to use an EventLog object to place an entry into a specific log (applications normally place entries into the Application log). The following code fragment uses an EventLog object to place an entry into the Application log:

```
Dim Log As New EventLog("Application")
Log.Source = "Program Name"
Log.WriteEntry("Message to place into the event log")
```

USE IT The following program, LogService.vb, creates a simple Windows service. The program directs the OnStart, OnStop, OnPause, OnContinue, and OnShutdown methods to place events into the Windows event log:

```
Protected Overrides Sub OnStart(ByVal args() As String)
    Try
        Dim Log As New EventLog("Application")
        Log.Source = "LogService"
        Log.WriteEntry("Service started at " & DateTime.Now)
        Log.Close()
    Catch E As Exception
    End Try
End Sub

Protected Overrides Sub OnPause()
    Try
        Dim Log As New EventLog("Application")
        Log.Source = "LogService"
        Log.WriteEntry("Service paused at " & DateTime.Now)
        Log.Close()
    Catch E As Exception
    End Try
End Sub

Protected Overrides Sub OnContinue()
    Try
        Dim Log As New EventLog("Application")
        Log.Source = "LogService"
        Log.WriteEntry("Service continued at " & DateTime.Now)
```

```
      Log.Close()
   Catch E As Exception
   End Try
End Sub


Protected Overrides Sub OnShutdown()
   Try
      Dim Log As New EventLog("Application")
      Log.Source = "LogService"
      Log.WriteEntry("Service shutdown at " & DateTime.Now)
      Log.Close()
   Catch E As Exception
   End Try
End Sub

Protected Overrides Sub OnStop()
   Try
      Dim Log As New EventLog("Application")
      Log.Source = "LogService"
      Log.WriteEntry("Service stopped at " & DateTime.Now)
      Log.Close()
   Catch E As Exception
   End Try
End Sub
```

Compile and build the service. Then use the InstallUtil program to install the service as shown here:

```
C:\> InstallUtil  C:\SomeDirectoryPath\LogService.exe  <Enter>
```

Next, using the Windows Services program, start, pause, continue, and stop the LogService service. Then view the application's events in the Windows Event Viewer program by performing these steps:

1. Select Start | Settings | Control Panel. Windows will open the Control Panel window.
2. In the Control Panel window, double-click the Administrative Services icon. Windows will open the Administrative Services window.
3. In the Administrative Services window, double-click the Event Viewer icon. Windows will open the Event Viewer window as shown in Figure 14-6.
4. In the Event Viewer window, click the Application log icon to view events in the Application event log.

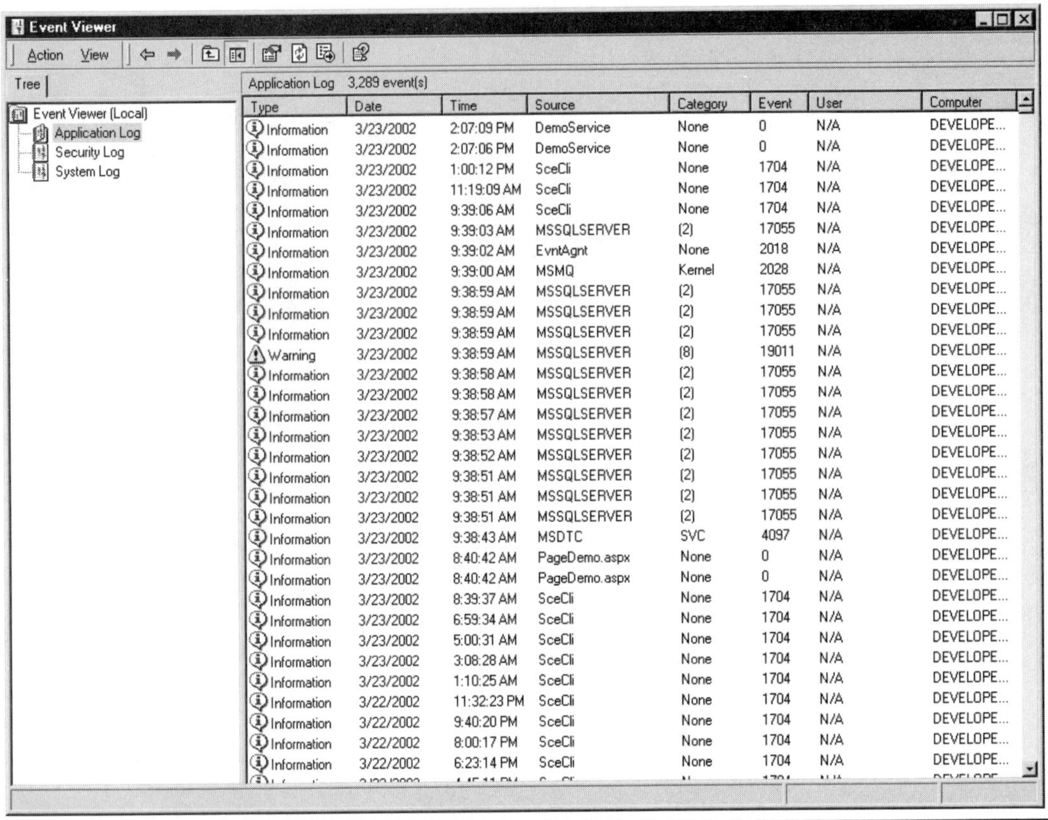

Figure 14-6   Viewing event log entries in the Windows Event Viewer

Directing a Service to Perform Operations at Specific Time Intervals

To reduce their overhead on the operating system, many Windows services will use the Sleep method to put the process into a wait state for a specific interval of time. Then the service will wake up, perform its processing, and go back to sleep. For example, assume that you have a service that monitors available disk space and notifies the system administrator when free space on the disk falls below a specific level. Under normal conditions, the service may only need to perform its processing every five minutes.

USE IT   In addition to using the Sleep method to direct a service to wake up at fixed time intervals, your code can use a Timer control. Chapter 10 examines the Timer control in detail. To use a Timer control in a Windows service is no different than using a timer in any application. To start, you simply create an instance of a Timer object. Then, in your code, you specify an event handler that runs each time the timer event occurs.

In a server environment, the number of files that reside in the root directory should remain constant. If files begin to accumulate in the root directory, the system may have a virus. The following program, ServiceTimer.vb, uses a timer to awaken the service every five minutes. When the service awakens, it will determine the number of files in the root directory on drive C and log the amount to the Windows event log:

```vb
Imports System.ServiceProcess
Imports System.Timers
Imports System.IO

Public Class Service1
    Inherits System.ServiceProcess.ServiceBase

#Region " Component Designer generated code "
  ' Code not shown
#End Region

    Private WithEvents Alarm As _
      Timer = New Timer(300000) ' 5 minutes

    Public Sub OnTimedEvent(ByVal source As Object, _
      ByVal e As ElapsedEventArgs) Handles Alarm.Elapsed

        Dim DirInfo As DirectoryInfo = New DirectoryInfo("C:\")

        Dim Log As New EventLog("Application")
        Log.Source = "ServiceTimer"
        Log.WriteEntry("Root files at " & Now() & " is " & _
                DirInfo.GetFiles("*.*").Length())
        Log.Close()
    End Sub

    Protected Overrides Sub OnStart(ByVal args() As String)
        Alarm.Enabled = True

        Try
            Dim Log As New EventLog("Application")
            Log.Source = "ServiceTimer"
            Log.WriteEntry("Service started at " & DateTime.Now)
            Log.Close()
        Catch E As Exception
```

```vbnet
        End Try
    End Sub

    Protected Overrides Sub OnPause()
        Alarm.Enabled = False

        Try
            Dim Log As New EventLog("Application")
            Log.Source = "ServiceTimer"
            Log.WriteEntry("Service paused at " & DateTime.Now)
            Log.Close()
        Catch E As Exception
        End Try
    End Sub

    Protected Overrides Sub OnContinue()
        Alarm.Enabled = True

        Try
            Dim Log As New EventLog("Application")
            Log.Source = "ServiceTimer"
            Log.WriteEntry("Service continued at " & DateTime.Now)
            Log.Close()
        Catch E As Exception
        End Try
    End Sub

    Protected Overrides Sub OnShutdown()
        Alarm.Enabled = False
        Try
            Dim Log As New EventLog("Application")
            Log.Source = "ServiceTimer"
            Log.WriteEntry("Service shutdown at " & DateTime.Now)
            Log.Close()
        Catch E As Exception
        End Try
    End Sub

    Protected Overrides Sub OnStop()
        Alarm.Enabled = False

        Try
            Dim Log As New EventLog("Application")
            Log.Source = "ServiceTimer"
```

```
            Log.WriteEntry("Service stopped at " & DateTime.Now)
            Log.Close()
        Catch E As Exception
        End Try
    End Sub
End Class
```

When a service uses a timer, your code must take into account the fact that an administrator can pause or stop the service. In the pause and stop handlers, the service code disables the timer:

```
Alarm.Enabled = False
```

If the administrator later restarts or continues the service, the code enables the timer:

```
Alarm.Enabled = True
```

As before, you must add installer software to your project and then configure the installers for the account context within which you want Windows to run the service. Then compile and build the service. Finally, use the InstallUtil program to install the service.

Taking Advantage of Threads to Process Service Operations

Admittedly, the processing that the services this chapter presents has been quite simplistic. As the complexity of the operations your services perform becomes more complex, your service should use threads to perform the operations. Chapter 8 examines thread operations in detail. Normally, in a service, the main thread will respond to events. For example, in a Web server, the main thread may listen for user requests. When a user requests a Web page from the server, the main thread can create a new thread to process the request. The main thread, in turn, can resume listening for the next request.

USE IT   The following program, MonitorSystem.vb, wakes up every five minutes and examines the number of files on drive C that have the .tmp file extension and the number of entries in the application event log. The actual processing the service performs using threads is not this Tip's focus. The service could have just as easily awakened to examine the amount of available disk space or the number of remote users connected to the system. To perform its processing, the program creates two separate threads. The first thread examines and logs the temporary files on the disk, and the second thread logs the number of event log entries:

```
Imports System.ServiceProcess
Imports System.Timers
Imports System.IO
Imports System.Threading
```

```
Public Class Service1
    Inherits System.ServiceProcess.ServiceBase

#Region " Component Designer generated code "
  ' Code not shown
#End Region

    Private WithEvents Alarm As _
      Timers.Timer = New Timers.Timer(300000) ' 5 minutes

    Function CountTree(ByVal Dir As String)
        Dim DirObj As New DirectoryInfo(Dir)

        Dim Files As FileInfo() = DirObj.GetFiles("*.tmp")
        Dim Dirs As DirectoryInfo() = DirObj.GetDirectories("*.*")
        Dim DirectoryName As DirectoryInfo
        Dim Count As Integer = 0

        For Each DirectoryName In Dirs
            Try
                Count = Count + CountTree(DirectoryName.FullName)
            Catch E As Exception
            End Try
        Next

        CountTree = Files.Length + Count
    End Function

    Public Sub LogTmpFiles()
        Dim Log As New EventLog("Application")
        Log.Source = "MonitorSystem"
        Log.WriteEntry("TMP files at " & Now() & " is " & _
              CountTree("C:\"))
        Log.Close()
    End Sub

    Public Sub LogEventEntries()
        Dim Log As New EventLog("Application")
        Log.Source = "MonitorSystem"
        Log.WriteEntry("Event log entries at " & Now() & " is " & _
              Log.Entries.Count)
        Log.Close()
    End Sub
```

```vb
Public Sub OnTimedEvent(ByVal source As Object, _
   ByVal e As ElapsedEventArgs) Handles Alarm.Elapsed
      Dim LogCheck, TmpFileCheck As Thread
      LogCheck = New Thread(AddressOf LogEventEntries)
      TmpFileCheck = New Thread(AddressOf LogTmpFiles)
      LogCheck.Start()
      TmpFileCheck.Start()
End Sub

Protected Overrides Sub OnStart(ByVal args() As String)
    Alarm.Enabled = True
    Try
        Dim Log As New EventLog("Application")
        Log.Source = "MonitorSystem"
        Log.WriteEntry("Service started at " & DateTime.Now)
        Log.Close()
    Catch E As Exception
    End Try
End Sub

Protected Overrides Sub OnPause()
    Alarm.Enabled = False
    Try
        Dim Log As New EventLog("Application")
        Log.Source = "MonitorSystem"
        Log.WriteEntry("Service paused at " & DateTime.Now)
        Log.Close()
    Catch E As Exception
    End Try
End Sub

Protected Overrides Sub OnContinue()
    Alarm.Enabled = True
    Try
        Dim Log As New EventLog("Application")
        Log.Source = "MonitorSystem"
        Log.WriteEntry("Service continued at " & DateTime.Now)
        Log.Close()
    Catch E As Exception
    End Try
End Sub

Protected Overrides Sub OnShutdown()
    Alarm.Enabled = False
```

```
      Try
            Dim Log As New EventLog("Application")
            Log.Source = "MonitorSystem"
            Log.WriteEntry("Service shutdown at " & DateTime.Now)
            Log.Close()
      Catch E As Exception
      End Try
   End Sub

   Protected Overrides Sub OnStop()
      Alarm.Enabled = False

      Try
            Dim Log As New EventLog("Application")
            Log.Source = "MonitorSystem"
            Log.WriteEntry("Service stopped at " & DateTime.Now)
            Log.Close()
      Catch E As Exception
      End Try
   End Sub
End Class
```

Again, use Visual Studio to add installers to the project and then compile and build the service. Next, use the InstallUtil program to install the service and, if necessary, the Windows Services application to start the service. Then periodically monitor the Windows Event Viewer for entries the application places in the event log.

Notifying the Administrator of Critical System Events

Several of the services this chapter presents have used the Windows event logs to record information. When a service monitors key events, there may be times when you will want the service to notify the system administrator when a specific event occurs. For example, if a service monitors available disk space and the space falls below 100MB, you may want the service to immediately notify the administrator. One of the simplest ways to notify the system administrator of an event is for the service to simply send an e-mail message describing the event to the administrator.

USE IT   In Chapter 5, you examined the MailMessage and smtpMail classes that let a program create and send e-mail messages. The following program, BigFileCheck.vb, monitors the files that reside on drive C. If a file's size exceeds 1MB, the service sends an e-mail message to the system administrator that contains the file's directory path:

```
Imports System.ServiceProcess
Imports System.Timers
```

```vb
Imports System.IO
Imports System.Threading
Imports System.Web.Mail

Public Class Service1
    Inherits System.ServiceProcess.ServiceBase

#Region " Component Designer generated code "
    ' Code not shown
#End Region

    Private WithEvents Alarm As _
      Timers.Timer = New Timers.Timer(300000) ' 5 minutes

    Private BigFileNames As String = ""

    Sub SearchTree(ByVal Dir As String)
        Dim DirObj As New DirectoryInfo(Dir)

        Dim Files As FileInfo() = DirObj.GetFiles("*.*")
        Dim Dirs As DirectoryInfo() = DirObj.GetDirectories("*.*")

        Dim Filename As FileInfo
        For Each Filename In Files
            If Filename.Length >= 1048576 Then
                BigFileNames = Filename.FullName & Chr(13) & Chr(10)
            End If
        Next

        Dim DirectoryName As DirectoryInfo
        For Each DirectoryName In Dirs
            Try
                SearchTree(DirectoryName.FullName)
            Catch E As Exception
            End Try
        Next
    End Sub

    Public Sub CheckBigFiles()
        SearchTree("C:\")

        If (BigFileNames.Length > 0) Then
            Dim Mail As New MailMessage()
            Dim SendMsg As SmtpMail
```

```vbnet
            Mail.To = "Admin@somesite.com"
            Mail.Subject = "Big Files"
            Mail.Body = BigFileNames

            SendMsg.Send(Mail)
        End If
    End Sub

    Public Sub OnTimedEvent(ByVal source As Object, _
      ByVal e As ElapsedEventArgs) Handles Alarm.Elapsed

        Dim FileCheck As Thread
        FileCheck = New Thread(AddressOf CheckBigFiles)
        FileCheck.Start()
    End Sub

    Protected Overrides Sub OnStart(ByVal args() As String)
        Alarm.Enabled = True
        Try
            Dim Log As New EventLog("Application")
            Log.Source = "BigFileCheck"
            Log.WriteEntry("Service started at " & DateTime.Now)
            Log.Close()
        Catch E As Exception
        End Try
    End Sub

    Protected Overrides Sub OnPause()
        Alarm.Enabled = False
        Try
            Dim Log As New EventLog("Application")
            Log.Source = "BigFileCheck"
            Log.WriteEntry("Service paused at " & DateTime.Now)
            Log.Close()
        Catch E As Exception
        End Try
    End Sub

    Protected Overrides Sub OnContinue()
        Alarm.Enabled = True

        Try
            Dim Log As New EventLog("Application")
            Log.Source = "BigFileCheck"
            Log.WriteEntry("Service continued at " & DateTime.Now)
```

```
            Log.Close()
        Catch E As Exception
        End Try
    End Sub

    Protected Overrides Sub OnShutdown()
        Alarm.Enabled = False
        Try
            Dim Log As New EventLog("Application")
            Log.Source = "BigFileCheck"
            Log.WriteEntry("Service shutdown at " & DateTime.Now)
            Log.Close()
        Catch E As Exception
        End Try
    End Sub

    Protected Overrides Sub OnStop()
        Alarm.Enabled = False

        Try
            Dim Log As New EventLog("Application")
            Log.Source = "BigFileCheck"
            Log.WriteEntry("Service stopped at " & DateTime.Now)
            Log.Close()
        Catch E As Exception
        End Try
    End Sub

End Class
```

To examine all the files on the disk, the service creates a thread that calls the SearchTree subroutine, which recursively examines the files in each directory. As the subroutine encounters files larger than 1MB, the service appends the file's path information and size to the string variable BigFileNames. After the subroutine completes its processing, the service uses the BigFileNames string as the body of the e-mail message that it sends to the system administrator:

```
Mail.To = "Admin@somesite.com"
Mail.Subject = "Big Files"
Mail.Body = BigFileNames
```

As before, in Visual Studio, you must define the installers that Windows will use to install the service. Then compile and build the service. Using the InstallUtil program, install the service. If you did not configure the service to automatically start, use the Windows Services application or the Visual Studio Server Explorer to start the service.

Integrating a FileSystemWatcher into a Web Service

USE IT   In Chapter 6, you learned how to use a FileSystemWatcher object to monitor a directory
for file or subdirectory changes. The following program, BackupService.vb, implements
a Windows service that uses a FileSystemWatcher object to monitor files in the C:\Data directory.
When the user changes a file in the directory, the service will create a backup copy of the file's
contents in the C:\Data\Backup directory:

```vb
Imports System.ServiceProcess
Imports System.IO

Public Class Service1
    Inherits System.ServiceProcess.ServiceBase

#Region " Component Designer generated code "
    ' Code not shown
#End Region

    Private WithEvents FileWatch As FileSystemWatcher

    Protected Sub OnChanged(ByVal From As Object, _
      ByVal e As FileSystemEventArgs) Handles FileWatch.Changed

        Dim Log As New EventLog("Application")
        Log.Source = "BackupService"
        Log.WriteEntry("File " & e.FullPath & _
           " changed at " & DateTime.Now)
        Log.Close()
        File.Copy(e.FullPath, "C:\Data\Backup\" & e.Name)
    End Sub

    Protected Sub OnCreated(ByVal From As Object, _
      ByVal e As FileSystemEventArgs) Handles FileWatch.Created
        Dim Log As New EventLog("Application")
        Log.Source = "BackupService"
        Log.WriteEntry("File " & e.FullPath & _
           " created at " & DateTime.Now)
        Log.Close()
        File.Copy(e.FullPath, "C:\Data\Backup\" & e.Name)
    End Sub
```

```vb
Protected Overrides Sub OnStart(ByVal args() As String)
    Try
        If Not Directory.Exists("C:\Data") Then
            Directory.CreateDirectory("C:\Data")
        End If

        If Not Directory.Exists("C:\Data\Backup") Then
            Directory.CreateDirectory("C:\Data\Backup")
        End If

        FileWatch = New FileSystemWatcher("C:\Data")
        FileWatch.Filter = "*.*"
        FileWatch.IncludeSubdirectories = False
        FileWatch.EnableRaisingEvents = True

        Dim Log As New EventLog("Application")
        Log.Source = "BackupService"
        Log.WriteEntry("Service started at " & DateTime.Now)
        Log.Close()
    Catch E As Exception
    End Try
End Sub

Protected Overrides Sub OnPause()
    Try
        FileWatch.EnableRaisingEvents = False
        Dim Log As New EventLog("Application")
        Log.Source = "BackupService"
        Log.WriteEntry("Service paused at " & DateTime.Now)
        Log.Close()
    Catch E As Exception
    End Try
End Sub

Protected Overrides Sub OnContinue()
    Try
        FileWatch.EnableRaisingEvents = True

        Dim Log As New EventLog("Application")
        Log.Source = "BackupService"
        Log.WriteEntry("Service continued at " & DateTime.Now)
        Log.Close()
    Catch E As Exception
    End Try
```

```
    End Sub

    Protected Overrides Sub OnShutdown()
        Try
            FileWatch.EnableRaisingEvents = False

            Dim Log As New EventLog("Application")
            Log.Source = "BackupService"
            Log.WriteEntry("Service shutdown at " & DateTime.Now)
            Log.Close()
        Catch E As Exception
        End Try
    End Sub

    Protected Overrides Sub OnStop()
        Try
            FileWatch.EnableRaisingEvents = False

            Dim Log As New EventLog("Application")
            Log.Source = "BackupService"
            Log.WriteEntry("Service stopped at " & DateTime.Now)
            Log.Close()
        Catch E As Exception
        End Try
    End Sub
End Class
```

As you can see, in the OnStart subroutine, the code creates a FileSystemWatcher object. The code then uses the object's attributes to specify the files and directories the object monitors. When a user creates or changes a file in a monitored directory, the code will call the OnCreated or OnChanged event handlers, which, in turn, back up the specified file.

Again, use Visual Studio to add installers to the project. Compile and build the service. Then use the InstallUtil program to install the service. If you did not set the service attributes to automatically start, use the Server Explorer or Windows Services application to start the service. Next, using a program such as Windows Notepad, create one or more files that you save in the C:\Data folder. Each time you create or change a file in the directory, the BackupService will detect the file operation and back up the corresponding file.

CHAPTER 15

Programming Web Forms

TIPS IN THIS CHAPTER

In Chapter 13, you learned how to create ASP.NET pages. Unlike traditional Active Server Pages that programmers create using VBScript, programmers create ASP.NET pages using a compiled programming language such as Visual Basic .NET or C#. Using Visual Basic .NET programs to drive ASP.NET pages, you learned, in Chapter 13, how to create pages that respond to events and exceptions, and that exploit multiple threads of execution.

In this chapter, you will learn how to build user interfaces for ASP.NET pages that leverage server-based controls that you drag and drop onto a special Web form. By taking advantage of Web forms, the ASP.NET pages you create can validate the data a user enters, as the user enters the data (as opposed to waiting for the user to submit the data to a remote script). Further, using Visual Studio, you can build your pages by dragging and dropping controls onto the page, just as you would place controls onto a form to build a user interface for a Visual Basic .NET application. Figure 15-1 illustrates the process of creating a Web form in Visual Studio.

Throughout this chapter, you will create a myriad of ASP.NET pages that utilize the Web forms interface. When you create an ASP.NET page that uses a Web form, Visual Studio will create several different files for the page that operate behind the scenes. Many of the files correspond to the standard ASP.NET files, such as Web.config, that you use to customize various page settings. In addition, when you use a Web form, Visual Studio will build what programmers refer to as the "code-behind page" file that contains the Visual Basic .NET statements (or C# statements if you are creating your page using C#) that the server will execute to handle the form's processing. The key to understanding the power of Web forms is to keep in mind that the server (as opposed to JavaScript-based scripts) executes code to interact with the controls you place onto the form. In fact, as you examine the HTML tags for the controls that you place onto a Web form, you will find that the controls contain the runat="server" attribute.

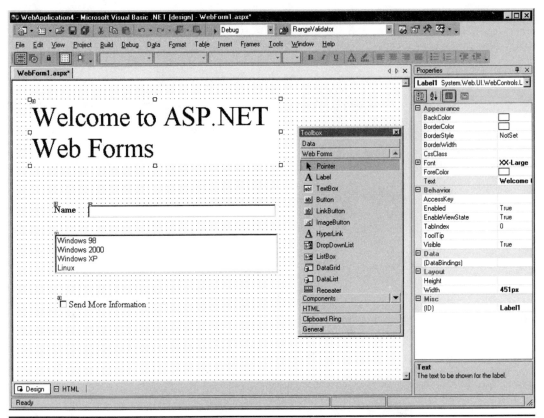

Figure 15-1   Using Visual Studio to drag and drop controls onto a Web form

Creating a Web form in Visual Studio is actually quite simple. To begin, you will direct Visual Studio to create an ASP.NET Web Application. Visual Studio will display a page grid onto which you can drag Web controls from the toolbox. Behind the scenes, when you create an ASP.NET Web form, Visual Studio will create the Visual Basic .NET code that implements the form (the code-behind page). To display the Visual Basic .NET statements, select View | Code. Also, Visual Studio will create the HTML tags (and scripts) that represent the ASP.NET page itself. To view the HTML statements, select View | HTML Source.

When an ASP.NET page uses a Web form, the page may interact with the server on a frequent basis. You can direct the server to respond to various events in the page, such a mouse click operation, a change in a control's value, and so on. When a page sends the server information about an operation, the page is said to "post back" data to the server. Throughout this chapter, the majority of the controls you place onto a Web form will support post-back operations. By default, when you place a control onto the form, the control disables post-back operations. As you can imagine, the continual interaction between controls and the server could lead to significant network and server overhead. As you design Web form solutions, you must determine which operations require server interactions and which are more efficiently performed using a client-side script. That said, to enable a control to perform post-back operations, you must set the control's AutoPostBack property to True. As you build the ASP.NET pages this chapter presents, you will drag and drop many controls onto Web forms. For the applications to work correctly, you must make sure you enable the control's AutoPostBack property.

Programming the asp:Button Control

In a Web form, the Button control displays a button the user can select to initiate a specific action. Often, forms use Button controls to submit data or to reset fields. However, a form might use a control to initiate a file upload, to direct the page to calculate the cost of items in a shopping cart, and so on.

USE IT   The following ASP.NET page, ASPClickDemo.aspx, creates a form that contains a button with the label Change Color. If the user clicks the button, the page changes the button's background and foreground colors, as shown in Figure 15-2:

```
Public Class WebForm1
    Inherits System.Web.UI.Page
    Protected WithEvents Button1 As System.Web.UI.WebControls.Button

#Region " Web Form Designer Generated Code "
  ' Code not shown
#End Region

    Private Sub Button1_Click(ByVal sender As Object, _
      ByVal e As System.EventArgs) Handles Button1.Click

        If (Equals(Button1.BackColor, Color.Red)) Then
            Button1.BackColor = Color.White
            Button1.ForeColor = Color.Black
        ElseIf (Equals(Button1.BackColor, Color.White)) Then
            Button1.BackColor = Color.Blue
            Button1.ForeColor = Color.White
        ElseIf (Equals(Button1.BackColor, Color.Blue)) Then
            Button1.BackColor = Color.Red
            Button1.ForeColor = Color.Black
        Else
            Button1.BackColor = Color.White
            Button1.ForeColor = Color.Black
        End If
    End Sub
End Class
```

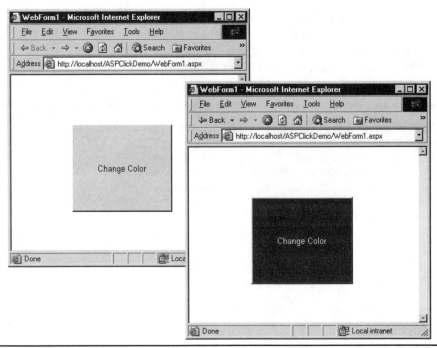

Figure 15-2   Using a server-side control to change a button's color in response to a click event

The page, in this case, does not initially set the button's background color. Instead, the final Else condition within the series of If-Else statements sets the color to white, regardless of the button's current color. Many programmers might want to set the initial color in the Page_Load handler. However, each time the page updates because of a button operation, the server executes the Page_Load handler. As a result, if you were to set the button's initial background color in the handler, the color would not change from one click to the next.

To create the page, drag and drop a Button control onto the page. In the control's properties, set the button text and set the AutoPostBack to True. Behind the scenes, Visual Studio will create HTML that uses the following <form> tag that connects the page to the server-side controls:

```
<form id="Form1" method="post" runat="server">
  <asp:Label id=Label1 style="Z-INDEX: 101; LEFT: 95px;
   POSITION: absolute; TOP: 119px" runat="server">Filename</asp:Label>

  <asp:TextBox id=TextBox1 style="Z-INDEX: 102; LEFT: 180px;
   POSITION: absolute; TOP: 116px" runat="server"></asp:TextBox>

  <asp:Button id=Button1 style="Z-INDEX: 103; LEFT: 148px; POSITION:
   absolute; TOP: 174px" runat="server" Text="Delete File"></asp:Button>
</form>
```

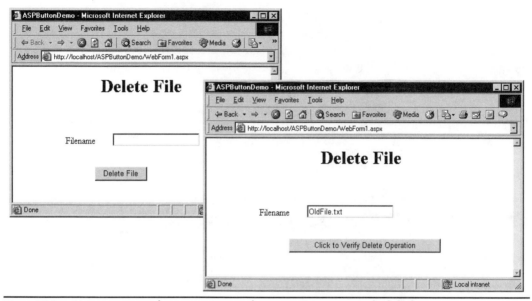

Figure 15-3   Using server-side processing to change a Button control's label in response to click operations

The following ASP.NET page, ASPButtonDemo.aspx, creates a form that prompts the user for the name of a file to delete (the page does not actually delete a file). As shown in Figure 15-3, when the user clicks the Delete File button, the form changes the button's label to read "Click to Verify Delete Operation." To create the page, drag and drop the Label, TextBox, and Button controls onto the page. You can use the Label control properties to increase the size of the Delete File font. Using the Button control properties, set the AutoPostBack property to True.

```
Private Sub Button1_Click(ByVal sender As Object, _
   ByVal e As System.EventArgs) Handles Button1.Click

   If Button1.Text = "Delete File" Then
     If TextBox1.Text.Length = 0 Then
       Button1.Text = "You must specify a filename to delete"
     Else
       Button1.Text = "Click to Verify Delete Operation"
     End If
   ElseIf Button1.Text = "Click to Verify Delete Operation" Then
     Button1.Text = "File to Delete: " & TextBox1.Text
   ElseIf Button1.Text = "You must specify a filename to delete" And _
     TextBox1.Text.Length <> 0 Then
     Button1.Text = "File to Delete: " & TextBox1.Text
   End If
End Sub
```

As you can see, the code uses the Button control's current text to determine the operation's status. As the page performs its processing, it changes the text the button displays to prompt the user to perform the next step. Behind the scenes, Visual Studio will create HTML statements that contain the following <form> tag that ties the page to the server-side control:

```
<form id="Form1" method="post" runat="server">
  <asp:Button id=Button1 style="Z-INDEX: 101; LEFT: 98px;
    POSITION: absolute; TOP: 77px" runat="server" Text="Change Color"
    Width="161px" Height="134px"></asp:Button>
</form>
```

Programming the asp:Checkbox Control

USE IT In an ASP.NET page, the asp:Checkbox control lets a user select an option. The following ASP.NET page, CheckBoxDemo.aspx, displays a form that contains checkboxes for several food items. Each time the user places or removes a check mark in a checkbox, the page updates the user's current bill, as shown in Figure 15-4.

To create the page, drag and drop the Label and CheckBox controls onto the page. Using the Label control's properties, you can increase the control's font size. In each CheckBox control's properties, set the AutoPostBack property to True:

```
Public Class WebForm1
    Inherits System.Web.UI.Page
    Protected WithEvents Label2 As System.Web.UI.WebControls.Label
    Protected WithEvents CheckBox1 As System.Web.UI.WebControls.CheckBox
    Protected WithEvents Checkbox2 As System.Web.UI.WebControls.CheckBox
    Protected WithEvents CheckBox3 As System.Web.UI.WebControls.CheckBox
    Protected WithEvents Label1 As System.Web.UI.WebControls.Label

#Region " Web Form Designer Generated Code "
  ' Code not shown
#End Region

    Public Shared Total As Double = 0.0

Private Sub CheckBox1_CheckedChanged(ByVal sender As _
        System.Object, ByVal e As System.EventArgs) _
        Handles CheckBox1.CheckedChanged
        If CheckBox1.Checked Then
            Total = Total + 1.99
        Else
            Total = Total - 1.99
        End If
```

```
        If Total < 0.01 Then
            Total = 0
        End If

        Label2.Text = "Total: $" & Total
    End Sub

    Private Sub CheckBox2_CheckedChanged(ByVal sender As _
        System.Object, ByVal e As System.EventArgs) _
        Handles Checkbox2.CheckedChanged
        If Checkbox2.Checked Then
            Total = Total + 0.99
        Else
            Total = Total - 0.99
        End If

        If Total < 0.01 Then
            Total = 0
        End If

        Label2.Text = "Total: $" & Total
    End Sub

    Private Sub CheckBox3_CheckedChanged(ByVal sender As _
        System.Object, ByVal e As System.EventArgs) _
        Handles CheckBox3.CheckedChanged
        If CheckBox3.Checked Then
            Total = Total + 0.99
        Else
            Total = Total - 0.99
        End If

        If Total < 0.01 Then
            Total = 0
        End If

        Label2.Text = "Total: $" & Total
    End Sub

End Class
```

To retain the total amount as the page executes, the code declares Total as Shared. Also note that each time the code updates the total, it tests to see if the value Total contains is less than one cent. If so, the code assigns Total the value 0. The code performs this processing to avoid rounding errors

Figure 15-4   Using a Checkbox control in an ASP.NET page

that result in Total containing a very small value, such as 0.00001. Again, behind the scenes, Visual Studio will create the following HTML statements that tie the page to the server-side controls:

```
<form id="Form1" method="post" runat="server">
  <asp:CheckBox id=CheckBox1 style="Z-INDEX: 101; LEFT: 82px;
  POSITION: absolute; TOP: 105px" runat="server" Text="Hamburger"
  AutoPostBack="True"></asp:CheckBox>

  <asp:CheckBox id=Checkbox2 style="Z-INDEX: 102; LEFT: 81px;
  POSITION: absolute; TOP: 147px" runat="server" Text="French Fries"
  AutoPostBack="True"></asp:CheckBox>

  <asp:CheckBox id=CheckBox3 style="Z-INDEX: 103; LEFT: 81px;
  POSITION: absolute; TOP: 189px" runat="server" Text="Soda"
  AutoPostBack="True"></asp:CheckBox>

  <asp:Label id=Label1 style="Z-INDEX: 104; LEFT: 33px; _
  POSITION: absolute; TOP: 32px" runat="server" Width="351px"
  Font-Size="XX-Large">Lunch Order</asp:Label>
```

```
<asp:Label id=Label2 style="Z-INDEX: 105; LEFT: 36px; POSITION:
 absolute; TOP: 234px" runat="server" Width="195px"
 Font-Size="Large" ForeColor="Black">Total: </asp:Label>
</form>
```

Programming the asp:CheckboxList Controls

USE IT   In an ASP.NET page, the asp:CheckBoxList displays a list of items, each preceded by a
          checkbox. When a user selects an item in the list, the control will precede the entry with
a checkbox. If the user selects more than one option, the control will return the first checked item in
the list as the selected item.

The following ASP.NET page, CheckBoxList.aspx, creates a form that contains a list of companies.
Each time you select a company from the list, the page displays a hyperlink that corresponds to the
company, as shown in Figure 15-5. If you remove a check mark, the page will remove the corresponding
hyperlink. To create the page, drag and drop the Label, CheckBoxList, and Hyperlink controls onto
the page. In the CheckBoxList properties, set the AutoPostBack property to True.

```
Public Class WebForm1
    Inherits System.Web.UI.Page
    Protected WithEvents HyperLink1 _
        As System.Web.UI.WebControls.HyperLink
    Protected WithEvents Label1 As _
        System.Web.UI.WebControls.Label
    Protected WithEvents CheckBoxList1 As _
        System.Web.UI.WebControls.CheckBoxList

#Region " Web Form Designer Generated Code "
  ' Code not shown
#End Region

    Private Sub Page_Load(ByVal sender As System.Object, _
      ByVal e As System.EventArgs) Handles MyBase.Load
        HyperLink1.Text = ""
        HyperLink1.Target = ""
    End Sub

    Private Sub CheckBoxList1_SelectedIndexChanged(ByVal sender _
      As Object, ByVal e As System.EventArgs) Handles _
      CheckBoxList1.SelectedIndexChanged
```

```
        If Not (CheckBoxList1.SelectedItem Is Nothing) Then
          If (CheckBoxList1.SelectedItem.Text = "Microsoft") Then
              HyperLink1.NavigateUrl = "http://www.microsoft.com"
          ElseIf (CheckBoxList1.SelectedItem.Text = _
            "McGraw-Hill/Osborne") Then
              HyperLink1.NavigateUrl = "http://www.osborne.com"
          ElseIf (CheckBoxList1.SelectedItem.Text = "Sybex") Then
              HyperLink1.NavigateUrl = "http://www.sybex.com"
          ElseIf (CheckBoxList1.SelectedItem.Text = _
            "Onword Press") Then
              HyperLink1.NavigateUrl = "http://www.onwordpress.com"
          End If

          HyperLink1.Text = HyperLink1.NavigateUrl
        End If
    End Sub
End Class
```

As you can see, when the user selects an item in the checkbox list, the code assigns the corresponding URL to the HyperLink control. Visual Studio will create HTML statements that use the following <form> tag to tie the page to the server-side controls:

```
<form id="Form1" method="post" runat="server">
  <asp:HyperLink id=HyperLink1 style="Z-INDEX: 101; LEFT: 92px;
  POSITION: absolute; TOP: 209px" runat="server">
  HyperLink</asp:HyperLink>

  <asp:CheckBoxList id=CheckBoxList1 style="Z-INDEX: 102;
  LEFT: 105px; POSITION: absolute; TOP: 90px" runat="server"
  AutoPostBack="True">

    <asp:ListItem Value="Microsoft">Microsoft</asp:ListItem>
    <asp:ListItem Value="McGraw-Hill/Osborne">McGraw-Hill/Osborne
    </asp:ListItem>
    <asp:ListItem Value="Sybex">Sybex</asp:ListItem>
    <asp:ListItem Value="Onword Press">Onword Press</asp:ListItem>

  </asp:CheckBoxList>

  <asp:Label id=Label1 style="Z-INDEX: 103; LEFT: 71px; POSITION:
  absolute; TOP: 28px" runat="server" Font-Size="X-Large">
  .NET Information Sources</asp:Label>

</form>
```

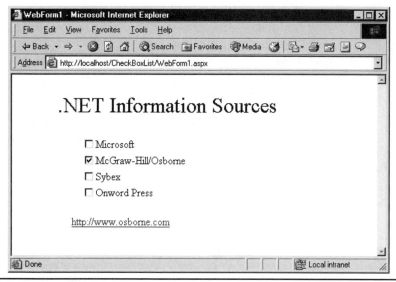

Figure 15-5   Processing CheckBoxList control events in an ASP.NET page

Programming the asp:RadioButton Control

USE IT   In a Web form, radio buttons let a user select one of two or more options. The following
ASP.NET page, RadioButtonDemo.aspx, displays a form that contains three radio buttons
that correspond to colors. When the user selects a color, the page changes the label's background using
the corresponding color, as shown in Figure 15-6. To create the page, drag and drop the Label and
RadioButton controls onto the page. In each RadioButton control's properties, set the AutoPostBack
property to True. Also, for each RadioButton control, set the group name to Color.

```
Public Class WebForm1
    Inherits System.Web.UI.Page
    Protected WithEvents RadioButton1 As System.Web.UI.WebControls.RadioButton
    Protected WithEvents RadioButton2 As System.Web.UI.WebControls.RadioButton
    Protected WithEvents RadioButton3 As System.Web.UI.WebControls.RadioButton
    Protected WithEvents Label1 As System.Web.UI.WebControls.Label

#Region " Web Form Designer Generated Code "
    ' Code not shown
#End Region
```

```
    Private Sub RadioButton1_CheckedChanged(ByVal sender As Object, _
      ByVal e As System.EventArgs) Handles RadioButton1.CheckedChanged
        If (RadioButton1.Checked) Then
            Label1.ForeColor = Color.Black
        End If
    End Sub

    Private Sub RadioButton2_CheckedChanged(ByVal sender As Object, _
      ByVal e As System.EventArgs) Handles RadioButton2.CheckedChanged
        If (RadioButton2.Checked) Then
            Label1.ForeColor = Color.Red
        End If
    End Sub

    Private Sub RadioButton3_CheckedChanged(ByVal sender As Object, _
      ByVal e As System.EventArgs) Handles RadioButton3.CheckedChanged
        If (RadioButton3.Checked) Then
            Label1.ForeColor = Color.Green
        End If
    End Sub
End Class
```

As you can see, the code simply responds to changes in each RadioButton control. Behind the scenes, Visual Studio will create a <form> tag that contains the following entries:

```
<form id="Form1" method="post" runat="server">

  <asp:RadioButton id="RadioButton1" style="Z-INDEX: 101; LEFT: 66px;
  POSITION: absolute; TOP: 99px" runat="server" Text="Black"
  AutoPostBack="True" GroupName="Color"></asp:RadioButton>

  <asp:RadioButton id="RadioButton2" style="Z-INDEX: 102; LEFT: 65px;
  POSITION: absolute; TOP: 135px" runat="server" Text="Red"
  AutoPostBack="True" GroupName="Color"></asp:RadioButton>

  <asp:RadioButton id="RadioButton3" style="Z-INDEX: 103; LEFT: 65px;
  POSITION: absolute; TOP: 172px" runat="server" Text="Green"
  AutoPostBack="True" GroupName="Color"></asp:RadioButton>

  <asp:Label id="Label1" style="Z-INDEX: 104; LEFT: 65px; POSITION:
  absolute; TOP: 29px" runat="server" Font-Size="XX-Large">
  Color Demo</asp:Label>

</form>
```

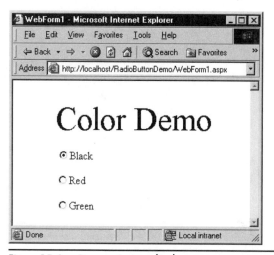 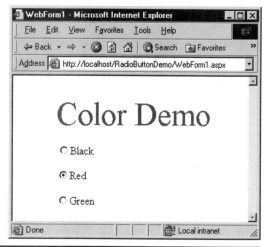

Figure 15-6   Processing radio button events in an ASP.NET page

Programming the asp:Hyperlink Control

USE IT   In a Web form, a hyperlink creates a link to another page. The following ASP.NET page, HyperLinkDemo.aspx, displays a form that contains three radio buttons. As the user selects a radio button, the page changes the hyperlink to match the user's selection, as shown in Figure 15-7. To create the page, drag and drop the Label, RadioButton, and HyperLink controls onto the page. For each RadioButton, set the AutoPostBack property to True and the group name to Sites.

```
Public Class WebForm1
    Inherits System.Web.UI.Page
    Protected WithEvents RadioButton1 As _
        System.Web.UI.WebControls.RadioButton
    Protected WithEvents RadioButton2 As _
        System.Web.UI.WebControls.RadioButton
    Protected WithEvents RadioButton3 As _
        System.Web.UI.WebControls.RadioButton
    Protected WithEvents Label1 As System.Web.UI.WebControls.Label
    Protected WithEvents HyperLink1 As _
        System.Web.UI.WebControls.HyperLink

#Region " Web Form Designer Generated Code "
 ' Code not shown
#End Region

  Private Sub Page_Load(ByVal sender As System.Object, _
```

```
      ByVal e As System.EventArgs) Handles MyBase.Load
         HyperLink1.Text = ""
   End Sub

   Private Sub RadioButton1_CheckedChanged(ByVal sender As Object, _
      ByVal e As System.EventArgs) _
      Handles RadioButton1.CheckedChanged, RadioButton2.CheckedChanged, _
      RadioButton3.CheckedChanged

         HyperLink1.NavigateUrl = "http://www." & _
            CType(sender, RadioButton).Text & ".com"
         HyperLink1.Text = HyperLink1.NavigateUrl

   End Sub
End Class
```

Visual Studio will create HTML statements that use the following <form> tag to connect the page to the server-based controls:

```
<form id="Form1" method="post" runat="server">

  <asp:RadioButton id=RadioButton1 style="Z-INDEX: 101;
   LEFT: 67px; POSITION:    absolute; TOP: 105px" runat="server"
   Text="Microsoft" GroupName="Sites" AutoPostBack="True">
   </asp:RadioButton>

  <asp:RadioButton id=RadioButton2 style="Z-INDEX: 102; LEFT: 66px;
   POSITION: absolute; TOP: 148px" runat="server" Text="Yahoo"
   GroupName="Sites" AutoPostBack="True"></asp:RadioButton>

  <asp:RadioButton id=RadioButton3 style="Z-INDEX: 103; LEFT: 66px;
   POSITION: absolute; TOP: 185px" runat="server" Text="Google"
   GroupName="Sites" AutoPostBack="True"></asp:RadioButton>

  <asp:Label id=Label1 style="Z-INDEX: 104; LEFT: 32px; POSITION:
   absolute; TOP: 29px" runat="server" Width="291px"
   Font-Size="XX-Large">Select a Site</asp:Label>

  <asp:HyperLink id=HyperLink1 style="Z-INDEX: 105; LEFT: 56px;
   POSITION: absolute; TOP: 238px" runat="server">
   HyperLink</asp:HyperLink>

</form>
```

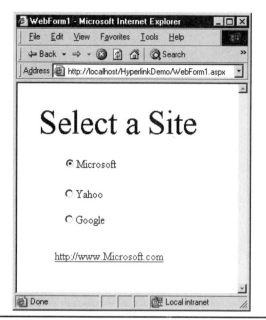 

Figure 15-7   Using an asp:Hyperlink control to change a Web page link

Programming the asp:Image Control

USE IT   In a Web form, the asp:Image control lets you display an image. When you display a
form, there may be times when you will want an image that appears on the form to
change, based on a user's current selection. In such cases, your pages can use the asp:Image control.
The following ASP.NET page, ImageDemo.aspx, displays a form with three radio buttons, each of
which corresponds to a book. When the user selects a radio button, the page changes its text and an
image, as shown in Figure 15-8. To create the page, drag and drop the Label, RadioButton, and Image
controls onto the page. For each RadioButton control, set the AutoPostBack property to True and the
group name to Books.

```
Public Class WebForm1
    Inherits System.Web.UI.Page

    Protected WithEvents RadioButton1 As _
        System.Web.UI.WebControls.RadioButton
Protected WithEvents RadioButton2 As _
        System.Web.UI.WebControls.RadioButton
    Protected WithEvents RadioButton3 As _
```

```vb
        System.Web.UI.WebControls.RadioButton
    Protected WithEvents Label1 As _
        System.Web.UI.WebControls.Label

  Protected WithEvents Image1 As _
        System.Web.UI.WebControls.Image

#Region " Web Form Designer Generated Code "
  ' Code not shown
#End Region

    Private Sub RadioButton1_CheckedChanged(ByVal sender As Object, _
      ByVal e As System.EventArgs) Handles RadioButton1.CheckedChanged
        If RadioButton1.Checked Then
            Image1.ImageUrl = "Book1.jpg"
            Image1.Visible = True
        End If
    End Sub

    Private Sub RadioButton2_CheckedChanged(ByVal sender As Object, _
      ByVal e As System.EventArgs) Handles RadioButton2.CheckedChanged
        If RadioButton2.Checked Then
            Image1.ImageUrl = "Book2.jpg"
            Image1.Visible = True
        End If
    End Sub

    Private Sub RadioButton3_CheckedChanged(ByVal sender As Object, _
      ByVal e As System.EventArgs) Handles RadioButton3.CheckedChanged
        If RadioButton3.Checked Then
            Image1.ImageUrl = "Book3.jpg"
            Image1.Visible = True
        End If
    End Sub

    Private Sub Page_Load(ByVal sender As System.Object, _
      ByVal e As System.EventArgs) Handles MyBase.Load
        If Image1.ImageUrl = "" Then
            Image1.Visible = False
        End If
    End Sub
End Class
```

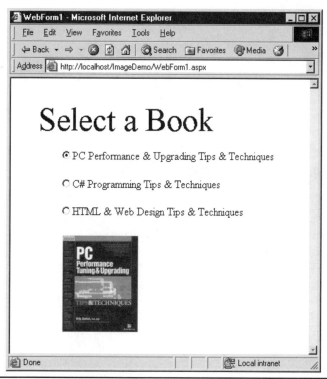

Figure 15-8 Using an asp:Image control to change the images a page contains based on a user's selections

As you can see, the code simply responds to changes in the RadioButton controls by changing the URL that corresponds to the image. Visual Studio will create HTML statements that use the following <form> tag to connect the page to the server-based controls:

```
<form id="Form1" method="post" runat="server">

  <asp:RadioButton id=RadioButton1 style="Z-INDEX: 101; LEFT: 73px;
    POSITION: absolute; TOP: 102px" runat="server"
    Text="PC Performance &amp; Upgrading Tips &amp; Techniques"
    AutoPostBack="True" GroupName="Books"></asp:RadioButton>

  <asp:RadioButton id=RadioButton2 style="Z-INDEX: 102; LEFT: 73px;
    POSITION: absolute; TOP: 143px" runat="server"
    Text="C# Programming Tips &amp; Techniques" AutoPostBack="True"
    GroupName="Books"></asp:RadioButton>

  <asp:RadioButton id=RadioButton3 style="Z-INDEX: 103; LEFT: 73px;
    POSITION: absolute; TOP: 183px" runat="server"
    Text="HTML &amp; Web Design Tips &amp; Techniques"
    AutoPostBack="True" GroupName="Books"></asp:RadioButton>
```

```
<asp:Label id=Label1 style="Z-INDEX: 104; LEFT: 42px; POSITION:
absolute; TOP: 33px" runat="server" Font-Size="XX-Large">
Select a Book</asp:Label>

<asp:Image id=Image1 style="Z-INDEX: 105; LEFT: 79px; POSITION:
absolute; TOP: 229px" runat="server"></asp:Image>
```

```
</form>
```

Programming the asp:ImageButton Control

USE IT In a Web form, the asp:ImageButton control lets a page display a button that contains an image. The following ASP.NET page, ImageButtonDemo.aspx, displays a form with two radio buttons. When the user selects a radio button, the page uses an asp:ImageButton to change the image that appears within the form's Submit button to match the user's selection, as shown in Figure 15-9. When the user clicks the image, the code will change the text of the label that appears at the top of the page. To create the page, drag and drop the Label, RadioButton, and ImageButton controls onto the page. For each RadioButton control, set the AutoPostBack property to True and the group name to Puppies. Also, set the ImageButton control's AutoPostBack property to True.

```
Public Class WebForm1
    Inherits System.Web.UI.Page
    Protected WithEvents Label1 As System.Web.UI.WebControls.Label
    Protected WithEvents RadioButton1 As System.Web.UI.WebControls.RadioButton
    Protected WithEvents RadioButton2 As System.Web.UI.WebControls.RadioButton
    Protected WithEvents ImageButton1 As System.Web.UI.WebControls.ImageButton

#Region " Web Form Designer Generated Code "
  ' Code not shown
#End Region

    Private Sub Page_Load(ByVal sender As System.Object, _
      ByVal e As System.EventArgs) Handles MyBase.Load
        If ImageButton1.ImageUrl = "" Then
            ImageButton1.Visible = False
        End If
    End Sub

    Private Sub RadioButton1_CheckedChanged(ByVal sender As Object, _
      ByVal e As System.EventArgs) Handles RadioButton1.CheckedChanged
        If RadioButton1.Checked Then
            ImageButton1.ImageUrl = "lab.jpg"
            ImageButton1.Visible = True
        End If
    End Sub

    Private Sub RadioButton2_CheckedChanged(ByVal sender As Object, _
```

```
    ByVal e As System.EventArgs) Handles RadioButton2.CheckedChanged
      If RadioButton2.Checked Then
          ImageButton1.ImageUrl = "dal.jpg"
          ImageButton1.Visible = True
      End If
    End Sub

    Private Sub ImageButton1_Click(ByVal sender As Object, _
      ByVal e As System.Web.UI.ImageClickEventArgs) _
      Handles ImageButton1.Click
      If RadioButton1.Checked Then
          Label1.Text = "Shopping for Labs"
      ElseIf RadioButton2.Checked Then
          Label1.Text = "Shopping for Dals and Beagles"
      End If
    End Sub
End Class
```

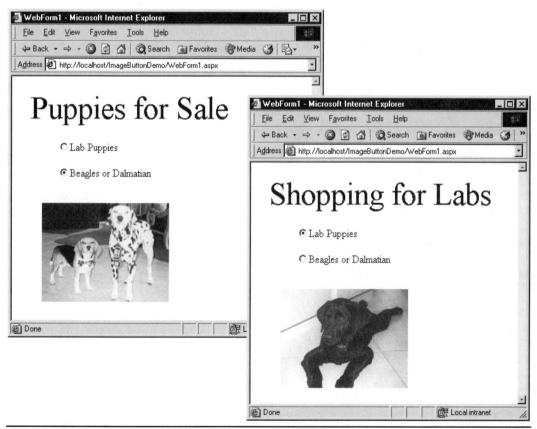

Figure 15-9   Changing a button's appearance using an asp:ImageButton control

When the user selects a radio button, the code will assign a related image to the ImageButton control. When the user clicks the ImageButton control, the code will respond by changing the main label. Behind the scenes, Visual Studio will create an HTML page that uses a <form> tag similar to the following to tie the page to the server-side control:

```
<form id="Form1" method="post" runat="server">

  <asp:Label id=Label1 style="Z-INDEX: 101; LEFT: 29px; POSITION:
  absolute; TOP: 21px" runat="server" Font-Size="XX-Large">
  Puppies for Sale</asp:Label>

  <asp:RadioButton id=RadioButton1 style="Z-INDEX: 102; LEFT: 71px;
  POSITION: absolute; TOP: 97px" runat="server" AutoPostBack="True"
  GroupName="Puppies" _ Text="Lab Puppies"></asp:RadioButton>

  <asp:RadioButton id=RadioButton2 style="Z-INDEX: 103; LEFT: 71px;
  POSITION: absolute; TOP: 136px" runat="server" AutoPostBack="True"
  GroupName="Puppies" Text="Beagles or Dalmatian"></asp:RadioButton>

  <asp:ImageButton id=ImageButton1 style="Z-INDEX: 104; LEFT: 47px;
  POSITION: absolute; TOP: 192px" runat="server"></asp:ImageButton>

</form>
```

Programming the asp:Label Control

USE IT   Normally, within a form, a Label control simply contains text that describes another control, such as a text box. In Web forms, you can think of an asp:Label control as a text holder. Using statements within your page's code, you can easily change the asp:Label's control's contents as the page executes. The following ASP.NET page, LabelDemo.aspx, uses an asp:Label control to display the current date and time. The page also contains a button the user can click to update the date and time displayed, as shown in Figure 15-10. To create the page, drag and drop the Label and Button controls onto the page. Using the Button control's properties window, set the AutoPostBack property to True.

```
Imports System.Timers

Public Class WebForm1
    Inherits System.Web.UI.Page
    Protected WithEvents Button1 As System.Web.UI.WebControls.Button
    Protected WithEvents Label1 As System.Web.UI.WebControls.Label

#Region " Web Form Designer Generated Code "
  ' Code not shown
#End Region
```

```
   Private Sub Page_Load(ByVal sender As System.Object, _
     ByVal e As System.EventArgs) Handles MyBase.Load
       Label1.Text = "Time: " & Now()
   End Sub

   Private Sub Button1_Click(ByVal sender As Object, _
     ByVal e As System.EventArgs) Handles Button1.Click
       Label1.Text = "Time: " & Now()
   End Sub
End Class
```

Visual Studio will create HTML statements that use a <form> tag similar to the following that ties the page to server-based controls:

```
<form id="Form1" method="post" runat="server">

  <asp:Label id=Label1 style="Z-INDEX: 101; LEFT: 67px; POSITION:
  absolute; TOP: 72px" runat="server" Font-Size="XX-Large">
  </asp:Label>

  <asp:Button id=Button1 style="Z-INDEX: 102; LEFT: 73px; POSITION:
  absolute; TOP: 172px" runat="server" Text="Update" Width="198px">
  </asp:Button>

</form>
```

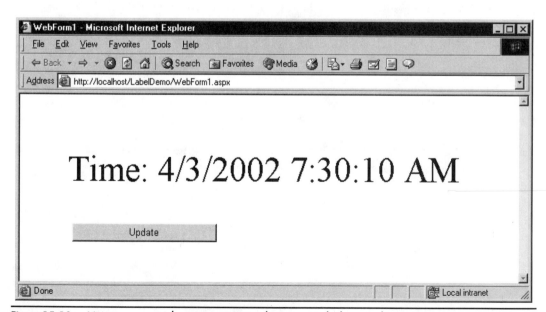

Figure 15-10   Using server-side processing to change a Label control's text

Programming the asp:TextBox Control

In a Web form, the asp:TextBox control lets you display read-only information or prompt the user for information. The following ASP.NET page, TextBoxDemo.aspx, creates a form that contains four TextBox controls. The first is a ReadOnly control that contains a quote. The second lets the user enter a single line of input. The third uses a password mode setting that directs the form to display an asterisk for each keystroke the user enters. The fourth lets the user enter multiple lines of text. As shown in Figure 15-11, each time the user enters, changes, or deletes text in a control and then leaves the control (selects another control), the page displays a message stating the number of characters the box contains. To create the page, drag and drop the Label and TextBox controls onto the page. For each TextBox control, use the properties window to set the ReadOnly, Password, or MultiLine attributes as the control requires.

```
Public Class WebForm1
    Inherits System.Web.UI.Page
    Protected WithEvents TextBox1 As System.Web.UI.WebControls.TextBox
    Protected WithEvents Label1 As System.Web.UI.WebControls.Label
    Protected WithEvents TextBox2 As System.Web.UI.WebControls.TextBox
    Protected WithEvents TextBox3 As System.Web.UI.WebControls.TextBox
    Protected WithEvents TextBox4 As System.Web.UI.WebControls.TextBox
    Protected WithEvents Label2 As System.Web.UI.WebControls.Label
    Protected WithEvents Label3 As System.Web.UI.WebControls.Label
    Protected WithEvents Label4 As System.Web.UI.WebControls.Label
    Protected WithEvents Label6 As System.Web.UI.WebControls.Label
    Protected WithEvents Label7 As System.Web.UI.WebControls.Label
    Protected WithEvents Label8 As System.Web.UI.WebControls.Label
    Protected WithEvents Label5 As System.Web.UI.WebControls.Label


#Region " Web Form Designer Generated Code "
  ' Code not shown
#End Region

    Private Sub Page_Load(ByVal sender As System.Object, _
      ByVal e As System.EventArgs) Handles MyBase.Load
        'Put user code to initialize the page here
    End Sub

    Private Sub TextBox2_TextChanged(ByVal sender As Object, _
      ByVal e As System.EventArgs) Handles TextBox2.TextChanged
        Label6.Text = TextBox2.Text.Length & " characters"
    End Sub
```

```
Private Sub TextBox3_TextChanged(ByVal sender As Object, _
   ByVal e As System.EventArgs) Handles TextBox3.TextChanged
     Label7.Text = TextBox3.Text.Length & " characters"
End Sub

Private Sub TextBox4_TextChanged(ByVal sender As Object, _
   ByVal e As System.EventArgs) Handles TextBox4.TextChanged
     Label8.Text = TextBox4.Text.Length & " characters"
End Sub

End Class
```

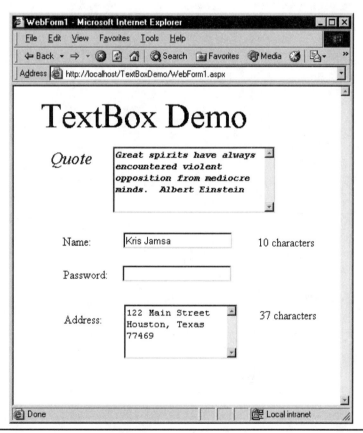

Figure 15-11   Programming an asp:TextBox control

Visual Studio creates HTML statements that use a <form> tag similar to the following to tie the page to the server-based controls:

```
<form id=Form1 method=post runat="server">

  <asp:TextBox id=TextBox1 style="Z-INDEX: 101; LEFT: 142px;
   POSITION: absolute; TOP: 84px" runat="server" Width="231px"
   Height="92px" Font-Italic="True" ReadOnly="True"
   TextMode="MultiLine" Font-Bold="True">Great spirits have
   always encountered violent opposition from mediocre minds.
   Albert Einstein</asp:TextBox>

  <asp:Label id=Label1 style="Z-INDEX: 102; LEFT: 53px; POSITION:
   absolute; TOP: 87px" runat="server" Font-Size="Large"
   Font-Italic="True">Quote</asp:Label>

  <asp:TextBox id=TextBox2 style="Z-INDEX: 103; LEFT: 157px;
   POSITION: absolute; TOP: 203px" runat="server"
   AutoPostBack="True"></asp:TextBox>

  <asp:TextBox id=TextBox3 style="Z-INDEX: 104; LEFT: 156px;
   POSITION: absolute; TOP: 249px" runat="server" TextMode="Password"
   AutoPostBack="True"></asp:TextBox>

  <asp:TextBox id=TextBox4 style="Z-INDEX: 105; LEFT: 158px;
   POSITION: absolute; TOP: 303px" runat="server" Width="162px"
   Height="75px" TextMode="MultiLine" AutoPostBack="True">
   </asp:TextBox>

  <asp:Label id=Label2 style="Z-INDEX: 106; LEFT: 39px; POSITION:
   absolute; TOP: 14px" runat="server" Font-Size="XX-Large">
   TextBox Demo</asp:Label>

  <asp:Label id=Label3 style="Z-INDEX: 107; LEFT: 70px; POSITION:
   absolute; TOP: 206px" runat="server">Name:</asp:Label>

  <asp:Label id=Label4 style="Z-INDEX: 108; LEFT: 71px; POSITION:
   absolute; TOP: 252px" runat="server">Password:</asp:Label>

  <asp:Label id=Label5 style="Z-INDEX: 109; LEFT: 72px; POSITION:
   absolute; TOP: 314px" runat="server">Address:</asp:Label>

  <asp:Label id=Label6 style="Z-INDEX: 110; LEFT: 348px; POSITION:
```

```
    absolute; TOP: 207px" runat="server"></asp:Label>

  <asp:Label id=Label7 style="Z-INDEX: 111; LEFT: 348px; POSITION:
    absolute; TOP: 251px" runat="server"></asp:Label>

  <asp:Label id=Label8 style="Z-INDEX: 112; LEFT: 351px; POSITION:
    absolute; TOP: 308px" runat="server"></asp:Label>

</FORM>
```

Programming the asp:Panel Control

USE IT   In a Web form, the asp:Panel control lets you visually group related controls. The following ASP.NET page, PanelDemo.aspx, uses two panels to visually group a series of controls. Using an asp:Panel control, you can display or hide a set of controls in one step. In each panel, the page places an Image control and a Label control. Using the On/Off button that appears beneath each panel, you can turn the panel's display on or off, as shown in Figure 15-12. To create the page, drag and drop the Label, Panel, and Button controls onto the page. Then drag and drop an Image and Label control into each panel. For each Button control, set the AutoPostBack property to True.

```
Public Class WebForm1
    Inherits System.Web.UI.Page
    Protected WithEvents Panel2 As System.Web.UI.WebControls.Panel
    Protected WithEvents Image1 As System.Web.UI.WebControls.Image
    Protected WithEvents Image2 As System.Web.UI.WebControls.Image
    Protected WithEvents Label1 As System.Web.UI.WebControls.Label
    Protected WithEvents Label2 As System.Web.UI.WebControls.Label
    Protected WithEvents Label3 As System.Web.UI.WebControls.Label
    Protected WithEvents Button1 As System.Web.UI.WebControls.Button
    Protected WithEvents Button2 As System.Web.UI.WebControls.Button
    Protected WithEvents Panel1 As System.Web.UI.WebControls.Panel

#Region " Web Form Designer Generated Code "
  ' Code not shown
#End Region

    Private Sub Page_Load(ByVal sender As System.Object, _
      ByVal e As System.EventArgs) Handles MyBase.Load
        Image1.ImageUrl = "dal.jpg"
        Image2.ImageUrl = "lab.jpg"
```

```
    End Sub

    Private Sub Button1_Click(ByVal sender As System.Object, _
      ByVal e As System.EventArgs) Handles Button1.Click
        If Panel1.Visible Then
            Panel1.Visible = False
        Else
            Panel1.Visible = True
        End If
    End Sub

    Private Sub Button2_Click(ByVal sender As System.Object, _
      ByVal e As System.EventArgs) Handles Button2.Click
        If Panel2.Visible Then
            Panel2.Visible = False
        Else
            Panel2.Visible = True
        End If
    End Sub
End Class
```

Visual Studio will create HTML statements that use the following <form> tag to tie the page to the server-based controls:

```
<form id="Form1" method="post" runat="server">

  <asp:Label id=Label3 runat="server" Font-Size="XX-Large">
   Panel Demo</asp:Label>

  <asp:Panel id=Panel1 runat="server" Width="447px" Height="166px"
BorderStyle="Double">Panel
    <asp:Image id=Image1 runat="server"></asp:Image>
    <asp:Label id=Label1 runat="server">Buddy & Happy</asp:Label>
  </asp:Panel>

  <asp:Button id=Button1 runat="server" Text="On/Off"></asp:Button>

  <asp:Panel id=Panel2 runat="server" Width="445px" Height="174px"
   BorderStyle="Groove">Panel
    <asp:Image id=Image2 runat="server"></asp:Image>
    <asp:Label id=Label2 runat="server">Raffles</asp:Label>
  </asp:Panel>
  <asp:Button id=Button2 runat="server" Text="On/Off"></asp:Button>
</form>
```

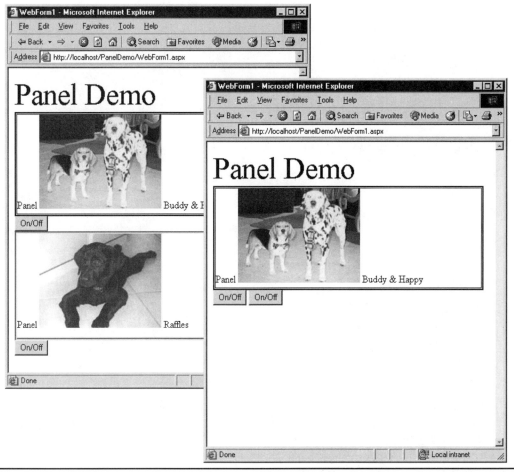

Figure 15-12   Using server-side processing to enable or disable a Panel control and the controls it contains

Programmnig the asp:DropDownList Control

USE IT   Like Windows forms, Web forms provide developers with several different ways to display a list of items. If the amount of space on your page is limited, you may find using a drop-down list lets you effectively display large amounts of information. The following ASP.NET page, DropDownListDemo.aspx, displays a list of pets. When the user selects an item in the drop-down list, the page changes the hyperlink to correspond to the user's selection, as shown in Figure 15-13. To create the page, drag and drop the Label, DropDownList, and HyperLink controls onto the page. Using the properties window, set the DropDownList control's AutoPostBack property to True.

```
Public Class WebForm1
    Inherits System.Web.UI.Page
    Protected WithEvents DropDownList1 As _
```

```
          System.Web.UI.WebControls.DropDownList
      Protected WithEvents HyperLink1 As _
          System.Web.UI.WebControls.HyperLink
      Protected WithEvents Label1 As System.Web.UI.WebControls.Label

#Region " Web Form Designer Generated Code "
  ' Code not shown
#End Region

      Private Sub Page_Load(ByVal sender As System.Object, _
        ByVal e As System.EventArgs) Handles MyBase.Load
          HyperLink1.NavigateUrl = "www.DogSite.com"
          HyperLink1.Text = HyperLink1.NavigateUrl
      End Sub

      Private Sub DropDownList1_SelectedIndexChanged(ByVal _
        sender As System.Object, ByVal e As System.EventArgs) _
        Handles DropDownList1.SelectedIndexChanged
          HyperLink1.NavigateUrl = DropDownList1.SelectedItem.Value
          HyperLink1.Text = HyperLink1.NavigateUrl
      End Sub
End Class
```

Visual Studio will create HTML statements that use a <form> tag similar to the following to tie the page to the server-side controls:

```
<form id="Form1" method="post" runat="server">

  <asp:DropDownList id=DropDownList1 style="Z-INDEX: 101; LEFT: 99px;
  POSITION: absolute; TOP: 149px" runat="server" Width="109px"
  Height="39px" AutoPostBack="True">
    <asp:ListItem Value="www.DogSite.com">Dogs</asp:ListItem>
    <asp:ListItem Value="www.CatSite.com">Cats</asp:ListItem>
    <asp:ListItem Value="www.HorseSite.com">Horses</asp:ListItem>
    <asp:ListItem Value="www.BirdSite.com">Birds</asp:ListItem>
    <asp:ListItem Value="www.FishSite.com">Fish</asp:ListItem>
  </asp:DropDownList>

  <asp:Label id=Label1 style="Z-INDEX: 102; LEFT: 60px; POSITION:
  absolute; TOP: 56px" runat="server" Font-Size="XX-Large">
  Pet Sites</asp:Label>

  <asp:HyperLink id=HyperLink1 style="Z-INDEX: 103; LEFT: 241px;
    POSITION: absolute; TOP: 151px" runat="server">HyperLink
  </asp:HyperLink>

</form>
```

Figure 15-13   Using an asp:DropDownList to change Web page links based on a user's selection

Programming the asp:ListBox

USE IT   In a Web form, the asp:ListBox control creates a box within which a user can select a list entry. Unlike a pull-down list that displays all of the list entries, the ListBox control lets the user scroll through entries within the same box. The following ASP.NET page, ListBoxDemo.aspx, displays a ListBox control that shows a list of topics. As the user selects a topic, the page displays a list of recommended books, as shown in Figure 15-14. To create the page, drag and drop the Label, ListBox, and TextBox controls onto the page. Using the properties window, set the ListBox control's AutoPostBack property to True.

```
Public Class WebForm1
    Inherits System.Web.UI.Page
    Protected WithEvents Label1 As System.Web.UI.WebControls.Label
    Protected WithEvents TextBox1 As System.Web.UI.WebControls.TextBox
    Protected WithEvents ListBox1 As System.Web.UI.WebControls.ListBox

#Region " Web Form Designer Generated Code "
  ' Code not shown
#End Region

    Private Sub Page_Load(ByVal sender As System.Object, _
      ByVal e As System.EventArgs) Handles MyBase.Load
        'Put user code to initialize the page here
    End Sub

    Private Sub ListBox1_SelectedIndexChanged(ByVal sender _
      As System.Object, ByVal e As System.EventArgs) _
      Handles ListBox1.SelectedIndexChanged
        If Not (ListBox1.SelectedItem Is Nothing) Then
```

```
            If (ListBox1.SelectedIndex = 0) Then
                TextBox1.Text = "Palm OS Programming: From the Ground Up" & _
                    vbCrLf & "Palm OS Developer's Guide" & vbCrLf & _
                    "Instant Palm OS Applications"
            End If

            If (ListBox1.SelectedIndex = 1) Then
                TextBox1.Text = "C# Programming Tips & Techniques" & _
                    vbCrLf & "C# The Complete Reference" & vbCrLf & _
                    "Rescued by C#"
            End If

            If (ListBox1.SelectedIndex = 2) Then
                TextBox1.Text = _
                    "Visual Basic .Net Programming Tips & Techniques" & vbCrLf & _
                    "Visual Basic .Net The Complete Reference" & vbCrLf & _
                    "Rescued by ASP & ASP.NET"
            End If
        End If
    End Sub
End Class
```

As you can see, based on the user's ListBox selection, the code assigns specific text to the TextBox control. Behind the scenes, Visual Studio will create HTML statements that use a <form> tag similar to the following to tie the page to the server-side controls:

```
<form id="Form1" method="post" runat="server">

  <asp:ListBox id=ListBox1 style="Z-INDEX: 101; LEFT: 53px; POSITION:
  absolute; TOP: 106px" runat="server" Width="201px" Height="61px"
  AutoPostBack="True">
    <asp:ListItem Value="Palm OS Programming">Palm OS Programming
    </asp:ListItem>
    <asp:ListItem Value="C# Programming">C# Programming</asp:ListItem>
    <asp:ListItem Value="Visual Basic .Net Programming">
    Visual Basic .Net Programming</asp:ListItem>
  </asp:ListBox>

  <asp:Label id=Label1 style="Z-INDEX: 102; LEFT: 32px; POSITION:
  absolute; TOP: 24px" runat="server" Font-Size="XX-Large">
  Book Information</asp:Label>

  <asp:TextBox id=TextBox1 style="Z-INDEX: 103; LEFT: 294px; POSITION:
  absolute; TOP: 105px" runat="server" Width="405px" Height="83px"
  TextMode="MultiLine"></asp:TextBox>

</form>
```

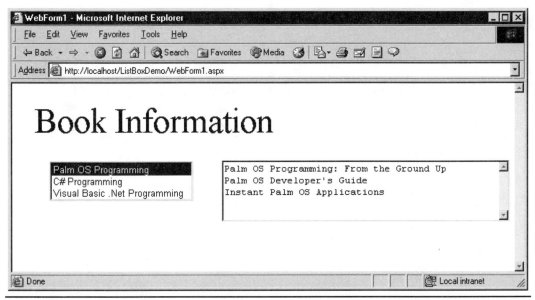

Figure 15-14   Responding to user ListBox selections in a Web page

Programming the asp:RadioButtonList Control

USE IT   In a Web form, radio buttons let a user select one item from two or more related options. In a similar way, an asp:RadioButtonList displays a list of items, each preceded by a radio button. Within the list, the user can only select one item. The following ASP.NET page, RadioButtonList.aspx, uses a RadioButtonList control to display a list of NBA teams. After the user selects a team, the code displays a hyperlink to the team's Web site, as shown in Figure 15-15. To create the page, drag and drop the Label, RadioButtonList, and HyperLink controls onto the page. Using the properties window, set the RadioButtonList control's AutoPostBack property to True.

```
Public Class WebForm1
    Inherits System.Web.UI.Page
    Protected WithEvents RadioButtonList1 As
System.Web.UI.WebControls.RadioButtonList
    Protected WithEvents HyperLink1 As System.Web.UI.WebControls.HyperLink
    Protected WithEvents Label1 As System.Web.UI.WebControls.Label

#Region " Web Form Designer Generated Code "
  ' Page not shown
#End Region

    Private Sub Page_Load(ByVal sender As System.Object, _
      ByVal e As System.EventArgs) Handles MyBase.Load
        HyperLink1.NavigateUrl = "www.nba.com"
```

```
            HyperLink1.Text = HyperLink1.NavigateUrl
      End Sub

   Private Sub RadioButtonList1_SelectedIndexChanged(ByVal _
      sender As System.Object, ByVal e As System.EventArgs) _
      Handles RadioButtonList1.SelectedIndexChanged
         If Not (RadioButtonList1.SelectedItem Is Nothing) Then
             If (RadioButtonList1.SelectedIndex = 0) Then
                 HyperLink1.NavigateUrl = "http://www.Lakers.com"
             ElseIf (RadioButtonList1.SelectedIndex = 1) Then
                 HyperLink1.NavigateUrl = " http://www.Kings.com"
             ElseIf (RadioButtonList1.SelectedIndex = 2) Then
                 HyperLink1.NavigateUrl = " http://www.Mavericks.com"
             ElseIf (RadioButtonList1.SelectedIndex = 3) Then
                 HyperLink1.NavigateUrl = " http://www.Knicks.com"
             End If
             HyperLink1.Text = HyperLink1.NavigateUrl
         End If
      End Sub
End Class
```

Visual Studio will create HTML statements that use a <form> tag similar to the following that ties the page to the server-side controls:

```
<form id="Form1" method="post" runat="server">

  <asp:RadioButtonList id=RadioButtonList1 style="Z-INDEX: 101;
   LEFT: 73px; POSITION: absolute; TOP: 113px" runat="server"
   AutoPostBack="True">

    <asp:ListItem Value="Lakers">Lakers</asp:ListItem>
    <asp:ListItem Value="Kings">Kings</asp:ListItem>
    <asp:ListItem Value="Mavericks">Mavericks</asp:ListItem>
    <asp:ListItem Value="Knicks">Knicks</asp:ListItem>

  </asp:RadioButtonList>

  <asp:Label id=Label1 style="Z-INDEX: 102; LEFT: 30px; POSITION:
   absolute; TOP: 31px" runat="server" Font-Size="XX-Large">
   Radio Button Demo</asp:Label>

  <asp:HyperLink id=HyperLink1 style="Z-INDEX: 103; LEFT: 219px;
   POSITION: absolute; TOP: 122px" runat="server">HyperLink
  </asp:HyperLink>

</form>
```

Figure 15-15   Using server-side processing to respond to selections in a RadioButtonList control

Programming the asp:Literal Control

USE IT   In an ASP.NET page, developers often use an asp:Label control to hold text. Using the Label control, the page can later change the text's formatting. In contrast, an asp:Literal control lets a page display text which can change, but the format cannot change. The following ASP.NET page, LiteralDemo.aspx, displays an asp:Literal control on a page with a button. When you click the button, the page will change the asp:Literal control's text. The page cannot, however, change the control's formatting:

```
Public Class WebForm1
    Inherits System.Web.UI.Page
    Protected WithEvents Button1 As System.Web.UI.WebControls.Button
    Protected WithEvents Literal1 As System.Web.UI.WebControls.Literal

#Region " Web Form Designer Generated Code "
    ' Code not shown
#End Region

    Private Sub Button1_Click(ByVal sender As System.Object, _
      ByVal e As System.EventArgs) Handles Button1.Click
        If Literal1.Text = "Hello" Then
            Literal1.Text = "Hello, World!"
```

```
        Else
            Literal1.Text = "Hello"
        End If
    End Sub
End Class
```

Behind the scenes, Visual Studio will create HTML statements that use a <form> tag similar to the following to tie the page to the server-side controls:

```
<form id=Form1 method=post runat="server">
  <asp:literal id=Literal1 runat="server" Text="Hello, World!"></asp:Literal>
  <asp:button id=Button1 style="Z-INDEX: 101; LEFT: 17px; POSITION: _
    absolute; TOP: 63px" runat="server" Text="Change Literal Text"></asp:Button>
</FORM>
```

Programming the asp:PlaceHolder Control

USE IT Depending on the processing an ASP.NET page performs, there may be times when you will want to add controls (such as buttons or text boxes) to the form as the page executes. In a Web form, the asp:PlaceHolder control lets you reserve space on the form into which your code can later place a control. The following ASP.NET page, PlaceHolderDemo.aspx, displays a page that contains two buttons. If the user clicks Add Button, the page will add a Button control to the PlaceHolder control. If, instead, the user clicks Add TextBox, the page will add a TextBox control to the page, as shown in Figure 15-16. To create the page, drag and drop the PlaceHolder and Button controls onto the page. For each Button control, set the AutoPostBack property to True.

```
Public Class WebForm1
    Inherits System.Web.UI.Page
    Protected WithEvents Button1 As _
      System.Web.UI.WebControls.Button
    Protected WithEvents Button2 As _
      System.Web.UI.WebControls.Button
    Protected WithEvents PlaceHolder1 As _
      System.Web.UI.WebControls.PlaceHolder

#Region " Web Form Designer Generated Code "
  ' Code not shown
#End Region

    Public DemoButton As HtmlButton = New HtmlButton()
    Public Message As HtmlTextArea = New HtmlTextArea()

    Private Sub Button1_Click(ByVal sender As System.Object, _
```

```
      ByVal e As System.EventArgs) Handles Button1.Click
        DemoButton.InnerText = "Demo"
        PlaceHolder1.Controls.Add(DemoButton)
    End Sub

    Private Sub Button2_Click(ByVal sender As System.Object, _
      ByVal e As System.EventArgs) Handles Button2.Click
        Message.InnerText = "Hello, world!"
        PlaceHolder1.Controls.Add(Message)
    End Sub

End Class
```

Visual Studio creates HTML statements that use a <form> tag similar to the following that ties the page to the server-side control:

```
<form id="Form1" method="post" runat="server">

  <asp:PlaceHolder id=PlaceHolder1 runat="server"></asp:PlaceHolder>

  <asp:Button id=Button1 style="Z-INDEX: 101; LEFT: 32px; POSITION:
   absolute; TOP: 78px" runat="server" Text="Add Button"></asp:Button>

  <asp:Button id=Button2 style="Z-INDEX: 102; LEFT: 151px; POSITION:
   absolute; TOP: 80px" runat="server" Text="Add TextBox"></asp:Button>

</form>
```

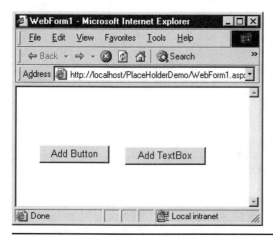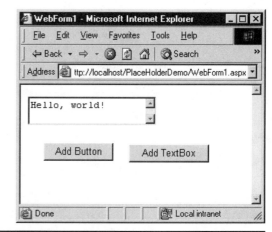

Figure 15-16 Adding controls dynamically to a PlaceHolder control

Programming the asp:Calendar Control

USE IT ▶ Across the Web, many pages prompt the user for date information, such as a travel date. To simplify the process of prompting the user for a date, the Web form interface provides the asp:Calendar control that displays a monthly calendar from which a user can select a date or a range of dates. The following ASP.NET page, the CalendarDemo.aspx, creates a page you can use to view the effect of different asp:Calendar control attribute settings. As the user selects a date, the page displays the corresponding date within a TextBox control, as shown in Figure 15-17. To create the page, drag and drop the Label, Calendar, and TextBox controls onto the page. Using the properties window, set the Calendar control's AutoPostBack property to True. For simplicity, the program does not trap errors. For example, if the user selects a range of dates, the existing program code will generate an exception.

```
Public Class WebForm1
    Inherits System.Web.UI.Page
    Protected WithEvents Label1 As System.Web.UI.WebControls.Label
    Protected WithEvents Calendar1 As System.Web.UI.WebControls.Calendar
    Protected WithEvents TextBox1 As System.Web.UI.WebControls.TextBox

#Region " Web Form Designer Generated Code "
  ' Code not shown
#End Region

    Private Sub Calendar1_SelectionChanged(ByVal sender As _
      System.Object, ByVal e As System.EventArgs) _
      Handles Calendar1.SelectionChanged
        TextBox1.Text = Calendar1.SelectedDate
    End Sub

End Class
```

Visual Studio will create HTML statements that use a <form> tag similar to the following that ties the page to server-side control:

```
<form id="Form1" method="post" runat="server">

  <asp:Label id=Label1 style="Z-INDEX: 101; LEFT: 81px; POSITION:
  absolute; TOP: 52px" runat="server" Font-Size="XX-Large">
  Calendar Demo</asp:Label>

  <asp:Calendar id=Calendar1 style="Z-INDEX: 102; LEFT: 82px;
  POSITION: absolute; TOP: 126px" runat="server">
  </asp:Calendar>

  <asp:TextBox id=TextBox1 style="Z-INDEX: 103; LEFT: 383px;
  POSITION: absolute; TOP: 132px" runat="server" Width="280px">
  </asp:TextBox>

</form>
```

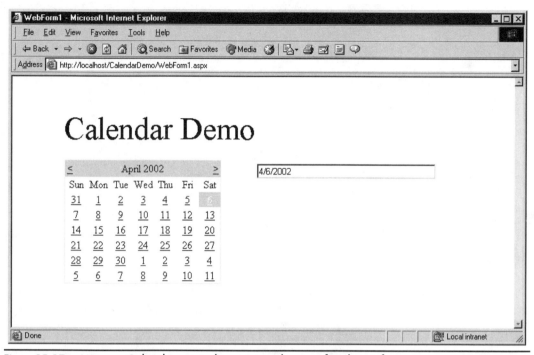

Figure 15-17   Using a Calendar control to prompt the user for date information

Programming the asp:Rotator Control

For years, Active Server Pages have used the Ad Rotator control to display banners at the top of Web pages that change from one user visit to the next. In a Web form, the asp:AdRotator control lets you place a similar control on a page. To use the AdRotator control, you must assign an XML file to the control that specifies information about each advertisement. Within the XML file that defines the advertisement, you use the XML tags similar to those shown here that specify the image the rotator is to display, the target URL if the user clicks the image, and so on:

```
<Ad>
<ImageUrl>http://www.SomeSite.com/banner1.gif</ImageUrl>
<NavigateUrl>http://www.SomeSite.com/Somepage.aspx</NavigateUrl>
<AlternateText>Some Image Description</AlternateText>
<Keyword>Books</Keyword>
<Impressions>100</Impressions>
</Ad>
```

The following ASP.NET page, AdRotatorDemo.aspx, places an AdRotator control on the page. The page uses the XML file, AdFile.xml, that contains the following two entries:

```
<Advertisements>
<Ad>
```

```
<ImageUrl>Banner1.gif</ImageUrl>
<NavigateUrl>http://localhost/AdRotatorDemo/WebForm1.aspx</NavigateUrl>
<AlternateText>Book Image</AlternateText>
<Keyword>Book Image</Keyword>
<Impressions>100</Impressions>
</Ad>

<Ad>
<ImageUrl>Banner2.gif</ImageUrl>
<NavigateUrl>http://localhost/AdRotatorDemo/WebForm1.aspx</NavigateUrl>
<AlternateText>Magazine Image</AlternateText>
<Keyword>Magazine Image</Keyword>
<Impressions>100</Impressions>
</Ad>

</Advertisements>
```

As you can see, the target URL for each ad is the AdRotatorDemo.aspx page, which lets you continue to click the banner ads to watch them change from page to page, as shown in Figure 15-18. To

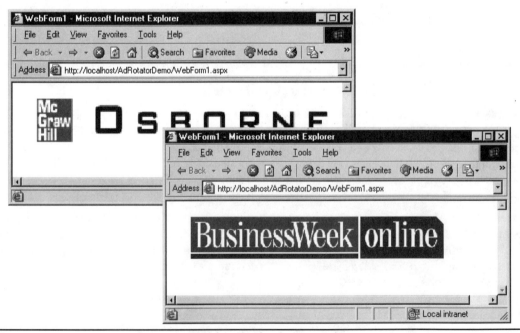

Figure 15-18   Using an AdRotator control to display banner ads

create the page, drag and drop the AdRotator control onto the page. Then create an XML file that contains the Advertising entries.

```
Public Class WebForm1
    Inherits System.Web.UI.Page
    Protected WithEvents AdRotator1 As _
      System.Web.UI.WebControls.AdRotator

#Region " Web Form Designer Generated Code "
  ' Code not shown
#End Region

    Private Sub Page_Load(ByVal sender As System.Object, _
      ByVal e As System.EventArgs) Handles MyBase.Load
        AdRotator1.AdvertisementFile = "AdFile.xml"
    End Sub

End Class
```

Visual Studio will create HTML statements that use a <form> tag similar to the following to tie the page to the server-side controls:

```
<form id="Form1" method="post" runat="server">
  <asp:AdRotator id=AdRotator1 style="Z-INDEX: 101; LEFT: 35px; _
   POSITION: absolute; TOP: 22px" runat="server" Width="468px" _
   Height="60px"></asp:AdRotator>
</form>
```

Programming the asp:XML Control

USE IT   Depending on the processing an ASP.NET page performs, there may be times when you will want the page to display XML-based data. In such cases, you can place an asp:XML control onto a Web form. In your code, you can later assign a string of XML-based content to the control, or you can assign the source of the XML data. The following ASP.NET page, XMLDemo.aspx, assigns a string of XML data to a control's DocumentContent field. When you display the page, your browser will display information about this book.

```
Public Class WebForm1
    Inherits System.Web.UI.Page
    Protected WithEvents Xml1 As System.Web.UI.WebControls.Xml

#Region " Web Form Designer Generated Code "
```

```
' Code not shown
#End Region

  Private Sub Page_Load(ByVal sender As System.Object, _
    ByVal e As System.EventArgs) Handles MyBase.Load
      Xml1.DocumentContent = "<book>" & _
        "<booktitle>Visual Basic .Net " & _
        "Programming Tips &amp; Techniques;</booktitle>" & _
        "<author>Kris Jamsa;</author>" & _
        "<publisher>McGraw-Hill/Osborne;</publisher>" & _
        "<price>$49.99</price>" & _
        "</book>"
    End Sub

End Class
```

Behind the scenes, Visual Studio will create HTML statements that use a <form> tag similar to the following to tie the page to the server-side controls:

```
<form id="Form1" method="post" runat="server">
  <asp:Xml id=Xml1 runat="server">
  </asp:Xml>
</form>
```

Programming the asp:RequiredFieldValidator Control

When your ASP.NET pages use a Web form to prompt the user for information, there will be many times when your forms will contain one or more required fields, for which the user must specify a value. Using the asp:RequiredFieldValidator control, you can easily integrate testing within your forms to ensure the user specifies a value for all required fields. If the user fails to specify a value, the program displays a prompt that directs the user to provide a value for the control, as shown in Figure 15-19.

 The following ASP.NET page, RequiredFieldDemo.aspx, creates a form that contains several fields. The form requires that the user specify his or her name and e-mail address:

```
Public Class WebForm1
    Inherits System.Web.UI.Page
    Protected WithEvents Label1 As System.Web.UI.WebControls.Label
    Protected WithEvents Label2 As System.Web.UI.WebControls.Label
    Protected WithEvents TextBox1 As System.Web.UI.WebControls.TextBox
```

```
    Protected WithEvents Label3 As System.Web.UI.WebControls.Label
    Protected WithEvents Label4 As System.Web.UI.WebControls.Label
    Protected WithEvents TextBox2 As System.Web.UI.WebControls.TextBox
    Protected WithEvents TextBox3 As System.Web.UI.WebControls.TextBox
    Protected WithEvents Label5 As System.Web.UI.WebControls.Label
    Protected WithEvents TextBox4 As System.Web.UI.WebControls.TextBox
    Protected WithEvents RequiredFieldValidator1 As _
        System.Web.UI.WebControls.RequiredFieldValidator
    Protected WithEvents Done As System.Web.UI.WebControls.Button
    Protected WithEvents RequiredFieldValidator2 As _
        System.Web.UI.WebControls.RequiredFieldValidator

#Region " Web Form Designer Generated Code "
  ' Code not shown
#End Region

    Private Sub Page_Load(ByVal sender As System.Object, _
      ByVal e As System.EventArgs) Handles MyBase.Load
        If (Not Page.IsPostBack) Then
            RequiredFieldValidator1.ControlToValidate = "TextBox1"
            RequiredFieldValidator1.ErrorMessage = _
              "Must specify your name"

            RequiredFieldValidator2.ControlToValidate = "TextBox4"
            RequiredFieldValidator2.ErrorMessage = _
              "Must specify your e-mail address"
        End If
    End Sub

    Private Sub Done_Click(ByVal sender As System.Object, _
      ByVal e As System.EventArgs) Handles Done.Click
        RequiredFieldValidator1.Validate()
        RequiredFieldValidator2.Validate()
    End Sub
End Class
```

Visual Studio will create HTML statements that use a <form> tag similar to the following to tie the page to the server-side controls:

```
<form id="Form1" method="post" runat="server">

  <asp:Label id=Label1 style="Z-INDEX: 101; LEFT: 41px; POSITION:
```

```
      absolute; TOP: 38px" runat="server" Font-Size="XX-Large">
    Required Field Demo</asp:Label>

  <asp:Label id=Label2 style="Z-INDEX: 102; LEFT: 73px; POSITION:
   absolute; TOP: 136px" runat="server">Name:</asp:Label>

  <asp:TextBox id=TextBox1 style="Z-INDEX: 103; LEFT: 147px; POSITION:
   absolute; TOP: 133px" runat="server" ></asp:TextBox>

  <asp:Label id=Label3 style="Z-INDEX: 104; LEFT: 72px; POSITION:
   absolute; TOP: 178px" runat="server">Phone</asp:Label>

  <asp:Label id=Label4 style="Z-INDEX: 105; LEFT: 72px; POSITION:
   absolute; TOP: 220px" runat="server">Fax</asp:Label>

  <asp:TextBox id=TextBox2 style="Z-INDEX: 106; LEFT: 148px; POSITION:
   absolute; TOP: 172px" runat="server" ></asp:TextBox>

  <asp:TextBox id=TextBox3 style="Z-INDEX: 107; LEFT: 149px; POSITION:
   absolute; TOP: 216px" runat="server" ></asp:TextBox>

  <asp:Label id=Label5 style="Z-INDEX: 108; LEFT: 75px; POSITION:
   absolute; TOP: 256px" runat="server">E-Mail</asp:Label>

  <asp:TextBox id=TextBox4 style="Z-INDEX: 109; LEFT: 149px;
   POSITION: absolute; TOP: 254px" runat="server" ></asp:TextBox>

  <asp:RequiredFieldValidator id=RequiredFieldValidator1
   style="Z-INDEX: 110; LEFT: 345px; POSITION: absolute; TOP: 137px"
   runat="server" ErrorMessage="RequiredFieldValidator">
  </asp:RequiredFieldValidator>

  <asp:RequiredFieldValidator id=RequiredFieldValidator2
   style="Z-INDEX: 111; LEFT: 348px; POSITION: absolute; TOP: 257px"
   runat="server" ErrorMessage="RequiredFieldValidator">
  </asp:RequiredFieldValidator>

  <asp:Button id=Done style="Z-INDEX: 112; LEFT: 183px; POSITION:
   absolute; TOP: 319px" runat="server" Text="Done"></asp:Button>
</form>
```

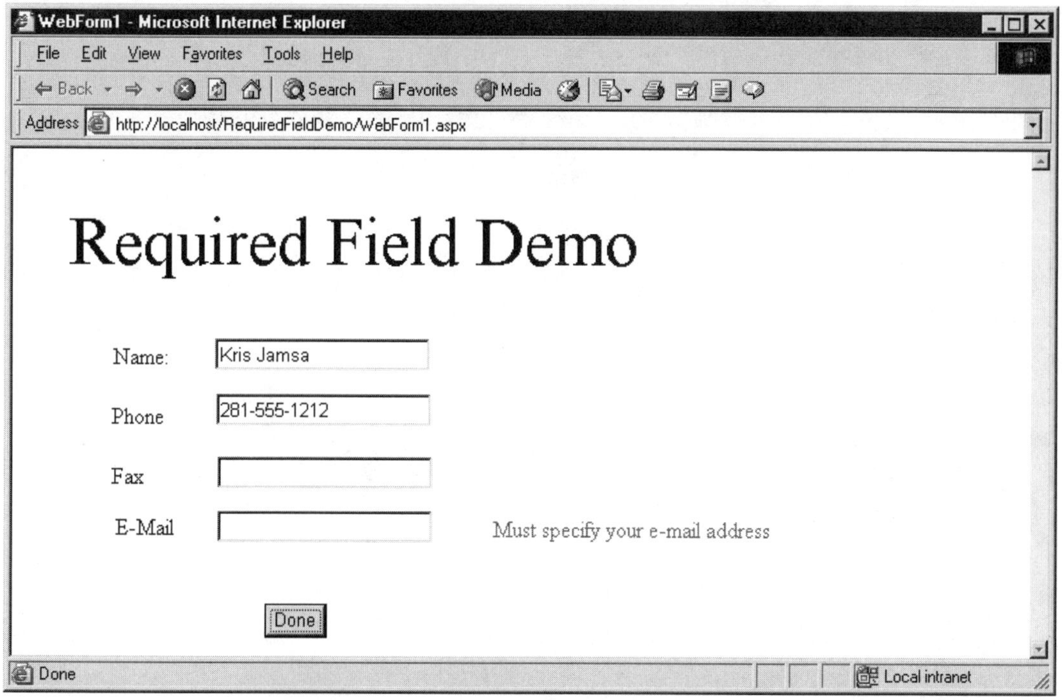

Figure 15-19   Using the RequiredFieldValidator control to prompt the user for required fields

Programming the asp:RangeValidator Control

When an ASP.NET page uses a form to prompt the user for information, there may be times when you will want the form to verify that the values a user enters fall into a specific range. For example, a form might validate that the number of hours per day a user watches TV falls in the range 0 to 24, or the number of days per week that the user surfs the Web falls in the range 0 to 7. To test if the value a user enters falls within a specific range, a Web form can assign an asp:RangeValidator control to a field.

USE IT   The following ASP.NET page, RangeValidator.aspx, creates a form that prompts the user to enter several fields. The page assigns an asp:RangeValidator control to each field to examine the user's input. If the user enters a value outside of the range, the page will display an error message, as shown in Figure 15-20, that describes the proper range of values.

```
Public Class WebForm1
   Inherits System.Web.UI.Page
   Protected WithEvents TextBox1 As System.Web.UI.WebControls.TextBox
   Protected WithEvents Label1 As System.Web.UI.WebControls.Label
   Protected WithEvents Label2 As System.Web.UI.WebControls.Label
```

```vb
    Protected WithEvents Label3 As System.Web.UI.WebControls.Label
    Protected WithEvents TextBox2 As System.Web.UI.WebControls.TextBox
    Protected WithEvents Label4 As System.Web.UI.WebControls.Label
    Protected WithEvents TextBox3 As System.Web.UI.WebControls.TextBox
    Protected WithEvents RangeValidator1 As _
       System.Web.UI.WebControls.RangeValidator
    Protected WithEvents RangeValidator2 As _
       System.Web.UI.WebControls.RangeValidator
    Protected WithEvents RangeValidator3 As _
       System.Web.UI.WebControls.RangeValidator

#Region " Web Form Designer Generated Code "
   ' Code not shown
#End Region

    Private Sub Page_Load(ByVal sender As System.Object, _
       ByVal e As System.EventArgs) Handles MyBase.Load
        If Page.IsPostBack Then
            RangeValidator1.Validate()
            RangeValidator2.Validate()
            RangeValidator3.Validate()
        Else
            RangeValidator1.Type = ValidationDataType.Integer
            RangeValidator1.MinimumValue = 18
            RangeValidator1.MaximumValue = 21
            RangeValidator1.ErrorMessage = "Enter age in the range 18 to 21"
            RangeValidator1.ControlToValidate = "TextBox1"

            RangeValidator2.Type = ValidationDataType.Integer
            RangeValidator2.MinimumValue = 0
            RangeValidator2.MaximumValue = 7
            RangeValidator2.ErrorMessage = "Enter days in the range 0 to 7"
            RangeValidator2.ControlToValidate = "TextBox2"

            RangeValidator3.Type = ValidationDataType.Integer
            RangeValidator3.MinimumValue = 0
            RangeValidator3.MaximumValue = 24
            RangeValidator3.ErrorMessage = "Enter hours in the range 0 to 24"
            RangeValidator3.ControlToValidate = "TextBox3"
        End If
    End Sub

End Class
```

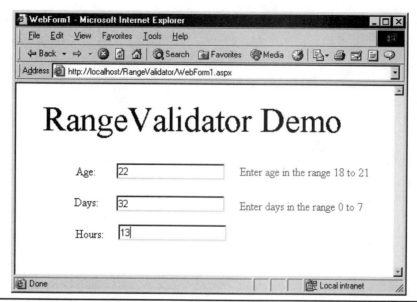

Figure 15-20   Using a RangeValidator control to restrict the range of values a user can assign to a field

Visual Studio will create HTML statements that use a <form> tag similar to the following to tie the page to the server-side controls:

```
<form id="Form1" method="post" runat="server">
  <asp:TextBox id=TextBox1 style="Z-INDEX: 101; LEFT: 144px;
   POSITION: absolute; TOP: 110px" runat="server" autoPostBack="True">
  </asp:TextBox>

  <asp:Label id=Label1 style="Z-INDEX: 102; LEFT: 86px; POSITION:
   absolute; TOP: 112px" runat="server">Age:</asp:Label>

  <asp:RangeValidator id=RangeValidator1 style="Z-INDEX: 103;
   LEFT: 320px; POSITION: absolute; TOP: 111px" runat="server"
   ErrorMessage="RangeValidator" ControlToValidate="TextBox1"
   MaximumValue="21" MinimumValue="18" Type="Integer">
  </asp:RangeValidator>

  <asp:Label id=Label2 style="Z-INDEX: 104; LEFT: 39px; POSITION:
   absolute; TOP: 22px" runat="server" Font-Size="XX-Large">
  RangeValidator Demo</asp:Label>

  <asp:Label id=Label3 style="Z-INDEX: 105; LEFT: 84px; POSITION:
   absolute; TOP: 155px" runat="server">Days:</asp:Label>
```

```
<asp:TextBox id=TextBox2 style="Z-INDEX: 106; LEFT: 144px; POSITION:
 absolute; TOP: 155px" runat="server" AutoPostBack="True">
</asp:TextBox>

<asp:RangeValidator id=RangeValidator2 style="Z-INDEX: 107; LEFT:
 320px; POSITION: absolute; TOP: 159px" runat="server"
 ErrorMessage="RangeValidator" ControlToValidate="TextBox2"
 MaximumValue="7" MinimumValue="0" Type="Integer">
</asp:RangeValidator>

<asp:Label id=Label4 style="Z-INDEX: 108; LEFT: 86px; POSITION:
 absolute; TOP: 199px" runat="server">Hours:</asp:Label>

<asp:TextBox id=TextBox3 style="Z-INDEX: 109; LEFT: 147px;
 POSITION: absolute; TOP: 195px" runat="server"
 AutoPostBack="True"></asp:TextBox>

<asp:RangeValidator id=RangeValidator3 style="Z-INDEX: 110;
 LEFT: 323px; POSITION: absolute; TOP: 201px" runat="server"
 ErrorMessage="RangeValidator" ControlToValidate="TextBox3"
 MaximumValue="24" MinimumValue="0" Type="Integer">
</asp:RangeValidator>

</form>
```

Programming the asp:CompareValidator Control

USE IT In the Tip titled "Programming the asp:RangeValidator Control," you learned how to use an asp:RangeValidator control to ensure the value a user enters falls within a specific range. In a similar way, using the asp:CompareValidator control, your page can validate if a value is equal to, greater than, or less than a specific value. The following ASP.NET page, CompareValidator.aspx, displays two fields, one that prompts the user to enter a year and one that prompts the user to enter a cost. The page uses asp:CompareValidator controls to validate the values the user enters. The user must enter a year less than 2003 and a cost greater than 50.00:

```
Public Class WebForm1
    Inherits System.Web.UI.Page
    Protected WithEvents Label1 As System.Web.UI.WebControls.Label
    Protected WithEvents TextBox1 As System.Web.UI.WebControls.TextBox
    Protected WithEvents Label2 As System.Web.UI.WebControls.Label
    Protected WithEvents TextBox2 As System.Web.UI.WebControls.TextBox
    Protected WithEvents Label4 As System.Web.UI.WebControls.Label
    Protected WithEvents CompareValidator1 As
```

```
System.Web.UI.WebControls.CompareValidator
    Protected WithEvents CompareValidator2 As
System.Web.UI.WebControls.CompareValidator

#Region " Web Form Designer Generated Code "
  ' Code not shown
#End Region

  Private Sub Page_Load(ByVal sender As System.Object, _
    ByVal e As System.EventArgs) Handles MyBase.Load
      If Page.IsPostBack Then
        CompareValidator1.Validate()
        CompareValidator2.Validate()
      Else
        CompareValidator1.Type = ValidationDataType.Integer
        CompareValidator1.ValueToCompare = 2003
        CompareValidator1.ErrorMessage = "Enter year less than 2003"
        CompareValidator1.ControlToValidate = "TextBox1"
        CompareValidator1.Operator = ValidationCompareOperator.LessThan

        CompareValidator2.Type = ValidationDataType.Double
        CompareValidator2.ValueToCompare = 50.0
        CompareValidator2.ErrorMessage = "Enter a cost greater than 50.00"
        CompareValidator2.Operator = ValidationCompareOperator.GreaterThan
        CompareValidator2.ControlToValidate = "TextBox2"
      End If
  End Sub

End Class
```

Visual Studio will create HTML statements that use a <form> tag similar to the following to tie the page to the server-side controls:

```
<form id="Form1" method="post" runat="server">
  <asp:Label id=Label1 style="Z-INDEX: 101; LEFT: 97px; POSITION:
  absolute; TOP: 103px" runat="server">Year:</asp:Label>

  <asp:TextBox id=TextBox1 style="Z-INDEX: 102; LEFT: 159px;
  POSITION: absolute; TOP: 100px" runat="server"></asp:TextBox>

  <asp:Label id=Label2 style="Z-INDEX: 103; LEFT: 96px; POSITION:
  absolute; TOP: 146px" runat="server">Cost:</asp:Label>

  <asp:TextBox id=TextBox2 style="Z-INDEX: 104; LEFT: 160px;
  POSITION: absolute; TOP: 143px" runat="server"></asp:TextBox>
```

```
<asp:Label id=Label4 style="Z-INDEX: 107; LEFT: 25px; POSITION:
 absolute; TOP: 18px" runat="server" Font-Size="XX-Large"
 Width="507px">CompareValidator Demo</asp:Label>

<asp:CompareValidator id=CompareValidator1 style="Z-INDEX: 108;
 LEFT: 336px; POSITION: absolute; TOP: 105px" runat="server"
 ErrorMessage="CompareValidator"></asp:CompareValidator>

<asp:CompareValidator id=CompareValidator2 style="Z-INDEX: 109;
 LEFT: 339px; POSITION: absolute; TOP: 144px" runat="server"
 ErrorMessage="CompareValidator"></asp:CompareValidator>
</form>
```

Programming the asp:CustomValidator Control

USE IT   In a Web form, your code can take advantage of validation controls to determine if a user specified a value for a field, if the field's value is in a specific range, and to compare one value to another. Depending on the form's contents and purpose, there may be times when you want to define specific processing the form performs to validate a field's value. In such cases, you can define the validation code that responds to the control's ServerValidate event. In addition to validating the data in the server, you can also specify a client-side subroutine that executes in a script to validate the value. The following ASP.NET page, CustomValidator.aspx, creates a form that prompts the user to enter his or her lucky number. The page uses an asp:CustomValidator control to force the user to enter the value 1, 7, or 11:

```
Public Class WebForm1
   Inherits System.Web.UI.Page
   Protected WithEvents Label1 As System.Web.UI.WebControls.Label
   Protected WithEvents Label2 As System.Web.UI.WebControls.Label
   Protected WithEvents TextBox1 As System.Web.UI.WebControls.TextBox
   Protected WithEvents CustomValidator1 As _
     System.Web.UI.WebControls.CustomValidator

#Region " Web Form Designer Generated Code "
   ' Code not shown
#End Region

   Sub ServerValidation(ByVal source As Object, _
     ByVal args As ServerValidateEventArgs) _
     Handles CustomValidator1.ServerValidate

       If (args.Value = "1") Then
           args.IsValid = True
```

```
        ElseIf (args.Value = "7") Then
            args.IsValid = True
        ElseIf (args.Value = "11") Then
            args.IsValid = True
        Else
            args.IsValid = False
        End If
    End Sub

    Private Sub Page_Load(ByVal sender As System.Object, _
      ByVal e As System.EventArgs) Handles MyBase.Load
        If Page.IsPostBack Then
            CustomValidator1.Validate()
        Else
            CustomValidator1.ErrorMessage = "Enter 1, 7, or 11"
            CustomValidator1.ControlToValidate = "TextBox1"
        End If

    End Sub

End Class
```

Behind the scenes, Visual Studio will create HTML statements that use a <form> tag similar to the following to tie the page to the server-side controls:

```
<form id="Form1" method="post" runat="server">

  <asp:Label id=Label1 style="Z-INDEX: 101; LEFT: 20px; POSITION:
  absolute; TOP: 14px" runat="server" Font-Size="XX-Large"
  Width="470px">Custom Validator Demo</asp:Label>

  <asp:Label id=Label2 style="Z-INDEX: 102; LEFT: 56px; POSITION:
  absolute; TOP: 92px" runat="server">Lucky Number:</asp:Label>

  <asp:TextBox id=TextBox1 style="Z-INDEX: 103; LEFT: 162px;
  POSITION: absolute; TOP: 89px" runat="server" AutoPostBack="True">
  </asp:TextBox>

  <asp:CustomValidator id=CustomValidator1 style="Z-INDEX: 104;
  LEFT: 334px; POSITION: absolute; TOP: 93px" runat="server"
  ErrorMessage="CustomValidator">
  </asp:CustomValidator>

</form>
```

Programming the asp:RegularExpressionValidator Control

USE IT When an ASP.NET page uses a Web form to prompt the user for information, there will be many times when you want the form to validate the format of the data the user entered. For example, if your form prompts the user to enter an e-mail address, the user should enter an address in the form name@somesite.com. Likewise, if your form prompts the user for a phone number, the user should enter data in the form 713-555-1212. To compare the data a user enters to a specific format, your code can use the asp:RegularExpressionValidator control. To use the control, you must specify a "regular expression" that contains the sequence of acceptable characters. For example, to require the user to enter a phone number in the form ###-###-####, you would use the following regular expression:

```
"\d{3}-\d{3}-\d{4}"
```

Across the Web, several sites examine regular expressions in detail. Normally, such sites will present examples you can use for such common items as Social Security numbers, credit card numbers, e-mail addresses, and so on.

The following ASP.NET page, RegularExpressionValidator.aspx, displays a page that prompts the user to enter a telephone number and e-mail address. The form assigns an asp:RegularExpressionValidator control to each field:

```
Public Class WebForm1
   Inherits System.Web.UI.Page
   Protected WithEvents Label1 As System.Web.UI.WebControls.Label
   Protected WithEvents TextBox1 As System.Web.UI.WebControls.TextBox
   Protected WithEvents Label2 As System.Web.UI.WebControls.Label
   Protected WithEvents Label3 As System.Web.UI.WebControls.Label
   Protected WithEvents TextBox2 As System.Web.UI.WebControls.TextBox
   Protected WithEvents RegularExpressionValidator1 As _
      System.Web.UI.WebControls.RegularExpressionValidator
   Protected WithEvents RegularExpressionValidator2 As _
      System.Web.UI.WebControls.RegularExpressionValidator

#Region " Web Form Designer Generated Code "
   ' Code not shown
#End Region

   Private Sub Page_Load(ByVal sender As System.Object, _
      ByVal e As System.EventArgs) Handles MyBase.Load
         If Page.IsPostBack Then
            RegularExpressionValidator1.Validate()
```

```
            RegularExpressionValidator2.Validate()
        Else
            RegularExpressionValidator1.ControlToValidate = "TextBox1"
            RegularExpressionValidator1.ErrorMessage = _
                "Use the format xxx-xxx-xxxx"
            RegularExpressionValidator1.ValidationExpression = _
                "\d{3}-\d{3}-\d{4}"

            RegularExpressionValidator2.ControlToValidate = "TextBox2"
            RegularExpressionValidator2.ErrorMessage = _
                "Use the format name@somesite.com"
            RegularExpressionValidator2.ValidationExpression = _
                "\w+([-+.]\w+)*@\w+([-.]\w+)*\.\w+([-.]\w+)*"
        End If
    End Sub

End Class
```

Visual Studio will create HTML statements that use a <form> tag similar to the following to tie the page to the server-side controls:

```
<form id="Form1" method="post" runat="server">

  <asp:Label id=Label1 style="Z-INDEX: 101; LEFT: 48px; POSITION:
  absolute; TOP: 47px" runat="server" Font-Size="X-Large">
  RegularExpressionValidator Demo</asp:Label>

  <asp:TextBox id=TextBox1 style="Z-INDEX: 102; LEFT: 129px;
  POSITION: absolute; TOP: 117px" runat="server" AutoPostBack="True">
  </asp:TextBox>

  <asp:Label id=Label2 style="Z-INDEX: 103; LEFT: 61px; POSITION:
  absolute; TOP: 118px" runat="server">Phone:</asp:Label>

  <asp:Label id=Label3 style="Z-INDEX: 104; LEFT: 64px; POSITION:
  absolute; TOP: 180px" runat="server">E-Mail:</asp:Label>

  <asp:TextBox id=TextBox2 style="Z-INDEX: 105; LEFT: 129px;
  POSITION: absolute; TOP: 177px" runat="server" AutoPostBack="True">
  </asp:TextBox>
```

```
<asp:RegularExpressionValidator id=RegularExpressionValidator1
  style="Z-INDEX: 106; LEFT: 311px; POSITION: absolute; TOP: 120px"
  runat="server" ErrorMessage="RegularExpressionValidator">
</asp:RegularExpressionValidator>

<asp:RegularExpressionValidator id=RegularExpressionValidator2
  style="Z-INDEX: 107; LEFT: 313px; POSITION: absolute; TOP: 179px"
  runat="server" ErrorMessage="RegularExpressionValidator">
</asp:RegularExpressionValidator>

</form>
```

Taking Advantage of HTML Server Controls

In addition to letting you use Web forms within programmable controls, ASP.NET also lets your page control several common HTML elements, which programmers refer to as HTML server controls. Table 15-1 briefly describes the HTML server controls.

USE IT To program an HTML server control in an ASP.NET page, you assign the control a unique ID using the id attribute and then specify the runat="server" attribute/value pair:

```
<a id="RemoteAnchor" runat= "server">Link Text</a>
```

Your program then provides code that manipulates the control's attributes. The following Page_Load subroutine, for example, assigns a URL to the link when the page loads:

```
<script language="vb" runat="server">
Sub Page_Load(sender as Object, e As EventArgs)
  RemoteAnchor.href = "http://www.osborne.com"
End Sub
</script>
```

The following ASP.NET page, HTMLButtonDemo.aspx, creates a simple form that contains a button with the value 1. Each time you click the button, the page increments the button's value:

```
<% @Page language="vb" %>
<script language="vb" runat="server">
Sub Button_Click(Sender As Object, E As EventArgs)
  Dim Value As Integer

  Value = Button1.InnerText
  Value = Value + 1
  Button1.InnerText = Value
```

```
End Sub
</script>

<html>
<head>
  <title>HTMLButton Demo</title>
</head>
<body>
<form runat="server">
    <button id="Button1" runat="server" OnServerClick="Button_Click">1</Button>
</form>
</body>
```

Control	Description
HTMLAnchor	Lets a program manipulate an anchor <a> tag's attributes.
HTMLButton	Lets a program manipulate a <button> tag's attributes.
HTMLForm	Lets a program manipulate a <form> tag's attributes.
HTMLGeneric	Lets a program manipulate a tag not specifically addressed by a different server control, such as the <font> tag.
HTMLImage	Lets a program manipulate an <image> tag's attributes.
HTMLInputButton	Lets a program manipulate a <input> tag's attributes for tags that use the button, submit, or reset types.
HTMLInputCheckbox	Lets a program manipulate an <input> tag's attributes for tags that use the checkbox type.
HTMLInputFile	Lets a program manipulate the attributes of an <input> tag for a file upload operation.
HTMLInputHidden	Lets a program manipulate an <input> tag's attributes for tags that use the hidden type.
HTMLInputImage	Lets a program manipulate an <input> tag's attributes for tags that use the image type.
HTMLInputRadioButton	Lets a program manipulate an <input> tag's attributes for tags that use the radio type.
HTMLInputText	Lets a program manipulate an <input> tag's attributes for tags that use the text type.
HTMLSelect	Lets a program manipulate a <select> tag's attributes.
HTMLTable	Lets a program manipulate a <table> tag's attributes.
HTMLTableCell	Lets a program manipulate the <td> and <th> tags.
HTMLTableRow	Lets a program manipulate the <tr> tag.
HTMLTextArea	Lets a program manipulate the <textarea> tag.

Table 15-1   A Summary of the HTML Server Controls

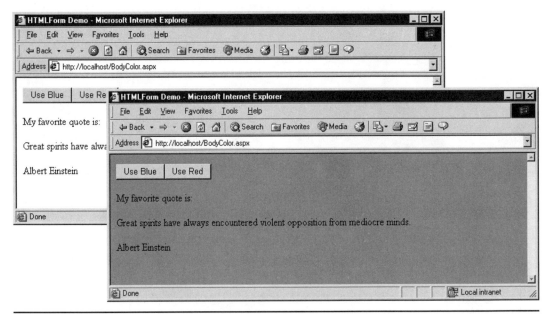

Figure 15-21   Using server-based HTML controls to change a page's background color

The following ASP.NET page, BodyColor.aspx, uses an HTMLGeneric control to set the background color for the body text, as shown in Figure 15-21.

```
<% @Page language="vb" %>
<script language="vb" runat="server">
Sub Button1_Click(Sender As Object, E As EventArgs)
  PageBody.Attributes("bgcolor") = "#0000ff"
End Sub

Sub Button2_Click(Sender As Object, E As EventArgs)
  PageBody.Attributes("bgcolor") = "#ff0000"
End Sub
</script>

<html>
<head>
  <title>HTMLForm Demo</title>
</head>
<body id="PageBody" runat="server">
<form id="Form1" runat="server">
  <button id="Button1" runat="server" OnServerClick="Button1_Click">Use
Blue</button>
```

```
    <button id="Button2" runat="server" OnServerClick="Button2_Click">Use
Red</button>
</form>
    <p>My favorite quote is:</p>
    <p>Great spirits have always encountered violent opposition from mediocre
minds.</p>
    <p>Albert Einstein</p>
</body>
</html>
```

Several of the HTML server controls are similar to Web form controls. In an ASP.NET page, you should use the control that best meets your needs. You can even use both types of control within the same ASP.NET page.

CHAPTER 16

Programming Web Services

TIPS IN THIS CHAPTER

Over the past ten years, applications have evolved to make extensive use of networks and to support remote operations. Normally, in a distributed environment, applications running on computer will access data stored on a remote computer, such as a company database. With the advent of Active Server Pages (and server-based scripts written in other languages such as Perl and PHP), applications could initiate processing that occurred on a remote server. When the server completed its processing, the server would return its result (typically an HTML-based page) to the user.

For years, many network operating systems have offered what programmers refer to as remote procedure calls (RPC). As you know, within an application, programmers make extensive use of subroutines and functions (which programmers collectively refer to as procedures) to perform specific tasks. Normally, the code for the subroutine or function resides in the program or in a library (such as a DLL file) that resides on the same system. In contrast, a remote procedure call is an invocation of a function or procedure that resides on a remote system (normally a server). Using a remote procedure, a program might, for example, authenticate a user, request a system date and time the program uses to synchronize an event, validate a credit card, and so on. In the program's source code, the call to the remote procedure looks very much like a standard procedure call, including the subroutine or function name and parameters.

Behind the scenes, however, the remote procedure call requires an exchange of messages between the program and the server. To start, the program must send the server a message that specifies the subroutine or function it wants to call. Further, if the procedure requires parameters, the program must send messages to the server that contain the parameter values. After the remote procedure completes its processing, the server must send messages back to the program that contain the procedure's result. The challenge in building an environment that supports remote procedure calls is in hiding the details of the underlying message exchange from the programmer (so he or she can simply call the procedure and use the result), while providing the flexibility to support error handling, a wide range of parameter types, and so on, and still maintain performance and security.

Across the Internet, Web services provide programmers with the ability to perform remote procedure calls. Although the .NET environment makes it easy to create Web services, you should not equate Web services to the .NET environment. As you might guess, other software companies beyond Microsoft offer Web service solutions. At Sun, for example, programmers make extensive use of Java-based Web services.

Although developers won't necessarily agree on whether it is best to create Web services using Visual Basic .NET, C#, Java, or yet another programming language, the development community has agreed on many of the underlying protocols that drive the behind-the-scenes message exchange that occurs between a program and the server that offers the Web service. As discussed, to call a remote procedure, a program must send to the server one or more messages that specify the procedure name and parameters. Likewise, the server must send messages back to the server that contain the result. Today, most Web services perform this message exchange using the Simple Object Access Protocol (SOAP). In general, SOAP is simply a protocol that defines the rules and data formats the server and an application must follow as they perform the message exchange. By sending SOAP-based messages to the server, an application describes the procedure it wants to call and the parameters it wants to use. Later, after the procedure ends, the server sends the application a SOAP-based message. Today, many programmers refer to Web services as XML Web Services. That is because the SOAP messages the application and server exchange are packaged within XML data.

As you might guess, creating a Web service could be quite similar to programming an Web-based program that must listen for and respond to messages. However, as briefly discussed, the power of a remote procedure call is that it hides the underlying details of the message exchange. In other words, to use a Web service, a programmer should not have to understand that the SOAP protocol and its XML-based messages exist. Instead, the programmer should simply be able to call the remote service, passing parameters and then using the result.

This chapter's Tips will introduce you to the steps you must perform to create and use Web services within the .NET environment. As you will learn, Visual Studio makes it very easy for you to create a service and to call a Web service. Throughout the Tips, you will periodically take a behind-the-scenes peak at the underlying SOAP and XML messages, not because you must interact with the technologies, but so that you can better appreciate the processing that occurs on your program's behalf each time you use a Web service.

Creating Your First Web Service

To help you get started programming with Web services, Visual Studio lets you create a Web Service project that provides a code template you can use to develop your own service.

USE IT   To create a simple Web service in Visual Studio, perform these steps:

1. Select File | New Project. Visual Studio will display the New Project dialog box.
2. In the New Project dialog box, click the ASP.NET Web Service icon. In the location field, enter the name **FirstWebService** (as http://localhost/FirstWebService). Click OK. Visual Studio will display your service in design mode, as shown in Figure 16-1.

In Visual Studio, click the hyperlink to the code view or select View | Code. Visual Studio will display the following code template, which it creates for each Web service you create:

```
Imports System.Web.Services

<WebService(Namespace := "http://tempuri.org/")> _
Public Class Service1
    Inherits System.Web.Services.WebService

#Region " Web Services Designer Generated Code "
    Public Sub New()
        MyBase.New()
```

```
        'This call is required by the Web Services Designer.
        InitializeComponent()

        'Add your own initialization code after the InitializeComponent() call
    End Sub


    'Required by the Web Services Designer
    Private components As System.ComponentModel.IContainer

    'NOTE: The following procedure is required by the Web Services Designer
    'It can be modified using the Web Services Designer.
    'Do not modify it using the code editor.
    <System.Diagnostics.DebuggerStepThrough()> Private Sub InitializeComponent()
        components = New System.ComponentModel.Container()
    End Sub


    Protected Overloads Overrides Sub Dispose(ByVal disposing As Boolean)
        'CODEGEN: This procedure is required by the Web Services Designer
        'Do not modify it using the code editor.
        If disposing Then
            If Not (components Is Nothing) Then
                components.Dispose()
            End If
        End If
        MyBase.Dispose(disposing)
    End Sub
#End Region

    ' WEB SERVICE EXAMPLE
    ' The HelloWorld() example service returns the string Hello World.
    ' To build, uncomment the following lines then save and build the project.
    ' To test this web service, ensure that the .asmx file is the start page
    ' and press F5.
    '
    '<WebMethod()> Public Function HelloWorld() As String
    'HelloWorld = "Hello World"
    ' End Function

End Class
```

As you can see in the Web service's template code, the actual service statements are commented out:

```
    '<WebMethod()> Public Function HelloWorld() As String
     'HelloWorld = "Hello World"
      ' End Function
```

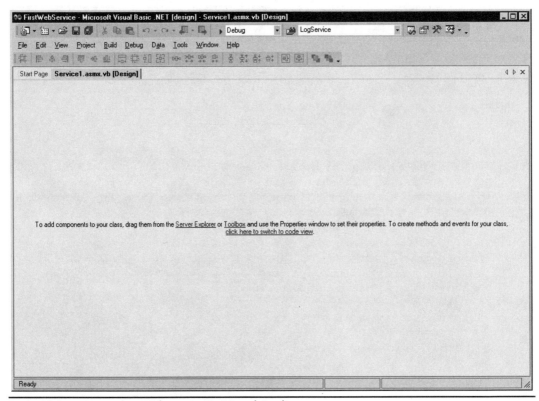

Figure 16-1   Creating a Web service in Visual Studio

In Visual Studio, remove the comments in front of the code. Then compile and build the service. Using the Debug menu Start option, run the service. Visual Studio will launch your browser, loading the page that describes your service, as shown in Figure 16-2.

In this page, click the HelloWorld link. Your browser will display a page that contains an Invoke button you can use to test the service. When you click the Invoke button, your browser will open a second window, as shown in Figure 16-3, within which it displays the service's XML result.

Regardless of the result a Web service provides, the Web service will package that result using XML. When you create programs that use Web services, software within your programs that runs behind the scenes (programmers call this proxy software) will unpack the result from within the XML data.

Next, close the browser windows you opened to display the service. Then, in Visual Studio, change the "Hello World" message in the service to display "Hello, Web Service World" as shown here:

```
<WebMethod()> Public Function HelloWorld() As String
    HelloWorld = "Hello, Web Service World"
End Function
```

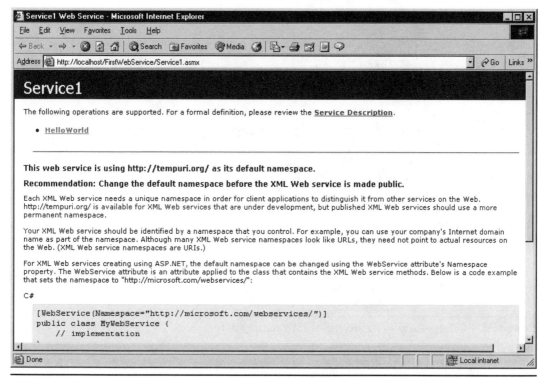

Figure 16-2   Running a simple Web service in Visual Studio

As before, build and start the service. This time, when you click the Invoke button, your service will display the new message. Again close the browser windows. In the Web service code, add the following function that returns the abbreviated name of this book:

```
<WebMethod()> Public Function BookTitle() As String
    BookTitle = "VB.NET Programming Tips & Techniques"
End Function
```

This time, when you build and run the service, the first page the browser creates will contain a BookTitle link and a HelloWorld link. If you click the BookTitle link, your browser will display a page that contains an Invoke button you can use to launch the service. When you click the Invoke button, your browser will open a window with the XML statements that contain the BookTitle function's result, as shown in Figure 16-4.

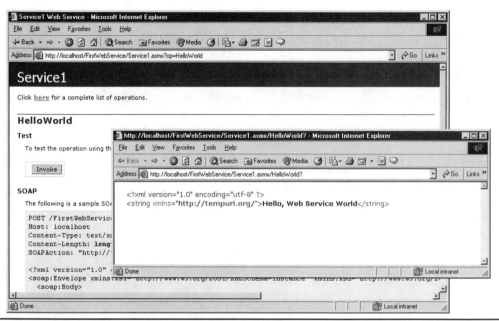

Figure 16-3   Displaying a Web service's XML-based result

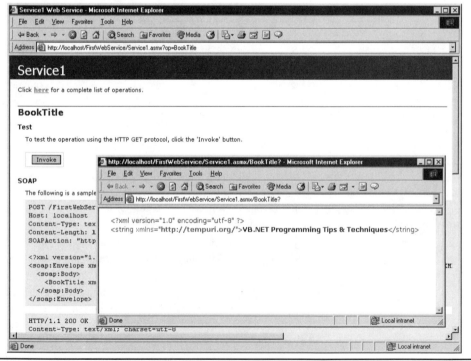

Figure 16-4   Using a Web service to display a book title

Creating a Simple Date/Time Web Service

Using the Visual Studio Web service template code, you can quickly build and test a simple Web service. However, the display of the "Hello World" message is not a very valuable service. In this Tip, you will create a simple date/time service a user can call to get date, time, and day of the week information, as shown in Figure 16-5.

 To create the service, perform these steps:

1. Select File | New Project. Visual Studio will display the New Project dialog box.

2. In the New Project dialog box, click the ASP.NET Web Service icon. In the location field, enter the name **DateTimeService** (as http://localhost/DateTimeService). Click OK. Visual Studio will display your service in design mode.

3. In Visual Studio, click the hyperlink to the code view or select View | Code. Visual Studio will display its Web service code template. In the code section, place the following statements that implement the methods the service provides:

```
<WebMethod()> Public Function DateTime() As String
    DateTime = Now()
End Function

<WebMethod()> Public Function DateOnly() As String
    Dim DT As New DateTime(Now.Ticks)

    DateOnly = Date.Today.Date
End Function

<WebMethod()> Public Function TimeOnly() As String
    TimeOnly = Now().TimeOfDay.ToString
End Function

<WebMethod()> Public Function DayOfWeek() As String
    Dim Days() As String = {"Sunday", "Monday", "Tuesday", _
        "Wednesday", "Thursday", "Friday", "Saturday"}

    DayOfWeek = Days(Now().DayOfWeek)
End Function
```

As you can see, the code defines four functions, each of which return String values (although, as you will learn, a Web service can return any type of value). Again, use Visual Studio to build and then run the service. Visual Studio will display a page that contains links for each function. When you click the link, your browser will display a page that contains an Invoke button you can use to run the service. When you click the Invoke button, your browser will open a new window that contains the Web service's XML result, as shown in Figure 16-6.

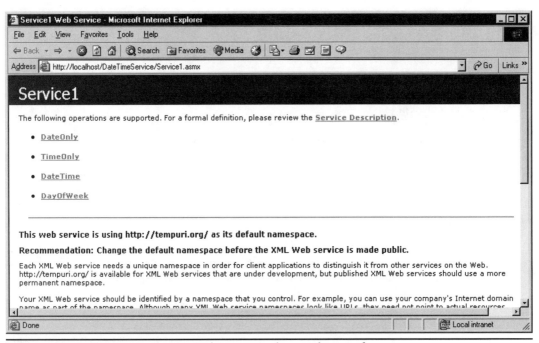

Figure 16-5   Creating a Web service that returns date and time information

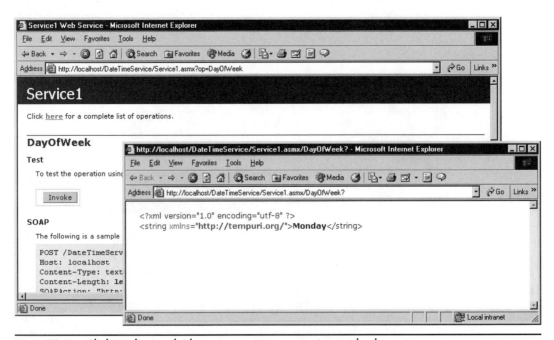

Figure 16-6   Clicking the Invoke button to execute a service method

Although this service provides only slightly more functionality than the standard Web service template demo, the service is still quite simplistic in that its methods do not receive parameters from the user.

Writing a Web Service that Uses Parameter-Based Methods

To perform useful work, a Web service will normally receive data from the client that is "consuming" the capability the service provides. In this Tip, you will create a Web service that calculates the monthly payment for a mortgage amount, given the number of years and interest rate, as shown in Figure 16-7.

To create the Web service, perform these steps:

1. Select File | New Project. Visual Studio will display the New Project dialog box.

2. In the New Project dialog box, click the ASP.NET Web Service icon. In the location field, enter the name **MortgagePayment** (as http://localhost/MortgagePayment). Click OK. Visual Studio will display your service in design mode.

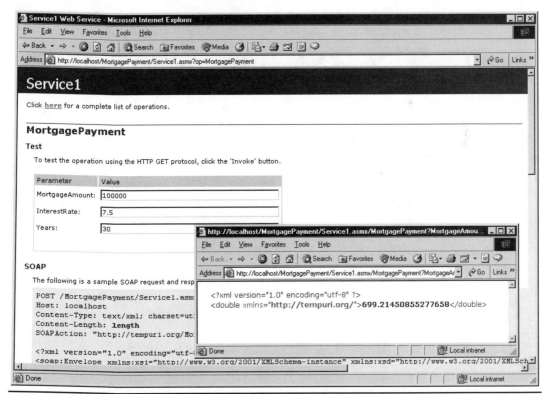

Figure 16-7   A Web service that returns mortgage payment amount

3. In Visual Studio, click the hyperlink to the code view or select View | Code. Visual Studio will display its Web service code template. In the code section, place the following statements that implement the method the service provides:

```
<WebMethod()> Public Function MortgagePayment(ByVal _
  MortgageAmount As Double, ByVal InterestRate As Double, _
  ByVal Years As Integer) As Double

  Dim MonthlyInterest = InterestRate / 12 / 100.0
  Dim Months = Years * 12

  MortgagePayment = MortgageAmount * _
    (MonthlyInterest/(1.0 - Math.Pow(1.0 + MonthlyInterest, -Months)))
End Function
```

As you can see, the MortgagePayment service requires three parameters. Using Visual Studio, build and run the service. Visual Studio will launch your browser, which will display a page that you can use to launch the service. In this case, your browser will display a page, as shown in Figure 16-8, within which you can specify values for the method's three parameters.

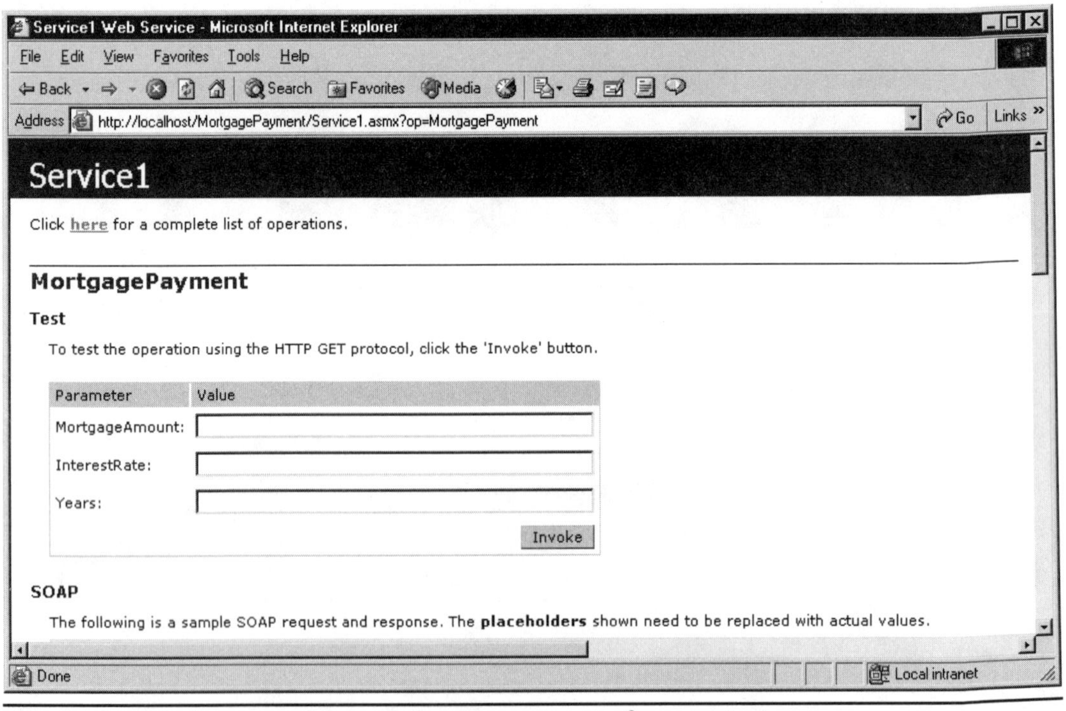

Figure 16-8 Displaying a Web page that prompts a user for a service's parameters

After you enter the parameter values and click the Invoke button, your browser will open a new window that contains the service's XML-based result:

```
<?xml version="1.0" encoding="utf-8" ?>
<double xmlns="http://tempuri.org/">699.21450855277658</double>
```

Note that the XML uses the <double> tag to indicate that the value the service returns is type Double.

Using an HTML Form to Interact with a Web Service

In the previous three Tips, you have run the Web services that you created from within Visual Studio. In this Tip, you will create an HTML-based form, as shown in Figure 16-9, which submits data to a Web service.

 USE IT To create the form, place the following HTML statements in the file ServiceDemo.html:

```
<html>
<head>
   <title>ServiceDemo</title>
</head>
<body>
  <center><h1>Demo MortgatePayment Web Service</h1></center><hr/>

  <form
   action="http://localhost/MortgagePayment/service1.asmx/MortgagePayment"
   method="GET">

  Mortgate Amount:
   <input type="text" maxlength="50" name="MortgageAmount"/><br/>

    Interest Rate:
    <input type="text" maxlength="50" name="InterestRate"/><br/>

    Years:
    <input type="text" maxlength="50" name="Years"/><br/>
    <br/></br>

    <input type="submit" value="Submit">
  </form>
</body>
</html>
```

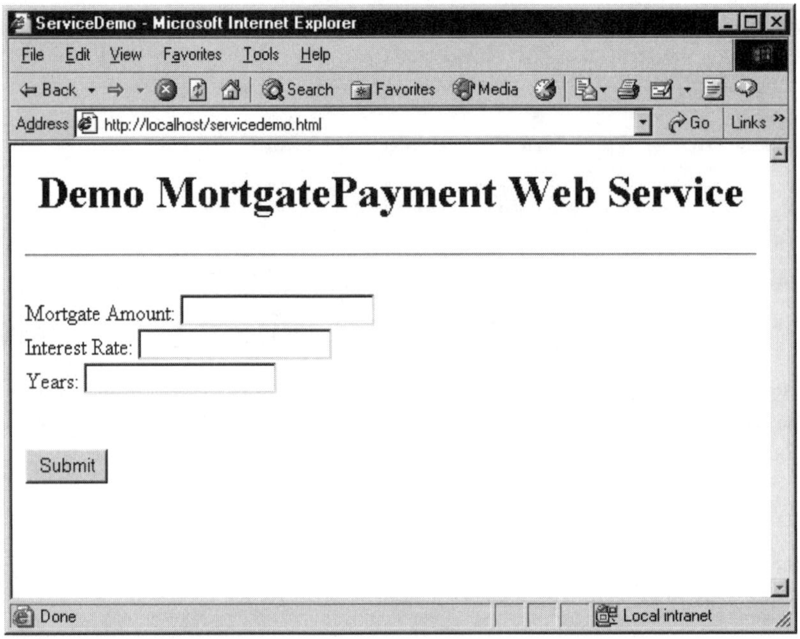

Figure 16-9   Using an HTML-based form to submit data to a Web service

The form, in this case, uses three variables whose names match the parameters that the Web service expects. When the user clicks the Submit button, the browser will send the form's data to the service using a GET operation. Note the URL the form uses to specify the MortgagePayment method in the service1.asmx file:

```
action="http://localhost/MortgagePayment/service1.asmx/MortgagePayment"
```

When you use the form to submit data to the Web service, the service will calculate its result and then package and return the result as an XML object, as shown in Figure 16-10.

Admittedly, although the XML contains the correct result, an application would ideally display the result in a more meaningful format. As you will learn in the next Tip, by creating special software programmers call a proxy, your applications can easily unpack a Web service's XML result.

Creating a Proxy for Your Web Service

As you have learned, when a Web service returns a result to a client, the Web service packages the result using XML. To process the data a Web service returns, you could write a program that performs HTTP and SOAP operations to interact with the service, and then parses the XML result. Fortunately, rather than having to write such complex code, you can use Visual Studio to create a proxy object that performs the processing on the client's behalf.

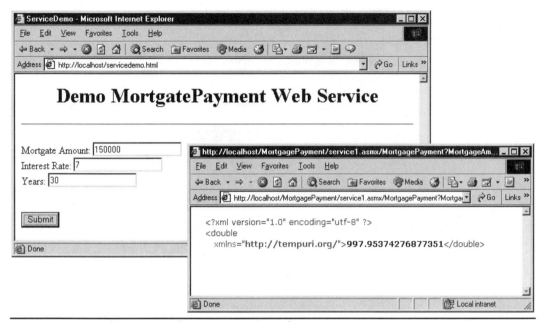

Figure 16-10   Displaying a Web service's XML result

In general, a proxy is an object specific to a Web service. Rather than directly accessing the Web service object, your program (or ASP.NET page) uses the proxy. The proxy, in turn, will interact with the Web service, making sense of the HTTP and SOAP protocols, and parsing the XML data to provide your code with the result it requires.

In a program that uses Web services, you must create a proxy for each Web service your code will use. The proxy essentially defines a class.

USE IT   The following program, UseWebService.vb, displays a form in which the user can enter mortgage information, as shown in Figure 16-11. When the user clicks the Calc Monthly Payment button, the code uses the Web service MortgagePayment method to determine the monthly payment.

To begin, use Visual Studio to create the UseWebService.vb program and to design the form previously shown. Then to create the proxy for the Web service, perform these steps:

1. In Visual Studio, select Project | Add Web Reference. Visual Studio will display the Add Web Reference dialog box.

2. In the Add Web Reference dialog box, you can browse for a Web reference (either on the Web or the local host) or you can type in the service's URL (which in this case is http://localhost/ MortgagePayment/Service1.asmx). After you select the service, Visual Studio will display specifics about the service. Click the Add Reference button.

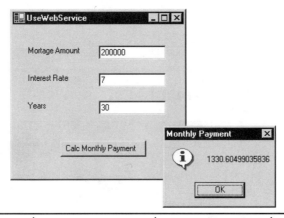

Figure 16-11 Using a Visual Basic .NET program that connects to a Web service

The proxy is now ready for use in your program. To use the proxy, you will create an object that corresponds to the service, as shown here:

```
Dim MortgageService As New localhost.Service1()
```

After you create the object, your code can then call the service's methods using the dot operator as shown here:

```
MonthlyPayment = MortgageService.MortgagePayment(100000, 7.5, 30)
```

In the UseWebService.vb program, place the following code for the Button1_Click event handler that uses the MortgagePayment service to determine the monthly payment based on the values the user enters:

```
Private Sub Button1_Click(ByVal sender As Object, _
   ByVal e As System.EventArgs) Handles Button1.Click

   If (TextBox1.Text.Length = 0) Then
     MsgBox("Must specify mortgage amount")
   ElseIf (TextBox2.Text.Length = 0) Then
     MsgBox("Must specify interest rate")
   ElseIf (TextBox3.Text.Length = 0) Then
     MsgBox("Must specify the number of years")
   Else
     Dim MortgageService As New localhost.Service1()

     MsgBox(MortgageService.MortgagePayment(TextBox1.Text, _
       TextBox2.Text, TextBox3.Text), MsgBoxStyle.Information, _
       "Monthly Payment")
```

```
      End If
End Sub
```

For simplicity, the code does not validate the values the user enters. The code's purpose is to demonstrate how easily you can integrate a Web service into your code.

Using a Web Service from Within an ASP.NET Page

After you create a Web service, you can easily use the service within a Visual Basic .NET program by using Visual Studio to add a Web reference to your project file. In a similar way, if you use Visual Studio to create an ASP.NET page, you again simply add a Web reference to your project to provide your script with access to a Web Service.

USE IT   The following ASP.NET page, Mortgage.aspx, creates a Web form, as shown in Figure 16-12, which prompts the user for mortgage information. Chapter 15 discusses Web forms in detail.

To begin, you must first create the ASP.NET page by performing these steps:

1. In Visual Studio, select File | New Project. Visual Studio will display the New Project dialog box.

2. In the New Project dialog box, click the ASP.NET Application icon and place the project in the location http://localhost/mortgage.

3. Create a form that contains the buttons shown in Figure 16-12.

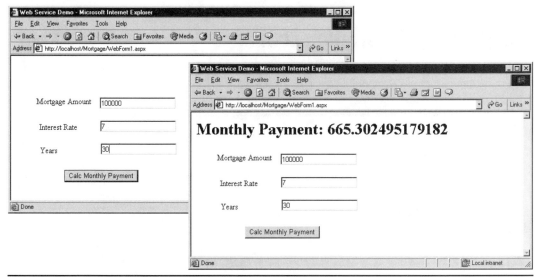

Figure 16-12   Connecting an ASP.NET page to a Web service

You are now ready to create the proxy that the page will use to interact with the MortgagePayment service. To create the proxy in Visual Studio, perform the following steps:

1. Select Project | Add Web Reference. Visual Studio will display the Add Web Reference dialog box.

2. In the Add Web Reference dialog box, you can browse for a Web reference (either on the Web or the local host) or you can type in the service's URL (which in this case is http://localhost/ MortgagePayment/Service1.asmx). After you select the service, Visual Studio will display specifics about the service. Click the Add Reference button.

Next, use Visual Studio to design the page's form. Finally, in the Button1_Click event handler, the code creates an object that corresponds to the Web service, which it uses to call the MortgagePayment method:

```
Private Sub Button1_Click(ByVal sender As Object, _
   ByVal e As System.EventArgs) Handles Button1.Click

      Dim MortgageService As New localhost.Service1()

      Response.Write("<h1>Monthly Payment: " & _
         MortgageService.MortgagePayment(TextBox1.Text, _
         TextBox2.Text, TextBox3.Text) & "</h1>")

End Sub
```

Looking Behind the Scenes at Your Service's Web Service Description Language

When you create a Web service using Visual Studio, Visual Studio will create a file with the .wsdl extension that uses the Web Service Description Language to describe how clients interact with the service. In other words, the WSDL file defines each of the methods, the parameters to each method, the type of value each method returns, and so on. WSDL is a metalanguage that describes a Web service using XML.

USE IT   Using your Web browser, you can view the WSDL statements that describe a Web service, as shown in Figure 16-13. To view a service's WSDL statements, you specify the service's URL followed by a question mark and the letters WSDL. For example, to view the WSDL for the MortgagePayment Web service, you would specify http://localhost/MortgagePayment/ Service1.asmx?wsdl.

If you examine the WSDL statements closely, you will find statements that describe the MortgagePayment function as well as its parameters, as shown here:

```
<s:element name="MortgagePayment">
 <s:complexType>
  <s:sequence>
    <s:element minOccurs="1" maxOccurs="1"
       name="MortgageAmount" type="s:double" />
    <s:element minOccurs="1" maxOccurs="1"
       name="InterestRate" type="s:double" />
    <s:element minOccurs="1" maxOccurs="1"
       name="Years" type="s:int" />
  </s:sequence>
 </s:complexType>
</s:element>
```

By examining a service's WSDL statements, a proxy can determine how to interact with a service using HTTP GET or POST operations, SOAP operations, and so on. In the WSDL statements, you can locate the message format that corresponds to such operations.

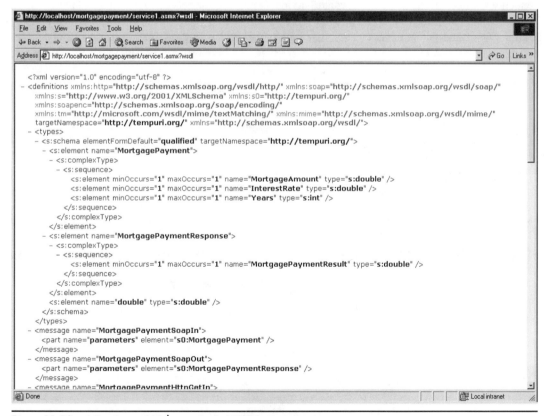

Figure 16-13   Viewing a Web service's WSDL statements

Handling Exceptions in Web Services

When you create a Web service, there may be times the service encounters an error that generates an exception. In such cases, the Web service should handle the exception itself. However, if the service fails to handle the exception, it will be forwarded to the calling program. The following Web Service, DivNumbers, provides the DivideTwoNumbers method, which divides two numbers and returns the integer result. If a division-by-zero error occurs, the function does not detect the exception:

```
<WebMethod()> Public Function DivideTwoNumbers(ByVal A _
    As Integer, ByVal B As Integer) As Integer

    DivideTwoNumbers = A / B

End Function
```

In Visual Studio, build and start the service. Visual Studio will display a page about the service in your browser. In this page, click the DivideTwoNumbers link. Your browser will display a page in which you can enter the values you want to divide and invoke the service. To start, test the service using two numbers such as 25 and 5. Your browser will open a window that contains the service's result. Next, enter the numbers 10 and 0 and invoke the service. Because the service does not handle the divide-by-zero exception, the service will crash and will not provide a result. Your browser will display a page that contains an error message.

The following code fragment illustrates the Web services used in a Visual Basic .NET program:

```
Private Sub Button1_Click(ByVal sender As Object, _
    ByVal e As System.EventArgs) Handles Button1.Click

    Dim DivNumbers As New localhost.Service1()

    MsgBox("<h1>Division Result: " & _
        DivNumbers.DivideTwoNumbers(10, 0) & "</h1>")
End Sub
```

When you execute this code, your screen will display an error message similar to that shown here.

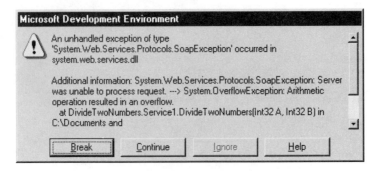

Within your code, you can handle the Web service's exception by using a Try-Catch statement similar to the following:

```
Try
    MsgBox("<h1>Division Result: " & _
       DivNumbers.DivideTwoNumbers(10, 0) & "</h1>")
Catch
    MsgBox("Exception occurred in Web service")
End Try
```

Leveraging the Web Service Configuration Files

When you use Visual Studio to create a Web service, Visual Studio will place the application in its own folder. In addition to a service's source file, Visual Studio will place several files in the folder that you can use to customize the application's processing. Table 16-1 briefly describes the various file types Visual Studio creates for a Web service.

USE IT   Depending on the processing a service performs, there may be times when you will want the service to perform specific operations each time a user requests service. In such cases, you can place a subroutine similar to the following in the Global.asax.vb file that executes each time a request begins. In this case, the service will create an entry in the Application log file that specifies when the session began:

```
Sub Application_BeginRequest(ByVal sender As Object, _
   ByVal e As EventArgs)
       Dim Log As New EventLog("Application")

       Log.Source = "Some Web Service"
       Log.WriteEntry("Service session at: " & Now())
       Log.Close()
End Sub
```

File	Contents
AppName.aspx, AppName.aspx.vb, AppName.aspx.resx	Contain the page's design template and the corresponding code-behind file that performs the form's processing. The .resx file is a resource file used by Web forms. The AppName corresponds to the page's application name.
AppName.vsdisco	Contains entries remote applications can use to discover the service.
Assembly.vb	Contains the assembly attributes. Visual Studio creates the Assembly.vb file for all .NET projects.

Table 16-1   Configuration Files You Can Use to Customize a Web Service

File	Contents
Global.asax, Global.asax.vb, Global.asax.resx	Provide support application (and error, request, response, and session) event handling.
Styles.css	Defines the application's cascading style sheet.
Web.config	Defines an application's runtime attributes.

Table 16-1 Configuration Files You Can Use to Customize a Web Service *(continued)*

Looking Behind the Scenes at Your Web Service's SOAP

Behind the scenes, to call a Web service, a proxy packages together the messages that specify the method to invoke and the parameters the method is to use. Later, after the service completes its processing, the service packages together a message that it sends to the proxy that contains the result. To format these messages, the proxy and the Web service use the Simple Object Access Protocol (SOAP). In general, the SOAP messages are simply XML-based entries.

USE IT To view the format of a Web service's SOAP messages, use your Web browser, type in the service's URL (such as http://localhost/DateTimeService/Service1.asmx). Your browser will display a page that describes the service's methods. Click one of the service links. Your browser will display a page in which you can call the service. If you scroll down the page, you can view the SOAP messages a proxy uses to interact with the service, as shown in Figure 16-14.

Building a Proxy Using WSDL.EXE

As you have learned, with respect to a Web service, a proxy is special software that your program can use to call a Web service. The proxy, in turn, takes care of packaging the messages that interact with the service and which later convert the XML-based data into types your programs can easily access. In addition to letting you create a proxy from within Visual Studio, you can also build a proxy using a command line program named WSDL.EXE that Visual Studio provides. For example, to create a proxy for the MortgagePayment service, you would use WSDL as follows (the following command assumes you have placed the program file WSDL.EXE into the command path):

```
C:\SomeDirectory> WSDL /l:vb /out:MortgageProxy.vb
   http://localhost/MortgagePayment/Service1.asmx?WSDL   <Enter>
```

In this case, the WSDL command will create a Visual Basic file named MortgageProxy.vb that contains the proxy's statements:

```
Option Strict Off
Option Explicit On
```

```
Imports System
Imports System.ComponentModel
Imports System.Diagnostics
Imports System.Web.Services
Imports System.Web.Services.Protocols
Imports System.Xml.Serialization


'
'This source code was auto-generated by wsdl, Version=1.0.3512.0.
'


'<remarks/>
<System.Diagnostics.DebuggerStepThroughAttribute(),  _
 System.ComponentModel.DesignerCategoryAttribute("code"),  _
 System.Web.Services.WebServiceBindingAttribute(Name:="Service1Soap",
 [Namespace]:="http://tempuri.org/")>  _
Public Class Service1
    Inherits System.Web.Services.Protocols.SoapHttpClientProtocol

    '<remarks/>
    Public Sub New()
        MyBase.New
        Me.Url = "http://localhost/MortgagePayment/Service1.asmx"
    End Sub

    '<remarks/>

<System.Web.Services.Protocols.SoapDocumentMethodAttribute _
    ("http://tempuri.org/MortgagePayment", _
    RequestNamespace:="http://tempuri.org/", _
    ResponseNamespace:="http://tempuri.org/", _
    Use:=System.Web.Services.Description.SoapBindingUse.Literal, _
    ParameterStyle := _
        System.Web.Services.Protocols.SoapParameterStyle.Wrapped)>  _

    Public Function MortgagePayment(ByVal MortgageAmount As Double, _
      ByVal InterestRate As Double, ByVal Years As Integer) As Double
        Dim results() As Object = Me.Invoke("MortgagePayment", _
          New Object() {MortgageAmount, InterestRate, Years})
        Return CType(results(0),Double)
    End Function

    '<remarks/>
    Public Function BeginMortgagePayment(ByVal _
```

```
        MortgageAmount As Double, ByVal InterestRate As Double, _
        ByVal Years As Integer, ByVal callback As System.AsyncCallback, _
        ByVal asyncState As Object) As System.IasyncResult

            Return Me.BeginInvoke("MortgagePayment", _
                New Object() {MortgageAmount, InterestRate, Years}, _
                    callback, asyncState)
        End Function


        '<remarks/>
        Public Function EndMortgagePayment(ByVal asyncResult _
            As System.IAsyncResult) As Double
                Dim results() As Object = Me.EndInvoke(asyncResult)
                Return CType(results(0),Double)
        End Function
    End Class
```

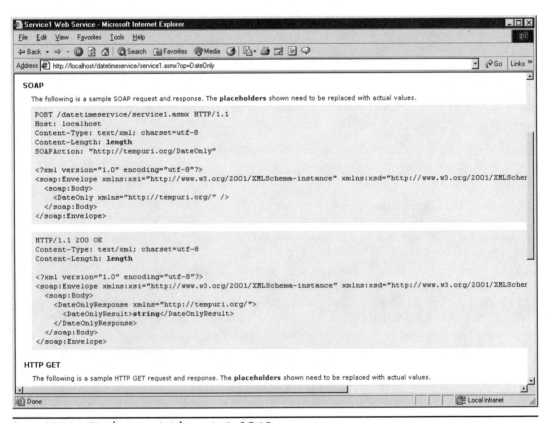

Figure 16-14 Displaying a Web service's SOAP messages

As you can see, the proxy inherits the SoapHttpClientProtocol class. The proxy provides a synchronous and asynchronous implementation of the MortgagePayment function. The synchronous method call uses HTTP to access the service (a GET or POST operation). The asynchronous method call uses SOAP to interact with the service. After you create a proxy file using the WSDL command, you can then include the file in your project (by selecting File | Add Existing Item), in order to access the Web service. Next, you must add a reference to the System.WebServices.dll file by selecting Project | Add Reference. Then, in your code, you can create an object that corresponds to the Web service as follows:

```
Dim MortgageService As New Service1()
Dim Payment As Double

Payment = MortgageService.MortgagePayment(100000, 7.5, 30))
```

In this case, the code creates an object of the class Service1 (as opposed to localhost.Service1 which you used earlier when you created the proxy in Visual Studio). If you examine the proxy source code, you will find that the code creates a class named Service1.

Changing the Web Service Namespace

Eventually, the Web may offer thousands (if not hundreds of thousands) of Web services. To avoid name conflicts between services, you must assign each service to a unique namespace. By default, when you create a Web service in Visual Studio, the code template that Visual Studio creates uses the namespace http://tempuri.org/, as shown here:

```
<WebService(Namespace := "http://tempuri.org/")> _
Public Class Service1
```

USE IT Although you can use this default namespace for testing, before you place a Web service on the Web for use, you should assign a namespace that corresponds to your site's URL. After you change the namespace in a service, you will need to update existing proxy code that may have referenced the old namespace.

Helping Others Discover Your Web Service

After you create a Web service, there may be times when you will want to publish the service for use by others across the Web. To help users (programmers, actually) discover the Web services that exist on the Web, several software companies created the Universal Description, Discovery, and Integration (UDDI) service. In general, the UDDI is a Web service you (and your applications) can use to discover other Web services that are available for use on the Web. For specifics on the UDDI protocol, visit http://www.uddi.org/. At this Web site, you can also register your company as a developer of Web services, which will help others find your services in the future.

Across the Web, a myriad of sites offer Web services. To help you locate specific Web services quickly, several sites, such as Microsoft, have created UDDI directories of available services. When you use the Visual Studio Add Web Reference dialog box to create a proxy for a Web service, you can search services that reside in the Microsoft UDDI directory. At the Microsoft UDDI Web site (http://www.uddi.microsoft.com/), you can register information about the services you create. To specify information about your Web services, you register the URLs that correspond to each service's discovery file, which as you will learn, Visual Studio automatically creates when you build a Web service.

USE IT   As you know, when you use Visual Studio to create a Web service, Visual Studio will create several different files you can use to customize your service's processing (see the Tip titled "Leveraging the Web Service Configuration Files"). One of the files Visual Studio creates for your Web service is a file with the .disco extension (short for discovery). Using your browser, you can view the file's XML contents, as shown in Figure 16-15. As you can see, the .disco file displays a URL a user can view to learn more about the service (such as the methods the service offers and the parameters to each—much like you did earlier in this chapter when you tested services in Visual Studio).

In addition to locating your files in a directory, programmers may use Web robots that visit servers in search of files with the .disco extension in order to locate Web services on the Web. If you do not want others to "discover" your services, simply delete the .disco files from your server.

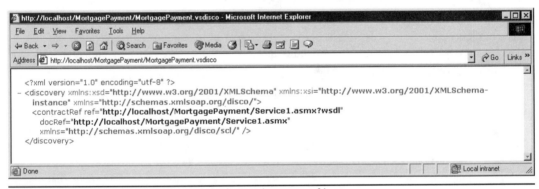

Figure 16-15   Viewing a Web service's disco (discovery) file

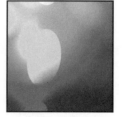

CHAPTER 17

Getting Started with ADO.NET

TIPS IN THIS CHAPTER

For years, programmers have made extensive use of Active Data Objects (ADO) to simplify database applications. The .NET environment brings with it a new model for database access called ADO.NET that provides significant function improvements over the ADO model. The ADO.NET model introduces the DataSet object, which replaces the RecordSet that programmers used in the past with ADO. Throughout this chapter, you will examine programs that use the DataSet object to perform operations without having to maintain a constant connection to the database, which is ideal for Web-based applications. Using a DataSet object, the application will query and then disconnect from a database, perform its processing, and later reconnect to the database to update the database with the changes to the data that it has made.

The ADO.NET model is very powerful and can be quite complex. Many outstanding books exist that focus purely on ADO.NET. This chapter's goal is to get you up and running with ADO.NET operations. You will learn how to connect to, query, and update databases. You will also examine how the ADO.NET model exploits XML to provide structure to the data the DataSet object contains. Finally, you will perform ADO.NET operations from within an ASP.NET page and you will map data stored in a table to a DataGrid control for display.

Specifying a Data Provider

In the ADO.NET model, the two key components are the data provider (the software that interacts with the database) and the data set that contains the data that results from the operation your code performs. The data provider software consists of four objects. The Connection object provides the software that connects (allows access to) the database. The Command object provides software that lets your programs perform queries against the database. The DataReader object is a stream-based read-only data source that provides better performance for applications that do not update data. Finally, the DataAdapter object provides the interface between the data source and the data set.

In general, the data provider is the software your program will use to connect and query a database. The ADO.NET environment supports the SQL Server .NET Data Provider and the OLE DB.NET Data provider. In the .NET environment, programmers often refer to the OLE DB.NET Data Provider as the ADO Managed Provider. Likewise, programmers often refer to the SQL data provider as the SQL Managed Provider. The ADO Managed Provider software should support most common OLE-based data providers (including ODBC-based databases).

As you examine the ADO.NET classes, you will find that the ADO Managed Provider class names begin with the letters OleDB, such as OleDBConnection, whereas the SQL Managed Provider class names start with the letters SQL, such as SqlConnection.

USE IT To connect to a database, your program first creates a Connection object. The following
statement, for example, creates a connection for an ADO Managed Provider, using the
ADOConnection class:

```
Dim Connect As New OleDBConnection("Provider=SQLOLEDB; " & _
    "Initial Catalog=Duwamish7vb; Data Source=(local); "& _
    "User ID=sa;password=;")
```

Likewise, the following statement creates a Connection object for a SQL Managed provider,
using the SqlConnection class:

```
Dim Connect As New SqlConnection("Initial Catalog=Duwamish7vb; " _
        & "Data Source=(local);User ID=sa;password=;")
```

Note that the OleDBConnection requires you to specify a Provider attribute, whereas the
SqlConnection does not.

After you create the Connection object, you actually establish the database connection by calling
the Connection class Open method. If the Open method encounters an error, it will raise an exception,
which your code should detect and handle using a Try-Catch statement as shown here:

```
Try
  Connect.Open()
Catch Ex As Exception
  Console.WriteLine("Exception: " & Ex.Message)
End Try
```

If the Open method is successful, your code can then perform queries against the database to
create a DataSet. After your code completes its processing, you should call the Connection class
Close method to end the connection, as shown here:

```
Connect.Close()
```

The following program, ConnectDB.vb, uses the SqlConnection class to establish a connection
to the Duwamish7vb database, provided with Visual Studio. If the program successfully connects to
the database, the program will display a message box so stating. If the program instead encounters an
error, the program will display a message box that describes the exception:

```
Imports System.Data.SqlClient

Module Module1

  Sub Main()
    Try
      Dim Connect As New SqlConnection("Initial Catalog=Duwamish7vb; " _
```

```
         & "Data Source=(local);User ID=sa;password=;")

      Connect.Open()
      Console.WriteLine("Database: " & Connect.Database)
      Console.WriteLine("Database: " & Connect.ServerVersion)
      Console.WriteLine("Database: " & Connect.DataSource)
      Connect.Close()

      Console.ReadLine()
   Catch Ex As Exception
      Console.WriteLine("Exception: " & Ex.Message)
      Console.WriteLine(Ex.ToString)
      Console.ReadLine()
   End Try

   End Sub

End Module
```

After you compile and execute this program, it should display output similar to the following:

```
Database: Duwamish7vb
Database: 08.00.0194
Database: (local)
```

Although the program's processing is quite simple, you may want to use the code to get you up and running with each database application you create. Using the code, you can quickly identify potential problems such as an invalid username and password for the account that provides access to the database.

Issuing a Query Using a DataReader Object

After your program uses a Connection object to successfully connect to a database, you are ready to issue a query against the data source that creates either a DataSet or DataReader object. When your program requires read-only access to a query result (meaning your program will not make changes to the query records and use the changes to update the database), you can improve performance by using a DataReader object. Unlike a DataSet object that buffers all the data a query returns, a DataReader object buffers one row of data at a time (one record), so the DataReader object does not place as much overhead on the server. The disadvantage of using a DataReader object, however, is that the object requires a constant connection to the database, which increases network overhead.

To issue a query against a data source, you will use a Command object (which, depending on your data provider type, will use the ADOCommand or SQLCommand class). When you create the command object, you can specify your SQL query in the object's constructor method. The following statement, for example, creates a SqlCommand that will query a table named Authors in the database that corresponds, in this case, to the Connect object for all the fields in the table:

```
Dim Command As New SqlCommand("SELECT * From Authors", Connect)
```

As you can see, the Command object specifies the actual query as well as the Connection object that corresponds to the data source. As discussed, depending on how you will use the data, you will create either a DataSet or DataReader object to hold the query result. The following statement, for example, creates a DataReader object:

```
Dim objDataReader As SqlDataReader
```

To actually perform the query operation, your code must call the Command class Execute method, as shown here:

```
ObjCommand.Execute(objDataReader)
```

USE IT The following program, QueryDB.vb, connects to the Duwamish7vb database and then performs a query using a DataReader object that retrieves all the fields in the table. The program then uses a While loop to display the resulting records:

```
Imports System.Data.SqlClient

Module Module1

  Sub Main()
    Try
      Dim Connect As New SqlConnection("Initial Catalog=Duwamish7vb;" _
        & " Data Source=(local);User ID=sa;password=;")

      Connect.Open()
      Console.WriteLine("Database: " & Connect.Database)
      Console.WriteLine("Database: " & Connect.ServerVersion)
      Console.WriteLine("Database: " & Connect.DataSource)

      Dim Command As New SqlCommand("SELECT * From Authors", Connect)

      Dim Reader As SqlDataReader = _
        Command.ExecuteReader(CommandBehavior.CloseConnection)
      While Reader.Read()
        Console.WriteLine(Reader.GetSqlValue(1))
      End While
```

```
      Console.ReadLine()
    Catch Ex As Exception
      Console.WriteLine("Exception: " & Ex.Message)
      Console.WriteLine(Ex.ToString)
      Console.ReadLine()
    End Try

  End Sub

End Module
```

As you can see, after the code creates the Reader object, it uses a While loop to read and display each of the records. The program does not have to close the connection in this case, because the ExecuteReader method uses the value CommandBehavior.CloseConnection to automatically close the connection after the program reads the last record.

Issuing a Query Using a DataSet Object

In the previous Tip, you used a DataReader object to query the Duwamish7vb database. As you learned, a DataReader object is ideal for read-only query operations. If you must update the database contents, your programs should instead use a DataSet object.

USE IT   The following program, DataSetQuery.vb, uses a DataSet object to query the Duwamish7vb database. The program uses the query to retrieve the list of names in the Authors table. Then the program moves through the DataSet object in a For loop to display the author names. This program does not change the contents of the database. You will learn how to update the database using a DataSet object in the next Tip. This program illustrates the steps you must perform to use a DataSet object to query a database:

```
Imports System.Data.SqlClient
Imports System.Data

Module Module1

  Sub Main()
    Try
      Dim Connect As New SqlConnection("Initial Catalog=Duwamish7vb;" _
        & "Data Source=(local);User ID=sa;password=;")

      Connect.Open()
      Console.WriteLine("Database: " & Connect.Database)
      Console.WriteLine("Database: " & Connect.ServerVersion)
      Console.WriteLine("Database: " & Connect.DataSource)
```

```
    Dim Command As String = "SELECT * From Authors"

    Dim DS As New DataSet()

    Dim Adapter = New SqlDataAdapter(Command, Connect)

    Adapter.Fill(DS)

    Dim I As Integer

    For I = 0 To DS.Tables(0).Rows.Count - 1
        Console.WriteLine(DS.Tables(0).Rows(I).Item(1))
    Next

    Console.ReadLine()
  Catch Ex As Exception
    Console.WriteLine("Exception: " & Ex.Message)
    Console.WriteLine(Ex.ToString)
    Console.ReadLine()
  End Try

  End Sub


End Module
```

Handling Data Set Updates Behind the Scenes

When you manipulate data using a data set, you will often make changes to data. Programmers refer to the data providers in the ADO.NET environment as managed providers because the providers, behind the scenes, will update the database contents based on the changes you make in a data set. To perform updates between your data set and the database, you must use a DataAdapter object. In general, the DataAdapter sits between the database and the data set. The DataAdapter performs the behind-the-scenes operations necessary to implement the changes you make to the data set back into the correct database locations.

The secret to updating a database using a DataAdapter is to create a SqlCommandBuilder object to which you pass the DataAdapter. The SqlCommandBuilder object, in turn, will monitor insert, delete, and update operations. Then, when your operations are complete, the SqlCommandBuilder object will create a query that the Update method uses behind the scenes to update the database tables with the changes you have made to the data set.

USE IT   The following program, ChangeAndUpdate.vb, queries the Duwamish7vb database to retrieve the list of authors. The code then converts each author name to uppercase. After the code has completed its processing, it calls the Update method to store the changes back into the

database. The key to the update's ease of use is the SqlCommandBuilder object, which builds the
query the program uses to update the database:

```
Imports System.Data.SqlClient
Imports System.Data

Module Module1

  Sub Main()
    Try
      Dim Connect As New SqlConnection("Initial Catalog=Duwamish7vb;" _
        " Data Source=(local);User ID=sa;password=;")

      Connect.Open()
      Console.WriteLine("Database: " & Connect.Database)
      Console.WriteLine("Database: " & Connect.ServerVersion)
      Console.WriteLine("Database: " & Connect.DataSource)

      Dim Command As String = "SELECT * From Authors"
      Dim DS As New DataSet()

      Dim Adapter As SqlDataAdapter = New SqlDataAdapter(Command, Connect)
      Dim CmdBuilder As SqlCommandBuilder = New SqlCommandBuilder(Adapter)

      Adapter.Fill(DS)

      Dim I As Integer

      For I = 0 To DS.Tables(0).Rows.Count - 1
        DS.Tables(0).Rows(I).Item(1) = UCase(DS.Tables(0).Rows(I).Item(1))
      Next

      Adapter.UpdateCommand = CmdBuilder.GetUpdateCommand()
      Adapter.Update(DS.Tables(0))
      Console.WriteLine("Update Complete")

      Console.ReadLine()
    Catch Ex As Exception
      Console.WriteLine("Exception: " & Ex.Message)
      Console.WriteLine(Ex.ToString)
      Console.ReadLine()
    End Try

  End Sub

End Module
```

Querying a Database about Its Tables

In the ADO.NET environment, a data set holds the results of a query. A data set actually consists of one or more tables. Data sets store each table's contents using a DataTable object. A data set can have one or more data tables. Further, a data set can maintain relationships between the data tables. In a DataSet object, the Tables collection tracks each DataTable object. A program can reference a table using an index into the Tables collection, or by name. The following code fragment, for example, uses a For Each loop to display the name of each data table in a DataSet object:

```
Dim TableObj As DataTable

For Each TableObj In DataSet.Obj.Tables
  Console.WriteLine(TableObj.TableName)
Next
```

USE IT   When you use a database, there may be times when you do not immediately know the specifics about the database, such as the tables it provides. In such cases, your programs can query the database schema information. The following query retrieves the names of the tables in the database:

```
Dim Command As String = "SELECT table_name From Information_Schema.Tables"
```

The following program, DatabaseTableNames.vb, queries the Duwamish7vb database about the tables it contains:

```
Imports System.Data.SqlClient
Imports System.Data

Module Module1

  Sub Main()
    Try
      Dim Connect As New SqlConnection("Initial Catalog=Duwamish7vb;" _
        & "Data Source=(local);User ID=sa;password=;")

      Connect.Open()
      Console.WriteLine("Database: " & Connect.Database)

      Dim Command As String = _
        "SELECT table_name From Information_Schema.Tables"

      Dim DS As New DataSet()
```

```
        Dim Adapter = New SqlDataAdapter(Command, Connect)

        Adapter.Fill(DS)

        Dim I As Integer

        For I = 0 To DS.Tables(0).Rows.Count - 1
            Console.WriteLine(DS.Tables(0).Rows(I).Item(0))
        Next

        Console.ReadLine()

        Catch Ex As Exception
            Console.WriteLine("Exception: " & Ex.Message)
            Console.WriteLine(Ex.ToString)
            Console.ReadLine()
        End Try

    End Sub
End Module
```

After you compile and execute this program, your screen will display the following output:

```
Database: Duwamish7vb
Database: 08.00.0194
Database: (local)
Tables:
Addresses
Authors
BookAuthor
Books
Categories
Customers
DailyPick
dtproperties
ItemCategory
Items
ItemType
OrderItems
Orders
Publishers
sysconstraints
syssegments
```

Querying a Table about Its Columns

In the previous Tip, you learned how to query a database about the tables it contains and how to move through the collection of tables returned by the DataSet class Tables property. After you know about a specific table, your programs may need to know about the specific data the table contains. To move through a table's columns, your code can use a For loop similar to the following:

```
Dim J As Integer

For J = 0 To TableList.Tables(0).Columns.Count - 1
   Console.WriteLine(TableList.Tables(0).Columns(J))
Next
```

USE IT   The following program, ListTables.vb, queries the Duwamish7vb database for the tables it contains. Then, for each table, the code uses a For loop to move through and display the name of each of the table's columns:

```
Imports System.Data.SqlClient
Imports System.Data

Module Module1

  Sub Main()
    Try
      Dim Connect As New SqlConnection("Initial Catalog=Duwamish7vb;" _
        & "Data Source=(local);User ID=sa;password=;")

      Connect.Open()
      Console.WriteLine("Database: " & Connect.Database)
      Console.WriteLine("Database: " & Connect.ServerVersion)
      Console.WriteLine("Database: " & Connect.DataSource)

      Dim Command As String = _
        "SELECT table_name From Information_Schema.Tables"

      Dim DS As New DataSet()

      Dim Adapter = New SqlDataAdapter(Command, Connect)

      Adapter.Fill(DS)

      Dim I As Integer

      For I = 0 To DS.Tables(0).Rows.Count - 1
        Console.WriteLine()
```

```
            Console.WriteLine(DS.Tables(0).Rows(I).Item(0))

            Dim Cmd As String = "SELECT * From " & _
              DS.Tables(0).Rows(I).Item(0)
            Dim TableList As New DataSet()

            Dim TableAdapter = New SqlDataAdapter(Cmd, Connect)

            TableAdapter.Fill(TableList)

            Dim J As Integer
              For J = 0 To TableList.Tables(0).Columns.Count - 1
                Console.WriteLine(TableList.Tables(0).Columns(J))
              Next
          Next

        Console.ReadLine()

      Catch Ex As Exception
        Console.WriteLine("Exception: " & Ex.Message)
        Console.WriteLine(Ex.ToString)
        Console.ReadLine()
      End Try

    End Sub

  End Module
```

Viewing the Underlying XML Content

In the ADO.NET environment, XML plays a major role behind the scenes to organize data. In fact, when a data set receives data from a database, it actually receives XML-based content. Likewise, if a data set updates its contents, it returns the new contents back to the database using XML.

USE IT   The following program, DataSetXMLDemo.vb, performs a simple query against a database. The program then uses the DataSet class GetXML method to display the data set's contents in an XML format:

```
Imports System.Data.SqlClient
Imports System.Data

Module Module1
```

```
    Sub Main()
        Try
            Dim Connect As New SqlConnection("Initial Catalog=Duwamish7vb;" _
                & "Data Source=(local);User ID=sa;password=;")

            Connect.Open()

            Dim Command As String = _
                "SELECT * From Authors Where Name Like 'Alf%'"

            Dim DS As New DataSet()

            Dim Adapter = New SqlDataAdapter(Command, Connect)

            Adapter.Fill(DS)

            Dim XMLContent As String = DS.GetXml()

            Console.WriteLine(XMLContent)

            Console.ReadLine()

        Catch Ex As Exception
            Console.WriteLine("Exception: " & Ex.Message)
            Console.WriteLine(Ex.ToString)
            Console.ReadLine()
        End Try

    End Sub

End Module
```

After you compile and execute this program, your screen will display output similar to the following:

```
<NewDataSet>
  <Table>
    <PKId>95</PKId>
    <Name>Alfred Cobban</Name>
  </Table>
  <Table>
    <PKId>112</PKId>
    <Name>Alfred Davidson</Name>
  </Table>
  <Table>
```

```
    <PKId>146</PKId>
    <Name>Alfred Duggan</Name>
  </Table>
  <Table>
    <PKId>246</PKId>
    <Name>Alfred Jarry</Name>
  </Table>
</NewDataSet>
```

Building a Data Set from an XML File

In the ADO.NET environment, the data that a data set and database exchange resides in the XML format. If you have an XML file that contains record-based data, you can use the file to create a database. The following XML file, BookInfo.xml, contains the records in an XML format:

```
<NewDataSet>
  <Table>
    <Title>C# Programming Tips &amp; Techniques</Title>
    <Author>Wright</Author>
    <Publisher>McGraw-Hill/Osborne</Publisher>
    <Price>49.99</Price>
  </Table>
  <Table>
    <Title>Visual Basic .Net Programming Tips &amp; Techniques</Title>
    <Author>Jamsa</Author>
    <Publisher>McGraw-Hill/Osborne</Publisher>
    <Price>49.99</Price>
  </Table>
  <Table>
    <Title>HTML &amp; Web Design Tips &amp; Techniques</Title>
    <Author>King</Author>
    <Publisher>McGraw-Hill/Osborne</Publisher>
    <Price>49.99</Price>
  </Table>
  <Table>
    <Title>PC Performance Tuning &amp; Upgrading Tips &amp; Techniques</Title>
    <Author>Jamsa</Author>
    <Publisher>McGraw-Hill/Osborne</Publisher>
    <Price>39.99</Price>
  </Table>
</NewDataSet>
```

To create a data set from an XML file, you first create a DataSet object:

```
Dim objDataSet As New DataSet()
```

Next, you can fill the DataSet object using the contents of the XML file by calling the ReadXML method:

```
ObjDataSet.ReadXML("filename.XML")
```

The following program, LoadXMLData.vb, creates a data set using the contents of the BookInfo.xml file. The program then displays the data set's contents one row at a time:

```
Imports System.Data.SqlClient
Imports System.Data

Module Module1

    Sub Main()
        Try
            Dim DS As New DataSet()

            DS.ReadXml("Authors.XML")

            Dim XMLContent As String = DS.GetXml()

            Dim I As Integer

            For I = 0 To DS.Tables(0).Rows.Count - 1
                Console.WriteLine(DS.Tables(0).Rows(I).Item("Title"))
                Console.WriteLine(DS.Tables(0).Rows(I).Item("Author"))
                Console.WriteLine(DS.Tables(0).Rows(I).Item("Publisher"))
                Console.WriteLine(DS.Tables(0).Rows(I).Item("Price"))
            Next

            Console.ReadLine()

        Catch Ex As Exception
            Console.WriteLine("Exception: " & Ex.Message)
            Console.WriteLine(Ex.ToString)
            Console.ReadLine()
        End Try

    End Sub

End Module
```

Next, the following program, ChangeDataSetXML.vb, loads the same XML file into the data set. Then the program changes each record by converting the author's name to uppercase. The code then uses the WriteXML method to create a new file that contains the data set's new contents:

```
Imports System.Data.SqlClient
Imports System.Data

Module Module1

    Sub Main()
        Try
            Dim DS As New DataSet()

            DS.ReadXml("Authors.XML")

            Dim XMLContent As String = DS.GetXml()

            Dim I As Integer

            For I = 0 To DS.Tables(0).Rows.Count - 1
                DS.Tables(0).Rows(I).Item("Author") = _
                  UCase(DS.Tables(0).Rows(I).Item("Author"))
            Next

            For I = 0 To DS.Tables(0).Rows.Count - 1
                Console.WriteLine(DS.Tables(0).Rows(I).Item("Title"))
                Console.WriteLine(DS.Tables(0).Rows(I).Item("Author"))
                Console.WriteLine(DS.Tables(0).Rows(I).Item("Publisher"))
                Console.WriteLine(DS.Tables(0).Rows(I).Item("Price"))
            Next

            DS.WriteXml("NewAuthors.xml")

            Console.ReadLine()

        Catch Ex As Exception
            Console.WriteLine("Exception: " & Ex.Message)
            Console.WriteLine(Ex.ToString)
            Console.ReadLine()
        End Try

    End Sub

End Module
```

After you compile and run this program, the XML file, NewAuthors.xml, will contain each author's name in uppercase.

When you import an XML file into a data set in this way, you can improve your program's performance by using an XML file that contains the database schema. For example, the following file, NewAuthors.xls, provides a schema for the BookInfo.xml database:

```
<?xml version="1.0" standalone="yes"?>
<xs:schema id="NewDataSet" xmlns=""
  xmlns:xs="http://www.w3.org/2001/XMLSchema"
  xmlns:msdata="urn:schemas-microsoft-com:xml-msdata">
  <xs:element name="NewDataSet" msdata:IsDataSet="true">
   <xs:complexType>
    <xs:choice maxOccurs="unbounded">
     <xs:element name="Table">
      <xs:complexType>
       <xs:sequence>
        <xs:element name="Title" type="xs:string" minOccurs="0" />
        <xs:element name="Author" type="xs:string" minOccurs="0" />
        <xs:element name="Publisher" type="xs:string" minOccurs="0" />
        <xs:element name="Price" type="xs:string" minOccurs="0" />
       </xs:sequence>
      </xs:complexType>
     </xs:element>
    </xs:choice>
   </xs:complexType>
  </xs:element>
</xs:schema>
```

If you do not have a schema file, the ReadXML method must determine the schema before it can successfully parse the data, which increases overhead. If you do not have a schema file, but you plan on using an XML-based database on a regular basis, you can create a schema file by opening the XML database and then using the WriteXMLSchema method to create a schema file.

Performing a Query Using an ASP.NET Page

USE IT   With ASP.NET applications, there will be many times when you must retrieve, update, or add data to a database. The following ASP.NET page, ViewBookInfo.aspx, displays a form that users can use to select a book by title. To simplify the processing, the code provides Button

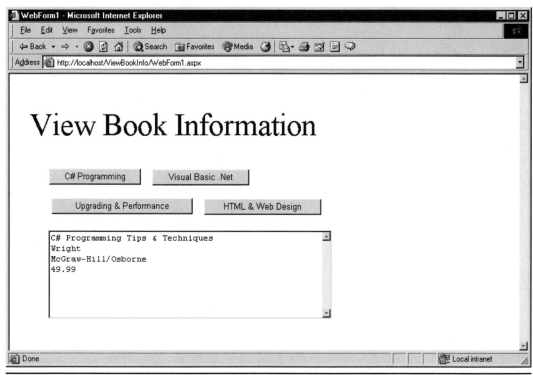

Figure 17-1   Using an ADO.NET DataSet object to drive an ASP.NET page

controls, as shown in Figure 17-1, from which the user can select the topic he or she desires. After the user clicks a button, the page will show the corresponding book information.

```
Public Class WebForm1
    Inherits System.Web.UI.Page
    Protected WithEvents Label1 As System.Web.UI.WebControls.Label
    Protected WithEvents Button1 As System.Web.UI.WebControls.Button
    Protected WithEvents Button2 As System.Web.UI.WebControls.Button
    Protected WithEvents Button3 As System.Web.UI.WebControls.Button
    Protected WithEvents Button4 As System.Web.UI.WebControls.Button
    Protected WithEvents TextBox1 As System.Web.UI.WebControls.TextBox

#Region " Web Form Designer Generated Code "
```

```vb
    ' Code not shown
#End Region

    Public Shared DS As DataSet

    Private Sub Page_Load(ByVal sender As System.Object, _
      ByVal e As System.EventArgs) Handles MyBase.Load

        If Not Page.IsPostBack Then
            DS = New DataSet()
            DS.ReadXml("http://localhost/Authors.XML")
        End If
    End Sub

    Private Sub Button1_Click(ByVal sender As Object, _
      ByVal e As System.EventArgs) Handles Button1.Click, _
      Button2.Click, Button3.Click, Button4.Click

      Dim I As Integer
        If (Equals(sender, Button1)) Then
            I = 0
        ElseIf (Equals(sender, Button2)) Then
            I = 1
        ElseIf (Equals(sender, Button3)) Then
            I = 2
        ElseIf (Equals(sender, Button4)) Then
            I = 3
        End If

        TextBox1.Text = DS.Tables("Table").Rows(I).Item("Title")
        TextBox1.Text += vbCrLf & _
          DS.Tables("Table").Rows(I).Item("Author")
        TextBox1.Text += vbCrLf & _
          DS.Tables("Table").Rows(I).Item("Publisher")
        TextBox1.Text += vbCrLf & _
          DS.Tables("Table").Rows(I).Item("Price")
    End Sub
End Class
```

As you can see, the code uses the data stored in the file Authors.xml. To read the file from the remote Web site, the code passes to the ReadXML method the file's remote URL. When the user clicks a button, the code determines the corresponding button and then creates an index into the DataSet object's table to access the corresponding row of data.

Displaying a Database Table in a DataGrid Control

In Chapter 11, you examined the various controls you can place onto a Windows form. At that time, the chapter did not examine DataGrid controls, which your programs can use to easily display a database table. Figure 17-2, for example, illustrates a DataGrid control in a Windows form that displays the contents of the Authors.xml database.

In general, you can think of a DataGrid control as a container that holds (and displays) the contents of a table. To use a DataGrid control, your code must simply bind a DataSet object to the control and specify which table in the data set you want the control to display:

```
DataGrid1.SetDataBinding(DS, "Table")
```

USE IT   The following program, DataGridDemo.vb, displays the DataGrid control with the database contents previously shown in Figure 17-2. To create the program, drag and drop a DataGrid control onto a form. Then place the following statements in the program's source code:

```
Public Class Form1
    Inherits System.Windows.Forms.Form

#Region " Windows Form Designer generated code "
    ' Code not shown
#End Region

    Private Sub Form1_Load(ByVal sender As System.Object, _
      ByVal e As System.EventArgs) Handles MyBase.Load
        Dim DS As New DataSet()

        DS.ReadXml("Authors.XML")

        DataGrid1.CaptionText = "Book Information"

        DataGrid1.SetDataBinding(DS, "Table")
    End Sub
End Class
```

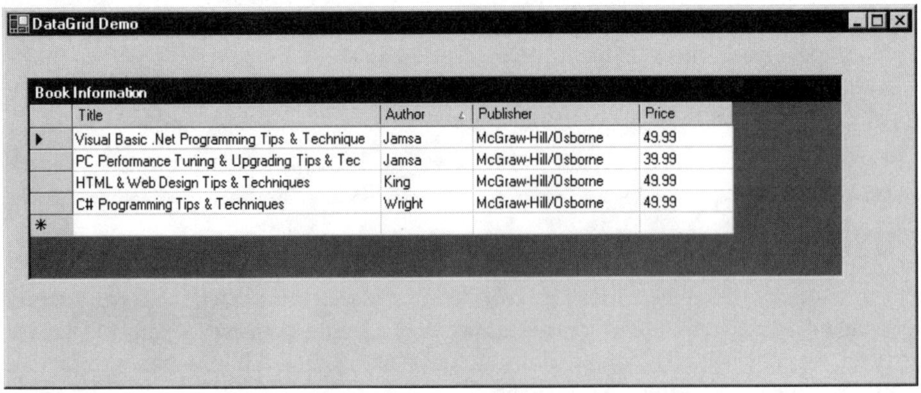

Figure 17-2 Displaying a DataSet object's table in a DataGrid control

As you can see, to display the data grid, the code simply binds the DataSet object to the DataGrid object and then specifies the table in the data set that the program wants to display.

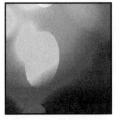

Programming .NET Reflection and Program Attributes

TIPS IN THIS CHAPTER

I n the .NET environment, objects make extensive use of metadata (data about data) to become self-describing. In other words, as a program executes, the program can query an object to learn about the capabilities the object provides. Programmers refer to the ability to query an object as reflection. When a program queries an object, the .NET Reflection application program interface (API) will examine the object's metadata to learn such information as the methods a class provides, the class members' variables, specifics about the class's base type, and more.

This chapter examines the steps you must perform to query an object's capabilities. You will learn how to query an assembly that contains an application or a class library about the classes it provides. Then, using the Reflection API, you will retrieve information about those classes. Next, you will examine the class methods in detail to determine the method's type (subroutine or function) as well as the number and type of parameters the method uses. With this information in hand, your programs can invoke the class methods, passing the methods the correct parameter values.

Using reflection, a .NET program, in theory, could search the assemblies on a system for a class that provides methods to sort an array. After the program locates the class, it can query the class for the specific methods the class provides and the parameter types for each method. Finally, after the program determines the method that will best meet its needs, the program can create an array of objects that contains the correct parameter values and then pass the array to the method.

To provide programs with more information about entities, such as a class, method, or even an assembly itself, Visual Basic .NET supports attributes which you can insert in your source code between left and right angle brackets: <attribute>. One set of attributes, for example, might influence compiler operations. A second set may influence how the debugger performs various operations. A third set of attributes might provide an application with specifics about class members. In this chapter, you will examine attributes Visual Studio inserts into your programs and ways you can create and use your own custom attributes.

Revisiting .NET Reflection

Throughout this book, several of the Tips have stated that .NET objects are self-describing—in other words, the objects contain metadata that programs can query to determine the capabilities the object provides. Programmers refer to the process of querying an object about its capabilities as reflection. To simplify the steps a program must perform to query an object, the Common Language Runtime provides the Reflection API. Using reflection, a program can ask an object to specify the methods it provides, as well as the type of value the method returns, and the number and type of parameters the method requires.

Behind the scenes, a key to .NET reflection is the Type class. In general, to determine an object's capabilities, a program calls the object's GetType method. The System.Object class, from which all .NET objects are derived, defines the GetType method. The program can then use the Type class methods to query the objects. Table 18-1 briefly describes the Type class methods.

USE IT The following program, FirstQuery.vb, uses the Type class GetType and GetTypeCode methods to retrieve information about several common data types you have used in

Method	Description
GetMethod	Returns a specific method in the current type. GetMethod is an overloaded method.
GetMethods	Returns the methods defined in the current type. GetMethods is an overloaded method.
GetNestedType	Returns a specific nested type in the current type. GetNestedType is an overloaded method.
GetNestedTypes	Returns the nested types in the current type. GetNestedTypes is an overloaded method.
GetProperties	Returns the properties of the current type. GetProperties is an overloaded method.
GetProperty	Returns the specified property from the current type. GetProperty is an overloaded method.
GetType	Returns the specified type. GetType is an overloaded method.
GetTypeArray	Returns an array containing the object types in the specified array.
GetTypeCode	Returns the type code of the specified type.
GetTypeFromCLSID	Returns the type associated with the specified class identifier. The GetTypeFromCLSID method is an overloaded method.
GetTypeFromHandle	Returns the type that corresponds to the specified type handle.
GetTypeFromProgID	Returns the type associated with the specified program identifier. The GetTypeFromProgID method is an overloaded method.
GetTypeHandle	Returns the handle for the type of the specified object.
InvokeMember	Invokes a specific method of the current type. InvokeMember is an overloaded member.
IsAssignableFrom	Returns a Boolean value that specifies whether an instance of the type can be assigned from an instance of the specified type.
IsInstanceOfType	Returns a Boolean value that specifies whether the object is an instance of the current type.
IsSubclassOf	Returns a Boolean value that specifies whether the current type was derived from the specified type.
ToString	Returns a string containing the current type's name. The ToString method is an overloaded method.

Table 18-1   Methods Defined in the Type Class

programs throughout this book. Later in this chapter, you will query a class about its methods, including the number and type of parameters the method requires. To determine a method's parameter-type information, you will perform operations similar to those shown here:

```
Module Module1

    Sub Main()
        Dim A As Integer
        Dim B As Double
        Dim C As String = "Hello, world"
        Dim D As DateTime = New DateTime(Now.Ticks)
        Dim E As Byte
        Dim F As Boolean

        Console.WriteLine("Type Codes:")
        Console.WriteLine("Integer: " & A.GetTypeCode() & _
            " " & A.GetType().Name & " " & _
            A.GetType().UnderlyingSystemType.ToString())

      Console.WriteLine("Double: " & B.GetTypeCode() & _
            " " & B.GetType().Name & " " & _
            B.GetType().UnderlyingSystemType.ToString())

        Console.WriteLine("String: " & C.GetTypeCode() & _
            " " & C.GetType().Name & " " & _
            C.GetType().UnderlyingSystemType.ToString())

        Console.WriteLine("DateTime: " & D.GetTypeCode() & _
            " " & D.GetType().Name & " " & _
            D.GetType().UnderlyingSystemType.ToString())

        Console.WriteLine("Byte: " & E.GetTypeCode() & _
            " " & E.GetType().Name & " " & _
            E.GetType().UnderlyingSystemType.ToString())

        Console.WriteLine("Boolean: " & F.GetTypeCode() & _
            " " & F.GetType().Name & " " & _
            F.GetType().UnderlyingSystemType.ToString())

        Console.ReadLine()
    End Sub
End Module
```

After you compile and execute this program, your screen will display the following output:

```
Type Codes:
Integer: 9 Int32 System.Int32
Double: 14 Double System.Double
```

```
String: 18 String System.String
DateTime: 16 DateTime System.DateTime
Byte: 6 Byte System.Byte
Boolean: 3 Boolean System.Boolean
```

Viewing Class Information in ILDASM

In the .NET environment, programs and class libraries do not hold native-mode code (the instructions that correspond directly to the CPU's instruction set). Instead, the assemblies that hold the program and class libraries store an intermediate language (IL) code. Before the code runs, a special program called the just-in-time (JIT) compiler converts the IL code into the native-mode code the CPU can execute.

Using a special command line utility named ILDASM (the intermediate language disassembler), you can view a program (or library's) intermediate language code. In addition, using metadata in the object, you can use ILDASM to view specifics about a class object, such as the methods the class provides, parameters to the methods, and more, as shown in Figure 18-1.

 The following program, SimpleClass.vb, creates a class named Person that contains member variables and methods:

```
Module Module1

    Class Person
        Public Name As String
        Public Age As Integer
        Public Phone As String

        Public Sub New(ByVal Name As String, _
          ByVal Age As Integer, ByVal Phone As String)
            Me.Name = Name
            Me.Age = Age
            Me.Phone = Phone
        End Sub

        Public Sub ShowPerson()
            Console.WriteLine("Name: " & Name)
            Console.WriteLine("Age: " & Age)
            Console.WriteLine("Phone: " & Phone)
        End Sub
    End Class

    Sub Main()
        Dim Employee As New Person("Buddy Jamsa", 21, "555-1212")
```

```
        Employee.ShowPerson()

        Console.ReadLine()
    End Sub

End Module
```

Using Visual Studio, compile the program. Then, to view the class specifics in ILDASM, run the ILDASM program from the command line as follows, replacing the directory path shown here with the directory in which the program file SimpleClass.exe resides on your disk:

```
C:\> ildasm  C:\SomeDirectoryPath\SimpleClass.exe  <Enter>
```

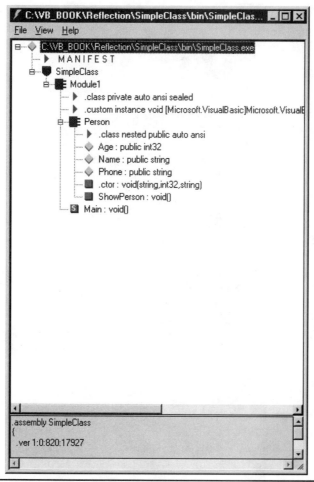

Figure 18-1   Using ILDASM to view class specifics

In the ILDASM program, click the Module1 entry. The program will open the module's branches. Next, click the Person class. The program will display the class members as previously shown in Figure 18-1. As you can see, the metadata the assembly stores describes the class in detail.

Revisiting an Object's Methods

USE IT In the .NET environment, the Reflection API lets programs query an object about the capabilities it provides. The following program, QueryClass.vb, creates a base class and then derives a second class from the base class. Each class defines member variables, methods, properties, and events. Further, the base class implements the IFormattable interface. The code then uses reflection to query each class:

```
Imports System.Reflection

Module Module1
    Class Base
        Public ProductID As String
        Public Weight As Double
        Private ProductPrice As Double

        Public Sub New(ByVal ProductID As String, _
          ByVal Price As Double, ByVal Weight As Double)
            Me.ProductID = ProductID
            Me.Price = Price
            Me.Weight = Weight
        End Sub

        Public Sub ShowProduct()
            Console.WriteLine("Product ID: " & ProductID)
            Console.WriteLine("Weight: " & Weight)
            Console.WriteLine("Price: " & Price)
        End Sub

        Public Property Price() As Double
            Get
                Return ProductPrice
            End Get
            Set(ByVal Value As Double)
                If (Value >= 0) And (Value <= 100) Then
                    ProductPrice = Value
                Else
                    Console.WriteLine("Invalid price for " & ProductID)
                    ProductPrice = 0
```

```vb
                End If
            End Set
        End Property
    End Class

    Class Derived
        Inherits Base
        Implements IFormattable

        Public Title As String
        Public Author As String
        Public Publisher As String

        Public Overridable Overloads Function ToString(ByVal _
           Format As String, ByVal Provider As IFormatProvider) _
           As String Implements IFormattable.ToString

            ToString = Title

        End Function

        Public Sub New(ByVal Title As String, ByVal Author As String, _
           ByVal Publisher As String, ByVal Price As Double, _
           ByVal Weight As Double)
            MyBase.New("11122", Price, Weight)

            Me.Title = Title
            Me.Author = Author
            Me.Publisher = Publisher
        End Sub

        Public Sub ShowBook()
            Console.WriteLine("Title: " & Title)
            Console.WriteLine("Author: " & Author)
            Console.WriteLine("Publisher: " & Publisher)
            ShowProduct()
        End Sub
    End Class

    Sub Main()
        Dim Book = New Derived("C# Programming Tips & Techniques", _
           "Wright", "McGraw-Hill/Osborne", 49.99, 4.3)

        Book.ShowBook()
```

```vb
        Dim Member As MemberInfo
        Console.WriteLine()
        Console.WriteLine("Members:")
        For Each Member In Book.GetType.GetMembers()
            Console.WriteLine(Member.Name & " " & Member.MemberType)
        Next

        Dim PropertyObj As PropertyInfo
        Console.WriteLine()
        Console.WriteLine("Properties:")
        For Each PropertyObj In Book.GetType.GetProperties()
            Console.WriteLine(PropertyObj.Name & " " & _
              PropertyObj.PropertyType.ToString())
        Next

        Dim MethodObj As MethodInfo
        Console.WriteLine()
        Console.WriteLine("Methods:")
        For Each MethodObj In Book.GetType.GetMethods()
            Console.WriteLine(MethodObj.Name & " " & _
              MethodObj.ReturnType.ToString())
        Next

        Dim EventObj As EventInfo
        Console.WriteLine()
        Console.WriteLine("Events:")
        For Each EventObj In Book.GetType.GetEvents()
            Console.WriteLine(EventObj.Name & " " & _
              EventObj.IsMulticast)
        Next

        Dim InterfaceObj As Type
        Console.WriteLine()
        Console.WriteLine("Events:")
        For Each InterfaceObj In Book.GetType.GetInterfaces()
            Console.WriteLine(InterfaceObj.Name)
        Next

        Console.ReadLine()
    End Sub
End Module
```

After you compile and execute this program, your screen will display the following output:

```
Title: C# Programming Tips & Techniques
Author: Wright
Publisher: McGraw-Hill/Osborne
Product ID:
Weight: 4.3
Price: 49.99

Members:
Title 4
Author 4
Publisher 4
ProductID 4
Weight 4
ToString 8
GetHashCode 8
Equals 8
ToString 8
ShowBook 8
ShowProduct 8
get_Price 8
set_Price 8
GetType 8
.ctor 1
Price 16

Properties:
Price System.Double

Methods:
ToString System.String
GetHashCode System.Int32
Equals System.Boolean
ToString System.String
ShowBook System.Void
ShowProduct System.Void
get_Price System.Double
set_Price System.Void
GetType System.Type

Events:

Events:
IFormattable
```

To display the various object members, the code uses a series of For Each loops that display the collections one of the reflection methods returns. In general, the processing is quite straightforward. You must, however, pay attention to the type of collection each routine returns.

Taking a Closer Look at an Object's Methods

Using the Type class GetMethods method, your programs can query a class about the methods (subroutines and function) it provides. The following code fragment, for example, queries an object named Employee for the methods it provides:

```
Dim MethodObj As System.Reflection.MethodInfo
Console.WriteLine("Methods:")
For Each MethodObj In Employee.GetType.GetMethods()
    Console.WriteLine(MethodObj.Name & " " & _
      MethodObj.ReturnType.ToString())
Next
```

To fully understand and later call an object's methods your program learns about using reflection, your program must know the method's type as well as the number and type of parameters the method requires.

 To determine a method's type and parameters, your program can use the GetParameters method that returns an array of ParameterInfo objects:

```
Dim Param As ParameterInfo
For Each Param In MethodObj.GetParameters()
    Console.WriteLine(Param.Name & " " & _
      Param.ParameterType.ToString())
Next
```

The following program, MethodInfo.vb, creates a class named Demo that contains several functions and subroutines. Using the GetMethods method, the code first determines the methods the class contains. The program further queries the object about each method's specifics:

```
Imports System.Reflection

Module Module1
    Class Demo
        Public Sub ShowMessage(ByVal Msg As String)
            Console.WriteLine("Message: " & Msg)
        End Sub

        Public Function AddTwoIntegers(ByVal A As Integer, _
          ByVal B As Integer) As Integer
```

```
            AddTwoIntegers = A + B
        End Function

        Public Sub ShowThreeDoubles(ByVal A As Double, _
          ByVal B As Double, ByVal C As Double)
            Console.WriteLine(A & " " & B & " " & C)
        End Sub
    End Class

    Sub Main()
        Dim SomeObj = New Demo()

        Dim MethodObj As System.Reflection.MethodInfo
        Console.WriteLine()
        Console.WriteLine("Methods:")
        For Each MethodObj In SomeObj.GetType.GetMethods()
            Console.WriteLine(MethodObj.Name & " " & _
              MethodObj.ReturnType.ToString())

            Dim Param As ParameterInfo
            For Each Param In MethodObj.GetParameters()
                Console.WriteLine(Param.Name & " " & _
                  Param.ParameterType.ToString())
            Next
            Console.WriteLine()
        Next

        Console.ReadLine()
    End Sub
End Module
```

After you compile and execute this program, your screen will display the following output:

```
Methods:
GetHashCode System.Int32

Equals System.Boolean
obj System.Object

ToString System.String

ShowMessage System.Void
Msg System.String

AddTwoIntegers System.Int32
```

```
A System.Int32
B System.Int32

ShowThreeDoubles System.Void
A System.Double
B System.Double
C System.Double

GetType System.Type
```

Contrasting Early and Late Binding

In a program, a subroutine name corresponds to the starting address of the set of instructions that perform the subroutine's processing. When the compiler compiles your program, the compiler (or linker if you are calling a subroutine that resides in a class library) binds (replaces) subroutine calls with statements that branch the program's execution to the corresponding address. Programmers refer to binding that occurs during compilation as early binding.

In contrast, in Chapter 10 you examined delegate objects that can store the address of one or more methods. As a program executes, the code can assign different addresses to the delegate. Later, when the code calls the delegate object's Invoke method, the .NET environment, during runtime, determines which method to invoke. Programmers refer to binding that occurs during runtime as late binding.

 The following program, BindingDemo.vb, illustrates early and late binding. The program defines two classes, one named Book and one named Software. Each class has multiple member variables and methods. The program calls the various class methods, each of which were bound by the compiler (early binding). Then the code will pass each object to the LateBindDemo subroutine that receives an Object parameter. Using the Object parameter, the subroutine invokes the ShowValues method, which both classes define. To determine which method to invoke, the LateBindDemo subroutine's code, behind the scenes, must determine the specific type of the Object parameter it receives and whether that type provides a ShowValues method. If the type implements the method, the code then determines the address of the method (binds the method) and calls the method to perform the corresponding operations. If the type the subroutine receives does not define the ShowValues method, the code will generate an exception:

```
Module Module1

    Class Book
        Public Title As String
        Public Author As String
        Public Publisher As String
        Public Price As Double

        Public Sub New(ByVal Title As String, _
```

```vb
           ByVal Author As String, ByVal Publisher As String, _
           ByVal Price As Double)
             Me.Title = Title
             Me.Author = Author
             Me.Publisher = Publisher
             Me.Price = Price
       End Sub

       Public Sub ShowAuthor()
           Console.WriteLine("Author: " & Author)
       End Sub

       Public Sub ShowValues()
           Console.WriteLine("Title: " & Title)
           Console.WriteLine("Author: " & Author)
           Console.WriteLine("Publisher: " & Publisher)
           Console.WriteLine("Price: " & Price)
       End Sub
   End Class

   Class Software
       Public Name As String
       Public Programmer As String
       Public Company As String
       Public Price As Double

       Public Sub New(ByVal Name As String, _
           ByVal Programmer As String, ByVal Company As String, _
           ByVal Price As Double)
             Me.Name = Name
             Me.Programmer = Programmer
             Me.Company = Company
             Me.Price = Price
       End Sub

       Public Sub ShowProgrammer()
           Console.WriteLine("Programmer: " & Programmer)
       End Sub

       Public Sub ShowValues()
           Console.WriteLine("Name: " & Name)
           Console.WriteLine("Programmer: " & Programmer)
           Console.WriteLine("Company: " & Company)
           Console.WriteLine("Price: " & Price)
```

```
            End Sub
        End Class

        Sub LateBinding(ByVal Obj As Object)
            Obj.ShowValues()
        End Sub

        Sub Main()
            Dim ComputerBook = New Book("ASP.NET", "Smith", _
               "Osborne", 49.99)

            Dim GameProgram As New Software("Avenger", "Jones", _
               "GameCO", 29.99)

            ComputerBook.ShowValues()
            Console.WriteLine()
            GameProgram.ShowValues()
            Console.WriteLine()

            LateBinding(GameProgram)
            Console.WriteLine()
            LateBinding(ComputerBook)
            Console.ReadLine()
        End Sub
End Module
```

After you compile and execute this program, your screen will display the following output:

```
Title: ASP.NET
Author: Smith
Publisher: Osborne
Price: 49.99

Name: Avenger
Programmer: Jones
Company: GameCO
Price: 29.99

Name: Avenger
Programmer: Jones
Company: GameCO
Price: 29.99

Title: ASP.NET
```

Author: Smith
Publisher: Osborne
Price: 49.99

Invoking an Object Method Using Invoke

In the Tip titled "Taking a Closer Look at an Object's Methods," you learned how to use .NET
reflection to query an object about the methods it provides, including the method's type (function
or subroutine) and the number and type of parameters the method requires. After your program
determines a method's specifics, your programs can invoke the method using MethodInfo.Invoke.

 USE IT To use the MethodInfo class Invoke method, your program passes to the method an array
of Object elements that correspond to the method's parameters:

```
Dim Parameters(MethodObj.GetParameters().Length - 1) As Object
```

Because all .NET types are based on the System.Object type, you can assign integers, strings,
floating-point values, classes, and so on to the array.

The following program, InvokeDemo.vb, creates a class with four methods, each of which uses a
different number and type of parameters. The code uses the Reflection API to query the class about
the capabilities it provides. Then the code examines each of the methods. Based on the information the
program learns about each method (the number and type of parameters), the program builds a parameter
array that contains values that match those the method supports. The program then invokes each
method, passing the method the array of parameter values:

```
Imports System.Reflection

Module Module1
    Class Demo
        Public Sub Hello()
            Console.WriteLine("Hello, World")
        End Sub

        Public Sub ShowMessage(ByVal Msg As String)
            Console.WriteLine("Message: " & Msg)
        End Sub

        Public Function AddTwoIntegers(ByVal A As Integer, _
          ByVal B As Integer) As Integer
            Console.WriteLine("In AddTwoNumbers with " & A & " " & B)
            AddTwoIntegers = A + B
        End Function
```

```vb
        Public Sub ShowThreeDoubles(ByVal A As Double, _
          ByVal B As Double, ByVal C As Double)
            Console.WriteLine(A & " " & B & " " & C)
        End Sub
    End Class


    Sub Main()
        Dim SomeObj = New Demo()
        Dim IntegerVar As Integer = 1
        Dim DoubleVar As Double = 100.0
        Dim StringVar As String = "Hello"
        Dim Param As ParameterInfo

        Dim MethodObj As System.Reflection.MethodInfo

        For Each MethodObj In SomeObj.GetType.GetMethods()
            Dim Parameters(MethodObj.GetParameters().Length - 1) _
                As Object

            Dim CallMethod As Boolean = True

            Dim I As Integer = 0

            For Each Param In MethodObj.GetParameters()
                If Equals(Param.ParameterType, IntegerVar.GetType()) Then
                    Parameters(I) = IntegerVar
                ElseIf Equals(Param.ParameterType, DoubleVar.GetType()) Then
                    Parameters(I) = DoubleVar
                ElseIf Equals(Param.ParameterType, StringVar.GetType()) Then
                    Parameters(I) = StringVar
                Else
                    CallMethod = False
                End If
                I = I + 1
            Next

            If (CallMethod) Then
                If MethodObj.GetParameters().Length = 0 Then
                    Console.WriteLine("Calling: " & MethodObj.Name)
                    Console.WriteLine(MethodObj.Invoke(SomeObj, Nothing))
```

```
                Else
                    Console.WriteLine("Calling: " & MethodObj.Name)
                    Console.WriteLine(MethodObj.Invoke(SomeObj, Parameters))
                End If
            End If

            Console.WriteLine()
        Next

        Console.ReadLine()
    End Sub

End Module
```

For simplicity, this program only supports parameters of type String, Integer, and Double. To support other data types, you would have to include additional processing. In this case, for each integer parameter, the code simply passes the value 1. Likewise, for each double parameter, the code passes the value 100.0. Finally, for each string parameter, the code passes the value "Hello". After you compile and execute this program, your screen will display the following output:

```
Calling: GetHashCode
4

Calling: ToString
InvokeDemo.Module1+Demo

Calling: Hello
Hello, World

Calling: ShowMessage
Message: Hello

Calling: AddTwoIntegers
In AddTwoNumbers with 1 1
2

Calling: ShowThreeDoubles
100 100 100

Calling: GetType
InvokeDemo.Module1+Demo
```

Taking a Closer Look at an Assembly

In the .NET environment, the assembly is the unit of program and class library deployment. To fully exploit reflection, your programs should start with an assembly. By using the Assembly class GetTypes method, your code can determine the classes the assembly contains. Then your code can retrieve the corresponding class members and methods. The following code fragment determines the classes that reside in the current assembly:

```
Dim ThisAssembly As [Assembly] = [Assembly].GetExecutingAssembly()
Dim TypeObj As Type

For Each TypeObj In ThisAssembly.GetTypes()
    Console.WriteLine(TypeObj.Name)
Next
```

USE IT   The following program, AssemblyQuery.vb, defines several (empty) classes. The code then uses the Assembly class GetTypes method to determine the types the program contains:

```
Imports System.Reflection

Class Person
End Class

Class Employee
End Class

Class Book
End Class

Class TVShow
End Class

Module Module1

    Sub Main()
        Dim ThisAssembly As [Assembly] = [Assembly].GetExecutingAssembly()
        Dim TypeObj As Type

        For Each TypeObj In ThisAssembly.GetTypes()
            Console.WriteLine(TypeObj.Name)
        Next

        Console.ReadLine()
    End Sub
End Module
```

After you compile and execute this program, your screen will display the following output:

```
Person
Employee
Book
TVShow
Module1
```

Making Sense of <Attributes>

As you examine Visual Basic .NET programs, you may encounter entries in the source code that reside in left and right angle brackets, which precede classes, variables, subroutines, as well as entries in an assembly. These entries are attributes. Programmers use attributes to specify information about an entity. The attributes may be used by the compiler as it compiles the program, the debugger, a profiler, or even the program itself.

If you examine the code Visual Studio creates for a form, you may encounter an attribute similar to the following, which, in this case, directs the debugger to step through the method:

```
<System.Diagnostics.DebuggerStepThrough()> Sub InitializeComponent()
   Me.TextBox1 = New System.Windows.Forms.TextBox()
   ' Other statements here
End Sub
```

An attribute consists of three parts: an optional modifier, a name, and optional parameters:

```
<modifier: name(parameters)>
```

The optional modifier exists to restrict the attribute's use to a specific module or the assembly. The attribute name corresponds to a class that implements the attribute. Finally, the optional parameter lets you assign specific values to the attribute class.

 USE IT In Chapter 12, you used the AssemblyInfo.vb file that Visual Studio creates for your application to customize the assembly's version and public key. As it turns out, the file actually contains Visual Basic .NET code, the majority of which are attributes:

```
Imports System.Reflection
Imports System.Runtime.InteropServices

' Comments removed

<Assembly: AssemblyTitle("")>
<Assembly: AssemblyDescription("")>
<Assembly: AssemblyCompany("")>
<Assembly: AssemblyProduct("")>
```

```
<Assembly: AssemblyCopyright("")>
<Assembly: AssemblyTrademark("")>
<Assembly: CLSCompliant(True)>

<Assembly: Guid("8205BCD6-7B9B-471D-8C81-3EFF8DA5FBA0")>
<Assembly: AssemblyVersion("1.0.*")>
```

Each of the attributes uses the Assembly modifier to apply attributes to the entire assembly. As discussed, each attribute corresponds to the class that implements the attribute. In this case, the System.Attribute namespace defines the attribute classes. Last, as you can see, different attributes support different parameters. When you build an application, the compiler uses these attributes to build the assembly.

Defining a Custom Attribute

In a Visual Basic .NET program, an attribute lets you specify information about an entity. The programs that use the attributes can vary. Normally, the attributes you encounter in a program's source code are generated by Visual Studio for use by the compiler or debugger. Programs for which the attributes were not intended ignore the attributes. Depending on your program's processing, there may be times when you will want to create one or more custom attributes.

USE IT To create an attribute, you must define a class that corresponds to the attribute. The class must inherit the Attribute class. The following program, CustomAttributes.vb, creates an attribute named ProgrammerName. The code then uses the attribute to specify the name of the programmer who created specific methods in the Demo class. Later, the code uses reflection to determine the methods the Demo class defines. For each method, the code uses the GetCustomAttributes methods to retrieve any attributes that may describe the method:

```
Imports System.Attribute

Class ProgrammerName
    Inherits Attribute

    Public Name
    Public Sub New(ByVal Name As String)
        MyBase.New()
        Me.Name = Name
    End Sub
End Class

Class Demo
    Public Msg As String

    <ProgrammerName("Kris Jamsa")> Sub DemoMsg()
```

```
            Console.WriteLine(Msg)
        End Sub

    <ProgrammerName("Phil Schmauder")> Sub Greet()
            Console.WriteLine("Hello, VB")
        End Sub

    Public Sub New(ByVal Message As String)
            Msg = Message
        End Sub
End Class

Module Module1
    Sub Main()
        Dim MethodObj As System.Reflection.MethodInfo
        Dim MessageDemo As New Demo("Hello, World")

        For Each MethodObj In MessageDemo.GetType.GetMethods()
            Dim Attr As Attribute
            For Each Attr In MethodObj.GetCustomAttributes(False)
                Console.WriteLine(MethodObj.Name)
                Console.WriteLine(Attr)
                Console.WriteLine(CType(Attr, ProgrammerName).Name)
                Console.WriteLine()
            Next
        Next
        Console.ReadLine()

    End Sub

End Module
```

Note that to display the attribute's value (the programmer name), the code uses the CType function to convert the Attribute object into a ProgrammerName object that contains the Name method:

```
Console.WriteLine(CType(Attr, ProgrammerName).Name)
```

After you compile and execute this program, your screen will display the following output:

```
DemoMsg
CustomAttributes.ProgrammerName
Kris Jamsa

Greet
CustomAttributes.ProgrammerName
Phil Schmauder
```

Displaying an Assembly's Attributes

Attributes exist to specify information about an entity. In a program's source code, various attributes may be used by different programs. Before a program can take advantage of an attribute, the program must know that the attribute exists and how the program uses the attribute.

 The following program, AssemblyAttributes.vb, uses the GetCustomAttributes method to retrieve attributes defined in the current assembly:

```
Imports System.Reflection

Module Module1
    Sub Main()
        Dim ThisAssembly As [Assembly] = _
          [Assembly].GetExecutingAssembly()

        Dim Attr As Attribute
        For Each Attr In ThisAssembly.GetCustomAttributes(False)
            Console.WriteLine(Attr)
        Next

        Console.ReadLine()
    End Sub
End Module
```

After you compile and execute this program, your screen will display the following output:

```
System.Diagnostics.DebuggableAttribute
System.Runtime.InteropServices.GuidAttribute
System.CLSCompliantAttribute
System.Reflection.AssemblyTrademarkAttribute
System.Reflection.AssemblyCopyrightAttribute
System.Reflection.AssemblyProductAttribute
System.Reflection.AssemblyCompanyAttribute
System.Reflection.AssemblyDescriptionAttribute
System.Reflection.AssemblyTitleAttribute
```

If you want to examine a specific value in an attribute and you know the member name of the value you desire, you can use the CType method (as shown in the previous Tip) to convert the Attribute object to a specific attribute type which you can then use to reference the member.

Index

INTERNATIONAL CONTACT INFORMATION

AUSTRALIA
McGraw-Hill Book Company Australia Pty. Ltd.
TEL +61-2-9417-9899
FAX +61-2-9417-5687
http://www.mcgraw-hill.com.au
books-it_sydney@mcgraw-hill.com

CANADA
McGraw-Hill Ryerson Ltd.
TEL +905-430-5000
FAX +905-430-5020
http://www.mcgrawhill.ca

**GREECE, MIDDLE EAST,
NORTHERN AFRICA**
McGraw-Hill Hellas
TEL +30-1-656-0990-3-4
FAX +30-1-654-5525

MEXICO (Also serving Latin America)
McGraw-Hill Interamericana Editores S.A. de C.V.
TEL +525-117-1583
FAX +525-117-1589
http://www.mcgraw-hill.com.mx
fernando_castellanos@mcgraw-hill.com

SINGAPORE (Serving Asia)
McGraw-Hill Book Company
TEL +65-863-1580
FAX +65-862-3354
http://www.mcgraw-hill.com.sg
mghasia@mcgraw-hill.com

SOUTH AFRICA
McGraw-Hill South Africa
TEL +27-11-622-7512
FAX +27-11-622-9045
robyn_swanepoel@mcgraw-hill.com

**UNITED KINGDOM & EUROPE
(Excluding Southern Europe)**
McGraw-Hill Education Europe
TEL +44-1-628-502500
FAX +44-1-628-770224
http://www.mcgraw-hill.co.uk
computing_neurope@mcgraw-hill.com

ALL OTHER INQUIRIES Contact:
Osborne/McGraw-Hill
TEL +1-510-549-6600
FAX +1-510-883-7600
http://www.osborne.com
omg_international@mcgraw-hill.com

About the Online Source Code

USE IT Throughout the Tips found in this book, you will examine the program source code for hundreds of Visual Basic .NET programs. Rather than typing the program code every time, you can quickly download a chapter's program files from the Osborne Web site at **www.osborne.com**. On the Web site, you will find a ZIP file that corresponds to each chapter's programs. After you download and "unzip" the file, you will find folders that correspond to each application. Within each folder, you will find the Visual Basic .NET project files, source code, and any graphics or supplemental files the program requires.